SONG OF THE SEASON

OUTSTANDING BROADWAY SONGS SINCE 1891

Thomas Hischak

methuen | drama
LONDON • NEW YORK • OXFORD • NEW DELHI • SYDNEY

METHUEN DRAMA
Bloomsbury Publishing Plc
50 Bedford Square, London, WC1B 3DP, UK
1385 Broadway, New York, NY 10018, USA
29 Earlsfort Terrace Dublin 2, Ireland

BLOOMSBURY, METHUEN DRAMA and the Methuen Drama logo are trademarks of Bloomsbury Publishing Plc

First published in Great Britain 2024

Copyright © Thomas Hischak, 2024

Thomas Hischak has asserted his right under the Copyright, Designs and Patents Act, 1988, to be identified as author of this work.

For legal purposes the Acknowledgments on p. x constitute an extension of this copyright page.

Cover design by Rebecca Heselton
Background image © jonbilous/ Adobe Stock
Neon signage © James Threw/ Adobe Stock

All rights reserved. No part of this publication may be reproduced or transmitted in any form or by any means, electronic or mechanical, including photocopying, recording, or any information storage or retrieval system, without prior permission in writing from the publishers.

Bloomsbury Publishing Plc does not have any control over, or responsibility for, any third-party websites referred to or in this book. All internet addresses given in this book were correct at the time of going to press. The author and publisher regret any inconvenience caused if addresses have changed or sites have ceased to exist, but can accept no responsibility for any such changes.

A catalogue record for this book is available from the British Library.

Library of Congress Cataloging-in-Publication Data
Names: Hischak, Thomas S., author.
Title: Song of the season : outstanding Broadway songs since 1891 / Thomas Hischak.
Description: New York : Bloomsbury Publishing, 2024. | Includes bibliographical references and index. | Summary: "Placing the score front and centre of the narrative, this is a critical historical survey of notable songs from Broadway musicals from 1891 to 2023"– Provided by publisher.
Identifiers: LCCN 2023036731 (print) | LCCN 2023036732 (ebook) | ISBN 9781350423725 (hardback) | ISBN 9781350423718 (paperback) | ISBN 9781350423732 (epub) | ISBN 9781350423749 (pdf)
Subjects: LCSH: Musicals–New York (State)–New York–History and criticism. | Musicals–New York (State)–New York–Chronology.
Classification: LCC ML1711.8.N3 H573 2024 (print) | LCC ML1711.8.N3 (ebook) | DDC 782.1/4097471–dc23/eng/20230818
LC record available at https://lccn.loc.gov/2023036731
LC ebook record available at https://lccn.loc.gov/2023036732

ISBN:	HB:	978-1-3504-2372-5
	PB:	978-1-3504-2371-8
	ePDF:	978-1-3504-2374-9
	eBook:	978-1-3504-2373-2

Typeset by Integra Software Services Pvt. Ltd.
Printed and bound in Great Britain

To find out more about our authors and books visit www.bloomsbury.com and sign up for our newsletters.

SONG OF THE SEASON

For Richard and Francine Fix,

who love Broadway songs

CONTENTS

Preface	viii
Acknowledgments	x
Guide to Musical Terms	xi
List of Seasons, Songs, and Musical Sources	xiv
1891–1899 Seasons	1
1900–1919 Seasons	21
1920–1939 Seasons	73
1940–1959 Seasons	131
1960–1979 Seasons	187
1980–1999 Seasons	243
2000–2023 Seasons	295
Afterword	348
Notes on Song Lyrics	349
Bibliography	355
Index of Songs	358
Index of Names and Titles	379
About the Author	422

PREFACE

Let's look at two Broadway opening nights.

It is the third of July 1902, and a warm night inside the Herald Square Theatre in New York City. The new musical, *The Defender*, is not actually new. It is a London transfer with an American cast. The plot has something to do with a yacht race between an American and a British ship and the efforts of a crooked soap manufacturer to fix the race. The opening night audience is mildly amused by the performers but little else. The English songs are routine at best. Then the third act curtain goes up and the saucy character of Millie Canvass steps forward and belts out "In the Good Old Summertime." The audience is enthralled by the melodic, rollicking song and insists on an encore. Soon they are singing along with her. The singer is Blanche Ring, a popular variety performer who sang "In the Good Old Summertime" a few times in vaudeville. When cast in *The Defender*, Ring insisted the song by George Evans (music) and Ren Shields (lyric) be put into the show for her to sing. It worked. The song stopped the show and soon the talk "on the Street" was "In the Good Old Summertime." It was *the* song of the 1902–03 season.

It is October 30, 2003, and the Gershwin Theatre is packed for the gala opening of the new musical *Wicked*. Although out-of-town notices were less than impressive and there have been major cast, script, and song changes over the previous weeks, the excitement is running high. From the first silhouette image of the Wicked Witch melting, the musical is playing like gangbusters. Despite what the critics write, this is an audience show and this audience is thrilled. As the end of the first act approaches, the green misfit Elphaba (Idina Menzel) realizes that "good" people like the Wizard are not at all good and she vows not to "play by the rules of someone else's game." The song is "Defying Gravity" by Stephen Schwartz. Elphaba rises off the ground, Menzel's voice rises into the stratosphere, and the theatre explodes with applause. Few were surprised the next day when the critics were not overwhelmed by *Wicked* but ticket sales soared and the songs were embraced by the public, none more so than "Defying Gravity." It was *the* song of the 2003–04 season.

This is a book about Broadway songs. There have been thousands of them since 1891 when the first American song leapt from the stage and into a wide public consciousness. These songs come from musical comedies, operettas, revues, music dramas, sung-through musicals, rock musicals, you name it. They incorporate ragtime, jazz, fox trot, swing, blues, country-western, R&B, rock and roll, pop, Latin, gospel, soul, hip hop, and rap. They are written by songwriters as diverse as Irving Berlin and Elton John. They have traveled from Broadway to sheet music, cylinders, phonograph records, radio, movies, television, cassette tapes, CDs, YouTube, downloads, and the Cloud. Some songs have become standards, being rediscovered again and again by later generations. Others were only briefly popular, fading away as tastes and musical styles changed. But a number of them shone so brightly, if only for a short time, that they could be labeled the "song of the season."

By season, I mean the Broadway season. It used to start in the fall when the cooler weather arrived and theatres that had been closed up for the summer reopened. As the theatres became "air cooled," the season started in June. Later, the season was determined by the dates announced by the Tony Awards. But no matter when it began, the Broadway season was and is a benchmark to chronicle the activity on Broadway. In the 1920s, it was not unusual for over 200 plays and musicals to open each season. By the 1970s, that number shrunk to twenty or thirty. At the same time, Off-Broadway and Off-Off-Broadway expanded and the theatre scene in New York was not so dismal as it sounded. But, regardless of the numbers, there have always been musicals and those shows introduced songs and often there was one that rose above the others. That is the focus of this book: that one song.

We have made the audacious decision to select a single song from each season, from 1891 to 2023, that we consider *the* song of the season. It may be the most popular song, or one of high quality, or one that was quickly discovered by the public at the time or later. The song may have been one that best captured the feeling in America at the time or it may have introduced a new sound or innovation. Choosing just one song was not an arbitrary choice. Many songs were considered but the selection could not help but be a somewhat personal and opinionated one. The resulting book is one that hopes to capture the variety and diversity of theatre songs. We have avoided songs that were originally heard in movies or elsewhere; the aim is to look at theatre songs that were introduced in America on Broadway or Off-Broadway or even Off-Off-Broadway. It is not possible that any one reader, no matter how informed, will agree with the choices we have made. But that is also an important aspect of this book. We have included "other notable songs" for each season to illustrate what else was of interest. Perhaps the reader will prefer one of these "also-rans" over the selected song of the season. That also is a vital part of this book. For the song of the season cannot be determined objectively. Sheet music sales or Grammy Awards or chart statistics are considered but are only part of the picture. Some songs are outstanding just by the impact they made then and, in many cases, now.

To clarify the terms used in the discussion, a Guide to Musical Terms is provided. Then each season, from 1891–92 to 2022–23, is summarized, followed by a description and discussion of the selected song. A list of other notable songs from the season ends each entry. The book concludes with a bibliography of works about theatre songs and popular music, and there is an index to help the reader locate musicals, songs, and people.

The Song of the Season hopes to inform, entertain, and even provoke anyone who loves Broadway musicals.

ACKNOWLEDGMENTS

I must first acknowledge Mark A. Robinson whose idea this book was. As he got involved with other projects, he kindly turned the project over to me. I also wish to thank Robbie Rozelle, Sam Nicholls, Dom O'Hanlon, Sophie Beardsworth, Kumaraguru Elangovan, and, most importantly, my wife Cathy for, well, many things.

GUIDE TO MUSICAL TERMS

arch rhyme When a word is mispronounced, usually for comic effect, in order to rhyme with another word. For example, rhyming "boil" with "goil" (girl) or "fickle with "partickle" (particular). A song in this book with arch rhymes: "Comedy Tonight!" from *A Funny Thing Happened on the Way to the Forum.*

ballad In modern popular music, any sentimental or romantic song, usually with the same melody for each refrain. Ballads are often the big sellers in a musical, the songs that can move listeners without the benefit of character or plot. A **narrative ballad** is more like poetry's definition of the term: a song that tells a story. An example of a ballad in this book: "My Funny Valentine" from *Babes in Arms.*

character song Any musical number that is concerned with revealing a character's personality or reaction to the events of the plot. A person's first character song in a musical is often his or her "I am" song. Character songs tend not to travel as well outside the context of the musical as ballads often do. An example of a character song in this book: "I'm Breaking Down" from *Falsettos.*

charm song A musical number less about character development than it is about utilizing the characters' warm and/or comic entertainment value. Charm songs are often expendable plot-wise but are usually audience favorites. Many charm songs feature children or songs sung to children. An example of a charm song in this book: "Do Re Mi" from *The Sound of Music.*

contrapuntal song Two distinct melodies and lyrics that are sung at the same time. Also called a **double song**, each section usually has a different tempo yet the two songs fit together musically. An example of a contrapuntal number in this book: "You're Just in Love" from *Call Me Madam.*

eleven o'clock number A special, show-stopping song that comes late in the last act of a musical. The actual time at which the number occurs is not as important as its powerful impact in bringing the show to life before the climax or finale. An example of an eleven o'clock number in this book: "Electricity" from *Billy Elliot.*

"I am" song Often a solo, but any song that introduces a character or group of characters early in a musical by revealing their wishes, dreams, confusions, and so on. Sometimes called an **"I wish" song**, "I am" songs became requisite with the advent of the integrated musical, but many musicals before *Oklahoma!* have "I am" songs that function in the same way. An example of an "I am" song in this book: "I Enjoy Being a Girl" from *Flower Drum Song.*

Guide to Musical Terms

integrated musical When the songs (and sometimes the dance) grow out of the characters and/or the plot. Although *Oklahoma!* (1943) is considered the first fully integrated musical, there are many musicals before that which had partially integrated scores. An example of an integrated musical discussed in this book: *Carousel*.

internal rhyme When two words or syllables in the same lyric line rhyme with each other. Such internal rhymes can be subtle, as with "You obvious*ly* do not adore *me*," or obvious for comic effect, as in "get that *ice* or else no *dice*." A song in this book with several internal rhymes: "Tea for Two" from *No No Nanette*.

interpolation A song added to a show, either before or after opening, that is not written by the same songwriters who wrote the rest of the score. Songs may be interpolated into a musical for a variety of reasons: to improve a weak score, to please a star, to take advantage of a hit Tin Pan Alley song, and so on. An example of an interpolated song in this book: "After the Ball" from *A Trip to Chinatown*.

list song Any song, serious or comic, that is structured as a list of examples or a series of items. Sometimes it is called a "laundry list" song, although the result, hopefully, is much more interesting than that. An example of a list song in this book: "A Little Priest" from *Sweeney Todd: The Demon Barber of Fleet Street*.

masculine and feminine rhymes When a rhyme in a lyric involves two one-syllable words, it is masculine. Words with two or more syllables that rhyme are considered feminine rhymes. Rhyming "take" and "make" is a hard, blunt masculine rhyme. "Follow" and "hollow" make for a softer, feminine rhyme.

pastiche song Any musical number that echoes the style, either musically or lyrically, of an earlier era. Such songs are written to spoof the past or to recapture the period of the setting of the new work. An example of a pastiche song in this book: "All That Jazz" from *Chicago*.

refrain The main body of a song; that is, the section that follows the verse and repeats itself with the same melody and/or lyric. The most familiar part of a popular song is usually the refrain section.

release A section of the song, usually after the second refrain, which departs musically and lyrically from the main theme of the refrain. Sometimes called the **bridge**, the release is often the most musically challenging part of a song.

reprise The repeating of part or all of a song later in the show, either by the same or by different characters. Reprises differ from an **encore** in that the latter are repeats that are sung immediately after a song is first sung. An example of a song in this book that has encores written in: "There's No Business Like Show Business" from *Annie Get Your Gun*.

score All of the songs (music and lyrics) written for one musical.

soliloquy A solo in which the character is alone on stage and reveals his or her thoughts, confusions, concerns, and so on. The most effective soliloquies are songs that show a character debating two sides of an issue or trying to come to a decision. An example of a soliloquy song in this book: "Michael in the Bathroom" from *Be More Chill*.

song structure The basic format of a song. While there are no set rules and songs vary in their structure, the standard format is:

verse
refrain 1
refrain 2
release or bridge
refrain 3

standard A song that remains popular over a long period of time, being discovered by later generations and receiving new recordings. An example of a song standard in this book: "Smoke Gets in Your Eyes" from *Roberta*.

Tin Pan Alley An old-fashioned term meaning the music business. The name came from the sound of upright pianos banging out tunes in the various music publishers' offices in lower Manhattan. A Tin Pan Alley song refers to one that did not come from the stage or the movies but was written directly for the music market.

torch song In popular music, a song, usually sentimental, involving unrequited love. In musical theatre, torch songs can be sarcastic or comic as well as serious. An example of a torch song in this book: "Send in the Clowns" from *A Little Night Music*.

verse The introductory section of a song. The melody is usually distinct from that of the refrain that follows, and verses tend to be shorter. While many songs are most known for their refrains, the musical number reaches its full potency from an effective verse.

LIST OF SEASONS, SONGS, AND MUSICAL SOURCES

1891–92	Oh, Promise Me—*Robin Hood*
1892–93	After the Ball—*A Trip to Chinatown*
1893–94	Old Before His Time—*The Passing Show of 1894*
1894–95	(Private) Tommy Atkins—*A Gaiety Girl*
1895–96	El Capitan's Song—*El Capitan*
1896–97	I Love Thee, I Adore Thee—*The Serenade*
1897–98	The Tattooed Man—*The Idol's Eye*
1898–99	My Wild Irish Rose—*A Romance of Athlone*
1899–1900	When Chloe Sings a Song—*Whirl-i-Gig*
1900–01	Tell Me, Pretty Maiden—*Florodora*
1901–02	Nancy Brown—*The Wild Rose*
1902–03	In the Good Old Summer Time—*The Defender*
1903–04	Toyland—*Babes in Toyland*
1904–05	Give My Regards to Broadway—*Little Johnny Jones*
1905–06	You're a Grand Old Flag—*George Washington, Jr.*
1906–07	The Streets of New York—*The Red Mill*
1907–08	I Love You So (The Merry Widow Waltz)—*The Merry Widow*
1908–09	Shine On, Harvest Moon—*Follies of 1908*
1909–10	Has Anyone Here Seen Kelly?—*The Jolly Bachelors*
1910–11	Ah, Sweet Mystery of Life—*Naughty Marietta*
1911–12	Be My Little Baby Bumble Bee—*The Winsome Widow*
1912–13	When Irish Eyes Are Smiling—*Isle o' My Dreams*
1913–14	Peg o' My Heart—*Ziegfeld Follies of 1913*
1914–15	They Didn't Believe Me—*The Girl from Utah*
1915–16	I Love a Piano—*Stop! Look! Listen!*
1916–17	Till the Clouds Roll By—*Oh, Boy!*
1917–18	I'm Always Chasing Rainbows—*Oh, Look!*
1918–19	Swanee—*Sinbad*
1919–20	A Pretty Girl Is Like a Melody—*Ziegfeld Follies of 1919*
1920–21	I'm Just Wild About Harry—*Shuffle Along*

List of Seasons, Songs, and Musical Sources

1921–22	April Showers—*Bombo*	
1922–23	Nellie Kelly, I Love You—*Little Nellie Kelly*	
1923–24	Charleston—*Runnin' Wild*	
1924–25	Indian Love Call—*Rose-Marie*	
1925–26	Tea for Two—*No No Nanette*	
1926–27	Someone to Watch Over Me—*Oh, Kay!*	
1927–28	Ol' Man River—*Show Boat*	
1928–29	I Wanna Be Love by You—*Good Boy*	
1929–30	Ain't Misbehavin'—*Hot Chocolates*	
1930–31	I Got Rhythm—*Girl Crazy*	
1931–32	As Time Goes By—*Everybody's Welcome*	
1932–33	Night and Day—*Gay Divorce*	
1933–34	Smoke Gets in Your Eyes—*Roberta*	
1934–35	I Get a Kick Out of You—*Anything Goes*	
1935–36	Begin the Beguine—*Jubilee*	
1936–37	My Funny Valentine—*Babes in Arms*	
1937–38	I'll Be Seeing You—*Right This Way*	
1938–39	September Song—*Knickerbocker Holiday*	
1939–40	All the Things You Are—*Very Warm for May*	
1940–41	Bewitched (Bothered and Bewildered)—*Pal Joey*	
1941–42	Everything I've Got (Belongs to You)—*By Jupiter*	
1942–43	Oh, What a Beautiful Mornin'—*Oklahoma!*	
1943–44	Speak Low—*One Touch of Venus*	
1944–45	If I Loved You—*Carousel*	
1945–46	There's No Business Like Show Business—*Annie Get Your Gun*	
1946–47	Almost Like Being in Love—*Brigadoon*	
1947–48	Papa, Won't You Dance with Me?—*High Button Shoes*	
1948–49	Some Enchanted Evening—*South Pacific*	
1949–50	Diamonds Are a Girl's Best Friend—*Gentlemen Prefer Blondes*	
1950–51	You're Just in Love—*Call Me Madam*	
1951–52	They Call the Wind Maria—*Paint Your Wagon*	
1952–53	It's All Right with Me—*Can-Can*	
1953–54	Stranger in Paradise—*Kismet*	
1954–55	Young and Foolish—*Plain and Fancy*	
1955–56	On the Street Where You Live—*My Fair Lady*	

List of Seasons, Songs, and Musical Sources

1956–57	The Party's Over—*Bells Are Ringing*
1957–58	Seventy-Six Trombones—*The Music Man*
1958–59	I Enjoy Being a Girl—*Flower Drum Song*
1959–60	Do Re Mi—*The Sound of Music*
1960–61	If Ever I Would Leave You—*Camelot*
1961–62	Comedy Tonight—*A Funny Thing Happened on the Way to the Forum*
1962–63	What Kind of Fool Am I?—*Stop the World—I Want to Get Off*
1963–64	People—*Funny Girl*
1964–65	Sunrise, Sunset—*Fiddler on the Roof*
1965–66	The Impossible Dream—*Man of La Mancha*
1966–67	Cabaret—*Cabaret*
1967–68	Aquarius—*Hair*
1968–69	Promises Promises—*Promises, Promises*
1969–70	The Ladies Who Lunch—*Company*
1970–71	Day By Day—*Godspell*
1971–72	I Don't Know How to Love Him—*Jesus Christ Superstar*
1972–73	Send in the Clowns—*A Little Night Music*
1973–74	In This Wide, Wide World—*Gigi*
1974–75	Time Heals Everything—*Mack & Mabel*
1975–76	All That Jazz—*Chicago*
1976–77	Tomorrow—*Annie*
1977–78	Old Friend—*I'm Getting My Act Together and Taking It on the Road*
1978–79	A Little Priest—*Sweeney Todd: The Demon Barber of Fleet Street*
1979–80	Don't Cry for Me Argentina—*Evita*
1980–81	Four Jews in a Room Bitching—*March of the Falsettos*
1981–82	And I'm Telling You I'm Not Going—*Dreamgirls*
1982–83	Memory—*Cats*
1983–84	I Am What I Am—*La Cage aux Folles*
1984–85	River in the Rain—*Big River*
1985–86	Don't Quit While You're Ahead—*The Mystery of Edwin Drood*
1986–87	The Lambeth Walk—*Me and My Girl*
1987–88	Music of the Night—*The Phantom of the Opera*
1988–89	Diva! (Hard to Be Diva)—*Starmites*
1989–90	Love Changes Everything—*Aspects of Love*
1990–91	Lily's Eyes—*The Secret Garden*

List of Seasons, Songs, and Musical Sources

1991–92	I'm Breaking Down—*Falsettos*
1992–93	Where You Are—*Kiss of the Spider Woman*
1993–94	Loving You—*Passion*
1994–95	As If We Never Said Goodbye—*Sunset Boulevard*
1995–96	Seasons of Love—*Rent*
1996–97	This Is the Moment—*Jekyll & Hyde*
1997–98	Ragtime—*Ragtime*
1998–99	And They're Off—*A New Brain*
1999–2000	Written in the Stars—*Aida*
2000–01	Alone in the Universe—*Seussical*
2001–02	Gimme Gimme—*Thoroughly Modern Millie*
2002–03	You Can't Stop the Beat—*Hairspray*
2003–04	Defying Gravity—*Wicked*
2004–05	Dividing Day—*The Light in the Piazza*
2005–06	I'm Here—*The Color Purple*
2006–07	96,000—*In the Heights*
2007–08	I Miss the Mountains—*Next to Normal*
2008–09	Electricity—*Billy Elliot*
2009–10	Go Back Home—*The Scottsboro Boys*
2010–11	I Believe—*The Book of Mormon*
2011–12	Something to Believe In—*Newsies*
2012–13	I'm Not My Father's Son—*Kinky Boots*
2013–14	Ring of Keys—*Fun Home*
2014–15	My Shot—*Hamilton*
2015–16	Everything Changes—*Waitress*
2016–17	You Will Be Found—*Dear Evan Hansen*
2017–18	Omar Sharif—*The Band's Visit*
2018–19	Michael in the Bathroom—*Be More Chill*
2019–20	Memory Song—*A Strange Loop*
2020–21	(no season because of the pandemic)
2021–22	Before I Go—*Kimberly Akimbo*
2022–23	Some Like It Hot—*Some Like It Hot*

Link to all the songs:

https://open.spotify.com/playlist/5qzZlWRM4Pm2pfSrXshHlr?si=28c30e8e50d745ee

1891–1892 SEASON

The American musical experienced a pivotal turning point with the 1891–92 Broadway season. After a century of British and French ballad operas, operettas, and musical comedies, two American works opened that were not only successful but helped define the future of the home-grown musical. *Robin Hood* was the first American operetta of note and *A Trip to Chinatown* was a musical comedy hit which foreshadowed the direction that genre would take. And, most importantly in regard to our subject, both musicals introduced some very popular songs.

Robin Hood and *A Trip to Chinatown* were not the first successful American musicals. There had been home-grown hits going back to *The Black Crook* in 1866. The composer, Connecticut-born Reginald De Koven, and the lyricist-librettist, Buffalo-born Harry B. Smith, were no Gilbert and Sullivan but they wrote seventeen musicals together and helped establish an American sound to Broadway shows. Their biggest hit, by far, was *Robin Hood*, which ran an impressive forty performances in its first New York engagement in 1891 and then was regularly revived over the next fifty years. It is a romanticized operetta based on the legend of the outlaw who stole from the rich and gave to the poor. The tuneful score included a rousing drinking song, "Brown October Ale," a jolly choral number called "Tinkers' Chorus," and the love song "Oh, Promise Me." Although revivals of *Robin Hood* are far from plentiful today, the operetta is generally acknowledged as the first masterwork of the American musical stage.

The biggest hit musical comedy of 1891 was *A Trip to Chinatown; or, an Idyl of San Francisco*, which ran on the Street for an astounding 657 performances. (At that time, a musical that ran 60 performances was a "hit" and one that ran over 100 was considered a "blockbuster.") Called a "farce-comedy" in its day, *A Trip to Chinatown* is actually a musical comedy as we know it today. Charles H. Hoyt wrote the book and lyrics and Percy Gaunt composed the music. The show has more than a few similarities to *Hello, Dolly!* (1964). The sportive plot concerns a group of young people who tell their guardian Uncle Ben that they are going sightseeing in Chinatown but they really plan a night on the town. Complications pile up when Ben also goes to town to woo the widow Mrs. Guyer and they all end up in the same restaurant hiding from each other. It was all light-hearted nonsense and the merry songs added to the enjoyment. Two hit songs came from the original production of *A Trip to Chinatown*. "The Bowery" is a standard that is still familiar to listeners today. You may not think you know "The Bowery" but you do. For over one hundred years its 3/4-time bouncing melody has been played by organ grinders, heard on carousels, and used in countless movies to set the scene in old New York City. To say that the melody is catchy is understatement. Once heard, the song is easily recalled and forever remembered. The other song, "Reuben and Cynthia," also has a catchy tune and can still be heard today, most commonly as background music in cartoons. It is a silly tune with a farcical lyric and an infectious, repetitive melody.

The rest of that season was rather lackluster after *Robin Hood* and *A Trip to Chinatown*. There were a few revivals of Gilbert and Sullivan operettas, the arrival of two minstrel show companies, a star turn by Lillian Russell in the musical *La Cigale* (*The Grasshopper*), and a farce-musical by Ned Harrigan titled *The Last of the Hogans* which ran four months. One of the more dramatic occurrences of the season was backstage. During the run of the musical *The Lion Tamer*, leading lady Marie Jansen was taken ill and the chorus girl Lulu Glaser took her place and was adulated by the press and public. It was not the first time for this sort of thing but Glaser's debut was so famous that many a fiction version of the tale was turned into plays and movies.

"Oh, Promise Me"
Music by Reginald DeKoven; lyric by Clement Scott
From *Robin Hood* (1891)
Sung by Jessie Bartlett Davis as Alan-a-Dale

The female star of *Robin Hood* was Jessie Bartlett Davis who did not play Maid Marion but the "trouser" role Alan-a-Dale, one of Robin's merry men. Davis got good notices when the operetta opened but she was not happy. She demanded a solo and so De Koven pulled from his files "Oh, Promise Me" with a lyric by Clement Scott written some years before and it was added during the run. In the second act, the evil Sheriff of Nottingham has captured Robin Hood and is going to force him to witness the marriage of Maid Marian to Guy of Gisbourne. The ceremony begins and Alan-a-Dale hides behind the bushes and sings to his sweetheart Annabel of her vow to marry him. Although Alan-a-Dale considers his hand might be "the most unworthy in this lonely land," he sees in Annabel's eyes a "vision of our paradise."[1] De Koven's music is not so much a waltz or march as it is a hymn. There is a gently flowing tempo (the sheet music is marked "con forza") that keeps the song from being sluggish. The vocal line is accompanied by a quiet series of repeated chords then some very subtle chromatic changes. The song has a narrow range until the climax which has a fortissimo high E. The lyric is far from clever but is sentimental without being too hyperbolic.

"Oh, Promise Me" immediately caught on, was added to the tours and the seven Broadway revivals of *Robin Hood*, and was sung at over a million weddings until the 1960s when it was considered an old-fashioned cliché. Davis claimed not to like the song but the audiences loved to hear her sing it so it was often requested throughout her career. In London, *Robin Hood* was retitled *Maid Marian* (1892) and the song was sung by Violet Cameron. An early popular recording of "Oh, Promise Me" was made by the Irish tenor John McCormack, followed by records by such diverse singers as the Neapolitan Trio, Tommy Dorsey's Orchestra, Nelson Eddy, Marie Rappold, Jan Peerce,

Jesse Crawford, Paul Robeson, Lauritz Melchior, Vaughn Monroe, and a duet version by Lucille Lawrence and Dick Leibert. There was even a popular pop version by the Platters in the 1950s. The song is also heard in dozens of movies, ranging from the Mickey Mouse cartoon *A Close Call* (1929) to *Harlem Nights* (1989), usually during a wedding scene. "Oh, Promise Me" was one of the first Broadway songs to find wide popularity outside of the theatre. The concept of a theatre song having a long life of its own was unique in 1891. But the success of the wedding song was noticed by music publishers and, for the first time, Broadway was seen as a source for Tin Pan Alley hits.

Other notable songs from that season: "Brown October Ale," "Tinkers' Chorus" from *Robin Hood*; "The Bowery," "Reuben and Cynthia," "Push Dem Clouds Away" from *A Trip to Chinatown*; "Molly O!" from *The Mavourneen*.

Song of the Season

1892–1893 SEASON

The most important event of the 1892–93 Broadway season did not take place on the Street. It happened in Milwaukee where the song "After the Ball" was interpolated into the touring production of *A Trip to Chinatown*. By the end of the season, the song was heard in New York and the rest, as they say, is history. It was a bustling but uneventful season. Of the fifty-two musicals that opened, two-thirds of them were revivals or return engagements. The most accomplished of the new works was the British operetta *The Mountebanks* with W. S. Gilbert writing the book and lyrics with composer Alfred Cellier rather than his usual partner Arthur Sullivan. The most successful of the new American musicals was *1492*, arriving in the spring one year late for the 400th anniversary of Columbus' crossing. Audiences didn't mind the late arrival and applauded the show for 354 performances.

"After the Ball"
Music and lyric by Charles K. Harris
From *A Trip to Chinatown* (tour) (1892)
Sung by J. Aldrich Libby

The first American popular song to sell over 5 million copies of sheet music was "After the Ball," one of the finest waltzes in the history of Tin Pan Alley. Charles K. Harris wrote the music and lyrics for the narrative ballad which tells a tale of lost love. An old man counsels his young niece in matters of love and explains to her why he never wed. Years earlier, at a fancy dress ball, he saw his sweetheart embrace and kiss another man, so he left the ball and never saw the woman again. It was only years later that he learned that the other man was her long-lost brother. The narrative is broken up by the famous refrain which uses a series of phrases beginning with the word "after." After the dance is over, after morning comes, after the dancers go home, after the stars disappear, and so on. One is left with an aching heart and hope is gone. The repetition of these "after" phrases supports the flowing nature of the music. The refrain climaxes with the title phrase and the notes jump an octave and conclude in a satisfactory manner which is a quiet marvel. While the tale is typical of the sentimental story-ballads prevalent at the time, "After the Ball" has such an unpretentious sense of power that the thirty-two-bar refrain still entrances even without the sixty-four-bar verses. The language may be antique ("Many a heart is aching") but Harris' sweeping waltz melody has not dated.[2]

The song has a unique history. Harris wrote the narrative ballad for Sam Doctor to sing in his vaudeville act but Doctor flubbed the long lyric and the audience was not impressed. When the tour of the Broadway hit *A Trip to Chinatown* came to Milwaukee, Harris paid the show's female star J. Aldrich Libby to sing it in the musical. Harris had to bribe orchestra conductor Frank Palma with a box of cigars to orchestrate the number for Libby. After she had completed singing the lengthy ballad, there was a moment of silence in the house and Harris thought the song had failed again. Then there was thunderous applause and audiences have been applauding "After the Ball" ever since. It was added to the still-running *A Trip to Chinatown* on Broadway and to subsequent tours and revivals. It became even more popular when John Philip Sousa played it at the Chicago World's Fair in 1893 and soon every band in the land was playing it. "After the Ball" has received hundreds of recordings over the decades ranging from Guy Lombardo and the Royal Canadians to Johnny Cash. Notable discs include those by Bing Crosby, Julie London, Nat King Cole, Bob Karnes, Lawrence Welk, the Kingsway Strings, Bob Crewe, and a duet version by Joan Morris and William Bolcom. Jerome Kern and Oscar Hammerstein interpolated "After the Ball" into their musical *Show Boat* (1927) when they needed a period song for Magnolia to sing on New Year's Eve; it is heard in every revival of that musical. Norma Terris sang it in the original Broadway production and Edith Day in the first London mounting of *Show Boat* in 1928. In the six Broadway revivals of *Show Boat*, "After the Ball" has been sung by such artists as Jan Clayton, Sheryl Woods, Barbara Cook, and Rebecca Luker. The song was first heard on screen in the short *After the Ball* (1929), followed by over fifty other films. In the screen versions of *Show Boat*, "After the Ball" was sung by Irene Dunne in 1936 and Kathryn Grayson in 1951. In the history of Tin Pan Alley, "After the Ball" remained the biggest song hit to come from the musical theatre for several decades. Harris earned some $10 million from "After the Ball," more than any songwriter had yet made off of one song. Music publishers thereafter looked to Broadway for possible songs that could make them a fortune as well.

Other notable songs from that season: "Ah Yes, I Love Thee" from *The Fencing Master*; "Put a Penny in the Slot," "High Jerry, Ho!" from *The Mountebanks*.

Song of the Season

1893–1894 SEASON

New American musicals outnumbered the imports this season, which was an encouraging sign. But none of the book musicals were of much value except as vehicles for popular performers. Two musical favorites appeared in two new American works: Marie Tempest in *The Algerian* and Lillian Russell in *Princess Nicotine*. Two male favorites returned to Broadway in familiar vehicles: Henry E. Dixie in *Adonis* and Chauncey Olcott in *The Mavoureen*. There were two astronomical musicals that season: *A Trip to Mars*, featuring a cast of "small people," and *Prince Kam; or, A Trip to Venus*, which came from Boston. The most profitable offerings were revivals, as with *A Trip to Chinatown, Erminie, The Black Crook*, and *Robin Hood*. *Utopia (Limited); or, The Flowers of Progress*, the last of the Gilbert and Sullivan operettas, arrived from London and, though it was not a top-drawer work in the team's impressive repertoire, it was still better than the American offerings of book musicals. Yet the most significant new work of the season was an American concoction: the first true "musical revue." *The Passing Show* introduced the new genre, calling itself a "revue" (from the French term) rather than a "review." Also from the French was the concept of a series of scenes and musical numbers in which various performers reappeared throughout the evening. Unlike the later vaudeville, the revue was put together as a single entertainment rather than a parade of individual acts. Sydney Rosenfeld wrote most of the lyrics and sketches and Ludwig Englander did the music, though there was a spoof of various operas that used the original music. Besides the opera world, *The Passing Show* also made fun of some dramas and musicals recently on the Street, current events presented sarcastically in a series of "living pictures" (tableaus), and two roundly applauded songs, "Hot Tamales" and "Old Before His Time." With a cast of 100 and high-quality production values, *The Passing Show* ran 121 performances and not only paved the way for other "Passing Shows" but for the development of the American musical revue itself.

"Old Before His Time"
Music by Ludwig Englander; lyric by Sydney Rosenfeld
From *The Passing Show of 1894* (1894)
Sung by members of the ensemble

A clever list song that captured the spirit of the new musical revue format, "Old Before His Time" might also be categorized as a novelty number. The lyric is a series of complaints about getting old but lyricist Rosenfeld's sense of humor keeps the song as light and carefree as Englander's sprightly, if predictable, music. The list song has fun with the many losses that come with old age: loss of wealth, health, hair, sleep, appetite, and even hope. Both Rosenfeld and Englander were mid-way through their prolific careers but were considered old-school songwriters in 1894. They were also opposed to the grim realism showing up in new plays and the non-romantic new style of acting. One of the verses of "Old Before His Time" addresses both issues, complaining "the heroine has consumption, the hero meningitis, the villain yellow jaundice" and the plays make the audience "themselves grow old before their time."[3] As entertaining as "Old Before His Time" was in *The Passing Show*, the song was neither a ballad nor a sentimental anthem so it did not enjoy a long life outside of the theatre. Sheet music sales were unimpressive and recordings were scarce. Yet there is something sassy (or maybe grumpy) about the tone of the song. This tone is what made the new-fangled genre of "musical revue" distinctive. Also, Rosenfeld's lyric foreshadows the kind of quick-witted language to be found in musical comedy songs in the next century.

Other notable songs from that season: "Hot Tamales," "The Fellow That Played the Drum" from *The Passing Show*; "Oh, Rapture Unrestrained," "Words of Love Too Loudly Spoken" from *Utopia (Limited)*; "A Leap from the Earth to the Sky" from *Prince Kam; or, A Trip to Venus*.

1894–1895 SEASON

The season was marked by a new British invasion and the debut of a major American composer. The London hit *A Gaiety Girl* not only repeated its success on Broadway but opened the door for a ten-year-long series of "Gaiety" musicals that were popular on both sides of the Atlantic. These musical comedies were different in that the characters, settings, and situations were modern, very satirical, and surprisingly coherent. Gone were the exotic locales and princes and princesses from operetta. The "Gaiety" characters were fun, far from stuffy, and dressed in the very latest fashions. This last attribute would turn the "Gaiety" musicals into an important trend-setter in London and New York. The series was produced by George Edwardes, most were written by Owen Hall, and the scores were usually by Sydney Jones (music) and Harry Greenbank (lyrics). *A Gaiety Girl* was a farce about the complications when some fun-loving Life Guards at Windsor barracks invite some theatre chorines to a party which is also attended by a bevy of high-class ladies, their chaperone, a judge, and a minister. Edwardes had difficulty with the Lord Chamberlain's office over some aspects of *A Gaiety Girl*, not the least of which was the very unmilitary-like behavior of the soldiers. Although *A Gaiety Girl* was thoroughly British, Broadway embraced the musical and was anxious to see more.

The other London import to find success on the Street this season was *Little Christopher Columbus*. But the longest-running show was an American product even if it was based on a Sir Walter Scott novel. *Rob Roy* had a score by Reginald De Koven, and it was as popular as his *Robin Hood*. Among the star turns that delighted audiences during the 1894–95 season were De Wolf Hopper in *Dr. Syntax*, Francis Wilson and Lulu Glaser in *The Devil's Deputy*, and Della Fox, who secured her stardom with her first musical lead in *The Little Trooper*. Historically speaking, the most important new American musical this season was the operetta *Prince Ananias* which introduced composer Victor Herbert to Broadway. It was his first of forty musicals which made Herbert the king of American operetta.

"Private Tommy Atkins"
Music by S. Potter; lyric by Henry Hamilton
From *A Gaiety Girl* (1894)
Sung by Charles Ryley as Charles Goldfield

Much as "G.I. Joe" is the general term for any American enlisted man, the name "Tommy Atkins" is used for English soldiers. "Tommy Atkins" was first used in 1815 as a generic name on War Office forms. The name caught on throughout the nineteenth century and was widely known during the Boer Wars (1880–1902). Rudyard Kipling published his poem "The Ballad of Tommy Atkins" in 1892, and the song "Private Tommy Atkins" was written soon after by Henry Hamilton (music) and C. Potter (lyric).

When producer George Edwardes was having trouble with the censors because of the way enlisted men behaved in *A Gaiety Girl*, he interpolated the patriotic number into the 1893 musical. It was the hit of the show and was retained when *A Gaiety Girl* opened on Broadway the next year. Surprisingly, the American audiences were equally thrilled by the very-British patriotic number. The sheet music for "Private Tommy Atkins" (sometimes listed simply as "Tommy Atkins") is marked *Tempo di Marcia*. The verses are a plodding kind of march but the refrain flows nicely even as it sticks to 4/4 time. The lyric is unabashedly patriotic and starry eyed, particularly in the repeated refrains in which Tommy is called "a good un, heart and hand" and "a credit to your calling, and to all your native land."[4] The verses get a bit more specific, sometimes listing the faraway places where British soldiers have fought. "Whether he's on India's coral strand/ Or pouring out his blood in the Soudan," Tommy Atkins is "every inch of him a soldier and a man." The song was originally sung by Charles Arnold in a London music hall program as part of a military sketch. With slight revision it was interpolated into *A Gaiety Girl* where it was sung by Hayden Coffin. On Broadway, it was performed by Charles Ryley and the chorus. A 1901 disc by baritone S. H. Dudley is believed to be the first recording. Other early records were made by Robert Howe and an orchestral version by the Victor Military Band in 1914. Interest in "Private Tommy Atkins" increased during the First World War, and it was a favorite years later during the Second World War. In addition to military band recordings, the song has been heard in many British films set during the two wars. There are about a half-dozen patriotic songs with "Tommy Atkins" in the title but none approach the popularity of the Potter/Hamilton work.

Other notable songs from that season: "Sunshine Above," "Beneath the Skies," "When Your Pride Has Had a Tumble" from *A Gaiety Girl*; "Rumpty Tumpty" from *Little Christopher Columbus*; "The Merry Miller" from *Rob Roy*; "Amaryllis" from *Prince Ananias*.

Song of the Season

1895–1896 SEASON

Business was booming on Broadway this season. Seven new musicals ran over 100 performances and another seven managed to turn a profit running less than that magic number. The nation was slowly recovering from the Panic of 1893 and it showed on Broadway. Unfortunately, of all the new offerings this season, only one musical is still revived on occasion: *El Capitan*. The comic opera is the best of composer John Philip Sousa's six musicals and "El Capitan's Song" lives on as one of his popular marches. The biggest hit of the year was *Excelsior, Jr.* in which Fay Templeton played the trouser role of an American heir who must scale a mountain in Switzerland to gain his inheritance. Other new musicals on the Street that ran over the 100-performance mark were *The Widow Jones, The Wizard of the Nile, A Black Sheep, The Lady Slavey,* and *In Gay New York*. In many cases, these (and several other) shows ran on star power. Among the favorites to trod the boards this season were Della Fox, Jefferson De Angelis, Francis Wilson, May Irwin, Marie Dressler, Lillian Russell, and De Wolf Hopper. Finally, a musical comedy titled *The Bicycle Girl* about the recent bicycling craze stopped in New York as part of its tour. It was a routine affair except when it came to the climatic bicycle race which was a movie projected on a screen. In a week, *The Bicycle Girl* was gone but it was clear the new-fangled "moving picture" was here to stay.

"El Capitan's Song"
Music by John Philip Sousa; lyric by Tom Frost
From *El Capitan* (1896)
Sung by De Wolf Hopper as the Viceroy of Peru, and the chorus

---

A few bars of Sousa's "El Capitan March" are enough for most listeners to recognize this very famous piece beloved by marching bands and concert orchestras. But few realize it was originally a song with lyrics and was first heard on Broadway. *El Capitan* is a 1896 operetta that was a vehicle for the stage favorite De Wolf Hopper who specialized in comic villains. He played Don Medigua, the seventeenth-century Viceroy of Peru, whose power is being threatened by a band of rebels led by El Capitan. The Viceroy manages to capture El Capitan, have him executed, then disguise himself as El Capitan and infiltrate the rebels. It all sounds rather heavy but *El Capitan* is a comic operetta and Hopper kept it light as he outwitted the rebels, got involved with sticky romantic complications, and managed a happy ending. "El Capitan's Song" was sung by Medigua (disguised as El Capitan) and the male chorus. At the operetta's finale, the music was heard as a robust march. Tom Frost's lyric is far from inspired but it does have panache and vigor. El Capitan boasts "Mile after mile I can lead the van, So follow me, El Capitan!"[5] His faithful followers are equally robust, admitting "What you can do any other man can do as well if his heart be true" and agree to follow El Capitan. While "El Capitan's Song" is definitely a march, it is not too fast. Sousa indicates "moderate march tempo" on the sheet music. Even as an instrumental piece, the music confidently builds to a series of climaxes, all of which add to the bravado. One must keep in mind that "El Capitan's Song" was a comic number sung by a popular character actor. Hopper introduced the song on Broadway and reprised his performance in London in 1899. Both times it was the musical highlight of the operetta. But the number would enjoy more fame as an orchestrated piece and, although some light opera companies still revive *El Capitan*, few singers made recordings of it. A rare 1898 disc by Harry Taft is an exception. Sousa arranged a band version and titled it "El Capitan March" and recorded it for the first time in 1896. The number remained in his band's repertory for the rest of his life and is now part of the standard repertory of many bands and orchestras. Early recordings by others include a 1904 disc by the Black Diamonds Band and a 1915 record by Pietro Deiro. Among the standout recordings over the years are those by Andre Kostelanetz, Band of the Grenadier Guards, Johnny Maddox, The New Orleans Syncopators, Warren Lubich, and The Alliance Orchestra of Gothenburg. A disc by the Mormon Tabernacle Choir is unique in that it has lyrics, though altered from the original. "El Capitan March" can be heard in dozens of movies and television shows.

Other notable songs from that season: "Sweetheart, I'm Waiting," "The Legend of the Frogs" from *El Capitan*; "The Bully Song" from *The Widow Jones*; "Star Light, Star Bright," "Stonecutters' Song" from *The Wizard of the Nile*; "Some Things Are Better Left Unsaid" from *A Black Sheep*; "The 20th Century Girl" from *Excelsior, Jr.*

1896–1897 SEASON

Three of the season's biggest hits came from London but the finest score heard on Broadway was an American one: Victor Herbert's *The Serenade*. It was the composer's fourth show and, at seventy-nine performances in repertory, his first hit. The British import *The Geisha*, which ran an astounding 760 performances in London, played a very profitable 161 showings on Broadway. *The Circus Girl* ran 172 performances in New York as opposed to 497 in London. More successful was *The Girl from Paris* which stayed for 281 showings. Originally titled *The Gay Parisienne*, it ran 369 performances in London and three years on tour. If the money was in English imports, much of the excitement that season was home grown. Young producer Florenz Ziegfeld created a sensation bringing the "French" beauty Anna Held to Broadway in a revival of *A Parlor Match*. The Polish-born Held lived up to all of Ziegfeld's hype and two significant careers were launched. Also making a splashy Broadway debut were "Dutch" comics Lew Fields and Joe Weber who took over a theatre on 29th Street, renamed it Weber and Fields' Music Hall, and started presenting a series of burlesques (parodies) of the latest shows in town. The Civil War drama *The Heart of Maryland* was spoofed in the first entry, *The Art of Maryland*. When *The Geisha* became a runaway hit, Weber and Fields altered the program and retitled their show *The Geezer*. For the next seventeen years, the duo thrilled New Yorkers with such fine foolery.

"I Love Thee, I Adore Thee"
Music by Victor Herbert; lyric by Harry B. Smith
From *The Serenade* (1897)
Sung by W. H. MacDonald as Alvarado,
and Jessie Bartlett Davis as Dolores, and chorus

The plot of *The Serenade* was as complicated as it was ridiculous. But every time the action stopped for a song, the music was glorious. The lyrics by the prolific Harry B. Smith were less so. But Smith knew what words allowed the singers to soar so Victor Herbert used the librettist-lyricist often. (Thirteen times, to be exact; Smith worked on some 300 musicals *in toto*.) The serenade of the title was a song that was supposedly taking Spain by storm and, once heard, you could believe it. The verse for "I Love Thee, I Adore Thee" is a "moderato" waltz that sets the atmosphere. In Seville, a cavalier "in sombrero and mantilla" courts a "fair Castillian lady" by playing a serenade on his guitar.[6] The refrain, to be sung "con fervore," is more robust but still romantic, the lyrics gushing without apology. "Thee" and "thou" and "thine" abound, adding to the archaic tone of the song. "I will worship thee forever," the cavalier sings, ending the serenade with "my dream and my star thou art." Herbert's music for "I Love Thee, I Adore Them" stays within a narrow range until the climax. One feels he is restraining himself, wanting to go more operatic but knowing the singers are not opera singers. Not until *Naughty Marietta* three years later, written for an opera company, does the music become difficult. Because it was limited by being part of a repertory by the theatre troupe The Bostonians, *The Serenade* remained on the Street for only seventy-nine performances but the operetta toured and returned to New York frequently over the next seven years. As for "I Love Thee, I Adore Thee," its popularity was later overshadowed by better Herbert ballads. There was a 1910 recording by the Columbia Light Opera Company but few discs after that even though the operetta was revived on occasion. In a memorable 1930 staging, the duet was sung by Lorna Doone Jackson and Greek Evans.

Other notable songs from that season: "Cupid and I," "The Angelus," "Song of the Carbine" from *The Serenade*; "I'll Wish Him a Polite Good-Day (The Toy Monkey)," "Chin Chin Chinaman" from *The Geisha*; "A Little Bit of String," "The Way to Treat a Lady" from *The Circus Girl*; "Miss Lucy" from *The Geezer*.

Song of the Season

1897–1898 SEASON

Once again the Broadway season was inundated with British works, both new and revivals, but the best music heard on New York stages was composed by Americans Reginald De Koven, John Philip Sousa, and Victor Herbert. The London hit *In Town*, a "Gaiety" musical comedy that ran 292 performances in the West End, survived only forty in New York. Similarly, *The French Maid* had chalked up 480 performances in London but had to settle for 175 on Broadway. A third London success, *Monte Carlo* amused Americans for only forty-eight showings. In an interesting reversal, the American musical *The Belle of New York* did not thrill New Yorkers but was later a hit in London, running an impressive 674 performances. De Koven's *The Highwayman* was the longest-running American musical of the season with 144 performances. Sousa's *The Bride Elect* and Herbert's *The Idol's Eye* were less fortunate but still turned a profit. They also included some delightful songs. There was a surge of patriotism after the battleship *Maine* was blown up in Havana harbor on February 15. It showed up in some of the season's later musicals, none so forcefully as in a minstrel show at the Grand Opera House where they sang the flag-waving "Uncle Sam, Tell Us Why You Are Waiting?" The government didn't wait long. The day after the song was first sung, the United States declared war on Spain and the Spanish American War began.

"The Tattooed Man"
Music by Victor Herbert; lyric by Harry B. Smith
From *The Idol's Eye* (1897)
Sung by Frank Daniels as Abel Conn, and chorus

The most talked about song of the season was a comic number sung by the clowning favorite Frank Daniels in *The Idol's Eye*. Not only did "The Tattooed Man" stop the show, it later inspired a whole new musical for Daniels. *The Idol's Eye* revolved around a ruby which is stolen from the eye of a Hindu idol by the hapless American balloonist Abel Conn (Daniels). The complications that follow allowed Daniels to show off his farcical talents. Halfway through the show, Daniels dropped the story and entertained the audience with "The Tattooed Man." It is a narrative number told by one who lost his sweetheart to a man covered with tattoos, a veritable "human picture gallery."[7] She marries the colorful fellow, saying she no longer wishes to go to Europe and see the sights; all the wonders of the world are displayed on her husband. But the tale ends unhappily, the "tattooed man" taking all the family money and running off never to be seen again. Victor Herbert's music is a sprightly march that maintains a moderate tempo so that Harry B. Smith's lyric is given full attention. And what a dandy lyric it is! The words "tattoo" and "design" are used throughout, playing off their double meanings. A tattoo is not only body art but an old military term referring to an evening drum or bugle signal recalling soldiers to their quarters. Design can refer to art but also to a plan with a specific purpose or intention in mind, as in the old expression "he had designs on her." Smith uses both meanings of the two words in his clever lyric: "He had designs upon himself, She had designs on him." Each refrain ends with similar foolishness, ending the lyric with the conclusion that "You can beat a tattoo/ But you can't beat a tattooed man!" One has to keep in mind that the comic Daniels made the best of this verbal buffoonery in his performance. He toured with *The Idol's Eye* for several years and throughout the rest of his life, Daniels was asked to sing "The Tattooed Man" and he often obliged. Ten years after *The Idol's Eye*, the song was still popular enough that Smith named his new musical *The Tattooed Man*. Herbert again wrote the music and Daniels was again the star, this time playing a Persian astronomer named Omar Khayyam, Jr., who sports a tattoo which can lead to his death sentence. The comic operetta ran a respectable fifty-nine performances thanks to Daniels' popularity. As for the song "The Tattooed Man," it has been recorded on occasion, usually in anthology recordings of Herbert's music.

Other notable songs from that season: "Talk about Yo' Luck (The Rabbit's Foot)" from *The Idol's Eye*; "I've 'er Portrait Nex' to My 'eart" from *The French Maid*; "Dreamless Rest" from *In Town*; "(She Is) The Belle of New York," "At Ze Naughty Folies Bergere" from *The Belle of New York*.

1898–1899 SEASON

New American works outnumbered British ones in this very profitable season. That said, many of the moneymakers were trumped-up vaudeville productions, garish spectaculars, and revivals. Twenty of the season's musicals were either return engagements or revivals of old favorites. The shows with the best songs only managed modest runs. The prime example was Victor Herbert and Harry B. Smith's *The Fortune Teller* with a superior score but a run of forty performances as part of a tour. Running twice as long was the Irish melodramatic musical *A Romance of Athlone* which introduced the American-Hibernian standard "My Wild Irish Rose." Other notable American works on the Street which fared modestly well at the box office included John Philip Sousa's *The Charlatan*, Ludwig Englander's *The Little Colonel*, and the May Irwin vehicle *Kate Kip, Buyer*. The only new British musical to chalk up an impressive total was *A Runaway Girl* at 216 performances. But the real runaway this season was the Joe Weber-Lew Fields musical burlesque *Hurly-Burly* that ran 264 performances thanks to its stars (Weber, Fields, Fay Templeton, David Warfield) and some catchy songs by in-house composer John Stromberg. During the summer there was a mini-musical titled *Clorindy; or, The Origin of the Cakewalk* which played at the rooftop venue atop the Casino Theatre. The raucous, unpretentious piece by poet Paul Laurence Dunbar (book and lyrics) and Will Marion Cook (music) was created and performed by African Americans, the first such musical to play in a theatre patronized exclusively by white audiences. *Clorindy* was the talk of the town and was held over several times throughout the summer.

"My Wild Irish Rose"
Music and lyric by Chauncey Olcott
From *A Romance of Athlone* (1899)
Sung by Chauncey Olcott as Dick Ronyane

"My Wild Irish Rose" is such a beloved and popular sentimental ballad that it is curious that the song did not catch on right away. But when it did find an audience, it became (and remains) one of the most famous of all Irish-American songs. It was written (music and lyric) by Chauncey Olcott who was born in Buffalo, New York, but whose mother's family came from County Cork in Ireland. Olcott was a singer-actor in musicals who was disappointed in the songs he was given to perform so he decided to write some himself. By the time he died in 1932, he had written or co-written three classic Irish favorites—"When Irish Eyes Are Smiling," "Mother Machree," and "My Wild Irish Rose"—and introduced a fourth: "Too-Ra-Loo-Ra-Loo Ral (That's an Irish Lullaby)." *A Romance of Athlone* had a complicated mess of a plot with abductions, gypsies, duels, and a purple love story. All this derring-do was interrupted by only five songs, all sung by Olcott, which is what the audience wanted. All five numbers have an Irish flavor and traffic in sentiment about anything Irish. The verse of "My Wild Irish Rose" tells of a girl who once gave a young man a rose then left him; ever since he dreams of her and that rose which is "now dropped and dead."[8] The title refers to both the girl and the rose, as in the celebrated refrain about "my wild Irish Rose, the sweetest flower that grows." The man's desire to "take the bloom" from the elusive lass may strike some as a bit carnal but the song is dripping with innocence. The music for the famous refrain of "My Wild Irish Rose" is not particularly Hibernian. It flows nicely within a narrow range and the waltz tempo is not sluggish. The lesser-known verse, on the other hand, has some Irish touches, particularly how some words encourage a lilting performance.

After singing "My Wild Irish Rose" for eighty-eight performances, Olcott had hoped it would catch on. A. C. Campbell had recorded the song during the run of *A Romance of Athlone*, followed by records by the Hayden Quartet in 1907 and the Brunswick Quartet in 1910. But still sheet music and record sales were sluggish. It was John McCormack's 1914 recording that turned the tide. Over a hundred recordings followed and no evening of Irish music was complete without "My Wild Irish Rose." Notable discs over the decades include those by Walter Van Brunt, Charles Harrison, Al Jolson, Leo Soileau's Four Aces, Glen Gray and the Casa Loma Orchestra (vocal by Kenny Sargent), Ray Noble (vocal by Larry Stewart), Kate Smith, the Mills Brothers, Joni James, Frankie Carle, Connie Francis and the Jordanaires, the Ink Spots, Dennis Day, the Moms and Dads, The Irish Tenors, Ciarán Sheehan, and Craig Duncan. The 1947 movie bio of Olcott was titled *My Wild Irish Rose* and the number was sung by Dennis Morgan as Olcott. It can be heard in dozens of other films with an Irish or Irish-American setting.

Other notable songs from that season: "Gypsy Love Song," "Romany Life," "Always Do as People Say You Should" from *The Fortune Teller*; "Emmaline," "Dinah" from *Hurly-Burly*; "Who Dat Say Chicken in Dis Crowd," "Darktown Is Out Tonight" from *Clorindy*; "The Boy Guessed Right," "The Soldiers in the Park" from *A Runaway Girl*.

Song of the Season

1899–1900 SEASON

Once again new American musicals outnumbered imports fifteen to two but, once again, the shows had mediocre scores and most ran on the fuel of stars, laughs, glitz, and girls. The up-and-coming Florenz Ziegfeld was proving himself a master of the last. The sixteen chorines in his musical *Papa's Wife* were cited by all the critics as the most impressive bevy of beauties on Broadway that season. A rivalry developed this season between the Theatrical Syndicate and the producers-comics Weber and Fields. For three seasons Joe Weber and Lew Fields had presented the biggest hits of the year with their burlesque revues which spoofed the musicals and plays currently on the boards. This year's entry had the usual nonsense title of *Whirl-i-Gig* and there was such a demand for tickets for opening night that an auction was held to distribute them. Millionaires William Randolph Hearst, Stanford White, and others paid between $750 and $1,000 for prime seating. Such gouging did not discourage patrons who kept the musical running for 264 performances at regular prices. The Syndicate wanted to cash in on the Weber and Fields gold mine and produced a similar satiric revue, *The Rogers Brothers in Wall Street*. Gus and Max Rogers came from vaudeville and were featured in eight musicals on the Street before Gus died in 1908. Their revues were popular enough but no threat to the Weber and Fields juggernaut. Other American musicals to enjoy profitable runs this season were the already-mentioned *Papa's Wife*, *The Rounders*, *The Singing Girl*, *Sister Mary*, *Broadway to Tokio*, and the holiday family attraction *Chris and the Wonderful Lamp*. The sole British success was *The Casino Girl* at 131 performances.

"When Chloe Sings a Song"
Music by John Stromberg; lyric by Harry B. Smith
From *Whirl-i-Gig* (1899)
Sung by Lillian Russell as Fifi Coocoo

Although minstrel shows were gradually losing their appeal in big cities, so-called "coon" songs remained popular and just about every new musical on Broadway featured one. This song genre with the unfortunate name goes back to the 1840s. They were written by white songwriters using a stereotypic, and often inaccurate, Black dialect. Some "coon" songs were highly derogatory while others just attempted to capture a nostalgic Southern flavor in the manner of Stephen Foster. In the 1890s, over 600 such songs were published and some sold in the millions. So it was very tempting to write them for Broadway where they were audience favorites. Some white female singers specialized in such songs and were known as "coon shouters." The classy Lillian Russell was not thought of as such an entertainer but even she could not resist singing at least one "coon" song in each of her shows. This season she stopped the musical *Whirl-i-Gig* each evening with the plantation number "When Chloe Sings a Song."

John Stromberg's music is light and sunny in the verses where the melody bounces up and down the scale. The refrain is more restrained but still a sprightly waltz within a slightly wider range. The lyric by Harry B. Smith is in an African American dialect but is not offensive. The verses list all the sounds heard on the plantation (banjos strumming, tambourines and fiddles playing, bees buzzing, a steamboat's whistle, and so on) but none can compare favorably to Chloe's singing. The refrain uses a series of feminine rhymes effectively, such as "tones a'comin' ... banjo a'strummin' ... bees dey stop dere hummin.'"[9] All this activity on the plantation cannot compare to the "sensation" when Chloe sings the "sweetes' music in creation."

Such a gentle "plantation ballad" is not to be shouted and Russell knew how to deliver it. The song was published and soon was on the sheet music sales charts. As with similar songs of this genre, recordings are scarce but "When Chloe Sings a Song" was performed in vaudeville, in concert, and on thousands of parlor pianos.

Other notable songs from that season: "I Wish I Really Weren't, But I Am" from *Papa's Wife*; "When the Cat's Away the Mice Will Play," "Ma Tiger Lily" from *Aunt Hannah*; "The Casino Girl," "How Actresses Are Made" from *The Casino Girl*.

1900-1901
SEASON

For the first time in several seasons, a London import was the runaway success of the year. *Florodora*, in fact, ran even longer in New York than it had in the West End. It was a fanciful musical comedy with fine songs, lovely production values, and a sextet of girls who became famous. The season's runner-up was the popular Weber and Fields piece of musical nonsense titled *Fiddle-Dee-Dee*. The usual expected (and anticipated) burlesque was stuffed with stars, Lillian Russell, Fay Templeton, De Wolf Hopper, David Warfield, and John T. Kelly, among them. Two future stars, comics Dave Montgomery and Fred Stone, caught the attention of critics and playgoers alike as they clowned around as pirates in *The Girl from Up There*. An even bigger talent arrived on Broadway this season: George M. Cohan. He took the family's vaudeville act, expanded it into the full-scale musical *The Governor's Son*, wrote the songs himself, and played the leading role. Before long, Cohan would add directing and producing to his duties. *The Governor's Son* ran only thirty-two performances but by season's end everyone had heard about the young musical dynamo who created it. Among the musicals that ran much longer than the Cohan show were *The Rogers Brothers in Central Park*, *The Giddy Throng*, *Garrett O'Magh*, *My Lady*, *The King's Carnival*, and the British import *San Toy*. The "Chinese musical comedy" ran 168 performances on Broadway, a far cry from the 778 performances in London.

"Tell Me, Pretty Maiden"
Music by Leslie Stuart; lyric by Frank Clement, Paul Rubens, Leslie Stuart
From *Florodora* (1900)
Sung by the clerks and the English girls

In the early years of the new century, you didn't have to be a theatregoer to have heard of *Florodora* because of the expression "Florodora Girls." At first this referred to six beautiful chorus girls in the original production, all of whom went on to marry millionaires. Later the term referred to any Broadway chorine who marries well—or is trying to. (Later the expression "gold digger" would replace "Florodora Girl.") The most famous of all the many girls from *Florodora* was Evelyn Nesbit, the wife of Pittsburgh steel tycoon Harry Thaw and the mistress of architect Stanford White. (Nesbitt was the center of the film *The Girl in the Red Velvet Swing* and the novel, film, and musical *Ragtime*.) Despite all the resulting gossip and scandal, *Florodora* was a very innocent affair with a ridiculous plot about a perfume factory on an island in the Philippines. In the second act, the action moves to a castle in Wales where a duet featuring one of the couples asked the musical question, "Are There Any More at Home Like You?" Legend has it that director-choreographer Sidney Ellison thought the number dull and decided to turn it into a chorus number for six girls and six gentlemen. He chose the six prettiest chorus girls, had them dressed in frills and parasols, and had the top-hatted men sing the song now titled "Tell Me, Pretty Maiden." The sextet (actually a double sextet since the girls sang their replies to the men) stopped the show with its gentle charm and coquettish innocence. The ladies (each weighing 130 pounds and measuring 5'4" tall) entered wearing pink dresses, a black-ostrich-plumed hat, and sporting a pink parasol. The men wore grey frock coats with top hats. The musical exchange had the young men inquire "Tell me, pretty maiden, are there any more at home like you?"[1] The girls reply in the affirmative but point out that "their manners are perfection, and the opposite of mine." So the men eventually declare that they "won't care a pin for your sisters if you love me" and vow their love on bended knee.

How such a simple, straightforward little ditty swept London and then New York is curious. Leslie Stuart's music is a plodding minuet with few flourishes and consisting almost entirely of eighth notes. Yet there is something very catchy about the melody as one can hear two distinct voices in the music. The lyric by Stuart, Frank Clement, and Paul Rubens is rather formal at times ("pretty maiden … kind sir") but is not afraid of slang ("girlies" and "I won't care a pin"). One must also remember how unusual it was for the hit song not to be sung by the star but the chorus. None of the twelve performers even has a character name; they are simply "pretty maidens" and "kind sirs." But that didn't stop them charming the audience in a surprisingly restrained manner. The six ladies in the original London production were Lydia West, Blanche Carlow, Beatrice Grenville, Nancy Girling, Fanny Dango, and LilyMcIntyre. In the Broadway mounting, the six "English" girls were Agnes Wayburn, Vaughn Texsmith, Daisy Green, Marie L. Wilson, Margaret Walker, and Marjorie Relyea; they all married millionaires. "Tell Me, Pretty Maiden" was quickly picked up by musicians in hotels, dance halls, and concerts. The original 1899 London cast recorded several songs from *Florodora* in 1900, including a chorus rendition of "Tell Me, Pretty Maiden." A 1902 record featured Byron G. Harlan and Joe Belmont singing it with a girls' chorus. Other early discs were made by the Columbia Light Opera Company, the Victor Light Opera Company, and the Brunswick Light Opera Company. In the 1930 film *The Florodora Girl*, Marion Davies portrayed one of the chorines and the entire double sextet number was recreated on screen, as it was in the 1955 movie *The Girl in the Red Velvet Swing*.

Other notable songs from that season: "The Silver Star of Love," "I Want to Be a Military Man," "The Shade of the Palm" from *Florodora*; "Ma Blushin' Rosie (Ma Poste Sweet)," "I'm a Respectable Working Girl" from *Fiddle-Dee-Dee*; "Love Has Come from Lotus Land," "The Petals of the Plum Tree" from *San Toy*; "Push Me Along in My Pushcart," "Yankee Doodle Doings" from *The Governor's Son*.

1901–1902 SEASON

Musicals were playing longer on the Street and this season eleven new shows ran over the milestone 100 mark. Four of them came from London, none more popular than *A Chinese Honeymoon*, the first West End musical to run over 1,000 performances. Its Broadway run of 364 performances paled in comparison but still made a bundle. The other London shows that proved to be hits in New York were *Dolly Varden*, *The Toreador*, and *The Messenger Boy*. The longest-running American musical was again a Weber and Fields burlesque, this year titled *Hoity-Toity*. Close behind was the holiday family entertainment *The Sleeping Beauty and the Beast*. Among the other new American works to pass 100 performances were *The Little Duchess*, *The Liberty Belles*, *Foxy Grandpa*, *The Hall of Fame*, and *The Wild Rose*. The *Robin Hood* sequel *Maid Marian* was a disappointment though even it managed to stay on the boards for two months. Despite some impressive numbers, critics felt that the quality of the scores, particularly in American musicals, was lacking. At the same time, it was a great season for outstanding performances. Among the star turns that called for encores each night were those by Marie Cahill, Lillian Russell, Sam Bernard, Harry Conor, Anna Held, Weber and Fields, Eddie Foy, May Irwin, Francis Wilson, Lulu Glaser, Henry Clay Barnabee, Eva Tanguay, Frank Daniels, Fay Templeton, De Wolf Hopper, and Marie Dressler. Such a selection was a treasure trove indeed!

"Nancy Brown"
Music and lyric by Clifton Crawford
From *The Wild Rose* (1902)
Sung by Marie Cahill as Vera van Lahn

Interpolating outside songs into Broadway scores was still common practice around the turn of the century. Some stars had it written into their contracts that they could interpolate any song they choose. Songwriters who wrote the show's score were not happy with interpolations, particularly when the outside song turned out to be the hit of the show. Such was the case with *The Wild Rose* with a score by Ludwig Englander (music), Harry B. Smith, and George V. Hobart (lyrics). The star was Marie Cahill and, when she wasn't pleased with the songs written for her, insisted on a handful of interpolations, including "Nancy Brown." The outside song was written by Clifton Crawford, an actor who was currently appearing on Broadway in *Foxy Grandpa*. The press reported that on opening night Cahill had to do six encores of "Nancy Brown" before the audience would let her go on with the show. Englander and his lyricists were not pleased.

"Nancy Brown" is self-described as a "bucolic wail" by the songwriter.[2] It is a sly comedy number about a young man who has fallen in love with Nancy Brown who has told him her father is a millionaire in New York City and she usually dines at Delmonico's. After she disappears, her admirer goes to the big city and wanders the streets looking for

Song of the Season

her. He has also looked up the name "Brown" in the city directory (an early version of a phone book) but can find no millionaire by that name. The naiveté of the man keeps the song humorous rather than heart-wrenching, yet there is something charming about it as well. Crawford's music for the refrain is not a "wail" at all but a light-footed melody that suggests traveling. Since the lyric is about the young man, the song can be sung by a man or woman. Cahill's rendition on Broadway was followed by early records by Rose Beaumont, Harry MacDonald, J. W. Myers, and William M. Redmond. Sheet music sales of "Nancy Brown" were strong enough to rank #31 in 1902. But the song was long associated with Cahill who commissioned a new musical in 1903 and titled it *Nancy Brown*.

Other notable songs from that season: "The Little Gypsy Maid" from *The Wild Rose*; "Keep Off the Grass," "Everybody Is Awfully Good to Me" from *The Toreador*; "True Love Is Not for a Day," "Tell Me Again, Sweetheart" from *Maid Marian*; "Maisie," "The Mummies" from *The Messenger Boy*; "I Want to Be a Lidy," "Mr. Dooley," "The a la Girl" from *A Chinese Honeymoon*.

1902–1903 SEASON

The two most exciting new offerings this season were both American and they couldn't have been more different. The musical version of *The Wizard of Oz* strayed far from the original book but, since author L. Frank Baum wrote both the libretto and the lyrics, who was there to complain to? In this version Dorothy (Anna Laughlin) is blown away to Oz with her pet cow, the witch helps Dorothy get back to Kansas, and the role of the Lion is minor. The chief attraction of the show was the clowning of Fred Stone and Dave Montgomery as the Scarecrow and the Tin Man who were enough entertainment in themselves to let the musical run 306 performances. The other season highlight ran far less—only fifty-three performances—but it made quite an impact. *In Dahomey* was written and performed solely by African Americans, the first such show to play in a major Broadway venue. (*Clorindy,* a few seasons earlier, had played at a rooftop venue in the summer.) Sometimes listed simply as *Dahomey,* the musical was a satiric affair about a scheme to found a community in Africa with out-of-work Black Americans. The plan depends on the hustler Rareback Pinkerton (George Walker) bamboozling the moneyed Shylock Homestead (Bert Williams) into financing the venture. The comedy team of Walker and Williams had refined their antics in vaudeville and proved they were polished professionals who could carry an entire musical. The score, by *Clorindy*'s Will Marian Cook (music) and Paul Laurence Dunbar (lyrics), certainly helped. Williams' rendition of "I'm a Jonah Man" introduced one of the American theatre's great tragi-comics to Broadway.

Much of the rest of the season was business as usual. The Weber and Fields burlesque *Twirly-Whirly* was a first-class affair with Lillian Russell singing what would become one of her signature songs, "Come Down, Ma Evenin' Star." Blanche Ring stopped the British import *The Defender* when she interpolated "In the Good Old Summer Time." American musicals with profitable runs included *The Billionaire, Sally in Our Alley, The Sultan of Sulu, When Johnny Comes Marching Home, The Mocking Bird, Nancy Brown, The Prince of Pilsen, The Jewel of Asia,* and *The Runaways.* Although none ran as long as they did in London, the musical imports *The Emerald Isle, Mr. Bluebeard, A Country Girl,* and *The Silver Slipper* had healthy runs on Broadway. George M. Cohan turned another family vaudeville act into the musical *Running For Office* which had a smart and funny book but no outstanding songs. All the same, the show ran five weeks and the Cohan style of musical comedy was getting noticed.

"In the Good Old Summer Time"
Music by George Evans; lyric by Ren Shields
From *The Defender* (1902)
Sung by Blanche Ring as Millie Canvass

Still one of the most recognized songs in popular culture, "In the Good Old Summer Time" is a nostalgic little gem. Hearing it today conjures up a bucolic time of innocence and young love. It had the same effect on audiences in 1902. The less-known verses by lyricist Ren Shields list the various activities associated with summer: relaxing in a field of clover, swimming in a pool of water rather than going to school, stealing cherries from an orchard, and so on. The familiar refrain is about summertime love as it recalls "strolling through a shady lane/ With your baby mine" who, if she returns your affection, is your "tootsey-wootsey."[3] George Evans, who could not read or write music, came up with the simple but catchy melody, a bubbly waltz that is quickly learned and easy to repeat. That is why the number has always been a favorite sing-along piece. Also, its straightforward nature makes the song ideal for harmonizing variations and has remained a staple for barbershop quartets.

"In the Good Old Summer Time" had trouble getting attention. Evans and Shields were vacationing at the shore with singer Blanche Ring when the idea for the song was spurred when Shields noted, "There's nothing like the good old summer time." Evans liked how the sentence scanned and came up with a tune. He needed to hum it to Ring who could read music and she notated the melody. Once Shields completed the lyric, the two men plugged the song for a few publishers but the consensus was that a song about summer would not be performed on stage or sung at the piano during the rest of the year. Ring sang it in vaudeville, as did J. W. Myers and the team of Stewart and Gillen, but nothing happened. When Ring was cast in the British import *The Defender,* she insisted the song be interpolated into the lackluster score. During the Boston tryout, she sang it at the top of Act Three and so many encores were called for that by the time she was finished, Ring had turned the number into a sing-along piece with the audience. "In the Good Old Summer Time" was soon published and being performed by everyone from John Philip Sousa to the Andrews Sisters. It not only sold over one million copies of sheet music but its success led to a crop of songs about the seasons or the months of the year. Broadway heard the song again in *In Posterland* (1902), *In the Good Old Summertime* (1904), and *By the Beautiful Sea* (1954). On screen it was heard several times in the musical *In the Good Old Summertime* (1949) and in a dozen other films, including *Doughboys* (1930), *One Sunday Afternoon* (1933), *Babes in Toyland* (1934), and *Jeepers Creepers* (1939). Of the numerous recordings over the decades, a 1952 disc by Les Paul and Mary Ford is highly prized. Early records that made the charts were those by William Redmond, Harry MacDonough, and J. W. Myers. Noteworthy discs were later made by Uncle Dave Macon, Chet Atkins, Gordon MacRae, Ace O'Donnell, Connie Francis, Bing Crosby, Fabian, Judy Garland, Nat King Cole, and many vocal quartets and Dixieland bands.

Other notable songs from that season: "Pinky Panky Poo" from *The Defender*; "I'm a Jonah Man" from *In Dahomey*; "Under the Bamboo Tree" from *Sally in Our Alley*; "Come Down, Ma Evenin' Star," "The Leader of Vanity Fair" from *Twirly-Whirly*; "Sammy," "Hurrah for Baffin's Bay" from *The Wizard of Oz*; "The Heidelberg Stein Song," "The Message of the Violet" from *The Prince of Pilsen*; "My Own United States" from *When Johnny Comes Marching Home*.

1903–1904 SEASON

The big event on Broadway this season was the debut of *Babes in Toyland*, Victor Herbert's most popular musical and one of the very few pre-First World War pieces still produced. It ran a profitable 192 performances but that was only the beginning for the light operetta that would return to Broadway often and across the nation it would be a Christmastime favorite for decades. The season's other long-run hits were the Eddie Foy vehicle *Piff! Paff!! Pouf!!!*; the Weber and Fields burlesque *Whoop-Dee-Doo*, and *The Yankee Consul*, which made the young comic Raymond Hitchcock a star. Three British imports repeated their success in New York: newcomer Paul Rubens' first full score in *Three Little Maids*; *The Girl from Kay's*, which introduced the comic character Mr. Hogenheimer (Sam Bernard); and the holiday family offering *Mother Goose*. Among the new American works to turn a profit this season were *Babette*, *The Tenderfoot*, *Undercover*, and *Peggy from Paris*. Revivals and return engagements were in evidence with such productions as *A Chinese Honeymoon, Wang, The Prince of Pilsen, Erminie*, and *The Wizard of Oz*. Of the thirty-two musicals which opened that season, only eight of them ran over 100 performances. The Panic of 1903 may have made money tight but it was an infamous fire in Chicago's Iroquois Theatre that discouraged playgoing for a while. The fire claimed hundreds of lives and New Yorkers knew that some Broadway theatres were just as dangerous. New fire codes and a crackdown on venues violating codes were encouraging but patrons were still wary.

"Toyland"
Music by Victor Herbert; lyric by Glen MacDonough
From *Babes in Toyland* (1903)
Sung by Bessie Wynn as Tom Tom, and the male chorus

While one can argue that Victor Herbert's *Naughty Marietta* or *The Red Mill* has a richer score, there is little doubt that *Babes in Toyland* is his most popular and beloved work. It has returned to the Street on four occasions and has been filmed for the big or small screen many times. Add to that regional and international productions and the numbers are impressive. But the operetta's real legacy is the annual return of the songs "Toyland" and "March of the Toys" each holiday season. Ironically, *Babes in Toyland* was never developed as a Christmas attraction (it opened on Broadway in October of 1903) and neither song makes a reference to Christmas. But both songs take one back to childhood and the nostalgia certainly has a holiday-like tone. Glen MacDonough wrote the *Babes in Toyland* libretto about two children who escape from a wicked uncle and find themselves on an enchanted island where Mother Goose lives with various fairy tale and nursery rhyme characters. The plot is an excuse for a series of delightful musical numbers, perhaps the lullaby "Toyland" being the most endearing and enduring.

Song of the Season

MacDonough's lyric for the verse is written from an adult point of view. If fact, the song begins as a memory ballad about childhood rather than a place filled with toys. The singer has "often ponder[ed] on the years/ That roll so swiftly by" and recalls "the best of all … the land your childhood knew."[4] Herbert's music for this section is stately and grand, getting a bit too close to grand opera. But the refrain relaxes and the notes tumble forth in a bewitching way. The music is soothing, as expected in a lullaby, yet keeps moving forward with very few rests. And the lyric is economically simple with no unnecessary words and few adjectives. "Toyland!" is described as "Little girl and boy land," a happy place "while you dwell within it." But the lyric ends with the somber line "Once you pass its borders, you can ne'er return again." The nostalgic number was sung in the original *Babes in Toyland* by Bessie Wynn, playing the boy Tom Tom, and the male chorus. Wynn reprised the song in the 1905 revival, Marcella Swanson sang it in the 1929 production, and Ruth Gillette in the 1930 revival.

The first recordings of "Toyland" were medleys of songs from the show played by the Victor Light Opera Company and a vocal by Corinne Morgan with the Haydn Quartet. Hundreds of discs followed, among them Jo Stafford, Bob Kames, Perry Como, Johnny Mathis, Risë Stevens, Don McLean, Maureen McGovern, KT Sullivan, Lorrie Morgan, Karen Mason, Charles Xavier, Natasha Stoll, Nina Miller, and Carolyn Lee Jones. Because it is associated with Christmas, the lullaby appears on dozens of holiday albums. "Toyland" was sung in the screen versions of *Babes in Toyland,* including Virginia Karns and the chorus in the 1934 *March of the Wooden Soldiers;* by Dennis Day and chorus in the 1955 television adaptation; by Tommy Sands, Annette Funicello, the children, and the singing trees in the 1961 movie version; by Drew Barrymore (dubbed by Linda Harmon) and the chorus in the 1986 TV version; and by Charles Nelson Reilly in the 1997 animated movie. "Toyland" can be heard in other films as well as many televisions specials.

Other notable songs from that season: "March of the Toys," "I Can't Do the Sum," "Don't Cry, Bo-Peep," "Slumber Deep" from *Babes in Toyland*; "Bedelia" from *The Jersey Lily*; "I'm on the Water Wagon Now" from *The Office Boy*; "My Alamo Love" from *The Tenderfoot*; "My San Domingo Maid" from *The Yankee Consul*; "Letters I Write All Day" from *Babette*; "She Was a Miller's Daughter" from *Three Little Maids.*

1904–1905 SEASON

Three important arrivals this season would eventually make quite an impact on Broadway but two were little noticed at the time. A great deal of attention was placed on the opening of the Hippodrome, the largest theatre in the history of New York City. Over the next thirty-four years, the 6,000-seat venue would house circuses, aquatic shows, grand opera, ballet, and horse races, but it opened with a "traditional" Broadway musical, *A Yankee Circus on Mars*. There was a plot but it was overshadowed by the horses diving into a tank of water, a ballet troupe of 200, a Civil War battle scene, circus acts, an airship from Mars, and some elephants pulling over-sized automobiles across the vast stage. There were songs but no one could distinguish the melodies no less the lyrics. It all seemed like the vision of a mad man but audiences came for 276 performances. They came for only forty-one performances of the quieter musical *Mr. Wiz of Wickham*, a British import that caused little commotion. For its New York version, eleven songs were written by young composer Jerome Kern. He would not remain unnoticed for long. Another modest run—fifty-seven performances—was earned by the new musical *Lady Teazle*. A chorus line of forty-eight beautiful girls helped keep the show on the boards but, more importantly, history relates that it was the first Broadway production produced solely by the Shubert Brothers. Over the next forty-two years, the brothers would produce over 500 shows and form an empire that included thirty-one theatres across America.

Nine new musicals this season ran over 100 performances (four of them ran twice that) but the show that caused the most excitement was George M. Cohan's *Little Johnny Jones*, the first full-fledged hit by the feisty composer-lyricist-librettist-director-actor. Weber and Fields continued their run of popular musical burlesques with *Higgledy-Piggledy* but it was to be their last. Joe Weber and Lew Fields had not been on speaking terms for over a year but managed to reunite for this show and some scattered projects for a few more years. Victor Herbert had another success with *It Happened in Nordland*; at 254 performances, it was one of his biggest hits. Running even longer was the musical comedy *Fantana* which boasted expert clowning by Jefferson De Angelis, a tuneful score, and promising debuts by Julia Sanderson and Douglas Fairbanks. London sent over the profitable *Sergeant Bru, The School Girl*, and *Humpty Dumpty*, a pantomime version of an old (1868!) American extravaganza.

"Give My Regards to Broadway"
Music and lyric by George M. Cohan
From *Little Johnny Jones* (1904)
Sung by George M. Cohan as Johnny Jones, and chorus

One of the most iconic musical numbers in early American theatre is the scene from *Little Johnny Jones* which introduced the song "Give My Regards to Broadway." In the second act, the American jockey Johnny Jones (George M. Cohan) has been wrongfully accused of "throwing" the Derby. He must remain in Britain to face the charges but he goes to the pier at Southampton to bid farewell to his New York City friends, asking in song to remember him to his beloved Manhattan. The ship departs, the lights dim, and Johnny is left alone on the pier watching the boat sail off into the distance. Suddenly a skyrocket is fired from the ship, the signal that evidence has been found on the boat that clears Johnny's name. The jubilant Johnny explodes into a high-kicking reprise of the song. In the 1929 screen version of *Little Johnny Jones*, the song was sung by Eddie Buzzell and Dan Dailey performed it in *Give My Regards to Broadway* (1948). The whole Southampton scene was accurately recreated in the 1942 Cohan film-bio *Yankee Doodle Dandy* with James Cagney as Johnny. The scene was also reprised on Broadway by Joel Grey in the musical *George M!* (1968) and by Donny Osmond in the too-brief 1982 revival of *Little Johnny Jones*.

Cohan was one of the first songwriters to use ragtime elements in his theatre songs. To "rag" notes in the melody was to place the emphasis on unexpected notes. This kind of syncopation broke up the regularly accented pattern and made for wonderful surprises. Early African American musicians developed the ragtime structure just as lyricists were forced to "rag" words as well. Often two syllable-words had the accent on the unexpected syllable. A ragtime song, as opposed to a ragtime composition, is doubly interesting and a break from the European-based chromatics Americans were used to. Cohan loathed European waltzes and similar patterns just as he refused to use poetic lyrics. No "thou" or "canst" in his songs; he preferred such adjectives as "swell" and "grand." "Give My Regards to Broadway" is not the slangiest of his songs but the informality is there. The verse is a patter section with a "tempo di marcia" that keeps it moving. Johnny describes the parting of two Americans overseas, one of whom is returning to the States. With "a tear-dimmed eye they say goodbye" then the "ship strikes out."[5] The refrain is a restrained march, never getting too fast because Cohan insisted that the lyrics be clearly heard. In addition to Johnny's instructions to "give my regards to Broadway" and "Herald Square," he also sends regards to the "gang at Forty-Second Street" and says "I'll be there ere long." The music relies on eighth and quarter notes so that the words are spit out rather than run together. And Cohan manages to match short and long vowels so the pattern is interrupted in an interesting way. While he insisted that his songs should be simple enough to be sung by the crowd, sometimes Cohan could be surprisingly sophisticated. It is believed that Billy Murray was the first to record "Give My Regards to Broadway" in 1905 (Cohan himself did not record it until 1911) followed by memorable discs by Al Jolson, Ella Logan, Jane Morgan, Maurice Chevalier, Bing Crosby, Jimmy Roselli, Russ Conway, Judy Garland, Terry Snyder, Barrel Fingers Barry, Frankie Vaughan, Barry Manilow, Robin Spielberg, and Patti LuPone. It can also be heard on the soundtracks for over 100 movies.

Other notable songs from that season: "Yankee Doodle Boy," "Life's a Funny Proposition After All" from *Little Johnny Jones*; "Under the Old Oak Tree" from *The Rogers Brothers in Paris*; "Absinthe Frappé" from *It Happened in Nordland*; "My Irish Molly-O" from *Sergeant Brue*; "A Great Big Girl Like Me" from *Higgledy-Piggledy*; "Hi-Ko, Hi-Ko" from *The Sho-Gun*; "Tammany" from *Fantana*.

1905–1906 SEASON

In the busiest season in years, Broadway saw fifty-six musical productions open on the Street, only two of which were revivals. A dozen of the new works managed to run over ninety performances. The Hippodrome spectacular A *Society Circus* ran an astounding 596 times. (Such large numbers were possible because the venue offered two showings most days.) Even better than the quantity of shows and the money they earned was the arrival of a handful of excellent musicals boasting coherent librettos, superior scores, and strong performances. George M. Cohan struck gold twice with two hits: *45 Minutes from Broadway* and *George Washington, Jr.* He appeared in the latter but the former ran a profitable ninety performances without him on stage. Victor Herbert was represented by three musicals this season: *Miss Dolly Dollars*, a routine affair that ran thanks to Lulu Glaser; *Wonderland*, a disappointing sequel of sorts to *Babes in Toyland*; and *Mlle. Modiste,* which remains a landmark musical for its integration of song, story, and character. It also boasted one of Herbert's best scores. Weber and Fields without Weber didn't seem to hurt *Twiddle-Twaddle*, a Fields-only burlesque that amused audiences 159 times. Of the four London imports, the most successful was *The Earl and the Girl* with several interpolated American songs. Jerome Kern's "How'd You Like to Spoon with Me?" was not only the hit of the show but it was his first commercially successful song. Kern had written it some years before and tried to get it done on stage but producers told him it was too "vulgar" to sell.

Even musicals that were not runaway hits had much to offer. Eva Tanguay stopped *The Sambo Girl* each night with her rendition of the feisty "I Don't Care." She not only sang it for the rest of her career but Tanguay became known as the "I Don't Care Girl." The African American artists behind *In Dahomey* returned to Broadway with *Abyssinia*. The comic repartee of George Walker and Bert Williams was better than ever and critics declared the libretto was one of the best of the season. Unfortunately, no memorable songs were heard and the musical lasted only a month. That was as long as *The Freelance* ran, a disappointing entry by composer John Philip Sousa. It was his first Broadway musical in six years; he would not return for another seven years. This season, there were notable star turns by Edna May in *The Catch of the Season* (where she sang three interpolated Kern songs), De Wolf Hopper in *Happyland*, Joseph Cawthorn in *Fritz in Tammany Hall*, Marie Cahill in *Moonshine*, and a little-known juggling comic billed W. C. Fields who ran off with the accolades in the musical *The Ham Tree*.

"You're a Grand Old Flag"
Music and lyric by George M. Cohan
From *George Washington, Jr.* (1906)
Sung by George M. Cohan as George Belgrave, and company

Song of the Season

Along with "Over There," "You're a Grand Old Flag" has secured George M. Cohan's reputation as our most patriotic songwriter. Yet as unwavering as he was in his love for his country, Cohan was not sentimental. These two songs are as brash, slangy even, as is much of his work. Sentiment is for operettas; his musicals prefer ragtime and ungrammatical street talk. When Cohan first made a splash on Broadway, audiences immediately took to his catchy melodies and conversational lyrics. But the critics dismissed his songs as simple tunes with unpoetic words. Cohan argued that his characters spoke with an everyday, common-folk language; so when they broke into song, the same kind of familiarity was there. But Cohan went a bit too far when he and the cast of *George Washington, Jr.* sang "You're a Grand Old Rag." He had heard a veteran of the Spanish American War refer affectionately to the US flag as an "old rag."[6] After opening night, complaints came from different patriotic organizations who were shocked at the disrespect for Old Glory. They even got President Theodore Roosevelt to send a disapproving memo from the White House. Cohan quickly changed the song to "You're a Grand Old Flag" and it has been sung that way ever since.

Although Cohan prefers brusk masculine rhymes, which are best for enunciating words, there are some interesting feminine rhymes in the verse. The lyric describes a "feeling comes a-stealing" and a sound that "sets my brain a-reeling" when patriotic music is played. The slangy couplet "Any tune like Yankee Doodle/Simply sets me off my noodle" is pure Cohan. The music for the verse is rapid, as befits a patter song. Then it slows down considerably in the famous refrain, although it is still a steady march tempo. The song's title phrase is joined by such sentiments as the flag being "the emblem of/ The land I love" and the "home of the free and the brave." There is the slightest hint of ragtime in the refrain, especially in the brief pauses in unexpected places: "you're a (beat) high-flying flag ... under (beat) red, white and blue." Interestingly, Cohan makes reference to the colonial song "Yankee Doodle" and quotes the first line of the Scottish favorite "Auld Lang Syne" ("Should old acquaintance be forgot") in the song. Such references are used to support the song's fervent patriotism. In *George Washington, Jr.*, Cohan defies his British-loving father by refusing to wed an aristocratic "lady" and pursues a "Yankee" gal, winning her hand and even changing his father's ways. So "You're a Grand Old Flag" is more than a patriotic anthem but a fight song full of grit. No wonder the melody has been used by sports teams as their own fight song.

The song quickly caught on, selling over a million copies of sheet music and picked up by marching bands. Billy Murray made an early recording as "You're a Grand Old Rag," but subsequent recording used the revised title, including those by the American Quartet, Dick Robertson and the Country Quartet, Bing Crosby, Fred Waring and the Pennsylvanians, the Mormon Tabernacle Choir, Willie Tyler Band, BeBe Winans, Joel Mabus, Ken Beebe, The Left Bank Bearcats, The Banjo Barons, Sam Vaughn, and David Phillips. James Cagney and the company sang it in the film *Yankee Doodle Dandy* (1942) and the number was heard in *Reds* (1981), *Born on the Fourth of July* (1989), *Primary*

Colors (1998), and several other movies. On Broadway, the song was performed by Joel Grey and company in *George M!* (1968) and by the cast of *Tintypes* (1980).

Other notable songs from that season: "I Was Born in Virginia" from *George Washington, Jr.*; "Forty-five Minutes from Broadway," "Mary's a Grand Old Name," "So Long, Mary," "I Want to Be a Popular Millionaire" from *Forty-five Minutes from Broadway*; "I Don't Care" from *The Sambo Girl*; "Kiss Me, Again," "The Mascot of the Troop," "I Want What I Want When I Want It" from *Mlle. Modiste*; "How'd You Like to Spoon with Me?" from *The Earl and the Girl*; "Good-bye, Sweet Old Manhattan Isle" from *The Ham Tree*; "Waltz Me Around, Willie" from *His Honor, the Mayor*.

Song of the Season

1906–1907 SEASON

It rarely seems to happen but this season's best musical was also its most popular. Victor Herbert's *The Red Mill* ran 318 performances, even more than the Hippodrome spectacle *Pioneer Days* (288 performances). Even better, *The Red Mill* has an amusing libretto, a superior score, and is still produced today by operetta companies. That cannot be said for any of the other new musicals. The Anna Held vehicle *The Parisian Model* and the Sam Bernard vehicle *The Rich Mr. Hoggenheimer* each fell short of 200 performances but enjoyed a healthy box office. Weber and Fields, now on their own, each crossed over the 100-performance milestone. Fields' *About Town* and Weber's *Dream City* demonstrated that there were enough fans to support each comic. Other profitable American shows included *The Tourists, Fascinating Flora*, and *The White Hen*. The last was not to be confused with *The Spring Chicken*, a British import that found an audience for 115 showings. Other successful London imports included *The Little Cherub, My Lady's Maid, The Belle of Mayfair, Blue Moon*, and *The Orchid*. The season's most notorious musical success was *Mamzelle Champagne*, a summer frolic staged at the Madison Square Garden Roof. On the opening night performance on June 25, the fashionable crowd included Pittsburgh millionaire Harry Thaw, his wife Evelyn Nesbit Thaw (a former Florodora Girl), and the famed architect Stanford White, who had been her lover. During the performance, Thaw fired three pistol shots into White, killing him on the spot. Morbid curiosity turned *Mamzelle Champagne* into a hit. Patrons lined up trying to get into the subsequent sixty performances and tickets to sit at White's table were sold at a premium.

"The Streets of New York"
("In Old New York")
Music by Victor Herbert; lyric by Henry Blossom
From *The Red Mill* (1906)
Sung by Fred Stone as Con Kidder, and
David Montgomery as Kid Connor, and chorus

Fred Stone and David Montgomery, the stars of *The Wizard of Oz* three years earlier, were featured in *The Red Mill* and were no small part of its success. They played penniless Americans Con Kidder and Kid Connor stranded in the Dutch port city of Katwyk-ann-Zee. In between donning disguises to escape creditors, the two help the daughter of the burgomaster escape an arranged marriage and wed her sea captain sweetheart. Henry Blossom wrote the clever libretto and the lyrics for Herbert's music and the score is a delightful mix of operetta arias and musical comedy songs. Con and Kid sang the praises of their hometown in "The Streets of New York" and before they were finished the audience was singing along. Also known as "In Old New York," the waltz favorite is one of the most recognized American tunes and has been used in dozens of movies to place the action in old-time New York City. It can also be heard on carousels, at skating rinks, ball games, parades, and summer band concerts. "The Streets of New York" just might be Herbert's most known melody. The lyric for the familiar refrain is uncluttered and straightforward. The praise for "old New York" is often directed to the women who are "sweet and fair and on the square" and rate higher than those from "gay Paree, London or in Cork."[7] The song even boasts "Lucky's the earl that can marry a girl/From Fifth Avenue New York." Just as Herbert kept the music within a narrow range so it could be sung by two comic actors with limited vocal abilities, Blossom breaks away from formal lyrics and gets a bit coarse, appropriate for comic characters. Con and Kid call the New York females a "peach crop" and dub them "queens." The lyric has fun with the alliteration of "maids of Manhattan for mine" and uses internal rhymes throughout. One of the earliest recordings of "The Streets of New York" was made by the Victor Light Opera Company and Herbert himself conducted the orchestra on a disc in 1909. Many orchestral and choral recordings followed. In the popular 1945 Broadway revival of *The Red Mill*, the song was sung by Eddie Foy, Jr., and Michael O'Shea.

Other notable songs from that season: "Moonbeams," "The Isle of Our Dreams," "Because You're You," "Everyday Is Ladies' Day to Me" from *The Red Mill*; "It's Delightful to Be Married," "I Just Can't Make My Eyes Behave" from *The Parisian Model*; "He Goes to Church on Sunday" from *The Orchid*.

Song of the Season

1907–1908 SEASON

While there were a good number of both British and American successes this season, they were overshadowed by the arrival of the Viennese operetta *The Merry Widow*. Not since *H.M.S. Pinafore* in 1879 had a musical caused such a commotion. There were Merry Widow hats, dresses, cigarettes, shoes, cocktails, and even corsets. And this was not just a passing fad. *The Merry Widow* has remained one of the most oft-produced musical works by both operetta and opera companies. The other fifty-four new works from this season have very rarely been heard of again. A few songs this season have survived, most memorably some numbers from *The Merry Widow* and "The Glow-Worm" and "Harrigan." This last was by George M. Cohan who wrote no less than four productions this season (and acted in two of them). His earlier *Running for Office* was revised and returned as *The Honeymooners*, finding an audience for seventy-two performances. His *The Talk of New York* and *The Yankee Prince* each ran twice as long but his *Fifty Miles from Boston* (which introduced "Harrigan") ran only a month. After *The Merry Widow*, the Hippodrome spectacular *The Auto Race* chalked up the most performances: 312. But not far behind was the British import *The Girl Behind the Counter* which Lew Fields revamped and starred in. The hit song from the show didn't come from London but was the interpolated "The Glow-Worm." Fields ex-partner Joe Weber had a modest success with *Hip! Hip! Hooray!* but a solid hit with *The Merry Widow Burlesque* which he produced and had on the boards only nine weeks after the Viennese operetta opened on the Street. Also from Vienna was the Oscar Straus operetta *A Waltz Dream* which ran over three months. Other imports to turn a profit this season included the London hits *Miss Hook of Holland*, *Tom Jones*, and *The Dairymaids*, which included six new songs by Jerome Kern.

If *The Merry Widow* and *A Waltz Dream* foreshadowed an era of European operettas on Broadway, Florenz Ziegfeld was ushering in a period of ornate musical revues with his *Follies of 1907*. Ziegfeld's wife Anna Held gave him the idea for a Parisian-like entertainment based on the Folies Bergere. This first edition was a relatively modest affair but it did feature some stars and a chorus of fifty beautiful girls. What distinguished the show from other expensive revues was the good taste Ziegfeld showed in everything from the sets and costumes to the comic sketches and dance numbers. Audiences flocked to this first *Follies* for seventy performances then Ziegfeld took it on the road, earning enough money to make sure his next edition was even more stunning. Later adding his name to the title, Ziegfeld presented his annual *Follies* for the next twenty-five years.

"I Love You So"
("The Merry Widow Waltz")
Music by Franz Lehár; English lyric by Adrian Ross
From *The Merry Widow* (1907)
Sung by Ethel Jackson as Sonia, and Donald Brian as Prince Danilo

The operetta *The Merry Widow* (*Die Lustige Witwe*) opened in Vienna in December of 1905. The music was by Franz Lehár and the German libretto and lyrics by Viktor Léon and Leo Stein who based it on a little-known French play by Henri Meilhac. *The Merry Widow* was an immediate success in Austria and productions in Berlin, Budapest, and London quickly followed. When the piece opened in New York City in October of 1907, it had an English book by Basil Hood (uncredited) and lyrics by Adrian Ross. The operetta was not a piece set in a distant time and place. The action occurs in present-day Paris where Prince Danilo is persuaded by the ministers of the bankrupt little nation of Pontevedro to woo and wed the wealthy young widow Sonia Sadoya and save his homeland. But Danilo and Sonia were once in love and parted when she married for money. It takes some time (and some beautiful music) before the couple is reconciled for a happy ending. The famous waltz from the operetta is heard in bits and pieces throughout the evening but "I Love You So" is not given a lyric until Danilo and Sonia sing it as a duet at the climax of the operetta. By that time the audience has been totally seduced by what many consider the finest waltz ever written.

There are so many different translations of the lyric that it seems the waltz song is never sung the same way twice. Adrian Ross's lyric, as heard in the first New York production, speaks of "love that hovers over lovers" and states that "Every touch of fingers tells me what I know ... it's true, you love me so."[8] Like many a translated lyric, there is a strained effort to sound poetic and, yet, somewhat conversational. But there is no getting around the beating heart, the clasping fingers, and the lips that "say no word." This is pure European operetta gushing. But no matter the language, the purple words are acceptable because of Lehár's music. The waltzes from the Strauss family are vigorous with the accent often placed heavily on the first of the three counts. Lehár diminishes this effect by giving the first note more counts and smoothing out the 1–2–3 pattern. The result is a waltz that never pounds but rather glides or sweeps along. (Lehár's signature is "allegretto moderato;" if one speeds up the tempo for "The Merry Widow Waltz," the whole thing falls apart.) This softer, more delicate, sound was very influential. Subsequent waltzes, particularly for theatre pieces, aimed for such a softly swaying effect. It is as if Lehár seduced the ears of the world.

In the first English-language production of *The Merry Widow* in London in 1907, the famous waltz was sung by Lily Elsie (Sonia) and Joseph Coyne (Danilo). The roles were played by Ethel Jackson and Donald Brian in the original Broadway production that same year. There have been over twenty Broadway revivals of the operetta and over twenty film and television adaptations in different languages. In the two Hollywood versions, Jeanette MacDonald and Maurice Chevalier sang the duet in the 1934 movie and Lana Turner (dubbed by Trudy Erwin) and Fernando Lamas performed it in the 1952 remake. *The Merry Widow* is one of the most oft-recorded operettas and there are plenty of duet versions and solo renditions of "I Love You So" in over thirty languages. The song has been covered by both opera and theatre artists, and it is a rare orchestra that has not made an instrumental version of the waltz.

Other notable songs from that season: "Maxim's (Girls! Girls! Girls!)," "Vilja," "Love in My Heart" from *The Merry Widow*; "The Glow-Worm" from *The Girl Behind the Counter*; "Harrigan" from *Fifty Miles from Boston*; "When a Fella's on the Level with a Girl That's on the Square" from *The Talk of New York*; "Yip-I-Addy-I-Ay" from *The Merry Widow Burlesque*; "Budweiser's a Friend of Mine" from *Follies of 1907*.

1908–1909 SEASON

Florenz Ziegfeld's idea of a classy revue was catching on. The *Follies of 1908* ran twice as long as the previous season's revue. Also, during the subsequent tour, the song "Shine On, Harvest Moon" was interpolated into the score and stopped the show each night. The other song standard introduced this season was "Cuddle Up a Little Closer, Lovey Mine" from *Three Twins*, the Broadway debut of the songwriting team of Karl Hoschna (music) and Otto Harbach (lyrics). The newcomers saw their first musical run 289 performances, the season's longest run after the Hippodrome spectacle *Sporting Days*. Other American works with long runs included Lew Fields' *The Midnight Sons* with Blanche Ring introducing "I've Got Rings on My Fingers (And Bells on My Toes)," the Elsie Janis college musical *The Fair Co-Ed*, the Can-Can-dancing *The Queen of the Moulin Rouge*, the Anna Held vehicle *Miss Innocence*, the Marie Cahill vehicle *The Boys and Betty*, composer Reginald De Koven's last success *The Beauty Spot*, and Victor Herbert's family entertainment *Little Nemo*. Herbert had two other entries this season—*Algeria* and *The Prima Donna*—but both had disappointing runs. George M. Cohan also had two offerings: the revue *Cohan and Harris Minstrels*, which failed to catch on, and *The American Idea*, which had a profitable run of sixty-four performances. *Havana* was the most successful British import (236 performances) followed by *Kitty Grey* and *The Girls of Gottenberg* which managed modest runs. There was one Viennese musical this season, *Mlle. Mischief*, which hoped to enthuse New Yorkers as *The Merry Widow* had the previous season. The operetta found an audience for three months on the Street, mostly on account of a vivacious star turn by Lulu Glaser.

"Shine On, Harvest Moon"
Music and lyric by Nora Bayes and Jack Norworth
From *Follies of 1908* (1908)
Sung by Nora Bayes

With hundreds of "moon" songs on the market, it is a challenge to come up with something original, particularly in the lyric. "Shine On, Harvest Moon" is unique enough to stand out and has remained a song standard over the last century. The premise is familiar: two sweethearts in a bucolic setting as the autumn evening approaches. But there is no moon. She is afraid of the dark and wants to go home; he pleads with the moon to come out and shine so that she'll stay and "spoon" with him. And not just any moon. He pleads for the harvest moon, the exceptionally bright moon that appears close to the time of the autumn equinox. It is an exceptionally theatrical lyric when both verse and refrain are sung. But over time the verse has been heard less and less and the song is simply about wanting moonlight for romance. The lyric is in casual shorthand, dropping articles and prepositions to get right to the point. The music is a bluesy patter composed mostly of eighth and quarter notes so that it moves along. The music for the famous refrain moves more slowly but never drags. There is a wailing quality to some of the long notes, reminding us that this is some kind of torch song. The boy sings "I ain't had no lovin'/ Since April, January, June or July."[9] For a romantic ballad, "Shine On, Harvest Moon" has a world-weary quality to it. This comes out in some of the solo recordings in which both verse and refrain are sung. When picked up by barbershop quartets or other choral ensembles, the tempo is often increased and that torchy feeling is gone.

The true authorship of the song has been a matter of conjecture for decades. We know for sure the number was interpolated into the tour of the *Follies of 1908* where it was sung by Nora Bayes. The sheet music lists Bayes and her recent husband (she had five) Jack Norworth as the songwriters. Norworth's only other notable music credit is the lyric for the standard "Take Me Out to the Ball Game" that same year; Bayes has no other songwriting credit. This raises the question of how such an inexperienced couple could write such a sophisticated popular song. During this time, songs were often sold outright to a performer who could be credited as the songwriter and collect the royalties. Bayes was a very popular vaudeville and Broadway performer and it is possible she bought "Shine On, Harvest Moon" and put her new husband's name with hers on the sheet music. A handful of other songwriters are possible authors of the song but one stands out. Dave Stamper contributed songs to over twenty editions of the *Ziegfeld Follies*, most memorably "Throw Me a Kiss" for Mary Eaton to sing in the *Ziegfeld Follies of 1922*. He was also Bayes' pianist from 1903 to 1908 (the year "Shine On, Harvest Moon" was published). Comic singer Eddie Cantor, many years later, wrote that it was common knowledge backstage that Stamper wrote the song. It is unlikely that the matter will ever be satisfactorily resolved.

Bayes and Norworth divorced in 1913 but each continued to sing "Shine On, Harvest Moon" as their signature song for many years after. The sheet music and piano player rolls sold in the many thousands. The first known recording of the song was in 1909 by Harry MacDonough and "Miss Walton" which climbed the charts. Other early successful discs include those by Billy Murray and Ada Jones, Frank Stanley and Henry Burr, Bob Roberts, and Arthur Pryor. Some of the many later recordings of note were those by Vernon Dalhart, Ethel Waters, Count Basie, Vera Lynn, the Ink Spots, the Boswell Sisters, Kate Smith, Vaughn Monroe, the Chordettes, the Four Aces, Teresa Brewer, Rosemary Clooney and Bing Crosby, the Isley Brothers, the Platters, Barbara Cook and Michael Feinstein, Liza Minnelli, Ken Beebe, and Christine Hitt. "Shine On, Harvest Moon" has been heard on Broadway on several occasions. Later in the 1908–09 season, Lillian Lorraine interpolated it into the musical *Miss Innocence*, the cast sang it in *Cochran's 1931 Revue*, and Ruth Etting revived it in the 1931 *Ziegfeld Follies*. In the West End, it was sung by the cast of the 1910 revue *Hullo, London!* The song has been used in many Hollywood movies. It was heard (and served as the title) for a 1932 Dave Fleischer cartoon, a 1938 Roy Rogers western, and a 1944 biographical film about Bayes with Ann Sheridan (dubbed by Lynn Martin) and Dennis Morgan performing it. Among the many other films where it can be heard: *Two against the World* (1936),

The Great Ziegfeld (1936), *The Flying Deuces* (1939), *Rose of Washington Square* (1939), *A Tree Grows in Brooklyn* (1945), *Look for the Silver Lining* (1949), *The Eddy Duchin Story* (1956), *Pennies from Heaven* (1978), *The Johnsons* (1992), *Transatlantic Coffee* (2012), and *Their Finest* (2016).

Other notable songs from that season: "Cuddle Up a Little Closer, Lovey Mine," "The Yama Yama Man" from *Three Twins*; "Rose of the World," "Twilight in Barakeesh" from *Algeria*; "I Wonder What's the Matter with My Eyes" from *Miss Innocence*; "I've Got Rings on My Fingers (And Bells on My Toes)" from *The Midnight Sons*; "Too Long from Long Acre Square" from *The American Idea*.

Song of the Season

1909–1910 SEASON

For the second season in a row, Nora Bayes got to introduce the best "new" song heard on Broadway. But "Has Anyone Here Seen Kelly?" had already become popular in Great Britain before Broadway heard an Americanized version of it in the musical *The Jolly Bachelors*. The numbers were down all across the board this season. Only thirty-three new, revived or returning musicals opened on Broadway. Of those, only seven ran past the magic 100-performance mark. Also disappointing was the number of songwriters, either established or recently promising, whose shows failed to run. Otto Harbach and Karl Hoschna, who had struck gold with *Three Twins* last season, had to settle for forty performances for their new work *Bright Eyes*. The ever-busy Victor Herbert had two offerings: *The Rose of Algeria* closed after forty showings and the well-received *Old Dutch* turned a modest profit running eleven weeks. George M. Cohan tried the revue format again with *Cohan and Harris Minstrels* but in two weeks it was gone. Cohan's musical comedy *The Man Who Owns Broadway* did much better with 128 performances. Audience favorite De Wolf Hopper couldn't keep *A Matinee Idol* on the boards for more than two months. Some of the African American talents who had brought *Clorindy* to Broadway could only keep *Mr. Lode of Koal* running for five weeks even though serio-comic Bert Williams was deemed better than ever. Even the opulent, starry *Ziegfeld Follies of 1909* closed after sixty-four performances then set out on a more lucrative tour. (For the first time, Ziegfeld added his name to the revue's title.) Disappointments were not limited to American works. *The King of Cadonia* had run a year in London only to close after two weeks on Broadway. Similarly, *The Belle of Brittany* ran 147 times in London but only half that in New York.

Once again it was the Hippodrome spectacular, this year titled *A Trip to Japan*, that chalked up the longest run: 447 performances. Also making a clear profit were three American "girl" musicals: *The Yankee Girl*, *The Motor Girl*, and *The Girl and the Wizard*. *The Old Town* ran fourteen weeks thanks to the clowning of Fred Stone and Dave Montgomery; Nora Bayes left the *Follies* to headline in the already-mentioned *The Jolly Bachelors* and kept it on the boards for 165 performances; and Marie Dressler helped *Tillie's Nightmare* run eight weeks, in large part because of her powerful rendition of "Heaven Will Protect the Working Girl." Three imports from Europe enjoyed long and profitable runs on Broadway this season. *The Dollar Princess* and *The Arcadians* didn't run as long as they had in London but still had a good showing. Even more popular was Oscar Straus' Viennese operetta *The Chocolate Soldier* which played 296 performances. It is the only musical from this season that is still regularly revived by opera and operetta groups.

"Has Anyone Here Seen Kelly?"
Music and lyric by C. W. Murphy, Will Letters;
revised lyric by William McKenna
From *The Jolly Bachelors* (1910)
Sung by Nora Bayes as Astarita Vandergould

In 1908, British songwriters C. W. Murphy and Will Letters wrote a song titled "Kelly from the Isle of Man" about an Irish couple who visit England and get separated in busy London. She is left wandering the streets and asking everyone if they have seen her dear Kelly. The song was introduced in a British music hall by singer Florrie Ford and quickly caught on. Broadway comic and producer Lew Fields heard the catchy number when he was visiting London, bought the American rights, and gave it to Norah Bayes to sing in his musical comedy *The Jolly Bachelors*. But, because of its many Irish and British references (Mona's Isle, Piccadilly, Isle of Man, old Antonio), it did not fit into the show's very Broadway score and New Yorkers were not impressed. With waning box office receipts, Fields closed *The Jolly Bachelors* after nine weeks. He then went to a music publisher to get the song put on sheet music but "Kelly from the Isle of Man" was deemed too foreign even for the Irish-American market. So the publisher gave the number to William McKenna to write a more American lyric. Fields was so pleased with the new version, titled "Has Anyone Here Seen Kelly?," that he reopened *The Jolly Bachelors*, Bayes sang it to great acclaim, and the show ran an additional three months.

The Broadway version of "Has Anyone Here Seen Kelly" is a fine example of an Irish-American song. It tells a story, offers an enigmatic character (did Kelly run off and leave his sweetheart or just get lost?), and has a very catchy refrain. Murphy's music for the narrative verses is a moderate patter section but the tempo picks up to "allegro vivace" for the familiar refrain. A series of eighth notes suggests an Irish jig and the lyric relies mostly on one-syllable words. In the original British lyric, "poor Kelly lost his little girl up Piccadilly way" and she ends up singing and spelling "Has anybody here seen Kelly?/ K-E-double L-Y."[10] She complains that "Kelly from the Isle of Man" has "left me on my ownio" McKenna reworked some of the original ideas but laid the action in New York where Michael Kelly and his sweetheart from the County Cork were "bent upon a holiday." This time he loses her somewhere on "the Great White Way" and she wanders from Herald Square up to 42nd Street shouting the title phrase. She even describes him as having red hair, blue eyes and being "Irish through and through." A later verse in the Broadway version has the girl attending the annual St. Patrick's Day parade on Fifth Avenue. "Has Anyone Here Seen Kelly?" soon joined the ranks of popular Irish-American songs even though it is far from sentimental and does not revolve around a yearning for the Emerald Isle.

Nora Bayes made the first recording of the revised song in 1910. On the disc she references her own Jewish heritage by "accidentally" singing "Has anybody here seen Levi ... I mean Kelly?" That same year, Ada Jones, Billy Murray, and Harry Fay each recorded it. Over the years there have been discs by several Irish singers as well as the Big Ben Banjo Band, Arthur Osmond, Bert Alvey, Paul Austin Kelly, Billie Milton, Christina Wilson, Charlie Kunz, Mitch Miller, and Mary Duff. The familiar refrain of "Has Anyone Here Seen Kelly?" can be heard in dozens of films, usually to provide an Irish-American atmosphere. It served as the title for a 1926 cartoon and a 1928 Bessie Love feature film. Also on screen, it was sung by Florrie Ford in *Say It with Flowers* (1934), Alice Faye and Jack Oakie in *Hello, Frisco, Hello* (1943), Pat Kirkwood

Song of the Season

in *Stars in Your Eyes* (1956), and Jonjo O'Neill in *The Ballad of Buster Scruggs* (2018). Also, the Mitch Miller Singers perform it on television in the movie *Catch Me If You Can* (2002).

Other notable songs from that season: "Stop That Rag" from *The Jolly Bachelors*; "All Down Piccadilly (Willy of Piccadilly)," "The Girl with the Brogue," "The Pipes of Pan (Are Calling)" from *The Arcadians*; "My Hero," "Sympathy" from *The Chocolate Soldier*; "Up! Up! Up! in My Aeroplane" from the *Ziegfeld Follies of 1909*; "Heaven Will Protect the Working Gil" from *Tillie's Nightmare*.

1910–1911 SEASON

The fallout from *The Merry Widow* was felt heavily on the Street this season in which operetta (particularly European operetta) was all the craze. Forty-four new and returning musicals opened this season; ten of them were imports. Four came from France, two from Germany, and four from Great Britain. With few exceptions they were in the Viennese manner; with fewer exceptions they failed at the box office. Only the French *Alma, Where Do You Live?*, Germany's *The Spring Maid,* and London's *The Balkan Princess* ran over the 100 mark. The three best (and very successful) American musicals this season were also operettas even if they were not billed as such. Victor Herbert's *Naughty Marietta* boasted his richest score and an operetta plot set in operetta land: eighteenth-century New Orleans. Otto Harbach and Karl Hoschna had a hit (*Madame Sherry*) and a miss (*Dr. De Luxe*), both of them with lots of operetta features. Similarly, *The Pink Lady* called itself a "musical comedy" but it was based on a French play and its superb score often flirted with operetta. For true American musical comedy, one had to turn to Lew Fields and his two hits—*The Summer Widowers* and *The Hen-Pecks*—or such popular (but questionable) shows as *Everywoman, He Came from Milwaukee, Girlies,* and *Up and Down Broadway*. It was a very good season for revues and special entertainments. Once again the Hippodrome spectacular, this year titled *The International Cup*, had the longest run: 333 performances. The *Ziegfeld Follies of 1910* ran only a third as long but it was a notable edition, welcoming comedienne Fanny Brice and African American comic Bert Williams to the cast. Another revue with an important debut was *La Belle Paree*; not a Parisian import but a Shubert Brothers extravaganza to celebrate the opening of their new Broadway playhouse, the beloved Winter Garden Theatre. The revue's program of performers was so long that many patrons and critics had left before newcomer Al Jolson came out to sing. From such an inauspicious debut came a famous fifteen-year teaming of Jolson and the Winter Garden.

"Ah, Sweet Mystery of Life"
Music by Victor Herbert; lyric by Rida Johnson Young
From *Naughty Marietta* (1910)
Sung by Emma Trentini as Marietta, and
Orville Harrold as Capt. Dick Warrington

Herbert's score for *Naughty Marietta* is more complex and expansive than any of his other works. This was no accident or arbitrary decision. The impresario Oscar Hammerstein loved opera and founded his own opera company in 1910. He commissioned Herbert to compose an operetta that would show off his troupe's vocal versatility, particularly his prima donna Emma Trentini. Not limited by the voices usually found on Broadway, Herbert composed more difficult and wide-ranged music not only for the singers but for the orchestra as well. Consequently, *Naughty Marietta* sometimes crosses the line between operetta and opera. The song "Ah, Sweet Mystery of Life" was used very dramatically in the story. The Louisiana beauty Marietta sings a few strains of the music at different times throughout the musical, recalling a dream song that could only be completed by a true love. We only hear the full composition at the finale when Captain Dick Warrington (Orville Harrold) joins her in a duet version. This device had been used effectively in *The Merry Widow* with the famous waltz but "Ah, Sweet Mystery of Life" is not a flowing waltz but a passionate declaration of love that soars upwards into a resounding climax. There is no verse; such an aggressive refrain needs no introduction. Because the number is so famous and something of a musical cliché today, it has often been parodied much like a familiar piece of classical music. The lyric by Rida Johnson Young is unabashed operetta rapture. Because Herbert starts the refrain with a long note to be held as long as one wishes, Young had little recourse but start her lyric with "Ah." To keep the song moving, the lyric uses a series of "-ing" endings ("All the longing, seeking, striving, waiting, yearning,/ The burning hopes") and makes sure each phrase ends with an open vowel sound.[11] The sentiments are not subtle: "For 'tis love and love alone the world is seeking." While such a lyric could never be conversational, Young still manages to avoid a "thee" and "thou" vocabulary, only resorting to that " 'tis" when it helps the lyric flow.

"Ah, Sweet Mystery of Life" perhaps represents American operetta more than any other single song. Ironically, Herbert and Young didn't think the song could be popular and in the program it was just listed as "Finale." *Naughty Marietta* is filled with wonderful music but this is the song that stuck with audiences and became a big hit. As popular as the operetta was in theatres, its fame redoubled with the 1936 film version in which Jeanette MacDonald and Nelson Eddy established themselves as Hollywood's premiere singing couple. Their recording from the film was a bestseller. But there had been dozens of recordings made before theirs was released. Robert Olsen, Richard Crooks, the Victor Salon Orchestra, and Jesse Crawford were among the first to record "Ah, Sweet Mystery of Life," followed by opera singers, pop singers, jazz artists, and even country western performers. Among the many notable discs are those by Dorothy Kirsten and Felix Knight, Vaughn Monroe, Mario Lanza, Les Harris, Ralph Flanagan, Gordon MacRae and Lucille Norman, Connie Boswell with Bob Crosby's Bob Cats, Wayne King, Maxine Sullivan, José Rastelli, Anna Moffo and Sergio Franchi, Sarah Vaughn, Slim Whitman, the Dick Meldonian Trio, and Kimmie Rhodes. The many movies in which the song is heard (not always with respect) include *Syncopation* (1929), *The Great Victor Herbert* (1939), *Thoroughly Modern Millie* (1967), *Bananas* (1971), *Young Frankenstein* (1974), *Magic* (1978), *The Ninth Configuration* (1980), *Mr. & Mrs. Bridge* (1990), and *Wild Card* (2015).

Other notable songs from that season: "'Neath the Southern Moon (for Thee)," "Italian Street Song," "I'm Falling in Love with Someone," "Tramp! Tramp!

Tramp!" from *Naughty Marietta*; "Every Little Movement (Has a Meaning of Its Own)," "Put Your Arms around Me, Honey," "The Butterfly" from *Madame Sherry*; "Donny Didn't, Donny Did," "(The Girl) By the Saskatchewan," "The Kiss Waltz" from *The Pink Lady*; "Chinatown, My Chinatown," "Sweet Italian Love" from *Up and Down Broadway*; "Mother Machree," "I Love the Name of Mary" from *Barry of Ballymore*; "Goodbye, Becky Cohen," "Lovie Joe" from *Ziegfeld Follies of 1910*.

Song of the Season

1911–1912 SEASON

Although forty-three new musicals (a new record) opened on Broadway this season, it was clear to all that there was not one outstanding show or even one exceptional score. Luckily there were some entertaining songs delivered with panache by top performers. *The Ziegfeld Follies of 1911* offered Bert Williams, Fanny Brice, Leon Errol, Lillian Lorraine, Bessie McCoy, and the Dolly Sisters. Elsewhere were Lillian Russell, Julia Sanderson, Donald Brian, Frank Tinney, Fritzi Scheff, Raymond Hitchcock, Laurette Taylor, Fay Bainter, Jefferson DeAngelis, Julian Eltinge, and Al Jolson who stopped the show in two revues: *Vera Violetta* and *Whirl of Society*. George M. Cohan also appeared twice, in his new hit *The Little Millionaire* and in a revival of his *Forty-five Minutes from Broadway*. Probably the most heart-warming event of the season was Joe Weber and Lew Fields reuniting with Lillian Russel for another wacky burlesque, this one titled *Hokey-Pokey*. Only two musicals came from London but no less than eleven came from Vienna or Germany. The most successful of them were the British *The Quaker Girl* and the Viennese operettas *Little Boy Blue, The Rose Maid,* and *The Siren*. There were three "widow" musicals this season, two of them (*The Red Widow* and *A Winsome Widow*) running well past the 100 milestone. Running only fifty-six times, *The Fascinating Widow* featured Broadway's favorite female impersonator, Julian Eltinge, and the last score by Karl Hoschna and Otto Harbach; 34-year-old Hoschna died before the year was out. The tireless Victor Herbert scored three musicals this season. *When Sweet Sixteen* and *The Duchess* quickly closed but *The Enchantress* ran 104 performances. Once again the longest run (443 performances) was at the Hippodrome where *Around the World,* true to its title, dazzled audiences with lavish scenes from across the globe.

"Be My Little Baby Bumble Bee"
Music by Henry I. Marshall; lyric by Stanley Murphy
From *The Winsome Widow.* (1912)
Sung by Elizabeth Brice as Isabel, and Charles King as Wilder Daly

---

A jaunty number that foreshadows a Roaring Twenties dance ditty, "Be My Little Baby Bumble Bee" is termed a "novelty" song. Such a number is built on some new (or novel) idea that is playful and often humorous. Novelty songs use a gimmick or vocal trick to make them unique. One of the most common devices is onomatopoeia, the use of words that sound like their meaning. The later songs "Splish Splash" and "Zing! Went the Strings of My Heart" are good examples. The hay-day of novelty songs was the 1920s with a resurgence in the 1950s. But there are novelty songs that go back to the nineteenth century. The vocal gimmick in "Be My Little Baby Bumble Bee" is the sound of buzzing. The lyric has a bee asking a sweetheart bee to "be my little baby bumble bee" then backs up the offer with "Buzz around, buzz around, keep a-buzzin' 'round."[12] This silliness is repeated with other repetitions ("cuddle up, cuddle up, cuddle up" and "you and me, you and me, you and me") and the lyric ends with the information that "I've got a dozen cousin bees" but he wants "you to be my bumble bee." Stanley Murphy wrote the clever lyric filled with "b" alliteration and Henry I. Marshall composed the animated music which stops for each of the parenthetical buzzing sounds. "Be My Little Baby Bumble Bee" was sung as a duet in *A Winsome Widow*, a Ziegfeld book musical with a thin plot interrupted by a series of vaudeville turns. (One of the vaudevillians appearing in a small role was a young Mae West.) The novelty song immediately charmed the audience and a recording was made by Billy Murray and Ada Jones which climbed the charts, as did sheet music sales. For a novelty song, it was recorded many times. Among the notable discs are those by Doris Day, Gordon MacRae and June Hutton, Bob Crosby and Marion Morgan, Benay Venuta, Jane Morgan, the Andrews Sisters, Teresa Brewer, Julie London, the Osmond Brothers, and Johnny Maddox. On screen, it was sung by Stan Freed and Pauline Loth in the animated feature film *Mr. Bug Goes to Town* (1941), Irene Manning in *Shine On Harvest Moon* (1944), Veda Ann Borg and chorus girls in *Irish Eyes Are Smiling* (1944), Doris Day, Gordon MacRae, and Russell Arms in *By the Light of the Silvery Moon* (1953), and Young Eddie (Richard Monda) and the kids in *The Eddie Cantor Story* (1953).

Other notable songs from that season: "Cupid, Tell Me Why" from *The Duchess*; "(To the) Land of My Own Romance," "Rose, Lucky Rose," "One Word from You" from *The Enchantress*; "Oh, You Beautiful Girl," "The Musical Moon" from *The Little Millionaire*; "Rum Tum Tiddle," "The Gaby Glide," "That Haunting Melody" from *Vera Violetta*; "Come to the Ball" from *The Quaker Girl*; "Woodman, Woodman, Spare That Tree" from *Ziegfeld Follies of 1911*.

Song of the Season

1912–1913 SEASON

With nine revivals or return engagements, the number of musicals on the Street this season totaled forty-three. Sadly, more than half of them closed within a month. But twelve musicals ran over 100 performances so there was still money to be made on Broadway; it was just a riskier proposition. After the Hippodrome spectacle *Under Many Flags*, the long-run winners were Victor Herbert's version of *Cinderella* titled *The Lady of the Slipper*; the British import *Oh! Oh! Delphine*; the reconfigured version of Johann Strauss' *Die Fledermaus* now called *The Merry Countess*; the new Franz Lehár operetta *The Count of Luxembourg*; *The Sunshine Girl* which cast a spotlight on the ballroom dance team of Vernon and Irene Castle; the Viennese operetta *The Purple Road*; and the Al Jolson vehicle *The Honeymoon Express* in which he sang "You Made Me Love You." Joining these hits was a new revue series that was to become an annual affair: *The Passing Show of 1912*. The Shubert Brothers were determined to come up with their own *Follies* so they sunk a lot of money into the production and hired several popular performers. But the stars of the evening turned out to be the vaudeville comics Willie and Eugene Howard in their Broadway debut. The revue ran 136 performances and the Shuberts promised future editions. As for the *Ziegfeld Follies*, this season's edition featured all of the audience favorites and ran nine weeks before setting out on tour. Also welcomed back this season were Joe Weber and Lew Fields in their latest burlesque *Roly Poly*, not to be confused with Fields' revue *Hanky-Panky* earlier in the season.

The finest new score heard on Broadway was newcomer Rudolf Friml's *The Firefly*. Otto Harbach, who had lost his collaborator Karl Hoschna, wrote the book and lyrics for *The Firefly*, the first of his ten musicals with Friml. Emma Trentini was the star but much attention was placed on Friml, a recent immigrant writing his first Broadway score. *The Firefly* would remain in the repertoire of opera and operetta groups for several decades. The two most popular songs of the season came from the melodramatic Irish musical *The Isle o' Dreams*. "Mother Machree" and "When Irish Eyes Are Smiling" were sung by co-author Chauncey Olcott and they eventually became audience favorites, not only on Broadway but across the United States and Ireland. Actually, "Mother Machree" had been introduced in *Barry of Ballymore* two seasons previous but failed to catch on. So Olcott reprised it in *The Isle o' Dreams* and this time it caught fire. Although *The Isle o' Dreams* stayed on Broadway for only a month, it set off on a long tour and introduced the two Irish-American classics to the nation.

"When Irish Eyes Are Smiling"
Music by Ernest R. Ball; lyric by Chauncey Olcott, George Graff, Jr.
From *The Isle o' Dreams* (1913)
Sung by Chauncey Olcott as Ivor Kelway

Considered a kind of Irish anthem, "When Irish Eyes Are Smiling" is actually an American song written by three American-born professional songwriters. The song conjures up romantic visions of Ireland and is beloved by millions who have never been there. And, depending on how it is performed, the number could be romantic, political, nostalgic, or even angry. A few years after the song became popular on both sides of the Atlantic, Ireland was plunged into a war for independence followed by a tragic civil war. "When Irish Eyes Are Smiling" became a watch-cry of sorts, turning sentiment into patriotism. But songwriter-singer Chauncey Olcott had none of this in mind when he came up with the highly poetic idea of eyes "laughing." He and George Graff, Jr., wrote the lyric as a "cheer up" song. The first verse urges a sad person (male or female) to smile, something so powerful that "a stone you'd beguile."[13] The famous refrain moves away from the personal "you" and reflects on the way any Irish person can smile through the look in one's eyes. Such smiling is "like the morn in Spring" and Irish laughter is like angels singing. The phrase "lilt of Irish laughter" and the concluding line "Sure, they steal your heart away" have been so often used that today they are clichéd but rarely unwelcome. Ernest R. Ball, who composed a handful of memorable Irish songs, uses a lullaby tone for the verse and the music is tentative as it moves slowly along. The celebrated refrain has a livelier waltz tempo and is unrestrained, particularly in the way the music builds to a climax in the final bars. While there is the flavor of an Irish folk ballad, the structure is pure Tin Pan Alley. "When Irish Eyes Are Smiling" has been sung as a robust drinking song but when Bing Crosby recorded it in 1939 and sang it in the 1949 film *Top o' the Morning* he slowed it down considerably and the number became a hymn of sorts. In fact, to this day the song is a favorite at Irish-American funerals.

Olcott made the first recording of the song in 1913, the same year Harry MacDonough made a disc but it was the 1917 record by the popular Irish tenor John McCormack that made the song a bestseller. Other artists who made recordings before the Second World War include George F. Murray, Maggie Stott, Justin Ring and his Orchestra, Bradley Kinkaid, Riley Puckett, and Glen Gray and the Casa Loma Orchestra. Over the years the song has been covered by a variety of performers, including Dennis Day, Kate Smith, the Buffalo Bills, Joni James, Connie Francis, John Gary, Jimmy Roselli, Frank Zappa, Finbar Wright, Perry Como, the Irish Tenors, and Maxine Linehan. "When Irish Eyes Are Smiling" became even more familiar in America when it was used as the theme song for Morton Downey's radio show; he sang it on the air more than 1,000 times. It was also the theme song for another popular radio serial, *Duffy's Tavern*. Either the song or just its music has been heard in dozens of movies, an effective way to add an Irish flavor to any film. In the Ernest Ball bio-pic *Irish Eyes Are Smiling* (1944), it was sung by Dick Haymes. Dennis Morgan sang it in the Olcott bio *My Wild Irish Rose* (1947). Other on-screen performances were made by Phil Regan, Pat O'Brien, and Edward Everett Horton in a cappella version in *In Caliente* (1935), Nelson Eddy in *Let Freedom Ring* (1939), Andrew Mack in *Vaudeville Days* (1942), and Betty Grable and an Irish quartet in *Coney Island* (1943). Among the dozens of movies in which the song can be heard on the soundtrack are *Stage Mother* (1933), *It All Came True* (1940), *Moonlight in Havana* (1942), *Doughboys in Ireland* (1943), *Nob Hill* (1945), *Starlift*

Song of the Season

(1951), *Painting the Clouds with Sunshine* (1951), *Sincerely Yours* (1955), *The Young Philadelphians* (1959), *Husbands* (1970), *We're No Angels* (1989), *Return to Me* (2000), and *Swimming Upstream* (2003).

Other notable songs from that season: "You Made Me Love You (I Didn't Want to Do It)," "Who Paid the Rent for Mrs. Rip Van Winkle?" from *The Honeymoon Express*; "Giannina Mia," "Love Is Like a Firefly," "Sympathy" from *The Firefly*; "Don't Turn My Picture to the Wall" from *The Girl from Montmartre*; "Row, Row, Row," "You're on the Right Road But You're Going the Wrong Way" from *Ziegfeld Follies of 1912*; "When It's Apple Blossom Time in Normandy" from *Roly Poly*.

1913–1914 SEASON

Of the thirty-four musicals seen on Broadway this season, most were either operettas or revues. It looked like musical comedy was in danger of going completely out of fashion. Nine of the operettas came from continental Europe and, of the eleven American works, the best of them were either revues or book musicals securely in the operatic mode. Victor Herbert offered the hit *Sweethearts* and the modest *The Madcap Duchess* and Rudolf Friml and Otto Harbach found success with *High Jinks*. Sigmund Romberg, who would eventually join their ranks as one of America's finest operetta composers, was represented on Broadway for the first time this season with *The Whirl of the World*, a Shubert Brothers revue. It joined such popular revues as *Ziegfeld Follies of 1913*, *The Passing Show of 1913*, the Hippodrome extravaganza *America*, and *All Aboard*, a summertime entertainment produced by Lew Fields. Where was George M. Cohan when you needed him? Jerome Kern provided songs for two musical comedies—*The Doll Girl* and *Oh, I Say!*—but both failed to run. Some of his songs interpolated into others' shows were starting to get attention, such as "You're Here and I'm Here" in *The Marriage Market*. But Kern had to wait another year before he finally mades a big splash. Happily, it would be with musical comedy.

"Peg o' My Heart"
Music by Fred Fisher; lyric by Alfred Bryan
From *Ziegfeld Follies of 1913* (1913)
Sung by José Collins

One of the most charming and popular comedies of the era was *Peg o' My Heart* (1912) by J. Harley Manners. The scruffy Irish girl Peg inherits a lot of money and the snobbish Chichester family has to accept her in order to get out of debt. Manners' wife Laurette Taylor played Peg and it made her a star. *Peg o' My Heart* was a hit in New York, London, and on the road where eight different companies toured the states. Prompted by the success of the play and Taylor's performance, composer Fred Fisher and lyricist Alfred Bryan wrote the song "Peg o' My Heart" about the spirited Irish girl and tried to get music publisher Leo Feist to buy it. Singer Irving Kaufman saw the sheet music in Feist's office and got permission to sing it in a New York eatery. Another singer, Charles Harrison, also found a copy and recorded it. With no singing star to put on the cover of the sheet music, "Peg o' My Heart" was published with a photograph of Laurette Taylor and her dog on the cover. Florenz Ziegfeld was not satisfied with the songs written for his 1913 *Follies* so he interpolated the song into the show where it was sung by José Collins. Finally the ballad caught on and sheet music sales soared.

The verse for "Peg o' My Heart" is not terribly interesting either musically or lyrically. The smitten singer tells the world that "I love her, I love her, yes, I do" and "I hope to make her mine someday."[14] The catchy refrain switches point of view and is sung directly to Peg: "I love you … I always knew it would be you … come make your home in my heart." For a gushing ballad, the music is unusual in that it is brisk and uses a march tempo. Even when slowed down and sung as a fervent ballad, "Peg o' My Heart" keeps moving in a jaunty manner. The music has a narrow range and gives the singer several rests along the way so it is not the most difficult to perform. Although the lyric refers to Peg's "Irish heart," there is nothing very Hibernian in the music. Two early recordings by Henry Burr and Walter Van Brunt helped popularize the song but it was the Taylor photo on the sheet music that did the trick. For decades "Peg o' My Heart" would be associated with Taylor even though she never sang it. The song was recorded by a variety of artists over the years and it was a particular favorite of dance bands, such as those by Bunny Berigan, Buddy Clark, Joe Loss, Gene Vincent, and Glenn Miller. Red Nichols and his Five Pennies made a jazz recording in 1930 that was very popular. An instrumental version of the song by the Harmonicats was a surprise hit in 1947 and went to the top of the charts; "Peg o' My Heart" was forever after a harmonica standard. Among the diverse artists who also recorded the song are Art Lund, Josephine Baker, Andy Williams, Phil Regan, Dean Martin, Joni James, Peggy Lee, Pat Boone, Ramina Lombard, Paul Finnerty, and the punk rock band Dropkick Murphys. On screen, "Peg o' My Heart" was sung by Ann Blyth in *Babes on Swing Street* (1944), by June Haver (dubbed by Bonnie Lou Williams) and Mark Reynolds (dubbed by Bill Shirley) in *Oh, You Beautiful Doll* (1949), and Lea Salonga in *Keanu* (2016). It was also heard in several movies, including *California Split* (1974), *Hop* (2011), and *Baby* (2020).

Other notable songs from that season: "Isle d'Amour" from *Ziegfeld Follies of 1913*; "Sweethearts," "Pretty as a Picture," "The Angelus" from *Sweethearts*; "You're Here and I'm Here" from *The Marriage Market*; "Something Seems Tingle-Ingleing," "All Aboard for Dixie" from *High Jinks*.

1914–1915 SEASON

The First World War, which broke out in Europe three weeks before the season began, would change the face of the world; so too, the nature of the Broadway musical would be altered by new sounds and new artists this year. Ragtime music became firmly established in musicals this season and the first sparks of jazz were heard, particularly in dance shows. The Broadway musical comedy got smarter, more contemporary, and further away from operetta with *Nobody Home,* the first of the Princess Musicals. These small-scale musicals laid the groundwork for the modern musical comedy. Newcomer Guy Bolton wrote the libretto for *Nobody Home* which made all the difference. Also making debuts this season were the dancing performers Marilyn Miller and Charlotte Greenwood. The petite Miller and the tall, lanky Greenwood could not have been more different. A different sort of debut was made by Irving Berlin with his syncopated musical *Watch Your Step* featuring the dancing Vernon and Irene Castle. Berlin had become famous back in 1911 with "Alexander's Ragtime Band" but this was the season in which he conquered Broadway. Also coming into the limelight was Jerome Kern whose songs were heard in a handful of shows, none more importantly than "They Didn't Believe Me" in the British import *The Girl from Utah.*

The biggest hit of the season, even surpassing the Hippodrome's timely titled *Wars of the World,* was the London import *Chin-Chin* which ran 295 performances. Much of the credit went to the American comics Fred Stone and David Montgomery who turned the musical into their own farcical showcase. Victor Herbert had a long-run hit with *The Only Girl* but had to settle for a six-week run for *The Debutante.* This season saw two editions of *The Passing Show,* the later one making Marilyn Miller a star. Other profitable revues included *Ziegfeld Follies of 1914,* the Shuberts' *Maid in America,* George M. Cohan's *Hello, Broadway,* and *Dancing Around* which was dominated by the tireless Al Jolson. Similarly, Charlotte Greenwood's performance as Letty Proudfoot in *Pretty Mrs. Smith* was such a sensation that the producers changed the name of the musical to *Long Legged Letty* for the tour. Greenwood would eventually return to Broadway in three more "Letty" shows.

"They Didn't Believe Me"
Music by Jerome Kern; lyric by Herbert Reynolds
From *The Girl from Utah* (1914)
Sung by Julia Sanderson as Una Trance,
and Donald Brian as Sandy Blair

If any one song can claim to have changed the direction of the Broadway ballad, that song would have to be "They Didn't Believe Me." The story behind the song goes back to the 1913 London musical *The Girl from Utah.* It was about Una Trance who runs away from an arranged Mormon marriage and ends up in London where she falls in love with an English actor, Sandy Blair. The charming story, fine cast, and pleasant British score allowed the musical to run 195 performances in the West End. American producer Charles Frohman liked the American aspects of *The Girl from Utah* and bought the Broadway rights to the musical even though he was cognizant of the flaws in the libretto and the lack of hits in the score. Also, with war eminent in Europe, Frohman feared that such a frivolous musical might seem suddenly dated. So the evening started with the three stars—Julia Sanderson (Una), Donald Brian (Sandy), and Joseph Cawthorn (as the Mormon Trimpel)—asking the audience to recall frivolous times past with the song "The Land of 'Let's Pretend.'" The song was by Jerome Kern and it was one of seven new numbers that he wrote for the Broadway version of *The Girl from Utah*. He had been providing the odd song here and there for Frohman's British imports for ten years but this was the closest that Kern had yet come to a full Broadway score. The musical launched his career not because of "They Didn't Believe Me" (that fame would come later) but because of the other six numbers in the score.

When Sanderson and Brian sang the duet "They Didn't Believe Me," it was warmly greeted by the audience but caused no excitement. In fact, hardly any of the New York critics even mentioned the song. So what makes this ballad so special? Consider first the lyric by Herbert Reynolds, a seemingly conventional piece of romantic gushing with such sentiments as "When I see your smile, Makes the living worth the while."[15] Without being slangy or ungrammatical, the lyric is conversational. Reynolds eliminates the pronouns in the verse. Instead of "I've got the cutest little way" and "I like to watch you" he begins with the verb: "Got the cutest ..." and "Like to watch ..." It is in the lyric for the refrain that things get more interesting. The male singer notes that "when I told them how beautiful you are,/ They didn't believe me, they didn't believe me." So he decides that "when I tell them,/ And I cert'nly am goin' to tell them,/ That I'm the man whose wife one day you'll be." That informal "And I cert'nly am goin' to tell them," is a parenthetical thought, commenting on itself and drawing attention to itself. It is the kind of casual comment that does not fit with a romantic lyric. Yet here it makes the romance more solid, less dreamy.

Kern's innovative music is more difficult to illustrate. Ever since the phenomenal success of *The Merry Widow*, popular songs were leaning more and more to operetta techniques and the waltz was again becoming the dominate style. Kern rebels against much of that in his music. "They Didn't Believe Me" has a 4/4 time but it isn't a march; it's a fox-trot. The four beats to a bar not only departed from the waltz-rhythms of European songs but it was ideal for the growing American passion for dance songs. Kern uses some unusual harmonics in "They Didn't Believe Me" that alter the melody slightly. He uses a triplet for that informal "cert'nly." The traditional way to handle that phrase would be "I'm certainly going to tell them" and some singers have sung it that way, wanting to follow the European pattern. Also remarkable about the music is the unexpected key changes throughout. A series of quarter notes in the refrain build up to a climax that is also a key change. All of these changes are subtle and audiences hearing "They Didn't Believe Me" didn't recognize any major musical development. They just liked the sound and the song became eventually a hit. Young songwriters like George Gershwin, Vincent Youmans, and Cole Porter—who all disliked the waltz—were encouraged to write for the musical stage where such ballads were possible. Kern's quietly revolutionary "They Didn't Believe Me" foreshadows the direction musical theatre would take as it moved away from European operetta.

The Girl from Utah was not a long-run hit and made a modest profit during its five months on the Street. Frohman made more money from the extended tour which became more and more attractive as the song "They Didn't Believe Me" caught on. The song was first heard on the London stage in 1915 when Haidee de Rance and George Grossmith sang it in *Tonight's the Night*. "They Didn't Believe Me" eventually sold millions of copies of sheet music on both sides of the Atlantic. The first recordings were made by the Victor Light Opera Company, Alice Green and Harry MacDonald, and Grace Kerns and Reed Miller, followed by hundreds of others. Among the notable discs are those by Red Nichols and His Five Pennies, Ambrose and His Orchestra, Dick Robertson, Nan Wynn, Johnny Mercer, Dick Haymes, Mario Lanza, Artie Shaw, Buddy Greco, Julie London, Lena Horne, Bernard Manning, Jane Powell, Bobby Troup, Oscar Peterson, Elvis Costello, André Previn, Charlie Byrd Quintet, Marvin Gaye, and Beegie Adair. On screen it was sung by Corinne Griffith in *Back Pay* (1930), Dinah Shore in the Kern biopic *Till the Clouds Roll By* (1946), a chorus of soldiers in *Oh! What a Lovely War* (1969), and Alison Jiear and Denzel Sinclaire in *Being Julia* (2004).

Other notable songs from that season: "Some Sort of Girl," "The Land of Let's Pretend," "You Never Can Tell" from *The Girl from Utah*; "Play a Simple Melody," "The Syncopated Walk," "When I Discovered You" from *Watch Your Step*; "Down By the Erie," "Barnum and Bailey Rag" from *Hello, Broadway*; "In Arcady," "You Know and I Know," "Another Little Girl" from *Nobody Home*; "Sister Susie's Sewing Shirts for Soldiers" from *Dancing Around*; "Goodbye Girls, I'm Through," "Ragtime Temple Bells" from *Chin-Chin*; "Long, Lean, Lanky Letty" from *Pretty Mrs. Smith*.

Song of the Season

1915–1916 SEASON

Thirty musicals opened on Broadway this season and, with only four of them revivals, there was plenty of new work to enjoy. Revues continued to thrive. There were two editions of the *Ziegfeld Follies*, one at the beginning of the season and another at the end. Comics W. F. Fields and Ed Wynn were the new faces at the *Follies*; Fields would become a regular, Wynn would go on to do his own shows on Broadway. The *Follies* were always known for their outstanding visuals but this season Ziegfeld topped himself. The reason was the addition of Austrian-born designer Joseph Urban who would supervise the look of the *Follies* for many years and bring revue design to new heights. Other successful revues included *The Passing Show of 1915* with Marilyn Miller as the top draw; *Town Topics* with newcomer Will Rogers getting attention; the Hippodrome attraction *Hip-Hip Hooray* which once again was the longest-running show at 425 performances; the Shubert Brothers' *A World of Pleasure*; and the *Cohan Revue of 1916*. Some "book" shows were mostly a revue, as with the Al Jolson vehicle *Robinson Crusoe, Jr.* Jerome Kern contributed songs to four musicals this season, by far the most important being *Very Good Eddie*, a Princess Theatre musical that ran 341 performances. Running a bit longer was Sigmund Romberg's *The Blue Paradise*, which made Vivienne Segal a star. Among the other shows running over the 100-performance mark were the French musical *The Girl Who Smiles*, the Rudolf Friml operetta *Katinka*, the Victor Herbert musical comedy *The Princess Pat*, and the Franz Lehár Viennese operetta *Alone at Last*.

Tin Pan Alley favorite Irving Berlin was getting more and more involved with Broadway this season. In addition to providing a song or two for different shows, he wrote the full score for *Stop! Look! Listen!* in which Harry Fox introduced two Berlin standards, "The Girl on the Magazine Cover" and "I Love a Piano." The musical ran a profitable 105 performances. For the next ten years, Berlin would score at least one show each season. A songwriter who would be a frequent presence on Broadway for the next forty years was Cole Porter who made a rather inauspicious debut this season. A few of his songs had been interpolated into other songwriters' shows but Porter was the sole composer and lyricist for *See America First*. The breezy musical comedy was nothing special but the songs were deemed promising by the critics. Inside of two weeks, *See America First* was gone but Porter was here to stay.

"I Love a Piano"
Music and lyric by Irving Berlin
From *Stop! Look! Listen!* (1915)
Sung by Harry Fox as Abel Connor, and chorus

Stop! Look! Listen! was Irving Berlin's second full score for Broadway and he was still writing songs in his celebrated Tin Pan Alley manner. Since the silly but entertaining libretto by the ever-busy Harry B. Smith did not call for an integrated score, Berlin was not yet forced to write character songs. He returned to his penchant for ragging words and notes, though even he himself admitted that none of his songs (including the phenomenally successful "Alexander's Ragtime Band") were true rags. Such is the case for "I Love a Piano." The plot of the musical comedy concerned a Broadway producer (Harlan Dixon) who searches high and low to find a replacement for his star who left the show to get married; he ends up hiring the chorus girl (Marion Sunshine) he had rejected in the first scene. Harry Fox played the press agent behind the search and he stopped the show with "I Love a Piano." With six pianos and pianists on a stage set that looked like a huge keyboard, the production number was far from subtle; but neither was the song. It is a gushing love song to the piano, a metaphor for a lovely woman and lovemaking. The verse is jaunty and straightforward, recalling how as a child the clarinet and the trombone thrilled him but today "there's one musical instrument that I call mine." The refrain simply states "I Love a piano," be it an upright or a "high-toned baby grand."[16] But the lyric gets intimate with tactile images such as "run my fingers" and "love to meddle" and even an orgasmic "p-i-a-n-o, oh, oh!"

The lyric is filled with internal rhymes ("bar is a jar ... fine way/Steinway ... delighted/invited ... stop right/upright") which push the words forward in time to the propulsive music. But more interesting is the way Berlin rags the words to let them sit on the ragged note. The three-syllable "piano" becomes the two-syllable "pyan-o." So the title phrase becomes "I love-a pyan-o" which goes directly against the expected. The lyric also has fun with the familiar phrase "a fine way to treat a lady," which becomes "a fine way to treat a Steinway," continuing the lady/piano metaphor. Perhaps the most memorable section of the song is the descending scale notes to go with the spelled out "p-i-a-n-o, oh, oh!" The song may not be a true ragtime composition but it is certainly in the spirit of ragtime.

"I Love a Piano" was first heard on the London stage in *Follow the Crowd* (1916) where it was sung by Ethel Levey. Billy Murray, Walter Van Brunt, M. J. O'Connell, and Levey each made a 1916 recording of "I Love a Piano" but the song did not become a *bona fide* hit until Arthur Shutt's 1934 chart-climbing disc. Over the decades notable recordings were made by Joe Bushkin, Benny Fields and Blossom Seeley, Burl Ives, Barbara Carroll Trio, André Previn, Joan Morris and William Bolcom, Dorothy Loudon, Barbara Cook, Michael Feinstein, Debbie Gravitte, Bebe Neuwirth, Ralph Sharon Trio, and Earl Rose. "I Love a Piano" was sung by Judy Garland in the movie musical *Easter Parade* (1948) and it was heard again on Broadway when it was sung by the cast of the dance revue *Fosse* (1999) and by Jeffrey Denman, Meredith Patterson, and the company in *White Christmas* (2008).

Other notable songs from that season: "The Girl on the Magazine Cover" from *Stop! Look! Listen!*; "Hello, Frisco, Hello," "Hold Me in Your Loving Arms," "When the Lights Are Low" from *Ziegfeld Follies* (two editions); "Auf Wiedersehn" from

Song of the Season

The Blue Paradise; "Neapolitan Love Song" from *The Princess Pat*; "Allah's Holiday," "Rackety Coo," "My Paradise" from *Katinka*; "Babes in the Wood," "Isn't It Great to Be Married," "Some Sort of Somebody" from *Very Good Eddie*; "Where Did Robinson Crusoe Go with Friday on Saturday Night?" from *Robinson Crusoe, Jr.*; "I've a Shooting Box in Scotland" from *See America First*.

1916–1917 SEASON

The United States entered the First World War in April of this season but repercussions were felt much earlier. Musicals with Austrian, Hungarian, and German roots were losing their appeal. Continental European operettas such as *Flora Bella, Follow Me, Miss Springtime,* and *Her Soldier Boy,* which opened in the first half of the season, managed to run over 100 performances before America declared war; similar shows that opened later did not have a chance. By the spring, patriotic songs were being written and/or added to American revues and book musicals. From various stages, you could hear "Can't You Hear Our County Calling?," "Goodbye Broadway, Hello France!," "Uncle Sam's Children," "I'll Be Somewhere in France," "I May Be Gone a Long Long Time," "When Uncle Sam Is Ruler of the Sea," "Let's All Be Americans Now," "Flag of My Country," "My Father Fights for Uncle Sam," and "We'll Stand by Our Country." Two familiar British songs—"It's a Long Way to Tipperary" and "Pack Up Your Troubles in Your Old Kit Bag"—were sung spontaneously in various theatres this season. By May, a revival of the 1902 "Patriotic Military Opera" *When Johnny Comes Marching Home* was on the boards. It was too soon to determine if war was good for business but Broadway wore its patriotism boldly.

Behind all the hoopla, some superior musicals arrived this season thanks to an impressive array of American songwriters. Jerome Kern contributed songs to five shows, most memorably *Have a Heart* and *Oh, Boy!,* both with books by Guy Bolton and lyrics by the transplanted Englishman P. G. Wodehouse. Finally there were lyrics that had the same punch as Bolton's librettos and the result was fresh and exciting musical comedy. Irving Berlin and Sigmund Romberg songs were also heard in five musicals, and also represented this season were Rudolf Friml and Otto Harbach with *You're in Love,* Victor Herbert with *The Century Girl* and *Eileen,* and newcomer George Gershwin with *The Passing Show.* Equally impressive was the number of stars for audiences to enjoy. Joining Will Rogers, Fanny Brice, W. C. Fields, Bert Williams, Ann Pennington, and Ina Claire at the *Ziegfeld Follies* was Eddie Cantor making a big splash. Ed Wynn moved from the *Follies* to *The Passing Show* where his popularity continued to flourish. Anna Held, Charlotte Greenwood, Raymond Hitchcock, Leon Errol, Irene Bordoni, Anna Pavlova, Eugene and Willie Howard, Marilyn Miller, Sam Bernard, Elsie Janis, Marie Dressler, Frank Tinney, Hazel Dawn, Edith Day, Blanche Ring, and others were on display elsewhere, along with newcomers Clifton Webb, Edna May Oliver, Charles Ruggles, and Marion Davies. For the first time within memory, a book musical chalked up more performances than the Hippodrome show, this year rather accurately titled *The Big Show.* It was outdistanced by a very little show, the Princess Theatre musical *Oh, Boy!* which delighted audiences 463 times. It was one of those rare occasions on Broadway when the best musical of the season was also the most popular.

Song of the Season

> "Till the Clouds Roll By"
> Music by Jerome Kern; lyric by P. G Wodehouse
> From *Oh, Boy!* (1917)
> Sung by Tom Powers as George Budd,
> and Anna Wheatley as Jackie Sampson

Perhaps no other song captures the breezy, melodic tone of the Bolton-Kern-Wodehouse Princess Musicals like "Till the Clouds Roll By." Musically and lyrically it is a sparkling number that actually comes from character and plot. George (Tom Powers) is hiding from his Aunt Penelope (Edna May Oliver) in a friend's apartment with the attractive Jackie (Anna Wheatley) who is hiding from a policeman who she socked in the eye. They both know they should get out of the apartment but it has started raining so they decide to stay and get better acquainted. P. G. Wodehouse wrote the lyric which has an unusual verse, conversational yet tentative. They agree they must respect the conventions of propriety but, since it is raining, they don't "mind a bit." Wodehouse prefers feminine rhymes but he doesn't put them in the expected places. The internal rhyme "gaining ... remaining" is not matched until much later in the verse with "explaining ... waning ... raining."[17] In the refrain, the rhyme "the rain comes a-pitter, patter" is not matched until the much later with "it is vain to remain and chatter." The lyric concludes with "Helter skelter" rhyming with "I must fly for shelter/ Till the clouds roll by." The feminine rhymes "weeping ... sleeping ... heaping" smooth out the refrain, lyrically following Kern's lilting music. Such music is surprisingly simple, particularly for Kern. There are no key changes in the refrain and Kern uses the notes sparingly, avoiding any flourishes or fussiness. The quarter notes on "pitter, patter" suggest raindrops while the whole notes on "clouds roll by" slow the song down to a floating sensation. Wodehouse was the finest lyricist Kern had yet worked with and their song collaboration was special. Unfortunately, Wodehouse did not remain in musical theatre; in 1928, he left off lyric writing to concentrate on comic novels, of which he had many.

"Till the Clouds Roll By" is an easily likable song but its charms are too subtle for some. None of the New York critics of *Oh, Boy!* singled out the number; there were splashier songs in the score. All the same, the song eventually caught on and has enjoyed many recordings over the years. Tom Powers reprised the song with Beatrice Lillie on the London stage where *Oh, Boy!* was retitled *Oh, Joy!* (1919). Wheaton, from the original Broadway cast, recorded it as a duet with James Harrod a month after opening. Most recordings eliminate the verse so that the ballad works as a solo. Among those to make distinctive discs were Mel Tormé, Gordon Jenkins, Helen Merrill, Sandy Stewart and Dick Haymes, Jesse Crawford, Paul Desmond, the Paragon Ragtime Orchestra, Sylvia McNair, the Charlie Byrd Quintet, Ronny Whyte, and Christian Jacob. The 1946 Kern biopic was titled *Till the Clouds Roll By* and the song was sung by Ray MacDonald to June Allyson before they danced with the chorus in the rain.

Other notable songs from that season: "You Never Knew About Me," "Nesting Time in Flatbush," "A Pal Like You" from *Oh, Boy!*; "Throw Me a Rose" from *Miss Springtime*; "Oh, Johnny, Oh, Johnny, Oh!" from *Follow Me*; "And I Am All Alone," "You Said Something" from *Have a Heart*; "I'll Be Somewhere in France," "Can't You Hear Our County Calling?" from *Ziegfeld Follies of 1917*; "Goodbye Broadway, Hello France!" from *The Passing Show*; "The Irish Have a Great Day To-Night," "Thine Alone" from *Eileen*; "When You Hear Jackson Moan on His Saxophone" from *So Long, Letty*; "I May Be Gone a Long Long Time" from *Hitchy-Koo*.

Song of the Season

1917–1918 SEASON

The effects a World War had on the Street were gradually becoming clear this season. The economic prosperity in America meant there was more money to invest in shows and patrons had more money in hand to spend on theatre. On the other hand, Broadway was in the midst of a building boom when the United States entered the war. With all labor and materials directed to the war effort, construction on new playhouses stopped and there was a theatre shortage. Producers had to wait longer to secure a venue and productions that were not selling out were prematurely closed so that more promising musicals could fill the space. Another effect of the war was the loss of German and Austrian works which had traditionally comprised a sizable portion of each season's offerings. Even American or British musicals based on such continental plays were not welcomed by a patriotic public. There were ways to get around that but it wasn't easy. The Sigmund Romberg operetta *Maytime* was the most successful musical of the season, running 492 performances, thirty-six more than the Hippodrome extravaganza *Cheer Up*. After providing songs here and there for the Shuberts, Romberg finally got to compose a full score for *Maytime* and it was superb. The libretto and lyrics by Rida Johnson Young were solid and the performances were superior. What was kept secret from the public and even much of the theatre community was that *Maytime* was based on a period German play, the characters' names were Americanized, and the setting was moved from Germany to New York City.

Half of the new musicals this season were revues. In addition to series such as the *Ziegfeld Follies*, Raymond Hitchcock decided to make last season's *Hitchy-Koo* an annual affair and presented *Hitchy-Koo of 1917*. George M. Cohan did likewise and offered *Cohan Revue of 1918*. Fred Stone's comedy partner David Montgomery had died suddenly in 1917 but Stone carried on solo and had a hit with his revue *Jack o' Lantern*. In fact, most of the revues were lucrative ventures this season, all of the above running well beyond 100 performances. Joining them were *Miss 1917, Odds and Ends, Doing Our Bit*, and *The Land of Joy*. To say that these revues were escapist entertainment would be understating the case. The same could be said for the musical comedies this season. But escapist did not mean that quality was low. There were some scintillating book musicals on hand, in particular the Bolton-Kern-Wodehouse Princess Musicals *Leave It to Jane* and *Oh, Lady! Lady!* The most successful musical comedy was *Going Up* by Louis Hirsch (music) and Otto Harbach (book and lyrics) inspired by the public's new fascination with airplanes. Other musical comedies running over 100 performances include *Flo-Flo, The Rainbow Girl, Fancy Free, The Kiss Burglar*, and *Sinbad*. This last was an Al Jolson vehicle that had a book but was mostly a one-man revue. *Over the Top*, a revue that lasted a modest seventy-eight performances, gave Broadway the first chance to see the young dancing duo Adele and Fred Astaire.

The big disappointment of the season fell to the producers who brought the London "Arabian Nights" musical *Chu Chin Chow* to Broadway. This comic musical version of *Ali Baba and the Forty Thieves* was just what war-weary Londoners wanted to see. It had a very funny libretto, a tuneful score, and top-notch performances. The 1916 show was so popular that it ran a staggering 2,238 performances, a West End record not broken for forty years. The American producers smelled big money and booked *Chu Chin Chow* into the mammoth Manhattan Opera House to handle the expected throng. The musical did modest business, rarely selling out the large venue during its 208 performances. London's five-year run would not be copied in New York until *Oklahoma!* twenty-six years hence.

"I'm Always Chasing Rainbows"
Music by Harry Carroll; lyric by Joseph McCarthy
From *Oh, Look!* (1918)
Sung by Harry Fox as Stephen Baird

With so many hit book musicals and revues this season, the modest little *Oh, Look!* might have been overlooked had it not produced the song of the season. The impoverished Stephen Baird (Harry Fox) borrows money from his rich friend Welch (Clarence Nordstrom) but soon finds that money doesn't bring true friends or the girl he pines for. Left alone on stage, Stephen laments his situation by singing the gentle, plaintive ballad "I'm Always Chasing Rainbows." Fox, who had introduced "I Love a Piano" two seasons earlier, brought just the right amount of pathos to the torchy number but also a hint of humor. The quiet song stopped the show. (Theatrical legend has it that the "foxtrot" was named after the singer-dancer Fox.) Ideas for songs come from all sorts of things. In this case, composer Harry Carroll was having an argument with a friend over how unrealistic songwriters could be. Carroll stated that composers and lyricists had to have their heads in the clouds. "We're always chasing rainbows," he said. Both Carroll and the friend immediately felt that phrase would make a hit song. He and his lyricist partner Joseph McCarthy liked the title "I'm Always Chasing Rainbows" and, while considering some musical ideas, Carroll discovered that the opening melody from Frederic' Chopin's "Fantasie Impromptu in C-Sharp Minor" fit the phrase exactly. The rest of the song was built around that enticing section from classical music. The verse introduces Stephen's dilemma with music that is somewhat sluggish, more a case of plodding along than flowing, and a lyric full of questions: "Why have I always been a failure? What can the reason be? I wonder if the world's to blame; I wonder if it could be me?"[18] The refrain, which uses the middle section of Chopin's "Fantasie Impromptu," settles into a graceful, yet not solemn, lullaby. The music now has a wider range and includes many whole notes for the singer to use effectively. "I'm always chasing rainbows," he sings. "Watching clouds drifting by ….My schemes are just like all my dreams,/ Ending in the sky." Both music and lyric are not so reverent as to become a hymn. The tone of the words is more familiar, best illustrated by the parenthetical "believe me" in the line "I never even make a gain, believe me" which is set to three descending quarter notes. The result is a thoroughly intoxicating song which can be appreciated and even remembered after one hearing.

Song of the Season

"I'm Always Chasing Rainbows" was hardly the first popular song to borrow heavily from the classics but it was the first to sell over a million copies of sheet music. *Oh, Look!* ran only two months on Broadway but the subsequent tour was very successful. In London, the ballad was sung by Phyllis Titmus in the musical *Bran Pie* (1919). The nationwide popularity of the song certainly helped. Harry Fox recorded the ballad in 1918, the same year there were discs by Charles Harrison and Harvey Wilson. After dozens of recordings, "I'm Always Chasing Rainbows" went to the top of the charts again in the late 1940s because of a best-selling recording by Perry Como and the Satisfiers. Among the many who have covered the song are Helen Forrest, Judy Garland, Dick Haymes, the Four Freshmen, Roger Williams, Barfota Jazzmen, Jo Stafford, Polly Bergen, Della Reese, Jane Olivor, Harry Nilsson, Barbra Streisand, Mandy Patinkin, Linda Eder, and Mark Lopeman. Garland and Charles Winninger performed it in the film *Ziegfeld Girl* (1941); in *The Merry Monahans* (1944) it was sung by Jack Oakie, Donald O'Connor, and Peggy Ryan; and Betty Grable and John Payne (as Harry Fox) performed it in *The Dolly Sisters* (1945). Instrumental versions of "I'm Always Chasing Rainbows" can be heard in several movies, such as *Suicide Fleet* (1931), *The Great Ziegfeld* (1936), *Rose of Washington Square* (1939), *The Shanghai Gesture* (1941), *Nobody's Darling* (1943), *Awakenings* (1990), and *Magic in the Moonlight* (2014). The song was heard again on Broadway when Debbie Reynolds sang it in the 1973 revival of *Irene*.

Other notable songs from that season: "Will You Remember?," "The Road to Paradise" from *Maytime*; "Rock-a-Bye Your Baby with a Dixie Melody," "My Mammy," "Chloe" from *Sinbad*; "Leave It to Jane," "The Crickets Are Calling," "Cleopatterer" from *Leave It to Jane*; "(Won't You) Wait Till the Cows Come Home?" from *Jack o' Lantern*; "The Land Where the Good Songs Go" from *Miss 1917*; "Going Up," "(Everybody Ought to Know How to Do) The Tickle Toe" from *Going Up*; "Not yet," "When the Ships Come Home" From *Oh, Lady! Lady!*; "Any Time's Kissing Time," "The Cobbler's Song" from *Chu Chin Chow*.

1918–1919 SEASON

There was a lot of musical theatre this season but, unfortunately, none of the thirty-six new shows were exceptional. Any excitement on Broadway came from the performers. For example, the routine musical comedy *Sometime* had little to offer except delightful comic turns by Ed Wynn and Mae West but they were enough to keep the musical on the boards for 283 showings. Star-making performances were seen this season by such up-and-coming artists as Ivy Sawyer, Adele and Fred Astaire, Frank Faye, Ned Sparks, Mitzi Hajos, Louise Groody, Hazel Kirke, Charles Coburn, Eleanor Painter, Charles Ruggles, Clifton Webb, Joseph Santley, and Tessa Kosta. The tide of the war had turned and America was already looking forward to a time of peace. But a new conflict arose when Prohibition went into effect and, in consequence, organized crime increased. Illegal booze would be the subject of many a musical in future. Nora Bayes got a head start on the trend when she added "Prohibition Blues" to her tour of *Ladies First*. Broadway had a crisis of its own when the struggling union Actors' Equity solidified its members and went on strike on August 6, 1919. The historic move halted twelve productions, less than half of the current Broadway shows, but by the time the strike was settled in September, actors were in a much better position.

The big moneymakers on the Street this season were revues. In addition to the series shows—*Ziegfeld Follies, The Passing Show, Hitchy-Koo of 1918*, the Hippodrome spectacular *Everything*—there were some other revues which had long runs, including *Listen Lester* and *Monte Cristo, Jr.* The most unique of the season was Irving Berlin's fundraiser *Yip Yip Yaphank*. He put together a cast of 350 enlisted men and booked the large Century Theatre for thirty-two performances The sketches were about Army life, as were most of Berlin's songs. The hit number was "Mandy" but the most memorable moment was when Sergeant Berlin delivered his wry lament "Oh! How I Hate to Get Up in the Morning." *Yip Yip Yaphank* raised thousands of dollars for the war effort and was fondly remembered for decades after. Considering how weak the scripts and scores were this season, several musical comedies had significant runs. *The Royal Vagabond* and *The Better 'Ole* each ran over 300 performances; *Somebody's Sweetheart* ran 224 times; and surpassing the 100 mark were *Head Over Heels, The Girl Behind the Gun, Ladies First, The Canary, Little Simplicity, Oh, My Dear!, The Velvet Lady, Tumble Inn, She's a Good Fellow,* and *La La Lucille*. (This last show marked the first full score by George Gershwin.) For the second time in two seasons, a huge London hit failed to run on Broadway. *The Maid of the Mountains* was a well-written operetta with a competent score and it pleased British audiences for an astounding 1,352 performances. On Broadway it was greeted with indifference and closed after thirty-seven performances.

"Swanee"
Music by George Gershwin; lyric by Irving Caesar
From *Sinbad* (1918)
Sung by Al Jolson as Gus

Song of the Season

The best song of the season did not debut on Broadway but during the tour of the Al Jolson vehicle *Sinbad*. Jolson was always on the lookout for new songs to interpolate into his shows, usually after the New York opening or on tour. But the story of "Swanee" starts two years before Jolson. Twenty-year-old George Gershwin was employed as a song plugger at the Remick Music Company and wrote his own songs after hours. Lyricist Irving Caesar suggested they write an uptempo number in 2/4 time. This was known as a "one step" song and was more likely to be heard in Harlem than on Broadway. Caesar based his lyric on the opening line of Stephen Foster's "Old Folks at Home": "Way Down upon the Swanee River." But instead of a sentimental Foster ballad, both men wanted a song that jazzed up the old form and had syncopation and even a touch of blues. It was a tall order but, because composer and lyricist were of a set mind, "Swanee" almost wrote itself. Gershwin and Caesar took the song to producer-director Ned Wayburn who liked it and wanted to use it in his new vaudeville entertainment at the Capitol, the largest movie house in New York. The trouble was, the theatre was still being built and, with war-times shortages, construction was slow. The songwriters waited nearly a full year before "Swanee" was performed as part of a revue titled *Demi-Tasse*. Wayburn staged a lavish production number with fifty chorines whose shoes lit up as they danced in the dark to Arthur Pryor's orchestra of sixty players. Suffice it to say that audiences loved the number but could barely recall the actual song. Sheet music was for sale in the lobby but no one was interested. Not until several months later, when Gershwin played the song at a party with Jolson in attendance, did something happen. Jolson had just finished a successful run on Broadway and was about to set off on tour. He offered to interpolate it into *Sinbad*, the songwriters agreed, and Jolson sang "Swanee" for the rest of his life.

"Swanee" cannot be termed a "coon song" even though it is Southern and can be "shouted." There is no Southern or "Negro" dialect in the lyric and the music is in a more slick, urban tone. The verse races ahead verbally and musically. "I've been away from you a long time" is not about a sweetheart but a place where "the birds are singing it is song time … the banjo's strumming soft and low."[19] The object of such affection is not revealed until the verse's final line,

"Swanee, you're calling me!" The refrain turns into a march of sorts (though the "allegro moderato" time has a signature of 2/4) as it gets more expansive even as it consists mostly of eighth or quarter notes. The repetition in the music is echoed in the lyric "how I love, how I love, My dear old Swanee" and one can feel the composition's propulsion in the "my mammy's/ Waiting for me,/ Praying for me/ Down by the Swanee." The lyric concludes with the decision "The folks up north will see me no more/ When I get to that Swanee shore." Although "Swanee" is not a difficult song to sing, it has subtleties that reveal Gershwin's sense of innovation. The key change from verse to refrain is felt, if not noticed, and the way the rhythm presses forward is technically complex. Caesar's lyric has its own clever touches, such as using the word "how" for the downbeat in "how I love you, how I love you" instead of the expected emphasis on the word "love." Spelling out "Dixie" but letting that final "e" turn into the word "Even" is the kind of playful lyric writing that Gershwin's music demands.

Because Jolson recorded "Swanee" in 1920 and the disc sold 2 million copies, the song has long been associated with him. But the sheet music sold a million copies, making it Gershwin's first and greatest hit. Other early recordings were made by Yerke's Novelty Five, the Peerless Quartet, the All-Star Trio, the Elliotts, and Al Bernard with Frank M. Kamplain. There have been hundreds of recordings since then, including covers by such diverse artists as the Hoosier Hot Shots, Georgie Stoll, Maurice Chevalier, Paul Anka, Sid Ramin, George Wright, Russ Conway, Jaye P. Morgan, Jackie Wilson, Aretha Franklin, Jim Nabors, The Temptations, Jimmy Roselli, Bing Crosby, Merle Travis, Charleston Chasers, Ruthie Henshall, Patti Austin, and Chie Ayado. Judy Garland recorded it in 1939 then sang it on screen years later in *A Star Is Born* (1954). Jolson can be heard singing "Swanee" on the soundtracks of *The Singing Kid* (1936), *Rhapsody in Blue* (1945), *The Jolson Story* (1946), *Jolson Sings Again* (1949), and *The Story of Will Rogers* (1952).

Other notable songs from that season: "Mandy," "Oh! How I Hate to Get Up in the Morning" from *Yip Yip Yaphank*; "Any Old Place with You" from *A Lonely Romeo*; "There's More to the Kiss Than XXX" from *Good Morning, Judge*; "When I Hear a Syncopated Tune" from *Ziegfeld Follies of 1918*; "The Real American Folk Son (Is a Rag)," "Prohibition Blues" from *Ladies First*; "Nobody But You" from *La La Lucille*; "A Paradise for Two," "Live for Today" from *The Maid of the Mountains*.

Song of the Season

1919–1920 SEASON

The new season started out awkwardly with the Actor's Equity strike which kept some theatres dark for a few weeks. But Broadway caught up and before the season was over, forty-seven musical productions opened. Once again, revues were plentiful (seventeen this season) and popular (nine were hits). Joining the established *Ziegfeld Follies*, *The Passing Show*, and the Hippodrome attraction, this year titled *Happy Days*, was a new series that would give Ziegfeld a run for his money. *George White's Scandals of 1919* was the first of fourteen productions which would introduce important songwriters and performers over the next two decades. White was a dancer/producer who had appeared in two editions of the *Ziegfeld Follies*. He was a shrewd and savvy producer and was able to woo major stars to his musicals. Also new this season were the profitable revues *As You Were*, the *Shubert Gaieties*, the *Greenwich Village Follies*, *What's in a Name*, and *The Ed Wynn Carnival*. Yet none of the revues on the Street were able to outshine this season's *Ziegfeld Follies*. Critics and playgoers at the time declared it the very best of the whole series and history can look back and agree with them. Instead of a handful of songwriters working on the show, most of the songs for the 1919 edition were by Irving Berlin. "A Pretty Girl Is Like a Melody," "You'd Be Surprised," "You Cannot Make Your Shimmy on Tea," "I've Got My Captain Working for Me Now," and "I Want to See a Minstrel Show" were the most applauded. The sketches were better than usual, the production values were outstanding, and most of the Ziegfeld favorites (Eddie Cantor, Bert Williams, Marilyn Miller, Van and Schenck, Eddie Dowling, the Fairbanks Twins, etc.) were back and were better than ever.

Irene was, by far, the most successful book musical of the season, running 675 performances. The score was by Harry Tierney (music) and Joe McCarthy (lyrics) and Edith Day starred as the Irish-American heroine of the title who is wooed by a Long Island millionaire. Other book musicals to have profitable runs include Victor Herbert's *My Golden Girl*, Sigmund Romberg's *The Magic Melody*, Jerome Kern's *The Night Boat*, and Rudolf Friml's *The Little Whopper*. Newcomer Oscar Hammerstein II (grandson of the impresario of the same name) wrote the book and lyrics for Herbert Stothart's music for *Always You* which lasted two months. Running much longer were *Buddies*, *Honey Girl*, *Monsieur Beaucaire*, *Lassie*, *Roly-Boly Eyes*, *A Lonely Romeo*, and *Apple Blossoms*, the last featuring Adele and Fred Astaire. The postwar slump in the economy and some inflation did not seem to affect Broadway greatly but one thing was getting obvious: production costs and ticket prices were rising considerably. Producers blamed the increase on the agreements made with Actors' Equity. The lavish *Ziegfeld Follies of 1917* cost $88,000, three times the amount for an average Broadway musical. For this season's edition, Ziegfeld had to pay $170,000. Over a two-year period, the top ticket price for a musical went from $2 to $3.50. These were the biggest jumps in prices since the Civil War! But soon the economy would recover, the most prosperous era of the century would begin, and the 1920s would be a golden time for Broadway.

> "A Pretty Girl Is Like a Melody"
> Music and lyric by Irving Berlin
> From *Ziegfeld Follies of 1919*
> Sung by John Steel

Usually described as the theme song for the *Ziegfeld Follies*, "A Pretty Girl Is Like a Melody" was showcased in the 1919 edition but was rarely used in later editions. One might better say the song captured the "philosophy" of the series and took Florenz Ziegfeld's notion of the idealized American female and put it to music. Although the ballad was the centerpiece of that year's *Follies*, it was actually a late addition. Irving Berlin had contributed songs to earlier editions but suggested to Ziegfeld he write all the songs for one *Follies*. Because singers often convinced Ziegfeld to let them interpolate a song that was promising, this wasn't possible. Berlin ended up contributing thirteen songs and the variety is remarkable: ballads, comedy songs, dance numbers, patriotic songs, rags, and even minstrel numbers. But Ziegfeld wasn't satisfied. He'd spent a fortune on six elaborate show girl costumes and there wasn't a song in the revue that was right for showing them off. He gave Berlin color sketches of the costumes and sent him home to come up with something. Looking at the six sketches, Berlin thought each might be companion to a piece of classical music. He selected Antonín Dvořák's "Humoresque" (op. 101, no. 7), Felix Mendelssohn's "Spring Song" (op. 62, no. 6), Jules Massenet's "Elegy" from *Les Érinnyes*, Jacques Offenbach's "Barcarolle" from *The Tales of Hoffman*, Franz Schubert's "Serenade" from *Schwanengesang*, and Robert Schumann's "Träumerei" from *Kinderszenen*. Berlin's plan was that a brief section of each piece of classical music would accompany each girl. Then he realized that the six selections needed to be united in some way and that led to "A Pretty Girl Is Like a Melody."

The verse introduces the metaphor of music being like a beautiful woman. The male singer claims to "have an ear for music" as well as "an eye for a maid."[20] With the claim that "they go together, like sunny weather goes with the month of May," the lyric solidifies the song's premise. The music is light and sprightly, using eighth and quarter notes to bounce up and down the scale. In fact, there is not a whole note anywhere in the verse. Berlin saves that for the refrain which begins with "A pretty girl is like a melody that haunts you night and day." Using "she" throughout, the lyric praises women and music interchangeably. She is a "marathon" that runs "around your brain" and one is unable to escape the memory of her. Perhaps the most potent idea is how "She will leave you and then come back again." The music turns stately in the refrain but is never sluggish. It flows effortlessly forward with very few rests. Such a tempo conjures up visions of beautifully bedecked show girls gracefully descending a staircase. Berlin had no trouble picturing this since it happened in every Ziegfeld show. The lyric is equally felicitous. Words or phrases with three counts are at every turn: melody, memory, marathon, run-around, back-again. Also, the metaphor introduced in the verse is further developed in the refrain. The phrase "a haunting refrain" is famous, now a cliché. Also, the idea of music (and a woman) running a marathon in your brain is certainly unique.

In the fifth spot in the *Follies*, John Steel sang "A Pretty Girl Is Like a Melody" then the five girls (the sixth costume representing Schumann was cut in rehearsal) enter, each accompanied by the appropriate classical music. The production number then concluded with Steel returning to Berlin's song. It was a highlight of the 1919 edition, a show filled with highlights. "A Pretty Girl Is Like a Melody" went to the number one spot in sheet music sales and early recordings were made by Steel, Ben Selvin's Novelty Orchestra, Sam Ash, and the Happy Six. Over the years there have been hundreds of discs made by such varied artists as Denny Dennis, Kenny Baker, Phil Brito, Vic Damone, Pat Boone, Eddie South, Guy Lombardo and His Royal Canadians, Claude Bolling, Bobby Vinton, Sonny Lester, Earl Hines, Tom Pletcher and the Classic Jazzband, and Adam Makowicz. Recordings by female singers are less common but there are discs by Vivian Blaine, Jane Morgan, Joni Janak, Beegie Adair, Margi Harrell, and others. "A Pretty Girl Is Like a Melody" was given a stunning Hollywood treatment in *The Great Ziegfeld* (1936) where it was sung by Dennis Morgan (dubbed by Allan Jones). It was also sung on screen by Ethel Merman in *Alexander's Ragtime Band* (1938), Fred Astaire in *Blue Skies* (1946), and Dan Dailey and Ethel Merman in *There's No Business Like Show Business* (1954). Over the years, the song has also been used for countless beauty pageants, debutante balls, fashion shows, and even strip-tease acts.

Other notable songs from that season: "You'd Be Surprised," "You Cannot Make Your Shimmy Shake on Tea," "I Want to See a Minstrel Show," "I've Got My Captain Working for Me Now" from *Ziegfeld Follies of 1919*; "When My Baby Smiles at Me," "I Want a Daddy Who Will Rock Me to Sleep" from *Greenwich Village Follies*; "Ida, Sweet as Apple Cider" from *Roly-Boly Eyes*; "I'm Forever Blowing Bubbles" from *The Passing Show of 1919*; "Alice Blue Gown," "The Last Part of Every Party," "Castle of Dreams" from *Irene*; "Left All Alone Again Blues," "Whose Baby Are You?" from *The Night Boat*; "Oh, By Jingo" from *Linger Longer Letty*; "Little Girls, Goodbye" from *Apple Blossoms*.

1920–1921 SEASON

Because so few musicals from the 1920s are revived today, one might come to the conclusion that there weren't many book musicals in that decade; or that they weren't very good. But there were more musicals on Broadway in the Roaring Twenties than any decade before or since. As for quality, many shows were critical and popular hits. But in those pre-*Oklahoma!* days, when musicals were not expected to be integrated, a musical comedy with a coherent book, some good jokes, a little romance, memorable songs, and star performances was all one needed. Take this season's *Sally* as an example. Guy Bolton's libretto was what is known as a Cinderella plot. The orphaned Sally Rhinelander (Marilyn Miller) works as a dish washer in Greenwich Village. The monied Blair Farquar (Irving Fisher) comes to the restaurant to hire workers for a party he's throwing and is smitten by Sally. The day of the party he is thrilled when the dancer that the theatrical agent Otis Hooper (Walter Catlett) has booked doesn't show and Sally gets to perform. Hooper is so impressed that he gets Sally into the *Ziegfeld Follies* where she becomes a star and wins the hand of Blair. Most of the songs in the score were by Jerome Kern, with P. G. Wodehouse and B. G. DeSylva doing the lyrics, and included the runaway hit "Look for the Silver Lining" and some other splendid songs. Add to that ballet music by Victor Herbert, masterful sets by Joseph Urban, and a glowing performance by Miller. The Ziegfeld production ran a year and a half, returned in 1923, and was revived in 1948. Just because *Sally* isn't revived any more doesn't diminish its impact and entertainment value in 1920.

There were forty-nine musicals this season, including some other *Sally*-like shows that ran well over 100 performances. Showing a tidy profit were *Mary, Tickle Me, Honeydew, Pitter Patter, Mecca, Lady Billy,* and *Two Little Girls in Blue*, the last offering the first full score by composer Vincent Youmans. But with rising production costs, the 100-mark was no longer a guarantee of success. This was particularly true of the expensive revues. The Hippodrome extravaganza *Good Times* ran 456 performances and, despite the huge overhead, made some money. But one wonders just how much profit there was with the *Ziegfeld Follies* (123 performances), *George White's Scandals* (134 performances), *Cinderella on Broadway* (126 performances), *The Century Revue* (150 performances), and *Jim Jam Jems* (105 performances). Even book musicals which hovered near the 100 mark were at risk, as with Sigmund Romberg's *Love Birds*, Herbert Stothart's *Jimmie*, and Percy Wenrich's *The Right Girl*. But then there were usually some surprises each season. The Oscar Straus operetta *The Last Waltz* was deemed far behind the times by the critics but it was a hit at 185 performances. Some revues without major stars sometimes ran and ran, as with *Mecca, Greenwich Village Follies of 1920, Afgar,* and *Tip-Top*. The biggest surprise of all was *Shuffle Along*, an African American musical that drew Broadway patrons up to 63rd Street for 484 performances. Many historians see the success of *Shuffle Along* as the beginning of the Harlem Renaissance.

"I'm Just Wild About Harry"
Music by Eubie Blake; lyric by Noble Sissle
From *Shuffle Along* (1921)
Sung by Lottie Gee as Jessie Williams, and chorus

Not only the first successful, full-length musical written, directed, and performed by African American artists, *Shuffle Along* was also one of the most joyous shows of the decade and it opened the door for all-Black musicals that could appeal to white and Black audiences. In the city of Jimtown, grocery store partners Steve Jenkins (Flourney Miller) and Sam Peck (Aubrey Lyles) are each running for mayor, each promising the other that the loser will be made chief of police. After Steve wins and Sam heads the police department, corruption sets in and the reform candidate Harry Walton (Roger Matthews) gets the people behind him and soon Steve and Sam are back in the grocery store. Flournoy Miller and Aubrey Lyles penned the risible libretto and Eubie Blake (music) and Noble Sissle (lyrics) wrote the scintillating score. The show tried out in various cities before getting a berth in a Broadway house far from the mainstream. Word slowly filtered down and soon the musical was a must-see sensation. Also, the song "I'm Just Wild About Harry" was soon sweeping the country. In the show it was sung by Jessie Williams (Lottie Gee) and the chorus encouraging Harry to run for office.

The number sounds like a campaign march but its lyric suggests something much more personal. After a brief verse, the refrain comes on strong with "I'm just wild about Harry/ And Harry's wild about me!"[1] Harry is described as sweet as "choc'late candy" and "honey from the bee." The music is a fast fox-trot that harkens back to the cake walk style of the nineteenth century. A series of short explosions of melody keep the music lively and varied even though it sticks mostly to a C-major scale. But the song didn't start like that. Blake had an eclectic ear for different kinds of music and wrote "I'm Just Wild About Harry" as a traditional European waltz. But during rehearsal the singer Lottie Gee pointed out that white audiences coming to an all-Black musical will find it disturbing to hear her singing a waltz. Lyricist Sissle agreed and so Blake rewrote the number into the high-stepping song everyone knows today. Gee was also worried about the love duet "Love Will Find a Way" which she was to sing with Roger Matthews. White audiences had never seen a sincere love song performed by African Americans. Such duets were usually comic or sarcastic. The whole company was greatly relieved when the duet was encored on opening night. "I'm Just Wild About Harry" was also a hit in London where it was sung by Florence Mills in the revue *Dover Street to Dixie* (1923).

Sheet music sales for "I'm Just Wild About Harry" flew off the shelves and the song remains in print. There were early recordings by Blake (conducting the show's orchestra for the Victor label), Marion Harris, Vincent Lopez, Benny Krueger, Vaughn De Leath, Louis Mitchell, and Paul Whiteman. Over the decades the song has appealed to a variety of singers and bands and it became a favorite of jazz musicians. Notable discs were made by Sidney Bechet, Billy Cotton, the Clark Sisters, Thelma Carpenter and Avon Long, Anita Ellis, Jimmy Mazzy, Red Nichols and His Five Pennies, Peggy Lee, Carmen Cavallaro, Willie "The Lion" Smith, Cleo Laine, the Bobby Gordon Sextet, Dick Hyman, Shani Wallis, Jessica Molaskey, Adam Swanson, and Rebecca Kilgore with the Harry Allen Quartet. Although the song never fell out of favor, it found a new wave of popularity in 1948 when President Harry Truman used it as the official song of his successful re-election campaign.

On screen, Judy Garland sang "I'm Just Wild About Harry" as part of a minstrel show in *Babes in Arms* (1939). That same year, Alice Faye sang it with Louis Prima's band in *Rose of Washington Square* and Priscilla Lane sang it in a nightclub in *The Roaring Twenties*. Nan Wynn performed it also in a nightclub in *A Shot in the Dark* (1941), as did Carmen Miranda in *Greenwich Village* (1944). Al Jolson dubbed the number for Larry Parks in *Jolson Sings Again* (1949); Jolson's recording later showed up on the charts. The song was also sung on screen by an unidentified singer in a nightclub in *So This Is Love* (1953), James Nesbitt in *Wild About Harry* (2000), Chiara Schoras with Ian Whitcomb and His Bungalow Boys in *The Cat's Meow* (2001), and Lilias White in *The Chaperone* (2018). "I'm Just Wild About Harry" was heard again on Broadway when sung by Janet Powell, Lynnie Godfrey, and the female cast of the revue *Eubie!* (1978), Loretta Devine in *Big Deal* (1986), and Audra McDonald, Adrienne Warren, and Curtis Holland in *Shuffle Along, or the Making of the Musical Sensation of 1921 and All That Followed* (2016).

Other notable songs from that season: "Love Will Find a Way," "I'm Craving for That Kind of Love," "Baltimore Buzz" from *Shuffle Along*; "Look for the Silver Lining," "Wild Rose," "Whip-poor-will," "The Church around the Corner" from *Sally*; "The Love Nest," "Tom Tom Toddle" from *Mary*; "I'm a Vamp from East Broadway," "I Was a Florodora Baby" from *Ziegfeld Follies of 1920*; "Rickety Crickety" from *Jimmie*; "Waiting for the Sun to Come Out" from *The Sweetheart Shop*; "The Moon Shines on the Moonshine" from *Broadway Brevities of 1920*; "If a Wish Could Make It So" from *Tickle Me*; "Dolly," "Oh Me! Oh My! Oh You!" from *Two Little Girls in Blue*.

Song of the Season

1921–1922 SEASON

With only two revivals this season, theatregoers had their choice of thirty-eight new works to patronize. But eighteen of them were revues so it limited one's choice for book musicals. Joining the *Ziegfeld Follies, George White's Scandals, Greenwich Village Follies*, and other familiar revues was a new series that would prove to be laudable entertainment for the next four years. The *Music Box Revues* were the brainchild of Irving Berlin who, with his producing partner Sam Harris, built a playhouse that was not as cavernous as the big venues but still had enough seats to turn a profit. They called their new house the Music Box Theatre and it opened with the *Music Box Revue of 1921–1922*. Berlin wrote the songs, which included two future standards: "Everybody Step" and "Say It with Music." The series would become known for its nimble-witted sketches but this first entry found more comedy in songs such as "I'm a Dumbell" and "They Call It Dancing." Whereas the *Follies* was lavish, expensive, and star-studded, the *Music Box Revues* were intimate, clever, and offered experienced performers delivering high-quality songs. The series was a hit from the start, this first edition running 440 times—more than all of the season's other revues.

It was an estimable year for book musicals as well. Sigmund Romberg adapted classical music by Franz Schubert for his score for *Blossom Time*, the season's biggest hit at 516 performances. Romberg had two other money-makers when he wrote his own music for *The Blushing Bride* and *The Rose of Stamboul*. The Astaires, now *bona fide* Broadway stars, kept *For Goodness Sake* on the boards, as did Irene Bordoni save *The French Doll*. Rudolf Friml had modest success with *The Blue Kitten* but Jerome Kern had a major one with *Good Morning, Dearie*. Comic Ed Wynn became his own producer for his vehicle *The Perfect Fool* and had no trouble filling seats for 275 performances. By this time, Al Jolson was so popular at the Winter Garden Theatre that the name of the show hardly mattered as long as his name was on the marquee. Sometimes Jolson even stopped the proceedings and asked the audience if it was all right to send the rest of the cast home and he'll just sing his favorite songs the rest of the night; the crowd always agreed. This year the Jolson show was titled *Bombo* and in it he introduced three song standards, "April Showers," "Toot, Toot, Tootsie," and (during the tour) "California, Here I Come."

"April Showers"
Music by Louis Silvers; lyric by B. G. DeSylva
From *Bombo* (1921)
Sung by Al Jolson as Gus

Is the profound observation that "April showers bring May flowers" one of the oldest and most tired clichés in English? Well, it is certainly old. The English farmer-poet Thomas Tusser (*c.* 1524–80) is best known for his poem "A Hundreth Good Pointes of Husbandrie," first published in 1557. In this lengthly piece he gives instructions to women for running an efficient household, particularly an Elizabethan garden. In this poem he notes, "Sweet April showers,/ Do spring May flowers." I doubt if Tin Pan Alley lyricist B. G. (Buddy) DeSylva was a follower of Elizabethan poets but he knew his clichés and how often a hit song can come from such overused expressions. DeSylva's lyric for the verse of "April Showers" is short but gives away the whole point of the song, that of April rain resulting in colorful blooms. Louis Silvers' music for the verse also gives a lot away. The way the singer can hold on to "bliss" and "flowers" foreshadows the way the refrain will provide a chance to warble. Within a narrow range, the music glides slightly up and down the scale then stops abruptly for a rest and then the song proper, beginning with "Though April showers may come your way,/ They bring the flowers that bloom in May."[2] The lyric cautions one not to complain about the cloudy and rainy weather since violets and daffodils will follow. And if that is not optimistic enough, one should "keep on looking for the bluebird" for his song will surely be heard soon. The lyric for the refrain is personal, supposedly speaking to a single person. "You" and "your" are used and, it is suggested, that the "you" is depressed and unhappy for reasons outside of the rain. So "April Showers" is not an observation of nature but a "cheer up" song with gushing optimism as the solution. If it had been written a decade later during the Depression, the song would be categorized as a "Depression chaser." In fact, when later sung in the 1930s, it became just that. DeSylva is unapologetic about the April/May cliché and goes so far as to introduce that old standby the Bluebird of Happiness into the mix. Imagining that the raindrops are violets is more of the same thing. "April Showers" is unrestrained optimism. Oddly, Louis Silvers' music is very restrained. A series of musical phrases carefully ascend the scale, only to just-as-carefully tumble down again. It is predictable but it works. Not so noticeable is the many key changes in the refrain.

Although "April Showers" was long associated with Jolson, it has been sung and recorded by hundreds of others. There were early discs by Arthur Fields, Ernest Hare, Charles Harrison, and Paul Whiteman. Among the many notable recordings after them were Abe Lyman and His California Orchestra (vocal by Louis Rapp), Arthur Prysock, Guy Lombardo (vocal by Dion Rodney), Cab Calloway, Ruth Etting, Bing Crosby, Judy Garland, Woody Herman, Patti Page, Bobby Rydell, Carol Burnett, Margaret Whiting, Leslie Uggams, Cynthia Sayer, Eddie Fisher, Julian Yeo, and Nicki Parrott. Jolson recorded "April Showers" for the first time in 1921, followed by discs in 1932 (with Guy Lombardo's Orchestra), 1946 (for the soundtrack of *The Jolson Story*), and 1949 (for *Jolson Sings Again*). A year before he made *The Jazz Singer* (1927), Jolson sang the song in the early sound short *A Plantation Act*. He reprised it on screen in the feature *The Singing Kid* (1936). "April Showers" has been performed on screen by Jeanne Crain (dubbed by Luann Hogan) in *Margie* (1946), Milton Berle and a boys choir in *Always Leave Them Laughing* (1949), Jerry Rees on the soundtrack for the animated *The Brave Little Toaster* (1987), Ian Whitcomb and His Bungalow Boys in *The Cat's Meow* (2001), and Max Casella, Danielle Ferland, Debi Mazar, and Bobby Slayton in *Wonder Wheel* (2017).

Other notable songs from that season: "Toot, Toot, Tootsie," "California, Here I Come" from *Bombo*; "Second Hand Rose," "Mon Homme (My Man)" from *Ziegfeld Follies of 1921*; "Song of Love," "Serenade" from *Blossom Time*; "Everybody Step," "Say It with Music" from *The Music Box Revue 1921-1922*; "Three O'Clock in the Morning" from *Greenwich Village Follies*; "Good Morning, Dearie," "Ka-lu-a," "Blue Danube Blues," "Way Down Town" from *Good Morning, Dearie*; "Do It Again" from *The French Doll*; "Drifting Along with the Tide" from *George White's Scandals*.

1922–1923 SEASON

Business was booming on the Street this season with more musicals opening and more of them running longer than usual. The fact that the quality of the shows was disappointing defines an era when audiences were willing and able to pay top dollar for mediocre work. Forty-seven musicals opened, a new record, and twenty-two of them showed a profit. Actually, several did much more than that. *Better Times*, the Hippodrome extravaganza, performed 415 times, but that was bested by the *Ziegfeld Follies of 1922* which (in two engagements) totaled 520 performances and the Vincent Youmans' book musical *Wildflower* with 477 showings. *The Music Box Revue of 1922–1923*, *The Gingham Girl*, and *Sally, Irene and Mary* each ran over 300; *The Lady in Ermine*, the *Greenwich Village Follies*, *Up She Goes*, *Molly Darling*, and *Little Nellie Kelly* all ran over 200; and another six shows ran over the 100 mark. The fact that none of the above-mentioned musicals are remembered or revived today says a lot. In some cases, a commendable libretto was weakened by a forgettable score. More often than not, a promising score was tied to a lackluster book. This situation was noted by commentators at the time; history has not proved them wrong.

Fond memories of the season might be attributed to wonderful star performances, some dizzily impressive sets and costumes, and a scattering of beloved songs. Joining the ranks of stage favorites this season were the comedy duo of Bobby Clark and Paul McCullough, Helen Ford, Fred Allen, James Barton, and George Jessel. With so many revues competing for attention, impressive scenery and costumes became more essential. Joseph Urban's exhilarating designs for the *Ziegfeld Follies* usually got the most praise but critics and playgoers were finding much to admire in the production values of the *Music Box Revues, George White's Scandals*, and other revues, not to mention the occasional book musical. While few of the season's musical scores were deemed first-rate, there were several songs that pleased even on first hearing. Sometimes they came from the hit shows, such as "Pack Up Your Sins (And Go to the Devil)" from *The Music Box Revue of 1922–1923*, "Bambalina" from *Wildflower*, and "Carolina in the Morning" from *The Passing Show of 1922*. Sometimes future song standards were heard for the first time in less successful ventures, as with "I'll Build a Stairway to Paradise" from *George White's Scandals of 1922* and "Way Down Yonder in New Orleans" from *Spice of 1922*. Perhaps the lack of outstanding scores this season might have had something to do with songwriters Cole Porter, Oscar Hammerstein, Richard Rodgers, Lorenz Hart, Dorothy Fields, Arthur Schwartz, and Howard Dietz all still struggling to get noticed. Once they were, the American musical theatre would not be lacking in great songs.

"Nellie Kelly, I Love You"
Music and lyric by George M. Cohan
From *Little Nellie Kelly* (1922)
Sung by Charles King as Jerry Conroy, and company

Song of the Season

George M. Cohan continued to be a significant force on Broadway despite the controversy that surrounded him after the Actors' Equity strike of 1919. As both a performer and a producer, Cohan found himself on both sides of the argument. When he decided to side with management, he was shunned by many in the theatrical community. Cohan performed less after that and concentrated on producing and writing. *Little Nellie Kelly*, which ran 276 performances, was one of his biggest hits. It is mostly remembered today for the unabashedly Irish ballad "Nellie Kelly, I Love You." It was sung by the wisecracking Irishman Jerry Conroy (Charles King) who loves the policeman's daughter Nellie but she is being wooed by the monied Jack Lloyd. So Jerry crashes a party thrown by Lloyd and sings the song to Nellie. The lyric in the verse is in the third person, singing about Nellie and how no one knows if there is one particular boy who she loves. The music is a sluggish Irish jig and more a tease than a resolved melody. The refrain has more expansive music, turning into a flowing waltz that is less Irish and more European than Cohan normally writes. The refrain's lyric begins "It's the same old song they sing,/ I love you!"[3] Cohan is not apologetic about using the "same old song" when the music is so entrancing. It seems all the boys are "mad about Nellie" and bring her "flowers all dripping with dew." In fact, they all sing to her, joining in "the chorus of Nellie Kelly, I love you!" Again the point of view is third person. One sings *about* Nellie rather than directly to her. But that doesn't keep the song from being very romantic in a slangy Cohan way. There are plenty of times in the song when the singer can hold a high note, warbling in the Irish tenor tradition. Also, sometimes the number is performed as a lively dance piece, other times as a slow ballad.

Sheet music sales for "Nellie Kelly, I Love You" sold very well and soon the song was sung or played by many Irish-American singers and bands. Charles Hart, the Bar Harbor Society Orchestra (vocal by Elliot Shaw), Billy Burton, the Majestic Dance Orchestra (vocal by Bob Thomas), Sam Ash, and Billy Murray with the American Quartet each made a record of the song in 1922. Later came discs by Phil Regan, Prince's Dance Band, William Reese, the Blue Amberol Quartette, the Emerson Dance Orchestra (vocal by Arthur Hall), Paul Renard, Arthur Lange's Orchestra, and the Wedderburn Oldtimers Orchestra. On screen, Douglas McPhail and a chorus of policemen sang "Nellie Kelly, I Love You" to Judy Garland in *Little Nellie Kelly* (1940), then later in the movie it was reprised by Garland, McPhail. George Murphy, and Charles Winninger. Frances Langford sang it as part of a medley in *Yankee Doodle Dandy* (1942). On Broadway, the number was sung by Joel Grey, Bernadette Peters, and the company in *George M!* (1968).

Other notable songs from that season: "You Remind Me of My Mother" from *Little Nelly Kelly*; "I'll Build a Stairway to Paradise" from *George White's Scandals of 1922*; "Mr. Gallagher and Mr. Shean" from *Ziegfeld Follies of 1922*; "Carolina in the Morning" from *The Passing Show of 1922*; "When Hearts Are Young" from *The Lady in Ermine*; "Pack Up Your Sins (And Go to the Devil)," "Lady of the Evening," "Crinoline Days" from *The Music Box Revue of 1922–1923*; "Wildflower," "Bambalina" from *Wildflower*; "Way Down Yonder in New Orleans," "An Old-Fashioned Cake Walk" from *Spice of 1922*.

1923–1924 SEASON

Once again, forty-seven musicals opened on Broadway this season. Nineteen of them were revues. New revues seem to come out of nowhere and some of them used the word "follies" in the title, which irritated Florenz Ziegfeld to no end. But because his *Ziegfeld Follies* got the word from a French revue, he couldn't copyright the title. So this year saw the *Grand Street Follies* and the *Greenwich Village Follies* among the many revues. Two new series, *Earl Carroll's Vanities* and *Artists and Models* quickly got a reputation for pushing the boundaries of nudity on stage. The two revues may not have had the most beautiful girls on Broadway but they surely had the least-dressed females. To no one's surprise, both shows enjoyed long runs. A new revue that was quite a sensation in its own way was *Andre Charlot's Revue* (often listed as *Charlot's Revue*) which didn't rely on sex appeal. Charlot had been presenting smart revues with some outstanding talents in London since 1912. He assembled the best songs and his favorite performers and introduced them to America with an intimate revue in which Gertrude Lawrence, Beatrice Lillie, and Jack Buchanan made their Broadway debuts. *Charlot's Revue* was a surprise hit at 298 performances; Buchanan would rarely return to New York but Lillie and Lawrence would each become enduring and endearing Broadway stars.

Among the other musicals noticeable this season for introducing new talent were: *Little Jessie James*, which featured Miriam Hopkins and Allen Kearns in supporting roles, and ran 385 performances, making it the longest run of the season now that the Hippodrome was temporarily dark; *Helen of Troy, New York*, the first Broadway libretto by celebrated playwrights George S. Kaufman and Marc Connelly and the first score by the team of Harry Ruby and Bert Kalmar; *I'll Say She Is*, which introduced vaudeville comics the Marx Brothers to Broadway where they delighted audiences with their shenanigans for over 300 performances; *The Greenwich Village Follies* marking the New York debut of dancer-choreographer Martha Graham; *Battling Buttler*, an English import which gave Charles Ruggles his first leading role; and *Stepping Stones*, in which comic Fred Stone performed with his daughter Dorothy, securing her Broadway career. Star comic W. C. Fields made a career change, leaving the revue format and starring in the book musical *Poppy* where he played the hilarious Eustace McGargle 346 times. Eddie Cantor also tried a book musical, *Kid Boots*, and it ran even longer. The season's finest score was the one Jerome Kern and P. G. Wodehouse wrote for the Princess Musical *Sitting Pretty*. Guy Bolton wrote the clever libretto and the young cast was very appealing. Although the critics sang the praises of the whole production, *Sitting Pretty* only managed to run three months and none of its excellent songs became popular. Such was not the case with *Runnin' Wild*, an all-Black book musical which also delighted the press and managed to run 228 times. This time there was an outstanding song and dance, "Charleston," which soon came to be the sound of the new Jazz Age.

Song of the Season

> "Charleston"
> Music and lyric by James P. Johnson, Cecil Mack
> From *Runnin' Wild* (1923)
> Sung by Elisabeth Welch as Ruth Little, and chorus

As sometimes happens with songs about a specific dance, the lyric for "Charleston" has pretty much disappeared and the piece is known today mainly as an instrumental number. So the question that comes up with "Charleston" is: which came first? The music or the dance? The movements involved in dancing the Charleston are based on the "Juba," a dance brought by enslaved people from Africa to Charleston, South Carolina. The Juba involved rhythmic stomping, kicking, and slapping; it was so physical that Juba became a challenge dance enjoyed by Americans at the turn of the twentieth century. The dance moved onto the stage in 1911 when an act called the Whitman Sisters performed it in Harlem. A decade later a form of the Charleston was first seen on Broadway in the all-Black musical *Liza*. There was a number in that show titled "That Brownskin Flapper" by Maceo Pinkard which was sung and danced by Gertrude Saunders and the "flappers." The following season, *Runnin' Wild* was trying out in Boston and Elisabeth Welch and the chorus performed for the first time the song and dance which was now listed as "Charleston." James P. Johnson, a composer and musician who favored the stride school of jazz piano, had heard the sounds of dock workers in the South Carolina city and used their driving rhythm for "Charleston." The music features a five-chord ragtime progression which would later become the standard harmonics in jazz. Johnson's composition not only lends itself to dancing but practically dictates where the kicks and slaps should occur. What Saunders and the chorus performed in *Runnin' Wild* on Broadway was probably much changed from the original Juba but, regardless of whatever it was, "Charleston" was an immediate success. Within a year the dance was sweeping the country and, thanks to dancer Josephine Baker, then spread to Europe.

One must not forget that "Charleston" started out as a song. The lyric was by Cecil Mark and it contributed greatly to the song's early success. The text is not in an African American dialect but it is slangy and jazzy all the same. The lyric praises the dance "made in Carolina" by exclaiming "there's nothing finer."[4] The Charleston is a "comer" that allows one to "shuffle" and lead "to something new." The highest compliment is the slangy line, "Man I'm telling you, it's a lapazoo!" Because it is a dance song, there is a good deal of repetition in the music but the lyric for every section differs. Unlike many dance songs, instructions on how the dance is performed are not found in the lyric. The words celebrate the dance itself as well as the city that inspired it all. Unfortunately, nearly all recordings of "Charleston" are instrumental and the lyric is rarely sung or heard.

Johnson recorded the music for "Charleston" in 1923 using the stride piano method. That same year, a disc by Paul Whiteman hit the charts. There were also early records of note by the Ambassadors and the Golden Gate Orchestra. Among the many notable recordings of "Charleston" are those by Isham Jones Orchestra, Arthur Gibbs and His Gang, Bob Wilson and His Varsity Rhythm Boys, Winifred Atwell, Louis Prima, the Ernie Fields Orchestra, Ben Selvin's Knickerbockers, and the Tennessee Tooters. On occasion, a recording includes a vocal. Bob Crosby sang it with his Bobcats in a 1958 disc and in 1961 Chubby Checker recorded the song with Mack's lyric. But recordings, piano rolls, and sheet music sales cannot fully illustrate just how popular this song was in the 1920s. It was in the repertoire of every dance band and was played many thousands of times. The music of "Charleston" so encapsulated the Roaring Twenties that over 100 movies used it to set the scene. In many cases the "Charleston" was danced to on the screen as well. The influence the song had on popular music is also considerable. "Charleston" introduced a new beat and a unique sound that could not be ignored. Soon any song using the same tempo and applicable to the same dance steps was called a "Charleston number." But perhaps the most lasting legacy of "Charleston" was in jazz music, particularly "hot jazz." Because the song was so popular, it paved the way for Americans to hear and open themselves up to jazz.

Other notable songs from that season: "What'll I Do?" from *The Music Box Revue of 1923-1924*; "Alibi Baby" from *Poppy*; "Dinah" from *Kid Boots*; "Limehouse Blues," "You Were Meant for Me," "Parisian Pierrot" from *Charlot's Revue*; "Bongo on the Congo," "The Enchanted Train" from *Sitting Pretty*; "Take, Oh Take Those Lips Away" from *Ziegfeld Follies of 1923*; "A Ring to the Name of Rosie" from *The Rise of Rosie O'Reilly*; "Once in a Blue Moon" from *Stepping Stones*.

Song of the Season

1924–1925 SEASON

Three runaway hits this season illustrated the transitions happening on Broadway with regards to book musicals. Representing the old European operetta style was Sigmund Romberg's greatest success: *The Student Prince*. The setting, story, characters, and score could only be described as old-fashioned but all elements were so well done that it greatly pleased a wide audience for over 600 performances. Also successful but in a very different style was the Gershwins' jazz musical *Lady, Be Good!* More than a vehicle for Adele and Fred Astaire, the jaunty, sassy musical introduced lyricist Ira Gershwin to Broadway and his sly words matched brother George Gershwin's up-to-date music masterfully. The season's third major success, the operetta *Rose-Marie*, was in the European mode yet was set in the Canadian Rockies and made strong efforts to integrate story, characters, songs, and dance. By modern standards, *Rose-Marie* is decidedly old fashioned, but composers Rudolf Friml and Herbert Stothart introduced American (even some Native American) sounds into the old format. The book and lyrics by Otto Harbach and Oscar Hammerstein were, in some ways, innovative and daring. The fact that three so very different musicals could prosper on Broadway was very encouraging.

Of the forty-eight musicals that opened this season, fifteen were revues. In addition to the expected return of series from previous seasons, there were some successful new entries in the genre, such as *Hassard Short's Ritz Revue*, *The Grab Bag*, and the *Garrick Gaieties*. This last show boasted the first full score by Richard Rodgers (music) and Lorenz Hart (lyrics) and it was roundly noticed, particularly the song "Manhattan." Except for a brief hiatus in Hollywood, Rodgers and Hart would have a musical on the Street every year through 1941. Just as their career was starting, another was ending. Victor Herbert had dominated the American musical since the 1890s. He died in May of 1924 but his last musical, *The Dream Girl*, opened in the fall and ran a respectable 117 performances. Several other book musicals fared well this season, including the all-African American show *Chocolate Dandies*, Romberg's *Marjorie* and *Louis the 14th*, the Gershwins' *Tell Me More!*, the jazz musical *Mercenary Mary*, the golf musical *Top-Hole*, the British import *Sky High*, and an European operetta, Offenbach's *The Love Song*.

"Indian Love Call"
Music by Rudolf Friml; lyric by Otto Harbach, Oscar Hammerstein
From *Rose-Marie* (1924)
Sung by Mary Ellis as Rose-Marie, and Dennis King as Jim Kenyon

---

Oscar Hammerstein and Otto Harbach firmly believed that songs and libretto could be better interconnected and they saw *Rose-Marie* as their chance to write an integrated musical play. They were only partially successful, much of the musical falling squarely into the world of romanticized operetta. There were the expected chorus numbers, arias, duets, comedy songs, and dance specialties performed by stock operetta characters. But there were differences as well, such as a murder that is wrongly placed on the hero and some songs that grew out of the situation. Such a number was "Indian Love Call," the musical's main romantic duet for the fur trapper Jim Kenyon (Dennis King) and the singer Rose-Marie La Flamme (Mary Ellis). The song grows out of the Canadian Rockies setting. In the verse, Jim tells Rose-Marie about an ancient legend of the mountains. Two Native Americans from rival tribes fell in love but were put to death by the community. The lovers live on in spirit and at certain times one can hear them calling to each other across the landscape. The refrain re-enacts the lovers' calling out to each other. The singers croon "Oo-Oo-Oo-Oo, Oo-Oo-Oo-Oo" before using words, acting out the Native legend. Those words are somewhat rudimentary ("When I'm calling you … Will you answer too? … If you refuse me I will be blue, waiting all alone") but all the "ooo" rhymes support the idea of the long-gone lovers calling each other over the landscape.[5] Friml's music is far from authentic Native American, yet it has unusual chromatics that make it very non-European. The actual call is somewhat primeval, the long notes ascending and descending without attempting to form a melody. The challenge facing Hammerstein and Harbach was to provide words with open vowels which still made sense when strung out for so many measures. The lyricists discovered that the "ah" sound turned nasal when sustained and the "ee" sound was more irritating than romantic. So they used the word "you" which turns into a haunting sound when held for several counts. The result is a resounding mating call, something basically primitive but still romantic.

"Indian Love Call" was the musical highlight of *Rose-Marie* as sung by King and Ellis. In London it was performed by Edith Day and Derek Oldham. But it seemed unlikely that such an unusual song would work out of the context of the musical. Yet that is what Hammerstein and Harbach had strived for: a song unique to the characters and situation. So you can imagine their surprise when "Indian Love Call" was a hit on sheet music, records, and (later) movies. The song has been performed as a duet as in the original but also as a solo, choral number, and instrumental piece. Early recordings by Leo Reisman, Paul Whiteman, Isham Jones, Willie Creager, and Yvette Rugelwere were followed by over 100 other discs. The most successful recordings include a 1936 duet version by Jeanette MacDonald and Nelson Eddy who sang it in the 1936 film version; a 1938 instrumental by Artie Shaw and His Orchestra that was the band's first hit; a version by whistler Fred Lowery released in 1939 that sold over 2 million copies; a 1952 solo version by yodeling cowboy singer Slim Whitman which was near the top of the charts in both the States and Great Britain; and a 1975 disc by country singer Ray Stevens. Other notable recordings over the decades were made by Chet Atkins, Karl Denver, Billy Vaughn, Anna Moffo and Sergio Franchi, Liberace, Gloria Lynne, Robert Merrill and Roberta Peters, Nino Tempo and April Stevens, Kenny Roberts, Ray Charles, Sara Davis Buechner, Charlie Thompson, Deborah Brown, and Wylie and the Wild West. There were also significant recordings in Norway, Germany, Spain, Sweden, and the Czech Republic. Like Victor Herbert's gushing duet "Oh! Sweet Mystery of Life," there have been many parodies or comic interpretations of "Indian Love Call," as in the movie *Dudley Do-Right* (1999) where it was lip-synced by Brendan Fraser and Sarah Jessica Parker to an old

Song of the Season

recording. In addition to the MacDonald-Eddy onscreen rendition of the song in *Rose-Marie* (1936), "Indian Love Call" was also sung by Ann Blyth and Fernando Lamas in the 1954 remake.

Other notable songs from that season: "Rose-Marie," "The Mounties," "Door of Her Dreams" from *Rose-Marie*; "Manhattan," "Sentimental Me" from *Garrick Gaieties*; "Golden Days," "Drinking Song," "Deep in My Heart, Dear," "Serenade (Overhead the Moon Is Beaming)" from *The Student Prince*; "Kickin' the Clouds Away" from *Tell Me More*; "Oh, Lady, Be Good," "Fascinating Rhythm" from *Lady, Be Good*; "Somebody Loves Me" from *George White's Scandals*; "Dixie Moon," "Jasmine Lane" from *The Chocolate Dandies*; "All Alone" from the *Music Box Revue of 1924–1925*; "A Houseboat on the Harlem" from *Dear Sir*; "Keep Smiling at Trouble" from *Big Boy*.

1925–1926 SEASON

Quantity and quality were both running high during this season with over fifty musicals opening and introducing first-rate songs by such masters as Vincent Youmans and Irving Caesar, Jerome Kern and Oscar Hammerstein, the Gershwins, the trio of DeSylva, Brown and Henderson, Rudolf Friml, Otto Harbach, Sigmund Romberg, and Rodgers and Hart. It was also a season of delectable star turns by such favorites as Marilyn Miller, Clifton Webb, Dennis King, Joe E. Brown, Will Rogers, Vivienne Segal, Beatrice Lillie, W. C. Fields, Gertrude Lawrence, Queenie Smith, Hazel Dawn, Jack Benny, Ann Pennington, Al Jolson, and the Marx Brothers. The longest-running shows were musical comedies, such as *Sunny, Tip-Toes, The Girl Friend, Dearest Enemy, The Cocoanuts,* and *No No Nanette.* Yet some operettas found success as well, as with *The Vagabond King, Song of the Flame,* and *Princess Flavia.* There were also some highly entertaining (and mostly profitable) revues, such as *Ziegfeld Follies, Artists and Models, Earl Carroll's Vanities, The Garrick Gaieties, Charlot's Revue of 1926,* and two editions of the *George White's Scandals.* It was a typical Roaring Twenties season with an abundance of riches as jazz musicals, operettas, imports, and revues all found an audience.

"Tea for Two"
Music by Vincent Youmans; lyric by Irving Caesar
From *No, No, Nanette* (1925)
Sung by Louise Groody as Nanette, and John Barker as Tom

Of the dozens of songs introduced this season, there is one that is still widely recognized by contemporary theatregoers: the simple and infectious ditty "Tea for Two." Why this narrow-range, lyrically witless song is so memorable is an intriguing question. Perhaps it is the music's catchy simplicity, similar to that heard on a TV commercial jingle. Or is it the childlike repetition of words using a limited vocabulary? Tom sings "picture you upon my knee" then uses the title phrase in both directions: "tea for two … two for tea." It is all so idiotically simple and charming. Perhaps the story behind the song will offer an explanation. Vincent Youmans had written the main melody years earlier when he was serving in the Navy in the First World War. The refrain is a series of dotted quarter notes and eighth notes that bounce back and forth like a metronome. It sounds like a finger exercise for a beginning pianist. He played it for Irving Caesar who, like many lyricists, did not read music so Youmans repeated the musical sequence and Caesar wrote a "dummy lyric." This is a rhythmic but nonsensical collection of words that a lyricist dashes off to help remember the cadence of the song. Listening to the pattern, Caesar sang "tea for two … two for tea.. etc." as he jotted down the words. Caesar then went and wrote a polished lyric. But Youmans liked the simple "tea for two" dummy lyric better and convinced Caesar to use it instead. So with a few slight revisions, that's how the song was created.

The verse for "Tea for Two" is not nearly so simple, having a longer melodic line and some tricky internal feminine rhymes: "discontented … rented … invented" and the delicious pairing of "this place is" with "lover's oasis" and "weary taste is unknown."[6] Such an introduction is needed to set up the premise of the song. It is an old but useful premise: two lovers imagine a simple but blissfully happy life together is a place very much different from where they presently are. The most clichéd example is "a castle in Spain." In *No No Nanette*, the young sweethearts Nanette (Louise Groody) and Tom (John Barker) sing the duet in the second act in a gentle, soft-shoe tempo. Then the ensemble joins them for a big tap number. "Tea for Two" was a late addition to the show. In fact, the score (with Otto Harbach writing the lyrics) was finished and being performed in Chicago when the producers requested two new numbers. The songs were needed right away so Youmans recalled the melody from his Navy days and thought it might make a charming duet. Caesar provided the lyrics for both "Tea for Two" and "I Want to Be Happy," ironically the two most popular songs to come out of *No, No, Nanette*. Audiences were very taken with "Tea for Two," as were some music scouts. While *No, No, Nanette* was still playing in Chicago, recordings were made by the Benson Orchestra of Chicago and by Marion Harris. Both records climbed the charts and by the time *No, No, Nanette* opened in New York, "Tea for Two" was a familiar hit. That same year, it was well received in the London production where the number was sung by Binnie Hale and Seymour Beard.

The 1925 London cast recorded most of the *No, No, Nanette* score, including "Tea for Two," and there were early discs by the Victor Light Opera Company, the Columbia Vocal Gem Chorus, and Binnie Hale. Other memorable recordings were made by Art Tatum, Doris Day, Jane Froman, Willie ("The Lion") Smith, Fats Waller, the Benny Goodman Quartet, Blossom Dearie, Duke Ellington, Artie Shaw, Thelonious Monk, the Mills Brothers, Django Reinhardt, duet versions by Frank Sinatra and Dinah Shore, Anita O'Day and Roy Eldridge, and April Stevens and Nino Tempo, and even a cha cha version by Warren Covington that was a hit in 1958. Later covers for "Tea for Two" include those by Nick DeCarlo, Offspring, Heather MacRae, Sarah McKenzie, and Stéphane Grappelli with Yehudi Menuhin. Over the decades there have been many foreign-language recordings as well. In the movies, "Tea for Two" was sung by Bernice Claire and Alexander Gray in *No, No, Nanette* (1930), Anna Neagle and Richard Carlson in *No, No, Nanette* (1940), and Doris Day and Gordon MacRae in *Tea for Two* (1950). The song can be heard in dozens of other films, ranging from *Sweethearts* (1938) to *Legend* (2015).

Other notable songs from that season: "No, No, Nanette," "I Want to Be Happy," "Too Many Rings Around Rosie" from *No, No, Nanette*; "Here in My Arms,"

"Bye and Bye" from *Dearest Enemy*; "Who?," "D'ye Love Me?" from *Sunny*; "Only a Rose," "Hugette's Waltz," "Song of the Vagabonds," "Love for Sale" from *The Vagabond King*; "Sweet and Low-Down," "That Certain Feeling" from *Tip-Toes*; "Mountain Greenery" from *The Garrick Gaieties*; "The Birth of the Blues," "Black Bottom," "Lucky Day" from *George White's Scandals*; "The Girl Friend," "The Blue Room" from *The Girl Friend*; "A Cup of Coffee, a Sandwich and You," "Poor Little Rich Girl" from *Charlot's Revue of 1926*.

Song of the Season

1926–1927 SEASON

It was a banner season on Broadway as forty-eight musicals opened and almost half of them ran over the 100 mark. (Thirteen ran over 200 performances.) There were hits in all categories. Musical comedy was represented by the Gershwins' *Oh, Kay!*, Rodgers and Hart's *Peggy-Ann*, Vincent Youmans' *Hit the Deck*, the Marx Brothers' *The Cocoanuts*, Harry Ruby and Bert Kalmar's *The Ramblers*, Jerome Kern's *Criss Cross*, B. G. DeSylva and Lewis Gensler's *Queen High*, and Eddie Dowling and James Hanley's *Honeymoon Lane*. The operetta hits were Sigmund Romberg's *The Desert Song*, Harry Tierney and Joe McCarthy's *Rio Rita*, and the Viennese imports *Countess Maritza*, *Katja*, and *The Circus Princess*. Long-running revues included *George White's Scandals*, *Earl Carroll's Vanities*, *Americana*, *Grand Street Follies*, *Merry-Go-Round*, *A Night in Spain*, and *Ziegfeld's American Revue* (in place of the annual *Follies*). Just as the economy was booming in America, business on the Street was boffo. Perhaps more important, the quality of many of the shows was commendable. Some of the above book musicals are still produced and many of the songs introduced this season are now part of the Great American Songbook.

"Someone to Watch Over Me"
Music by George Gershwin; lyric by Ira Gershwin
From *Oh, Kay!* (1926)
Introduced by Gertrude Lawrence as Kay

For reasons too complicated (and silly) to go into, the British aristocrat Kay (Gertrude Lawrence) is disguised as a maid working in the Long Island mansion of Jimmy Winter (Oscar Shaw) in the musical comedy *Oh, Kay!* When Kay learns that Jimmy is engaged to marry another, it is time for a torch song: nothing too tragic or passionate—something more wistful and touching. Alone on stage in her maid's uniform and clutching a little rag doll, Kay/Lawrence gently sings, in her thin but expressive voice, "Someone to Watch Over Me." For a generation or two of Broadway playgoers, this remained one of the most cherished theatrical moments of the era. *Oh, Kay!* doesn't get done much these days (there was an all-Black version in 1990 and a much-revised revival called *Nice Work If You Can Get It* in 2012) but the song is everywhere. It is probably the most performed and recorded of all Gershwin ballads. So it is interesting to contemplate that "Someone to Watch Over Me" might have become a forgotten Twenties dance number. George Gershwin composed the music as an uptempo tune and Ira Gershwin planned an innocuous lyric not necessarily heard during a vigorous Charleston or other two-step production number. Happily, when George was playing variations of the music, he tried a slower foxtrot rhythm and both brothers realized it worked better as a ballad.

Ira then went and wrote a lyric inspired by the lullaby-like music. The result is a song that is both musically and lyrically very restrained. That, of course, is what makes it so powerful.

The verse is unusually long for a twentieth-century popular song. Also atypical of verses, the melody is repeated once, leading one to think this is the refrain. The lyric sets up the character's determination to find love. Kay has heard that "love is blind" and that one must "seek and ye shall find."[7] Although there is "a certain lad I've had in mind," she can't find him and wonders where "is the shepherd for this lost lamb?" Musically the verse is a series of undulating scales then breaks off suddenly for the final three lines which are less rangy and more pointed. The music for the refrain is beautifully constructed, carefully climbing the scale in a direct force, then gently descending with a kind of resigned resolution. The repetition of the title phrase works effectively, ending each refrain with it. The lamb metaphor is repeated when Kay describes herself as "a little lamb who's lost in the wood." Also repeated is the "eee" sound: speed, lead, need. The music for the release ("Although he may not be the man some ...") has a narrow range, also unusual for a refrain where the highest notes can be found. The lyric is not showy or clever, though there are some nice touches such as rhyming "man some" with "handsome." All the other rhymes are masculine without being too abrupt. The lyric is also more conversational than flowery. That interjection "Oh, how I need" provides just the right touch.

Legend has it that George Gershwin saw the rag doll in a Philadelphia toy shop when *Oh, Kay!* was trying out there and he bought it for Lawrence to sing to in "Someone to Watch Over Me." Because so much of *Oh, Kay!* is farce with bootleggers, revenue officers, identical twins, and lots of dancing, such a quiet moment as Lawrence singing hopefully to a doll was all the more effective. Lawrence recorded the song in 1927 and it went to #2 on the charts. That same year she reprised her performance in the London production of *Oh, Kay!* and introduced the song to Great Britain. This was followed by, according to recent data, 2,000 other recordings, most in the slow ballad format but some in the uptempo style. (In 2007 alone, there were twelve new recordings released in English.) The song is a particular favorite of jazz singers and musicians. Most would agree that among the finest recordings of "Someone to Watch Over Me" are those by Lee Wiley, Margaret Whiting, Frank Sinatra, Lena Horne, Ella Fitzgerald, Chet Baker, Blossom Dearie, Ray Charles, Sarah Vaughn, Willie Nelson, Barbra Streisand, Linda Ronstadt, Ricky Lee Jones, Elton John, and Amy Winehouse. Instrumental versions of "Someone to Watch Over Me" are heard in dozens of movies and it was sung onscreen (or on the soundtrack) by Frank Sinatra in *Young at Heart* (1954), Ann Blyth (dubbed by Gogi Grant) in *The Helen Morgan Story* (1957), Julie Andrews in *Star!* (1968), Dinah Shore in *A Safe Place* (1971), Nikka Costa in *Deal of the Century* (1983), Yves Montand in *Beyond Therapy* (1987), Michelle Pfeiffer and Susan Sarandon in *The Witches of Eastwick* (1987), Sting in *Someone to Watch Over Me* (1987), Willie Nelson in *Jennifer 8* (1992), Jean Louisa Kelly in *Mr. Holland's Opus* (1995), Benny Carter and His Orchestra in *Return to Me* (2000), Julia Deakin in *Liam* (2000), Kay Panabaker and Asher Monroe in *Fame*

Song of the Season

(2009), and Jana Kramer in *Heart of the Country* (2013). On Broadway, the song was performed by Julia Sanderson in the 1928 revival of *Oh, Kay!*, and Angela Teek in the 1990 revival, Jodi Benson in *Crazy for You* (1992), the cast of *The Gershwins' Fascinating Rhythm* (1999), Hershey Felder in *George Gershwin Alone* (2001), and Kelli O'Hara in *Nice Work If You Can Get It* (2012).

Other notable songs from that season: "Do Do Do," "Maybe," "Clap Yo' Hands" from *Oh, Kay!*; "Blue Skies," "This Funny World" from *Betsy*; "The Desert Song," "The Riff Song," "One Alone" from *The Desert Song*; "Rio Rita," "The Kinkajou," "The Rangers' Song," "If You're in Love, You'll Waltz" from *Rio Rita*; "Sometimes I'm Happy," "Hallelujah" from *Hit the Deck!*; "Where's That Rainbow?" from *Peggy-Ann*; "Cross Your Heart" from *Queen High*; "All Alone Monday" from *The Ramblers*; "That Lost Barbershop Chord," "Sunny Disposish" from *Americana*; "The Little White House (At the End of Honeymoon Lane)," "Half a Moon" from *Honeymoon Lane*.

1927–1928 SEASON

The 1927–28 Broadway season was one for the history books and most people at the time knew it. Some things were obvious. More plays and musicals opened that season than in any before (or since). A record number of 270 productions arrived; fifty-nine of them musicals. On the evening of December 26, 1927, eleven new productions opened (another record never approached again). There were more musical hits than in any previous season (an estimated twenty-seven shows) and arguably more famous songs that had yet been introduced in one season. It certainly helped that many of the finest librettists and songwriters in the American musical theatre were very active this season. Rodgers and Hart had two hits—*A Connecticut Yankee* and *Present Arms*—as did DeSylva, Brown, and Henderson, with *Good News!* and *Manhattan Mary*, the team of Ruby and Kalmar, with *The Five O'Clock Girl* and *She's My Baby*, and Sigmund Romberg, with *My Maryland* and *Rosalie*. This last also had contributions by the Gershwins who had another hit with *Funny Face*. Irving Berlin was represented by the *Ziegfeld Follies*, George M. Cohan with *The Merry Malones*, and newcomers Jimmy McHugh and Dorothy Fields with *Blackbirds of 1928*. Rudolf Friml, at the end of his career, had a hit with *The Three Musketeers* and a near-miss with *The White Eagle*. Most important, in the long run, was *Show Boat* with Oscar Hammerstein and Jerome Kern writing an outstanding libretto and score and introducing the "musical play" to Broadway. It was a season whose like has never been seen again.

If only the most near-sighted commentators did not recognize the season of all seasons as it was happening, hardly anyone saw the full significance of another event of that season. On October 6, 1927, the talkie *The Jazz Singer* premiered in Manhattan's Warner Theatre starring Al Jolson who was noticeably absent on Broadway this season. The film was only partially a talking picture, with only the songs and some bits of dialogue heard. But it would change the history of Hollywood and, indirectly, Broadway. Not only would stage musicals be brought out to California, but with them Broadway composers, lyricists, writers, directors, choreographers, and, of course, stars. How many in 1927 foresaw all that is questionable. And with the Depression just around the corner, it would happen sooner and faster than anyone thought possible. The 1927–28 season was indeed a last hurrah.

"Ol' Man River"
Music by Jerome Kern; lyric by Oscar Hammerstein
From *Show Boat* (1927)
Sung by Jules Bledsoe as Joe, and the African American male chorus

---

"Ol' Man River" is an atypical Broadway song, just as *Show Boat* was an atypical musical in its day. Rarely has the atmosphere, tone, setting, and theme for a musical been captured so completely in one song. "Ol Man River" is heard several times throughout *Show Boat*, serving as a kind of leitmotif. The African American stevedore Joe (Jules Bledsoe) sings it early in the musical when he contemplates the river and how it moves forward without concern for man, beast, or vegetable. The verse asks, "What does he care if de world's got troubles?" followed by the deeper question, "What does he care if de land ain't free?" Kern's music here is a casual Dixie tune, something lively that would be played on a banjo. Then there is a purposeful shift for the release. The music seems to churn out like the paddle-wheel on a riverboat, moving forward majestically but also with a solemn air. Hammerstein's lyric uses few rhymes but multi-syllabic phrases: "He mus' know sumpin' … But don't say nuthin' … He keeps on rollin' along."[8] When there is finally a true rhyme, it is a soft feminine one: "don' plant cotton … soon forgotten." The repetitive use of "he" at the start of each line supports Kern's musical idea of a slow, grinding pattern. The release is, musically, a section of the verse repeated, unifying the song thematically as well as audibly. Joe sings "Tote dat barge! Lift dat bale!" then wryly notes, "Git a little drunk,/ An' you land in jail." The final refrain does not repeat an earlier idea but moves on to the personal. All the "he's" are replaced with "ah's" and we hear the voice of Joe once again. He laments "Ah gits weary/ An' sick of tryin'," then sings the famous fatalistic couplet "Ah'm tired of livin'/ An' skeered of dyin'." When the dock workers join Joe for a repeat of the refrains and release, the solo voice becomes the voice of a people. The African American lament their oppression, yet they can't help feeling in awe of the mighty river that is indifferent to mankind's troubles. Later in the musical, Joe reprises the song a few times as commentary on the events of the plot.

"Ol Man River" was sometimes mistaken as an authentic Negro spiritual because Kern's music has a Southern folk flavor rarely found in theatre songs. In some ways the music is not complex. It uses the pentatonic-scale and has no major jumps in the melody. It does have a wide range (an octave and a sixth) with a high ending that has always proven a challenge to baritones and bases who usually sing it. Kern goes beyond finding unity within the song. The opening number of *Show Boat*, the light and frivolous "Cotton Blossom" uses the same notes as those in the refrain of "Ol' Man River" but inverted. A white chorus is contrasted with a black chorus; so different, and yet so close to the same. Lyrically, it is Hammerstein's master achievement. He avoids lengthy phrases and hard endings (sumpin', nuthin', livin', rollin', dyin') and uses the African American dialect carefully, giving the uneducated Joe a way of expressing himself with dignity and even eloquence. Hammerstein considered "Ol' Man River" a folk song but also a protest song. It is this ambiguity that makes the song so haunting. Although Bledsoe introduced the number in the original *Show Boat*, it is most associated with the actor-singer Paul Robeson who sang "Ol' Man River" in the London production, in revivals, in the 1936 film, and in concerts for many years. Later in his career, Robeson altered some of the lyric to make the song a more potent form of protest. A change made by all who recorded or produced *Show Boat* after 1936 is the opening of the verse: "Niggers all work on de Mississippi,/Niggers all work while de white folks play." The offensive "niggers" was replaced by "darkies" for the 1936 screen version; later, less offensive, replacements include "colored folks work" or "here we all work."

The first successful recording of "Ol' Man River" was by Paul Whiteman's Orchestra with a vocal by Bing Crosby and featuring Bix Beiderbecke on cornet. It was an uptempo rendition, as with Whiteman's later disc with Robeson. Of the hundreds of subsequent recordings, special note should be made of discs by Lennie Hayton, Frank Sinatra, the Ames Brothers, Ruth Brown, Delta Rhythm Boys, Oscar Peterson, Sam Cooke, Earl Grant, Sammy Davis, Jr., Pete Fountain, Maynard Ferguson, Gloria Lynne and the Earl May Trio, Ray Charles, the Flamingos, Aretha Franklin, The Temptations, Lawrence Winters, Johnny Nash, Jim Croce, Samuel Ramey, James Taylor, and Flymo and The Vershons. There have been three screen versions of *Show Boat*. Jules Bledsoe and the Dixie Jubilee Singers sang "Ol' Man River" in the prologue of the 1929 film which was a partial talkie. Later in the movie it was sung by Laura La Pante (dubbed by Eva Olivetti). Robeson sang "Ol' Man River" in the 1928 London production and in the 1932 Broadway revival. The number was performed by Robeson in the 1936 film and by William Warfield in the 1951 version. In the Kern biopic *Till the Clouds Roll By* (1946) Caleb Peterson played Joe and sang the song in the context of *Show Boat*; then Frank Sinatra did a concert version at the end of the movie. Actors who have played Joe in Broadway revivals and sang "Ol' Man River" include Kenneth Spencer in 1946, William C. Smith in 1948, Lawrence Winters in 1954, William Warfield in 1966, Bruce Hubbard in 1983, and Michel Bell in 1994.

Other notable songs from that season: "Can't Help Lovin' Dat Man," "Make Believe," "Bill," "You Are Love," "Why Do I Love You?," "Life Upon the Wicked Stage" from *Show Boat*; "Good News," "The Best Things in Life Are Free," "The Varsity Drag," "Lucky in Love" from *Good News!*; "Thou Swell," "My Heart Stood Still," "On a Desert Island with You" from *A Connecticut Yankee*; "Funny Face," "'S Wonderful," "He Loves and She Loves" from *Funny Face*; "How Long Has This Been Going On?" from *Rosalie*; "My Sword and I," "Your Eyes," "March of the Musketeers," "Ma Belle" from *The Three Musketeers*; "Shaking the Blues Away" from *Ziegfeld Follies of 1927*; "Your Land and My Land" from *My Maryland*; "I Can't Give You Anything But Love," "Doin' the New Low Down," "Diga, Diga, Doo" from *Blackbirds of 1928*; "Thinking of You" from *The Five O'Clock Girl*; "You Took Advantage of Me" from *Present Arms*; "Crazy Rhythm" from *Here's Howe*.

Song of the Season

1928–1929 SEASON

Although there were far fewer new musicals opening this season, so many shows from the previous season were still running so Broadway seemed to be bustling. Sad to say, the new works were less than commendable even though some turned a tidy profit. Of the thirty new book musicals that arrived on the Street, only one is ever revived today: Sigmund Romberg's operetta *The New Moon*. Happily, several of the season's new songs have survived. One can still hear on occasion such standards as Cole Porter's "Let's Do It!," the Gershwins' "I've Got a Crush on You," Rodgers and Hart's "With a Song in My Heart," Gus Kahn and Walter Donaldson's "Love Me or Leave Me," DeSylva, Brown, and Henderson's "Button Up Your Overcoat," Noel Coward's "A Room with a View," Romberg's "Lover, Come Back to Me," the Harry Ruby-Herbert Stothard-Bert Kalmar favorite "I Wanna Be Loved By You," and others. Some of these came from unsuccessful productions but sometimes a good song has a way of finding an audience and sticking around.

Some tried-and-true songwriters had a difficult season. Rodgers and Hart stumbled badly with *Chee-Chee* (thirty-one performances) but recovered with the modest success *Spring Is Here* (104 performances). The Gershwins came a cropper with *Treasure Girl* (sixty-eight performances) even with Gertrude Lawrence in top form. Vincent Youmans' *Rainbow* was deemed quite adventurous by some but it could not find an audience for more than three weeks. On the other hand, DeSylva-Brown-Henderson contributed songs to three hits—*Hold Everything*, *Follow Thru*, and *George White's Scandals*—as did Ruby-Kalmar with *Good Boy*, *Three Cheers*, and *Animal Crackers*. After years of struggling, Cole Porter finally had a *bona fide* hit with *Paris*. Howard Dietz and Arthur Schwartz had better luck, finding gold their first time on Broadway with *The Little Show*. Also finally finding success on Broadway were Tin Pan Alley veteran songwriters Gus Kahn and Walter Donaldson with *Whoopee*. Eddie Cantor was the star and, as often happened this season, performers were sometimes largely responsible for keeping a show on the boards. W. C. Fields can be credited with the long run of *Earl Carroll's Vanities*, Irene Bordoni for *Paris*, the Marx Brothers for *Animal Crackers*, Fanny Brice and Leon Errol for *Fioretta*, and Libby Holman and Clifton Webb for *The Little Show*. Two of America's favorite comics found their first recognition this season: Bert Lahr in *Hold Everything* and Bob Hope in *Ups-a-Daisy*. So maybe it wasn't such a disappointing season after all.

"I Wanna Be Loved By You"
Music by Harry Ruby, Herbert Stothard; lyric by Bert Kalmar
From *Good Boy* (1928)
Sung by Helen Kane as Pansy McManus,
and Dan Healy as Bobby D'Arnell

It's not often that a song solidifies a performer's career and inspires a popular cartoon character as well, but that is the story of "I Wanna Be Loved by You." The novelty number was by Harry Ruby and Herbert Stothard collaborating on the music that was set to a lyric by Bert Kalmar for the musical *Good Boy*. The number was not written for any of the principal characters but for the comic supporting roles of Pansy McManus, a chorus girl in the backstager, and the tap-dancing Bobby D'Arnell. The duet was meant to be a comedy special with a twenties kind of frivolity. In the verse, Pansy and Bobby claim not to want much out of life except to be loved by each other. The refrain is a simple declaration of love but kept farcical by adding a very particular piece of slang: "I want to be loved by you, alone! Boop-boop-a-doop!"[9] The release continues with the slang expression with "Boop-boop, I couldn't aspire,/ To anything higher." The silly lyric is set to a surprisingly restrained tempo, moving forward not as a furious dance piece but as a gentle soft-shoe. The song might have served as a pleasant diversion in *Good Boy* except for the fact that Helen Kane was cast as Pansy. She was a vaudeville singer with a squeaky, high pitched voice that turned everything she said and sang into a kind of baby talk. After years of touring the vaudeville circuits, Kane finally got to Broadway in the revue *A Night in Paris* where she got the attention of Arthur Hammerstein who was producing *Good Boy*. Paired with hoofer Dan Healy as Bobby, the couple stopped the show with "I Wanna Be Loved By You." Soon Kane was the talk of the town, labeled the "Boop-Boop-a-Doop Girl," and she set off on a long and successful career with the number as her signature song. So popular was her recording of "I Wanna Be Loved by You" that there were many imitations of her singing style. At this time the Fleischer Studios animators were creating the cartoon character of Betty Boop, a flapper who sounded an awful lot like Kane. In fact, Betty Boop sang "I Wanna Be Loved By You" in some cartoon shorts. Kane attempted unsuccessfully to sue the studio for stealing her signature "boop-oop-a-doop" style. (Betty Boop was voiced by five different actresses between 1930 and 1937, most famously by Mae Questel, all imitating Kane.)

As much as "I Wanna Be Loved by You" is associated with Kane, the song has been recorded by a variety of artists in different styles not at all like the original baby-talk squeal. There have been discs by Vaughn De Leath, the High Hatters, Annette Hanshaw, Jack Lemmon, Eydie Gorme, Frank Sinatra, Skeeter Davis, Rose Murphy, Sinéad O'Connor, Stephanie Lawrence, Jinx Titanic, Shiina Ringo, Claire Johnston, Asha-Louise, and a duet version by Barry Manilow singing with the Marilyn Monroe recording. "I Wanna Be Loved By You" was performed in a handful of movies. In the Kalmer-Ruby biopic *Three Little Words* (1950), it was sung by Debbie Reynolds (dubbed by Kane) to Carleton Carpenter in a farcical recreation of the scene from *Good Boy*. In *Gentlemen Marry Brunettes* (1955), Jane Russell, Jeanne Crain (dubbed by Anita Ellis), and Rudy Vallee sang it, as did Jane Horrocks in *Little Voice* (1998), John Turturro in *Monkeybone* (2001), and Ana de Armas (dubbed by Vanessa Lemonides) in *Blonde* (2022). But the most famous screen version of "I Wanna Be Loved by You" is the sexy rendition Marilyn Monroe gave the number in *Some Like It Hot* (1959).

Song of the Season

Other notable songs from that season: "Let's Do It" from *Paris*; "My Lucky Star," "Button Up Your Overcoat," "You Wouldn't Fool Me, Would You?" from *Follow Thru*; "You're the Cream in My Coffee" from *Hold Everything*; "Softly, as in a Morning Sunrise," "Stouthearted Men," "One Kiss," "Wanting You," "Lover, Come Back to Me" from *The New Moon*; "Love Me or Leave Me," "Makin' Whoopee" from *Whoopee*; "I've Got a Crush on You," "Feeling I'm Falling" from *Treasure Girl*; "Moanin' Low," "Can't We Be Friends?," "I Guess I'll Have to Change My Plan" from *The Little Show*; "With a Song in My Heart" from *Spring Is Here*; "World Weary," "A Room with a View" from *This Year of Grace*; "Hooray for Captain Spaulding" from *Animal Crackers*; "Out of Breath (And Scared to Death of You)," "I Am Only Human After All" from *Garrick Gaieties*; "The One Girl" from *Rainbow*.

1929–1930 SEASON

Any season in which the Gershwins, Cole Porter, and Rodgers and Hart all had two new musicals open must be worth something. And if one considers the Broadway debuts of songwriters Vernon Duke, Jay Gorney, E. Y. Harburg, and Johnny Mercer were also this season, things were looking up. The number of shows dropped but the quality of the songs was high. Add to the above songwriters Noel Coward, Thomas "Fats" Waller, Andy Razaf, Harry Brooks, Vincent Youmans, Gus Kahn, Jerome Kern, Oscar Hammerstein, Dorothy Fields, Jimmy McHugh, Harry Ruby, and Bert Kalmar who contributed songs to this season and it ends up being pretty impressive. Even some of the librettos were commendable, with the likes of George S. Kaufman, Morrie Ryskind, Herbert Fields, William Anthony McGuire, Guy Bolton, and Moss Hart turning out strong books for such musicals as *Strike Up the Band, Sweet Adeline, Fifty Million Frenchmen, Flying High, Heads Up!*, and *Sons o' Guns*. It is worth noting that some musicals boasted not just one song to become a standard but two or three. Even Vincent Youmans' *Great Day*, which struggled to run a month, introduced "More Than You Know," "Without a Song," and the title number. Other musicals with two or three outstanding songs include Noel Coward's *Bitter Sweet*, the Gershwins' *Strike Up the Band*, Kern and Hammerstein's *Sweet Adeline*, Fields and McHugh's *International Revue*, Cole Porter's *Fifty Million Frenchmen*, and the Waller-Razaf-Brooks revue *Hot Chocolates*. In a time when musicals have been mostly forgotten except for their scores, this season left a treasure trove for future generations.

The season was not half gone when the Stock Market Crash in October created a dark cloud over Broadway that would not clear away for a dozen years. The Wall Street disaster didn't affect Broadway immediately but by the end of the season it was evident a golden era was over and it didn't seem likely to ever return again.

"Ain't Misbehavin'"
Music by Thomas "Fats" Waller,
Harry Brooks; lyric by Andy Razaf
From *Hot Chocolates* (1929)
Sung by Margaret Simms, Paul Bass,
and Russell Wooding's Jubilee Singers

Perhaps the most fondly remembered all-African American revues of the era was *Hot Chocolates*. It began as a nightclub show at Connie's Inn in Harlem and went over so well that brothers Connie and George Immerman turned it into a full-scale Broadway revue with sixty African American singers, dancers, "tumblers," and a full orchestra. The Immermans also hired the young trumpeter Louis Armstrong to conduct the orchestra. The songs by Thomas "Fats" Waller, Harry Brooks (music), and Andy Razaf (lyrics) included several dance numbers but the score's best-known songs are the sobering "(What Did I Do to Be So) Black and Blue?" and the jaunty "Ain't Misbehavin'." Armstrong's trumpet rendition from the pit of the latter song was such a crowd pleaser that he was given a solo and was featured in the Entr'acte. *Hot Chocolates* opened at the Hudson Theatre, a mainstream Broadway venue, and ran 219 performances before setting out on a successful tour. It is today considered a landmark production and one of the highlights of the Harlem Renaissance.

Like any jazz classic, "Ain't Misbehavin'" is open to many musical interpretations and the question of tempo and even which notes to play/sing is variable. The sheet music sometimes calls for "rhythm: foxtrot or swing" while vocal scores often just indicate "moderately." Waller recorded different vocal and piano versions of the song and even they vary greatly. When he sings it, the number has a definite 4/4 beat that never wavers, plodding along with purpose and emphasizing the lyric. But when he does an instrumental version, honky tonk piano and what was called "jungle rhythm" is used. The music, a collaboration by Waller and Harry Brooks, does not have a wide range or any extreme sections, though when basses sing it they can go as low as they want on "just me and my radio."[10] Razaf's lyric is conversational but not terribly slangy. With "no one to talk with" and "no one to walk with," the singer claims he "ain't misbehavin'" while "savin' my love for you." The lyric drops any unnecessary words ("no one to talk to" instead of "there's no one to talk to") as well as any punctuation. Razaf takes the poetic approach that "less is more" and the whole song is a lesson in minimalist, effective writing. The release is particularly sparse with short phrases, such as "like Jack Horner ... don't go no where ... What do I care?" In *Hot Chocolates*, the number was sung as a duet by Margaret Simms and Paul Bass, then later in the show was reprised by Russell Wooding's Jubilee Singers. Most of the reviews mentioned "Ain't Misbahavin'" as the hit of the revue and it quickly was heard in nightclubs and saloons.

Thirteen recordings of "Ain't Misbehavin'" were released in 1929 and six of them were in the Top 20 charts. A disc by Leo Reisman and His Orchestra (vocals by Lew Conrad) reached #2, but following close behind were recordings by Armstrong, Bill Robinson with Irving Mills and His Hotsy Totsy Gang, Gene Austin (with Leonard Joy and His Orchestra), Ruth Etting, and Waller's instrumental version. Among the many who later recorded the song are Anita O'Day, Sarah Vaughn, Bing Crosby, Dinah Washington, Billie Holiday, Eartha Kitt, Ella Fitzgerald, Carol Channing, Django Reinhardt, Miles Davis, Kay Starr, Frankie Laine, Art Tatum, Maxine Sullivan, Sonny Stitt, Sam Cooke, Johnnie Ray, Sidney Bechet, Ray Charles, Willie Nelson, Kermit Ruffins, Leon Redbone, Dave Brubeck, Hank Williams Jr., Tony Bennett, Robson Green and Jerome Flynn, Bill Haley and His Comets, Leslie Vincent, and Loudon Wainwright III with Vince Giordano and The Nighthawks. "Ain't Misbehavin'" is heard in over fifty films, including vocal performances on screen or on the soundtrack by Teddy Brown and his Orchestra in *Elstree Calling* (1930), Mary Beth Hughes in *Follow the Band* (1943), Waller himself at the piano in *Stormy Weather* (1943), Louis Armstrong in *Atlantic City* (1944), the team of Patterson and Jackson in *Killer Diller* (1948), Charlotte Austin in *Rainbow 'Round My Shoulder* (1952), Alan Young, Jane Russell, and Jeanne Crain (dubbed by Anita Ellis) in *Gentlemen Marry Brunettes* (1955), Liza Minnelli and Burt Reynolds in *Lucky Lady*

(1975), Dick Shawn in *Good-bye Cruel World* (1982), Hank Williams, Jr. in *In Country* (1989), The Benny Goodman Sextet in *Mr. Saturday Night* (1992), Jack Black in *Be Kind Rewind* (2008), Cliff Jackson in *The Curious Case of Benjamin Button* (2008), and Chad Selph in *The Forty-Year-Old Version* (2020). "Ain't Misbehavin'" was heard on Broadway again when sung by the cast of the award-winning 1978 revue *Ain't Misbehavin'*.

Other notable songs from that season: "(What Did I Do to Be So) Black and Blue" from *Hot Chocolates*; "You Do Something to Me," "You've Got That Thing," "Find Me a Primitive Man" from *Fifty Million Frenchmen*; "Ten Cents a Dance" from *Simple Simon*; "Strike Up the Band," "Soon" from *Strike Up the Band*; "On the Sunny Side of the Street," "Exactly Like You" from *The International Review*; "Get Happy" from *9:15 Revue*; "Liza" from *Show Girl*; "Why Was I Born?," "Don't Ever Leave Me" from *Sweet Adeline*; "Great Day," "More Than You Know," "Without a Song" from *Great Day*; "I'll See You Again," "If Love Were All" from *Bitter Sweet*; "A Ship Without a Sail" from *Heads Up*; "What Is This Thing Called Love?" from *Wake Up and Dream*; "Thank Your Father," "Red Hot Chicago" from *Flying High*.

Song of the Season

1930–1931 SEASON

The first full season during the Depression was an accurate indication of how things would be on Broadway for the foreseeable future. Fewer shows opened, more musicals closed within a few weeks, and the hits didn't run as long as they did in the recent past. It was also clear that audiences were losing interest in operetta, particularly European models. Sigmund Romberg, the last of the great American operetta composers, had three entries this season: revivals of *The Student Prince* and *Blossom Time*, and a new work, *Nina Rose*. The revivals struggled and *Nina Rose* ran four months because it was advertised by the Shuberts' as a "musical play." The season's other six operettas failed to run very long. It seemed playgoers who could still afford the luxury of theatre wanted modern musical comedies. They certainly got one with the Gershwins' jazz musical *Girl Crazy*, the hit of the season at 272 performances. Other book musicals that turned some kind of profit were Cole Porter's *The New Yorkers*, Rodgers and Hart's *America's Sweetheart*, Harold Arlen and Jack Yellen's *You Said It*, and *Fine and Dandy*, a jazz musical with a sparkling score by Kay Swift (music) and Paul James (lyrics). Al Jolson, back on Broadway after some blockbuster films, couldn't keep *Wonder Boy* on the boards beyond ten weeks, just as Adele and Fred Astaire could not overcome weak material and keep *Smiles* running past sixty-three performances.

Musical revues had a better track record this season. In fact, the Depression would turn out to be a golden era for the genre with Howard Dietz and Arthur Schwartz as the songwriters associated with the best revues. This season they provided songs for the hit show *Three's a Crowd* and the moderately successful *The Second Little Show*. Most revues had multiple songwriters, as in the case of the *Garrick Gaieties, Earl Carroll's Vanities, Crazy Quilt*, and *Sweet and Low*—all of them hits. The last two were presented by Broadway's newest impresario Billy Rose and featured his then-wife Fanny Brice. Because of the success of the previous season's *Hot Chocolates*, there were a handful of all-African Americans revues and even some all-Black book musicals: *Lew Leslie's Blackbirds of 1930, Change Your Luck, Hot Rhythm, Rhapsody in Black,* and *Brown Buddies*. This last show ran fourteen weeks, the longest run that any of them enjoyed. And this was despite such talents as Eubie Blake, Andy Razaf, Flournoy Miller, James C. Johnson, and Shelton Brooks writing the songs, and such on-stage favorites as Ethel Waters, Bill Robinson, Adelaide Hall, the team of Buck and Bubbles, Alberta Hunter, Minto Cato, Arthur Bryson, and Mae Barnes. Talented performers and star appeal were not in short supply on Broadway this season. In addition to those already mentioned, the musicals offered such current and future stars as Ed Wynn, Jack Benny, Marilyn Miller, Jimmy Savo, Victor Moore, Ginger Rogers, Imogene Coca, Clifton Webb, Libby Holman, Hildegarde, Ethel Merman, Ray Heatherton, Jimmy Durante, Patsy Kelly, Rosalind Russell, Guy Robertson, Fred Allen, Norma Terris, James Barton, Joe Cook, Robert Halliday, Evelyn Herbert, Willie Howard, Howard Marsh, Eddie Foy, Jr., Tamara Geva, Joe Penner, Ann Pennington, Marie Cahill, Walter Slezak, Bettina Hall, Lyda Roberti, Jack Whiting, Ann Sothern, Ted Healy, and George Jessel. It is quite a line-up; sad to think how many of them would soon head west for Hollywood.

"I Got Rhythm"
Music by George Gershwin; lyric by Ira Gershwin
From *Girl Crazy* (1930)
Sung by Ethel Merman as "Frisco" Kate Fothergill, and chorus

The Gershwin brothers' "I Got Rhythm" is one of their simplest songs—basically a four-note riff that climbs and descends the pentatonic scale—and one of their most complex, with unusual rhythm changes and a lyric that is full of surprises. But when it was introduced in *Girl Crazy*, the song was all about Ethel Merman. She did not play the leading lady (that went to Ginger Rogers) but the supporting role of the western prairie gal "Frisco" Kate Fothergill who had three songs in the show. Merman blasted her way into stardom with "I Got Rhythm" with full confidence and little subtlety. At one point in the performance, she belted out a high C for sixteen bars while the ensemble sang a full version of the refrain. Merman recorded and performed the number throughout her long career, making it her signature song. But aside from Merman, "I Got Rhythm" has enjoyed a busy life as a jazz standard and open to seemingly endless variations. That is because the music is so unlikely. Although it seems to simply ascend and descend four of the five basic notes, the music's main melodic line is a beat behind the primary pulse of the accompaniment. This means the lyric is sometimes syncopated to fall where least expected. The structure of "I Got Rhythm" is the standard 32-bar AABA form yet the chord progressions are unique, later labeled "rhythm changes" by musicians and used in countless other jazz numbers. The music was written first so Ira Gershwin had to experiment with different lyric choices before he realized that traditional rhyming would not work for this composition. He opted instead to reduce the rhymes altogether and rely on short, blunt lyric phrases. In the verse, the opening has an unexpected cut-off phrase: "Don't need what money/ Can buy."[11] That abrupt "Can buy" is surprising and intriguing. Such a quirk is repeated twice in the verse and a different tact is taken in the refrain. The short phrases "I got rhythm … I got music … I got my man" are answered by "Who could ask for anything more?" Lyrically, the surprise is in an opposite manner. One expects the fourth line to be a short, abrupt phrase but instead it's a full melodic and lyrical question. Singers sometime adjust this by breaking up "Who can ask for anything more?" with rests or holding certain notes. The release returns to the verse's structure of short phrases— "Old Man Trouble … I don't mind him … you won't find him/ 'Round my door." The song "I Got Rhythm" cries out for improvisation and from the start it has provided endless opportunities for variation. George Gershwin knew this and in 1934 he composed a concert piece for piano and orchestra which he titled "Variations on 'I Got Rhythm.'" The composition runs about eight minutes and is as thrilling as it is inventive.

There have been well over 200 vocal and instrumental recordings of "I Got Rhythm" and the variety of approaches is remarkable. Before 1930 had passed, there were discs by Red Nichols (vocal by Dick Robertson), the Victor Arden-Phil Ohman Orchestra (vocal by Frank Luther), Kate Smith, Ethel Waters, and the orchestras of Fred Rich and

Song of the Season

Luis Russell. Other early records were made by Gershwin himself, Louis Armstrong, the Ballyhooligans, and Joe Daniels and His Hot Shots. Every decade since has seen numerous recorded versions, perhaps most surprisingly a 1967 disc by the Happenings which sold over 1 million copies. Other memorable recordings include those by Duke Ellington, Jimmy Dorsey, Benny Goodman, Willie "The Lion" Smith, Pete Fountain, Joe Venuti, Stephane Grappelli and McCoy Tyner, Chris Connor, "Scat Man" Crothers, Thelonious Monk, Charlie Parker, Judy Garland, Zoot Sims, Barbra Streisand, Mike Oldfield, Tony Orlando, The Yellowjackets, Maureen McGovern, Bobby Darin, Ruthie Henshall, John Pizzarelli, Andre Watts, Manhattan Jazz Quintet, and Michael Feinstein with Brad Paisley. In the screen versions of *Girl Crazy*, "I Got Rhythm" was sung by Kitty Kelly in 1932 and by Judy Garland and Mickey Rooney with Six Hits and a Miss, the Music Maids, and Tommy Dorsey with his Orchestra in the 1943 remake. The number has been sung on screen or on the soundtrack by Gene Kelly and some French children in *An American in Paris* (1951), Harve Presnell and Connie Francis in *When the Boys Meet the Girls* (1965), Hazel Scott in *Rhapsody in Blue* (1945), and Teddy Wilson in *Celebrity* (1998). On Broadway, Jodi Benson, Harry Groener, and the company sang "I Got Rhythm" in the revised revival of *Girl Crazy* retitled *Crazy for You* (1992), by the cast of *The Gershwins' Fascinating Rhythm* (1999), and by Henri Baurel, Adam Hochberg, Gerry Mulligan, and company in *An American in Paris* (2015).

Other notable songs from that season: "But Not for Me," "Embraceable You," "Bidin' My Time," "Could You Use Me?" from *Girl Crazy*; "Fine and Dandy," "Can This Be Love?," "I'll Hit a New High" from *Fine and Dandy*; "I Found a Million Dollar Baby (In a Five and Ten Cent Store)" from *Billy Rose's Crazy Quilt*; "I Happen to Like New York," "Take Me Back to Manhattan," "Let's Fly Away," "Love for Sale" from *The New Yorkers*; "Body and Soul," "Something to Remember You By" from *Three's a Crowd*; "Memories of You" from *Lew Leslie's Blackbirds of 1930*; "I've Got Five Dollars" from *America's Sweetheart*; "Time on My Hands" from *Smiles*.

1931–1932 SEASON

Looking at the numbers, the 1931–32 season was promising. Forty-seven musicals opened and six of them ran over 200 performances. But looking more closely, one sees that eighteen of those shows were revivals and seventeen musicals this season closed inside of three weeks. And if it wasn't clear that there was a Depression, one had only to look at the empty theatres (or worse, theatres turned into movie houses) and the exodus of talent heading to Hollywood. So the situation was grim; unless, of course, you were enjoying one of season's hits, of which there were several. The long-run champ was the musical satire *Of Thee I Sing*. George S. Kaufman, who claimed "satire is what closes on Saturday night," and Morrie Ryskind wrote the nimble-witted libretto and the Gershwins provided a full comic operetta score a la Gilbert and Sullivan. Kaufman notwithstanding, *Of Thee I Sing* ran 441 performances and was the first musical to be awarded the coveted Pulitzer Prize. The season's other successful book musical was *The Cat and the Fiddle* by Jerome Kern and Otto Harbach. It was, in essence, an operetta, but a modern one that billed itself as "a musical love story." Whatever it was, the score was superior, the story engaging, and the production lovely. *The Cat and the Fiddle* managed a very profitable run of 395 performances.

All the other musicals with long runs were revues, the best being Howard Dietz and Arthur Schwartz's *The Band Wagon*. Many consider it the finest revue of the era. With a bouquet of outstanding songs, dandy sketches, captivating scenery and lighting, and a top-notch cast headed by the Astaires, Frank Morgan, and Helen Broderick, it was hard to imagine a better show than *The Band Wagon*. Nearly as good was *Face the Music* with songs by Irving Berlin, sketches by Moss Hart, and a cast that featured Joseph McCauley, Mary Boland, Andrew Tombes, Katherine Carrington, and David Burns. Florenz Ziegfeld, always a step away from bankruptcy because of his expensive productions, presented his last *Ziegfeld Follies* and it ran 197 performances, not long enough to get him out of debt. He died in 1932 owing everybody. Other revues to have substantial runs were *George White's Scandals*, *The Third Little Show*, *Shoot the Works*, *Earl Carroll's Vanities*, *Hot-Cha!*, and Ed Wynn's *The Laugh Parade*. Some of Broadway favorite songwriters came up with quality products but Depression-era audiences just weren't interested. Vincent Youman's tragic musical *Through the Years*, Sigmund Romberg and Oscar Hammerstein's operetta *East Wind*, and Hammerstein and Richard Whiting's *Free for All* were the most notable examples. If Hammerstein was having a bad season, at least his *Show Boat* was revived with success. Most of the original cast returned and this time Paul Robeson played Joe. One couldn't help wondering what would have happened if *Show Boat* had premiered in such a tough season.

"As Time Goes By"
Music and lyric by Herman Hupfield
From *Everybody's Welcome* (1931)
Sung by Frances Williams as Polly Bascom

Song of the Season

"As Time Goes By" is considered a Hollywood song. It was voted Number 2 on the American Film Institute's 100 Top Songs to come from the movies. (It was right behind "Over the Rainbow.") Although it is inaccurate to say that "As Time Goes By" came from *Casablanca* (1942), had it not been used so effectively in that film who knows how or when or even if the ballad would have been discovered. Certainly not from its source: the Broadway musical comedy *Everybody's Welcome*. Ten years had elapsed between that show and *Casablanca* and the song was, at best, a modest success. After *Casablanca*, it became one of the most beloved, performed, and recorded ballads in American music. Herman Hupfield, who wrote both the music and the lyric, wrote over 100 songs during his career but he is remembered for "As Time Goes By." *Everybody's Welcome* was a domestic musical comedy about a husband (Oscar Shaw) who quits his job to become a writer while his wife (Ann Sothern still using the name Harriette Lake) goes to work in the theatre and becomes the family breadwinner. The plan nearly destroys their marriage and they end up going back to their old roles. It was all a rather innocent trifle with songs by a handful of different songwriters. Hupfield's "As Time Goes By" was his only contribution and it was sung by Frances Williams, as one of the wife's friends, as a solo mid-way through the first act. It caused little stir, was rarely mentioned in the reviews, and didn't even click with Tommy and Jimmy Dorsey who played in the orchestra pit. *Everybody's Welcome* ran a profitable 139 performances and was never heard of again.

As for "As Time Goes By," it was first recorded by Rudy Vallée in July of 1931, three months before *Everybody's Welcome* opened on Broadway. Other early discs were made by Jacques Renard and his Orchestra, Fred Rich, and Binnie Hale. The African American singer Elisabeth Welch was among the first to include the song in her cabaret act. Sheet music sales were sluggish but the records sold well enough to be termed a modest hit. Ten years later the song was sung by Dooley Wilson in *Casablanca* and the music was used as a kind of leitmotif for the romance between Rick (Humphrey Bogart) and Ilse (Ingrid Bergman). Warner Brothers, who bought the rights to the song, wanted Wilson to record it but a musicians' strike kept him out of the studio so the ten-year-old Vallée recording was re-released and it shot to the top of the charts. It has never fallen out of favor.

Hupfield's verse for "As Time Goes By" sets up the refrain nicely but Wilson doesn't sing it in the film so it is not so well known. The lyric notices that there is a lot of "apprehension" in the world and instead of worrying about "Mr. Einstein's theory," one should "get down to earth" and face the facts of life that "cannot be removed."[12] Those facts of life are outlined in the famous refrain which states "You must remember this: A kiss is just a kiss,/ A sigh is just a sigh." Daringly, Hupfield uses the unromantic word "fundamental" to describe all these emotional things such as a kiss and a sigh. Then he uses another unromantic word—"apply"—in the title lines "The fundamental things apply/ As time goes by." The release and the final verse mention "passion" and a "fight for love and glory" but concludes that the "world will always welcome lovers." It is a vigorous lyric yet the music is a slow jazz composition that the effect is a resigned commentary on love. A series of musical phrases which repeat themselves at a different pitch also suggests a low-key blues number. Sometimes marked "moderately" and other times "freely," the sheet music was originally published in the key of E-flat major but in the version Wilson sang in *Casablanca* it is in D-flat major. But there are many interpretations of the song. Often it is played in C major but B-flat major has also been frequently used, as in Frank Sinatra's 1962 recording. It is estimated that over 600 recordings of "As Time Goes By" exist just in English. Special mention must be made of those by Adelaide Hall, Billie Holiday, Sammy Kaye (vocal by Judy Johnson), Barbra Streisand, Jimmy Durante, Louis Armstrong, Lee Wiley, Pat Suzuki, Petula Clark, Lillian Roth, Billy Eckstine, Peggy Lee, Ace Cannon, Harry Nilsson, the Platters, Vera Lynn and Bryan Ferry, Boots Randolph and Richie Cole, Bobby Short, Natalie Cole, Steve Tyrell, Barry Manilow, and the Jeff Steinberg Jazz Ensemble. "As Time Goes By" can be heard in over thirty movies, mostly instrumental versions but sometimes old recordings of the song are heard on the soundtrack.

Other notable songs from that season: "Dancing in the Dark," "New Sun in the Sky," "I Love Louisa," "High and Low" from *The Band Wagon*; "Life Is Just a Bowl of Cherries," "The Thrill Is Gone" from *George White's Scandals*; "Mad Dogs and Englishmen" from *The Third Little Show*; "She Didn't Say Yes (She Didn't Say No)," "The Night Was Made for Love," "Try to Forget" from *The Cat and The Fiddle*; "Love Is Sweeping the Country," "Who Cares?," "Because," "Wintergreen for President" from *Of Thee I Sing*; "Through the Years," "Drums in My Heart" from *Through the Years*; "Let's Have Another Cup of Coffee," "Soft Lights and Sweet Music," "I Say It's Spinach" from *Face the Music*.

Song of the Season

1932–1933 SEASON

Most historians consider 1932 and 1933 the worst years of the Depression and this was reflected on the Street where thirty-one musicals opened and only seven showed a profit. Revues dominated the season with eleven such shows opening and four of them making substantial money: *Strike Me Pink*, *Ballyhoo of 1932*, *Flying Colors*, and *Walk a Little Faster*. Top songwriters contributed to the scores and some excellent songs were introduced. *Music in the Air*, an operetta disguised as a romantic musical play, ran the longest of the book musicals. Oscar Hammerstein did the libretto and the lyrics to Jerome Kern's music and it was an old-fashioned pleasure for 342 performances. Cole Porter's *Gay Divorce* was quite different in tone and a hit at 248 performances even though Fred Astaire was appearing without his sister Adele for the first time. *Take a Chance*, with songs by various songwriters, was the other book musical to run over the 200-mark. The Gershwins' couldn't keep their *Pardon My English* on the boards for more than six weeks. An array of such talented songwriters as Harold Arlen, E. Y. Harburg, Johnny Mercer, Irving Caesar, Burton Lane, Vernon Duke, Jay Gorney, and Ted Koehler found their efforts for the revues *New Americana* and *George White's Music Hall Varieties* each close after nine weeks. Looking back at the season with hindsight, the most interesting failure was Kurt Weill and Bertolt Brecht's German import *The Threepenny Opera* which folded after twelve showings. With a better translation and production, the expressionistic music-theatre piece would return twenty-five years later and become a legendary Off-Broadway success. With the old Hippodrome currently dark, the largest venue in New York was Radio City Music Hall which opened at Rockefeller Center this season. Never considered a Broadway theatre, Radio City showed films as well as spectacular live productions and has managed to survive to this day.

"Night and Day"
Music and lyric by Cole Porter
From *Gay Divorce* (1932)
Sung by Fred Astaire as Guy,
and Claire Luce as Mimi

Of the handful of song standards introduced this season, perhaps none approaches the popularity of Cole Porter's "Night and Day." It was sung and danced by Fred Astaire and Claire Luce as a couple involved in a plot to get her a divorce, hence the title *Gay Divorce*. (Hollywood argued that no divorce can be a happy occasion and changed the title to *The Gay Divorcee*.) The musical was a variation on the traditional bedroom farce but the songs and the sterling cast turned the whole thing into a sophisticated but slaphappy delight. Reviewers were not thrilled about seeing Fred without Adele Astaire since she had always been a critics' darling. But when he took to the dance floor with Luce and they introduced "Night and Day," all was well. So well that Hollywood whisked Astaire to California and he never appeared on Broadway again. (He did reprise his performance in the 1933 London production of *Gay Divorce*.) When RKO filmed the musical in 1934, Astaire danced to "Night and Day" with his new partner, Ginger Rogers.

There is a hypnotic quality in both the music and the lyric for "Night and Day." At different times during his life, Porter said the song was inspired by Moroccan calls to prayer, the dripping of raindrops on the eves of a restaurant, and the mosaics in an Italian church. What is known is that Porter breaks away from several popular song conventions in "Night and Day" so everything feels different and exotic. Most songs are composed of thirty-two bars and have an AABA pattern in the refrain. This number runs forty-eight bars and has the structure of ABABCB, the C section being the release which comes late and goes in a surprising direction. Porter makes several key changes throughout the song, starting with B flat, moving into E, G, C, and F, and ending with B flat major. Also, the release is unusual in the way it departs from a syncopated series of descending chords and suddenly soars in an operatic way. The verse is a monotone series of the same note repeated thirty-five times, supporting the lyric's "beat beat beat of the tom-tom" and the "drip-drip-drip of the raindrops."[13] This recitative-like teasing is then broken with the first refrain, which begins with "Night and day, you are the one,/ Only you beneath the moon and under the sun." The second refrain offers such contrasting images as "the roaring traffic's boom" and "the silence of my lonely room." The most passionate lyric is found in the expansive release and final refrain. The singer confesses that "under the hide of me" there is "an, oh, such a hungry yearning burning inside of me." These feelings are described as a "torment" that can only be relieved if he can "spend my life making love to you." It is a very turbulent love song in both its heated words and its hypnotic music.

Fred Astaire recorded "Night and Day" with the Leo Reisman Orchestra in 1933 and it went to #1 spot on the charts, eventually becoming the most popular disc of the year. After Astaire, the song is most associated with Frank Sinatra who recorded it five times between 1942 and 1977. Among the hundreds of other discs are those by Eddy Duchin (vocal by Lew Sherwood), Paul Whiteman (vocals by Phil Dewey and the Pickens Sisters), Bing Crosby, Billie Holiday, Mel Tormé, Paul Evans, Ella Fitzgerald, Pee Wee Hunt, Mario Lanza, Joe Henderson, Sergio Mendes & Brasil '66, Shirley Bassey, Ringo Starr, Dionne Warwick, U2, Oscar Peterson, Samuel Ramey, Eartha Kitt, the Temptations, Rod Stewart, Bradley Walsh, Diana Krall, Stan Getz, Willie Nelson, Charlie Parker, Django Reinhardt, Dina Blade, and Tony Bennett and Lady Gaga. Astaire and Rogers performed "Night and Day" on the screen in *The Gay Divorcee* (1934) and the 1946 Porter biopic was titled *Night and Day* and the song was performed by Bill Days. In the 2004 Porter biopic *De-Lovely*, Kevin Kline and John Barrowman sang it. Among the times the number was sung on screen or on the soundtrack are: Frank Sinatra in *Reveille with Beverly* (1943), Julie Bishop (dubbed by Martha Mears) in *Action in the North Atlantic* (1943), Katharine Hepburn in *The Desk Set* (1957), Rick Riso in *Mafia!*

Song of the Season

(1998), Tom Burlinson in *All the Way* (2003), Cathi Ogden in *These Foolish Things* (2006), Patrick Peronne in *The Monuments Men* (2014), and Mark Jonathan Davis in *Batman v Superman: Dawn of Justice* (2016).

Other notable songs from that season: "After You, Who?," "Mister and Mrs. Fitch" from *Gay Divorce*; "Brother, Can You Spare a Dime?" from *New Americana*; "April in Paris" from *Walk a Little Faster*; "I Gotta Right to Sing the Blues" from *Earl Carroll's Vanities*; "Alone Together," "A Shine on Your Shoes," "Louisiana Hayride" from *Flying Colors*; "I've Told Ev'ry Little Star," "The Song Is You," "We Belong Together," "When the Spring Is in the Air" from *Music in the Air*; "You're an Old Smoothie," "Eadie Was a Lady," "Rise n' Shine" from *Take a Chance*; "Thrill Me" from *Ballyhoo of 1932*; "Isn't It a Pity?" from *Pardon My English*.

1933–1934 SEASON

The number of musicals continued to shrink: a total of twenty-seven shows and twelve of them revivals, mostly of Gilbert and Sullivan and other operettas from the distant past. More distressing, only eight musicals ran over 100 performances, a number which no longer guaranteed a profit. There was no question of the revue *As Thousands Cheer* ending up in the black. This Irving Berlin musical treat boasted an outstanding score including three standards ("Easter Parade," "Supper Time," and "Heat Wave"), a brilliant cast (Marilyn Miller, Clifton Webb, Ethel Waters, Helen Broderick, etc.), and estimable production values. In these dark days of the Depression, *As Thousands Cheer* was able to run 400 performances. The most successful book musical was Jerome Kern and Otto Harbach's *Roberta* (295 performances) followed by *Murder at the Vanities* (207 performances) and *All the King's Horses* (120 performances). Florenz Ziegfeld's widow Billie Burke joined forces with the Shubert Brothers and offered a new edition of the *Ziegfeld Follies*. Critics thought it paled in comparison to the *Follies* of the past but audiences wanted to see Fanny Brice, Willie and Eugene Howard, Jane Froman, and Buddy and Vilma Ebsen and kept the revue on the boards for twenty-three weeks. A new revue series was launched with Leonard Sillman's *New Faces of 1934* in which two dozen young performers were featured in sketches and original songs. None of the songs enjoyed much of a future but cast members Imogene Coca and Henry Fonda went on to notable careers. Audiences were curious, Sillman's revue ran five months, and future editions would follow irregularly over the next four decades. The major disappointment of the season was *Let 'Em Eat Cake*, a sequel to the Gershwins' long-running *Of Thee I Sing*. All the creative staff and cast were reassembled for this severe musical satire with a wicked sense of humor. Perhaps too wicked because some critics and playgoers thought it unpleasant and unfunny. Only the large advance allowed *Let 'Em Eat Cake* to run ninety performances. The curiosity of the season was the premiere of the opera *4 Saints in 3 Acts* in a Broadway house. The Gertrude Stein (libretto) and Virgil Thomson (music) piece was definitely in the avant-garde mode and probably belonged in an intimate opera venue with a discerning clientele. The opera ran forty-eight performances in two engagements.

"Smoke Gets in Your Eyes"
Music by Jerome Kern; lyric by Otto Harbach
From *Roberta* (1933)
Sung by Tamara as Princess Stephanie

It is not very often that one song turns a struggling musical production into a long-run hit but that was the case with "Smoke Gets in Your Eyes" and *Roberta*. Kern wrote the melody as a soft-shoe number for *Show Boat* (1927) but it was never used. The music was then used as the theme song for an NBC-Radio series that never got on the air. For *Roberta*, Kern gave the song a brisk, march-like beat in keeping with the rest of the swinging 1930s musical, but in rehearsals it was a failure. Harbach suggested that it be played at a more leisurely tempo and wrote the enchanting lyric which was based on an ancient Russian proverb. In *Roberta*, "Smoke Gets in Your Eyes" was sung by the expatriate Russian princess Stephanie (Tamara) to sing as she accompanied herself on the guitar. Despite a first-rate cast and a score filled with wonderful songs, *Roberta* met with mixed notices and the box office take was waning and it looked like the show would close. A recording of "Smoke Gets in Your Eyes" by Gertrude Niesen was released first but it was Paul Whiteman's disc with a vocal by Bob Lawerence that climbed the charts and made the song a national hit. The producers then billed *Roberta* as the "Smoke Gets in Your Eyes Show" and business picked up, running nearly ten months.

"Smoke Gets in Your Eyes" is not a traditional Broadway song. The Princess Stephanie accompanies herself on the guitar and sings it as an old Russian folk song so there is no verse and the structure is not in the usual AABA form. The number is rangy but not so much in an operatic way but in a lullaby manner. The flowing melody jumps up the scale at times and in the release there is a key change that is hypnotic. It is Harbach's finest lyric, a mysterious piece with the unforgettable image of lost love being like a dying fire with smoke that stings your eyes. The final refrain is particularly potent, ending with the entrancing couplet "When a lovely flame dies,/ Smoke gets in your eyes."[14] The release is rather archaic with the phrase "So I chaffed/ Them and gaily laughed" which is in the operetta style but much of the charm of "Smoke Gets in Your Eyes" is its old-fashioned quality. Surprisingly, this did not keep it from being a chart hit in different decades; a rock and roll version by the Platters in 1958 sold a million records and there was a 1972 best-selling disc by the English group Blue Haze. Among the other memorable discs were those made by Tamara, Sarah Vaughn, Jeri Southern, Louis Armstrong, Andrea Marcovicci, Billie Holiday, jazz pianist Beegie Adair, Billy Eckstine, Joan Roberts, Peggy Lee, Sonny Rollins, Judy Garland, Benny Goodman, Eartha Kitt, Cher, Kiri Te Kanawa, The Four Preps, Edith Piaf, Harry Belafonte, Elaine Paige, Dinah Shore, and Thelonious Monk. "Smoke Gets in Your Eyes" was heard during the opening credits of the 1935 screen version of *Roberta*, then was sung by Irene Dunne, then reprised as a dance by Fred Astaire and Ginger Rogers. In the 1952 remake titled *Lovely to Look At*, the ballad was first heard when Marge and Gower Champion danced an elegant pas de deux to the music then later in the movie Kathryn Grayson sang it as a solo. "Smoke Gets in Your Eyes" was sung by a chorus and danced to by Cyd Charisse and Gower Champion in the Kern biopic *Till the Clouds Roll By* (1945). The popular ballad has also been heard on the soundtrack of over thirty movies. On stage, Elisabeth Welch performed the number in the revue *Jerome Kern Goes to Hollywood* in London in 1985 and on Broadway in 1986.

Other notable songs from that season: "Yesterdays," "The Touch of Your Hand," "You're Devastating," "I'll Be Hard to Handle" from *Roberta*; "Easter Parade," "Supper Time," "Heat Wave," "Harlem on My Mind," "How's Chances?" from *As Thousands Cheer*; "Mine" from *Let 'Em Eat Cake*; "I Like the Likes of You," "The Last Round-Up," "Wagon Wheels" from *Ziegfeld Follies of 1933–1934*; "Weep No More, My Baby" from *Murder at the Vanities*.

Song of the Season

1934–1935 SEASON

If it were not for the eleven Gilbert and Sullivan revivals, the number of musicals this season would shrink down to twenty-one. And of those, only four ran more than 100 performances. This dismal statistic doesn't show that three of those shows were major long-running ventures. Cole Porter's *Anything Goes* was a resounding hit at 420 performances; it is also one of the few musicals from the 1930s that is revived frequently today. This is due to the funny, solid libretto as much as for the renowned score, one of the best in American musical comedy. The other book musical to run this season was *The Great Waltz*, a far-from-accurate musical biography of Johann Strauss Senior and Junior that used their waltzes for the songs. A magnificently mounted production made this the show of choice for Depression-weary audiences. *The Great Waltz* ran over a year and would have continued on except that a national tour was already booked. Howard Dietz and Arthur Schwartz, the go-to songwriters for revues, offered a book musical this season titled *Revenge with Music*. It was a modest success and added a few more standards to the great American Songbook. Noel Coward also returned to the book musical but *Conversation Piece* only lasted seven weeks. There were eight revues on the Street this season but only two were clear-cut hits. *Life Begins at 8:40* boasted some fine songs by Harold Arlen, E. Y. Harburg, and Ira Gershwin but it probably ran eight months on the strength of its gifted cast: Bert Lahr, Ray Bolger, Luella Gear, Brian Donlevy, Frances Williams, Dixie Dunbar, and Earl Oxford. *Thumbs Up!* offered the risible Bobby Clark, Paul McCullough, Ray Dooley, Eddie Dowling, and others but the material wasn't as strong so it ran only five months.

"I Get a Kick Out of You"
Music and lyric by Cole Porter
From *Anything Goes* (1934)
Sung by Ethel Merman as Reno Sweeney

The first musical number in *Anything Goes* is the wistful "I Get a Kick Out of You" sung by the wise-cracking Reno Sweeney (Ethel Merman). This is an odd place for such a torchy song sung by the star without any build-up. It is also a more serious ballad than most of what follows in the musical comedy. Perhaps the librettists didn't know where else to put it or thought it might slow things down later in the show. Regardless, it is one of Cole Porter's most beloved ballads and Merman made it a hit by the end of the first scene of *Anything Goes*. The verse is one of his finest and when the song is performed without it, the number loses much of its richness. The singer has a past that "is much too sad to be told" and it has left her "totally cold."[15] Only when she sees the "fabulous face" of an old love is she able to rise from the "old ennui." The rhyme scheme in the verse is formally constructed with the first and last lines rhyming (case … face) but all of the interior lines using the same feminine rhyme (quiet spree ... old ennui ... turn and see). The tone throughout "I Get a Kick Out of You" has a world-weary feeling and the rhymes fall in unexpected places but it is the restless rhumba-like music that drives the verse. The refrain offers examples of what does not impress: alcohol, drugs, riding in an airplane. The music suddenly gets more rhythmic as it ascends and descends the scale to underline the character's indecision. It is only in the release that the true nature of the songs is revealed. A quiet frustration is suggested in "I get a kick though it's clear to me/ You obviously don't adore me." Under the sense of "ennui" that runs throughout the song is a potent torch song. Notice how Porter never uses the word "love" anywhere in the song; the more casual "get a kick" replaces it. Also, the internal rhyming throughout the lyric adds to the carefree point of view, climaxing in one of his most famous internal rhymes: "Flying too high with some guy in the sky/ Is my idea of nothing to do." Originally the lyric referenced "Mrs. Lindbergh" in the flying metaphor but after the infamous kidnapping of the Lindbergh baby in 1932, Porter rewrote the lyric, ending up with the classic line.

Several hit songs came out of *Anything Goes* but none has been recorded as often as "I Get a Kick Out of You." Because of the lyric "I get no kick from cocaine," many radio stations would not broadcast the song without the sanitized alternative ("perfumes from Spain") which Porter never authorized. Merman recorded "I Get a Kick Out of You" with Johnny Green's Orchestra in 1934, the same year there were discs by Paul Whiteman (vocal by Ramona), the Dorsey Brothers (vocal by Kay Weber), and the orchestras of Leo Reisman and Bob Causer. There are close to 300 recordings since then, including those by Frank Sinatra, Mary Martin, Vaughn Monroe, Ella Fitzgerald, Louis Armstrong, Jeri Southern, Dolly Parton, Rod Stewart, Matt Forbes, Van Morrison, and Tony Bennett with Lady Gaga. "I Get a Kick Out of You" was sung by Jeanne Aubert in the 1935 London production of *Anything Goes*. New York revivals of the musical have included such Reno Sweeneys as Eileen Rogers in 1962, Patti LuPone in 1987 and 2002, and Sutton Foster in 2011. In the 1936 film version of the musical the song was sung by Merman. Also on screen, "I Get a Kick Out of You" was performed by Zizi Jeanmarie in *Anything Goes* (1956), Ginny Simms in *Night and Day* (1946), Billy Daniels in *Sunny Side of the Street* (1951), Cleavon Little and the chain gang in *Blazing Saddles* (1974), Sarah Chrétien in *The Knife* (1991), Diana Krall in *De-Lovely* (2004), and Henry Hall and The BBC Dance Orchestra in *Being Julia* (2004).

Other notable songs from that season: "Anything Goes," "You're the Top," "All Through the Night," "Blow, Gabriel, Blow" from *Anything Goes*; "Autumn in New York," "Zing! Went the Strings of My Heart!," "Words without Music" from *Thumbs Up!*; "You're a Builder-Upper," "Fun to Be Fooled," "Let's Take a Walk Around the Block" from *Life Begins at 8:40*; "You and the Night and the Music," "If There Is Someone Lovelier Than You" from *Revenge with Music*; "I'll Follow My Secret Heart" from *Conversation Piece*.

1935–1936 SEASON

As if Broadway didn't already have enough to worry about, a new threat came this season in the form of "swing." This new sound was unofficially launched when Benny Goodman and his orchestra opened the Palomar Ballroom in Los Angeles in August of 1935 and the band and the sound were resounding hits. This evolving trend in music was considered anathema to the traditional Broadway musical. Whereas jazz musicals were well established, the new Big Band sound was played in ballrooms where patrons could dance rather than just sit and observe. And although most bands had vocalists, they only sang for a portion of the song, the emphasis being on the band itself. The only encouraging aspect of the swing invasion was the practice of Big Band arrangers taking Broadway songs and fashioning them into band numbers, often turning obscure songs into nationwide hits. This season, for example, Cole Porter's "Begin the Beguine" did not become popular until a recording by Artie Shaw three years after it was introduced on Broadway.

If the Broadway musical was not swinging, it was certainly thriving this season. The number of productions was not impressive but the quality of the shows was, with both the revues and the book musicals. Howard Dietz and Arthur Schwartz returned to the revue format and had success with *At Home Abroad*. Beatrice Lillie, Eddie Foy, Jr., Eleanor Powell, Ethel Waters, and Reginald Gardner shone in the roguish sketches and/or proficient songs. The Shuberts offered another *Ziegfeld Follies* and it also boasted an outstanding cast that included Fanny Brice, Bob Hope, Josephine Baker, Eve Arden, Judy Canova, Gertrude Niesen, and the Nicholas Brothers. The other successful revues were *Earl Carroll's Sketch Book*, *George White's Scandals*, and *New Faces of 1936*. A revue titled *The Illustrator's Show* was a quick failure so few got to hear some early songs by Frederick Loewe and Frank Loesser. It was a remarkable season for book musicals, even though there were so few of them. Oscar Hammerstein and Sigmund Romberg were still betting on the operetta form and found audiences liked their *May Wine* enough to let it run 213 performances. Cole Porter's *Jubilee* didn't run as long but it offered a superb score. Richard Rodgers and Lorenz Hart returned from Hollywood with a vengeance, scoring two major hits. Their circus musical *Jumbo* was that rare occasion when a Broadway musical was presented in the reopened Hippodrome Theatre. Some critics complained it was more circus than musical, and some of the songs were lost in the huge venue, but audiences like it and *Jumbo* ran 233 times. Rodgers and Hart's other show was even better. *On Your Toes* had a superior score, a splendid cast headed by Ray Bolger, a solid book and direction by George Abbott, and stunning choreography by George Balanchine. It rightfully ran longer than any other show that season.

And then there was *Porgy and Bess*. The Gershwins had been absent from Broadway for a few seasons as the brothers collaborated with DuBose Heyward on this ambitious opera based on Heyward's novel *Porgy* and its stage version by DuBose and Dorothy Heyward. *Porgy and Bess* premiered in a Broadway venue even though it was billed as an "American folk opera." Both theatre and music critics covered the new work; it was better appreciated by the former. George Gershwin not only composed three hours of music, but also orchestrated the opera himself. It was given a superlative production by director Rouben Mamoulian and was sung by a venerable cast of mostly African Americans. Today *Porgy and Bess* is considered the great American opera but in Depression-era New York it only survived fifteen weeks. The brothers then headed to Hollywood; George Gershwin never returned.

"Begin the Beguine"
Music and lyric by Cole Porter
From *Jubilee* (1935)
Sung by June Knight as Karen O'Kane

Before one can "Begin the Beguine," it helps to know that a "beguine" was a popular dance, much like a fox trot or slow rhumba, from the French West Indies. Like some other dances from Latin America, it was making the rounds in North America in the 1930s. Some believe the fad began with "The Carioca" by Gus Kahn, Edward Eliscu (lyric), and Vincent Youmans (music) in the film *Flying Down to Rio* (1933). Cole Porter used Latin rhythms in various songs throughout his career but nowhere as effectively as in "Begin the Beguine." Yet Porter claimed that he got the inspiration for the music from an Indonesian war dance that he heard while sailing around the world. He later said the song was based on a dance he saw Martinique natives perform in a Parisian nightclub. One thing is certain: "Begin the Beguine" was first sung by June Knight then danced by Knight and Charles Walters in the Broadway musical *Jubilee*. It is understandable why the song didn't catch on. It is over three times as long as the standard thirty-two-bar popular song of the time. The structure departs so far from the conventional AABA pattern that both singer and listener can get lost in its many tangents. Yet for all that, the music is driven forward and builds to a passionate climax that satisfies. There is no verse. We are thrown into the pulsating flow of the music with no warning with "When they begin the beguine/ It brings back the sound of music so tender."[16] Also recalled is a night of "tropical splendor" and a "memory ever green." More images of music coming back to haunt one follow, then a release that is not radically different from the first two refrains. After returning to the music of the original refrain, a whole new release, more expressive and fervent follows. The singer pleads "don't let them begin the beguine!" because he prefers the let these thoughts "sleep like a dead desire I only remember." Then instead of returning to the refrain, the release is repeated with more fervor before coming to an original ending that ties it all together with "we suddenly know what heaven we're in/ When they begin the beguine."

Although *Jubilee* ran almost six months, nothing much happened to "Begin the Beguine." A recording Xavier Cugat made with vocalist Don Reid a month before the show opened on Broadway was released at the time of the premiere and it sold well enough to

Song of the Season

get on the charts. Then two years of little or no activity. Artie Shaw was trying to establish a sound for his orchestra and wanted to record an instrumental swing version of the song. RCA balked but a compromise was reached: "Begin the Beguine" would be the B side of a record featuring "Indian Love Call." The 1938 disc was a bestseller peaking in #3 spot and securing the future of Shaw and the song. The Andrews Sisters' 1939 recording was the first vocal version to sell well but it was bested by a record by Joe Loss (vocalist Chick Henderson) which sold a million copies. Since then, there have been hundreds of discs by Big Bands, singers, jazz musicians, Latin bands, and rock groups. Among the many memorable discs are those by Mildred Bailey, Harry James, Billy Cotton, Adelaide Hall, Benny Goodman, Connee Boswell, Delta Rhythm Boys, Tommy Dorsey, Glenn Miller, Frank Sinatra, Ella Fitzgerald, Charlie Parker, Elvis Presley, Steve Ross, Oscar Peterson, Dizzy Gillespie, Peter Townsend, Michael Nesmith, Harry Connick, Jr., Michael Feinstein, Steven Herring, and Earl Rose. There was no film version of *Jubilee* but in *Broadway Melody of 1940* the song was sung by Carmen D'Antonio (dubbed by Lois Hodnott) and danced by Eleanor Powell and Fred Astaire. "Begin the Beguine" was sung on screen or on the soundtrack by Deanna Durbin in *Hers to Hold* (1943), Carlos Ramírez and chorus in *Night and Day* (1946), Sammi Davis in *Hope and Glory* (1987), Sammy Davis, Jr. in *Moon Over Parador* (1988), Melora Hardin in *The Rocketeer* (1991), Sheryl Crow in *De-Lovely* (2004), and Leslie "Hutch" Hutchinson in *The Brothers Bloom* (2008). Instrumental versions of "Begin the Beguine" can be heard on the soundtracks in many movies, from *Everybody's Hobby* (1939) to *The Survivor* (2021).

Other notable songs from that season: "Just One of Those Things," "A Picture of Me Without You," "Why Shouldn't I?" from *Jubilee*; "Summertime," "It Ain't Necessarily So," "Bess, You Is My Woman Now," "My Man's Gone Now," "I Loves You, Porgy" from *Porgy and Bess*; "On Your Toes," "Glad to Be Unhappy," "There's a Small Hotel," "It's Got to Be Love" from *On Your Toes*; "I Can't Get Started with You," "He Hasn't a Thing Except Me" from *Ziegfeld Follies of 1936*; "My Romance," "Little Girl Blue," "The Most Beautiful Girl in the World" from *Jumbo*; "Thief in the Night," "Love Is a Dancing Thing" from *At Home Abroad*; "Red Sails in the Sunset" from *Provincetown Follies*.

1936–1937 SEASON

The Depression continued to devastate Broadway despite Franklin Roosevelt's re-election to a second term in the fall of 1936. Only thirteen new musicals opened on Broadway and only three of those managed to turn a profit. The two musical comedy hits were Cole Porter's *Red, Hot and Blue!* and Rodgers and Hart's *Babes in Arms*. The anti-war musical *Johnny Johnson* had a strong score by composer Kurt Weill but it was not what audiences wanted. They did want musical revues and the 1930s continued to be a Golden Age for that genre. *The Show Is On* and *Ziegfeld Follies* offered such popular stars as Bobby Clark, Beatrice Lillie, Fanny Brice, Bert Lahr, and Gypsy Rose Lee. Add to that a trio of favorites—Ethel Merman, Jimmy Durante, Bob Hope—in *Red, Hot and Blue!* and the cast of young unknowns in *Babes in Arms* and Broadway was filled with talent that season. Operetta continued to decline during the Depression and even Sigmund Romberg and Otto Harbach, two old hands at the genre, could not find success with *Forbidden Melody*. The large spectacle *The White Horse Inn* was also an operetta and it ran 223 performances but still lost a bundle. The visiting D'Oyly Carte Opera Company from England presented the entire Gilbert and Sullivan repertoire on Broadway and managed to keep the Martin Beck Theatre busy. But operetta in any form was already becoming museum-piece theatre. A final distressing sign of the times: the New Amsterdam Theatre, once the home of the glittering *Ziegfeld Follies*, was revamped into a movie house. It would not return as a legitimate Broadway theatre until 1997.

"My Funny Valentine"
Music by Richard Rodgers; lyric by Lorenz Hart
From *Babes in Arms* (1937)
Sung by Mitzi Green as Billie Smith

Very few musicals have introduced as many song standards as *Babes in Arms*. But the song that is probably most beloved and most recorded is "My Funny Valentine." Lorenz Hart's lyric for the verse uses archaic language (thy, knowest, hast) but turns to slangy intimacy in the refrain. The song is unique in the way the singer manages to take gentle insults ("your looks are laughable.. unphotographical") and turn them into highly romantic compliments ("You're my favorite work of art").[17] Richard Rodgers' melody for the verse is simple and unaccompanied; the refrain is a brilliant variation of the same six-note phrase that climaxes quietly and beautifully. The Hart lyric is less showy in the refrain, with such straightforward sentiments as the wish "don't change a hair for me" paired with "not if you care for me." As with many of his other compositions, Rodgers states the main musical phrase right at the beginning of the refrain with the title phrase. He then repeats the melody and embellishes it, raising the key slightly. In the release, the

Song of the Season

prominent note also rises gently. ("Is your figure less than Greek ... ?") It is a song only Rodgers and Hart could have written and a marvel by any standards.

As wonderful as the songs in *Babes in Arms* are, they have little to do with plot or character. Yet "My Funny Valentine" is somewhat integrated. *Babes in Arms* is a Depression-era musical comedy about the young offspring of out-of-work vaudevillians who put on a show to raise enough money to keep them from being sent to a work farm. The leading man is named Valentine so when Billie sings "My Funny Valentine" she is not referring to the holiday but to her dear Val. (The character's name was changed to Val after the song was completed.) That reference has not stopped the song from working outside the context of the show. There have been over one thousand recordings over the years. "My Funny Valentine" has been a particular favorite of jazz musicians. Gerry Mulligan's 1945 jazz recording was the first to hit the charts and later Chet Baker made it his theme song. Among the many others to record "My Funny Valentine" are such diverse artists as Margaret Whiting, Sammy Davis, Jr., Bobby Troup and his Trio, the Four Freshmen, Manhattan Jazz Quintet, Tony Bennett, Frank Sinatra, Miles Davis, Kenny Rogers, Judy Collins, Leon Russell, Chris Botti, Linda Ronstadt, Carly Simon, and Michael Bublé. Inexplicably, "My Funny Valentine" was not used in the 1939 film version of *Babes in Arms* but it has been sung or heard in dozens of other movies over the years.

Other notable songs from that season: "Babes in Arms," "Johnny One-Note," "Where or When," "I Wish I Were in Love Again," "Way Out West," "The Lady Is a Tramp" from *Babes in Arms*; "Johnny's Song (Listen to My Song)" from *Johnny Johnson*; "Down in the Depths (On the 90th Floor)," "It's De-Lovely," "Ridin' High" from *Red, Hot and Blue!*; "You Were There" from *Tonight at 8:30*; "Song of the Woodman" from *The Show Is On*.

1937–1938 SEASON

There were a lot of empty theatres on the Street this season; only sixteen musicals opened and nine of them ran less than 100 performances. Producers were frustrated because five musicals this season were presented as non-profit productions, offering low ticket prices and creating unfair competition for commercial ventures. Four of these sponsored musicals were part of the Federal Theatre Project, a branch of the Works Progress Administration (WPA) which offered free or modestly priced theatre of all kinds across the country. Providing free productions for the unemployed Hoosiers in Indiana was one thing; presenting shows on Broadway at low prices was something else. Three of the WPA productions—*Swing It, A Hero Is Born,* and *No More Peace*—had limited runs and limited box office receipts but it didn't matter. The controversial *The Cradle Will Rock* got so much publicity that it ran 108 performances. Whether it made money or not was a moot point. Another sponsored musical, *Pins and Needles*, was produced and performed by the International Ladies Garment Workers Union. By definition, it was an amateur production but the songs by Harold Rome and some of the performers were very skillful. *Pins and Needles* updated its material to keep up with events in the news so, in different editions, it chalked up 1,108 performances.

Commercial Broadway continued to struggle through the Depression, the musicals sometimes commenting on current events. Rodgers and Hart's *I'd Rather Be Right* had the current US president as its main character and the libretto by George S. Kaufman and Moss Hart did not steer away from issues in the news. The musical was probably more didactic than playgoers wanted but with George M. Cohan playing FDR it was highly entertaining and ran a surprising 290 performances. Also filled with commentary on the outside world was *Hooray for What!*, a vehicle for the popular comic Ed Wynn. The libretto by Howard Lindsey and Russel Crouse, as well as the songs by Harold Arlen and E. Y. Harburg, was highly satiric as the show lampooned international arms build-up and spies trying to get the formula for a powerful laughing gas. The conservative Wynn censored much of the most potent material but *Hooray for What!* ended up being enjoyable and somewhat pointed. It managed to run 200 performances. Even more successful was a second Rodgers and Hart entry: *I Married an Angel*. The romantic fantasy was escapist entertainment, to say the least, and it pleased playgoers 338 times. The other two profitable book musicals were the musical melodrama *The Fireman's Flame* and the Strauss operetta *Three Waltzes*. Howard Dietz and Arthur Schwartz returned to the book musical with *Between the Devil* but, despite some splendid songs, it was a near miss at ninety-three performances. That was much more than *Right This Way* managed to run. This book musical with songs mostly by Sammy Fain and Irving Kahal closed inside of two weeks but left behind two song standards: "I Can Dream, Can't I?" and "I'll Be Seeing You."

Song of the Season

> "I'll Be Seeing You"
> Music by Sammy Fain; lyric by Irving Kahal
> From *Right This Way* (1938)
> Sung by Tamara as Mimi

Possibly no other song captured the heartache of lovers separated during the Second World War as potently as "I'll Be Seeing You." And for two generations after the war, the song conjured up nostalgic feelings for those times. Ironically, "I'll Be Seeing You" was written four years before America entered the war and the song was almost lost forever. Sammy Fain (music) and Irving Kahal (lyric) wrote the ballad as a Tin Pan Alley possibility in 1938 but before they could do anything with it they were asked to provide six songs for the upcoming Broadway musical *Right This Way*. One of the songs, "I'll Be Seeing You," was given to Tamara who sang it in the second act. Reviews for the show were dismissive, next to nothing was written about the songs, and *Right This Way* closed after fifteen performances. None of the score was published and "I'll Be Seeing You" was not recorded until 1940 when a disc was made by Dick Todd, followed by another by Tommy Dorsey with a vocal by Frank Sinatra that got on the charts. Still nothing came of the song and Kahal died in 1942 never seeing his lyric find a wide audience. It was a 1944 recording by Bing Crosby with the John Scott Trotter Orchestra that reached the Number 1 spot. By then America had been in the war for two years and thousands of G.I.s were separated from loved ones. "I'll Be seeing You" resonated so strongly that many still believe it is the Second World War song. "I'll Be Seeing You" has a brief verse in which the memory evoked is very specific. The lyric describes an April morning in Paris when the cathedral bells are heard. The refrain is a list of other images and memories: a small cafe, the park, a children's carousel, the chestnut trees, and a wishing well. There is no distinct release. Fain's music is a slow lullaby that carefully climbs the scale with no apparent jumps. After repeating the main theme, the music goes in a new direction and sits on the final lyric with firm resolve: "I'll be looking at the moon,/ But I'll be seeing you."[18] It has been pointed out that there is a resemblance between the music for the first four lines of the refrain and a passage from Gustav Mahler's Third Symphony (1896). But it has also been shown that the Mahler section was derived from the overture to Daniel Auber's opera *Marco Spada* (1852).

In 1944, when the Crosby record caught on, there were other discs by Billie Holiday, Jo Stafford, Anne Shelton, and Rita Marlowe. Over the decades there were memorable recordings by Tony Bennett, the Four Sergeants, Vera Lynn, Carol Bruce, Rosemary Clooney, Charlie Cochran, Brenda Lee, the Lettermen, Lionel Hampton, Robert Goulet, Boots Randolph, Ray Charles, Hildegarde, Maxine Sullivan, Mandy Patinkin, Neil Sedaka, Max Bygraves, Etta Jones, Ruth Brown, Stan Whitmire, Willie Nelson, Engelbert Humperdinck, Linda Eder, Nancy Wilson, and Carlos Franzetti. The song was used throughout the film *I'll Be Seeing You* (1944) with a vocal by Louanne Hogan. It was also sung or heard on movie soundtracks by Yvette in *See My Lawyer* (1945), the Five Satins in *Let the Good Times Roll* (1973), Anne Shelton in *Yanks* (1979), Billie Holiday in *Bad Timing* (1980) and several other movies, Jo Stafford in *Swing Shift* (1984) and *Crazy Moon* (1987), Liberace in *Crimes and Misdemeanors* (1989) and *Misery* (1990), Kate Smith in *The Good Girl* (2002), Carmen Twillie in *Children on Their Birthdays* (2002), Martha Wainwright in *The Aviator* (2004), Frank Sinatra in *Louise's Diary* (2010), the Skyliners in *Since I Don't Have You* (2013), Brenda Lee in *Out of Blue* (2018), and Audra McDonald in *Respect* (2021). On the New York stage, "I'll Be Seeing You" was sung by the cast of *The 1940's Radio Hour* (1979), the company of *Swingtime Canteen* (1995), and Ann Hampton Callaway in *Swing!* (1999).

Other notable songs from that season: "I Can Dream, Can't I?" from *Right This Way*; "I Married an Angel," "Spring Is Here," "At the Roxy Music Hall" from *I Married an Angel*; "Have You Met Miss Jones?," "Off the Record" from *I'd Rather Be Right*; "Sunday in the Park," "Nobody Makes a Pass at Me," "Sing Me a Song with Social Significance," "Four Little Angels of Peace" from *Pins and Needles*; "Down with Love," "God's Country" from *Hooray for What!*; "I See Your Face Before Me," "By Myself," "Triplets" from *Between the Devil*; "The Cradle Will Rock," "Nickel Under the Foot" from *The Cradle Will Rock*.

Song of the Season

1938–1939 SEASON

If Gilbert and Sullivan's *The Mikado* was your cup of tea, this season gave you a rare chance to see it three times on Broadway in three very different forms. London's D'Oyly Carte Opera Company brought a repertory of nine G&S favorites to Broadway including the popular *The Mikado* with Martyn Green as Ko-Ko. The British company prided itself on recreating the original staging from the Victorian era. Not so with the Federal Theatre Project which used the original plot and songs but had the music rearranged for the Big Band sound and called it *The Swing Mikado*. The show was set in tribal Africa with an all-Black cast and it was a huge hit in Chicago. Producer Michael Todd tried to bring it to Broadway but failed to come to terms with the government-sponsored company so he put together his own all-Black version and called it *The Hot Mikado*. With Bill "Bojangles" Robinson in the title role, the Todd production was glitzy and modern. When *The Swing Mikado* arrived on Broadway, there were two competing *Mikado*'s playing across the street from each other. The Chicago version and *The Hot Mikado* each ran about eleven weeks but Todd made a higher profit by moving his show to the New York World's Fair in the summer. And if three *Mikado*'s were not enough, Oscar Hammerstein penned a biographical musical about Gilbert and Sullivan, called it *Knights of Song*, and used selections from the operettas as the score. Maybe it was more G&S than Broadway could handle because *Knights of Song* folded after two weeks.

The Federal Theatre Project, a branch of the New Deal's WPA, also brought to Broadway the family musical entertainment *Pinocchio* and a patriotic revue titled *Sing for Your Supper*. That title also served for one of the sparkling songs Rodgers and Hart wrote for *The Boys from Syracuse*, a rough-and-tumble musical farce that George Abbott adapted from Shakespeare's *A Comedy of Errors*. From its sportive cast and story to its clever sets, costumes, and dances, *The Boys from Syracuse* was the best musical of the season, but even it struggled to run 235 performances. Cole Porter had two book musicals this season. The witty *You Never Know* was a period piece that only occasionally came to life despite some fine songs. It ran only ten weeks. More to the audience's liking was the contemporary musical *Leave It to Me* which satirized the newspaper industry, foreign affairs, and Soviet Russia. In addition to some top-notch songs, *Leave It to Me* is most remembered as the debut of Mary Martin who stopped the show 307 times with "My Heart Belongs to Daddy." Composer Kurt Weill collaborated with distinguished playwright Maxwell Anderson on the musical *Knickerbocker Holiday*, a satire on early New Amsterdam politics with peg-legged Pieter Stuyvesant (Walter Huston) seen as a colonial Franklin Roosevelt. It was an uneven musical but with Huston's popularity and the hit number "September Song," *Knickerbocker Holiday* managed to run 168 performances.

Eight revues opened on Broadway this season and most of them were able to edge over the 100-performance mark and make a modest profit. Gone were the days of the lavish *Follies*, *Scandals*, and *Vanities*, but there were some noteworthy songs and fine performances to be found in *Sing Out the News*, *Set to Music*, *One for the Money*, and

Stars in Your Eyes. The long-run champ was not so much a revue as an inflated vaudeville comedy act. The Depression was killing off old-time vaudeville so comics Ole Olsen and Chic Johnson put together a series of skits, songs, and dances, called it *Hellzapoppin*, and opened in one of Broadway biggest houses. The humor was loud and juvenile, the songs forgettable, and the comedy stunts filled (literally) with bells, whistles, and sirens. *Hellzapoppin* was castigated by the critics but it appealed to Depression-weary audiences and, with the unabashed ballyhooing by the powerful columnist Walter Winchell, the show became a hit. Like the previous season's *Pins and Needles*, *Hellzapoppin* kept changing material, performers, and even the title to encourage repeat business. By the time it closed, the curiosity had played 1,414 times.

"September Song"
Music by Kurt Weill; lyric by Maxwell Anderson
From *Knickerbocker Holiday* (1938)
Sung by Walter Huston as Pieter Stuyvesant

The German-Jewish composer Kurt Weill emigrated to America in 1935 and brought his music drama ideas to Broadway with the anti-war musical *Johnny Johnson* in 1936. It was not what Broadway audiences wanted and did not run but Weill was not discouraged. For his second Broadway musical, Weill teamed up with the dramatic playwright Maxwell Anderson who wrote the libretto and lyrics for *Knickerbocker Holiday*. Anderson was critical of some of FDR's New Deal ideas and thought the president was moving the nation into a fascist state. His libretto was about the seventeenth-century governor Pieter Stuyvesant who uses his power to make New Amsterdam a totalitarian state. A councilman offers his young daughter Tina as a wife for the aged governor even though she is in love with the radical "American" Brom Broeck. Stuyvesant is charmed by Tina and asks her to make his last days special. Brom is set to be hung for treason but an attack by native tribes makes him a hero and the governor lets the couple reunite. It was a sly and knowing libretto and the parallels to Franklin D. Roosevelt were not hidden. But *Knickerbocker Holiday* lost most of its political potency when Walter Huston was cast as Stuyvesant. The venerable actor of stage and film was so funny and enjoyable as the governor that most of the satire dissolved. Stuyvesant was a comic villain and Huston was afraid he would lose the audience's sympathy and requested a solo that showed a tender side of the aging dictator. Huston had never done a musical and knew he had a very limited singing range so Weill and Anderson wrote "September Song" with the actor in mind. Houston's wistful rendition of the ballad was one of the highlights of the season. It was so moving that the audience sided with the governor in the political debate and *Knickerbocker Holiday* was weakened as a satire.

Not surprisingly, "September Song" has a narrow musical range and plenty of opportunities for a non-singer to shine because the song must be acted. Although it has the traditional AABA structure and stays within the thirty-two-bar form, Weill's music rarely repeats a phrase, subtly changing some notes so that there is a haunting quality to the song. Also, the tempo is as slow as a lullaby so there is a soothing sensation throughout. Anderson's lyric is provocative but restrained, using few rhymes and letting the seasons of the year provide the imagery. The verse is very personal as Stuyvesant recalls his romantic conquests in the past. As a young man, he courted girls who eventually "as time came around, she came my way."[19] But in the refrain he admits that he is too old for such wooing. Noting that "it's a long, long while from May to December," he realizes the "days grow short when you reach September" and "one hasn't got time for the waiting game." The short release is not a wide-ranged declaration but a somber observation that "the days dwindle down to a precious few." The song ends with a heartfelt invitation: "These few precious days I'll spend with you." The music does not completely resolve at the end of the song. Rather it is suspended in space with a question mark, making "September Song" so beguiling.

Knickerbocker Holiday ran less than six months but Huston recorded "September Song" so his performance was widely known and enjoyed. Because the ballad is best interpreted by an aged singer, the song did not get many recordings right after *Knickerbocker Holiday*. Then in 1945 Huston recorded it again with the Victor Young Orchestra and Artie Shaw had a popular instrumental version. The first female vocalist to record "September Song" was Sarah Vaughn with the Teddy Wilson Quartet in 1947. Soon the number was established as a standard and hundreds of records followed, among them discs by Sammy Kaye, Bing Crosby, the Ravens, Dave Brubeck Trio, "Scat Man" Crothers, Larry Adler, Coleman Hawkins, Lotte Lenya, Dion and the Belmonts, Eileen Farrell, the Platters, Tex Ritter, Jimmy Durante, Patti Page, Chet Baker, James Brown, Faron Young, Diahann Carroll, Zoot Sims, Marilyn Michaels, Wesla Whitfield, Jessica Lange, Lou Reed, and Jimmy Felts. In the 1944 movie version of *Knickerbocker Holiday*, Charles Coburn played Stuyvesant and sang "September Song." It can be heard in dozens of other films, including Huston's recording in *September Affair* (1950), Maurice Chevalier in *Pepe* (1960), Django Reinhardt in *Catch-22* (1970), Willie Nelson in *Texasville* (1990), Bob Swenson and Steve Hatzai in *A Trip to Swaddades* (2008), and heard throughout *Radio Days* (1987) as a recurring theme song.

Other notable songs from that season: "It Never Was You" from *Knickerbocker Holiday*; "Falling in Love with Love," "Sing for Your Supper," "This Can't Be Love," "Dear Old Syracuse," "Oh, Diogenes" from *The Boys from Syracuse*; "My Heart Belongs to Daddy," "Most Gentlemen Don't Like Love," "Get Out of Town" from *Leave It to Me!*; "You Never Know," "At Long Last Love" from *You Never Know*; "F.D.R. Jones" from *Sing Out the News*; "Mad About the Boy," "The Stately Homes of England," "(I've Been to a) Marvelous Party" from *Set to Music*; "Ballad of Uncle Sam (Ballad for Americans)" from *Sing for Your Supper*.

1939–1940 SEASON

Just before the new season got underway, the New York World's Fair opened on April 30 after much ballyhoo and high expectations. "Dawn of a New Day" was the theme and international cooperation was the hope of the two-year exhibition. But this dream was shattered four months later when Hitler's troops invaded Poland on September 1 and within days the Second World War began. Broadway, like most of America, tried to ignore the war in Europe and concentrate on the struggling domestic economy. Pointed political satire, left-wing commentary, and foreign caricatures all but disappeared from musicals on the Street. The new shows were not only softened but often drained of vitality. Respected songwriters Cole Porter, Rodgers and Hart, Jerome Kern and Oscar Hammerstein, and others all produced mediocre book musicals and the season's revues were not much better. Only Irving Berlin came up with a lively score to go with the spoof of big business and government that was *Louisiana Purchase*. It certainly helped to have William Gaxton, Victor Moore, Vera Zorina, and Irene Bordoni in the cast. But weak librettos hindered Porter's *DuBarry Was a Lady*, Kern and Hammerstein's *Very Warm for May*, and both of Rodgers and Hart's two entries: *Too Many Girls* and *Higher and Higher*. Each show offered a laudable song or two but mostly the scores were as disappointing as the librettos. Happily, Bert Lahr, Ethel Merman, Jack Haley, Jack Whiting, Shirley Ross, Eddie Bracken, Eve Arden, Betty Grable, and others used their star power to help these shows run. Only one other book musical enjoyed a profitable run: *Yokel Boy*, which first brought attention to comic Phil Silvers. The most successful revue of the season was *The Streets of Paris* which is most remembered for introducing the "Brazilian bombshell" Carmen Miranda. The stars were Bobby Clark, Abbott and Costello, and Luella Gear, but Miranda got the best song: "South American Way." *Folies Bergere* from France found an audience, as did the revue *Two for the Show*. *George White's Scandals* managed to run 120 performances, not enough to pay expenses; it was the last *Scandals*. This season marked the end of the *Earl Carroll's Vanities* as well; this last edition folded after three weeks and the *Vanities* never returned. It is sad to consider that the World's Fair was demonstrating air conditioning, electric razors, 3-D movies, electric typewriters, and early forms of television and computers as a look into the future, but the musicals on Broadway were mostly old hat, predictable, and irrelevant.

"All the Things You Are"
Music by Jerome Kern; lyric by Oscar Hammerstein
From *Very Warm for May* (1939)
Sung by Hiram Sherman as Ogden Quiler, Frances Mercer as
Liz Spofford, Hollace Shaw as Carroll, and Ralph Stuart as Charles

Song of the Season

How ironic that one of the most dismal of Broadway seasons would produce one of the finest of all popular songs. And also ironic that it came from a flop show. *Very Warm for May* was a very promising Kern and Hammerstein musical but it was fraught with difficulties from the start, underwent many changes, met with unenthusiastic notices, and closed after seven weeks. Happily "All the Things You Are" survived the ordeal. In 1964, a poll of American composers listed "All the Things You Are" as their all-time favorite American song, and the decades since then have done little to diminish the high opinion people have of it. In *Very Warm for May*, the ballad was sung as a quartet but "All the Things You Are" works best as a vocal solo and that is how dozens of singers have recorded it over the years. There have been many instrumental versions as well but the ballad needs Hammerstein's indelible lyric for the song to truly soar.

"All the Things You Are" is a straightforward love song, enthrallingly romantic without crossing over to mawkishness. The lyric of the verse sets up the premise of one longing for "adventure" and finding it in one person, concluding "all that I want in all of this world is you."[20] The refrain offers a list of metaphors. The loved one is "the promised kiss of springtime/ That makes the lonely winter seem long" as well as "the breathless hush of evening/ That trembles on the brink of a lovely song." The release goes even further, using "angel" and "star" as additional images. The final refrain ties it all together and the word "divine" caps it with "that that moment divine/ When all the things you are, are mine!" Like many of Hammerstein's lyrics, it can only be truly appreciated when set to Kern's music. For example, the double "are" in the final line seems awkward on the page but when the first "are" reaches up and the second one descends, the effect is radiant. "All the Things You Are" has been endlessly analyzed by musicologists because of its subtle yet effective modulations, key changes, and unexpected twists and turns not at all usual in popular songs of the era. The way the music in the refrain gently descends for sixteen bars then rises for the release is one of the song's notable features. Kern wrote the odd but striking key and tempo changes for his own satisfaction and never thought the song would catch on. (It is a difficult song to sing correctly.) But it is those surprises that appeal to singers and musicians. The unexpected quirks in the music are particularly attractive to jazz musicians who find the song provides the opportunity for endless variations.

Only a few of the critics mentioned "All the Things You Are" in their dismissive reviews of *Very Warm for May*, but it did not take long for the ballad to be noticed and recorded. In 1939, there were discs by Artie Shaw (vocal by Helen Forrest), Mildred Bailey, Tommy Dorsey (vocal by Jack Leonard), Paul Whiteman (vocal by Bob Hannon), and Frankie Masters (vocal by Harlan Rogers). These were followed by hundreds of recordings over the years by such artists as Adelaide Hall, Kenny Baker, Dennis Day, Frank Sinatra, Miles Davis, Chet Baker, Allan Jones, Jo Stafford, Barbra Streisand, Michael Jackson, Dave Brubeck, Willie Nelson, Gerry Mulligan, Keith Jarrett, Larry Cordell, Carly Simon, Tony Bennett and Bill Charlap, Down for the Count, Scott Bradlee, and Renée Fleming. No film version of *Very Warm for May* was made but the song was sung by Ginny Simms in *Broadway Rhythm* (1944) and was performed or heard on the soundtrack by Tony Martin in *Till the Clouds Roll By* (1946), Mario Lanza in *Because You're Mine* (1952), Jo Stafford in *Tin Men* (1987), Art Tatum and the Ben Webster Quartet in *Deconstructing*

Harry (1997), Sarah Vaughn in *Anja & Viktor* (2001), and Will Young in *Mrs. Henderson Presents* (2005). On Broadway, "All the Things You Are" was sung by the cast of the revue *Jerome Kern Goes to Hollywood* (1986).

Other notable songs from that season: "In the Heart of the Dark," "Heaven in My Arms" from *Very Warm for May*; "Louisiana Purchase," "You're Lonely and I'm Lonely," "It's a Lovely Day Tomorrow," "What Chance Have I with Love?" from *Louisiana Purchase*; "I Didn't Know What Time It Was" from *Too Many Girls*; "South American Way" from *The Streets of Paris*; "Are You Havin' Any Fun?" from *George White's Scandals of 1939-1940*; "Darn That Dream" from *Swingin' the Dream*; "Friendship," "Katie Went to Haiti," "Well, Did You Evah?" from *DuBarry Was a Lady*; "How High the Moon" from *Two for the Show*; "It Never Entered My Mind" from *Higher and Higher*.

1940–1941 SEASON

The numbers might have been pathetic (only sixteen new musicals and seven of them revues, only two of which ran very long) but this season saw three innovative book musicals that would make any season look productive. *Cabin in the Sky*, with a score by Vernon Duke (music) and John LaTouche (lyrics), was that rare thing: a musical about African Americans that was funny, touching, and tasteful. Even better, performers such as Ethel Waters, Dooley Wilson, Rex Ingram, Todd Duncan, Katherine Dunham, and J. Rosamund Johnson got to play characters who were beyond the stereotypic. It was a fantasy but it had more to do with real people and emotions than was usually seen in such ethnic shows. *Lady in the Dark* was an original. Moss Hart's libretto about a magazine editor (Gertrude Lawrence) undergoing psychoanalysis was new and different and the score by Kurt Weill and Ira Gershwin was resplendent. The third notable new musical was Rodgers and Hart's *Pal Joey*, an adult piece with an anti-hero (Gene Kelly) and an uncompromising score by Rodgers and Hart. The fact that there was an audience (though different audiences) for these three adventurous musicals boded well for the future. Cole Porter's *Panama Hattie* and *Hold On to Your Hats*, with a score by Burton Lane (music) and E. Y. Harburg (lyrics), were the other two book musicals that turned a profit. The former was helped by the star power of Ethel Merman while the latter benefitted from having Al Jolson, Martha Raye, and Jack Whiting in the cast. The season's two most successful revues were *Meet the People,* featuring unknowns Jack Albertson, Nanette Fabray, and Jack Gilford, and *Boys and Girls Together* with Ed Wynn top-billed. Revues were getting smaller and, sometimes, smarter. As the decade progressed, they would get patriotic as well.

"Bewitched (Bothered and Bewildered)"
Music by Richard Rodgers; lyric by Lorenz Hart
From *Pal Joey* (1940)
Sung by Vivienne Segal as Vera Simpson

Pal Joey has been called the first "adult" musical as well as an anti-sentimental show with Joey Evans as the first leading character in a Broadway musical who is an absolute heel. Lorenz Hart, who was more than familiar with the seamy side of life, wrote his most caustic and non-romantic lyrics for *Pal Joey*. They are in keeping with the tough-as-nails libretto by John O'Hara and George Abbott. But it is not just Joey who is amoral and self-serving. The rich Vera Simpson (Vivienne Segal) is the same, only she is smarter than Joey. So when she finds herself falling in lust with him, her reaction is one of mixed emotions. This is what Hart captures so vividly in "Bewitched, (Bothered and Bewildered)," perhaps the most cynical and jaded lyric he ever wrote. The verse sets up Vera's predicament. She points out that "Men are not a new sensation" for her but the "pint-sized imitation" Joey has her "on the blink."[1] She sees through him, calls him a fool, but admits "a fool can have his charms." Rodgers' music here is playful as it bounces up and down the scale. But the refrain is a simple three-note phrase that creeps up warily, creating a languid or even bored tone. The lyric uses internal rhymes ("wild again, beguiled again … simpering, whimpering child again") and the alliteration in the title phrase flows effortlessly. The rhymes get a bit lusty with the sequence "Couldn't sleep and wouldn't sleep/ Until I could sleep where I shouldn't sleep." The music for the release takes the same three-note pattern but this time descends the scale, ending up with a rise on "the laugh's on me." "Bewitched" has three refrains, an encore, and a totally original repeat to be sung as a reprise later in the show. Later singers tend to pick and choose from the song, meaning it is rare for any two recordings to be exactly alike. Also, the lyric is sometimes too promiscuous for radio broadcast so many versions soften the images, often making for lame lyric phrases that do not sound at all like Hart. The above phrase "I could sleep where I shouldn't sleep" has been changed to "love came and told me I shouldn't sleep." In a later refrain, Vera says that she "worship(s) the trousers that cling to him" but the lyric is often altered to "I long for the day I can cling to him." Her sly observations that "horizontally speaking, he's at his best" is rarely retained. When Vera finally dumps Joey, her reprise of "Bewitched" includes a sigh of relief: "Those ants that invaded my pants—finis!" This also has very rarely been recorded.

There was no original cast recording of *Pal Joey* so "Bewitched" was first put on disc by Benny Goodman (vocal by Helen Forrest), followed soon after by Leo Reisman (vocal by Anita Boyer) and Bob Chester (vocal by Betty Bradley). A musicians' strike delayed further recordings and "Bewitched" was being played in France and Great Britain before an American disc by Doris Day and the Mellowmen was circulated in 1949. The song finally took off in a big way in the 1950s, remaining on *Your Hit Parade* longer than any other song that decade. Pianist Bill Snyder and his orchestra cut a disc in 1950 that sold over a million records and in June of 1950, six different recordings of "Bewitched" made the Top 20 list of most-played records on the radio. There have been over 400 versions of the ballad but special mention must be made of those by Mel Tormé, Sarah Vaughn, Larry Green, Les Paul and Mary Ford, Frank Sinatra, Nancy Wilson, Ruth Brown, Anita O'Day, Buddy Greco, Dinah Washington, Judy Collins, Diana Ross and the Supremes, Boz Scaggs, Celine Dion, Sinéad O'Connor, Jeff Lynne, Barbra Streisand, Carly Simon, Ella Fitzgerald and Lady Gaga; Rod Stewart and Cher, Sugarpie and the Candymen, Tom Cubis, and the Richard Lennox Trio.

Pal Joey was not produced in London until 1954 when Carol Bruce played Vera and sang "Bewtiched" but it was already well known in Britain. In the 1957 film version of *Pal Joey*, "Bewitched" was sung by Rita Hayworth (dubbed by Jo Ann Greer) and reprised by Frank Sinatra. The song was also performed or heard on the soundtrack by Lloyd Nolan and Maureen O'Sullivan in *Hannah and Her Sisters* (1986), Ella Fitzgerald in *Love! Valour! Compassion!* (1997) and *Paris-Manhattan* (2012), Katalina in *Simply Irresistible* (1999), Les Paul and Mary Ford in *Speed Racer* (2006), and Kamilah Marshall, Shayna Steele, and Jordan Ballard in *Sex in the City 2* (2010). In Broadway revivals of *Pal Joey*, "Betwitched" has been sung by Vera Simpson as played by Vivienne Segal in 1952, Viveca Lindfors in 1963, Joan Copeland in 1976, and Stockard Channing in 2008.

Other notable songs from that season: "I Could Write a Book," "Take Him," "Zip," "You Mustn't Kick It Around" from *Pal Joey*; "Cabin in the Sky," "Honey in the Honeycomb," "Taking a Chance on Love" from *Cabin in the Sky*; "My Ship," "Tschaikowsky," "The Saga of Jenny" from *Lady in the Dark*; "There's a Great Day Coming, Mañana," "Don't Let It Get You Down" from *Hold on to Your Hats*; "Let's Be Buddies," "Make It Another Old-Fashioned, Please," "I've Still Got My Health" from *Panama Hattie*.

Song of the Season

1941–1942 SEASON

In the middle of the season, the United States was plunged into war and even Broadway had to take notice. By the end of the season, the many men enlisting or being drafted created a casting problem, particularly when established stars opted to go overseas to entertain American troops. The first patriotic revue of the war, *Of V I Sing*, opened late in the season; it would be far from the last. The portrayal of German and Japanese characters on stage was unabashedly propagandistic once war was declared. A revival of *The Mikado* this season changed the opening lyric from "We are gentlemen of Japan" to "We are gangsters of Japan." The hostilities overseas provided new material for songs and sketches in revues and even some book musicals would gradually include the war. This season's Cole Porter hit *Let's Face It* was based on an older play with the central characters changed from three gigolos to three contemporary soldiers. The Eddie Cantor vehicle *Banjo Eyes* added the flag-waving number "We Did It Before (We'll Do It Again)" for the finale when the show was trying out in Philadelphia. Similarly, Sophie Tucker sang a ditty titled "Army and Navy Song" in *High Kickers*. Two of the season's long-running hits were far removed from the war. Rodgers and Hart's *By Jupiter* was about the battle of the sexes set in ancient Greece and *Best Foot Forward*, by newcomers Hugh Martin and Ralph Blane, was set in a boys high school at prom time. Ole Olsen and Chic Johnson followed up their successful *Hellzapoppin* with *Sons o' Guns*, another low-brow comedy revue and, at 742 performances, another giant hit. This time there were some laudable songs and Olsen and Johnson were joined on stage by such talents as Carmen Miranda, Ella Logan, Joe Besser, and the Blackburn Twins. Another revue, titled *Priorities of 1942*, was a surprise hit late in the season. With so many young performers going off to war, a group of too-old-for-service vaudevillians were assembled to do some vintage and new routines. Audiences were nostalgic enough to want to see Lou Holtz, Willie Howard, Hazel Scott, Phil Baker, Paul Draper, Helen Merrill, and other past favorites that the show chalked up 353 performances.

It was a season of disappointments for some respected songwriters. Oscar Hammerstein re-teamed with Sigmund Romberg for the operetta *Sunny River* but the old genre seemed more out-of-date than ever once war broke out. It closed in a month. *Sunny River* was the latest in a long line of flops for Hammerstein and he was considered by many to be all washed up. Vernon Duke and John LaTouche's *Banjo Eyes* was doing brisk box office but when Cantor decided to leave the show early; the musical had to close after a modest run of 126 performances. Later in the season, Duke and LaTouche's *The Lady Comes Across* did much worse, playing only three times before closing. On the other hand, the Gershwins' *Porgy and Bess* returned to the Street, was greeted with better reviews this time around, ran 286 performances, then toured successfully. The great American opera was finally accepted as such but George Gershwin was not there to see it; he had died in Hollywood in 1937.

"Ev'rything I've Got (Belongs to You)"
Music by Richard Rodgers; lyric by Lorenz Hart
From *By Jupiter* (1942)
Sung by Ray Bolger as King Sapiens,
and Benay Venuta as Queen Hippolyta

In several Rodgers and Hart musicals, there is a comic duet in which two characters trade insults, complaints, or back-handed compliments with each other. Some of the more familiar examples include "I Wish I were in Love Again," "What Can You Do with a Man?," "Too Good for the Average Man," "He and She," and "Take Him." The duet "Ev'rything I've Got (Belongs to You)" from this season's *By Jupiter* is the last such number the team wrote. It was sung by King Sapiens (Ray Bolger) and his wife Queen Hippolyta (Benay Venuta) who leads the Amazons in battle while the men stay home and keep house. The marriage of Sapiens and Hippolyta, forced on her by his wealthy mother, is not a happy one, as witnessed in this combative duet. Both he and she have their own verses in which Sapiens is criticized for his "attitude that just stinks" and Hippolyta's yelling "smells."[2] There are three refrains (one is reprised later in the show) in which insults are traded back and forth but always conclude with the sarcastic title line. Such barbs as "eyes for you to give you dirty looks" and "words that do not come from children's books" are pure Hart, as is the alliterative "I've a terrible tongue and a temper for two." In the release, the couple's sex life is mocked: "Off to bed we will creep/ Then we'll sleep and sleep and sleep." All the references to physical violence may not go down with a modern audience but the tone of the song is more one-upmanship than actual threats. There is actually a playful kind of affection implied in the lyric. Of course, there are different ways the actors can interpret the song. Ray Bolger and Benay Venuta were expert comics and the duet stopped the show. Rodgers wrote one of his most contagiously catchy melodies for the refrains. It is a series of jazz riffs jumping up and down before reaching a silly height then descending down on the title phrase. Because the music is so nimble, one cannot take all the lyric insults too seriously. Although little known and rarely revived today, *By Jupiter* enjoyed the longest run of any Rodgers and Hart musical: 427 performances. No one knew it at the time, but *By Jupiter* would be the team's last new Broadway show. Hart's drinking problem was interfering more and more with any productivity the team had. When Hart declined to do the lyrics for *Oklahoma!*, Rodgers turned to Oscar Hammerstein. The runaway success of that landmark musical spelled the end of Hart's career. But Rodgers did not want to give up entirely on Hart. They worked together again on the 1943 revival of *A Connecticut Yankee* (1927) for which they wrote six new songs. It was a hit but Hart hardly had time to enjoy it; he died five days after opening night.

Song of the Season

There was no movie version of *By Jupiter* and it has never received a Broadway revival. There was a delightful Off-Broadway production in 1967 that ran 118 performances. Bob Dishy and Jackie Alloway played Sapiens and Hippolyta and sang "Ev'rything I've Got." Considering the way *By Jupiter* has faded away and the fact that the number is not a love ballad, the song has enjoyed quite an active recording history. Since there was no original cast album for the show, it took a while for "Ev'rything I've Got" to catch on. Betty Garrett and Milton Berle did a duet version with Lehman Engel's Orchestra in 1947 and there was a disc by the Herb Geller Quartet in 1953, but it was Ella Fitzgerald's 1956 recording that finally brought recognition to "Ev'rything I've Got." It is usually recorded as a solo vocal but the song has long been a favorite of jazz musicians. Among the many notable discs are those by Blossom Dearie, the Barbara Carroll Trio, Morgana King, Woody Herman, Nancy Walker, Lester Lanin, Peter Nero, Johnny Pace with the Chet Baker Quintet, Annie Ross with Zoot Sims, Buddy Greco, Vikki Carr, Mary Clare Haran, Andrea Marcovicci, Malcolm Gets, Sara Gazarek, Cécile McLorin Salvant, Nicki Parrott, and the Harry Allen Quartet. On screen, the Blackburn Twins performed "Ev'rything I've Got" in the Rodgers and Hart bio-pic *Words and Music* (1948).

Other notable songs from that season: "Nobody's Heart (Belongs to Me)," "Wait Till You See Her" from *By Jupiter*; "Buckle Down, Winsocki," "Just a Little Joint with a Juke Box" from *Best Foot Forward*; "Let's Not Talk About Love," "Ace in the Hole" from *Let's Face It*; "We're Having a Baby (My Baby and Me)" from *Banjo Eyes*; "Of V We Sing," "You Can't Fool the People" from *Of V We Sing*.

1942–1943 SEASON

The 1942–43 season begins and ends with *Oklahoma!* for no other musical of such significance opened on Broadway during that time. *Oklahoma!* constitutes a landmark in the American musical theatre more important than a season of hits. The history of the Broadway musical can accurately be divided into what came before *Oklahoma!* and what came after it. It is the first fully integrated musical play and its blending of song, character, plot, and even dance would serve as the model for Broadway shows for decades to follow. Oscar Hammerstein, who wrote the libretto and lyrics, had attempted to integrate all the elements of a musical into a cohesive, unified whole with *Rose-Marie* (1924) and *Show Boat* (1927) but not until *Oklahoma!* did he fully succeed. Richard Rodgers' music for *Oklahoma!* was in a different vein than in his previous works with Lorenz Hart. Some of the songs are in the operetta style, others in a folk medium, and still others in the musical comedy tradition. *Oklahoma!* also has the first fully integrated score rather than a collection of songs. As different as all this was, audiences had no trouble accepting a new kind of musical theatre. It helped that the original production, directed by Rouben Mamoulian and choreographed by Agnes de Mille, was extraordinary and the performances by a young, unknown cast were remarkable. *Oklahoma!* opened to the most glowing raves within memory and the Theatre Guild production ran a record-breaking 2,212 performances. It remains the most frequently revived of all the Rodgers and Hammerstein shows.

The rest of the season paled in comparison to *Oklahoma!* None of the thirteen other musicals were very memorable and, except for a few songs, have disappeared. The only book musicals to turn a profit were Cole Porter's *Something for the Boys* and the operetta *Rosalinda*. The former had a weak, joke-filled libretto but a strong cast (Ethel Merman, Paula Laurence, Betty Garrett, Bill, Johnson, etc.) and some vivacious songs. It was exactly what audiences wanted so it ran 422 performances. *Rosalinda* was the old favorite *Die Fledermaus* (1874) by Johann Strauss given a new translation and less intimidating title. It ran a surprising 521 times. Of the thirteen revues that season were nine that made money. New York City burlesque houses had been closed by Mayor Fiorello LaGuardia so the enterprising producer Michael Todd gathered some of the popular strippers (Gypsy Rose Lee, Georgia Sothern, etc.) and comics (Bobby Clark, Professor Lamberti, etc.) from the genre and put them into the Broadway revue *Star and Garter*. The show appealed to more than just G.I.s passing through New York for it was performed 609 times. Later in the season, another burlesque revue titled *Wine, Women and Song* managed to run four months. The last *Ziegfeld Follies* to appear on Broadway opened this season and it was able to run 533 times. It was less lavish than the past revues but it boasted some talented performers, including Milton Berle, Ilona Massey, Jack Cole, Arthur Treacher, and Jack McCauley. Other revues to pass the 100 mark this season were Irving Berlin's patriotic show *This Is the Army*, the Yiddish musical *Oy, is Dus a Leben!* (*Oh, What a Life!*), and the George Jessel vaudeville-like revue *Show Time* which played twelve times a week and soon chalked up 342 performances. And for those tourists and locals not inclined to theatre, the ice-skating spectacular *Stars on Ice* also performed a dozen times weekly in the large Center Theatre and, in two editions, played 830 times. With such alternatives, no wonder *Oklahoma!* looked so good.

"Oh, What a Beautiful Mornin'"
Music by Richard Rodgers; lyric by Oscar Hammerstein
From *Oklahoma!* (1943)
Sung by Alfred Drake as Curly McLain

The songs in *Oklahoma!* continue the plot and characterization, rather than interrupting them. No song from the score could be reassigned to another actor, no less another show, because each was drawn from the character so fully that it became an integral piece of the character's development within the plot. Also unusual about the songs in *Oklahoma!* is their placement. Traditionally a musical before 1943 opens with a chorus number. But *Oklahoma!* begins with a solo. Curly (Alfred Drake) begins singing "Oh, What a Beautiful Mornin'" offstage, then enters, singing to himself but for the benefit of Aunt Eller (Betty Garde), who is churning butter, and Laurie (Joan Roberts), who is inside the house. This delicate opening not only works for the characters but also sets the tone for the non-glitzy musical to follow.

Rodgers' music "Oh, What a Beautiful Mornin'" is a gentle waltz with the flavor of a cowboy song. The number does not use the conventional AABA structure of a popular song but rather the alternating pattern of ABABAB of a folk song. The verses are as melodic as the refrains so there is variety but there is no release. This means there is no climatic section and the song remains restrained and down-to-earth. While "Oh, What a Beautiful Mornin'" has a leisurely, even lazy, feel to it, it has its own subtle dynamics. In the refrains, the melody climbs up to accent the "morn" of "mornin'." Then it descends in the next line to rest firmly on the word "day." On paper this couplet—"Oh, what a beautiful mornin',/ Oh, what a beautiful day"—looks boring and unnecessarily repetitive.[3] But with Rodgers music, the lyric is potent. Considering the fact that Hammerstein wrote the lyric first, he must have trusted Rodgers to turn a simple folk lyric into something exciting. The lyric for "Oh, What a Beautiful Mornin'" is drawn from Lynn Riggs' poetic stage directions for the first scene of his play *Green Grow the Lilacs* (1931) which served as the basis for *Oklahoma!* The opening verse is simple but evocative with pictures of "a bright, golden haze on the meadow" and the "corn is as high as an elephant's eye." In the refrains, Hammerstein clips off the "g" endings (mornin' instead of morning; standin' instead of standing) not only to capture the mid-western colloquialisms but also to soften the words and allow for a smooth, dreamy line of verse. It is so gentle that the lyric could easily serve as the text for a lullaby, something suggested in Rodgers' music. The third verse has the lullaby-like lyric "The breeze is so busy it don't miss a tree." This is poetry but rural, unfussy poetry. In the third refrain, Hammerstein gives Curly a simple statement—"All the sounds of the earth are like music"—which sums up everything that the song wants to say. Nature is music and that's why a Broadway musical can be set on the prairie and still be true to itself.

The full-voiced Alfred Drake sang "Oh, What a Beautiful Mornin'" in the original *Oklahoma!* production and Howard Keel introduced it in the 1947 London mounting. Because the Broadway version was the first musical to have an original cast album (on a series of 78's), Drake's baritone rendition of the number was put on a disc. But the song has been recorded by many kinds of voices in many kinds of styles over the decades. A 1943 disc by Bing Crosby and Trudy Erwin peaked at Number 4 on the charts and that same year Frank Sinatra had a hit single. Subsequent recordings of note were made by Gracie Fields, Ray Charles with the Count Basie Orchestra, Nelson Riddle, the Dardanelle Trio, Dick Hyman, James Taylor, Rosemary Clooney, Lou Rawls, Placido Domingo, Marilyn Horne, Jennifer Nettles, Samuel Ramey, Judy Kuhn, Ben Monder, and the Mormon Tabernacle Choir. In the 1955 film version of *Oklahoma!*, Gordon MacRae played Curly and sang "Oh, What a Beautiful Mornin'." Actors who have played Curly and sung the song in Broadway revivals include Ridge Bond in 1951 and 1953, Laurence Guittard in 1979, Patrick Wilson in 2002, and Damon Daunno in 2019. Hugh Jackman was Curly in an acclaimed 1998 London revival of *Oklahoma!* which was preserved on video.

Other notable songs from that season: "Oklahoma," "People Will Say We're in Love," "The Surrey with the Fringe on Top," "I Cain't Say No," "Out of My Dreams," "Many a New Day," "Kansas City," "Pore Jud Is Daid" from *Oklahoma!*; "Hey, Good-Lookin'," "By the Mississinewah" from *Something for the Boys*; "This Is the Army, Mr. Jones," "I Left My Heart at the Stage Door Canteen," "I'm Getting Tired So I Can Sleep" from *This Is the Army*; "I Did It for Defense," "It's Fun to Be Free" from *Let Freedom Sing*.

Song of the Season

1943–1944 SEASON

Escape from events in the headlines continued to be the operative motivation on Broadway as the Second World War dragged on. Nothing could be more escapist than the season's runaway hit, *Follow the Girls*, a broad, shallow musical comedy that often slipped into burlesque. Audiences (especially G. I.s in town) didn't mind and the girly show ran 888 performances. Far more sophisticated was *One Touch of Venus*, a rare musical comedy by composer Kurt Weill, which featured Mary Martin in her first starring role. It also had the finest score of the season. Cole Porter's musical farce *Mexican Hayride* was also a star vehicle. Bobby Clark's shenanigans help keep the show on the boards for 481 performances. Of the more serious musicals, the most accomplished and successful was *Carmen Jones*, Oscar Hammerstein's reworking of Bizet's opera *Carmen* with a modern setting and an all-African American cast. It was a season filled with revivals of old works going as far back as the D'Oyly Carte days. The Gilbert and Sullivan Opera Company offered a selection of the beloved English operettas while other producers brought in revivals of *The Student Prince*, *The Vagabond King*, *The Merry Widow*, *Blossom Time*, *The New Moon*, and a return engagement of *Porgy and Bess*. The best revival of the season was Rodgers and Hart's 1927 *A Connecticut Yankee,* a slightly altered musical comedy with a superb cast and a new song: "To Keep My Love Alive." (It was the last lyric Lorenz Hart wrote before his death in 1943.) Despite favorable reviews, the new *A Connecticut Yankee* ran only 136 performances.

"Speak Low"
Music by Kurt Weill; lyric by Ogden Nash
From *One Touch of Venus* (1943)
Sung by Mary Martin as Venus, and Kenny Baker as Rodney Hatch

---

The melancholy ballad "Speak Low" with a Cole Porterish beguine quality was written by the German immigrant Kurt Weill (music) and the American humorist-poet Ogden Nash (lyric) as the love duet for *One Touch of Venus*. The fantasy musical was about the barber Rodney Hatch (Kenny Baker) who accidentally brings a statue of the goddess Venus (Mary Martin) to life and it looks like romance is in the air. But Venus realizes she does not care for living in the New York suburbs in 1943 and returns to stone. Venus sings "Speak Low" as a way of seducing Rodney away from his possessive, obnoxious fiancée. Not only does it work but soon Rodney is singing it with her. As romantic as the ballad is, there is a brooding quality to the music. Although it is written in 4/4 time, Weill labeled the sheet music "moderate Latin feel." Also, the way the song subtly shifts rhythms is unique. Weill repeats not only notes but some patterns of notes which adds to the haunting quality. The song is unusually long (fifty-six measures) and that allows the music to take its time in building to a climax. The lyric, suggested by a line in *Much*

Ado about Nothing, has lovely imagery but there is something fatalistic about the tone of the words. Love is "a spark lost in the dark" and the inevitable approach of tomorrow is "always too soon."[4] With its mournful music and its sorrowful subtext, "Speak Low" comes across more as a torch song than a love ballad. Yet the effect is so hypnotic that one believes it comes from a goddess.

A 1944 recording of "Speak Low" by Guy Lombardo with a vocal by Billy Leach was the first of many recordings over the years. Billie Holiday, Anita O'Day, Tony Bennett, Sarah Vaughn, the Miracles, Lotta Lenya, the Four Freshmen, Ella Fitzgerald, Carmen McRae, the Hi-Lo's, Jeri Southern, Dee Dee Bridgewater, Anthony Newley, Eartha Kitt, Barbra Streisand, Boz Scaggs, Smokey Robinson, and Kurt Weill himself are among those who later recorded it. "Speak Low" has long been a favorite of jazz singers and musicians with notable covers by Gerry Mulligan, Sonny Clark, Bill Evans, Al Caiola, Donald Byrd, John Coltrane, Roy Hargrove, Coleman Hawkins, Walter Bishop, Jr., Woody Shaw, Bobby Shew, Eumir Deodato, and Brian Bromberg. The screen version of *One Touch of Venus* cut most of the Weill-Nash score but retained "Speak Low" which was sung by Ava Gardner (dubbed by Eileen Wilson) and Dick Haymes. On stage, it was sung by the ensemble in the Off-Broadway revue *Berlin to Broadway with Kurt Weill* (1972) and by Donna Murphy and Michael Cerveris in the Broadway bio-musical *LoveMusik* (2007).

Other notable songs from that season: "That's Him," "Foolish Heart," "I'm a Stranger Here Myself" from *One Touch of Venus*; "There Must Be Someone for Me," "Count Your Blessings," "I Love You" from *Mexican Hayride*; "I Wanna Get Married" from *Follow the Girls*; "To Keep My Love Alive" from *A Connecticut Yankee* (revival); "Ladies Who Sing with the Band" from *Early to Bed*.

1944–1945 SEASON

The last months of the Second World War were a prosperous time for Broadway, particularly for musicals. Of the ten new book musicals that opened on the Street, five ran over 400 performances. Even better, all five were of some quality with laudable librettos and exceptional scores. None ran longer than Rodgers and Hammerstein's *Carousel*, which is remarkable because it was the team's darkest musical and far from escapist. *Carousel* owed much to operetta, as did *Song of Norway*, using Edvard Grieg's music for its songs, and *Up in Central Park*, the last successful musical by the operetta veteran Sigmund Romberg. Jazz infiltrated Leonard Bernstein's music for *On the Town* which had a sprightly libretto and nimble-witted lyrics by Betty Comden and Adolph Green. It was a sensational Broadway debut for the three songwriters and for choreographer Jerome Robbins. Another surprise hit was *Bloomer Girl* with a score by Harold Arlen and E. Y. Harburg. For a musical about women's rights, slavery, and religious hypocrisy, *Bloomer Girl* was a farcical romp that pleased audiences for 657 performances. Of the season's seven revues, five ran pass the 100 mark: Cole Porter's smart and sassy *The Seven Lively Arts*; a celebration of American folk music titled *Sing Out, Sweet Land*; the Olsen and Johnson comedy free-for-all *Laffing Room Only*; and the vaudeville program *Show Time*. Tourists and New Yorkers were not yet tired of ice shows and *Hats Off to Ice* offered multiple showtimes which resulted in 890 performances.

There were disappointments as well. Kurt Weill and Ira Gershwin stumbled badly with *The Firebrand of Florence*, Vernon Duke and Howard Dietz could not make *Sadie Thompson* work, and the operetta *Rhapsody*, with John LaTouche lyrics set to Fritz Kreisler's music, was a quick failure. In a bizarre coincidence, there were two musical spoofs of Gilbert and Sullivan's *H.M.S. Pinafore* this season. *Memphis Bound* reset the Victorian operetta in present-day Tennessee where a show boat full of African American performers hits a sandbar on the river. Led by Pops Meriwether (Bill "Bojangles" Robinson), the troupers try to raise money by putting on their version of *Pinafore* only to be arrested for performing without a license. *Hollywood Pinafore* set the action in a movie studio with George S. Kaufman providing a hilarious libretto and satirical lyrics set to Arthur Sullivan's music. Neither of the musical parodies ran very long but they represented the high spirits on Broadway as the season and the war came to an end.

"If I Loved You"
Music by Richard Rodger; lyric by Oscar Hammerstein
From *Carousel* (1945)
Sung by Jan Clayton as Julie Jordan,
and John Raitt as Billy Bigelow

"If I Loved You" is not only the most remembered ballad from *Carousel* but also one of the most innovative and remarkable musical numbers in the history of the American theatre. Mostly recorded as a standard ballad in which a lover relates what it would be like to be in love, the song is used as part of an integrated musical scene in *Carousel*. Often referred to as the "bench scene," it runs about fourteen minutes and consists of dialogue, underscoring, and four distinct musical ideas. Carousel barker Billy Bigelow (John Raitt) and mill worker Julie Jordan (Jan Clayton) have met that evening and, in this musical sequence, we see their relationship develop in a way that is dangerous and exciting. The inspiration for the song comes from *Carousel*'s source material, Ferenc Molnar's play *Liliom*, in which the carousel barker Billy asks Julie if she would marry such a rough fellow as himself and she responds, "Yes I would—if I loved you, Mr. Liliom."

The musical number begins with Billy briefly reprising "You're a Queer One, Julie Jordan," a song Carrie (Jean Darling) sang previously, but with a different lyric. He asks "Ain't you sorry that you didn't run away?" and Julie answers with a new musical idea that is youthful and frolicsome. She claims that he couldn't take her money because she hasn't any but if she did, and he asked her, she'd give it to him. After a duologue sung as a kind of recitative, Julie repeats the same musical idea as she explains "I ain't never goin' to marry" which angers Billy because she has put marriage in his mind. He tells Julie that she doesn't know what it would be like to be married to him and her response is the famous "If I Loved You" section of the scene. The title phrase is followed by possible consequences if she loved him: "words wouldn't come in an easy way" and "round in circles I'd go."[5] Rodgers' music for this section sweeps up the scale majestically then winds down carelessly on "round in circles I'd go." It is a felicitous composition in the operetta tradition but the Hammerstein's lyric is direct and fearless. Julie foresees the tragedy that will come if she loves such a person as Billy. "Soon you'd leave me," she sings, and he'd never "know how I loved you." In a traditional musical, such an indirect declaration of love would result in softening Billy. But instead of his repeating the "If I Loved You" idea, he instead gets angry then reflective. In a totally different musical idea, Billy becomes a cynical poet. "The tide's creepin' up on the beach like a thief,/ Afraid to be caught stealin' the land," he notes "On a night like this I start to wonder/ What life is all about." Such reflection scares him and he turns on Julie with "What are we? A couple specks of nothin'" and returns to his restless musical motif, declaring "two little people, you and I/ We don't count at all." In the dialogue that follows, Billy gets angry at Julie for trying to get him to marry her. She denies it so he asks, "So what's puttin' in into my head?" It is indeed on his mind and he quickly realizes that marriage for him would "be awful!" A new musical idea is used as Billy contemplates marriage with disgust, the music turning into a frivolous gavotte. He pictures himself "kinda scrawny, and pale,/ Picking at my food" and "love-sick like any other guy." Even though Julie assures Billy that they are not in love, he can't help wondering. He finally sings his part of the "If I Loved You" section using the same lyric, but this time it would be her who deserts him. In a bold move, Rodgers and Hammerstein do not end the scene with the two singing together operetta style. Instead the music continues and the "bench scene" ends with dialogue and then an embrace that is desperate and terrifying because both know what dangers come from such a love. The "If I Loved You" scene is the fulfillment of Hammerstein's dream of song, story, and character coming together in one sustained piece of musical drama.

Although "If I Loved You" is woven into the "bench scene" so well, it has been removed and stands on its own as a romantic ballad. There are over twenty cast recordings of *Carousel* but only the more recent ones include the entire "If I Loved You" sequence. Even the version on the original cast album is abbreviated. The song has had a busy life on record and in concert as a solo or duet. Frank Sinatra and Perry Como each recorded it in 1945, followed by many discs by others, including Bing Crosby, Harry James, Helen Merrill, Roy Hamilton, Robert Merrill and Patrice Munsel, Barbra Streisand, Jane Morgan, the Skyliners, Etta Jones, Alfred Drake and Roberta Peters, Sammy Davis, Jr., Samuel Ramey and Barbara Cook, Nancy LaMott, Bernadette Peters, Julie Andrews, Elaine Paige, Marie Osmond, Chad and Jeremy, and Robin Spielberg. The song was first sung on the London stage in 1950 by Iva Withers (Julie) and Stephen Douglass (Billy). In the 1956 film version *Carousel*, Gordon MacRae and Shirley Jones sang "If I Loved You," as did Robert Goulet and Mary Grover in the 1967 television adaptation. To date, there have been five Broadway revivals of *Carousel*. Stephen Douglass and Iva Withers sang "If I Loved You" in the 1949 production, Jo Sullivan and Chris Robinson in 1954, Barbara Cook and Howard Keel in 1957, Sally Murphy and Michael Hayden in 1994, and Jessie Mueller and Joshua Henry in 2018. Victoria Clark sang a solo version in the Broadway revue *A Grand Night for Singing* (1993).

Other notable songs from that season: "You'll Never Walk Alone," "June Is Bustin' Out All Over," "When the Children Are Asleep," "Soliloquy," "What's the Use of Wond'rin'?" from *Carousel*; "New York, New York," "I Can Cook, Too," "Come Up to My Place," "Lonely Town," "Lucky to Be Me," "Some Other Time" from *On the Town*; "Right as the Rain," "The Eagle and Me," "Sunday in Cicero Falls" from *Bloomer Girl*; "Close as Pages in a Book," "April Snow" from *Up in Central Park*; "Strange Music" from *Song of Norway*; "Ev'ry Time We Say Goodbye" from *The Seven Lively Arts*.

1945–1946 SEASON

With so many long-run hits from previous seasons still filling major playhouses, Broadway looked busy and productive during the 1945–46 season but successful new entries were far and few between. It was the season of one giant hit—*Annie Get Your Gun*—and many giant flops. A musical that ran less than 200 performances was a modest success at best. When big expensive shows closed in a few weeks, the losses were record-breaking. This season saw such embarrassments as *Nellie Bly* (sixteen performances), *The Duchess Misbehaves* (five performances), *The Girl from Nantucket* (twelve performances), and *Mr. Strauss Goes to Boston* (twelve performances). Losing even more money was a behemoth musical *Around the World*, Orson Welles' version of *Around the World in Eighty Days* with a cast of more than 100 and thirty-six different settings all converging to bury a score by Cole Porter. The operating costs were so high that the three-month run of *Around the World* lost an undisclosed bundle. But there was still big money to be made on Broadway. Rodgers and Hammerstein produced Irving Berlin's *Annie Get Your Gun* with Ethel Merman as Annie Oakley. It ran 1,147 performances, by far the greatest success of Berlin and Merman's careers. Two revues—*Call Me Mister* and *Three to Make Ready*—ran 734 and 327 performances, respectively. Even some book musicals that received mixed to poor reviews managed to run, as with *Polonaise* (113 performances), *Marinka* (165 performances), *Billion Dollar Baby* (220 performances), and *Are You with It?* (267 performances). Unfortunately there were some commendable musicals that were praised by the critics but couldn't find an audience, as with *The Lute Song, The Day Before Spring*, and *St. Louis Woman*. There were six revivals this season and two were old musicals that became surprise hits: *Show Boat* and *The Red Mill*. All in all, it was a season of questionable contrasts: expensive winners and expensive losers.

"There's No Business Like Show Business"
Music and lyric by Irving Berlin
From *Annie Get Your Gun* (1946)
Sung by William O'Neal as Buffalo Bill, Ray Middleton as Frank Butler,
Marty May as Charlie Davenport, and Ethel Merman as Annie Oakley

---

Even though it is a slightly sarcastic, tongue-in-cheek song, "There's No Business Like Show Business" is the unofficial anthem for theatre; and that's the way it ought to be. This salute to any kind of entertainment business is a merry march in which Irving Berlin tips his hat at the same time he winks at his colleagues in show business. The song is the centerpiece of *Annie Get Your Gun* so it is curious to learn that it was added to the musical very late in the rehearsal process. Theatre folklore has it that there was a major set change needed behind the curtain and it could not be accomplished very quickly. In the old "in one" production style, a short scene was presented in front of the curtain

Song of the Season

while a bigger scene was set up behind. But this set change was substantial and having the orchestra vamp or reprise some music wasn't going to work. So producers Rodgers and Hammerstein asked Berlin if he would compose a new song to be performed in front of a curtain or drop. It came at the point of the musical in which Buffalo Bill (William O'Neal) tries to convince Annie Oakley (Ethel Merman) to join his Wild West Show. Because Annie/Merman already had many musical numbers to carry, the producers suggested that Berlin write a number to be sung to Annie to urge her to go into show business. Berlin agreed, went home, and quickly wrote "There's No Business Like Show Business." When he showed it to Rodgers and Hammerstein the next day, they were preoccupied with production problems and were rather unenthusiastic about the song. Berlin was crushed because he thought it was a catchy number. He took the song home and forgot about it until a few days later when the producers and director Joshua Logan wanted to rehearse "There's No Business Like Show Business" and asked Berlin for the song. The songwriter was elated at first but then panic set in because he went home and could not find the sheets of paper he had scribbled down the lyric and some chords. After an anxiety-filled search, Berlin's secretary found the sheets tucked inside a phone book. The song was finished, polished, rehearsed, and put in *Annie Get Your Gun* where it stopped the show every performance.

How much of the above story is apocryphal or exaggeration will never be determined as different people tell the tale differently. What is known is that it was not meant to be Annie/Merman's number. It was sung by Buffalo Bill, Frank Butler (Ray Middleton), and Charlie Davenport (Marty May) to Annie and she joined in later in the number. Also, it was clear the song was going to be a hit so it was reprised twice later in the musical, once by Merman and then by the entire company at the finale. "There's No Business Like Show Business" is a simple song to sing with a limited range and no tricky transitions or chord changes. Berlin wrote three verses and three refrains which could be used for reprises or encores. The first verse lists "The butcher, the baker, the grocer, the clerk" and how they are not happy in their work because they never get any applause.[6] That realization leads into the familiar refrain. The title phrase is augmented by such satisfaction as "that happy feeling when you are stealing that extra bow." The music here is a forceful march with some effective repetition of a four-note phrase. The lyric then lists the pleasing aspects of the business (other show people, a star on your dressing room door, your billing) and the negative (no customers, stranded out in the cold, the "turkey you know will fold"). By the third verse, Berlin includes "The cowboys, the tumblers, the wrestlers, the clowns/ The Roustabouts who move the show at dawn." Each refrain ends with the call to arms: "Let's go on with the show!" As bombastic as many of the images are in the song, Berlin believes it all and there is a sincerity not usually found in a pep song like this.

Dolores Gray played Annie in the first London production of *Annie Get Your Gun* and in that 1947 production the song was sung to her by Bill Johnson, Ellis Irving, and Hal Bryan. Merman recorded "There's No Business Like Show Business" a handful of times (including a disco version), sang it in concerts and on television, and performed it in the 1954 film *There's No Business Like Show Business*. An early disc of the number was made by Bing Crosby with Dick Haymes and the Andrews Sisters which climbed the charts.

Other recordings of note include those by Mary Martin and John Raitt, the Four Lads, Judy Garland, Rosemary Clooney, Frank Sinatra, Connie Boswell, Vivian Blaine, Harry Connick, Jr., Susannah McCorkle, Brian Stokes Mitchell, and Earl Rose. In the 1950 screen version of *Annie Get Your Gun*, "There's No Business Like Show Business" was sung by Betty Hutton, Howard Keel, and the ensemble. Mary Martin, John Raitt, and the cast sang it in the 1957 television adaptation. In other movies, it was sung by or heard on the soundtrack by Ethel Merman in *All That Jazz* (1979) and *Little Voice* (1998), Warren Beatty and Dustin Hoffman in *Ishtar* (1987), Niki Harris in *Noises Off* (1992), Nathan Lane and the chorus in *Love's Labour's Lost* (2000), Ken Barry, Bob Saker, and Carl Wayne in *Lucky Break* (2001), Rosemary Clooney in *Confessions of a Dangerous Mind* (2002) and *Ovation* (2015), Albert Brooks in *Looking for Comedy in the Muslim World* (2005), and Adam Sandler in *Sandy Wexler* (2017). In the Broadway revivals of *Annie Get Your Gun*, "There's No Business Like Show Business" was sung by Rufus Smith, Jerry Orbach, Bruce Yarnell, and Ethel Merman in 1966 and by Tom Wopat, Ron Holgate, Peter Marx, and Bernadette Peters in 1999.

Other notable songs from that season: "You Can't Get a Man with a Gun," "They Say It's Wonderful," "I Got the Sun in the Morning," "Anything You Can Do (I Can Do Better)," "Moonshine Lullaby," "Doin' What Comes Natur'lly," "The Girl That I Marry," "I Got Lost in His Arms" from *Annie Get Your Gun*; "Come Rain or Come Shine," "I Had Myself a True Love," "Any Place I Hang My Hat Is Home" from *St. Louis Woman*; "Mountain High—Valley Low" from *Lute Song*; "Face on a Dime," "South America, Take It Away" from *Call Me Mister*; "Nobody Else But Me" from *Show Boat* (revival).

Song of the Season

1946–1947 SEASON

Only twenty-two productions opened on the Street this season and two of those were ice shows, one was an opera double bill, and another was Maurice Chevalier's one-man show. Take away four revivals and you have one of the thinnest seasons in memory. Happily, three of the eleven book musicals were significant and are still revived today. Granted, Kurt Weill's *Street Scene* is done by opera companies rather than theatre groups because of its difficult vocal demands. Based on Elmer Rice's play of the same title and filled with piquant lyrics by Langston Hughes, *Street Scene* was exhilarating and still is when done in opera houses. The other two celebrated shows were that tricky thing called musical fantasy. *Finian's Rainbow* was a satirical piece in which magic was used to make its point, such as turning a bigoted Southern senator into an African American so he could experience the Jim Crow laws of Dixie. A thrilling score by Burton Lane and E. Y. Harburg both softened and heightened the musical's socio-political agenda. Such things usually close on Saturday night; *Finian's Rainbow* ran 725 performances. *Brigadoon* used fantasy for romantic reasons, offering a love story that could traverse time and place. It was the first hit by Alan Jay Lerner (book and lyrics) and Frederick Loewe (music) who wrote one of the finest scores of the decade. *Brigadoon* ran 581 performances without benefit of stars and has been consistently revived ever since. Most of the rest of the season's entries were of limited value. In fact, only those two ice shows made a profit. Some smart and sassy songs by Duke Ellington and John LaTouche could not save *Beggar's Holiday*; the vibrant Nancy Walker could not overcome the problems in *Barefoot Boy with Cheek*; a trunkful of recycled Victor Herbert tunes could not bring *Gypsy Lady* to life; and such pros as George S. Kaufman, Ira Gershwin, and Arthur Schwartz could not make *Park Avenue* work. A double bill of Carlo Menotti's short operas *The Medium* and *The Telephone* managed to run seven months but, like *Street Scene*, their future would be in opera houses. So the 1946–47 season came down to three musicals. But such a trio of classics would make any season proud.

"Almost Like Being in Love"
Music by Frederick Loewe; lyric by Alan Jay Lerner
From *Brigadoon* (1947)
Sung by David Brooks as Tommy Albright,
and Marion Bell as Fiona

The German-born composer Frederick Loewe was one of Broadway's great chameleon artists, able to write music in so many ethnic and cultural styles that he seemed to have no distinct style himself. For *Brigadoon,* he composed Scottish music so authentic that many mistake some of the melodies for traditional Gaelic folk tunes. An essential element in the musical is the possibility that a 1940s New Yorker and an eighteenth-century Scottish lassie can fall in love and connect musically as well as emotionally. Earlier in the musical, Tommy (David Brooks) joined Fiona (Marion Bell) in the Scottish-flavored duet "The Heather on the Hill" so Lerner and Loewe needed a duet for them in the brash Broadway style. "Almost Like Falling in Love" is the most "American" song in the score; perhaps that is why it is also the most popular number from a musical filled with exceptional songs. Loewe moves from rural Gaelic music in "The Heather on the Hill" to a jazzy, urban sound for "Almost Like Being in Love." Lerner's lyric is a very contemporary, direct declaration with flowery distractions. There is a very brief verse in which Tommy feels so empowered that he claims "I could swim Loch Lomond and be home in half an hour."[7] Then in the refrain he expresses himself with a series of short phrases: "a rare mood I'm in ... a smile on my face ... why, it's—almost like being in love!" That "why" keeps the romantic lyric conversational. Yet as exuberant as he is, Tommy does not sing about being in love. Instead he hesitates and then sings about a feeling that is "almost" like love. Loewe's music, which is an uptempo swing, stops for a rest before Tommy sings the word "almost." Is this hesitation a lack or sincerely or is he being cautious? Fiona sings the third refrain and, although she doesn't sound like a New Yorker, her lyric flows from his: "your arm linked in mine/ Made the world kind o' fine." By the end of the song, that pronounced rest is gone and Tommy and Fiona sing "I could swear I was falling ... in love!" Considering the fact that the two of them only met that morning, this cautious approach is not only acceptable but more convincing.

David Brooks (Tommy) and Marion Bell (Fiona) introduced the song in the original Broadway production of *Brigadoon* and it was sung by Philip Hanna and Patricia Hughes in the 1949 London mounting which ran even longer than the New York original. After the Broadway cast recording, the first disc of "Almost Like Being in Love" was made by Jo Stafford with Paul Weston's Orchestra. In 1947 three other records were on the charts: Mildred Bailey with Julian Working, Frank Sinatra with Axel Stordahl, and Mary Martin with Guy Lombardo and His Royal Canadians. Other memorable recordings over the decades include those by Nat King Cole, Earl "Fatha" Hines, the Mary Kaye Trio, Bobby Scott, Judy Garland, Bud Powell, Shirley Bassey, Chet Baker, Ella Fitzgerald with Dizzy Gillespie, Erroll Garner, Seth MacFarland, Diana Krall, Karen Mason, Julie Wilson, Jermaine Jackson, James Taylor, and the Shaymus Hanlin Quartet. In the movie version of *Brigadoon*, "Almost Like Being in Love" was performed by Gene Kelly and Cyd Charisse and in the 1966 television adaptation by Robert Goulet and Sally Ann Howes. The Nat King Cole recording was used on the soundtrack of *Groundhog Day* (1993) and the song was sung by Woody Allen in the animated film *Antz* (1998), Rick Riso in *Relative Values* (2000), Nick D'Egidio in *The Cooler* (2003), Paul Anka in *Confetti* (2006), and Gerry Mulligan in *The Lake House* (2006). There have been five Broadway revivals of *Brigadoon* and the song was sung by Phil Hanna and Virginia Oswald in 1950, David Atkinson and Virginia Oswald in 1957, Peter Palmer and Sally Ann Howes in 1963, Martin Vidnovic and Meg Bussert in 1980, and Jason Danieley and Melissa Errico in 2010.

Other notable songs from that season: "The Heather on the Hill," "Come to Me, Bend to Me," "I'll Go Home with Bonnie Jean," "There But for You Go I" from *Brigadoon*; "How Are Things in Glocca Moora?," "If This Isn't Love," "Old Devil Moon," "Look to the Rainbow," "Something Sort of Grandish," "When I'm Not Near the Girl I Love (I Love the Girl I'm Near)" from *Finian's Rainbow*; "Moon-Faced, Starry-Eyed," "I Got a Marble and a Star," "Lonely House," "What Good Would the Moon Be?" from *Street Scene*.

1947–1948 SEASON

The number of musical productions on Broadway continued to drop this season and the only shows of interest were three revues and three book musicals. The long-run champ of the latter was the daffy musical farce *High Button Shoes* which introduced composer Jule Styne to Broadway. He had been very successful in Hollywood with lyricist Sammy Cahn but yearned for recognition in the theatre. The team provided a set of delightful songs for *High Button Shoes* which also boasted a first-class cast (Phil Silvers, Nanette Fabray, Jack McCauley, Joey Faye), tight direction by George Abbott, and some outstanding comic choreography by Jerome Robbins. Although Cahn soon returned to Hollywood, Styne mainly stuck to Broadway where he scored sixteen more musicals. *High Button Shoes* ran 727 performances, the kind of run one expected from a Rodgers and Hammerstein musical. But that team's *Allegro* ran only half as long as the Styne-Cahn musical and only that long because of the huge advance. With *Allegro*, Rodgers and Hammerstein moved from being innovators to experimenters. Hammerstein's original tale followed one man from childhood to middle age, questioning the decisions made along the way regarding family, love, career, and self-fulfillment. Audiences and critics were divided in their response and, with no stars or hit songs, the musical had limited appeal. Less lofty was the musical comedy *Look, Ma, I'm Dancin'* in which Nancy Walker thrilled playgoers as a beer heiress who dabbles in the world of ballet. Despite Walker's expert clowning, some enjoyable songs, and clever Jerome Robbins' dances, the musical was too thin to sustain itself and closed after 188 performances, a number that would have spelled success in the prewar years but no more.

The three profitable revues of the season were no match for the glittering shows of the distant past or even the smaller, lucid revues of the 1930s. But each one was a crowd pleaser and each ran over 300 performances. Arthur Schwartz and Howard Dietz, who had scored some of the very best past revues, returned to Broadway with *Inside U.S.A.* The songs were more pleasant than memorable but the sketches were facile and the performances by Beatrice Lillie, Jack Haley, Herb Shriner, Carl Reiner, and others were first-rate. While the theme of *Inside U.S.A.* was a cross-country tour of the nation, *Make Mine Manhattan* focused its songs and sketches on contemporary life in New York City. The material might have been uneven but the gap was filled by such nimble performers as Sid Caesar, Sheila Bond, David Burns, Joshua Shelley, Danny Daniels, and Eleanor Bagley. There was no set theme for *Angel in the Wings* and there was only one song that caught everyone's attention: "Civilization (Bongo, Bongo, Bongo)." It was sung by a young but fearless Elaine Stritch at the beginning of her sixty-three-year career on Broadway. Of the many revivals on the Street this season, the D'Oyly Carte Opera Company's repertory of nine Gilbert and Sullivan operettas was the only prosperous venture. Return engagements of the controversial *The Cradle Will Rock*, Noel Coward's anthology program *Tonight at 8:30*, and the 1920 favorite *Sally* each ran a month. There were also a few curiosities this season worth mentioning. Jerome Moross wrote the music for *Ballet Ballads*, an evening of three one-act dance pieces written by John LaTouche.

Song of the Season

Music by Pyotor Tchaikovski was used in *Music in My Head*, a musical biography of the famed Russian composer. *Caribbean Carnival* was billed as a "calypso musical revue" featuring "native songs and dance." The craze for "South-of-the border" music had weakened after the war and the revue closed inside of two weeks.

"Papa, Won't You Dance With Me?"
Music by Jule Styne; lyric by Sammy Cahn
From *High Button Shoes* (1947)
Sung by Nanette Fabray as Mrs. Longstreet,
Jack McCauley as Papa Longstreet, and chorus

Not too many polka songs have come from Broadway shows and it is even rarer for one to become a hit. But "Papa, Won't You Dance with Me?" from *High Button Shoes* caught on and still can be found in the repertoire of polka ensembles and dance bands. In the musical, the middle-aged couple Henry (Jack McCauley) and Sara Longstreet (Nanette Fabray) are watching the young people dancing and she tries to get "Papa" to take to the dance floor with her. Sammy Cahn's lyric is simple and direct. "Papa, won't you dance with me? … take a chance with me … dance with me tonight!"[8] Jule Styne's vivacious music is indeed a polka but not too fast as it repeats some catchy musical phrases. The release comes quickly and is even more expansive than the refrain and speeds up somewhat. "When you whirl me/ Round and round we'll go,/ Right off the ground we'll go!" "Papa" then sings his own refrain about being too old to dance but he relents, the two join the dancing, and the chorus sings the song. Styne's music is so contagious that once heard it is easily remembered. It has some substantial leaps up the scale but is, for the most part, not difficult to sing. For this reason the number has proven to be an enticing sing-along song.

"Papa Won't You Dance with Me?" was sung by Kay Kimber and Sidney James in the 1948 London version of *High Button Shoes*. After the Broadway cast recording of the musical in which Fabray and McCauley sing the song, the first disc was made by Skitch Henderson and His Orchestra (vocal by Nancy Reed). Another early record was made by Guy Lombardo and His Royal Canadians with a chorus doing the vocals. The most successful disc was that by Doris Day, the vocal version most Americans heard and remembered. It was her first hit single as a solo vocalist after breaking away from the Big Bands. Other recordings of note were made by Ray Bolger, Magic Organ, Gale Storm, Alice Faye, Evelyn Knight, Maxine Sullivan, Roger Williams, and Vivian Blaine. "Papa, Will You Dance with Me?" has been recorded and performed live by numerous polka bands and became a staple on television programs such as *The Lawrence Welk Show*. There was no movie version of *High Button Shoes* but two television adaptations were broadcast. Nanette Fabray and Joey Faye reprised their Broadway performances for a 1956 television version in which "Papa, Won't You Dance with Me?" was sung by

Fabray and Don Ameche. The song was sung by Maureen O'Hara and Garry Moore in a 1966 broadcast. On Broadway, Faith Prince and Jason Alexander recreated the original 1947 staging in *Jerome Robbins' Broadway* (1989).

Other notable songs from that season: "I Still Get Jealous," "On a Sunday by the Sea," "There's Nothing Like a Model T" from *High Button Shoes*; "Allegro," "The Gentleman Is a Dope," "So Far," "You Are Never Away" from *Allegro*; "Civilization (Bongo Bongo Bongo)" from *Angel in the Wings*; "Saturday Night in Central Park," "Anything Can Happen in New York" from *Make Mine Manhattan*; "Haunted Heart," "Rhode Island Is Famous for You," "We Won't Take It Back" from *Inside U.S.A.*

Song of the Season

1948–1949 SEASON

Any season that produces not one or two but three musical theatre classics is one for the books. Add to that some resplendent musicals that, although no longer done, were highly satisfying for their time and place. All of which means there were several outstanding songs this season. Rodgers and Hammerstein's score for *South Pacific* is remarkable not because it is filled with chart hit songs but because each number became famous for what it is in the context of the musical. Singers are not going to record "You've Got to Be Carefully Taught" as if it was a Tin Pan Alley bestseller. It is a superlative theatre song and, like every other number in *South Pacific*, it is character and plot-driven. Cole Porter's score for *Kiss Me, Kate* is an ingenious example of a musical comedy score. Actually, it is two scores: a modern, sportive set of songs for backstage and a collection of anachronistic pseudo-Elizabethan numbers for onstage. *Kiss Me, Kate* is Porter's finest work because he finally got to score a first-class libretto (by Bella and Samuel Spewack). Frank Loesser's score for *Where's Charley?* was his first for Broadway and a delicious surprise. Loesser had written many songs for the movies and Tin Pan Alley but nothing prepared him to write the songs for a Victorian farce. Yet the numbers in *Where's Charley?* are very British while staying within the Broadway sound. It must be pointed out that in each case, these three musicals were fortunate to have sturdy librettos, masterful directors, and exceptional casts.

Some of the other book musicals this season had much to recommend even if they cannot rank as classics. With *Love Life*, Kurt Weill and Alan Jay Lerner experimented with history as told through a marriage and it was filled with exciting ideas and fine songs. The musical farce *As the Girls Go* was a vehicle for comic Bobby Clark and did not disappoint his fans. But there were also some felicitous songs by Jimmy McHugh (music) and Harold Adamson (lyrics). Similarly, some expert songs were to be found in *Lend an Ear, All for Love, Along Fifth Avenue*, and *Small Wonder*, all of which had substantial runs. If one could not get a ticket to *South Pacific*, there were splendid revivals this season of Hammerstein's earlier hits *Show Boat* and *Carousel*. Failing that, there were two editions of the skating extravaganza *Howdy, Mr. Ice*, each one playing over 400 times. Broadway in the 1940s didn't get more eclectic than that.

"Some Enchanted Evening"
Music by Richard Rodgers; lyric by Oscar Hammerstein
From *South Pacific* (1949)
Sung by Ezio Pinza as Emile de Becque

Sung early in the musical *South Pacific*, "Some Enchanted Evening" is a love song but also a plot and character song. Oscar Hammerstein's lyric provides exposition, letting us know that the middle-aged planter Emile (Ezio Pinza) first saw the American nurse Nellie (Mary Martin) at a party crowded with people. Emile also says that he heard her laugh. Emile's confession that he immediately sensed that he would see her again and forever remember that laughter makes it a character song. Finally, his decision to "fly to her side" makes the song a proposal of love and, implied, marriage.[9] Few love songs cover so much in so short a time. But there are other aspects of "Some Enchanted Evening" that are unusual. The lyric is written in the second person. On that special night, "*you* may see a stranger ... somehow *you* know, *you* know even then,/ That somehow *you'll* see here again and again." The *you* is not Nellie, of course; but is it Emile? For a love song sung to the object of one's affection, "Some Enchanted Evening" is removed by that second person perspective. In fact, the lyric sometimes sounds like an old and wise man giving advice to a smitten young man who is hesitating on acting on his feelings. There is even a sense of warning in the lyric, urging one to "fly to her side and make her your own" otherwise forever after "you may dream all alone." The lyric ends with the clear directive "once you have found her, never let her go." Perhaps the gulf that exists between Emile and Nellie—the difference in age, education, breeding, nationality—is why Hammerstein allows Emile to be so restrained in the song. There are no references to one's heart or passion. Even the word *love* is only used once and it is as a noun ("when you find your true love") and not a verb. "Some Enchanted Evening" has no verses; it starts with the direct refrain. The release is very short, a couplet that looks at the situation philosophically: "Who can explain it, who can tell you why?/ Fools give you reasons— wise men never try." Rodgers' music up to this point has been flowing and definite. (The sheet music calls for "slowly, with expression.") But for the release it gets tentative with eighth notes that are uncertain until the music expands on "wise men never try."

"Some Enchanted Evening" is reprised near the end of the musical by Nellie who knows Emile is in great danger and fears she will never see him again and accept the proposal he offered in the first scene. The words about never letting go once you have found that special person take on a new meeting when sung by Nellie; she foolishly let him go and now regrets it. "Some Enchanted Evening" is Rodgers and Hammerstein's most-recorded song despite the way it is tied to these two characters. Sung out of context, it can mean many other things. It has the tone of a torch song if performed in such a manner. It can be done effectively as a romantic duet. (Because Pinza was a bass and Martin a mezzo-soprano, the two rarely sang together in *South Pacific*; Rodgers and Hammerstein thought it too unusual a combination.) Of course, the song remains highly romantic in instrumental versions and it even works as a jazz piece. Martin reprised her Nellie in the 1951 London version of *South Pacific* in which Wilbur Evans sang "Some Enchanted Evening" to her. Pinza's rendition of the ballad from the original Broadway cast recording of *South Pacific* was released as a single and climbed to Number 7 in the charts in 1949 but it was Perry Como's disc that same year that reached Number 1. Among the hundreds of other recordings are notable ones by Frank Sinatra with Rosemary Clooney, Gordon MacRae, Fred Waring and the Pennsylvanians, Richard Kiley, Jay & The Americans, Ace Cannon, Ray Charles, Frankie Vaughan, José Carreras, Florence Henderson, Mandy Patinkin, the Temptations, Jane Olivor, Bryn Terfel, Philip Quast, Christine Andreas, Art Garfunkel, Bob Dylan, Harry Connick, Jr., Jenn Gambatese, and Grahame Stuart Booth. In the

Song of the Season

1958 screen version of *South Pacific*, "Some Enchanted Evening" was sung by Rossano Brazzi (dubbed by Giorgio Tozzi) and Rade Serbedzija sang it in the 2001 television adaptation. In Broadway revivals of *South Pacific*, Richard Collett played Emile and sang the ballad in the 1955 production, as did Giorgio Tozzi in 1967 and Paulo Szot in the 2008 revival.

Other notable songs from that season: "A Wonderful Guy," "Younger Than Springtime," "There Is Nothin' Like a Dame," "Bali Ha'i," " I'm Gonna Wash That Man Right Outa My Hair," "This Nearly Was Mine" from *South Pacific*; "Wunderbar," "Brush Up Your Shakespeare," "So in Love," "Too Darn Hot," "Always True to You in My Fashion," "Another Op'nin', Another Show," "Why Can't You Behave?," "Where Is the Life That Late I Led?" from *Kiss Me, Kate*; "I Got Lucky in the Rain," "You Say the Nicest Things, Baby" from *As the Girls Go*; "Once in Love with Amy," "At the Red Rose Cotillion," "My Darling, My Darling" from *Where's Charley?*; "Green-Up Time," "Here I'll Stay" from *Love Life*.

1949–1950 SEASON

There were some very ambitious musicals this season and there were some pretty frivolous shows. Oddly enough, there were hits in both categories. Kurt Weill's powerful musical drama *Lost in the Stars*, for example, found enough patrons to run over nine months. Dramatic playwright Maxwell Anderson wrote the libretto and lyrics for this tale of racial unrest and domestic tragedy in South Africa. The vibrant score demanded opera-quality voices which is why today *Lost in the Stars* lives on in opera houses. Running nearly as long was Irving Berlin's *Miss Liberty*, a fictional account about the creation of the famous statue in New York harbor. While not a tragedy, it was Berlin's most serious musical and a valiant attempt to write a musical play in the Rodgers and Hammerstein mold. Marc Blitzstein's *Regina* was a musical version of Lillian Hellman's acclaimed drama *The Little Foxes* and it also was more an opera than a Broadway musical. It only lasted seven weeks in its initial offering but *Regina* has been revived by opera companies around the world. The same is true for Carlo Menotti's political tragedy *The Consul*, but in this case the opera enjoyed a run of 269 performances on Broadway.

Of the lighter musicals, the most popular was *Gentlemen Prefer Blondes* with a sprightly score by Jule Styne and Leo Robin and a star-making performance by Carol Channing. It ran two years while the political satire *Texas, Li'l Darling* had to settle for ten months. The only other book musical to chalk up that many performances on the Street was the colonial period comedy *Arms and the Girl* with some merry songs by Morton Gould (music) and Dorothy Fields (lyrics). Not many notable songs came from the season's revues but *Touch and Go, Alive and Kicking*, and *Tickets, Please!* each had substantial runs. As often happens, some splendid performers first got noticed in revues, as with this season's Nancy Andrews, Nathaniel Frey, Peggy Cass, Bobby Van, Helen Gallagher, Gwen Verdon, and Bob Fosse. A Broadway entry that was and wasn't a musical was a revival of the fantasy play *Peter Pan* featuring Jean Arthur as the boy who didn't want to grow up and Boris Karloff as Captain Hook. Leonard Bernstein wrote six songs for Hook and Wendy (Marcia Henderson) to sing (Peter never sang) but most commentators did not consider this *Peter Pan* to be a musical. Audiences weren't concerned either way and kept the show on the boards for 320 performances.

"Diamonds Are a Girl's Best Friend"
Music by Jule Styne; lyric by Leo Robin
From *Gentlemen Prefer Blondes* (1949)
Sung by Carol Channing as Lorelei Lee

Character songs from musicals become famous far less often than ballads, torch songs, or romantic numbers but "Diamonds Are a Girl's Best Friend" is the exception. Gold digger Lorelei Lee (Carol Channing) is alone on stage when she sings this cunning credo in *Gentlemen Prefer Blondes*, expressing her philosophy of life in a smart and slapstick manner. The music by Jule Styne is a lively march with a swinging flavor and Leo Robin's hilarious lyric still delights with its sassy attitude and clever rhymes. The number has a short verse in which Lorelei states her case: men who fight duels are not as valuable as men who give women expensive jewelry. The refrains are specifically about diamonds providing the kind of security a girl needs in this world. "A kiss on the hand," Lorelei argues, "May be quite continental,/ But diamonds are a girl's best friend."[10] The lyric rarely uses "I" or gets very personal. Instead the song is a cautionary number that is both callous and charming: "Men grow cold/ As girls grow old/ And we all lose our charms in the end." There is even a reference to a gold digger's need to survive after an affair with a sugar daddy ends and "those louses go back to their spouses." Robin has fun with some of the rhymes, pairing "stiff knees" with "Tiff'ny's" and "strictly platonic" with affairs that "you must keep liaisonic." It is believed that Robin invented the word "liaisonic" meaning an understanding or willingness to be discreet. It is unlikely the uneducated Lorelei would know such a word but it would be in character for her to make it up.

Although "Diamonds Are a Girl's Best Friend" is a specific character song, it can be sung by a male or female as a wry observation or a droll piece of advice. Consequently, the number had been recorded by a wide variety of performers. Channing sang it on the *Gentlemen Prefer Blondes* original cast recording and then a few months later as a single. It became her signature song and she performed it often on the radio, in concert, and on television programs. The musical was not seen in London until 1962 when Dora Bryan played Lorelei and sang the song. When *Gentlemen Prefer Blondes* was revised and revived on Broadway in 1974 as *Lorelei*, Channing reprised her role and sang it again. In the 1995 revival of *Gentlemen Prefer Blondes*, KT Sullivan sang the number. When the screen version of *Gentlemen Prefer Blondes* was made in 1953 with Marilyn Monroe as Lorelei Lee, Monroe sang it with some dubbing help from Marni Nixon. The sequence in the movie was so sensational that for many "Diamonds Are a Girl's Best Friend" was forever after associated with Monroe. Among the roughly 150 recordings of the song are memorable ones by Pearl Bailey, Ethel Merman, Lena Horne, Harry Pitch, Della Reese, Eartha Kitt, Bertice Reading, Emmylou Harris, Anna Nicole Smith, T-Bone Burnett, Shirley Bassey and Paloma Faith, Susannah McCorkle, Blue Harlem, Karen Mason, Jane Krakowski, Blue Champagne, and Steve Yarrington. The Monroe rendition of the song was used in the films *Guilty by Suspicion* (1991), *Calendar Girl* (1993), and *Town and Country* (2001), and it was sung by Alan Cumming in *Company Man* (2000), Rachel Griffiths in *Blow Dry* (2001), Nicole Kidman in *Moulin Rouge!* (2001), Salaam Remi in *Sex in the City* (2008), and Christina Aguilera in *Burlesque* (2010).

Other notable songs from that season: "A Little Girl from Little Rock," "Bye Bye, Baby" from *Gentlemen Prefer Blondes*; "Lost in the Stars," "Cry, the Beloved Country," "Trouble Man" from *Lost in the Stars*; "Let's Take an Old-Fashioned Walk," "Falling Out of Love Can Be Fun" from *Miss Liberty*; "There Must Be Somethin' Better Than Love," "Nothin' for Nothin'" from *Arms and the Girl*; "The Best Thing of All," "Lionnet (Birdie's Aria)" from *Regina*.

1950–1951 SEASON

Any season which introduced new musicals by Rodgers and Hammerstein, Irving Berlin, Cole Porter, and Frank Loesser is promising, to say the least. Then add to that list new works by songwriters Arthur Schwartz, Dorothy Fields, Harold Rome, E. Y. Harburg, Sammy Fain, and Hugh Martin; and add to them such performers as Ethel Merman, Sam Levene, Gertrude Lawrence, Shirley Booth, Robert Alda, Barbara Cook, Yul Brynner, Nanette Fabray, Vivian Blaine, Jules Munshin, Charlotte Greenwood, Pearl Bailey, and Stubby Kaye—then it looks like a sure thing. Not all of the above were associated with hit shows but a large percentage of them were. It was a season in which long-run successes like *Guys and Dolls, Call Me Madam,* and *The King and I* were in such demand for tickets that the Broadway audience base was spread thin and lesser musicals had difficulty attracting patrons even if they got enthusiastic notices. The Schwartz-Fields musical *A Tree Grows in Brooklyn* (270 performances), Porter's *Out of This World* (157 performances), Hugh Martin's *Make a Wish* (102 performances), the Harold Rome revue *Bless You All* (eighty-four performances), and even the oddball Fain-Harburg musical *Flahooley* (forty performances) all deserved to run much longer than they did. Perhaps in another season they would have. Some have become cult favorites even if none of them ever got a Broadway revival.

Call Me Madam has also failed to get revived on Broadway. It boasted a superb Irving Berlin score and a slick political satire for its libretto. But *Call Me Madam* was created as an Ethel Merman vehicle and is still thought of as a Merman show. There is no question her performance helped the musical run 644 times. Yet *Guys and Dolls* ran twice as long and it was not a star vehicle. The "stars" were Frank Loesser's brilliant score and Abe Burrows' sterling libretto and the hundreds of productions of *Guys and Dolls* each year are a testament to those songs, characters, and story. Rodgers and Hammerstein's *The King and and I* also ran well over one thousand performances and it also receives hundreds of productions each year. Yet it was written with a star in mind: the beloved British actress Gertrude Lawrence with limited vocal prowess and unlimited charm. Ironically, the unknown Yul Brynner became a star playing the King and today we think of *The King and I* as a two-star musical. Or a no-star musical because, unlike *Call Me Madam*, *The King and I* doesn't have to fight against the memory of Gertrude Lawrence. The 1950s is considered a golden decade for the Rodgers and Hammerstein-model book musical. The era begins, appropriately, with these three beloved classics.

"You're Just in Love"
Music and lyric by Irving Berlin
From *Call Me Madam* (1950)
Sung by Ethel Merman as Sally Adams, and
Russell Nype as Kenneth Gibson

Song of the Season

So many outstanding songs were added to the Great American Songbook this season that just mentioning some of them is an embarrassment of riches. But no one song stopped the show and demanded encores like the contrapuntal number "You're Just in Love" from *Call Me Madam*. Several songs from *The King and I* and *Guys and Dolls* have been recorded far more frequently than "You're Just in Love" and there certainly are more moving or funnier songs from this season. But Irving Berlin's "double-song" is inspired theatricality and perhaps the very essence of Broadway showmanship. Different artists working on *Call Me Madam* have told somewhat different stories about how "You're Just in Love" came to be. Director George Abbott, choreographer Jerome Robbins, performer Ethel Merman, and Berlin himself each have their own version of the truth with conflicting details. What it generally thought is that the young actor Russell Nype, who was playing Kenneth, the assistant to diplomat Sally Adams (Merman), was proving to be one of the show's charming assets in rehearsal and tryouts. His song and dance number "It's a Lovely Day Today" with Princess Maria (Galina Talva) was going over very well and *someone* (Abbott? Robbins?) suggested that he be given a second number to do in the second act. One must remember that this was an Ethel Merman vehicle and drawing attention away from the star was not going to go over very well with her. So *someone* (Merman herself?) suggested that Berlin write a duet for Nype and Merman. At this point the story goes in different directions. Possibly Berlin was stuck for an idea for a duet since the two characters were not at all romantically involved with each other. Also, Nype's singing voice was higher than Merman's so having them sing together would be tricky. Again, there are various versions of what happened next but some sources say that Abbott heard on the radio a new recording of Berlin's 1914 hit "(Play a) Simple Melody" by Bing Crosby and his son Gary and he had an idea. The catchy "A Simple Melody" was a contrapuntal number; that is, two distinct melodies and lyrics that can be sung together. Abbott (maybe) asked Berlin if he could write such a double song for Merman and Nype. It was just the kick-start Berlin needed and in a few days he completed "You're Just in Love," the best song in the *Call Me Madam* score and the last great song of Berlin's career.

A contrapuntal number or "double song" has two distinct music and lyrics which can be performed independently and together. The best of such songs also have separate tempos and musical styles. "You're Just in Love" has all of these and is considered by many to be Broadway's finest "double song." The first section is a flowing, operatic piece for Kenneth who hears "singing and there's no one there" and smells "blossoms and the trees are bare."[11] Kenneth elaborates in his naive and facile manner: He cannot sleep, he's lost his appetite, he has stars in his eyes. Sally replies with her section which has a swing tempo and a clipped, no-nonsense lyric. "You don't need analyzing," she bluntly states. "It is not so surprising/That you feel very strange but nice." Sally recognizes the symptoms because she's "been there once or twice." Being older and more experienced, she concludes that there is no medicine because Kenneth is not sick but is "just in love." Each of the sections is musically and lyrically very pleasing but each also leaves you wanting more. So instead of a release section, Kenneth and Sally repeat their refrains together. Her section is twice as long as his but hers is twice as fast. Also, he may hold one note for four beats while she might sing four quarter notes. The test of a good double song is how it sounds when both parts are sung together and "You're Just in Love" sound great. The opening night audience at *Call Me Madam* called for seven encores of the number and a similar reaction met the song every night. In the 1952 London production, the duet was performed by Billie Worth and Jeff Warren and it also was a showstopper.

Being a song that can only be performed as a duet, one might assume that there might be a limited number of recordings over the years. But "You're Just in Love" has an impressive history of top-selling discs. A 1950 recording by Perry Como and the Fontane Sisters with Mitchell Ayres' Orchestra was on the charts for seventeen weeks. Other early discs that sold well include Rosemary Clooney and Guy Mitchell, Ethel Merman and Dick Haymes, Harry Babbitt and Martha Tilton, Dinah Shore and Russell Nype, and Per and Ulf Lindqvist. Over the decades, "You're Just in Love" has also been recorded as a solo, an instrumental, and as a choral piece. Among the many memorable discs are those by Sarah Vaughn and Billy Eckstine, Chet Atkins, Della Reese and Kirt Stuart, Louis Prima, Kay Starr, Bing Crosby, Louis Armstrong, Liberace, Helen Reddy, Joanne O'Brien and Lee Lessack, the New Deal Rhythm Band, Lois Zann, Ewan McGregor and Jane Horrocks, and Roger Marks' Armada Jazz Band. Merman got to reprise her Sally Adams in the 1953 screen version of *Call Me Madam* and sang the duet with Donald O'Connor.

Other notable songs from that season: "It's a Lovely Day Today," "I Like Ike," "The Hostess with the Mostes' on the Ball" from *Call Me Madam*; "Hello, Young Lovers," "Shall We Dance?," "Getting to Know You," "We Kiss in a Shadow," "Something Wonderful," "I Have Dreamed" from *The King and I*; "Guys and Dolls," "Luck Be a Lady," "Sit Down, You're Rockin' the Boat," "A Bushel and a Peck," "I'll Know," "The Oldest Established," "Fugue for Tinhorns," "I've Never Been in Love Before," "Take Back Your Mink," "Adelaide's Lament," "Marry the Man Today," "If I Were a Bell" from *Guys and Dolls*; "He Had Refinement," "Look Who's Dancing," "I'll Buy You a Star" from *A Tree Grows in Brooklyn*; "Here's to Your Illusions," "The World Is Your Balloon," "The Springtime Cometh" from *Flahooley*; "I Am Loved," "Use Your Imagination," "Nobody's Chasing Me," "They Couldn't Compare to You" from *Out of This World*.

Song of the Season

1951–1952 SEASON

There was no embarrassment of riches this season as both the number of shows and the quality dropped noticeably. Only five new book musicals opened and none of them made a profit. That did not mean that they didn't have respectable runs. The slight but enjoyable *Top Banana,* with an estimable cast led by Phil Silvers, chalked up 350 performances and still lost money. This was a new record and a frightening sign of things to come. Lerner and Loewe's rustic musical *Paint Your Wagon* boasted the finest score of the season and had much to recommend in its cast and libretto but even at 289 performances it ended up in the red. Running far less and floundering in the economics of Broadway were such promising musicals as *Seventeen, Courtin' Time,* and *Three Wishes for Jamie.* Two small-scale revues that were highly entertaining—*New Faces of 1952* and *Two on the Aisle*—were able to pay with runs no longer than 365 and 276 performances each. The latter was a showcase for the savvy veteran Bert Lahr and the fiery Dolores Gray who were helped by some prankish songs by Jule Styne, Betty Comden, and Adolph Green. For his revue, producer Leonard Sillman came up with "faces" that were not only "new" but often very gifted. Paul Lynde, Carol Lawrence, Robert Clary, Eartha Kitt, and Alice Ghostley would all go on to substantial careers. If new works were far and few between this season, there were a total of seven musical revivals for audiences to choose from. In fact, the long-run champ was an excellent revival of Rodgers and Hart's *Pal Joey* which opened to better reviews than it had in 1940 and ran longer (542 performances) than the original. Harold Lang was Joey, Vivienne Segal reprised her Vera, and there were expert supporting performances by Helen Gallagher, Elaine Stritch, Lionel Stander, and Pat Northrop. Also well received by the press were revivals of the Gershwins' *Of Thee I Sing* and the Kern-Hammerstein operetta *Music in the Air* but they ran only a few months each ended up deep in the red. From the producers', players', and the playgoers' points of view, it was a difficult season indeed.

"They Call the Wind Maria"
Music Frederick Loewe; lyric by Alan Jay Lerner
From *Paint Your Wagon* (1951)
Sung by Rufus Smith as Steve Bullnack, and the male chorus

Nothing could seem further from the Lerner and Loewe musical fantasy *Brigadoon* than the rough-and-tumble Gold Rush musical *Paint Your Wagon.* Both have superior scores which also could not have been more different. The German-born Loewe composed songs rich in the sounds of Americana and Lerner's lyrics were both plain speaking and bucolic. Two hit songs came from this unlikely source: "They Call the Wind Maria" and "I Talk to the Trees," both in the folk song idiom. Of the two, the former is the more complex and stirring. In the 1941 novel *Storm* by George Rippey Stewart, the local name for a stormy wind is Maria. The word is pronounced "Mariah" (as in the singer Mariah Carey, who was named after the song) with the accent on the middle syllable. This pronunciation gives the name a poetic form which inspired both the music and the lyric. "They Call the Wind Maria" has a folk song structure of AABAABAAB with no definite release. Yet the song never gets repetitive because of Loewe's driving music that feels oppressive but also restless. The song is sung by Steve Bullnack (Rufus Smith), a minor character in *Paint Your Wagon* but a memorable one. Bullnack has left his young wife hundreds of miles away as he tries to make his fortune prospecting for gold in California. Not only is he weary and discouraged but he misses his wife. In some ways, Bullnack curses the wind yet he also asks Maria to "blow my love to me."[12] Lerner's lyric introduces in the first verse the idea of naming aspects of mother nature: "The rain is Tess, the fire Joe,/ And they call the wind Maria." In the following verse he describes the power of the wind, so strong that "Maria makes the mountains sound/ Like folks were up there dying." Bullnack is joined by the other miners in the brief but haunting refrain. Because of the lift of the three syllables in "Maria," the repetition of the word creates a moaning or wailing sound and the lyric needs no other words. Not until later in the song does Bullnack tell us how he left his girl behind and how he is lonely and lost, so lost that "Not even God can find me." The lyric concludes with the miners asking Maria to use her power to bring "my love to me." Lerner's lyric has a sense of emptiness implied in the miners. Loewe's music adds to this in the accompaniment which is a series to strident notes which drive the song forward. As much as "They Call the Wind Maria" is like a cowboy song, it is also theatrical in the Broadway manner. Coming at the end of the first act of *Paint Your Wagon*, the number makes for a thrilling finale. Sung out of the context of the musical, the ballad becomes a torch song of sorts with its sad and lonely expression of loss. Rufus Smith sang the ballad in the original Broadway production and James Mitchell led the dancing miners. In the 1953 London version, "They Call the Wind Maria" was sung by Joseph Leader and Veit Bethke led the dance.

After the original Broadway cast recording of *Paint Your Wagon*, the song's first discs were made by Vaughn Monroe and by Gil Huston with the Victor Young chorus and orchestra. Other early recordings include those by John Raitt, George London, the Kingston Trio, and David Hill. While there have been female vocal covers of the song, most versions are by men. With the rising popularity of "They Call the Wind Maria" came the assumption by many that it was an authentic folk song from the past. In fact, members of the Western Writers of America chose it as one of the Top 100 Western songs of all time. In addition to vocal and instrumental versions, the number has also been popular with choral groups. Among the notable discs over the years are those by Sam Cooke, the Smothers Brothers, Pernell Roberts, the Ray Bloch Singers, Vic Damone, Jim Nabors, Roy Clark, Art Blakey and the Jazz Messengers, Frankie Laine, P. J. Proby, Zoot Sims, Bryn Terfel, Robert Goulet, Stan Wilson, Squeek Steele, and Bobby Osborne. In the greatly altered 1969 movie version of *Paint Your Wagon*, the ballad was sung by the character Rotten Luck Willie (Harve Presnell) and the miners.

Other notable songs from that season: "I Talk to the Trees," "Another Autumn," "Wand'rin' Star," "I Still See Elisa" from *Paint Your Wagon*; "Monotonous," "Boston Beguine," "I'm in Love with Miss Logan" from *New Faces of 1952*; "Summertime Is Summertime," "I Could Get Married Today," "After All, It's Spring" from *Seventeen*; "Give a Little, Get a Little," "If You Hadn't, but You Did" from *Two on the Aisle*; "Top Banana," "I Fought Every Step of the Way" from *Top Banana*.

1952–1953 SEASON

If it were not for nine musical revivals, this season would have been slim indeed with only two revues and eight new book musicals. Yet none of those revivals stayed very long except *Porgy and Bess* which further secured its place in the American musical by running 305 performances in one of the biggest houses on the Street. The two revues were star vehicles. *An Evening with Beatrice Lillie* found an audience for 275 performances but *Two's Company*, featuring Bette Davis, struggled to run eleven weeks. Half of the new book musicals enjoyed long runs. The summer camp musical *Wish You Were Here* was given a media blitz and everyone in town was talking about the full-sized swimming pool on stage. The songs by Harold Rome were commendable and the large cast more than proficient, turning the show into an audience favorite. *Wish You Were Here* ran 598 performances; since then, it has rarely been done elsewhere. Running almost as long was the resplendent musical comedy *Wonderful Town* which had a lot going for it. The popular play *My Sister Eileen* (1940) was adapted into a musical by Betty Comden and Adolph Green who also wrote some expert lyrics to go with Leonard Bernstein's jazz-flavored score. *Wonderful Town* also had Rosalind Russell in one of her best roles, yet business continued to be strong when Carol Channing took over. The longest-running musical of the season (892 performances) was Cole Porter's *Can-Can* with a problematic script but a fine collection of songs and a first-class cast to perform them. The most-anticipated musical of the season was Rodgers and Hammerstein's *Me and Juliet* and the advance was so hefty that the show ran 358 performances even after the dismal reviews came out. The backstage musical was criticized as being rather unimaginative in story and song, only Jo Mielziner's evocative sets and lights getting approval. Since its initial Broadway run, *Me and Juliet* has rarely been heard of again. Another disappointment was *Hazel Flagg*, a facile musical based on the screwball film comedy *Nothing Sacred* (1937). After memorable supporting performances, Helen Gallagher finally got to star in her own Broadway musical and she was deemed effervescent by the press. The score by Jule Styne (music) and Bob Hilliard (lyrics) had some first-rate songs but *Hazel Flagg* was riddled with problems and closed after 190 performances.

"It's All Right with Me"
Music and lyric by Cole Porter
From *Can-Can* (1953)
Sung by Peter Cookson as Aristide Forestier

One of Cole Porter's finest torch songs, "It's All Right with Me" is unique in the fact that it is delivered to a person one doesn't love about a person one does love. It was introduced in *Can-Can* by Peter Cookson as the young Parisian judge Aristide Forestier who ought to arrest the dance hall proprietress La Mome Pistache (Lilo) for allowing the illegal dance known as the Can-Can. Instead Aristide has fallen in with La Mome and when the flirtatious chorus girl Mimi (Dania Krupska) puts the moves on Aristide, he replies with this melancholy rebuke. There is no verse as he begins the refrain with a dispassionate observation. "It's the wrong time, and the wrong place,/ Though your face is charming, it's the wrong face."[13] The reason is simple: "it's not her face." Yet he wryly notes, "it's all right with me." The suggestion is that Aristide might sleep with the willing Mimi at some point but for now he is haunted by La Mome. The lyric continues to list feminine attributes (her lips, her smile) and comparing the two women. In the release he admits that "There's someone I'm trying so hard to forget" and asks her, "Don't you want to forget someone, too?" The song ends with a decision: if she is free one night, Mimi will do.

It is a sensual lyric but Porter's music is so morose that there is nothing very sexy about the song. Like many Porter composition, there is an insistent rhythm pushing the music forward. Porter shifts expertly from major to minor keys which gives the music a haunting quality as well. The melody sometimes goes in surprising direction, such as the way the notes climb on "it's not *her* face," reaching a peak on *her*, then descending warily on "but such a charming face." "It's All Right with Me" is one of Porter's most finely crafted and emotional songs and it remains a beguiling piece. In the 1954 London production of *Can-Can*, Edmund Hockridge played Aristide and sang the ballad.

Since Peter Cookson recorded "It's All Right with Me" for the *Can-Can* cast album, there have been over 200 discs of the ballad. Early records by Bob Manning, Kay Thompson, and Edmund Hockridge were followed by covers by such diverse artists as Bing Crosby, Sonny Rollins, Buddy Greco, Ella Fitzgerald, Dinah Shore, Harry James, Jeri Southern, Lionel Hampton with Sylvia Bennett, Brenda Lee, Crystal Gayle, Tom Waits, Harry Connick, Jr., Mel Tormé, George Michael, Nat King Cole, Natalie Cole, KT Sullivan, Seth MacFarlane, Ann Hampton Callaway, Jocelyn Gould, and Kari Kirkland. In the 1960 film version of *Can-Can*, Frank Sinatra sings the song to dancer Juliet Prowse. In the 1981 Broadway revival of *Can-Can*, "It's All Right with Me" was sung by Ron Husmann to Donna King, and in the 1998 Cole Porter Broadway musical *High Society*, it was sung by Melissa Errico.

Other notable songs from that season: "Can-Can," "C'est Magnifique," "I Love Paris" from *Can-Can*; "Ohio," "A Little Bit in Love," "Conga!," "One Hundred Easy Ways (To Lose a Man)," "A Quiet Girl" from *Wonderful Town*; "Wish You Were Here," "Where Did the Night Go?" from *Wish You Were Here*; "Every Street's a Boulevard in Old New York," "How Do You Speak to an Angel?" from *Hazel Flagg*; "No Other Love," "Marriage Type Love," "That's the Way It Happens" from *Me and Juliet*.

1953–1954 SEASON

The number of new musicals on Broadway this season shrunk to nine and three of those were one-person shows. Off-Broadway, on the other hand, had more productions than ever before and they included two very significant musicals. It was a season of contrasts, not only in its hits and failures but in subject matter and style. There were operetta, ballad-opera, musical revues, and musical comedy; they were about everything from the *Arabian Nights* to a labor dispute in present-day Cedar Rapids, Iowa. These are references to the two biggest hits on Broadway this season: *Kismet* and *The Pajama Game*. But in the record books they were eclipsed by the Off-Broadway sensation *The Threepenny Opera* which ran seven years. There was much disappointment when three musicals that looked so promising failed. *Carnival in Flanders*, based on a famous French film, lasted only a week but left one superior song: "Here's that Rainy Day." Sigmund Romberg's posthumous operetta *The Girl in Pink Tights*, about the "first musical" *The Black Crook* in 1866, struggled for five months and departed, not even leaving one good song. There was nothing disappointing about the sparkling musical *The Golden Apple*, a transfer from Off-Broadway with a clever retelling of episodes from Homer's *The Iliad* and *The Odyssey*, except that it failed to find an audience on Broadway. The season's only revue of note was *John Murray Anderson's Almanac*, a delightful evening of comedy and silly songs. Despite vibrant performances by Hermione Gingold, Billy DeWolfe, Orson Bean, Polly Bergen, and Harry Belafonte, the show could not run long enough to make a profit. Similarly, popular favorite Shirley Booth couldn't turn *By the Beautiful Sea* into a success even though it had much to recommend. What did turn a quick profit? The one-person shows *At Home with Ethel Waters* and *Comedy in Music* with Victor Borge. Such were the economics of Broadway in the postwar years.

"Stranger in Paradise"
Music by Alexander Borodin; lyric by Robert Wright, George Forrest
From *Kismet* (1953)
Sung by Richard Kiley as the Caliph, and Doretta Morrow as Marsinah

Over the years there have been many popular songs based on melodies taken from classical music. Two early examples are "I'm Always Chasing Rainbows" (taken from Chopin) and "Serenade" (based on a Schubert piece). Both songs were concert and recording favorites for decades. But the most popular classical-to-Broadway song is "Stranger in Paradise" from this season's *Kismet*. Lyricists Robert Wright and George Forrest took an exotic Alexander Borodin melody and turned it into what is by far the most recognized song based on a classical source. All of the music in *Kismet* comes from Borodin's symphonies, string quartets, and his unfinished opera *Prince Igor* (1890).

Song of the Season

The Russian composer's rich harmonies and vibrant melodies were ideal for a musical version of the 1911 play *Kismet*, a rousing adventure with an *Arabian Nights* setting, and Wright and Forrest provided fanciful lyrics that made for highly satisfying songs. A highlight in the score is the duet "Stranger in Paradise" sung by the young Caliph (Richard Kiley) and the maiden Marsinah (Doretta Morrow) when they first meet in a romantic garden. The lyric is unashamedly rhapsodic, the Caliph's declaration of love being "a fervent prayer" and how he hangs "suspended … somewhere in space" waiting for her to his return love before he falls into "dark despair."[14] Such purple poetry would come across as banal but for the soaring music that accompanies it. That music is adapted from Borodin's "The Gliding Dance of the Maidens," one of the "Polovtian Dances" from *Prince Igor*. "Gliding" is the operative word here; the melody glides up and down the scale before climaxing in the upper register. This is operetta in its truest form yet "Stranger in Paradise" has managed to have an appeal far beyond that supposedly old fashioned genre. Such a memorable melody had not been ignored before *Kismet*. In 1940, Artie Shaw recorded a song titled "My Fantasy" that also used "The Gliding Dance of the Maidens." The vocalist was Pauline Byrne and the lyric was totally different from the later "Stranger in Paradise." In the Broadway production of *Kismet*, Doretta Morrow sang the duet with Richard Kiley. Morrow reprised her performance in the 1955 London version in which she sang the number with Peter Grant.

Of the many recordings of "Stranger in Paradise" over the years, the two biggest sellers were those by Tony Bennett and by the Four Aces, both in 1953. (Bennett also made a duet version of the song with Andrea Bocelli in 2011.) Other covers of note were made by Tony Martin, Bing Crosby, Don Cornell, Sammy Davis, Jr., Al Hirt, the Ink Spots, Jack Jones, Isaac Hayes, Johnny Mathis, Keely Smith, Engelbert Humperdinck, Toots Thielemans, Ruth Ann Swenson and Jerry Hadley, Della Reese, Sarah Brightman, William Ash, Sierra Boggess and Julian Ovenden, and Linda Gentille. In the 1955 film version of *Kismet*, "Stranger in Paradise" was sung by Ann Blyth and Vic Damone, and in the 1967 television adaptation, the duet was performed by Anna Maria Alberghetti and George Chakiris.

Other notable songs from that season: "Baubles, Bangles and Beads," "And This Is My Beloved," "Night of My Nights" from *Kismet*; "Mack the Knife," "Pirate Jenny," "Jealousy Duet" from *The Threepenny Opera* (Off Broadway); "Hey, There," "Steam Heat," "Hernando's Hideaway," "I'll Never Be Jealous Again," "I'm Not at All in Love" from *The Pajama Game*; "Here's That Rainy Day" from *Carnival in Flanders*; "Lazy Afternoon," "Windflowers," "It's the Going Home Together" from *The Golden Apple*; "Alone Too Long," "Coney Island Boat," "The Sea Song" from *By the Beautiful Sea*; "Hold 'Em, Joe," "Merry Little Minuet," "Which Witch?" from *John Murray Anderson's Almanac*.

1954–1955 SEASON

With the advantage of hindsight, one can look back on this season and see how deceptive a hit show or a flop musical on Broadway can be. For example, of all of the season's new musicals, the one that is arguably the most revived today is *Peter Pan*. Because of its television broadcasts starring Mary Martin and its many Broadway revivals and tours, this show must have been a classic from the start. Yet the original production of *Peter Pan* ran only an unprofitable 152 performances. On the other hand, one might assume that the mostly forgotten and rarely revived musical *Fanny* was a less-than-successful curiosity when it opened. But with a lot of hype from new producer David Merrick and good word of mouth, *Fanny* ran 888 times. It was a season full of such surprises. No one produces *Silk Stockings* or *Plain and Fancy* today, and probably for good reasons. Yet they ran a lucrative 478 and 461 performances each in 1954–55. What is not surprising is that *Damn Yankees* was a giant hit then (1,019 performances) and remains an audience favorite. To a lesser extent, so was the British import *The Boy Friend*. It had been decades since a London musical did very well on the Street so the charming pastiche musical running 483 times was news indeed. Many thought then (and now) that the Truman Capote-Harold Arlen musical *House of Flowers* should have run longer than 165 times. At the same time, one wonders how such a piece of fluff like *Ankles Aweigh* could last 176 performances. When the famed movie composer Victor Young wrote some lovely music for *Seventh Heaven*, the stars were Ricardo Montalban and Gloria DeHaven but only one of the critics noticed Chita Rivera in a small part. We repeat: it was a season of surprises.

Hits or flops, there were many stellar performances this season. One could see such established stars as Mary Martin and Cyril Ritchard in *Peter Pan*, Walter Slezak and Ezio Pinza in *Fanny*, Pearl Bailey and Juanita Hall in *House of Flowers*, Don Ameche and Hildegarde Neff in *Silk Stockings*, and Ray Walston in *Damn Yankees*. Just as exciting was to see new talent either making their debut or getting their first major roles, as with Julie Andrews (*The Boy Friend*), Florence Henderson (*Fanny*), Diahann Carroll (*House of Flowers*), and Gwen Verdon (*Damn Yankees*). There were seven revivals or return engagements this season and, while none of them stayed very long, it gave audiences a chance to see Jo Sullivan and Barbara Cook in *Carousel*, Bobby Van and Vera Zorina in *On Your Toes*, Walter Matthau and Helen Gallagher in *Guys and Dolls*, and Merv Griffin and Helen Gallagher in *Finian's Rainbow*. And for those with higher brows, Carlo Menotti brought his latest opera, *The Saint of Bleecker Street*, to a Broadway house and stayed for eleven weeks.

"Young and Foolish"
Music by Albert Hague; lyric by Arnold B. Horwitt
From *Plain and Fancy* (1955)
Sung by Gloria Marlowe as Katie, and David Daniels as Peter

Song of the Season

Plain and Fancy is set in an Amish community in rural Pennsylvania where two city dwellers come to sell some land to a local farmer. There is a love triangle involving Katie (Gloria Marlowe), her fiancé Ezra (Douglas Fletcher), and Ezra's brother Peter (David Daniels) who left the community years ago. Peter's return rekindles a romance between Katie and himself, culminating in the lovely duet "Young and Foolish." Albert Hague (music) and Arnold B. Horwitt (lyrics) wrote a pleasing score for *Plain and Fancy* but most of the songs were so integrated into the plot and characters that they don't "travel" well. The exception is "Young and Foolish" which is open to many interpretations as well as musical styles, from an operatic duet to a cool jazz wail. The structure of the song is unusual. There is a short verse in which Peter recalls how as children he and Katie played at being in love. Although they are older and wiser now, he admits that he wishes he was still young and foolish. There follows two refrains but no release. This works because the music slowly builds in each refrain, steadily rising without becoming bombastic. In the second refrain the musical climax comes on "rain" in the couplet "Smiling in the sunlight,/ Laughing in the rain."[15] Then the music descends with a resigned feeling on the last two lines. It is a simple, tightly constructed song and the music is both romantic and wistful. That is why "Young and Foolish" has been recorded so effectively as a torch song or a melancholy lament for lost youth. Gloria Marlowe and David Daniels introduced the song in the original Broadway production and in London it was sung by Grace O'Connor and Jack Drummond.

In the same year as the original cast recording of *Plain and Fancy* was made, there were discs of "Young and Foolish" by Jo Stafford with Paul Weston's Orchestra, Billy Fields, Dean Martin, and the Maguire Sisters. Of the dozens of recordings over the years, special mention must be made of those by Nat King Cole, Paul Anka, Johnny Mathis, Chris McNulty, Brad Mehldau, Nancy Wilson, the Lettermen, Mabel Mercer, Lesley Gore, Bill Evans, the Four Preps, Joe Williams, Gloria Lynne, Eve Boswell, Sacha Distel, Bill Henderson, Andrea Marcovicci, Laura Welland, Claudio Chiara and Barbara Raimondi, Nancy Kelly, Wesla Whitfield, and Chris Flory. There was no movie version of *Plain and Fancy* but a 1956 television adaptation featured Jack Drummond and Grace O'Connor as Peter and Katie who sang "Young and Foolish."

Other notable songs from that season: "This Is All Very New to Me" from *Plain and Fancy*; "(You Gotta Have) Heart," "Whatever Lola Wants," "A Little Brains—A Little Talent," "Two Lost Souls," "Near to You," "Shoeless Joe from Hannibal, MO" from *Damn Yankees*; "Fanny," "Be Kind to Your Parents," "Why Be Afraid to Dance?" from *Fanny*; "Never, Never Land," "I've Gotta Crow," "Tender Shepherd," "I'm Flying," "I Won't Grow Up" from *Peter Pan*; "The Boy Friend," "A Room in Bloomsbury," "It's Never Too Late to Fall in Love," "I Could Be Happy with You," "Fancy Forgetting," "Safety in Numbers," "Won't You Charleston with Me?" from *The Boy Friend*; "A Sleepin' Bee," "Two Ladies in the Shade of de Banana Tree," "I Never Has Seen Snow" from *House of Flowers*; "All of You," "Paris Loves Lovers" from *Silk Stockings*.

1955–1956 SEASON

Because *My Fair Lady* dominated the season, both at the time and in retrospect, other shows in 1955–56 were sometimes left in the shadows. It is understandable since *My Fair Lady* was a surprise hit and some kind of high-water mark for the American musical theatre. It also broke many of the rules of the successful Broadway musical. It had no overt love story, the action is that of a drawing room comedy, there is more talk than music, dancing is secondary, the characters are more comic than romantic, and there is absolutely nothing American about it. None of this mattered with Lerner's intelligent and ingenious libretto, outstanding performances, an exquisite production, and the sterling Lerner and Loewe score. But what about all those patrons (and there were thousands) who could not get tickets to *My Fair Lady*? They turned to Frank Loesser's *The Most Happy Fella* and were not disappointed. In any other season the Italian opera-flavored musical would have gotten more attention but all the same it managed to run a very successful 678 performances. The Sammy Davis, Jr. vehicle *Mr. Wonderful* had its own appeal and ran 383 times yet somehow ended up in the red. The major disappointment of the season was Rodgers and Hammerstein's *Pipe Dream*. The tale of a lonely prostitute (Judy Tyler) finding love with a marine biologist (William Johnson) thanks to the help of a kindly brothel madame (Helen Traubel) was problematic, to say the least. Not only was opera singer Traubel out of her league, one might say that Rodgers and Hammerstein were also miscast. It was not their kind of show and it had the shortest run of any R&H musical: 246 performances. Time has shown that the score for *Pipe Dream* is quite good but revivals of the musical are extremely rare.

"On the Street Where You Live"
Music by Frederick Loewe; lyric by Alan Jay Lerner
From *My Fair Lady* (1956)
Sung by John Michael King as Freddie Eyensford-Hill

My Fair Lady seems like the perfect musical so it is not apparent how many problems and changes occurred during its preparation. It was not an easy creative process, to say the least. A good example is "On the Street Where You Live," arguably the most popular song in the score. It was written for the character of Freddie Eyensford-Hill (John Michael King), a secondary character in the story who is far from interesting. He appears briefly in the opening scene, trying to get a taxi for his mother and sister, and then again at the races at Ascot where he is charmed by Eliza (Julie Andrews). When he calls on her at Professor Higgins' residence, Freddie is turned away by the housekeeper Mrs. Pearce. But Freddie is nonplussed and remains on the sidewalk and sings about how contented he is just to be near Eliza. Although he is very familiar with the street and has often walked down the thoroughfare, the "pavement always stayed beneath my feet before."

Song of the Season

Now the street is something special. He continues in this manner then gets even more rhapsodic in the release. "Oh, the towering feeling,/ Just to know somehow you are near," he sings, then glories in the "overpowering feeling/ That any second you may suddenly appear."[16] Freddie expresses himself in rather bombastic terms and Loewe's music soars at the appropriate times. "On the Street Where You Live" is in the operetta mode and the only direct "I love you" song in the score. The music in each refrain is a gradual ascending of phrases which climax and descend on the title lyric. Lerner writes the words with an educated British dialect in mind. For example, he rhymes "bother" with "rather" which is not a true rhyme in American English but a comfortable one in London. There has been some criticism over the years about the song's title. In British parlance, a shop is said to be *in* the Tottenham Road or a person resides *in* Leadenhall Street instead of *on* those thoroughfares. This means that Freddie should sing "In the Street Where You Live." But to a Broadway audience, it sounds like he is singing in the middle of traffic and Lerner was right to keep it in the American vernacular.

When *My Fair Lady* began tryout performances, the song did not go over very well. Instead of being a showstopper, it left the audience restless and inattentive. When the same thing happened each performance, Lerner was stymied because he thought it the finest ballad in the show. Loewe, who didn't like his own music for the piece, was all for cutting the number. But Lerner was adamant and inquired from friends attending the previews about the song. He discovered that Freddie, having only briefly appeared previously, was all but forgotten by the audience by the time he re-entered to sing the song. To interrupt the Eliza–Higgins plot for a pretty ballad sung by a stranger put the audience in an unreceptive mood for the number. So Lerner re-wrote some of the dialogue with Mrs. Pearce and gave Freddie a verse to help the audience remember him, recalling how "my heart went on a journey to the moon/ When she told about her father and the gin." The next time "On the Street Where You Live" was performed with the alterations, it was met with vigorous applause. Such is the fragile nature of the Broadway musical that the placement or the set-up for a song can make all the difference.

John Michael King introduced "On the Street Where You Live" on Broadway and in the 1958 London version of *My Fair Lady* it was sung by Peter Gilmore. Because the original cast album of *My Fair Lady* was such a giant hit, most people first heard King's rendition of "On the Street Where You Live." But a Vic Damone recording soon after went to the Number 4 spot on the charts. Other early hit discs were made by Eddie Fisher, Lawrence Welk and His Orchestra, and Andy Williams. Of the hundreds of subsequent recordings were those by Bing Crosby, Doris Day, Bobby Darin, the Miracles, Shirley Horn, George Shearing, Count Basie, Mario Lanza, Chet Baker, Nat King Cole, Perry Como, Pat Suzuki, Harry Connick Jr., Gene Pitney, Bryn Terfel, Ed Townsend, Quincy Jones, Billy Porter, Ilse Huizinga, Scott Hamilton, Richard Clayderman, Ricki Lee Jones, Carrie Jackson, Pete Fountain, Roberta Flack, Blue Champagne, and Spencer Day. In the 1964 movie version of *My Fair Lady*, the song was sung by Jeremy Brett (dubbed by Bill

Shirley). Among the actors who have played Freddie in Broadway revivals and sung the ballad are Jerry Lanning in 1976, Nicholas Wyman in 1981, Robert Sella in 1993, and Jordan Donica in 2018.

Other notable songs from that season: "The Rain in Spain," "I Could Have Danced All Night," "Wouldn't It Be Loverly?," "Get Me to the Church on Time," "A Hymn to Him," "With a Little Bit of Luck," "Show Me," "I'm an Ordinary Man," "I've Grown Accustomed to Her Face" from *My Fair Lady*; "All at Once You Love Her," "The Man I Used to Be," "Everybody's Got a Home but Me" from *Pipe Dream*; "The Most Happy Fella," "My Heart Is So Full of You," "Joey, Joey, Joey," "Big D," "Warm All Over," "Standing on the Corner" from *The Most Happy Fella*; "Mr. Wonderful," "Too Close for Comfort" from *Mr. Wonderful*.

Song of the Season

1956–1957 SEASON

For various reasons, the season's four top musicals have—over the years—fallen under the radar and are rarely revived today. *Bells Are Ringing* has a serviceable libretto by Betty Comden and Adolph Green, who also wrote some commendable lyrics for Jule Styne's first-rate music. It was a star vehicle for Judy Holliday and she stayed with the show (except for brief vacations) for all of its 924-performance run. The season's runner-up was *Li'l Abner* at 693 performances. There was no star except for the popular Al Capp comic strip itself. Again the score, by Gene De Paul (music) and Johnny Mercer (lyrics), was splendid. The star for *New Girl in Town* was Gwen Verdon who was able to make a serious libretto, based on a Eugene O'Neill drama, palatable thanks to her dancing abilities. The admirable score was by Bob Merrill and Bob Fosse provided the spirited choreography. It received mixed notices (except for Verdon) but still ran a profitable 432 performances. The Ethel Merman vehicle *Happy Hunting* had a run just shy of that. The libretto and score were not nearly as accomplished as the other three shows but Merman was still box office insurance. Does this mean that *Bells Are Ringing*, *New Girl in Town*, and *Happy Hunting* are no longer produceable without stars? And is the world of *Li'l Abner* totally lost on modern audiences? Or were these four musicals for 1956–57 and not for the ages?

Ironically, the season's biggest disappointment turned out to be a musical that is frequently revived today. *Candide* was a highly anticipated musical boasting impressive credentials: a libretto by distinguished playwright Lillian Hellman, music by Leonard Bernstein, lyrics by acclaimed poet Richard Wilbur and others, all under the direction of the internationally celebrated Tyrone Guthrie. But Voltaire's novella was much trickier source material than anyone had anticipated and the libretto, trying to combine eighteenth-century satire and Broadway musical comedy, failed to work and *Candide* closed in nine weeks. The score was so brilliant that over the years efforts were made to revive and repair the musical but not until 1974 were the difficulties solved and *Candide* was finally a hit. Until that time, the show was a beloved cast album and an overture that was favored around the world.

The rest of the season was mostly revues, two of which ran. Leonard Sillman's *New Faces of 1956* featured some performers who went on to notable careers: Jane Connell, John Reardon, Maggie Smith, Tiger Haynes, Inga Swenson, Virginia Martin, and Bill McCutcheon. Also with a future were some of the writers and composers, as with Dean Fuller, Marshall Barer, Arthur Siegel, and Neil Simon. The revue ran 221 performances, one of the longest in the *New Faces* series. A cast of more familiar faces could be found in *Ziegfeld Follies of 1957*, an attempt to recall the most famous revue series of all. But this was not a lavish affair and the material was routine so it fell to such performers as Beatrice Lillie, Billy De Wolf, Harold Lang, Carol Lawrence, and Jane Morgan to keep this *Follies* on the boards for 123 performances.

> "The Party's Over"
> Music by Jule Styne; lyric by Betty Comden, Adolph Green
> From *Bells Are Ringing* (1956)
> Sung by Judy Holliday as Ella Peterson

When Betty Comden and Adolph Green were writing a torch song for Ella Peterson (Judy Holliday) to sing in *Bells Are Ringing*, they decided to use a party as a metaphor. Ella has long been in love with the writer Jeff Moss (Sydney Chaplin) but just as it looked as if things were going her way, the romance exploded. This is a very traditional set-up for a musical comedy torch song; not tragic but hurtful enough that the show can get serious for three minutes. Instead of taking the "my heart is breaking" path, Ella looks at the affair that wasn't as if it were a wonderful party and everything was bliss. Then comes the let-down. The brief verse sets up the party motif by telling one (herself?) to throw away the confetti, put away the horns and funny hats, and face the facts. The refrain continues the metaphor also addressing the *you*: "Just make, your mind up/The piper must be paid."[17] Other party images follow: candles burning out, dancing coming to an end, the need to stop dreaming about it all. The release is even more direct, addressing "my friend" which could only be herself. "Take off your makeup," she sings; "it's all over, my friend." It is a clever lyric but not too gimmicky or contrived. Jule Styne's music is not too somber but has enough minor chords that one suspects heartbreak under self-aware words. Styne does something unusual in the music for the release. The first three phrases ("Now you must wake up, all dreams must end,/ Take off your makeup") echo each other musically but when he comes to the title phrase, he changes key, drops down quickly, and then remains in the lower register for "It's all over, my friend." Ending the song with the blunt word "friend" instead of an open vowel is also unusual. It gives a finality to the song that is as harsh as it is engaging.

Judy Holliday introduced "The Party's Over" on Broadway and in the 1957 London version of *Bells Are Ringing* it was sung by Janet Blair. Holliday recorded "The Party's Over" for the Broadway cast album and for the soundtrack for the 1960 movie version of *Bells Are Ringing*. Carmen McRae made a disc of the song before the show opened on Broadway but it was Doris Day's recording with Frank De Vol's Orchestra that stayed on the *Billboard* chart for eleven weeks. Of the 100 or so recordings are notable ones by Nat King Cole, Lonnie Donegan, Shirley Bassey, Bobby Darin, Robie Lester, Lesley Gore, Seth MacFarlane, the Lettermen, Polly Bergen, Wynton Marsalis, Matt Monro, Willie Nelson, Judy Kuhn, Helen Reddy, Kelli O'Hara, Van Morrison, Leslie Odom, Jr., and Johanna Pettersson. Faith Prince sang the number in the 2001 Broadway revival of *Bells Are Ringing*.

Other notable songs from that season: "Just in Time," "Drop That Name," "It's a Perfect Relationship," "I'm Going Back," "Long Before I Knew You" from *Bells Are Ringing*; "The Best of All Possible Worlds," "Glitter and Be Gay," "Make Our Garden Grow," "Oh, Happy We!," "What's the Use?," "I Am Easily Assimilated" from *Candide*; "Mutual Admiration Society" from *Happy Hunting*; "The Country's in the Very Best of Hands," "If I Had My Druthers," "Jubilation T. Cornpone," "Namely You" from *Li'l Abner*; "It's Good to Be Alive," "Sunshine Girl," "Flings" from *New Girl in Town*.

1957–1958 SEASON

Could there be two musicals (and two scores) as different as *The Music Man* and *West Side Story*? Those were the two most significant musicals of the season, a season filled with very diverse options for Broadway playgoers. Because of its nostalgic look at the past, *The Music Man* is sometimes inaccurately described as old-fashioned and even corny. Yet Meredith Willson's re-creation of life in a small Iowa town early in the century is satiric in many ways. The view of River City is from decades later and the characters and situations are comic rather than naively nostalgic. Willson's score is a masterly handling of the sounds of Americana. What other musical has used barbershop quartets, piano lesson scales, auctioneer patter, square dancing, ragtime, and march music all in one score? Leonard Bernstein's music for *West Side Story* is also very diverse: jazz, Latin, blues, vaudeville, swing, and opera. The *Romeo and Juliet*-based libretto is tragic and firmly set in the urban 1950s. *The Music Man* is musical comedy and set so far in the past that no one can recall it first hand. That is why it never dates. It ran for 1,375 performances; *West Side Story* ran only half that. A final comparison: young Stephen Sondheim made his Broadway debut with his lyrics for *West Side Story*; veteran musical director Meredith Willson also made his debut that season, writing the score and co-writing the libretto for *The Music Man*. For Sondheim, it was the start of a brilliant career; for Willson, it was his only long-run hit.

There were other profitable musicals that season but, because they are very rarely revived, are little known today. The Lena Horne vehicle *Jamaica* was not just a star turn but a caustic look at tropical island living. The songs by Harold Arlen and E. Y. Harburg are expert but so satiric they were little recorded. All the same, *Jamaica* played 558 times. Another satiric show, *Say, Darling,* is only a footnote in musical theatre history but the Jule Styne-Betty Comden-Adolph Green backstager ran 332 performances without benefit of stars. It was a slightly disguised recreation of the making of the hit musical *The Pajama Game* with names changed to protect the not-so-innocent. There was much to recommend in: Langston Hughes' African American folk comedy *Simply Heavenly*; the merry *Oh, Captain!* with Tony Randall leading a double life; the Nancy Walker vehicle *Copper and Brass*; and the boxing musical *The Body Beautiful* with the first full score by Jerry Bock (music) and Sheldon Harnick (lyric). None ran long enough to pay the bills.

"Seventy-Six Trombones"
Music and lyric by Meredith Willson
From *The Music Man* (1957)
Sung by Robert Preston as Harold Hill, and townspeople;
reprised by Barbara Cook as Marion Paroo

Song of the Season

The familiar march "Seventy-Six Trombones" has been around long enough that most assume the composition to be an old march piece going back to the days of John Philip Sousa. Composer Meredith Willson actually did go back that far (as a young man he played flute in Sousa's legendary band) and he drew on his experiences with performing marches to create Broadway's most famous march. In the world of marching bands, the arranger is the star. Most marches don't even have lyrics and, if they do, they have long fallen by the wayside. For example, two of Broadway's most popular marches—Sousa's "El Capitan March" and Victor Herbert's "March of the Toys"—have quite accomplished lyrics but are rarely heard. Such is the case with "Seventy-Six Trombones." Willson's lyric is compelling but the song is often an instrumental outside of *The Music Man*. On Broadway, marches are usually sung by a male chorus. In *The Music Man*, "Seventy-six Trombones" is a complete mini-musical that builds from a solo to a choral song and dance. It is also important to the plot, as it should be in an integrated musical. "Professor" Harold Hill (Robert Preston) needs to inform the citizens of River City, Iowa, that their youth is in danger and a boys' band is the solution. He creates panic with the song "(Ya Got) Trouble" soon after he arrives. At the Fourth of July festivities in the school gym, Hill comes forward again and reprises "Trouble" with a new lyric that sets up his idea for a boys' band. "I can deal with the trouble, friends, with a wave of my hand," he promises. The solution? "I'm here to organize a River City's boys' band." Soon Hill is recalling the great bands in the nation, conjuring up a vision of the day he saw the greatest conference of marching bands ever. Such legendary band conductors as Gillmore, Liberati, Pat Conway, The Great Creatore, W.C. Handy, and John Phillip Sousa are listed. All of the mentioned men are real but the possibility of all of them together in one place and time is hyperbole. In fact, the whole song is exaggeration grown from the excitement of the moment. Just the numbers alone in the lyric are laughable. The refrain starts with such impressive numbers as seventy-six trombones and 110 cornets, "followed by rows and rows of the finest virtuosos,/ The cream of ev'ry famous band."[18] In the succeeding refrains, the list of instruments and the big numbers continue with lively imagery: "There were more than a thousand reeds springing up like weeds." Hill imitates the sounds of some of the instruments, as with the tympani "thundering, thundering, all along the way" and each bassoon "having his big fat say!" There are even descriptions of the orchestrations, as with the trumpets "who'd improvise a full octave higher than the score" and those trombones playing in "counter point." It is a vigorous and stimulating lyric that one believes could mesmerize an entire town. As for Willson's music, it has the qualities of the very best marches: strong on melody, forceful climbing and descending notes, a clear shift in the release ("There were copper bottom tympani in horse platoons …") for variety sake, and a finale that easily leads into a repetition of previous music. In *The Music Man*, the townspeople pick up the song and that eventually leads into a zesty dance by the younger members of the crowd. In all, it is a potent scene of musical theatre.

A few minutes before this rigorous scene, Marian (Barbara Cook) sings the wistful lullaby "Goodnight, My Someone." It has the same melody as "Seventy-Six Trombones" but is played in 3/4 time at a slower tempo. Willson links Hill and Marian musically (and very subtly) from the beginning but it is rarely noticed by the audience. Near the end of the musical, things are more obvious as Marion and Hill sing lines from "Seventy-Six Trombones" and "Goodnight My Someone" in alternation with each other. This is not a new idea. The technique is frequently used in opera, but one must look far and wide for such a musical device used in a Broadway musical. Such is the musical prowess of Willson. Robert Preston's rendition of "Seventy-Six Trombones" was a highlight of the original Broadway production. In the 1961 London production, Van Johnson played Hill and sang the number. The original cast album of *The Music Man* was released in early 1958 and was a big seller; even more so was the 1962 movie soundtrack also featuring Preston. Vocal and choral versions of "Seventy-Six Trombones" are not as numerous as orchestra and marching band recordings but the song has been well covered by a variety of artists, including Fred Waring and the Pennsylvanians, the Four Saints, Ethel Smith, Michael Bond, Jimmy McPartland's All-Stars, Edmund Hockridge, Henry Mancini, Howard Keel, André Rieu, the Cliff Adams Singers, Dick Wickman, Tom Hazelton, the Dixieland Ramblers, and Dave Ruffner. In the 2003 television adaptation of *The Music Man*, Matthew Broderick played Hill and led the ensemble in the song. On Broadway there have been three revivals of the musical and "Seventy-Six Trombones" has been sung by such Harold Hills as Dick Van Dyke in 1980, Craig Bierko in 2000, and Hugh Jackman in 2022.

Other notable songs from that season: "Till There Was You," "Goodnight, My Someone," "(Ya Got) Trouble," "Lida Rose/Will I Ever Tell You?," "Marian the Librarian," "My White Knight" from *The Music Man*; "Tonight," "Somewhere," "Maria," "I Feel Pretty," "Something's Comin'," "The Jet Song," "Gee, Officer Krupke," "Cool," "America," "A Boy Like That/I Have a Love" from *The West Side Story*; "Push De Button," "Cocoanut Sweet," "Monkey in the Mango Tree," "Ain't It the Truth" from *Jamaica*.

Song of the Season

1958–1959 SEASON

Although *Gypsy* was the crowning achievement of the 1958–59 season, two long-forgotten musicals ran longer than the Arthur Laurents-Jule Styne-Stephen Sondheim classic. At the time, *Gypsy* was classified as an Ethel Merman vehicle but time has shown that this musical was outstanding in every element. While it still needs a star to survive on Broadway, *Gypsy* has been successfully presented everywhere without one. The two shows that ran longer than *Gypsy*'s 702-performance run were the French revue *La Plume de Ma Tante* and the Harold Rome musical *Destry Rides Again* based on the vibrant 1939 film. Both were highly entertaining but of little substance, relying on some fine performances, clever staging, and raucous choreography to run so long. Much more satisfying was *Flower Drum Song*, Rodgers and Hammerstein's musical comedy with a mostly Asian cast and a highly proficient score. After the regretful *Me and Juliet* and *Pipe Dream*, R&H had a solid hit with *Flower Drum Song* at 600 performances. Almost as entertaining were the musical murder mystery *Redhead* staring Gwen Verdon and the Hollywood spoof *Goldilocks* featuring Elaine Stritch. Both musicals had some commendable songs but problematic librettos. One was hard pressed to find competent songs, or much else, in the unsuccessful musicals *Whoop-Up* and *First Impressions*. The former was an unfunny comedy set on a Montana reservation for Native Americans and the latter was an unnecessary adaptation of Jane Austen's *Pride and Prejudice*. Another adaptation, *Juno* based on the Sean O'Casey tragedy *Juno and the Paycock*, was a compelling musical play with a top-notch score by Marc Blitzstein and powerful performances by Shirley Booth and Melvyn Douglas. Too grim for mainstream tastes, *Juno* closed after two weeks but has been revived on occasion—something which could not be said for almost all of this season's offerings.

As the 1950s came to a close, rock and roll had firmly established itself on the music scene and both country-western and rhythm and blues moved out of the specialty category to become more mainstream. Yet there were still many recordings of Broadway songs by various artists and orchestras. Show tunes may not have appeared on many charts but there was still a viable audience for such recordings. Theatre songs were also a staple on television variety shows. It was a situation that would fade away during the next decade.

"I Enjoy Being a Girl"
Music by Richard Rodgers; lyric by Oscar Hammerstein
From *Flower Drum Song* (1958)
Sung by Pat Suzuki as Linda Low

While *Gypsy* had by far the best score of the season and all of the songs are now familiar Broadway icons, the Styne-Sondheim score is so efficiently integrated into the plot and characters that few numbers have found wide success away from the show. Rodgers and Hammerstein's score for *Flower Drum Song*, on the other hand, produced a popular ditty that was heard everywhere. In the context of *Flower Drum Song*, "I Enjoy Being a Girl" is a boastful celebration by Asian-American Linda Low (Pat Suzuki) of her assimilation into American culture. Outside of the musical, the vivacious number is a more a list of superficial feminine attributes used to dazzle men. The song bubbles with an enthusiasm that many women might consider cloying today but, for a 1950s woman discovering her New World charms as she tosses off ancient Chinese views, it is quite appropriate. "I Enjoy Being a Girl" is Linda's "I am" song in *Flower Drum Song* but the number soon became a kind of anthem for femininity and for decades was used thousands of times for beauty pageants and fashion shows.

Like much of the score for *Flower Drum Song*, the song is contemporary and jazzy. There is no trace of the Asian musical motifs that Rodgers uses so effectively in some of the other songs. In fact, "I Enjoy Being a Girl" is a very American-sounding march, a tune propelled forward so confidently that it might be a political rally sing-along or a college fight song. It also has one of Rodgers' most catchy melodies with musical phrases that stick in the head like a television jingle. (Not surprisingly, the song has been used in radio and television commercials.) Hammerstein's lyric is so playful that it borders on mockery. In the verse, Linda uses such expressions as curvy, swivelly, and swervy to describe her shape and compares herself to "a filly who is ready for the race."[19] The refrains list clichés about women's efforts to look beautiful (a new hairdo, curling one's eyelashes, cold cream on the face, etc.) and the results (teeth like pearls, silky curls of hair, a shape which causes men to whistle). As much as Linda enjoys all this, she has a goal. "My future I hope will be/ In the home of a brave and free male/ Who'll enjoy being a guy, having a girl like me!" Today all this can be considered politically incorrect and an insult to the empowerment of women but in 1950s context the lyric expresses ideas that were very familiar to many women. Of course, the manner in which "I Enjoy Being a Girl" is delivered makes all the difference. Pat Suzuki's rendition in the original Broadway production was frivolous but self aware. The song was sung in a similar manner by Yama Suki in the 1960 London production. Nancy Kwan (dubbed by B. J. Baker) does not take herself too seriously in the 1961 movie version of *Flower Drum Song*. In a much-revised revival on Broadway in 2002, the song was turned into a nightclub act and Sandra Allen sang it with merry sarcasm. There have been a few dozen recordings of "I Enjoy Being a Girl" with memorable disks by Doris Day, Barbara McNair, Florence Henderson, Yama Saki, Diana Trask, Roseanne Barr, Lea Salonga, the Studebakers, Deborah Gibson, Ena Baga, Helena Blackman, and Debbie Gravitte. In the late 1960s, the transgender activist Christine Jorgenson performed "I Enjoy Being a Girl" in nightclubs and it has become a favorite of drag queens in clubs and revues.

Other notable songs from that season: "You Are Beautiful," "Love, Look Away," "A Hundred Million Miracles," "Grant Avenue," "Don't Marry Me" from *Flower Drum Song*; "Everything's Coming Up Rose," "Some People," "You Gotta Have a Gimmick," "Small World," "Let Me Entertain You," "All I Need Is the Girl," "If Mamma Was Married," "You'll Never Get Away from Me," "Together Wherever We Go" from *Gypsy*; "I Know Your Kind," "Respectability" from *Destry Rides Again*; "We're Alive," "I Wish It So," "Bird Upon the Tree" from *Juno*; "The Beast in You," "I Never Know When to Say When," "Who's Been Sleeping in My Chair?" from *Goldilocks*; "(I Feel) Merely Marvelous," "Look Who's in Love" from *Redhead*.

1959–1960 SEASON

The 1950s went out with one of the strongest seasons on record. There were only twenty-four musicals on Broadway, nine of them revivals, but the quality was thrilling. Even some of the unprofitable also-rans had some laudable songs, solid librettos, and estimable performances. Looking over the list of veteran and new songwriters represented this season may help explain why musical theatregoing was such a joy in 1959–60. The seasoned professionals Rodgers and Hammerstein, Harold Arlen, Johnny Mercer, Frank Loesser, Bob Merrill, Sammy Fain, Paul Francis Webster, and Albert Hague were joined by newcomers Mary Rodgers and Marshall Barer, Jerry Bock and Sheldon Harnick, Charles Strouse and Lee Adams, Tom Jones and Harvey Schmidt, and Fred Ebb. They didn't all score hit shows but the uncommon talent was evident. Rodgers and Hammerstein were once again on top, their *The Sound of Music* running 1,443 performances. Sadly, it was the team's last Broadway production; Hammerstein died nine months after *The Sound of Music* opened. Their second time out, Bock and Harnick struck gold with *Fiorello!* about the beloved New York City Fiorello La Guardia who had passed away in 1947. So many New Yorkers recalled La Guardia with affection that *Fiorello!* played 795 times. As memories of the "Little Flower" faded, so did the musical. Despite its many attributes, *Fiorello!* is rarely produced today. That cannot be said about *Bye Birdie Birdie,* the Strouse and Lee musical which gently satirized the power that rock and roll had over American teenagers. It ran 607 performances on the Street and forever in schools, community theatres, and summer stock. Jackie Gleason helped the Bob Merrill musical *Take Me Along* run over a year but stars couldn't save the mammoth epic musical *Saratoga*, based on Edna Ferber's novel *Saratoga Trunk*. The Arlen-Mercer score and director Morton DaCosta's libretto were riddled with problems and, despite fine performances by Carol Lawrence, Howard Keel, and Carol Brice, and an eye-popping production designed by Cecil Beaton, *Saratoga* struggled to run ten weeks before closing deep in the red. Perhaps more frustrating was *Greenwillow* which boasted one of Frank Loesser's best scores. The charming rural story was perhaps too thin to sustain a full-length musical and, despite heartfelt performances throughout, *Greenwillow* also had to close after ten weeks. While the revues *A Thurber Carnival, At the Drop of a Hat,* and *Billy Barnes Revue* enjoyed decent runs, the star-studded *The Girls Against the Boys* featuring Bert Lahr and Nancy Walker closed within two weeks. Running no longer was the revue *From A to Z* which had such performers as Hermione Gingold, Paula Stewart, Bob Dishy, Stuart Damon, Virginia Vestoff, and Alvin Epstein. In the 1960s, it would be more and more difficult for a revue to run on Broadway and turn a profit.

Some of this season's hits came from Off-Broadway, a sign that Broadway would someday be only a portion of the musical activity in New York City. The operetta pastiche *Little Mary Sunshine* pleased audiences for 1,143 performances. Mary Rodgers' delightful fairy tale musical *Once Upon a Mattress* sold out its Off-Broadway run and came to Broadway this season where it had to move from theatre to theatre because it kept selling tickets beyond its limited engagements. By the time it closed, *Once Upon a*

Song of the Season

Mattress had run 460 times and made Carol Burnett a star. The legendary little musical *The Fantasticks* began its forty-two-year run this season. Besides bringing recognition to creators Jones and Schmidt and providing the first small musical to be produced around the world, *The Fantasticks* put Off-Broadway on the musical map, so to speak. Never again would it be ignored or overlooked and before long Broadway would find itself depending more and more on Off-Broadway.

"Do Re Mi"
Music by Richard Rodgers; lyric by Oscar Hammerstein
From *The Sound of Music* (1959)
Sung by Mary Martin as Maria, and the Von Trapp children

Ask any person—adult or child—on the street if they have ever heard of any of the songs in this book, the one ditty that they would recognize most likely would be "Do Re Me." It is not thought of as a theatre song but rather a silly little tune that one just knows. It is difficult to imagine a world before "Do Re Mi" and *The Sound of Music*. How would one understand anything about music without this song? If one told you "Do Re Mi" was an old children's song going back to the Middle Ages, you might believe it. It is so simple and unpoetic it must have come from the time of the plagues. And like those ancient children's ditties, "Do Re Mi" is hopelessly convoluted. The female deer for Doe (musically Do), "the drop of holden sun" for Ray (musically Re), and calling oneself Me make some kind of sense, as does Sew (for So) involving a needle and thread.[20] But how did "Fa" become "Far"? And is there no other way to describe "La" except to say it follows "So"? And where else but in a children's nursery rhyme in England does "tea" immediately call to mind jam and bread? Is this the stupidest song Rodgers and Hammerstein ever wrote?

Actually, it is not. "Do Re Mi" is an example of a solfège, a method used in Western music education to teach such things as aural skills, voice pitch, and sight-reading of music. In English the pattern is given the sounds of do, re, mi, fa, so la, and ti. Because in each foreign language the sounds differ, the solfèges are quite different. And in each case the effort to give a word meaning to each sound is, well, stupid. At best it is nonsense, but Maria (Mary Martin) is a nun-in-training and when she finds out the Von Trapp kids don't know music at all, she whips out her guitar and starts to teach them. It may sound like an excuse to say that Hammerstein's lyric is supposed to sound like a nun improvising on the spot but that probably was what was going through his mind when he wrote the song. Some believe that the feeble "la—a note to follow sew" was a dummy lyric, something temporary to be polished later. Hammerstein was dying of cancer at the time so maybe there was no "later." In any case, "Do Re Mi" is a lyric that fulfills the primary concern of the lesson: it's easy to remember. But what of Rodgers' music? It must have been easy to take the lyric, place each sound word on the appropriate note and you've got a song. Actually, what you've got is a scale and Rodgers felt so hemmed in by having to return to a scale that he turned to dance music arranger Trude Rittman to help him. Rittman was some kind of genius who fully understood dance and music and had worked on many Rodgers shows. (It was Rittman who composed most of the music for "The Small House of Uncle Thomas" number in *The King and I*.) She came up with the embellishments that Maria magically creates using the scale for an actual tune. Hammerstein's lyric is another piece of childish nonsense: "When you know the notes to sing,/ You can sing most anything." From this point, Rodgers is able to move far enough from the scale and turn Rittman's variations into a merry march. It is a remarkable musical number and does more for *The Sound of Music* than fill in a musical spot. If the average American knows anything at all about music, it probably stems from "Do Re Mi."

For such a simplistic ditty, "Do Re Mi" has been recorded many times by very different artists. Percy Faith and his Orchestra made a disc the same month that *The Sound of Music* opened on Broadway. The original cast album of the musical came out soon after and it was a bestseller. Other early recordings were made by Anita Bryant with Monty Kelly's Orchestra, John Senati (vocal by Bill Jacob), Jimmie Dodd, and the actual Von Trapp Singers now middle-aged adults and still singing professionally. Other recordings of note include those by Doris Day with Jimmy Joyce, Benny Goodman, the Cliff Adams Singers, Dinah Shore, the Merrymen, Connie Francis, Blackwater Junction, Bob McGrath, Dusty Springfield, Harry Connick, Jr., Jenn Gambatese, John Bucchino, and the Harry Allen Quintet. The song is most remembered as Julie Andrews singing it with the children in the 1965 film version of *The Sound of Music*. Rebecca Luker played Maria and sang it in the 1998 Broadway revival of the musical and Carrie Underwood sang it in the 2013 television adaptation.

Other notable songs from that season: "The Sound of Music," "Climb Every Mountain," "Edelweiss," "My Favorite Things" from *The Sound of Music*; "Shy," "In a Little While," "Normandy" from *Once Upon a Mattress*; "Try to Remember," "Soon It's Gonna Rain," "They Were You," "Much More," "I Can See It" from *The Fantasticks* (Off-Broadway); "Take Me Along," "Staying Young," "I Get Embarrassed" from *Take Me Along*; "Colorado Love Call," "Look for a Sky of Blue" from *Little Mary Sunshine* (Off-Broadway); "Politics and Poker," "Little Tin Box," "When Did I Fall in Love?" "Till Tomorrow" from *Fiorello!*; "The Music of Home," "Never Will I Marry," "Faraway Boy," "Summertime Love," "Walking Away Whistling" from *Greenwillow*; "Put on a Happy Face," "Kids," "A Lot of Livin' to Do," "Baby, Talk to Me," "One Boy" from *Bye Bye Birdie*; "A Game of Poker," "Love Held Lightly" from *Saratoga*.

1960–1961
SEASON

Most of the musicals this season suffered from libretto problems but that didn't keep five shows from running 400 performances or more. Despite various imperfections, several musicals had much to offer. The long-run champ this season was *Camelot*, which is surprising since it opened to unenthusiastic reviews. Because so much of the musical's personnel had worked on *My Fair Lady*, expectations were high—probably unreasonably high. Most of the complaints were about Alan Jay Lerner's libretto which tried to put so much of T. H. White's massive novel *The Once and Future King* on stage. The press was also negative about the score by Lerner and Frederick Loewe, though time has shown it to be an exceptionally fine set of songs. Playgoers were not so critical and enjoyed Richard Burton and Julie Andrews (and their replacements) and the sumptuous production for 873 performances. The only musical this season that was wholeheartedly approved of by the critics was *Carnival*. The poignant story and fragile characters were matched by Bob Merrill's delicate songs resulting in a beautifully understated musical that pleased audiences for 719 performances. Also getting a critical drubbing but finding success anyway were Meredith Willson's robust and rural musical *The Unsinkable Molly Brown* starring Tammy Grimes; the amusing take on the juke box business titled *Do Re Mi* with a score by Jule Styne, Betty Comden, and Adolph Green, and some first-class clowning by Phil Silvers and Nancy Walker; and the French musical *Irma la Douce* which arrived on Broadway in a London production. Then there were those musicals that didn't quite work but had some high-quality elements. Such was the case with the satiric *Tenderloin* with a superb score by Jerry Bock and Sheldon Harnick; the Lucille Ball vehicle *Wildcat* with songs by Cy Coleman (music) and Carolyn Leigh (lyrics); the musical version of the ancient comedy *Lysistrata* retitled *The Happiest Girl in the World* which used Jacques Offenbach music for its score; and the revue *Show Girl* starring Carol Channing. Because of ever-rising costs, musicals had to run close to a year to earn a profit so producers were pulling the plug on faltering shows earlier than ever. This resulted in more musicals closing after a few weeks (or, in some cases, a few days) than in the past. Show business was becoming more and more of a risky business on Broadway.

"If Ever I Would Leave You"
Music by Frederick Loewe; lyric by Alan Jay Lerner
From *Camelot* (1960)
Sung by Robert Goulet as Sir Lancelot

Song of the Season

A favorite device of lyricist Alan Jay Lerner is to structure a song in three or four parts, each section an example or about a particular person. He did it in "There but for You Go I" in *Brigadoon*, in "A Hymn to Him" and "With a Little Bit of Luck" in *My Fair Lady*, and in this season's *Camelot* with "Then You May Take Me to the Fair" and "What Do the Simple Folk Do?" But Lerner's most famous song using this format is "If Ever I Would Leave You" sung by Sir Lancelot (Robert Goulet) to Queen Guenevere (Julie Andrews) at the top of Act Two of *Camelot*. The structure of the song is the conventional AABA pattern with a season of the year used in each section. There is no verse and the lyric gets to the point in the first refrain. Lancelot could never leave Guenevere in summer with "Your hair streaked with sun-light,/ Your lips red as flame,/ Your face with a lustre that puts gold to shame!"[1] This is followed by reasons he cannot leave her in autumn, winter, and spring, concluding with "Summer, winter or fall!/ No, never could I leave you at all!" Lerner's imagery in the song is highly poetic but, as is often the case, more intelligent than gushing. Lancelot sings of how Guenevere "sparkles/When fall nips the air" and how in winter her face catches "the fire's glow." Loewe's music is in the flowing operetta mode with each section starting low then, using a series of ascending musical phrases, climaxes at the end of each refrain. The release is unusual in the way it is confined to a narrow range in the lower register. "If Ever I Would Leave You" made a strong first impression on audiences, no doubt helped by newcomer Goulet who sang it so beautifully. In the tradition of Broadway baritones Alfred Drake and John Raitt and Hollywood's Howard Keel and Gordon MacRae, Goulet was the dashing leading man that musicals depended on. Also, since Richard Burton was not a singer, King Arthur never gets the kind of sweeping ballad like this.

Close to the time that the original cast album of *Camelot* was released, Goulet made a pop version of "If Ever I Would Leave You" and there were discs by Vic Damone and Gordon MacRae. These were followed by approximately eighty other recordings, including those by Billy Eckstine, Mel Tormé and Margaret Whiting, Aretha Franklin, Chuck Mangione Quintet, Jan Peerce, Ed Ames, Tom Jones, Roger Whittaker, Chris Bennett, Colm Wilkinson, Beegie Adair, Sharon Reuben, Shoshana Bean, Brian Stokes Mitchell, Eric Wyatt, and Jessamyn Anderson. In the 1964 London production of *Camelot*, Lancelot was played by Barry Kent who sang "If Ever I Would Leave You." It was sung by Franco Nero (dubbed by Gene Merlino) in the 1967 movie version of the musical. There have been five Broadway revivals of *Camelot* in which the song was sung by Richard Muenz in 1980 and again in 1981, Steve Blanchard in 1993, James Barbour in 2011, and Jordan Donica in 2023.

Other notable songs from that season: "Camelot," "The Lusty Month of May," "The Seven Deadly Virtues," "Before I Gaze at You Again," "What Do the Simple Folk Do?," "I Loved You Once in Silence" from *Camelot*; "Love Makes the World Go Round," "Always, Always You," "Her Face" from *Carnival*; "Our Language of Love,"

"Dis-Donc" from *Irma la Douce*; "Little Old New York," "Artificial Flowers," "The Picture of Happiness" from *Tenderloin*; "I Ain't Down Yet," "I'll Never Say No," "Belly Up to the Bar, Boys" from *The Unsinkable Molly Brown*; "What Takes My Fancy," "Hey, Look Me Over" from *Wildcat*; "Make Someone Happy," "Adventure" from *Do Re Mi*; "Adrift on a Star" from *The Happiest Girl in the World*.

Song of the Season

1961–1962 SEASON

There were more new musicals this season (seventeen, three of which were revues) and, even better, most of them were quite pleasing. So it is sad to report that only three made money. The reason: the average age of the Broadway theatregoer was getting higher and higher and so were tickets prices. Possibly Broadway no longer had enough playgoers to keep more than a limited number of shows running a long time. The two biggest hits, both with long-running titles as well, were *A Funny Thing Happened on the Way to the Forum* and *How to Succeed in Business without Really Trying* (hereafter *Forum* and *How to Succeed*). They were not only hits in their day but quickly entered the repertoire of oft-revived musicals. The third profitable musical was Richard Rodgers' *No Strings* with top-notch performances (Richard Kiley and Diahann Carroll), a fine score (music and lyrics by Rodgers), and an intelligent book about an interracial romance. *Kwamina* was also about a mixed couple and it too had a skillful book and a masterful score but audiences were not interested and it closed in a month. Other admirable musicals that ran only a few months were *The Gay Life, Sail Away, Kean, A Family Affair, All American,* and *Bravo, Giovanni*. It used to be that a musical that ran 100 performances was a moneymaker. Several shows this season ran that or twice that and still couldn't turn a profit. *Milk and Honey, I Can Get It for You Wholesale,* and *Subways Are for Sleeping* fell into this category. On the bright side, it was a season that introduced some notable songwriters and librettists: Jerry Herman, John Kander, James and William Goldman, Peter Stone, Mel Brooks, Stephen Sondheim (as a composer), and Richard Rodgers (as a lyricist).

"Comedy Tonight"
Music and lyric by Stephen Sondheim
From *A Funny Thing Happened on the Way to the Forum* (1962)
Sung by Zero Mostel as Pseudolus, and company

Although Stephen Sondheim found respect, if not much recognition, writing the lyrics for *West Side Story* (1957) and *Gypsy* (1959), he did not get to compose for Broadway until *Forum*. Even then, the critics were more enamored of his lyrics in the musical farce than his music. It took years before the composer Sondheim was acknowledged and today there is great appreciation for his music in *Forum*. The opening number, "Comedy Tonight," is a good example of this late recognition. It was sung by the slave Pseudolus (Zero Mostel) as an exposition piece that introduced the characters and the comic situation. The music is a sportive march that actually sounds funny. The lyric is a series of short phrases that keep in step with the 4/4 time. Included are things that the show is not (kings, crowns, tragedy, anything portentous or polite, a Trojan horse) as well as what is in store ("lovers, liars and clowns" and "a happy ending of course").[2] "Comedy Tonight" is a mock military march that speeds up on occasion. By the time the song climaxes, the phrases (musically and lyrically) get shorter and Sondheim uses a Cole Porter-like devise as the number moves into a list song filled with delightful feminine rhymes: "tunics/eunuchs … panderers/philanderers … tumblers/grumblers//bumblers/fumblers." Included is a famous arch rhyme—"gaudy/bawdy/everybawdy"—that is reminiscent of Lorenz Hart at his silliest. The lyric is a marvel but the music is also superior. The song remains one of Sondheim's most recognized tunes. "Comedy Tonight" starts the musical off with a bang but it didn't come easily. Sondheim wrote a highly satiric piece for the opening titled "Invocation" but director George Abbott thought it too esoteric. So Sondheim wrote a sweet soft-shoe number titled "Love Is in the Air" that was quietly engaging but all wrong for the farce that followed. When Jerome Robbins was brought in during the out-of-town tryouts, he pointed out the inconsistency and urged Sondheim to go back to a rhythmic march but one that was simple and straightforward. "Comedy Tonight" is far from simple and its humor is sometimes tricky but it certainly works. Legend has it that by changing the opening number, *Forum* played like gangbusters. Of course things were improved by Robbins' staging of the number, adding low humor and high style.

In the 1963 London production of the musical, Pseudolus was played by British comic Frankie Howerd. The 1966 film version of *Forum* jettisoned most of the score but "Comedy Tonight" was retained and it was again sung by Mostel. Jason Alexander sang it in the Broadway revue *Jerome Robbins' Broadway* (1989), Julia McKenzie, Millicent Martin, and David Kernan performed it in the revue *Side by Side by Sondheim* (1977), and the cast of *Sondheim on Sondheim* (2010) sang it as well. In various Broadway revivals of *Forum* it was sung by Phil Silvers, Nathan Lane, and Whoopie Goldberg. Because it is not a ballad, "Comedy Tonight" has not received a large number of recordings. In addition to cast albums, the song was recorded by Bob Gunton, Frankie Howerd, the Tony Hatch Singers, Jackie Cain and Roy Kral, Jill Perryman, and the Trotter Trio.

Other notable songs from that season: "Everybody Ought to Have a Maid," "I'm Calm," "Lovely" from *A Funny Thing Happened on the Forum*; "Once Upon a Time" from *All American*; "I Believe in You," "Brotherhood of Man," "Grand Old Ivy," "A Secretary Is Not a Toy" from *How to Succeed in Business without Really Trying*; "No Strings," "The Sweetest Sounds," "Nobody Told Me" from *No Strings*; "Magic Moment," "Come A-Wandering with Me" from *The Gay Life*; "Milk and Honey," "Shalom" from *Milk and Honey*; "Miss Marmelstein," "Have I Told You Lately?," "The Sound of Money" from *I Can Get It for You Wholesale*; "Nothing More to Look Forward To," "Another Time, Another Place" from *Kwamina*; "Sail Away," "Why Do the Wrong People Travel (While the Right People Stay at Home)?" from *Sail Away*; "Be a Santa," "Ride through the Night" from *Subways Are for Sleeping*.

Song of the Season

1962–1963 SEASON

One had to look back to the pre-First World War days to find a season in which the only two hits on Broadway were British imports. But there was no other way to describe the situation this season when *Oliver!* thrilled audiences for 774 performances and the offbeat *Stop the World—I Want to Get Off* intrigued New Yorkers enough to run 556 times. Both had been giant successes in London but it had been so long since West End musicals had dominated Broadway that everyone was very surprised, except maybe David Merrick who produced both shows in New York. Despite the darker elements in Charles Dickens' tale, *Oliver!* was a family show in a day when there was rarely such a thing. The radiant score by Lionel Bart helped the musical join the ranks of the oft-revived musicals in America. *Stop the World* was more demanding theatre fare with its Everyman plot and circus tent presentation. Anthony Newley, who co-wrote the libretto and score with Leslie Bricusse, was very popular in the States so his performance as the central character of Littlechap was a boon to business. It certainly helped that the score produced three chart hits: "Gonna Build a Mountain," "Once in a Lifetime," and "What Kind of Fool Am I?"

While a few American musicals inched past the nine-month mark on the Street, none made any money. The best of the lot was *She Loves Me* with a scintillating score by Bock and Harnick, a charming book by Joe Masteroff, an exceptional cast headed by Barbara Cook and Daniel Massey, and skillful direction by Harold Prince. It was only producer Prince's second Broadway directing stint but *She Loves Me* already hinted that he would go on to stage some of the finest musicals of the next fifty years. A sillier musical but a very satisfying one was *Little Me* with a farcical libretto by Neil Simon and delightful songs by Cy Coleman and Carolyn Leigh. Television favorite Sid Caesar was not only the star but he played multiple roles so his fans were not disappointed. But 257 performances did not mean success for *Little Me*. Running only one week longer was *Mr. President*, the highly anticipated Irving Berlin musical about a fictitious POTUS. The critics disparaged the show's dull plot, uninteresting characters, and even Berlin's songs. It was, admittedly, a less-than-stellar score but the savagery of the reviews convinced Berlin to retire from Broadway. Also disappointing was the Judy Holliday vehicle *Hot Spot* with a score by Mary Rodgers (music) and Martin Charnin (lyrics) but a hopeless libretto about an American in the Peace Corps. Hollywood's Vivien Leigh was the highlight of the musical *Tovarich* which struggled to run nine months. For those who wanted to see stars without the hindrance of a plot, there were one-man's shows this season featuring Danny Kaye, Maurice Chevalier, Eddie Fisher, and Jack Benny. And if that didn't satisfy, this season also saw a puppet show, a dance concert, and thirteen revivals.

"What Kind of Fool Am I?"
Music and lyric byAnthony Newley and Leslie Bricusse
From *Stop the World—I Want to Get Off* (1962)
Sung by Anthony Newley as Littlechap

With such distancing effects as clown makeup, a circus tent setting, and a lot of mime instead of dancing, *Stop the World—I Want to Get Off* was not an easy sell for those coming to see the popular singer Anthony Newley. Also, the character of Littlechap is not very nice, being a terrible husband and father. Yet Newley was able to use humor and sentiment to get the audience on his side and at the end of the musical, when he breaks down and sings "What Kind of Fool Am I?," it was a cathartic moment. The lyric is a series of unanswered question climaxing with the title phrase. Littlechap wonders why he never fully loved anyone. He realizes that "I'm the only one/ That I have been thinking of."[3] He compares himself to "an empty shell" with an "empty heart" and, taking his exterior guise literally, asks "What kind of clown am I?" The lyric has some powerful rhetoric such as lips that "lied with every kiss" and all the "whispered empty words of love." The music is in the pop song mode rather than a Broadway one as its phrases express a strong musical idea then repeats it with variations. The release continues the main melodic theme but climbs up the scale for a punch, something that is repeated at the end of the song. "What Kind of Fool Am I?" is meant to be acted as well as sung and the song has been subjected to some overacting by some artists. The Newley recording was a success but Tony Bennett had a bigger hit with it, as did Sammy Davis, Jr. In 1963, "What Kind of Fool Am I?" was the first British song to win the Grammy Award for Song of the Year. Other notable discs were made by Andy Williams, the Cordials, Shirley Bassey, Lesley Gore, Robert Goulet, Keely Smith, the Hampton Hawes Trio, James Brown, Vince Guaraldi, Sergio Franchi, Perry Como, Regine Velasquez, Linda Eder, the folk rock band Deer Tick, Maria Friedman, Clay Aiken, and P. J. Proby. In a 1966 British television version of *Stop the World*, Tony Tanner played Littlechap and sang "What Kind of Fool Am I?" A 1979 American TV adaptation titled *Sammy Stops the World* starred Sammy Davis, Jr., as Littlechap, and a 1996 version on TV featured Peter Scolari as Littlechap.

Other notable songs from that season: "Gonna Build a Mountain," "Once in a Lifetime" from *Stop the World—I Want to Get Off*; "She Loves Me," "Ice Cream," "A Trip to the Library," "Dear Friend," "Will He Like Me?" from *She Loves Me*; "Consider Yourself," "Where Is Love?," "You've Got to Pick a Pocket or Two," "I'd Do Anything," "As Long As He Needs Me," "Who'll Buy?" from *Oliver!*; "Hey, Love" from *Hot Spot*; "Empty Pockets Filled with Love," "This Is a Great Country," "Let's Go Back to the Waltz" from *Mr. President*; "Real Live Girl," "I've Got Your Number," "Be a Performer!" from *Little Me*.

Song of the Season

1963–1964 SEASON

Just as the nation went through an emotional period with the assassination of John F. Kennedy, Broadway was in turmoil in the weeks following the tragedy. The season started late but there were a number of shows running by the time November 22 arrived and the country was thrown into shock. The next day two Broadway musicals closed and others struggled or adapted. Noel Coward's *The Girl Who Came to Supper* was on its tryout tour where the sarcastic song "Long Live the King (If He Can)," about an attempted assassination, had to be cut. When the musical opened on Broadway it received some complimentary notices but the story, about a middle-aged crown prince (José Ferrer) and an American chorus girl (Florence Henderson), was too glib for wary audiences in the weeks following Kennedy's death. After the holidays the temperament of the audience changed so when *Hello, Dolly!* opened on January 16 they were ready to be entertained and that's what the Jerry Herman musical did so very well. Yet when something demanding or outright strange came along, such as the experimental *Anyone Can Whistle*, playgoers stayed away. By the time the season ended, the tally showed five musicals breaking even or, in the case of *Hello, Dolly!* and *Funny Girl*, going far beyond that.

Most of the season's musicals boasted an established star's name above the title. It didn't guarantee success, as was the case with Mary Martin in *Jennie*, Bert Lahr in *Foxy*, and Angela Lansbury in *Anyone Can Whistle*. Pop singer Steve Lawrence had a strong enough following to keep *What Makes Sammy Run?* on the boards for 540 performances but somehow it still lost money. The same with Carol Burnett in *Fade Out—Fade In* which ran 271 times in two engagements and closed in the red. Carol Channing was the undisputed star of *Hello, Dolly!* and during the show's long run other stars were needed to keep the big musical running. Beatrice Lillie was featured in *High Spirits* and her clowning certainly helped that musical run after receiving favorable but not glowing reviews. The next best thing to having a star is to introduce one, as in the case of Barbra Streisand and *Funny Girl*. Two musicals that managed decent runs without stars were Meredith Willson's *Here's Love* and *110 in the Shade* with songs by Tom Jones and Harvey Schmidt. Both opened early in the fall and managed to keep running in the weeks following the assassination. *Here's Love* was a Christmas musical, based on the film *Miracle on 34th Street* (1947), that provided family entertainment for the holiday season. *110 in the Shade* was based on the popular play and film *The Rainmaker* and offered strong performances by Robert Horton and Inga Swenson. Both musicals ran eleven months.

"People"
Music by Jule Styne; lyric by Bob Merrill
From *Funny Girl* (1964)
Sung by Barbra Streisand as Fanny Brice

By the 1960s, the pop songs on the charts were not coming from Broadway as they had in the past. Yet this season had two songs that defied the odds and became bestsellers: the title song from *Hello, Dolly!* and "People" from *Funny Girl*. Because it is a ballad, "People" was more frequently performed and recorded. It is by far the most famous song from *Funny Girl* yet the songwriters had to fight to get it into the show. Composer Jule Styne and composer-lyricist Bob Merrill were both seasoned Broadway songwriters when they were hired to write the score for *Funny Girl*. Merrill had been writing both music and words since he wrote novelty songs in the 1950s. Yet in 1962 he agreed to collaborate with Styne, writing lyrics only for a planned musical about Fanny Brice. "People" was the first song they wrote and both lyric and music came easily and successfully. Merrill ad-libbed "People ... people who need people ... are the luckiest people in the world" and the melody quickly came to Styne. The music has a two-note motif on the word "People" that introduces the refrain then repeats at different octaves. Later the two-notes are reversed for the word "lovers" which is very effective. Merrill's lyric is simple but potent as it moves from general observations ("We're children, needing other children") into a romantic one ("Lovers, very special people").[4] In the release, the lyric becomes more flowery as the music gets more passionate. With regards to "one very special person," one realizes "you were half, now you're whole" and the need to "first be a person who needs people." The song ends with "the luckiest people in the world" which Styne turns into a suspended, incomplete musical chord which lets the final note linger rather than climax.

"People" was planned as the love song for Fanny (Barbra Streisand) and Nick Arnstein (Sydney Chaplin) but it was decided early on that it should not be a duet. Styne and Merrill wrote a brief verse that was more character specific. Fanny and Nick come from different worlds but, she argues, perhaps they are not all that different. The song came early in their relationship so Fanny expresses her thoughts about people in general rather than directed to Nick as a love ballad. When the score for *Funny Girl* was played for director Garson Kanin, he liked all of the songs except "People" and wanted it cut. The songwriters insisted that they see how it played in rehearsals but by the time the musical started tryouts "People" was gone. Without telling Kanin, Merrill arranged for Streisand to sing the ballad one night in previews and she stopped the show with it. From that point on, "People" was not only in *Funny Girl* but it became Streisand's signature song and has always been associated with her. It was Streisand's first disc to make it to the Top Ten and over the decades she recorded it six times, including a duet version with Stevie Wonder in 2014. Although "People" was considered Streisand's property, it did not keep many others from performing and recording it. The first to do so was Nat King Cole with a disc in 1964. Over the years there have been notable recordings by Ella Fitzgerald, the Tymes, Little Anthony and the Imperials, Vic Damone, Billy Eckstine, Dionne Warwick, the Village Stompers, Count Basie, Stan Whitmire, George Benson, Aretha Franklin, the Oscar Peterson Trio, Johnny Mathis, the Supremes, Patti LaBelle and the Bluebelles, Jennifer Lopez, and the Alvin Queen Trio. Streisand reprised her Fanny Brice in the 1966 London production, singing it to Michael Craig, and in the 1968

Song of the Season

movie version of *Funny Girl* where she sang it to Omar Sharif. In the 2022 Broadway revival of the musical, Beanie Feldstein was Fanny and sang it, as did her replacement Lea Michele.

Other notable songs from that season: "The Music That Makes Me Dance," "Don't Rain on My Parade," "You Are Woman," "Who Are You Now?" from *Funny Girl*; "Hello, Dolly!," "Put on Your Sunday Clothes," "Before the Parade Passes By," "Ribbons Down My Back," "It Only Takes a Moment," "So Long, Dearie" from *Hello, Dolly!*; "Love, Don't Turn Away," "Simple Little Things" from *110 in the Shade*; "A Room without Windows," "My Home Town" from *What Makes Sammy Run?*; "Anyone Can Whistle," "With So Little to Be Sure Of," "Me and My Town," "A Parade in Town" from *Anyone Can Whistle*; "You Mustn't Be Discouraged," "Call Me Savage" from *Fade Out—Fade In*; "Here's Love," "Pine Cones and Holly Berries" from *Here's Love*; "Waitin' for the Evening Train," "Before I Kiss the World Goodbye" from *Jennie*; "Talking to You," "The Bicycle Song" from *High Spirits*.

1964–1965 SEASON

When *Fiddler on the Roof* opened this season, expectations were modest. Joseph Stein's libretto was a Jewish folk tale filled with ethnic characters and expressions, and the songs by Jerry Bock (music) and Sheldon Harnick (lyrics) were rarely in the Broadway mode. Producer Harold Prince and director-choreographer Jerome Robbins thought the appeal of the musical to be limited to Jewish audiences and were hoping for a one-year run to break even. Instead, *Fiddler on the Roof* went on to break the record set by *My Fair Lady* and then *Hello, Dolly!* and ran seven years. For those waiting to get tickets, the season offered forty-four other musical productions, an impressive number until one subtracted a complete Gilbert and Sullivan repertory, many other revivals, specialty acts, a burlesque show, the French *Folies Bergere*, and a handful of revues. That left twelve new book musicals which is also impressive. The British were all over the Street this season. The First World War-era songs were sung in the London revue *Oh, What a Lovely War!*, *Half a Sixpence* and *The Roar of the Greasepaint—The Smell of the Crowd* were both full-scale book musicals. The clever First World War revue ran 125 times, *The Roar of the Greasepaint* played 232 performances, and *Half A Sixpence* chalked up 512 performances. The American shows included the Sammy Davis, Jr. vehicle *Golden Boy*, the Sherlock Holmes musical *Baker Street*, Richard Rodgers' *Do I Hear a Waltz?* with Stephen Sondheim as his lyricist, *I Had a Ball* featuring the broad comedics of Buddy Hackett, *Bajour* about gypsies (Chita Rivera, in particular) in contemporary New York City, Robert Preston as *Ben Franklin in Paris*, and *Flora, the Red Menace* which brought the first wide attention to Liza Minnelli and songwriters John Kander and Fred Ebb. Some of these ran over a year but very few of them made money. The era of the modest Broadway success that paid off after 200 performances had passed. The risks in producing on Broadway were illustrated by this season's big-budget musical *Kelly*. It closed on opening night and lost $650,000.

In the 1960s, it was still possible to produce a musical Off-Broadway without breaking the bank. Two revues and two book musicals this season enjoyed substantial runs and modest-to-considerable profits. Producer Julius Monk had been presenting smart, intimate revues since the mid-1950s, often putting a number in the title to indicate the order of the shows. This season's *Bits and Pieces, XIV* was his fourteenth revue and one of Monk's most popular ones, running over a year. *The Game Is Up* was Ron Warren's second revue and, with Marian Mercer leading the small cast, sketch material by an unknown Joan Rivers, and some songs by undiscovered Marvin Hamlisch, the show ran 620 performances. The two book musicals were not lucky enough to run so long but each had its merits. *The Secret Life of Walter Mitty* expanded the famous James Thurber short story into a full-length musical with some delightful songs and fantasy sequences. Rick Besoyan, who wrote book, music, and lyrics for the long-running *Little Mary Sunshine*, turned his hand to Shakespeare's *A Midsummer Night's Dream* and musicalized it as *Babes in the Woods*. It struggled to run six weeks and concluded Besoyan's career; he died prematurely six years later.

Song of the Season

> "Sunrise, Sunset"
> Music Jerry Bock; lyric by Sheldon Harnick
> From *Fiddler on the Roof* (1964)
> Sung by Zero Mostel as Tevye, Maria
> Karnilova as Golde, and the ensemble

Ever since 1891, the song of choice for weddings was "Oh, Promise Me." The operetta ballad was falling out of favor by the 1960s and was replaced by "Sunrise, Sunset" from *Fiddler on the Roof*. It is sung at the wedding of Tzeitel (Joanna Merlin) and Motel (Austin Pendleton) while the Rabbi performs the marriage ritual. Tzeitel's parents Tevye (Zero Mostel) and Golde (Maria Karnilova) begin the number, each singing their thoughts, then other characters join them until it is a stirring chorale number. For a wedding song, it is more reflective and somber than joyous. Jerry Bock's music is hymn-like with a waltz tempo in a minor key yet still has traces of lively klezmer music. There is repetition in the music, somewhat like the sound of a metronome that indicates the passage of time. It is a simple tune, easily played and sung, but one that needs to be acted. "Sunrise, Sunset" has a beautifully restrained lyric by Sheldon Harnick. The point of view is that of a parent dealing with the fact that a child has grown up so quickly and one hardly noticed the time go by. Much of the verses are a series of unanswered questions: Is this the girl one carried? Is this the boy at play? When did she grow up to be beautiful? When did he grow so tall? And the sobering realization that "I don't remember growing older; when did they?"[5] The familiar refrain moves from a question to an observation and here the music repeats, just as the lyric does, to suggest time passing: "Seedlings turn overnight to sunflowers,/ Blossoming even as we gaze." There is nothing in the lyric or the music that makes "Sunrise, Sunset" obviously Jewish in sound or words. That is why the song is appropriate for most any wedding and has been used for that purpose thousands of times. There have been about 200 recordings of "Sunrise Sunset." It may not be a bestseller on the charts but it is probably the most non-professionally performed song to come from Broadway.

The original cast album of *Fiddler on the Roof* was a big seller so millions of Americans knew "Sunrise, Sunset" well. Because the musical was translated and performed around the world, the songs all became familiar and "Sunrise, Sunset" resonated with people everywhere. Solo vocal, chorale, and instrumental versions of the song have been recorded internationally. In the States, the earliest discs were made by Johnny Hartman, Eddie Fisher, Sammy Davis, Jr., Eddie Hazell, the Barry Sisters, and Robert Goulet. Among the many other singers and musicians to record "Sunrise, Sunset" are Roger Williams, Jerry Vale, Guy Lombardo, Mike Douglas, Harry James, Mickey Katz, Steve Lawrence and Eydie Gormé, the Ray Charles Singers, Leontyne Price, Louis Armstrong, Neil Sedaka, Michael Ball with Alfie Boe, Wendy Goodwin, and Ada Jones. The Israeli actor Topol played Teyve and sang "Sunrise Sunset" with Miriam Karlin in the 1967

London production and he sang the song with Norma Crane in the 1971 film version of *Fiddler on the Roof*. There have been five Broadway revivals of the musical and the song has been sung by Zero Mostel and Thelma Lee in 1976, Herschel Bernardi and Maria Karnilova in 1981, Topol and Marcia Lewis in 1990, Alfred Molina and Randy Graff in 2004, and Danny Burstein and Jessica Hecht in 2015.

Other notable songs from that season: "Tradition," "If I Were a Rich Man," "Matchmaker, Matchmaker," "Far from the Home I Love," "(L'Chaim) To Life" from *Fiddler on the Roof*; "Who Can I Turn To (When Nobody Needs Me)?," "A Wonderful Day Like Today," "Feeling Good," "Nothing Can Stop Me Now" from *The Roar of the Greasepaint—The Smell of the Crowd*; "A Quiet Thing," "Sing Happy," "You Are You," "Dear Love" from *Flora, the Red Menace*; "I Want to Be with You," "Night Song" from *Golden Boy*; "To Be Alone with You" from *Ben Franklin in Paris*; "Where Is the Tribe for Me?," "Love-Line" from *Bajour*; "Half a Sixpence," "If The Rain's Got to Fall," "Money to Burn," "Flash Bang Wallop" from *Half a Sixpence*; "A Married Man" from *Baker Street*; "Do I Hear a Waltz?," "Moon in My Window" from *Do I Hear a Waltz?*

Song of the Season

1965–1966 SEASON

It was a season of extremes. Four book musicals (*Pousse-Café, The Yearling, La Gross Valise,* and *Drat! The Cat!*) closed in a week or less. Yet three book musicals (*Man of La Mancha, Sweet Charity,* and *Mame*) each ran over two years and are still frequently revived. It was a season with some once-in-a-lifetime performances (Richard Kiley in *Man of La Mancha,* Gwen Verdon in *Sweet Charity,* Angela Lansbury in *Mame,* and Barbara Harris in *On a Clear day You Can See Forever*) and yet a cast of eight unknowns from South Africa propelled the revue *Wait a Minim!* for 457 performances. This season also saw fifteen revivals of everything from *The Merry Widow* to *Oklahoma!* to *Annie Get Your Gun*. Fifty-eight-year-old Ethel Merman played Annie, causing some to christen the show "Granny Get Your Gun," but audiences came for 124 performances and were treated to a new number by Irving Berlin, the double song "An Old-Fashioned Wedding." It was Berlin's last Broadway contribution and a memorable one. New Yorkers also had to say goodbye to the dazzling Ziegfeld Theatre which had been designed by the great scenographer Joseph Urban in 1927. After the two-week run of *Anya,* the theatre was closed and eventually demolished. On the other hand, the glorious Palace Theatre, considered the shrine of vaudeville, was reopened this season as a legit playhouse and had a hit with its first tenant, *Sweet Charity*.

While *Man of La Mancha* was a very serious and powerful musical, most shows that succeeded this season were lightweight affairs. When the subject or the tone was highly dramatic, audiences were not interested, as with *Anya, The Yearling, Pousse-Cafe,* and *A Time for Singing*. Not that being a comedy was any guarantee. Two musical spoofs arrived this season with unhappy results. *Drat! The Cat!* was a parody of a nineteenth-century crime thriller penned by mystery writer Ira Levin. Sadly, the crime was not interesting enough, the humor was strained, and most of the songs forgettable. After one week, it was gone. Probably losing more money but much more satisfying was *It's a Bird ... It's a Plane ... It's Superman!* It was a gentle mockery of the popular comic strip with a bright and bouncy score by Charles Strouse and Lee Adams and a fine cast adept at playing the tongue-in-cheek humor. The reviews were mostly enthusiastic so producer-director Harold Prince kept the show running hoping it would catch on. This was just before America got interested in pop cartoon culture (such as the television show *Batman*) so the musical struggled on for 129 performances before calling it quits. Another musical that deserved a longer run was *Pickwick,* a musical version of Charles Dickens' *The Pickwick Papers* which had run two years in London; the Broadway version closed after seven weeks. Of all the star turns this season, the most curious one was that of Julie Harris, one of the American theatre's most distinguished actresses. Harris gave a sparkling performance in *Skyscraper* despite her limited singing talents and, along with the eccentric Charles Nelson Reilly, entertained audiences for 248 (unprofitable) performances.

> "The Impossible Dream (The Quest)"
> Music by Mitch Leigh; lyric by Joe Darion
> From *Man of La Mancha* (1965)
> Sung by Richard Kiley as Don Quixote

This hymn-like ballad and its lofty ideas have been performed (and mocked) so much over the years that one has to put it in context of *Man of La Mancha* to recall what a powerful number it is. The eccentric knight errant Don Quixote (Richard Kiley) is spending a night's vigil in preparation for his dubbing when the sluttish Aldonza (Joan Diener), who he sees as the virtuous lady Dulcinea, asks him about "The Quest," as the song was titled at that time. Quixote describes the quest with a series of goals: to fight antagonists who are "unbeatable"; to withstand sorrow; to go where even "the brave dare not go"; to right wrongs and love "pure and chaste from afar"; and finally to reach for what is "unreachable."[6] Joe Darion's lyric is indeed bombastic, as is the character of Quixote. Because he is not in his right mind, Quixote has "impossible" visions of a better world. Yet he is not blind enough not to see the cruelty of the real world. He knows his cause is a lost cause which makes his determination all the more admirable and pathetic. In the release, Quixote vows "to march into hell/ For that heavenly cause" and the song concludes with him forever reaching for "the unreachable star." Mitch Leigh's music has a subtle Spanish bolero running under the melody which propels the song forward. This restless undercurrent also helps the music build until the explosive climax is justified.

From the first preview, "The Impossible Dream" stopped the show, helped by Kiley's full-voiced rendition. Parts of the song are reprised three more times in *Man of La Mancha*, most potently at the end of the musical when sung by prisoners in the dungeon as Miguel de Cervantes and his manservant go off to face trial by the Spanish Inquisition. Few musicals end on such a dramatic note. Because *Man of La Mancha* played at a small out-of-the-way theatre, it took a little while to catch on even with the exemplary reviews. After the original cast album, the first recording of "The Impossible Dream" was made by Roy Hamilton, closely followed by discs by Johnny Mathis, Gordon MacRae, Jim Nabors, and Mel Carter. Shirley Bassey was the first female vocalist to record the ballad and over the years "The Impossible Dream" has been covered by a wide variety of artists, including Ed Ames, the Temptations, Matt Monro, Roger Williams, the Hesitations, the Imperials, the Vogues, Glen Campbell, Cher, the Smothers Brothers, Shani Wallis, Roberta Flack, Elvis Presley, the Mormon Tabernacle Choir, Colm Wilkinson, Luther Vandross, José Carreras, Linda Eder, Susan Boyle, Ramon Jacinto, and Josh Groban. There have also been several foreign language versions. Keith Michell played Quixote and sang the ballad in the 1968 London production and Peter O'Toole (dubbed by Simon Gilbert) did likewise in the 1972 film adaptation. During the Broadway run of *Man of La Mancha*, Quixote

Song of the Season

was played by John Cullum, José Ferrer, David Atkinson, and Charles West. Raul Julia was Quixote in the 1992 revival and Brian Stokes Mitchell played him in the 2002 revival.

Other notable songs from that season: "Man of La Mancha (I, Don Quixote)," "To Each His Dulcinea," "What Does He Want of Me?," "Dulcinea" from *Man of La Mancha*; "Mame," "If He Walked into My Life Today," "We Need a Little Christmas," "Open a New Window," "Bosom Buddies" from *Mame*; "Hey, Big Spender," "If They Could See Me Now," "I'm a Brass Band," "Baby, Dream Your Dream" from *Sweet Charity*; "On a Clear Day You Can See Forever," "Come Back to Me," "Hurry! It's Lovely Up Here," "What Did I Have That I Don't Have?" from *On a Clear Day You Can See Forever*; "If I Ruled the World" from *Pickwick*; "You've Got Possibilities," "You've Got What I Need" from *It's a Bird ... It's a Plane ... It's Superman*; "Little Hands" from *Anya*; "Everybody Has a Right to Be Wrong" from *Skyscraper*; "An Old-Fashioned Wedding" from *Annie Get Your Gun* (revival); "The Boy from ...," "Looking for Someone" from *The Mad Show* (Off-Broadway).

1966–1967 SEASON

With a series of classic musicals presented at the City Center and a full repertory of Gilbert and Sullivan favorites, there ended up being fourteen revivals on the Street this season. That was nearly twice as many as new book musicals. Happily, several of those new works had much to recommend even if only three musicals made a profit. *Cabaret* was much more than a hit. It brought songwriters John Kander and Fred Ebb, as well as director-producer Harold Prince, to the forefront of the American musical theatre. Here was a musical that was conventional in some ways but wildly different in other aspects. How a musical about the beginning of the Holocaust could also be entertaining is one of the wonders of *Cabaret*. Another wonder is how the musical has remained potent over the decades with new interpretations and formats. This is arguably the defining musical of the decade.

The other two hits seem lightweight in comparison. Jerry Bock and Sheldon Harnick's charming *The Apple Tree* was skillfully done and provided another indelible performance by Barbara Harris but lacks substance and, consequently, has seen few revivals. Tom Jones and Harvey Schmidt thought a two-person musical based on the domestic comedy *The Fourposter* (1951) was a terrible idea until producer David Merrick told them that the two people were Mary Martin and Robert Preston. Both of these legends of the musical stage had been in unsuccessful vehicles of late but in *I Do! I Do!* they shone because they were given solid material. Leslie Uggams, a younger and less established performer, proved to be a star in the unconventional *Hallelujah, Baby!* As an African American woman who lives through decades of American history, Uggams was everything one wanted in a Broadway musical. Sadly, the libretto and score were not up to the intriguing premise and Uggams was ultimately defeated by weak material. *Hallelujah, Baby!* ran 295 performances, closing a few months before it won the Tony Award. Other disappointments with short or unprofitable runs but memorable lead performances were *Walking Happy* (featuring Norman Wisdom), *Sherry!* (Clive Revill), *A Joyful Noise* (John Raitt), and *Illya, Darling* (Melina Mercouri). Finally, it was a good season for Jewish "entertainments." *Sing, Israel, Sing!*, *Let's Sing Yiddish*, and *Hello, Solly!* weren't exactly *Fiddler on the Roof* but offered a kind of escapism from the nightmare conjured up by *Cabaret*.

"Cabaret"
Music by John Kander; lyric by Fred Ebb
From *Cabaret* (1966)
Sung by Jill Haworth as Sally Bowles

The seemingly jubilant title number from *Cabaret* is the most popular song from the musical and is oft recorded, though rarely in the fashion that songwriters John Kander and Fred Ebb intended. Near the end of the musical, Sally Bowles (Jill Haworth) has ended her relationship with the British writer Cliff (Bert Convy), has aborted their unborn child, and decided to remain in Berlin, being blind to what is happening around her. She returns to her old job at the Kit Kat Klub and sings "Cabaret," a song of defiance, arguing that life can only be endured by celebrating it without cares or worries. Sally's call to "come hear the music play" and her stating "life is a cabaret, old chum" are delivered to the cabaret patrons, to those not present (like Cliff) whom she has abandoned, and even to herself.[7] Does Sally actually believe what she says? Is she still trying to convince herself? Or, as some interpret the song, is she having an emotional breakdown on stage? The structure of "Cabaret" is unusual. It has two refrains, a release, then after the third refrain it moves into a patter section with a different tempo and melody. It is one of the many narrative lyrics Ebb wrote during his career, telling a story as part or all of a lyric. (The song "Meeskite" in *Cabaret* is another example.) Elsie is old and decrepit and living a life of "too much pills and liquor" but she enjoys herself with no regrets until she drops dead. But when Sally "sees her laid out like a queen," she admits "she was the happiest ... corpse ... I'd ever seen." So Sally is determined to live life like Elsie: "When I go, I'm going like Elsie." The song returns to the opening lyric and ends with the steadfast philosophy "Life is a cabaret!" The whole song is a dramatic little scene and serves as the musical's eleven o'clock number. A song with such a dark subtext is not likely to become popular but Kander's vivacious music, which is in a hot jazz mode with a touch of Dixieland in it, is contagious. With the Elsie section removed, the lyric can be performed at face value as a party song. In fact, most vocal recordings do just that. Out of context of *Cabaret*, the song holds up as a vibrant uptempo number; but in the musical, it should be devastating.

"Cabaret" is most associated with Liza Minnelli who played Sally in the 1972 movie version of *Cabaret*. Of all the recordings, the most popular was that by Louis Armstrong in 1966. Among the 100-plus other discs were versions by such notable artists as Frankie Vaughan, Herb Alpert and the Tijuana Brass, Marilyn Maye, Steve Lawrence and Eydie Gormé, Brenda Lee, Max Bygraves, the Ray Charles Singers, Ella Fitzgerald, Vikki Carr, Lester Lanin, Bing Crosby, Russ Conway, Nelson Riddle, Julius LaRosa, Tennessee Ernie Ford, Frankie Carle, and Kristina Bach. Judi Dench played Sally and sang the title number in the 1968 London production. For the Broadway revivals of *Cabaret*, Sally Bowles was played by Alyson Reed in 1987, Natasha Richardson in 1998, and Michelle Williams in 2014. Among the many actresses to replace these on Broadway were Penny Fuller, Anita Gillette, Mary Munger, Jennifer Jason Leigh, Susan Egan, Deborah Gilson, Milena Govich, Gina Gershon, Molly Ringwald, Brooke Shields, Sienna Miller, and Emma Stone.

> Other notable songs from that season: "Wilkommen," "Tomorrow Belongs to Me," "Two Ladies," "Married," "If You Could See Her" from *Cabaret*; "Being Good Isn't Good Enough," "My Own Morning" from *Hallelujah, Baby!*; "My Cup Runneth

Over," "I Love My Wife," "What Is a Woman?," "The Honeymoon Is Over" from *I Do! I Do!*; "What Makes Me Love Him?" "Oh, to Be a Movie Star/Gorgeous" from *The Apple Tree*; "Happiness," "My Blanket and Me," "Book Report" from *You're a Good Man, Charlie Brown* (Off-Broadway); "Walking Happy" from *Walking Happy*; "Love, Love, Love" from *Illya, Darling*; "Sherry" from *Sherry!*; "(Come to the) Masquerade," "Hulla-Baloo-Balay," "Little Rag Doll" from *Man with a Load of Mischief* (Off-Broadway).

1967–1968 SEASON

There was so much drama, not to mention tragedy, in the news that Broadway musicals sometimes seemed superfluous. The escalation of the war in Vietnam, the equally increasing anti-war protests, the assassinations of Martin Luther King and Robert Kennedy, and fiery events in the Civil Rights movement made 1968 one of the most turbulent years in American history. Yet there was little evidence of any of this on the musical stage. For over ten years, Broadway had done a pretty thorough job of ignoring the new trends in popular music. Early rock-and-roll, urban folk, gospel, rhythm and blues, as well as the Beatles and 1960s rock—none could be found on Broadway. The gap between Broadway songs and popular music had been getting wider and wider and younger generations were turning their back on Broadway-style musicals. When rock finally arrived on the Street, it had to do so by way of Off-Broadway. Producer Joseph Papp presented *Hair* in his Off-Broadway venue the Public Theatre and it was an immediate sensation. Several changes were made (including a new director, Tom O'Horgan) for the Broadway edition, most memorably a brief nude scene in the shadows that got a lot of publicity. *Hair* ran 1,750 performances and toured extensively for years. Everything else on Broadway that season was fully conventional unless one considered an African American cast in *Hello, Dolly!* as innovative. Perhaps it was a gimmick but with Pearl Bailey remaking the role of Dolly in her own distinctive style it was not to be missed. The only other new musical to have a long run was *George M!*, a bio-musical about George M. Cohan (Joel Grey) using songs that were at least a half a century old. The patriotic, bombastic Cohan score was perhaps Broadway's response to *Hair*. The other book musicals were decidedly old hat. The Steve Lawrence-Eydie Gormé vehicle *Golden Rainbow* ran the longest (385 performances) because of the stars' popularity. The musical adaptation of John Steinbeck's novel *East of Eden*, re-titled *Here's Where I Belong*, ran the shortest (one performance). In between were such unsatisfying ventures as *I'm Solomon*, *The Education of H*Y*M*A*N K*A*P*L*A*N*, *How Now, Dow Jones*, and *Henry, Sweet Henry*. Two new musicals deserved better than they got. *Darling of the Day* had an intelligent libretto, a competent score, and a compelling performance by Patricia Routledge. *The Happy Time* had a sentimental libretto but an outstanding score by John Kander and Fred Ebb. The appeal of Robert Goulet and David Wayne helped keep the musical on the boards for 286 (unprofitable) performances.

Hair was not the only Off-Broadway musical of note this season. The entries Off-Broadway were far from old hat, sometimes intriguing, often enthralling. The anti-war musical *Now Is the Time for All Good Men* introduced the songwriters Nancy Ford and Gretchen Cryer, the first notable female team of the American theatre. Al Carmines' tapestry-like musical *In Circles* was as unorthodox as it was thrilling. The Shirley Temple satire *Curly McDimple* was deliciously vicious. The mock rock musical *Your Own Thing* played fast and loose with Shakespeare's *Twelfth Night* and the pop music industry. Audiences laughed for 933 performances. The scintillating songs of the Belgian singer-composer Jacques Brel were collected and performed in a highly imaginative revue titled

Jacques Brel Is Alive and Living in Paris. Like *Your Own Thing*, it enjoyed a long run but, unlike *Hair*, stayed Off-Broadway where it ran 1,847 performances. With such vital productions Off-Broadway and so little new life on Broadway, it was clear where the future of the American musical could be found.

"Aquarius"
Music Galt MacDermot;
lyric by Gerome Ragni, James Rado
From *Hair* (1968)
Sung by Ron Dyson and ensemble

Not every song in *Hair* is in the rock idiom. "Aquarius," the most popular song from the musical, is not rock in its music, which is hymn-like and also like a gospel number. But its lyric has the dreamy, mystical quality that one associates with some powerful rock numbers. Gerome Ragni and James Rado took some basic astronomy and a bit of astrology and came up with the entrancing lyric. The opening lines quickly set up the celestial image of the moon "in the seventh house" and Jupiter and Mars aligning, marking the "dawning of the age of Aquarius" when "love will steer the stars."[8] The "seventh house" refers to the constellation Libra and the moon can be seen in that cluster of stars. The planets of Jupiter and Mars, when viewed from Earth, seem to line up. Such an arrangement bodes well for the future. Aquarius is the eleventh sign of the zodiac and, astrologically speaking, those born under this sign tend to have a social conscience and wish to make the world a better place. The new age under this zodiacal sign will bring "Harmony and understanding,/ Sympathy and trust abounding." For a protest musical, *Hair* starts out on a very optimistic note.

In the original Off-Broadway production of *Hair*, the song "Aquarius" was sung by the ensemble, called the Tribe, in the middle of the second act. By the time the show moved to Broadway, "Aquarius" had started to catch on so it was changed to the opening of the musical with Ron Dyson leading the Tribe in singing it. The song not only set the tone for the production but encapsulated the whole youth movement of the 1960s. The Broadway cast album of *Hair* was a big seller but by itself "Aquarius" was considered too short and too repetitive to stand as a single record. The group known as the Fifth Dimension mashed the song up with *Hair*'s "Let the Sunshine In" and the disc was a huge hit. Most subsequent recordings used the same double song format. Among the many notable discs were those by Diana Ross and the Supremes, the Ventures, Andy Williams and the Osmond Brothers, Dizzy Gillespie, Engelbert Humperdinck, Charlie Byrd, Moog Machine, John Rowles, the Ray Conniff Singers, Boots Randolph, and Rachel Eckroth. "Aquarius" was sung by Renn Woods and the Tribe in the opening of the 1979 movie version of *Hair*. Sasha Allen led the Tribe in singing it in the 2009 Broadway revival. "Aquarius" and all the songs in the original production of *Hair* were miked. It

Song of the Season

was the first show in which the musicians were amplified which meant all the performers were obviously miked and there was no pretense that they weren't. Before long, musical theatre amplification became the norm. So *Hair* changed the sound of Broadway in more ways than one.

Other notable songs from that season: "Hair," "Easy to Be Hard," "Let the Sunshine In (The Flesh Failures)," "Good Morning Starshine," "Frank Mills," "Where Do I Go?" from *Hair*; "The Happy Time," "I Don't Remember You," "A Certain Girl," "The Life of the Party" from *The Happy Time*; "Not on Your Nellie," "Sunset Tree," "Let's See What Happens" from *Darling of the Day*; "Poor Little Person," "In Some Little World," "Nobody Steps on Kafritz" from *Henry, Sweet Henry*; "The Middle Years" from *Your Own Thing* (Off-Broadway); "Step to the Rear" from *How Now Dow Jones*; "I've Got to Be Me" from *Golden Rainbow*; "Tea in the Rain," "What's in the Air?" from *Now Is the Time for All Good Men* (Off-Broadway).

1968–1969 SEASON

The melodramatic attraction in the fall of 1968 was not on Broadway but was the hotly debated presidential election in which Richard M. Nixon defeated George McGovern, a decision that further fueled anti-war protests across America. Very little of this showed up in Broadway musicals. In fact, one of the season's biggest hits was the patriotic *1776* which managed to be as engrossing as it was entertaining. The score was by the history teacher-turned-songwriter Sherman Edwards. Peter Stone wrote one of the finest of all musical librettos for *1776* which had its anti-war ("Momma, Look Sharp") and anti-slave ("Molasses to Rum") moments. Also making their Broadway debuts (and farewells) with a giant hit were pop songwriters Burt Bacharach (music) and Hal David (lyrics) with *Promises, Promises*. The vibrant musical may have sounded more pop than Broadway but nobody seemed to mind for 1,281 performances. These were the only two Broadway musicals to turn a profit. Coming close was John Kander and Fred Ebb's *Zorbá*, based on the novel and film *Zorbá the Greek*, which had an amiable Greek-flavored score and superb performances by Herschel Bernardi and Maria Karnilova. But at 305 performances, *Zorbá* ended up in the red. A substantial (but unprofitable) run was earned by the allegorical musical *Celebration* with an intriguing score by Tom Jones and Harvey Schmidt. Unlike their recent glossy Broadway ventures, *Celebration* was closer to their Off-Broadway hit *The Fantasticks*. Some critics felt the show belonged Off-Broadway but they praised it all the same. It was one of those few cases in which the press liked a show more than the audience did.

The British import *Canterbury Tales*, which had run 2,082 performances in London, could only survive 122 times on Broadway. It had its merits, in particular a spirited performance by George Rose, but Chaucer was a hard sell on Broadway no matter what form it took. Other outstanding performances could be enjoyed this season but often their vehicles closed much too soon. Such was the case with Shirley Jones and Jack Cassidy in *Maggie Flynn*, Richard Kiley and Leslie Uggams in *Her First Roman*, Dorothy Loudon in *The Fig Leaves Are Falling*, Angela Lansbury in *Dear World*, and Ray Bolger in *Come Summer*. This last ran only one week, which was more than *But Never Jam Today*, an African American take on *Alice in Wonderland*, and *Billy*, based on Herman Melville's *Billy Budd*, both of which closed on opening night. As was becoming more and more common, some of the most exciting musicals were Off-Broadway. *Dames at Sea*, a delightful spoof of 1930s Hollywood musicals, not only ran 575 performances but introduced Bernadette Peters to New York audiences. Al Carmines' expressionistic *Promenade* was in the Bertolt Brecht style and took on war, race, and big business. Also finding an audience away from Broadway were the racial revue *Walk Down Mah Street!*, the political satire *How to Steal an Election*, and the symbolist musical *Peace*. One was never far from the real world with Off-Broadway.

By the end of the 1960s, songs from Broadway were designated to the occasional Easy Listening or Instrumental Favorites categories for an ever-shrinking audience. There were fewer artists recording such songs and it seemed only aging listeners were

Song of the Season

interested. Original Cast Albums were still popular enough that record companies made them but often it was a tradition of preserving Broadway scores rather than for financial profits. The new generation of songwriters, even those not in the pop-rock mode, were not interested in writing for the theatre. Even when popular songwriters crossed over to Broadway, as Bacharach and David did with *Promises, Promises*, they rarely returned. In the music business, Broadway was "not where it's at."

"Promises, Promises"
Music by Burt Bacharach; lyric by Hal David
From *Promises, Promises* (1968)
Introduced by Jerry Orbach as Chuck Baxter

From its catchy melodies to its brassy orchestrations, *Promises, Promises* had a very different sound than usually heard on Broadway. Burt Bacharach and Hal David had penned several pop hits for such beloved singers as Dionne Warwick, Tom Jones, the Carpenters, and Dusty Springfield, but *Promises, Promises* was their first (and only) Broadway musical and they were successful in writing character and chorus numbers. The surging title song is sung by Chuck Baxter (Jerry Orbach) near the end of the musical when he discontinues his practice of loaning his apartment to company executives needing a trysting place. Free from guilty responsibility and embracing that new-found freedom, Chuck joyously sings "I'm all through with promises" because he "got the nerve to walk out."[9] Hal David's lyric bubbles with enthusiasm ("Every night I sleep now, no more lies") and optimism ("My kind of promises/ Can lead to joy and hope and love!") and the words are supported by Bacharach's pulsating music which seems to rush ahead with Chuck barely keeping up. The tempo feels like a double-time march which is difficult to sing unless the words flow efficiently. Removed from the context of *Promises, Promises*, the song holds up on its own, being an uptempo number about letting go and being free. It was Warwick's recording that was the top seller but there were other noteworthy discs by Connie Francis, Jerry Vale, Al Hirt, the Charlie Byrd Quartet, Billy Vaughn, Herb Alpert and the Tijuana Brass, Naked Eyes, Mario Said, Liz Callaway, and Erik Friedlander. In the 1969 London production of *Promises, Promises*, Anthony (later Tony) Roberts played Chuck and sang the title number. There was no film version of *Promises, Promises* but Sean Hayes was Chuck and sang the song in the 2010 Broadway revival.

Other notable songs from that season: "I'll Never Fall in Love Again," "Knowing When to Leave," "Whoever You Are" from *Promises Promises*; "Momma, Look

Sharp," "He Plays the Violin," "Molasses to Rum" from *1776*; "Life Is," "No Boom Boom," "Only Love" from *Zorbá*; "Each Tomorrow Morning," "I Don't Want to Know" from *Dear World*; "Dames at Sea," "Raining in My Heart," "The Echo Waltz," "Choo Choo Honeymoon" from *Dames at Sea* (Off-Broadway); "Celebration," "I'm Glad to See You've Got What You Want," "It's You Who Makes Me Young" from *Celebration*; "Love Will Conquer All" from *Canterbury Tales*.

Song of the Season

1969–1970 SEASON

The arrival of the landmark musical *Company* at the very end of the season helped put the many earlier casualties behind one, concentrating on a show so unique, so exciting, and so important. George Furth's libretto, Stephen Sondheim's score, producer Harold Prince's direction, Boris Aronson's scenic design, Jonathan Tunick's orchestrations, and Michael Bennett's musical staging all supported each other in the first true "concept" musical in which theme overrode chronological plot and realistic portrayal of events. *Company* was the first in a decade of extraordinary Sondheim-Prince musicals, the likes of which have not been repeated. For all its unorthodox elements, *Company* was surprisingly entertaining and, at 690 performances, modestly popular. Much more conventional, but also highly satisfying, was the season's other long-run, *Applause*. Because it was based on the short story "The Wisdom of Eve" and not the celebrated film *All about Eve*, *Applause* had a disappointing libretto but a playful score by Charles Strouse and Lee Adams and a stellar performance by Lauren Bacall. The non-singing, non-dancing film favorite carried the musical by pure star quality. Similarly, the musically challenged Katharine Hepburn carried the musical *Coco* by mere personality, keeping it alive for 333 performances on Broadway and then on tour. The only other musical with a substantial run was the vibrant *Purlie*, a rousing musical with a sly sense of humor as it mocked race relations in the deep South. It also boasted a sparkling score by Gary Geld (music) and Peter Udell (lyrics) and risible performances by Cleavon Little and Melba Moore.

The rest of the reason was dismal. Three musicals (*Gantry*, *Blood Red Roses* and *La Strada*) closed on opening night and four others (*Cry for Us All*, *Georgy*, *Park*, and *Buck White*) lasted a week or less. Stars could not save two other musicals—*Look to the Lilies* with Shirley Booth and *Minnie's Boys* with Shelley Winters—and *Jimmy*, about "gentleman" Jimmy Walker (Frank Gorshin) was unfavorably compared to that other "mayor of New York" musical *Fiorello*. *Jimmy* had a forced run of ten weeks, losing more money than all the other casualties. There were only two revivals this season—*Oklahoma!* and *The Boy Friend*—but both lost money running longer than *Jimmy*. Off-Broadway offered a handful on interesting musicals, two of which would later transfer to Broadway. The disarming musical *The Me Nobody Knows* was taken from the writings of inner-city teenagers and was well received by the press and the public. The erotic musical revue *Oh, Calcutta!* was not generally recommended by the critics but it had no difficulty finding an audience. It also moved to Broadway where it stayed a shockingly long time. The best of the Off-Broadway offerings was the rock-pop musical *The Last Sweet Days of Isaac* about the way humans do and do not communicate. The lucid score by Gretchen Cryer and Nancy Ford was enjoyed for 485 performances. Other shows with substantial runs Off-Broadway were the satirical rock musical *Salvation* about religious fervor, the American premiere of Kurt Weill's expressionistic *Mahagonny*, and the musical "mellerdrammer" spoof *The Drunkard* with some tuneful songs by Barry Manilow.

> "The Ladies Who Lunch"
> Music and lyric by Stephen Sondheim
> From *Company* (1970)
> Sung by Elaine Stritch as Joanne

There are many sterling songs in *Company* but the number which resonates in one's memory is "The Ladies Who Lunch," the eleven o'clock tour de force originally sung by Elaine Stritch. At a nightclub with her third husband Larry (Charles Braswell) and their friend Robert (Dean Jones), Joanne (Stritch) drinks too much and gets rather testy and a bit noisy. Some fellow patrons stare at her which prompts Joanne to comment on the useless upper-class women of Manhattan. As she starts her commentary, there are unsettling chords under her opening lyric. The song is a series of mocking toasts. The first is "Here's to the ladies who lunch—Everybody laugh" at those women "lounging in their caftans and planning a brunch … On their own behalf."[10] In this first section, the target of Joanne's mockery is the idle and monied women whose idea of a difficult day is "sitting/ Choosing a hat." With her toast "I'll drink to that," the melody comes in with a chilly bossa nova beat, quite in tempo but a bit slurred or perhaps drunken. In the second section of the song, Elaine ridicules the "smart" wealthy women who take "classes in optical art," attend formidable plays by Harold Pinter and go to concerts where Gustave Mahler is performed. (At the mention of "a piece of Mahler's," the accompaniment quotes a phrase from Mahler's Fourth Symphony.) Next are the women who try to be the super housewife and mothers, "Keeping house but clutching/ A copy of *Life*" magazine, trying to stay informed as they chauffeur their kids to and from school. In the final section, Joanne turns on her own kind, "the girls who just watch" and disapprove. "When they get depressed,/ It's a bottle of Scotch," she sings and contemplates "another vodka stinger." She then turns on all of the ladies and comes to the fateful conclusion "Everybody tries … Everybody dies." Just as her tone has gotten more and more harsh, so too the music speeds up then suddenly stops, allowing Joanne's series of "Everybody rise … rise!" to echo *a cappella*.

Although Sondheim's music is in the key of D Major, the song feels like it's in a minor mode, dissonant even. The lyric always takes precedent in "The Ladies Who Lunch" which is why it is such a theatrical piece and requires more acting talent than sonorous tones. Stritch's performance was indeed a showstopper and the song has always been associated with her. (She also played Joanne in the 1972 London production.) Yet other performers playing Joanne have found their own special approaches. During the run of *Company*, Stritch was replaced by Vivian Blaine and then Jane Russell. In the Broadway revivals of the musical, "The Ladies Who Lunch" was sung by Debra Monk in 1995, Barbara Walsh in 2006, and Patti LuPone in 2021. For a character song, it has had more recordings than one might suppose. The first disc was made by Eydie Gormé, followed by recordings by such artists as Cleo Laine, Barbra Streisand, Julie Wilson, Ute Lemper,

Song of the Season

Blossom Dearie, Alice Ripley, Cheryl Bentyne, Anthony de Mare, and Dana Russell with Emile Pandolfi. There was no movie version of *Company* but Anna Kendrick and Alana Allen sang "The Ladies Who Lunch" in the 2003 film *Camp*.

Other notable songs from that season: "Company," "Being Alive," "Getting Married Today," "Another Hundred People," "Side by Side by Side," "Barcelona," "You Can Drive a Person Crazy," "Sorry-Grateful" from *Company*; "Applause," "But Alive," "Who's That Girl?" from *Applause*; "Purlie," "Walk Him Up the Stairs," "I Got Love," "New Fangled Preacher Man," "First Thing Monday Morning" from *Purlie*; "When Your Lover Says Goodbye," "The Money Rings Out Like Freedom" from *Coco*; "Mama, a Rainbow" from *Minnie's Boys*; "My Most Important Moments Go By," "Somebody Died Today," "I Want to Walk to San Francisco" from *The Last Sweet Days of Isaac* (Off-Broadway); "Dream Babies," "If I Had a Million Dollars," "Let Me Come In" from *The Me Nobody Knows* (Off-Broadway); "Seagull, Starfish, Pebble" from *La Strada*; "Something Good Will Happen Soon," "Have Another Drink" from *The Drunkard* (Off-Broadway).

1970–1971 SEASON

The season's two most memorable new musicals could have not have been more different. The dark Harold Prince-Stephen Sondheim-James Goldman show *Follies* was a searing musical drama with lavish production values, costing a record-breaking $800,000. The Off-Broadway musical *Godspell* was a playful retelling of the *Gospel of St. Matthew* requiring only ten actors and a chain-link fence. The two scores were also vastly different. Newcomer Stephen Schwartz wrote a vibrant set of songs for *Godspell* that utilized rock, gospel, old-time vaudeville, folk, and pop. Veteran Sondheim wrote two scores for *Follies*: sparking pastiche numbers for the *Follies* and incisive contemporary songs for the various characters in the present. *Follies* opened to mixed reviews, ran 522 performances, and lost a bundle. *Godspell* met with enthusiastic notices, ran 2,651 performances, and turned into a gold mine with hundreds of productions nationally each year. But time has been kind to *Follies*, now regarded as one of the glories of the American Musical theatre.

The surprise hit of the season was a bubbly revival of *No No Nanette* that ran nearly two years, toured extensively, and put the 1925 musical back into the repertory of revived works. Another surprise was the transfer of the Off-Broadway youth musical *The Me Nobody Knows* to Broadway where it remained for 578 performances. Another transfer, the adult musical revue *Oh, Calcutta!*, brought explicit nudity to the Street and no one was surprised when it ran for four years. Danny Kaye helped the weak Richard Rodgers musical *Two By Two* run 351 times. But a glittering cast of senior citizens, led by Mildred Natwick, could not keep *70, Girls, 70* on the boards for more than a month. This was unfortunate as the John Kander-Fred Ebb score was a sunny delight. Also unfortunate was *The Rothschilds*. The musical ran a very respectable 505 performances but its preparation was so stressful that songwriters Sheldon Harnick and Jerry Bock quarreled and never worked together again. It was a major Broadway loss. There were a number of promising musicals that closed quickly, such as the one-performance *Frank Merriwell*. *Soon*, *Ari*, *Earl of Ruston*, and *Lovely Ladies, Kind Gentlemen* all folded within two weeks. Even the Yiddish musicals *The President's Daughter* and *Light, Lively and Yiddish* managed to run a few months.

The Theatre District in Manhattan was in dismal shape during the 1970s. Crime in New York City was rampant and Times Square was littered with drug dealers and prostitutes, particularly on 42nd Street. All the legit theatres on that fabled street were now either boarded up or turned into porn movie houses. More police were assigned to the district during performance times and Broadway tried different curtain times to make theatregoing more convenient. But patrons were hesitant to go into midtown at night and only a sensational hit show would convince them to risk it. Ironically, the Seventies produced some of the most innovative and rewarding musicals, from *A Chorus Line* (1975) to *Sweeney Todd: The Demon Barber of Fleet Street* (1979). So it was a matter of surviving the hard times and hoping for better days.

Song of the Season

> "Day By Day"
> Music and lyric by Stephen Schwartz, etc.
> From *Godspell* (1971)
> Introduced by Robin Lamont and company

As brilliant as the Sondheim songs from *Follies* are, none had the simple and catchy quality of "Day By Day" from *Godspell*. It is one of the very few musical theatre songs to be a hit on the charts and in churches and synagogues. Schwartz composed the music, a gentle folk-rock tune with a touch of gospel revival in it. He also wrote the lyric based on the librettist-director John-Michael Tebelak's original which was, in turn, based on a prayer by the thirteenth-century bishop Saint Richard of Chichester that, in turn, was based on a twelfth-century prayer. That is an awful lot of authors for one of the musical theatre's simplest and most repetitive song lyrics. "Day By Day" is a prayer which lists the three things one hopes to carry out every day: to "See thee more clearly, Love thee more dearly, Follow thee more nearly."[11] It was sung by cast member Robin Lamont who was joined by the rest of the company. It was also reprised at the end of the musical. The title phrase lends itself to Schwartz's contagious music so "day by day by day" can be repeated almost indefinitely. The song also lends itself to an easy-to-learn sing-along number. Despite its obvious religious content, "Day By Day" was oft recorded. The track from the original cast album was on the charts, as were discs by the Fifth Dimension, Colleen Hewitt, and Judy Stone. Among the other artists to record the song are Judy Collins, Hot Butter, Jackie & Roy, the Diamond Five, Shirley Bassey, the Second Generation, Sunny Phillips, Anita Bryant, Cliff Richard, Sarah Vaughn, Cher and Gene Kloser, Pat Lundy, and Michael Bluestein. Lamont reprised her rendition of "Day By Day" with the cast of the 1973 movie version of *Godspell* and again in the 1976 Broadway production. Verity-Anne Meldrum sang it in the 1971 London production and Anna Maria Perez de Tagle sang it in the 2011 Broadway revival.

Other notable songs from that season: "All for the Best," "By My Side," "Turn Back, O Man," "We Beseech Thee" from *Godspell*; "Losing My Mind," "I'm Still Here," "Broadway Baby," "Could I Leave You?," "Who's That Woman?," "Too Many Mornings," "Waiting for the Girls Upstairs," "The Road You Didn't Take," "In Buddy's Eyes" from *Follies*; "In My Own Lifetime," "One Room" from *The Rothschilds*; "I Do Not Know a Day I Did Not Love You" from *Two By Two*; "Home," "Yes," "See the Light," "Coffee in a Cardboard Cup," "Go Visit Your Grandmother" from *70, Girls, 70*.

1971–1972 SEASON

The season's longest-running musical was not a surprise hit. *Jesus Christ Superstar* had been around long enough that many wondered what took so long for it to arrive on Broadway. It had started with the rock song "Superstar" by Andrew Lloyd-Webber (music) and Tim Rice (lyric) with a vocal by Murray Head which first hit the charts in 1969. Its popularity encouraged Decca/MCA in 1970 to finance the double-album *Jesus Christ Superstar* which was self-described as a "rock opera" about the last days of Jesus. The album was also on the charts and prompted a series of rock concerts in which the sung-through piece was performed with different singers playing various roles. A stage musical version was expected but some were surprised to see *Jesus Christ Superstar* premiere on Broadway rather than London. The New York production was given an over-the-top staging by Tom O'Horgan which did not please some of the critics and the fans of the album. All the same, *Jesus Christ Superstar* ran a very profitable 711 performances. (In London, it ran a record-breaking 3,358 performances.)

The season's other long run was also a rock musical of sorts. *Two Gentlemen of Verona* was a rough-and-tumble version of Shakespeare's play with a multi-ethnic cast and a score by Galt MacDermot (music) and John Guare (lyrics) that used pop, rock, Latin, and Broadway sounds. The musical had been first presented for free in Central Park and was embraced by the public and the press so it transferred to Broadway for 628 performances. The only conventional musical to find any success on Broadway this season was *Sugar*, an uneven version of the 1959 movie classic *Some Like It Hot*. Much more experimental and powerful were two African American pieces by songwriter Melvin Van Peebles. *Ain't Supposed to Die a Natural Death* and *Don't Play Us Cheap* used anger, humor, poetry, songs, and speeches to illustrate life in Black America. Each musical was popular enough to run 325 and 164 performances. Two musicals about Jewish life were less intense and also found an audience. *To Live Another Summer, to Pass Another Winter* was an Israeli revue and *Only Fools Are Sad* was a book musical also from Israel. Six musicals this season lasted less than a week, the most unfortunate victim being *The Grass Harp*, a charming Southern-flavored musical based on the Truman Capote novel and boasting a fine performance by Barbara Cook. The show would later become a cult favorite. There were three revivals of note. *Lost in the Stars* and *On the Town* opened to mixed notices and ran five weeks and ten weeks. The first Broadway revival of *A Funny Thing Happened on the Way to the Forum* received a better welcome and lasted 156 performances The slapstick cast included Phil Silvers, Larry Blyden, and Reginald Owen, and the production was directed by co-author Bert Shevelove. Ironically, Silvers had been the first choice to play Pseudolus back in 1962 but he turned it down and the role went to Zero Mostel.

Song of the Season

> "I Don't Know How to Love Him"
> Music by Andrew Lloyd Webber; lyric by Tim Rice
> From *Jesus Christ Superstar* (1971)
> Introduced by Yvonne Elliman as Mary Magdalene

Just as the score for the rock musical *Hair* is not all rock, so too the songs in the "rock opera" *Jesus Christ Superstar* are not all in the rock mode. "I Don't Know How to Love Him," arguably the most popular number in the show, is a pop ballad with a few operatic jumps but mostly in a comfortable range for pop singers. It is sung by Mary Magdalene (Yvonne Elliman) who, in this version, is a prostitute who has fallen in love with Jesus (Jeff Fenholt). This creates an interesting dilemma for Mary and her confusion is expressed near the end of the first act in this song. The lyric by Tim Rice is a series of questions—"Should I bring him down? ... Should I scream or shout? ... Let my feelings out?"—as well as some contradictions, such as "I'd turn my head ... I'd back away ... I wouldn't want to know."[12] Mary admits "He scares me so" yet "I want him so." The only reference to her as a sex worker is indirect—"I've had so many men before/ In very many ways"—so the song can be sung as a torch number out of the context of the musical. Andrew Lloyd Webber's music presents a considerable jump on the word "love" in the lyric's title phrase. The technique is reminiscent of the same kind of jump in the "where" in the first line of "Over the Rainbow" though the notes are not the same. After this attention-getting device, the music settles into a mid-range pattern with some minor chords to characterize Mary's indecisive language. Also, the song does not end with a climatic push but rather a resigned "I love him so" with repetitive notes. The number had originally been written as the pop song "Kansas Morning" but Rice wrote a whole new lyric for the rock opera.

"I Don't Know How to Love Him" had been part of *Jesus Christ Superstar* from the concept album where it was sung by the unknown American singer Elliman who was attempting to jump-start her career in London. She played Mary and sang it on Broadway and in the 1973 film version of *Jesus Christ Superstar*. Elliman's 1970 recording of the ballad was immediately on the charts, only to be joined by Helen Reddy's version the next year. Other early discs were made by Peggy Lee, Robin Wilson, Jerry Vale, Julie Budd, Percy Faith, Jill Kirkland, and Pilita. These were followed by 100+ recordings by such artists as Shirley Bassey, Four Jets, Peter Matz, Jackie Trent, Bobby Darin, Max Greger, Mulgrew Miller, Laurie Beechman, Emily Skinner, Pieces of 8, and Spencer Day. Dana Gillespie played Mary in the 1972 London production. In the 1977 Broadway revival of *Jesus Christ Superstar*, the ballad was sung by Barbara Niles, by Maya Days in 2000, and by Chilina Kennedy in 2012. Sara Bareilles played Mary and sang it in the 2018 live television version of the rock musical.

Other notable songs from that season: "Superstar," "Herod's Song," "Hosanna," "Everything's All Right" from *Jesus Christ Superstar*; "Yellow Drum," "Marry with Me," "Chain of Love" from *The Grass Harp*; "Put a Curse on You," "Just Don't Make No Sense" from *Ain't Supposed to Die a Natural Death*; "Night Letter," "Who Is Sylvia?," "Bring All the Boys Back Home" from *Two Gentlemen of Verona*; "We Could Be Close," "It's Always Love," "November Song" from *Sugar*.

Song of the Season

1972–1973 SEASON

The season's four long-run musicals were wildly different. *A Little Night Music* was a waltzing comedy of manners with a rich and sophisticated score by Stephen Sondheim. *Pippin* was an anachronistic anything-goes romp with a pop-rock score by Stephen Schwartz. *Grease* was an irreverent pastiche of 1950s music and manners. *Don't Bother Me, I Can't Cope* was a sassy revue about being African American in the 1970s with an eclectic score that used blues, R&B, gospel, and honky tonk. Each, in their own way, was very accomplished and each found an audience, though not the same audience. The more traditional musical *Seesaw* should have joined the other four but, struggle as it did, it couldn't find long-run success. Many of the season's other new musicals had short runs and, according to many, deserved to close early. Two of the most ballyhooed, the rock musicals *Via Galactica* and *Dude*, tried to repeat the popularity of *Hair* and were, in fact, by the creators of *Hair*; together, they ran only twenty-three performances. Other short runs included *Smith, Nash at Nine, Ambassador, Tricks, Mother Earth, Shelter, Cyrano, Dear Oscar,* and *Hurry, Harry*. For the ever-aging Broadway audience looking backward was the revised revival of *Irene* from 1919 which offered movie star Debbie Reynolds as its main attraction. It ran 605 performances but, because of some corrupt book-keeping, still lost money. There was a scandal, of course. But *Irene* took to the road and made another bundle. Off-Broadway was very active this season with fifteen new musicals. Two revues, each celebrating a songwriter of the past, not only had successful runs but enjoyed a long life regionally and in colleges. *Berlin to Broadway with Kurt Weill* and *Oh, Coward!* each had a small cast who sang a trunk load of famous and obscure songs. Original scores were heard in four shows which also had substantial runs: the silly *El Grande de Coca-Cola*, which was sometimes spoken in pidgin Spanish; the musical revue *What's a Nice Country Like You Doing in a State Like This?*, which was filled with up-to-the-minute political songs and sketches; and *Doctor Selavy's Magic Theatre*, a unorthodox musical about psycho-therapy.

"Send in the Clowns"
Music and lyric by Stephen Sondheim
From *A Little Night Music* (1973)
Sung by Glynis Johns as Desiree Armfeldt

Since the 1960s, it is a rare occasion when a theatre song takes off like "Send in the Clowns" has. The enticing ballad is now considered a "standard," something you can say about only a few Broadway songs since 1970. "Send in the Clowns" was a late addition to *A Little Night Music* but the Stephen Sondheim song quickly established itself as the centerpiece of the celebrated waltz score. The ballad was sung by the scandalous actress

Desiree (Glynis Johns) after she has been rejected by her old flame, the lawyer Fredrik (Len Cariou). The number is a torch song yet the unsentimental lyric allows it to be interpreted in various ways, from a wistful statement on the frivolity of love to a deeply cynical ballad about the futility of life. At the end of the musical, "Send in the Clowns" is reprised, with a different lyric, by Desiree and Fredrik and becomes a subdued love duet. Johns had a very limited vocal range and Sondheim wrote the song with this in mind. It is actually one of his least difficult compositions to sing, having no sustained notes and having several musical interludes for the singer to rest. But the number is rich in both melody and harmony, being disconcerting and satisfying at the same time. The masterful lyric is understated, with short questioning phrases: "Isn't it rich? ... Are we a pair? ... Don't you approve?"[13] As through most of the lyric, each phrase ends with a consonant so sustained notes are not needed. Sondheim uses random details to paint vivid pictures and, Desiree being an actress, the song is filled with theatre metaphors, as with "making my entrance ... sure of my lines ... don't you love farce?" There has been much discussion over the years over the song's title. The clowns mentioned are not necessarily circus clowns. The theatrical expression "send in the clowns" refers to any time things are not going well on stage and it is necessary to cut to the jokes to win the audience back. Desiree knows this show biz expression and applies it to her dissolving relationship. Of course, the lyric can be interpreted on another level. The song ends with "Send in the clowns ... Don't bother, they're here." Perhaps Desiree means she is the clown and we are all fools. This is why the song can be effectively performed outside of the context of *A Little Night Music*.

All of the songs in *A Little Night Music* use variations of 3/4 time. "Send in the Clowns" has a slow, lazy even, waltz tempo that uses a rare and complicated 12/8 and 9/9 meter. The melody has a fairly narrow range and the music tends to descend rather than ascend at the most important moments. This appeals particularly to jazz singers and musicians. But as musically enthralling as the song is, "Send in the Clowns" is a ballad that needs to be acted as well as sung. That is why Sondheim and others were so surprised that the song became a chart hit; it is still Sondheim's most well-known song. Frank Sinatra recorded it in 1973 but even wider recognition came two years later when a Judy Collins recording climbed the charts in every English-speaking nation. Among the 300+ artists to record "Send in the Clowns" are Barbra Streisand, Lou Rawls, Kenny Rogers, Count Basie, Roger Whittaker, Blossom Dearie, Jack Jones, Rosemary Clooney, Barbara Carroll, Karen Akers, Hue and Cry, Joe Venuti and Dave McKenna, Cleo Laine, Danny Wright, Olivia Newton John, Bucky and John Pizzarelli, José Carreras, Déja Vu, Susan Boyle, Ruthie Henshall, Matthew Morrison, Betty Buckley, Melissa Errico, and Amanda McBroom. Jean Simmons sang "Send in the Clowns" in the 1975 London production of *A Little Night Music* and Elizabeth Taylor in the 1977 film version. In Broadway revivals, it was sung by Sally Ann Howes in 1990 and Catherine Zeta Jones in 2009, who was replaced by Bernadette Peters during the run.

Song of the Season

Other notable songs from that season: "The Miller's Son," "The Glamorous Life," "A Weekend in the Country," "Every Day a Little Death," "Remember?" from *A Little Night Music*; "No Time at All," "Magic to Do," "Corner of the Sky," "Morning Glow" from *Pippin*; "We Go Together," "Summer Nights," "Freddy, My Love," "Beauty School Dropout" from *Grease*; "It's Not Where You Start (It's Where You Finish)," "Welcome to Holiday Inn" from *Seesaw*; "Don't Bother Me, I Can't Cope" from *Don't Bother Me, I Can't Cope*.

1973–1974 SEASON

The most thrilling new musical on the Street this season was neither new nor from Broadway. Leonard Bernstein's *Candide* had been a glorious failure back in 1956 with a celebrated score but a dismal libretto. The Chelsea Theatre Center of Brooklyn put together a new version of the Voltaire musical with a libretto by Hugh Wheeler and some new or reused songs with new lyrics by Stephen Sondheim. Harold Prince staged the revised revival in the unconventional Off-Broadway space with actors, musicians, and audience all mixed together on different levels. The reviews for the new *Candide* were propitious so the show moved to Broadway. In order to retain Prince's inventive staging, set designer Eugene Lee took most of the existing seats out of the Broadway Theatre and filled the space with platforms, bridges, and steps which allowed the actors full access to the entire space. The reviews were again exemplary and *Candide* ran 788 performances. Even better, the new version placed the musical in the repertory of theatre and opera companies around the world. So after twenty-eight years, *Candide* was finally a hit.

Much of the rest of the season paled in comparison. The Broadway musicals were mostly lackluster with stars used to punch up mediocre material. Carol Channing returned to the role of Lorelei Lee with *Lorelei*, a bland reworking of *Gentlemen Prefer Blondes*. The two surviving Andrews Sisters were the appeal for the Second World War musical *Over Here!* Kay Ballard couldn't keep *Molly* afloat but the popular magician Doug Henning kept *The Magic Show* on the boards for 1,859 performances. Some stars didn't bother with librettos and did their one-person shows on Broadway much as they would in Las Vegas. Bette Midler, Josephine Baker, Sammy Davis, Jr., and Liza Minnelli were all able to attract audiences for successful runs. A musical that ran 847 performances without stars was *Raisin*, a faithful if watered down version of Lorraine Hansberry's landmark drama *A Raisin in the Sun*. Aside from *Candide*, the season's revivals failed to catch on. *The Pajama Game* with a multi-racial cast was commendable but audiences weren't interested. Neither did they patronize *The Desert Song* or *The Beggar's Opera*. The stage version of the beloved movie musical *Gigi* felt like a revival for it was a copy of the screen classic with a half dozen new songs by Frederick Loewe and Alan Jay Lerner. Despite a superior cast, *Gigi* struggled to run three months. Regardless, the musical joined *Candide* in becoming an appealing new/old Broadway musical picked up by regional theatres. It was not apparent at the time, but *Gigi* was the beginning of a trend for turning renowned movie musicals into Broadway shows. Only rarely did the transition succeed.

"In This Wide, Wide World"
Music by Frederick Loewe; lyric by Alan Jay Lerner
From *Gigi* (1974)
Introduced by Karin Wolfe as Gigi

Song of the Season

Frederick Loewe came out of retirement to write six new songs with Alan Jay Lerner for *Gigi*. The movie already had nine songs so the new score was perhaps a matter of more is less. While all the news songs were commendable, the critics felt they lacked theatricality. This might have been due to the way they were staged because even the superb songs from the movie failed to work effectively on stage. Also, Karin Wolfe was cast as Gigi and she was charming but did not have the star quality that was needed for the role. Since the 1973–74 season produced no outstanding score, it was not surprising that the Tony Award for Best Score went to *Gigi*. The best of the new numbers was Gigi's soliloquy "In This Wide, Wide World" in which she is tossed and turned about her affections for the older and more sophisticated Gaston Lachaille (Daniel Massey). The structure of the song is more stream of consciousness than conventional song format. She sings to Gaston but he isn't there, asking him questions and telling him things she cannot bring herself to say to him in person. "I'm sorry you wounded me so," she sings but quickly comes back with "No, please, again, Don't try to explain!" as if he is actually there.[14] In the refrain, Gigi feels that she is not the woman he wants: "In this wide, wide world,/ There is someone who is more ideal for you … Someone who is more your world." She goes on to list the qualities that she lacks, such as "charm galore … finesse and style," and the most important aspect of being his mistress, someone "who can love and still not hope too high." Yet Gigi confesses that, "If you find her I'll die." The song ends with the realization, "I would rather be miserable with you/ Than without you." Loewe's music is a lovely, flowing composition but it has several rests for the singer to stop and find the courage to move on. Also, the music seems to sweep in a circle on the words "wide, wide world," a graceful effect worthy of the veteran songwriter. The *Gigi* revival was recorded but the album was not a big seller. "In This Wide, Wide World" has received few recordings. In 2015, there was another stage version of *Gigi* on Broadway with a revised libretto that tried to sanitize the French tale. In this version, "In This Wide, Wide World" was given an awkward new lyric and was sung as a duet by Gigi (Vanessa Hudgens) and Gaston (Cory Cott) for the happy ending. This did nothing to create interest in the song and "In This Wide, Wide World" remains to be discovered.

Other notable songs from that season: "Paris Is Paris Again," "I Never Want to Go Home Again" from *Gigi*; "The Best of All Possible Worlds," "The Sheep Song," "Life Is Happiness Indeed," "This World" from *Candide* (revival); "Measure the Valleys," "Sidewalk Tree," "A Whole Lotta Sunlight" from *Raisin*; "West End Avenue," "Style," "Lion Tamer" from *The Magic Show*; "Men," "I Won't Let You Get Away" from *Lorelei*; "Over Here," "The Big Beat," "We Got It" from *Over Here!*

1974–1975 SEASON

Not for the first time nor the last, the big excitement this season came from Off-Broadway. *A Chorus Line* opened at the Public Theatre will little advance hoopla, no stars, little scenery, no multiple costumes, and it immediately was the talk of the town. Its limited engagement quickly sold out and plans were made to move uptown. *A Chorus Line* was not the first musical with a lot of dance but it was the first that was exclusively *about* dance. Developed in workshops held by director-choreographer Michael Bennett and using taped interviews with actual Broadway dancers, the concept musical focused on characters and their shared emotions rather than plot. James Kirkwood and Nicholas Dante shaped the material into a libretto using the framework of an audition, and Marvin Hamlisch (music) and Edward Kleban (lyrics) wrote songs that built on the ideas expressed in the interviews. *A Chorus Line* had such wide appeal and struck a nerve with audiences that it ran fourteen years and remains an emotional favorite for many.

The season's two Broadway hits—*The Wiz* and *Shenandoah*—each ran over one thousand performances fueled by popular demand. The new version of *The Wizard of Oz*, with an African American cast of characters and a Motown sound, had a troubled tryout tour but was whipped into shape by opening night and was a joyous affair. The reviews were mixed but it was an audience show from the start. The critics were more harsh with *Shenandoah*, a sentimental tale about a Virginia farmer (John Cullen) trying to retain his pacifist beliefs as the Civil War wages around him. Some pleasant songs and performances were mildly praised by the press but audiences were not so particular and the show ran nearly three years. The musical that should have run as long was *Mack and Mabel*, a stylish musical bio about silent film director Mack Sennett and his star Mabel Normand. The show had everything going for it—brilliant songs by Jerry Herman, an uncompromising libretto by Michael Stewart, star turns by Robert Preston and Bernadette Peters, and inventive staging by Gower Champion—except a happy ending. (Mabel dies of tuberculosis in the end.) The critics were surprisingly dismissive of a Jerry Herman musical that went into Harold Prince-Stephen Sondheim territory and audiences were wary. *Mack and Mabel* closed in two months but has enjoyed many productions elsewhere ever since.

There were the usual number of musicals than ran a week or less, such as the rock musical *The Lieutenant*, set during the Vietnam War; *Man on the Moon*, about warfare in space; and *Doctor Jazz*, a fictional tale about the development of jazz music. Ann Reinking and Joel Grey played Joan of Arc and her French king in *Goodtime Charley* for three months. Familiar Beatles songs couldn't help *Sergeant Pepper's Lonely Hearts Club Band* last more than two months. The London import *The Rocky Horror Show* stirred up little interest and folded after forty-five performances; the sci-fi rock spoof would not become a stage favorite until after the 1975 movie version. There were three notable revivals this season. After playing Mama Rose in *Gypsy* in London to great acclaim, Angela Lansbury brought the show to Broadway for fifteen weeks before setting out

Song of the Season

on tour. Her interpretation of the role was unique and thrilling. Raul Julia shone as the cross-dressing Charley in a revival of Frank Loesser's *Where's Charley?* and the revival did brisk business during its ten-week engagement. A revival of the 1927 favorite *Good News!* had been touring the nation with aging movie stars Alice Faye and John Payne as the box office draw. When the show arrived on Broadway, it was castigated by the press and closed two weeks later. Two Off-Broadway musicals somewhat lost in the shadows after *A Chorus Line* were *Philemon* and *Diamond Studs*. The later was a clever Western spoof that used new songs and old cowboy favorites. *Philemon* was a tragic-comic piece about a Roman slave (Dick Latessa) who discovers Christianity with dire results. Tom Jones and Harvey Schmidt, after three glossy Broadway productions, returned to the Off-Broadway of their still-running *The Fantasticks*. *Philemon* had a limited one-month run while *Diamond Studs* found an audience for 232 performances.

"Time Heals Everything"
Music and lyric by Jerry Herman
From *Mack and Mabel* (1974)
Sung by Bernadette Peters as Mabel Normand

The finest score of the season, most would agree, was Jerry Herman's songs for *Mack and Mabel*. Many also consider it Herman's best score. Yet when *Mack and Mabel* was nominated for eight Tony Award nominations, including Best Musical, there was no nomination for the score. The show's failure on Broadway has been attributed to everyone from the press, who were championing a more "modern" sound at the time, to producer David Merrick who didn't care for the musical and did little to promote it. Although *Mack and Mabel* closed after only eight weeks, the score immediately started to catch on and the song that was most embraced was "Time Heals Everything." Mabel (Bernadette Peters) sings the number after one of the break-ups in her rocky romance with the anti-romantic Mack (Robert Preston). For a torch song from a rather emotional character, "Time Heals Everything" is remarkably restrained. In fact, the singer is not as passionate or overwrought as she is numb. Herman's lyric is a series of sequences of time passing. The title phrase is followed by days, months, seasons, and even "next year." The music is a series of repeated two-note phrases which suggest a clock ticking or a metronome keeping time. The tempo increases in the last refrain as all the units of time are repeated: "Some Tuesday, Thursday, April, August, Autumn, winter, next year, some year."[15] The title phrase is ironic. It is quite clear that nothing has healed. The song ends with a sobering realization that "time heals everything/ But loving you." The whole number is simplicity itself. Herman avoids rhymes and relies on identities or repeated sounds. The vocal range is not terribly wide. The music even has rests that allow for hesitation between ideas. Perhaps the reason "Times Heals Everything" is so potent is that it is not striving for effect. By this time in his career, Herman could trust himself to do more with less. Although there was a production of *Mack and Mabel* in British regional theatre in 1981, the musical did not play in London until 1995 with Caroline O'Connor as Mabel. Her rendition of "Time Heals Everything" is preserved on the cast recording. Since its short Broadway run, *Mack and Mabel* has caught on and there are many productions in England, Australia, Canada, and the States each year. "Time Heals Everything" is a favorite in concerts and cabarets and there have been many recordings, including those by Barbara Cook, Liza Minnelli, Michael Feinstein, Audrey Morris, Georgia Brown, Celia Lipton, Julia McKenzie, Paige O'Hara, Debbie Gravite, Louise Dearman, and Katie Birtill.

Other notable songs from that season: "I Won't Send Roses," "Tap Your Troubles Away," "Hundreds of Girls," "Look What Happened to Mabel" from *Mack & Mabel*; "What I Did for Love," "One," "I Can Do That," "The Music and the Mirror," "Nothing" from *A Chorus Line* (Off-Broadway); "Believe in Yourself," "Home," "Ease On Down the Road," "Be a Lion" from *The Wiz*; "The Pickers Are Comin'," "Next to Lovin' (I Like Fightin')," "Violets and Silverbells" from *Shenandoah*; "Time Warp," "Sweet Transvestite," "What Ever Happened to Saturday Night," "Science Fiction Double Feature" from *The Rocky Horror Show*.

Song of the Season

1975–1976 SEASON

When *A Chorus Line* transferred from the Public Theatre to the Street, it dominated the season. There was not much competition. Only two new book musicals shone; one a hit and the other a miss. *Chicago* was a stylish pastiche jazz musical by John Kander and Fred Ebb about notorious "merry murderesses" in the Roaring Twenties. Gwen Verdon, Chita Rivera, and Jerry Orbach were the nominal stars but it was still considered a "Fosse show" because of Bob Fosse's direction and choreography. *Chicago* ran a profitable 947 performances. The very inventive *Pacific Overtures*, about the history of Japan in the nineteenth century, was a hard sell on Broadway. With a fascinating libretto by John Weidman, a superlative score by Stephen Sondheim, and masterful direction by Harold Prince, *Pacific Overtures* was as ingenious as it was unique, but patrons were afraid of it so the musical struggled to run 193 performances. The season's other book musicals were uneven except for *The Robber Bridegroom*, a backwoods musical that stopped on Broadway for two weeks as part of The Acting Company's national tour. Four giants of the American musical theatre were saddled with problematic librettos which sabotaged their scores. Richard Rodgers' *Rex* told the familiar story of King Henry VIII without anything new to add except some fine songs with lyrics by Sheldon Harnick. Leonard Bernstein and Alan Jay Lerner wrote a rich score for *1600 Pennsylvania Avenue*, an historic cavalcade about various presidents and their first ladies. The script was a muddled mess but the score was admirable and Patricia Routledge was outstanding as the presidents' wives. The expensive musical folded after seven performances. Also closing inside a week were *Boccaccio*, *Rockabye Hamlet*, and *Home Sweet Homer*. Running only marginally longer was *So Long, 174th Street* which had a fun score but a problematic book. *Something's Afoot*, a charming and unpretentious spoof of Agatha Christie whodunnits, only lasted two months on Broadway but became a favorite regionally.

It was an interesting season regarding revues and revivals. The African American revue *Bubbling Brown Sugar* consisted of song standards and delighted audiences for 766 performances. Old songs were also heard in *Me and Bessie* in which Linda Hopkins dazzled as singer Bessie Smith for 453 performances. Music by Scott Joplin was used to create *Treemonisha*, a ragtime musical that played sixty-four times. The most controversial musical of the season was a revival of Kurt Weill's *The Threepenny Opera* with a new translation and avant-garde staging by Richard Foreman. Critics and patrons debated its merits during its 306-performance run. The more conventional revivals of *My Fair Lady* and *Hello, Dolly!* had substantial runs. Pearl Bailey returned as Dolly in the latter and Ian Richardson and Christine Andreas headed the cast of the former. The most surprising revival of the season was *Very Good Eddie*, the 1915 Princess Musical which had rarely been produced since then. This production from the Goodspeed Opera House in Connecticut was endorsed by the press and ran 307 performances. Two lightweight Off-Broadway musicals ran over 400 performances. *Boy Meets Boy* spoofed 1930s musicals with one major gender change and the revue *Tuscaloosa's Calling Me ... but I'm

Not Going was a tribute to (and ribbing of) living in New York City. A decade later, after the advent of AIDS and further urban decay, such scatter-brained musicals would not be possible.

"All That Jazz"
Music by John Kander; lyric by Fred Ebb
From *Chicago* (1975)
Sung by Chita Rivera as Velma Kelly, and ensemble

All of the songs in *Chicago* are pastiche numbers echoing 1920s jazz. Some are nods to specific songs, such as "Mr. Cellophane" and Bert Williams' signature song "Nobody." But it is "All That Jazz" that is the centerpiece of the score and the most popular number from the show. John Kander and Fred Ebb wrote it knowing that Bob Fosse was going to choreograph it and the music alone conjures up Fosse's distinctive style: slow and sensual movement, arms and torso featured over the footwork, and contortions that border on the sideshow look. *Chicago* is set in the mid-1920s when jazz was just starting to go mainstream. Many Americans (particularly the older generations) considered the sound of jazz to be much too sexy, too tribal, even animal like. Uptempo jazz, as in Dixieland jazz, was thought to be too wild but slow jazz was worse. "All That Jazz" starts with a restrained beat but is seething with energy. As the music progresses, it builds, climbing in half-steps. This semi-tone advancement gives the song lift and, to use the obvious metaphor of physical sex, the number climaxes with "But, oh, I love my life" right before the releasing of tension with the title phrase.[16]

The expression "all that jazz" has been a cliché since the 1920s. Before "jazz" became widely associated with a kind of music, "jazzing" was slang for the sexual act. Such a lascivious connotation never completely disappeared and it is in the subtext of Ebb's lyric. Velma Kelly (Chita Rivera) introduces *Chicago* with "All That Jazz," setting up the period and the carefree new lifestyle of era's flappers. The lyric mentions alcohol ("the gin is cold"), speakeasies ("a whoopee spot ... just a noisy hall"), dancing ("shimmy shake ... bunny hug"), drugs ("aspirin down at United Drug"), and hot music ("Father Dipp is gonna blow the blues"). One of the many nicknames for trumpeter Louis Armstrong was "Father Dip." The lyric has several such 1920s slang expressions which may or may not be familiar to modern audiences. Yet it doesn't matter because the hedonism in the air pervades the whole song. The lyric has a few references to being "high," including a nod to Lindbergh: "I betcha Lucky/ Lindy never flew so high." In order to get a more sassy pronunciation of the word "jazz," Kander sometimes gives the word two notes, allowing for the pronunciation "jay-azz." Like many of the pastiche numbers in *Chicago*, "All That Jazz" sounds so authentic that it might pass as a 1920s jazz song. Of course Ebb's lyric is perhaps too direct for the period. Irving Berlin's "Everybody's Doing It" and Cole

Song of the Season

Porter's "Let's Do It" got by as long as "it" could mean falling in love or a new dance step. "All That Jazz" leaves little to the imagination.

Rivera's rendition of "All That Jazz" is indelible but several performers have sung the number on stage with success. Ute Lemper was Velma in the 1979 London production of Chicago and Bebe Neuwerth was the first of many Velmas in the long-running 1996 Broadway revival. Catherine Zeta Jones played Velma in the 2002 film version. While the song has been heard on television shows, Las Vegas spectaculars, and dance competitions, there are only a handful of recordings. Liza Minnelli, Shirley Bassey, Niki Evans, Kate Hudson, Lea Michele, Camila Mendes, Madelaine Petsch, and Vanessa Morgan are among those who have performed "All That Jazz" on TV or in concerts that were filmed. Karen Ziemba, Jim Walton, and Bob Cuccioli sang "All That Jazz" in the Off-Broadway Kander and Ebb revue *And the World Goes 'Round* (1991). The title "All That Jazz" was used for the 1979 film by Bob Fosse but the song was not among the numbers heard on the soundtrack.

Other notable songs from that season: "Cell Block Tango," "Nowadays," "All I Care About (Is Love)," "Class," "Razzle Dazzle," "Mr. Cellophane" from *Chicago*; "Pretty Lady," "Someone in a Tree," "A Bowler Hat," "Please, Hello," "Poems" from *Pacific Overtures*; "Sleepy Man," "With Style," "Love Stolen" from *The Robber Bridegroom*; "Away from You," "No Song More Pleasing" from *Rex*; "Take Care of This House," "Lud's Wedding/I Love My Wife," "Duet for One (The First Lady of the Land)" from *1600 Pennsylvania Avenue*.

1976–1977 SEASON

It was a busy season with lots of variety, from family-friendly fare to erotic revues, but when the dust settled, it all came down to only one long-run hit—*Annie*—which joined the repertory of oft-produced musicals. The mostly forgotten comic strip *Little Orphan Annie* was crafted into a conventional but effective musical comedy with a bright score, playful performances, and a solid production. By the time *Annie* closed, it had chalked up 2,377 performances; there are still hundreds of productions each year. The season's other shows with substantial runs are pretty much forgotten today. *I Love My Wife*, a coy musical about wife swapping, ran 857 times and was hopelessly dated by the time it closed. The vibrant *Your Arms Too Short to Box with God*, a retelling of St. Matthew's gospel in the context of a religious revival meeting, ran 429 performances then disappeared. And there were two revues with plenty of nudity that had insanely long runs. *Let My People Come*, a transfer from Off-Broadway which left little to the imagination, played in a small venue for 1,273 performances. A revival of *Oh! Calcutta!* also found an intimate berth and played for locals and tourists for 5,959 performances. Better shows with shorter runs included the London revue *Side by Side by Sondheim*, the 1929 Kurt Weill-Bertolt Brecht music-drama *Happy End* finally making its New York debut, the South African revue *Ipi-Tombi*, and a musical version of Shakespeare's *Twelfth Night* titled *Music Is* which certainly deserved to run more than a week.

It was a bountiful season for first-class revivals. Zero Mostel returned in *Fiddler on the Roof* and Yul Brynner did likewise in *The King and I*. The Jewish-themed musical played 167 times but the Siamese-flavored musical ran for 719 performances. An all-Black version of *Guys and Dolls* sounded like a gimmick but the Frank Loesser show played very well with an African American sensibility. The rarely revived 1917 musical *Going Up!* was resurrected with the hopes of catching on as *No No Nanette* and *Very Good Eddie* had recently done. It had to settle for six weeks. The backwoods musical *The Robber Bridegroom* returned from its tour and this time stayed on Broadway for eighteen weeks. The Houston Grand Opera's stirring revival of *Porgy and Bess* was roundly praised and remained on Broadway for 122 performances before continuing on its tour. Musicals Off-Broadway this season were also diverse. The revue *Starting Here, Starting Now* introduced the team of David Shire (music) and Richard Maltby, Jr., and their evening of smart, incisive songs pleased patrons for fifteen weeks. Tommy Tune staged the offbeat musical *The Club* in which cigar-smoking Victorians males (played by women) sang period songs in their men-only club. The quasi-revue ran nearly two years. Although it had been around since 1968, the playful biblical musical *Joseph and the Amazing Technicolor Dreamcoat* was finally given a professional production in New York and was so well received that after three weeks the producers moved it to Broadway.

Song of the Season

> "Tomorrow"
> Music by Charles Strouse; lyric by Martin Charnin
> From *Annie* (1977)
> Sung by Andrea McArdle as Annie

"Tomorrow" is the Broadway song people love to hate; or perhaps, hate to love. The unabashedly optimistic ballad is quite appropriate in the context of *Annie*. Charles Strouse and Martin Charnin wrote what was once called a Depression-chaser, the kind of song sung in the 1930s that offered bright blue skies and better days. Shirley Temple sang a bunch of such numbers in her movies during the Depression. The young Annie sings it to her dog Sandy but really to boost up her own spirits. The lyric is uncomplicated and direct, pointing out that you can "bet your bottom dollar/ That tomorrow/ There'll be sun."[17] Charnin's lyric is filled with clichés of optimism: "clear away the cobwebs … stick out my chin and grin … ya gotta hang on." The rhymes are mostly masculine and simple, as one would expect from the young uneducated Annie (Andrea McArdle). Strouse's melody is a moderately paced march with repeated musical phrases. The word "tomorrow" becomes a clarion call, especially when sung in the higher register. Then the music descends for the "day away" line in "You're only/ A day / Away!" It is not the easiest song to sing effectively because of its high reaches and the need to not get shrill. That is why male vocalists are not drawn to the number. But even when sung well by kids and women, "Tomorrow" is a bit overpowering outside of the context of *Annie*. The number is reprised later in the musical by Annie, President Roosevelt, and members of his cabinet. "Tomorrow" quickly became the hit of the show and is familiar to many who have never seen *Annie*. Strouse first wrote the song's music back in 1970 for the short film *Replay*, providing a lyric as well. He must have thought it too good a melody to waste so he wrote a new lyric and included it in his score for the stage musical *Charlie and Algernon* but ended up not using it. When working on *Annie*, Strouse played the tune for Charnin who wrote the cheery lyric that became "Tomorrow."

Cissy Houston, Johnny Mathis, and Grace Jones recorded "Tomorrow" the year *Annie* opened, followed by 100+ discs by such artists as Barbra Streisand, Alvin and the Chipmunks, Jackie Trent, Lou Rawls, the Manhattans, Lea Salonga, Nikka Costa, André Kostelanetz, Elaine Paige, Paige O'Hara, Kim Criswell, Robin Spielberg, the Midnite String Quartet, and Jennifer Nettles. On screen, Aileen Quinn played Annie and sang "Tomorrow" in the 1982 movie version and Quvenzhané Wallis played her in the 2014 remake. On television, Alicia Morton played Annie in a 1999 version and Celina Smith in a 2021 live broadcast. McArdle also played Annie in the 1978 London production, Brittny Kissinger sang "Tomorrow" in the 1997 Broadway revival and by Lilla Crawford in the 2012 revival.

Other notable songs from that season: "It's a Hard-Knock Life," "Easy Street," "You're Never Fully Dressed Without a Smile" from *Annie*; "Hey There, Good Times," "Lovers on Christmas Eve" from *I Love My Wife*; "Your Arms Too Short to Box with God," "We're Gonna Have a Good Time" from *Your Arms Too Short to Box with God*; "Should I Speak of Loving You," "I Am It" from *Music Is*; "Surabaya Johnny," "The Bilbao Song," "Sailors' Song" from *Happy End*; "Starting Here, Starting Now," "Watching the Parade Go By," "I Don't Remember Christmas" from *Starting Here, Starting Now* (Off-Broadway); "Any Dream Will Do," "Close Every Door" from *Joseph and the Amazing Technicolor Dreamcoat* (Off-Broadway).

Song of the Season

1977–1978 SEASON

The precarious ways of Broadway were on display this season in which highly anticipated musicals failed to run long enough to turn a profit and sleepers ran for years. Business was booming but not where you expected. For example, *The Act* looked like a sure winner. Liza Minnelli, at the peak of her popularity, was teamed up with John Kander and Fred Ebb for the score and George Furth providing the book. Or consider *On the Twentieth Century* with Madeleine Kahn and John Cullum, a libretto and lyrics by Betty Comden and Adolph Green, and music by Cy Coleman, all under the direction of Harold Prince. Ticket brokers and theatre parties could just about smell the money. But Martin Scorsese had little experience directing for the stage and *The Act* went through so many revisions that by the time it opened it was little more than a Las Vegas show with a few good songs. When word got out that Minnelli's singing-dancing was so strenuous that in one number she was lip-synching to a recording, there was a big stink and a lot of bad press, leaving *The Act* losing a bundle when it closed after seven months. Much more satisfying was *On the Twentieth Century* with dazzling performances, a merry mock operetta score, and glittering art deco sets and costumes by Robin Wagner and Florence Klotz. The reviews were widely divided and two months after opening Kahn mysteriously left the show and her understudy, the unknown Judy Kaye, took over. The expensive production soldiered on but at 460 performances it did not pay. So what did run? The Off-Broadway revue *Ain't Misbehavin'*, celebrating the music of Thomas "Fats" Waller, transferred to Broadway, received rave reviews for the five-member cast and the way the famous and not-so-famous songs were presented, and ran 1,652 performances. Running a few months longer was *Dancin'*, Bob Fosse's revue in which the cast did not sing but were radiant in the Fosse-choreographed dances. The other Broadway production to run over one thousand performances was *Beatlemania*, a concert with a Beatles tribute band. How odd that the three big hits of the season had no story, characters, or original songs.

The Off-Broadway musical *Runaways*, featuring the voices of teens who escape abusive homes and try to make it on their own, transferred from the Public Theatre to a Broadway house and found an audience for over eight months. The other new Broadway musicals—*Working*, *A History of the American Film*, and *Angel*—had much to recommend but each closed inside of three weeks. Two revivals allowed theatregoers the opportunity to see two classic portrayals: Richard Kiley in *Man of La Mancha* and Carol Channing in *Hello, Dolly!* Also back on Broadway was *Jesus Christ Superstar* for three months but, like *Beatlemania*, it was in a concert format rather than a theatre production. Thoroughly theatrical was a revival of *Kismet* re-set in Africa and titled *Timbuktu!* Some tribal music was added but much of the score remained and was delivered mellifluously by the African American cast. The lavish production found an audience for seven months. Once again, one had to turn to Off-Broadway for the season's best new score. *I'm Getting My Act Together and Taking It on the Road* had delectable songs by Nancy Ford and Gretchen Cryer and a thin plot to hang them on. During a dress rehearsal for her cabaret act, former soap opera actress Heather (Gretchen Cryer) demonstrates for her manager

(Joel Fabiani) how she has changed her image and wants to sing more truthful songs about herself and about being a woman. The script is mostly a debate but the pop-rock songs were resplendent. *I'm Getting My Act Together and Taking It on the Road* was a surprise success, running three years in its intimate Off-Broadway venue.

"Old Friend"
Music by Nancy Ford; lyric by Gretchen Cryer
From *I'm Getting My Act Together
and Taking It on the Road* (1978)
Sung by Gretchen Cryer as Heather

The songs in *I'm Getting My Act Together and Taking It on the Road* cover a variety of topics, from empty marriages with smiling facades to the downside to the empowerment of women. "Old Friend" is about platonic friendships that disregard gender. Heather's manager Joe is a friend in whom she has confided in over the years. Heather tells Joe that she wrote this song about them and she sings it to him at her dress rehearsal. Cryer's lyric is casual yet potent. Throughout the song is a short refrain that returns, commenting on what preceded it: "Love is rare, life is strange; Nothing lasts, people change."[18] The verses set up the situation: the two friends sitting in bar late at night after she has "lost another lover" and she needs someone she trusts to talk to. The "old friend" listens to "my sad story/ And wonders at my taste" in choosing a lover. Despite the "pain of getting through it," both know that "You'll do it again." In the following verses, the two reminisce about "life and love, as old friends do." The friend admits that he has learned to love despair "(be)cause that's really all part of it." The two even consider taking off together to "travel the world as old friends do." But they soon realize it is all wishful thinking and not solving anything. It is late, the bartender is "dozing," and it is decided that she will "go out on my own" and the refrain about how life changes is repeated once more. Like all the lyrics in *I'm Getting My Act Together and Taking It on the Road*, "Old Friend" is incisive, honest, and very engaging. Ford's music is a moderately paced folk ballad in 4/4 time with a narrow range for the verses and a flowing, expansive quality for the refrains. The composition is also the kind of gentle music one might hear in a quiet bar late at night. Because "Old Friend" is not about a romantic relationship, it can apply to all kinds of friendships. It also is very effective whether sung by male or female vocalists. A handful of effective recordings of "Old Friend" over the years include those by Liz Robertson, Betty Buckley, Sean Ray, the New York City Gay Men's Chorus, Salena Jones, Paul Baker, and Nathan Temby, as well as duet versions by Emily Skinner and Alice Ripley, and Michael Feinstein and Cheyenne Jackson. Diane Langton was Heather in the 1981 London production of the musical and her rendition of "Old Friend" is preserved on the cast recording.

Other notable songs from that season: "Strong Woman Number," "Natural High," "In a Simple Way I Love You" from *I'm Getting My Act Together and Taking It on the Road* (Off-Broadway); "Our Private World," "Repent," "Babette," "Never" from *On the 20th Century*; "All the Livelong Day," "Just a Housewife," "It's an Art," "Fathers and Sons," "Nobody Tells Me How" from *Working*; "City Lights," "Shine It On," "Arthur in the Afternoon" from *The Act*; "We Are Not Strangers," "Lonesome on the Road," "Where Are Those People Who Did 'Hair'?" from *Runaways*.

1978–1979 SEASON

While this season introduced *Sweeney Todd: The Demon Barber of Fleet Street*, one of Stephen Sondheim's crowning achievements, it also saw failed efforts by such established songwriters as Jerry Herman, Charles Strouse and Lee Adams, Alan Jay Lerner, and Richard Rodgers. This last was the most unfortunate as *I Remember Mama* was Rodgers' last project; he died three months after the show closed with 108 unprofitable performances. Strouse and Adams scored *A Broadway Musical*, a supposed inside look at the making of a musical. After it ran three weeks Off-Broadway, the producers transferred it to the Street where it closed opening night. Lerner's and Herman's shows deserved to run longer for they boasted fine scores and top-notch performances. Herman's *The Grand Tour* held on for two months whereas Lerner's *Carmelina* closed in two weeks. Time has shown both scores to be much better than initially thought and both musicals have been revived on occasion. The power of the critics and the economics of Broadway made it more and more difficult for a show to take its time to find an audience. Even *Sweeney Todd*, with favorable reviews and a slew of awards, could only stay on the boards for 557 performances. Today it is considered a masterpiece and audiences have gotten used to the macabre tale. Besides dozens of productions each year, *Sweeney Todd* has already returned to Broadway on three occasions. The two long-run hits on Broadway were *They're Playing Our Song* and *The Best Little Whorehouse in Texas*, both running over one thousand performances. The latter began Off-Broadway but had no trouble finding an audience on Broadway. Michael Bennett's *Ballroom* met with mixed notices and had to settle for fifteen weeks. Running only a few weeks longer was *Savará*, a musical based on the popular 1976 Brazilian film *Dona Flor and Her Two Husbands*. *Zoot Suit*, the first musical created by Latinx artists, got a lot of attention but not the kind of reviews to let it run beyond five weeks. Similarly, *Platinum*, *King of Hearts*, and *The Utter Glory of Morrissey Hall* failed to run, the last closing after its first performance. *Up in One*, a revue featuring Peter Allen, did not catch on, but *Eubie!*, a musical tribute to African American composer Eubie Blake, entertained audiences for 439 performances. There were several revivals this season, the most successful being *Whoopee!*, the 1928 musical comedy which ran seven weeks.

"A Little Priest"
Music and lyric by Stephen Sondheim
From *Sweeney Todd: The Demon Barber of Fleet Street* (1979)
Sung by Len Cariou, as Sweeney Todd,
and Angela Lansbury, as Mrs. Lovett

The duet "A Little Priest" is the most overtly comic number in *Sweeney Todd*; it is also the most diabolical. The song is the first finale, which is unusual. Often a chorus number or a dramatic solo is preferred to close the act and send the audience into the intermission. The number that comes right before "A Little Priest" is Sweeney's explosive "Epiphany" in which he decides to murder without reason or restraint. Such a powerful moment would certainly provide an Act One climax. But Sondheim and librettist High Wheeler (and perhaps director Harold Prince) decided to end the act with a comedy duet, albeit a very dark kind of comedy. When one realizes that the theme of the whole musical, the dog-eat-dog mentality of cruel survival, is expressed vividly in the duet, one sees that "A Little Priest" is the ideal song for this act closer. Like many Sondheim songs, "A Little Priest" is a mini-musical in itself. The scene begins with Sweeney (Len Cariou) and Mrs. Lovett (Angela Lansbury) contemplating what to do with the body of the blackmailing Señor Pirelli whom Sweeney has just murdered. Sweeney says he will wait until dark to dispose of the body but Mrs. Lovett has a better idea. Without ever coming out and saying that Pirelli would provide the substance for several meat pies, she hints at her idea, commenting that it "seems an awful waste" to just dispose of such a "plump" corpse.[19] Mrs. Lovett has to provide a few more hints ("business needs a lift … think of it as thrift … the price of meat") before Sweeney catches on and immediately likes the idea. He has been such a morose person since his first appearance in the musical that to see him suddenly joyously excited about something is striking. Also, for the first time he acts with a little affection for Mrs. Lovett, which she craves. The excitement builds for Sweeney as he sees such cannibalism as an apt metaphor for the human condition. "It's man devouring man," he notes and reasons "who are we to deny it in here?" Both of them are actually slaphappy at the thought of their new venture and they start play acting. Mrs. Lovett offers various dishes, identified by the profession of the deceased, and Sweeney plays the customer who considers her suggestions and comments on them. She offers him "a little priest" which he questions with, "Is it really good?" "Too good," she sings, because priests "don't commit sins of the flesh … So it's pretty fresh." And so begins one of the most ingenious list songs of the American musical theatre. Sondheim's catalogue of professions and how they translate into dishes is filled with puns and other so-called low comedy. For example, Mrs. Lovett sings about how one can identify the "grocer" dish because "it's green." Sondheim has a field's day with rhymes. At one point in the song, Sweeney attempts to find a rhyme for each profession that Mrs. Lovett offers: "Tinker/something pinker … tailor/something paler … butler/something subtler … potter/something hotter" but she stumps him with "Locksmith" for which Sweeney (and maybe Sondheim?) cannot come up with a rhyme. Throughout the duet, Sondheim returns to the theme of "The history of the world, my sweet … Is who gets eaten, and who gets to eat!" The song ends with a double-meaning joke: "we'll serve anyone—Meaning anyone—And to anyone at all!"

Sondheim's music for "A Little Priest" changes from one section to another, sometimes filled with harsh chords and other times a sprightly waltz. Yet the sheet music is marked 4/4 with the direction for 120 beats per minute and the notation "rubato." This is a musical instruction to temporary disregard the strict tempo when necessary to allow the singers to pick up the pace or slacken it, in this case for comic effect. Also, the song starts with several contemplative rests while Mrs. Lovett lets Sweeney figure out what she is suggesting. As the song builds and the two of them get more and more excited about their new enterprise, the music expands and ends up being a sweeping waltz. The score for *Sweeney Todd* is filled with extraordinary songs, from sublime ballads to fiery chorale numbers, but "A Little Priest" is a piece that sticks with the audience in an odd and macabre way. That said, it has not had much of a life outside of the context of the musical. How could it? It is not only character driven but also thematically linked to *Sweeney Todd* and only *Sweeney Todd*. The only recordings of note are those in the various original cast albums. During the original Broadway run, Cariou and Lansberry were replaced by George Hearn and Dorothy Loudon. In the 1989 revival, Sweeney and Mrs. Lovett were played by Bob Gunton and Beth Fowler, as were Michael Cerveris and Patti LuPone in 2005 and Josh Groban and Annaleigh Ashford in 2023. In the 2007 film version of *Sweeney Todd*, "A Little Priest" was sung by Johnny Depp and Helena Bonham Carter. *Sweeney Todd* is very popular in Great Britain. The original 1980 London production featured Denis Quilley and Sheila Hancock.

Other notable songs from that season: "The Ballad of Sweeney Todd," "(I'll Steal You) Johanna," "Pretty Women," "Not While I'm Around," "Green Finch and Linnet Bird," "The Worst Pies in London" from *Sweeney Todd*; "The Bus to Amarillo," "Hard Candy Christmas," "The Sidestep," "Twenty-Four Hours of Lovin'" from *The Best Little Whorehouse in Texas*; "They're Playing Our Song," "I Still Believe in Love" from *They're Playing Our Song*; "I'll Be Here Tomorrow," "One Extraordinary Thing," "Marianne" from *The Grand Tour*; "Fifty Percent," "I Love to Dance" from *Ballroom*; "One More Walk Around the Garden" from *Carmelina*; "Nothing, Only Love" from *The King of Hearts*.

Song of the Season

1979–1980 SEASON

The number of new musicals continued to climb this season and eight shows (new and revivals) had long and profitable runs. The anxiously awaited London import *Evita*, with an American cast, had no trouble settling down for a long run. Another British import, *A Day in Hollywood / A Night in the Ukraine*, was greatly altered and was actually better than the London original. It ran over a year. Running twice as long was the circus-style musical *Barnum*. As a musical biography of P. T. Barnum (Jim Dale), it was pretty thin but as solid entertainment it was a winner. Another long run this season, both on Broadway and on the road, was the quasi-burlesque show *Sugar Babies* which filled houses as long as stars Mickey Rooney and Ann Miller were in it. Among the new musicals that floundered and then closed were *Happy New Year, Comin' Uptown, Strider, The 1940s Radio Hour, Black Broadway, Billy Bishop Goes to War, King of Schnorres*, and *Musical Chairs*. Efforts to bring non-Broadway music to Broadway failed to find an audience, as with *But Never Jam Today, Got Tu Go Disco, Reggae*, and *Broadway Opry '79*. Three revivals that had significant runs were: *West Side Story* with Debbie Allen as a fiery Anita; *Peter Pan* with Sandy Duncan as the boy hero; and *Oklahoma!* with a superior cast led by Laurence Guittard, Christine Andreas, Mary Wickes, and Christine Ebersole. There were several other revivals which either had limited runs or just couldn't find an audience to keep them on the boards: *Babes in Toyland, Canterbury Tales, The Most Happy Fella, Naughty Marietta, Street Scene*, and *The Merry Widow*. Depending on the "person," one-person shows sometimes made a lot of money in a short time. This season saw *Gilda Radnor: Live from New York, Bette Midler: Divine Madness, Bruce Forsythe on Broadway*, and the magician *Blackstone!* Three revues of interest played Off-Broadway this season. *Tintypes* looked at America at the turn of the twentieth century using period songs. It was received with enough enthusiasm that after four months it transferred to Broadway. The intimate revue managed to survive three months in one of Broadway's smallest venues then went on to become a popular choice for theatres across the country. The other two revues wisely decided to remain Off-Broadway where they had very long runs. The farcical *Scrambled Feet* parodied and lampooned the current New York theatre scene. During its 831 performances, the material was altered to keep up with the times. Running even longer was *One Mo' Time*, a recreation of African American vaudeville with authentic songs and sketches. The revue ran 1,372 times without any needed alterations.

"Don't Cry for Me Argentina"
Music by Andrew Lloyd Webber; lyric by Tim Rice
From *Evita* (1979)
Introduced by Patti LuPone as Eva Peron

Because *Evita* had been playing in London for more than a year before it opened on Broadway, the Andrew Lloyd Webber-Tim Rice score was already familiar to Americans and "Don't Cry for Me, Argentina" was already on the charts. The number was the signature song of the musical, heard near the beginning of *Evita* when the deceased Eva Peron (Patti Lupone) sings it to the people of Argentina. In the second act, Eva reprises it with altered lyrics when she appears on a balcony of the presidential palace in Buenos Aires and sings to the people that she will not forget them now that she and her husband are in power. "Don't Cry for Me, Argentina" is heard one last time when Eva sings it during a radio broadcast soon before her death. The music is graceful and regal, being appropriate for a funeral or a coronation. (As with a lot of Lloyd Webber's music, some music critics have found similarities to classical pieces; in this case, Gounod's "Ave Maria" and Bach's "Prelude in C Major.") There is something about the music that signifies sincerity yet the lyric is emotionally suspect. It is a political banality but with such engaging music one believes it could move a nation to tears. Eva reminds her subjects that regardless of her social standing, "I kept my promise. Don't keep your distance."[20] The lyric ends with the shameless declaration, "All you have to do is look at me to know/ That every word is true." Highlighting the ironic tone of the song, the melody of "Don't Cry for Me, Argentina" is very close to Che's very critical song "Oh, What a Circus!," sung during Eva's funeral and questioning what all the fuss is about.

The title of the song comes from the plaque on Eva Peron's grave in Buenos Aires which reads: "Don't cry for me, Argentina. I remain quite near you." Because the lyric is more political than romantic, it is surprising how popular the song became. Julie Covington, who sang the role of Eva on the 1976 concept album of *Evita*, made a single which quickly climbed the charts, first in Britain and then in every English-speaking nation on the planet. When the concept album was being turned into a West End musical in 1978, Covington decided to opt out and director Harold Prince convinced the producers to go with newcomer Elaine Paige to play Eva. Another relatively unknown actress-singer, Patti LuPone was cast as Eva in the 1979 Broadway production. "Don't Cry for Me, Argentina" was a kind of signature song for LuPone for a time. Madonna played Eva in the 1996 film version and Elena Roger played her in the 2006 London revival and in the 2014 Broadway revival. There have been many cover versions of "Don't Cry for Me, Argentine" beginning with early records by the Carpenters, the Shadows, Olivia Newton-John, Shirley Bassey, Tom Jones, Paloma San Basilio, and the American disco group Festival. Over the years there have been notable versions by Sinéad O'Connor, the Mike Flowers Pops, Nacha Guevara, the punk rock band Me First and the Gimme Gimmes, Judy Collins, Nicole Scherzinger, Donna Summer, Richard Clayderman, Sharon Campbell, Alice Heywood, Blonde Ambition, and Lea Michele and Chris Colfer from *Glee*.

Song of the Season

Other notable songs from that season: "On This Night of a Thousand Stars," "High Flying Adored," "Another Suitcase in Another Hall," "A New Argentina," "And the Money Keeps Rolling In (and Out)" from *Evita*; "The Colors of My Life," "Love Makes Such Fools of Us All," "Come Follow the Band," "The Museum Song" from *Barnum*; "Just Go to the Movies," "The Best in the World," "I Love a Film Cliché" from *A Day in Hollywood / A Night in the Ukraine*; "Theatre Party Ladies," "Makin' the Rounds," "Composer Tango" from *Scrambled Feet* (Off-Broadway).

1980-1981 SEASON

Broadway was not the place to hear new songs this season. Instead the shows offered 1930s movie tunes, Shakespeare songs, turn-of-the-century oldies, Duke Ellington favorites, French classic chansons, and Gilbert and Sullivan numbers. And when there was a new score, the disappointment was great. Songwriters John Kander and Fred Ebb had a hit with the Lauren Bacall vehicle *Woman of the Year* but it had what most consider the weakest score of their career. Charles Strouse and Lee Adams also stumbled badly, not only for trying to resurrect their *Bye Bye Birdie* with a sequel, *Bring Back Birdie*, but for what can be safely called their worst score together. New songs were heard in *Charlie and Algernon, Copperfield, Fearless Frank, It's So Nice to Be Civilized,* and *Onward Victoria*, the last closing on opening night and the others folding before two weeks had passed. (Also running only one performance were *The Mooney Shapiro Songbook* and *Broadway Follies*.) So what were patrons hearing on Broadway? Most memorably Harry Warren (music) and Al Dubin (lyrics) songs from the 1933 film classic *42nd Street* which producer David Merrick turned into the season's biggest hit. In *Sophisticated Ladies* one heard a treasure trove of Ellington songs performed by a dynamite cast that included Gregory Hines, Judith Jamison, Hinton Battle, and Gregg Burge. One heard gems from early in the century in *Tintypes*, Elizabethan verse set to music in *Shakespeare's Cabaret*, Edith Piaf (Jane Lapotaire) standards in *Piaf*, and the ever-vibrant score from *The Pirates of Penzance* given new life thanks to a delicious staging by Wilford Leach and standout performances by Kevin Kline, Linda Ronstadt, Rex Smith, George Rose and Estelle Parsons. The revival was first presented in Central Park then later moved to Broadway where, at 772 performances, it broke the record for the longest-running Gilbert and Sullivan production in New York on record. Familiar songs were also heard in the nine revivals this season. Richard Burton in *Camelot* and Dick Van Dyke in *The Music Man* got the most attention, if not the most praise. The only new score of any vigor this season came from Off-Broadway. William Finn had written the book, music, and lyrics for a quirky little musical called *In Trousers* back in 1978. This season Finn took that show's incorrigible hero Marvin (Michael Rupert) and continued his story in the longer and more satisfying *March of the Falsettos*. From the first notes of the score, one knew this was an exciting new voice in the musical theatre. Off-Broadway patrons agreed and kept the eccentric musical on the boards for 268 performances. The only other Off-Broadway musical to run that long was *Really Rosie*, a delightful piece about kids (but to be enjoyed by everyone) based on characters created by Maurice Sendak and musicalized by Carole King. These two shows were a bright spot in a season with very little new to sing about.

Song of the Season

> "Four Jews in a Room Bitching"
> Music and lyric by William Finn
> From *March of the Falsettos* (1981)
> Introduced by Michael Rupert as Marvin, Chip Zien as Mendel,
> Stephen Bogardus as Whizzer, and James Kushner as Jason

Has a musical ever started out on such a furious note as *March of the Falsettos* does? Make that sixty-four rapid eighth notes before the four male characters in the musical jump into "Four Jews in a Room Bitching." Here is a musical number that begins mid-staccato and never lets go. William Finn's music is in 4/4 time and it is indicated there are 175 beats per minute. That, in plain English, is fast. The lyric consists of mostly one-syllable words which have to be spit out rather than sung. The opening line, "Four Jews in a room bitching," is followed by the rapid "Four Jews in a room plot a crime." The words "bitch" and "funny" are then repeated like a manic mantra. The four Jews are the hapless hero Marvin (Michael Rupert), his young son Jason (James Kushner), his lover Whizzer (Stephen Bogardus) who (he tells us) is only half Jewish, and Marvin's psychiatrist Mendel (Chip Zien). They are "bitching" about life, love, each other, and being Jewish. In regards to the last, they sing about Pharaoh chasing the Jews across the Red Sea and being destroyed. "We got our miracle," they sing but they are still unhappy, they are still "itching for answers" as they are "bitching their whole life long."[1] The foursome use words like neurotic, nauseous, manipulating, and loose screws to introduce themselves. The music repeats phrases as swiftly as the lyric repeats words. Both lyric and music are so frantic that the number is over before the audience could take it all in. "Four Jews in a Room Bitching" is the opening chorus number for the 1980s. (The title of the musical was originally *Four Jews in a Room Bitching* until James Lapine refused to direct a show with such an off-putting name.) Not until the number is over and things settle down does Marvin calmly explain to the audience what the situation is. But the opening number has done its job: set the tone for the musical. Without resorting to rock, Finn musically presents a contemporary world of urban angst. It is an untidy world and so is *March of the Falsettos*. The episodic plot is messy as it jumps about, mostly sung. It's a wild ride, to say the least. Nine years later, Finn wrote the sequel *Falsettoland* which was more conventionally structured because Lapine served as co-author of the "book." The two musicals were later combined to make *Falsettos* and in 1992 the double-bill arrived on Broadway. In that production "Four Jews in a Room Bitching" was again sung by Rupert, Zien, and Bogardus, with Jonathan Kaplan as Jason. In the 2016 Broadway revival of *Falsettos*, the opening number was sung by Christian Brole (Marvin), Brandon Uranowitz (Mendel), Andrew Rannells (Whizzer), and Anthony Rosenthal (Jason).

Other notable songs from that season: "March of the Falsettos," "Trina's Song," "The Games I Play," "I Never Wanted to Love You," "Father to Son" from *March of the Falsettos* (Off-Broadway); "The Grass Is Always Greener," "One of the Boys," "When You're Right, You're Right" from *The Woman of the Year.*

Song of the Season

1981–1982 SEASON

It was a case of feast or famine on Broadway this season, four shows running beyond the 500-performance mark but seven musicals closing within a month, three of them lasting less than a week. Some, such as *Merrily We Roll Along, Is There Life After High School?*, and *Oh, Brother!*, had excellent scores that deserved to be heard. And did a revival of George M. Cohan's *Little Johnny Jones* deserve to close on opening night? Or what of *Do Black Patent Leather Shoes Reflect Up?* It had broken records in Chicago and Philadelphia but folded after five performances on Broadway. The economics of theatre producing in New York had gotten so brutal that it was next to impossible for audiences to discover a show. Of course, if a musical did get noticed, the results could be financially plentiful. *Dreamgirls* was the season's champ, running 1,522 performances. *Nine* overcame mixed notices to run 732 times, and the Off-Broadway transfers *Joseph and the Amazing Technicolor Dreamcoat* and *Pump Boys and Dinettes* found a lucrative welcome on Broadway, running 747 and 573 performances. Starry Broadway revivals this season were no guarantee of success. An aged Rex Harrison returned to *My Fair Lady* and patrons came for fifteen weeks, but Herschel Bernardi in *Fiddler on the Roof*, Richard Harris in *Camelot*, Donny Osmond in *Little Johnny Jones,* and Victor Garber and James Coco in *Little Me* all failed to run. Even the return of the provocative *This Was Burlesque* closed inside of four weeks.

In addition to the Off-Broadway productions *Pump Boys and Dinettes* and *Joseph and the Amazing Technicolor Dreamcoat* successfully transferring to Broadway, there was a notable little musical that chose to remain where it was. *Cotton Patch Gospel* told Bible stories reset in rural Georgia with bluegrass songs by Harry Chapin. It ran six months then later enjoyed a long life in regional theatres. During the 1970s, many small theatre groups had sprung up in small venues around New York that did not use Off-Broadway contracts, allowing them to put on productions for pittance. At some point they were labeled Off-Off-Broadway and by the end of the decade there were over one hundred such theatres coming into existence and disappearing with little record. When an Off-Off-Broadway production looked promising and found an audience, the company sometimes moved to an Off-Broadway house or stayed put and rewrote its contract to become an Off-Broadway production. Musicals developed Off-Off-Broadway sometimes went on to fame and fortune. This season, the WPA Theatre presented a small musical called *Little Shop of Horrors* for three weeks. It would be heard of more in the near future.

"And I Am Telling You I'm Not Going"
Music by Henry Krieger; lyric by Tom Eyen
From *Dreamgirls* (1981)
Sung by Jennifer Holliday as Effie White

Dreamgirls had a lot going for it: an engrossing story and characters (inspired by various African American singing groups), riveting performances, resplendent staging by Michael Bennett, and a pastiche Motown score by Henry Krieger (music) and Tom Eyen (lyrics). The songs were not Broadway songs but they were certainly theatrical. A case in point is "And I Am Telling You I'm Not Going." The overweight, temperamental singer Effie White (Jennifer Holliday) is fired and replaced in the act and her manager/lover Curtis Taylor, Jr. (Ben Harney) deserts her. In most musicals this would be the opportunity for a torch song. But Effie is not going to go quietly and instead of lamenting her situation, she turns on those who have hurt her and declares "I'm not going!" Her musical retort declares "No, no, no, no way I'm livin' without you" and vows "you, and you, you're gonna love me!"[2] With such a powerful lyric, Kreiger keeps his music steady but not rangy, letting the words land and allowing the singer to improvise both musically and emotionally. In the release, the song reaches a plateau of sorts and the lyric consists of short, blunt phrases. One can "tear down the mountains,/ Yell, scream and shout" but "I'm not walkin' out!" The song climaxes with a series of "love me" shouts. This is not a pop Motown ballad but a musical screech of pain and anger that is pure theatre. That said, "And I Am Telling You I'm Not Going" has been performed and recorded outside of the context of *Dreamgirls*. Holliday's first record was a single of the song and it climbed the charts, as did one by Jennifer Hudson who played Effie in the 2006 film version of *Dreamgirls*. Other discs were made by such artists as Koffie, Bonnie Tyler, Whitney Houston, Sutton Foster, Jack Vidgen, Donna Giles, Jermain Jackman, Dami Im, and Sheridan Smith. Lilias White played Effie and sang it in the 1987 return engagement on Broadway. "And I Am Telling You I'm Not Going" was sung by John Cho in the movie *Down to Earth* (2001), Joanna Chilcoat in *Camp* (2003), and a parody version by David Alan Grier in *Dance Flick* (2009).

Other notable songs from that season: "One Night Only," "Cadillac Car," "When I First Saw You," "I Am Changing" from *Dreamgirls*; "Be Italian," "My Husband Makes Movies," "Only with You," "Be on Your Own," "Simple" from *Nine*; "Merrily We Roll Along," "Good Thing Going," "Not a Day Goes By," "Our Time," "Now You Know," "Like It Was," "Franklin Shepard, Inc." from *Merrily We Roll Along*; "I, To the World," "Everybody Calls Me by My Name" from *Oh, Brother!*; "Be Good or Be Gone," "Sister," "Highway 57" from *Pump Boys and Dinettes*; "The Kid Inside," "Diary of a Homecoming Queen," "Things I Learned in High School" from *Is There Life After High School?*

Song of the Season

1982–1983 SEASON

Although many feel that the British invasion really started back in 1971 with *Jesus Christ Superstar*, this season's mega-hit *Cats* made it clear that London hits were dominating Broadway. A quasi-revue and dance show with Andrew Lloyd Webber's music set to feline poems by T. S. Eliot, *Cats* was both embraced and scorned by Americans when it opened and things didn't change during its record-breaking eighteen-year run. The fact that new American musicals of quality were not to be seen on Broadway this season didn't help matters. The best of the lot was *My One and Only* which was actually a greatly rewritten revival of the 1927 musical *Funny Face* with a score of Gershwin brothers songs from various sources. Helped by the charms of Tommy Tune and Twiggy singing and tapping away, the stylish production ran 767 performances. The only show to come close to that was a highly entertaining revival of Rodgers and Hart's *On Your Toes* staged by its original author and director George Abbott. Despite being vilified by the *New York Times*, *On Your Toes* chalked up 505 performances, more than the original production in 1936. The season's other two notable revivals were not so lucky. *Show Boat*, with Donald O'Connor as the draw, and *Your Arms Too Short to Box with God*, with Patti LaBelle, each ran two months. Also falling short was the dance musical *Manhattan Rhythm* and the revue *Blues in the Night*.

Efforts to bring country music to Broadway failed when *Play Me a Country Song* closed on opening night. Rock-and-Roll didn't do much better. *Rock 'n' Roll! The First 5,000 Years* lasted a week. Magician Doug Henning hoped for another *The Magic Show* with his new bag of tricks titled *Merlin* but 199 performances were enough to satisfy his fans. Similarly, the producers of *Seven Brides for Seven Brothers* must have hoped for another *42nd Street* when they put the classic film musical on stage. It closed after five showings. More discouraging was the quick closing of two musicals by veteran artists. *A Doll's Life*, an imagined sequel to Henrik Ibsen's landmark drama *A Doll's House*, had book and lyrics by Betty Comden and Adolph Green, music by Larry Grossman, a fine cast, and elegant staging by Harold Prince. Surely it deserved more than five performances. *Dance a Little Closer*, a misguided musicalization of Robert Sherwood's comedy-drama *Idiot's Delight* had an exceptional score by Alan Jay Lerner and Charles Strouse. Despite its many flaws, it shouldn't have closed on opening night, ending Lerner's forty-year Broadway career on a sad note.

It was a lively season Off-Broadway with sixteen musicals, two of them going on to run over 2000 performances. *Little Shop of Horrors* moved from Off-Off-Broadway to a larger Off-Broadway venue and wisely stayed there instead of risking Broadway. After a long London run and a tour, *Little Shop of Horrors* became one of the most-produced modern musicals with all kinds of theatre groups. A clever spoof of New York theatre using musical theatre songs with altered lyrics, *Forbidden Broadway* also stayed Off-Broadway, going through several new "editions" as the theatre changed over the next six years. Another sharp-witted revue, *Upstairs at O'Neals'*, satirized New York City, politics, and Off-Broadway revues and their inevitable "Stools." Also noteworthy for their playful scores were the Victorian melodrama burlesque *Charlotte Sweet* and the Charles Schulz musical *Snoopy*. Although both had substantial runs, neither enjoyed the kind of regional future that *Little Shop of Horrors* had.

"Memory"
Music by Andrew Lloyd Webber;
lyric by Trevor Nunn, T. S. Eliot
From *Cats* (1982)
Sung by Betty Buckley as Grizabella

It is perhaps ironic that of the twenty songs in *Cats*, the one to find wide success was the only one not taken from directly from a T. S. Eliot poem. When composer Andrew Lloyd Webber and director Trevor Nunn were putting together a musical using a series of plotless poems from Eliot's *Old Possum's Book of Practical Cats*, they needed a song for the aging feline Grizabella to sing. There was a poem *about* the former glamour cat but not one in her voice. Lloyd Webber had a piece of music in mind for a Grizabella solo, something he had written earlier and had been considered for a handful of musicals. Lyricists Don Black and Tim Rice each wrote a lyric to fit the music but Lloyd Webber preferred one that Nunn himself wrote using some phrases from Eliot's poems "Rhapsody on a Windy Night" and "Preludes." From the poem came such passages as "the moon has lost her memory" and "Every street lamp that I pass/Beats like a fatalistic drum."[3] For the *Cats* score, Lloyd Webber had to compose to lyrics already set in stone. For "Memory" the music came first and the lyric was fitted to it. It is a morose melody that moves from B-flat major to G-flat major to D-flat major, a comfortable transition for the singer whom he thought should not be a soprano. In fact, Judi Dench was originally cast as Grizabella for the 1981 London production and hers was a mezzo voice. Part of the song turns into a duet with the kitten Jemima who is a soprano and the contrast of voices is very powerful. While *Cats* was still in development, guitarist Garry Moore recorded an instrumental version of "Memory" and it was heard on the radio, generating interest from several individuals. Singer Elaine Paige heard it and requested permission to record it. Not only did Lloyd Webber approve but, when Dench was injured and had to leave the project, he offered the role of Grizabella to her. In *Cats*, the song is heard in fragments before it is sung in its entirety. The famous introduction, a series of descending notes that suggests a floating to the ground, is heard when Grizabella is first introduced. At the end of the first act, she then sings a prelude to the song proper. Later Jemima sings some parts of the song an octave higher than Grizabella. Not until the second act does Grizabella sing the complete song. By then the audience has been musically teased but are not disappointed when the full number is heard.

Nunn's lyric has an unusual structure: AABABA. The song is divided into four major sections, each starting with key words: Midnight, Memory, Daylight, and Touch Me. The first refrain is sung by lamplight, Grizabella wondering "has the moon lost her memory" as "withered leaves collect at my feet." In the next refrain, she recalls her glamorous past when she "knew what happiness was." In the first release, the music drops an octave as Grizabella realizes "soon it will be morning." In the "Daylight" refrain she waits for the dawn, knowing "Tonight will be a memory too." In a second release the "street lamp dies" and it is dawn. The final refrain changes point of view and Grizabella pleads "touch me" to an unseen observer. "If you touch me," she sings, "You'll understand what happiness is." The lyric ends with the observation "Look, a new day has begun." As with any of Lloyd Webber's popular compositions, musicologists argue over where the music was stolen from or inspired by. He purposely wanted a tune that sounded like Giacomo Puccini and when he finished the song he took it to a Puccini expect to make sure he had not inadvertently taken something that was actually by the Italian composer. Assured that it wasn't, Lloyd Webber proceeded with *Cats* and "Memory" was an instant hit. Over the years, some musicologists insist the music for the song comes from Maurice Ravel's *Boléro*. Others have argued that the chord progression, tone, and time signature (12/8) are not at all Ravel-like and more in keeping with pop song composition. The debate rages on as "Memory" continues to be one of the most popular of all theatre songs … ever. There are over 300 recordings of "Memory" in English with new ones added each year. Among the many notable ones are discs by Barry Manilow, Barbara Streisand, Judy Collins, Marti Webb, Johnny Mathis, the Shadows, Shirley Bassey, Barbara Dickson, Michael Crawford, Sarah Brightman, Mirage, Debbie Gravitte, Wing, Susan Boyle, the Midnite String Quartet, and Whitney Phoenix. Betty Buckley played Grizabella in the 1982 Broadway production of *Cats* and during the long run she was succeeded by such singers as Loni Ackerman, Linda Balgord, Laurie Beechman, Liz Callaway, and Diane Fratantoni. Paige reprised her Grizabella in the 1998 television adaptation of *Cats*, Leona Lewis sang "Memory" in the 2016 Broadway revival, and Jennifer Hudson played Grizabella in the 2019 movie version.

Other notable songs from that season: "Old Deuteronomy," "Macavity," "Grizabella," "Bustopher Jones," "Gus: the Theatre Cat" from *Cats*; "Little Shop of Horrors," "Somewhere That's Green," "Suddenly Seymour," "Skid Row" from *Little Shop of Horrors* (Off-Broadway); "Dance a Little Closer," "Another Life," "He Always Comes Home to Me," "Mad," "There's Always One You Can't Forget" from *Dance a Little Closer*; "Learn to Be Lonely," "There She Is" from *A Doll's Life*; "A-Weaving," "Lonely Canary" from *Charlotte Sweet* (Off-Broadway); "I Know Now," "Dime a Dozen" from *Snoopy* (Off-Broadway); "Boy, Do We Need It Now," "Stools" from *Upstairs at O'Neals'* (Off-Broadway).

1983–1984 SEASON

There were some splendid scores heard on and Off-Broadway this season but they did not always translate to substantial runs. John Kander and Fred Ebb wrote a masterful set of songs for *The Rink* and they were delivered with panache by Liza Minnelli and Chita Rivera. But the story and characters were not what Minnelli fans were expecting and the musical ran only six months, far from what was needed to turn a profit. David Shire and Richard Maltby, Jr., came up with a laudable score for *Baby* but it also only survived half a year. At the Public Theatre Off-Broadway, Galt MacDermot (music) and William Demaresq (lyrics) wrote a beautiful set of songs for *The Human Comedy*, a small-town musical based on the William Saroyan novella. It was so well received that after eight weeks producer Joseph Papp moved it to Broadway. But *The Human Comedy* was too gentle and intimate for a Broadway house and it folded after thirteen performances. Happily, the two of the best scores heard on Broadway this season did find success. Jerry Herman's songs for *La Cage aux Folles* may not have ranked as high as his other efforts but the musical version of the popular French film was solid entertainment and ran over four years. Conversely, Stephen Sondheim's score for *Sunday in the Park with George* was one of his finest achievements. Not nearly the audience pleaser that *La Cage aux Folles* was, the musical, based on a George Seurat painting, was designed, staged, and performed with rare brilliance and was able to find interested patrons for 604 performances. Dance overshadowed songs in *The Tap Dance Kid* but its score was also commendable. The family-friendly musical ran 669 performances. The rest of the Broadway entrees did not fare so well. The political comic strip *Doonesbury* was turned into a droll musical but fans of Mike Doonesbury (Ralph Bruneau) and friends could only keep the show on the boards for three months. Running a month or less were the musicals *Marilyn: An American Fable, Amen Corner,* and *Peg,* this last being an autobiographical piece about and by Peggy Lee. Some of the season's many revivals also had surprisingly short runs. Angela Lansbury returned to *Mame* and found herself at liberty after five weeks. Ron Moody and Patti LuPone were starred in *Oliver!* only to find themselves in a similar situation after two weeks. Stephanie Mills, the original Dorothy in *The Wiz* and now a recording star, came back to Broadway in a revival of the hip *Wizard of Oz* musical but she also was only needed for two weeks. A revival that did pay was *Zorbá* starring Anthony Quinn and Lila Kedrova who had been in the original non-musical movie *Zorbá the Greek*. It found an audience for 362 performances, nearly the same number as the 1968 original.

The Human Comedy was not the only Off-Broadway musical of quality this season. Gary William Friedman and Will Holt, who had musicalized the voices of young people in *The Me Nobody Knows*, turned their attention to senior citizens in *Taking My Turn*. Margaret Whiting and Marni Nixon headed a cast of very-seasoned performers and kept patrons entertained for 395 performances. Running just as long was the smart, so-called "feminist" musical *A … My Name Is Alice* which addressed women's issues with both pathos and joy. In a very different vein was the satiric *Nite Club Confidential* about

Song of the Season

five desperate performers in a smokey 1950s hangout who are going through trauma on and backstage. The bizarre little musical ran five months then was picked up by theatre groups for some years after.

"I Am What I Am"
Music and lyric by Jerry Herman
From *La Cage aux Folles* (1983)
Sung by George Hearn as Albin

La Cage aux Folles, the first Broadway musical to center on gay characters, was a rather mild affair in terms of socio-political ideas. In fact, if the center of the story were not a gay couple, *La Cage aux Folles* could pass for a pleasant 1950s musical comedy. But there is one number that attempts to say something about homosexuals and their mindset. "I Am What I Am" is a direct declaration of self worth, an anthem of sorts for all LGBTQ+ people. It does not take a socio-political stance but, rather, a personal one. In *La Cage aux Folles*, Georges (Gene Barry) demands that his long-time lover Albin (George Hearn) not be around when George's son Jean-Michel brings his future in-laws to visit. Albin, who is highly temperamental on a good day, explodes with emotion in "I Am What I Am." The song is not delivered to Georges, who is gay and does not require convincing, but to the audience: "I am what I am,/ I am my own special creation."[4] Because Albin is a drag performer in a French cabaret, the lyric has references to "each feather and each spangle" and his inability to remain silent. "Your life is a sham," he sings, "till you can shout out loud: 'I am what I am'!" Coming at the end of the first act, "I Am What I Am" is a dramatic finale of sorts even though the number is a solo. Yet *La Cage aux Folles* opens with another version of the song. The dragline at the club sings "We Are What We Are," a more sassy version of the same lyric and melody. This campy number moves into a big tap number so the lyric is diminished. Yet when Albin later sings "I Am What I Am," there are defiance and pride. The music in "We Are What We Are" is a dainty soft-shoe but when Albin sings "I Am What I Am" the 4/4 time signature is more definite. The song is not only an anthem but also a march which builds musically and lyrically. "Life's not worth a damn," it says, "till you can say, 'Hey world, I am what I am'!" During the long Broadway run, George Hearn was replaced by Walter Charles, Keene Curtis, and Jack Davison. In the 2004 Broadway revival of *La Cage aux Folles*, Gary Beach played Albin and Douglas Hodge played him in the 2010 revival. Both male and female vocalists, as well as musicians, have made effective recordings of "I Am What I Am." Among the notable discs are those by Gloria Gaynor, Sandra Mihanovich, Shirley Bassey, Pia Zadora, Marti Webb, the Gay Men's Chorus of Los Angeles, Murray Ross, Anthony Warlow, Linda Eder, John Barrowman, the San Francisco Gay Men's Chorus, Hermes House Band, Karen Mulder, and Nathan Temby.

Other notable songs from that season: "The Best of Times," "Look Over There," "Song on the Sand" from *La Cage aux Folles*; "Sunday in the Park with George," "Children and Art," "Finishing the Hat," "Color and Light," "Sunday," "Move On," "Beautiful" from *Sunday in the Park with George*; "I Want It All," "Fatherhood Blues," "The Story Goes On" from *Baby*; "Fabulous Feet," "Four Strikes Against Me," "William's Song" from *The Tap Dance Kid*; "Long Past Sunset," "Everything Has Changed" from *The Human Comedy*; "All the Children in a Row," "Colored Lights," "The Apple Doesn't Fall Very Far" from *The Rink*; "Angels on Your Pillow" from *Peg*; "Good Thing I Learned to Dance," "At My Age" from *A ... My Name Is Alice* (Off-Broadway).

Song of the Season

1984–1985 SEASON

The number of Broadway musicals this season dropped to a new low: thirteen new and old works, and only three original book musicals. It would be nice to report that those three were critical and popular successes but that was not the case. The critics were mixed in their reactions to *Big River: The Adventures of Huckleberry Finn* but audiences liked it and it stayed on Broadway for over one thousand performances. Country music singer-songwriter Roger Miller wrote an animated score which effectively used country songs as theatre songs. Also, *Big River* had a stunning production with fine performances. Some very old songs from Broadway were mixed with new ones for *Harrigan 'n Hart* about the two early musical comedy pioneers Edward Harrigan and Tony Hart who were active in the 1880s. The idea was intriguing but the production was plagued with problems and, after dismissive reviews, closed after five showings. Better executed but perhaps too dark for Broadway playgoers was *Grind* which showed the unseemly side of burlesque as it was dying during the Depression. First-rate performances by Ben Vereen, Stubby Kate, Joey Faye, Leilani Jones, Timothy Nolan, and Lee Wallace and a striking production directed by Harold Prince made for an uncompromising show. But audiences were curious for only ten weeks. There were two revues of note on Broadway. *Leader of the Pack*, considered the first jukebox musical by many, offered no new songs but old favorites by singer-songwriter Ellie Greenwich. Fans came for 120 performances. Mostly old songs were also featured in the revue *Haarlem [sic] Nocturne* put together by and featuring Andre de Shields. It managed to run six weeks. Of the handful of revivals on Broadway this season, the shortest run was for *Take Me Along*, which closed on opening night, and the longest was *The King and I* with Yul Brynner yet again playing the King of Siam to Mary Beth Peil's Anna. Brynner in his most famous role was appealing enough to playgoers that the revival ran twenty-four weeks.

The numbers Off-Broadway were also low (fifteen musicals including revivals) but the quality was higher and two shows ran over nine months. *Kuni-Leml* was based on a popular Yiddish farce and translated into a silly but likable musical. Despite a title that was a hard sale, *Kuni-Leml* found appreciative patrons for 298 showings. An evening at the Cotton Club in the 1920s was recreated in *Shades of Harlem* which offered familiar classics and some new songs performed by a cast of four. Only two singers and a pianist were needed for *A Kurt Weill Cabaret*. It ran sixteen weeks, as did *Diamonds*, a collection of songs and sketches about baseball. The musical *3 Guys Naked from the Waist Down* was about three struggling stand-up comics in New York City. Possibly helped by its provocative title (which is slang for stand-up performers), the intimate show ran 160 times. Finally, there were two shows that had fun lampooning political figures currently in office. *Rap Master Ronnie* satirized the standing US President Reagan (Reathel Bean) for six weeks and the current mayor of New York, Ed Koch (Lenny Wolpe), was kidded in *Mayor*, amusing New Yorkers for 185 performances. When that musical transferred to Broadway in October of 1985, it managed to run two months.

> "River in the Rain"
> Music and lyric by Roger Miller
> From *Big River* (1985)
> Sung by Daniel Jenkins as Huck,
> and Ron Richardson as Jim

Roger Miller's songs for *Big River* embrace bluegrass, country, blues, comic ditties, and occasionally Broadway. "River in the Rain," for example, is a true Broadway ballad even as it cannot hide its country roots. The evocative song about the Mississippi River is sung by the adolescent Huck (Daniel Jenkins) and the runaway slave Jim (Ron Richardson) as they float downstream on a raft in a gentle rain. It is one of those rare things, a Broadway nature song. The uneducated Huck and Jim describe the Mississippi in simple terms. In the rain at night, it sometimes looks "like a long white train/ Winding your way away somewhere."[5] As in the classic "Ol' Man River," the two runaways wonder if the river notices them at all: "River I love you, don't you care?" Miller's lyric ends on a bittersweet note: "Winding your way away from me,/ River, I've never seen the sea." The music is written in 4/4 time and marked "slow," sounding like a country-western lullaby. Besides being a quiet song, "River in the Rain" has few jumps in the music and ends with a gentle drop rather than a soaring climax. Only in the release ("sometimes in a time of trouble") does the music reach high but it doesn't stay there for long. In *Big River*, the image of Huck and Jim huddled under a tarp as the rain falls is a transcendent one. As originally staged by Des McAnuff, the last note of the song was the cue for the rain to stop and for the stars suddenly appear. It was a magical moment in this top-notch production. Possibly because of its rural folk tone, few Broadway singers have recorded "River in the Rain" but country-western artists have, including Paula Nelson, Alison Krauss, Corey Cott, and Miller himself. In the 1985 Broadway revival *Big River* by the Deaf West Theatre, Jenkins returned to the musical and voiced Huck while deaf actor Tyrone Giordano was Huck's physical presence, and Jim was played by Michael McElroy.

Other notable songs from that season: "Waiting for the Light to Shine," "Muddy Water," "World's Apart," "Leaving's Not the Only Way to Go" from *Big River*; "This Must Be the Place," "All Things to One Man" from *Grind*; "The Boys of Summer," "Diamonds Are Forever," "What You'd Call a Dream" from *Diamonds* (Off-Broadway); "Don't Worry Darling," "Nothing Counts but Love" from *Kuni-Leml* (Off-Broadway); "How'm I Doin'?" from *Mayor* (Off-Broadway).

Song of the Season

1985–1986 SEASON

More musicals opened on Broadway this season than in recent years but very few were home-grown shows. Instead more and more entries each season were from Off-Broadway, London, regional theatres, and from such far-off places as Italy and Argentina. Broadway was slowly becoming a showcase for works developed and polished elsewhere. For example, the season's biggest hit was *The Mystery of Edwin Drood* which was created as a two-week summer attraction in Central Park. But *Drood* (as it was later sometimes titled) was so well received by both the press and the public that producer Joseph Papp moved it to Broadway where it won all the awards and ran 608 performances. The second-longest entry this season was the unusual double musical *Song and Dance* which came from London but featured the American favorite Bernadette Peters giving a tour de force performance. From Argentina was the dance program *Tango Argentino* and from Italy was the puppet attraction *Pipino il Breve* (*Pippin the Short*) and the musical fable *La Gatta Cenerentola* (*Cinderella the Cat*). While the Italian shows were limited runs, the South American program was an open run and found an audience for twenty-five weeks. The American Dance Machine, which re-created and preserved classic dances from past Broadway shows, stopped in New York for two weeks as part of its tour. Coming from regional theatre were *The News* from Florida and *Wind in the Willows* from Washington, DC, both closing after four performances. The four-singer *Jerome Kern Goes to Hollywood* was a hit in London but closed inside of two weeks on Broadway. (Coincidentally, there was an Off-Broadway revue, *Ladies and Gentlemen, Jerome Kern*, covering a lot of the same songs which also closed quickly.) And coming from "Old Hollywood" was a stage version of *Singin' in the Rain* which was roasted by the critics but pleased audiences for a year.

So what exactly did Broadway come up with this season? A revival of *Sweet Charity* featuring Debbie Allen, which ran 368 times, and a handful of short-run musicals. The revue *Uptown ... It's Hot*, created by and starring Maurice Hines, folded in two weeks. *Jerry's Girls*, in which an all-female cast headed by Dorothy Loudon, Chita Rivera, and Leslie Uggams performed numbers from Jerry Herman shows, was successful on tour but struggled to run four months on Broadway. The biggest disappointment of all was *Big Deal*, the Bob Fosse musical based on the Italian film *Big Deal on Madonna Street* (1958) about some small-time crooks. Fosse decided to eliminate songwriters and authors from the project and wrote the libretto himself, used song standards for the score, and directed and choreographed the show. Aside from some vivacious dance numbers, *Big Deal* was all muddled and ineffective and closed inside of two months. Sadly, the expensive fiasco was Fosse's last production; he died a year later.

The number of Off-Broadway musicals also rose, as did the quality of the scores. Carol Hall, who had written the songs for *The Best Little Whorehouse in Texas*, came up with a very different, and very engaging, score for *To Whom It May Concern* about the thoughts of individuals during a church service. Polly Pen set some of Christina Rossetti's poems to music resulting in a beguiling little musical titled *Goblin Market*.

Some very farcical songs by various writers could be found in the comic revue *Personals* about the world of personal ads. While the Hall and Pen musicals only ran their three-month engagements, *Personals* caught on and played 265 performances. Running even longer were two revues that were fueled by nostalgia. *The Golden Land* collected songs from early in the century and performed them in English and Yiddish. More recent music was recalled in *Beehive*, a revue of songs by girl groups of the 1960s. While both shows had long runs, the hands-down champ for the season was *Nunsense*, a revue-of-sorts performed by five actresses playing nuns from the order of the Little Sisters of Hoboken and singing about the Catholic religion and being nuns. The satire was broad and harmless, the songs pastiches of various musical styles, and from the start audiences loved it all. *Nunsense* not only ran nine years and toured but then saw (and still sees) hundreds of regional productions each year. It was still profitable Off-Broadway to revive a musical, have it run for nine months, and make a profit. Such was the case with *What's a Nice Country Like You Doin in a State Like This?* and *Dames at Sea*. But it was also possible Off-Broadway to lose big time, as with *Yours, Anne*, a musical based on the Holocaust drama *The Diary of Anne Frank*. The critics were light in their dismissal of the musical drama but *Yours, Anne* struggled to run six weeks and lost a bundle.

"Don't Quit While You're Ahead"
Music and lyric by Rupert Holmes
From *The Mystery of Edwin Drood* (1985)
Sung by Cleo Laine as Princess Puffer, and company

Because Charles Dickens died before he could complete *The Mystery of Edwin Drood*, any stage, film, or television adaptations of the novel has to deal with somehow bringing the plot to some kind of satisfactory conclusion. Rupert Holmes solved the problem by letting the audience decide on who murdered Edwin Drood. It is a gimmick and not a new one in the theatre. (As far back as 1935, Ayn Rand's courtroom drama *Night of January 16* let the theatre audience be the jury and vote on the outcome of the trial.) Holmes, who wrote the libretto, music, lyrics, and orchestrations for *The Mystery of Edwin Drood*, uses a Victorian music hall format to tell the story, a loose structure that allowed for balloting the audience. It also permitted the show to have rousing musical numbers that were outside of the plot or characters. On more than one occasion, the cast steps out of character and sings a song that is a specialty of the company, no matter how far afield it is to the murder in question. Arguably the best of these entertaining diversions is the merry ditty "Don't Quit While You're Ahead." Late in the second act, Princess Puffer (Cleo Laine) leads the company in singing the song and it conveniently serves as the eleven o'clock number for the musical. All of Holmes' songs for *The Mystery of Edwin Drood* are pastiches of Victorian popular music, ranging from parlor songs to rapid patter numbers. "Don't Quit While You're Ahead" is in the spirited music hall style in both music and lyric. Although the song is in 4/4 time and in the key of D Major, the verse is marked moderately and works best starting off slowly. But as the refrain is picked up by various characters, the music builds, eventually reaching 125 beats per minute. Also distinctive about the composition are the rests Holmes puts in, punctuated with percussion accents, that provide opportunity for kicks by the performers. This is dance music with built-in flourishes. That doesn't take away from the excellent lyric. Princess Puffer sings the verse which introduces the song's premise: having once won ten pence, she risked it and bet it all again. In the first refrain, she sings the theme of the number. "If you've won, don't quit while you're ahead," she argues, "Just press your blessed luck instead!"[6] Other characters pick up on this, using a maritime metaphor. They sing "I see my dream ship fin'lly comin' in/ Like a steam ship anch'rin in to win!" By the time the whole company is singing, the lyric emphasizes the percussion with onomatopoeia: "Ta-ray—ta-rah!Boom! … Bang it, bash it, Hoo-ray-ha-rah! … Clang it, clash it, oo-la-dee-dah!" The lyric ends on a high note of optimism with "Sing out, 'There's more in store for me!'" Holmes, a pop songwriter who was born in Great Britain but has worked mostly in the States, captures the authentic sound of Victorian songs in *The Mystery of Edwin Drood* so well that, unfortunately, the score has not produced any hits outside of the musical. So it is with "Don't Quit While You're Ahead." Yet the musical is produced many times each year so this wonderful score is often heard. On Broadway, Cleo Laine was replaced by Loretta Swit and Karen Morrow, both of whom led the cast in singing "Don't Quit While You're Ahead." In the 2013 Broadway revival of *The Mystery of Edwin Drood*, Chita Rivera played Princess Puffer and sang it with the company.

Other notable songs from that season: "Moonfall," "Off to the Races," "The Wages of Sin," "Perfect Strangers" from *The Mystery of Edwin Drood*; "Unexpected Song," "Tell Me on a Sunday" from *Song and Dance*; "I Could've Gone to Nashville," "Growing Up Catholic" from *Nunsense* (Off-Broadway); "Come Buy, Come Buy," "Sleep, Laura, Sleep" from *Goblin Market* (Off-Broadway); "To Whom It May Concern," "My Sort of Ex-Boyfriend" from *To Whom It May Concern* (Off-Broadway).

1986–1987 SEASON

Although the authors were French and it originated in Paris, *Les Misérables* was a big part of the British invasion of the 1980s. London producer Cameron Mackintosh and the Royal Shakespeare Company commissioned the translation and assembled a British staff of designers and directors to turn the Victor Hugo novel into a West End hit musical. When it was brought to New York this season, it remained a very-British production with the only Americans involved to be found in the cast. The advance sale was considerable and *Les Misérables* settled in for a sixteen-year run. Adding to Broadway's woes, the only other two long-runs this season were also from London: the 1937 musical comedy *Me and My Girl,* produced for the first time in New York, and the train musical *Starlight Express,* which was so expensive it didn't show a profit after 761 performances. *Me and My Girl* ran twice that and not only made a profit but a new-old musical was added to the repertory of oft-produced works. Such a deluge of London musicals might have been easier to swallow if any American works had made an impressive showing. Instead, four new musicals— *Raggedly Ann, Honky Tonk Nights, Rags,* and *Into the Light*—didn't last even one week. The Off-Off-Broadway revue *Stardust* transferred to Broadway and became the American champ at only 177 performances. Even the much-anticipated Marvin Hamlisch-Howard Ashman musical *Smile* with an exceptional score struggled to run eight weeks.

All of the major Off-Broadway musicals this season were American and, while there was no long-run hits like *Nunsense,* the quality was high. *Lady Day at Emerson's Bar and Grill* was perhaps more a play with songs but when Lonette McKee as Billie Holiday sang fourteen standards, it was enough to please patrons 281 times. Original songs were the highlight of the daffy farce *Olympus on My Mind*, another retelling of the myth of Zeus and Alcmene with a lot of anachronistic touches. It ran 207 performances; in better days, it deserved to be a hit on Broadway. Audiences kept a few other shows running six months or more, such as *Angry Housewives, Sex Tips for Modern Girls*, and *Staggerlee*. But in the opinion of some, the two finest new scores heard this season were in two limited-run Off-Broadway musicals: Craig Carnelia's tender character musical *Three Postcards* and Douglas J. Cohen's sly murder mystery musical *No Way to Treat a Lady*. The boldest musical of the season was *The Knife* at the Public Theatre, about a married chef (Mandy Patinkin) who undergoes a sex change operation. The British rock musical could not find a producer in England who would present *The Knife* so the authors turned to Joseph Papp who never dismissed a challenging idea. So the British invasion was so evasive this season that it even reached the Public Theatre.

"The Lambeth Walk"
Music by Noel Gay; lyric by Douglas Furber
From *Me and My Girl* (1986)
Sung by Robert Lindsay as Bill Snibson,
Maryann Plunkett as Sally Smith, and the company

Song of the Season

The most applauded song of the season was nearly fifty years old by the time it was heard on Broadway in the British musical comedy *Me and My Girl*. Although that 1937 show ran 1,646 performances in London, was turned into the popular 1939 British film *The Lambeth Walk*, and saw many revivals in the UK over the years, *Me and My Girl* never came to Broadway and was virtually unknown in the States. There had been only a few American recordings of the show's hit song "The Lambeth Walk," most memorably a vocal version by the Mills Brothers. But "The Lambeth Walk" became popular in the States not so much as a song but as a dance. The star of *Me and My Girl* was Lupino Lane, a comic singer and dancer. He is credited for coming up with a dance step, a kind of high-kicking strut, which was inspired by the way proud Cockneys walk. The dance was performed in the musical by Lane and his female lead Teddie St. Denis and soon the Lambeth Walk was being danced in Britain, France, and Germany. (The Nazi Party saw the dance as a crude Jewish dance and later outlawed it.) Within a year of the opening of *Me and My Girl*, the dance showed up in the States. Boston bandleader Joe Rines is thought to have introduced it in New York City when his band was playing at a nightclub there. Popular recordings of "The Lambeth Walk" by Russ Morgan and Duke Ellington helped spread the dance and the song, though it was rarely sung. A slightly revised revival of *Me and My Girl* opened in London in 1984 to rave reviews and it ran four years. Broadway was finally interested and the London production was presented this season to similar praise and success.

In the new version of *Me and My Girl*, the Cockney-turned-aristocrat Bill Snibson (Robert Lindsay) is at a gathering of all the blue-bloods of London society and when his Cockney sweetheart Sally (Maryann Plunkett) shows up, he proudly celebrates his lower-class neighborhood of Lambeth in the song. The upper-class set are amused then thrilled and soon join in for a raucous song and dance finale for the first act. Because the song by Noel Gay (music) and Douglas Furber (lyric) is so contagious in melody and rhythm, one believes that Bill could mesmerize this crowd so thoroughly. It is a rambunctious song that moves in a sprightly fashion (some versions of the sheet music say "with bounce") in 4/4 time. Several times in the music there is a percussive bang in which the singer shouts "Oi!" The lyric is simple with lots of repetition, as wanted in a dance song. The title sounds like a dance number but the song is inspired by an actual street in London with the name Lambeth Walk. The phrases "Lambeth Walk" and "Lambeth way" are repeated throughout, giving the lyric a rhythm of its own. In the short verse, it is admitted that Lambeth has no green grass and "hasn't got the Mayfair touch" but when the residents gather for "a bit of fun," it is a hopping place.[7] The refrains are about the dance step with "Ev'ry little Lambeth gal/ With her little Lambeth pal … You'll find 'em all doin' the Lambeth walk!" In the releases, the music gets more jaunty and the lyric uses the Cockney slang: "Ev'rything's free and easy,/ Do as you darn well pleasey." The structure of the song is ABBCBBCBBC, the alternating refrains and releases allowing for a continuous melodic line except for the "Oi!" after each "Doin' the Lambeth Walk!"

There was an original cast recording of the score for *Me and My Girl* with Lane and St. Denis leading the cast in "The Lambeth Walk." Other early recordings were made by Ronnie Munro and His Orchestra, Ray Ellington and Harry Roy with Roy's Tiger Ragamuffins, Gracie Fields, Leslie Carew with Ambrose and His Orchestra, and Billy

Cotton. During the following decades there were notable discs by Pat Dodd and His Boys, Big Ben Banjo Band, Chet Atkins, Acker Bilk, Annie Windsor and David Rayner, Norman Wisdom, the Blue Bird Society Orchestra, Wild Billy Childish and the Blackhands, and Twiggy. The 1939 film version of *Me and My Girl* was titled *The Lambeth Walk* and Lane and St. Denis reprised their stage performances and sang the song. Also on film, people at a dance hall sang it in *The Key* (1958) and British soldiers sang it in *The Longest Day* (1962).

Other notable songs from that season: "Me and My Girl," "Leaning on a Lamppost," "Once You Lose Your Heart" from *Me and My Girl*; "One Day More," "I Dreamed a Dream," "Empty Chairs at Empty Tables," "Bring Him Home," "On My Own," "Do You Hear the People Sing?" from *Les Misérables*; "Rags," "Blame It on the Summer Night," "Children of the Wind" from *Rags*; "Starlight Express," "Only You" from *Starlight Express*; "Smile," "Disneyland" from *Smile*; "The Gods on Tap," "Heaven on Earth" from *Olympus on My Mind* (Off-Broadway); "The Picture in the Hall," "Cast of Thousands" from *Three Postcards* (Off-Broadway); "So Far, So Good," "Only a Heartbeat Away" from *No Way to Treat a Lady* (Off-Broadway).

Song of the Season

1987–1988 SEASON

Just as last season's surprise revival hit was the British *Me and My Girl* from the 1930s, this season it was the return of an American musical from the 1930s to make a splash. Cole Porter's *Anything Goes* was slightly revised by Timothy Crouse and John Weidman and staged by Jerry Zaks at Lincoln Center with Patti LuPone heading the cast as Reno Sweeney, all of them set to marvelous dancing by choreographer Michael Smuin. The limited run quickly sold out so the 1934 musical comedy stayed around for 804 performances. The season's other big surprise was *Sarafina!*, a musical featuring teenagers from South Africa in song and dance about life under Apartheid. The musical opened Off-Broadway early in the season, ran ten weeks, then transferred to Broadway where it found an audience for 597 performances. A surprise of a different kind was the much-anticipated London musical *Chess* which was substantially altered for Broadway, failed to please the press or the public, and closed in eight weeks. Revised versions of *Chess* later found life in regional and educational theatres. The one Broadway musical that was no surprise was Andrew Lloyd Webber's *The Phantom of the Opera*. The massive, high-powered operetta had been playing in London for two years before it opened on Broadway so audiences were not only familiar with it but bought enough tickets to break records for advance sales. The critics carped about the grandiose musical thriller but they were drowned out by public acclaim. *The Phantom of the Opera* stayed on Broadway for thirty-five years. Some reviewers also criticized the new Stephen Sondheim musical *Into the Woods* but again it was embraced by the public. Not only did the thought-provoking fairy tale musical run 764 performances, it became one of Sondheim's most produced works regionally, as well as in London and beyond. Only three other Broadway productions had substantial (but unprofitable) runs: revivals of *Cabaret* and *Dreamgirls*, and the two-part musical *Romance, Romance* which originated Off-Broadway and moved to Broadway for nine months. Running only a month or less this season were *Roza*, *Late Nite Comic*, *Mail*, and *Carrie*. Running a few months without getting out of the red were the gospel musicals *Don't Get God Started* and *The Gospel at Colonus*, the Brazilian revue *Oba Oba*, and *Teddy and Alice*, about T. R. Roosevelt and his daughter using John Philip Sousa music for the songs.

    Off-Broadway did what it does best this season: producing small, smart shows in intimate venues with lively scores and young talent. The most successful of the offerings was *Oil City Symphony*, a hilarious spoof of a small Ohio town band giving a concert with diligent naiveté. The musical ran 626 times in New York then enjoyed productions across the country. Three revues ran only half as long but were applauded by the press and satisfied patrons. *No-Frills Revue* mostly satirized the theatre, and *Bittersuite* poked fun at the cycle of dating, marriage, parenthood, and old age with a caustic sense of humor. The title of the *Ten Percent Revue* referred to the portion of the population that is not heterosexual and it too was sharp as well as tender in its songs and sketches. Two book musicals had superior scores and skillful librettos but did not run very long. *Birds of Paradise*, about a summer theatre putting on Chekhov's *The Sea Gull*, was totally captivating but was gone after three weeks. *Lucky Stiff*, a broad musical farce by Lynn Ahrens (book and lyrics) and Stephen Flaherty (music), closed inside of two weeks. Happily, *Lucky Stiff* did catch on regionally and the musical launched the career of one of the premiere songwriting teams of the era.

"Music of the Night"
Music by Andrew Lloyd Webber;
lyric by Charles Hart, Richard Stilgoe
From *The Phantom of the Opera* (1988)
Sung by Michael Crawford as the Phantom

How ironic that the most popular musical at the end of the twentieth century was an operetta in the nineteenth-century style. *The Phantom of the Opera* is unabashedly old-fashioned, inspired by European operas, musically rhapsodic and lyrically grandiose. Except for the title song, nothing in the operetta is remotely pop or rock. Instead Andrew Lloyd Webber goes for a lush romanticism with a touch of gothic horror in the music. Nowhere is this more effective than in the Phantom's seduction song "Music of the Night." Having kidnapped Christine (Sarah Brightman) and taken her down to his lair beneath the opera house, the Phantom (Michael Crawford) sings to her using music as a metaphor for sex. It is both romantic and chilling. The lyric by Charles Hart and Richard Stilgoe utilizes several purple clichés ("let your spirit start to soar … journey through a strange new world … savor each sensation") but in this kind of operetta, words are to be caressed rather than punctuated.[8] There are some intriguing images ("the garish light of day … Turn your thoughts away from cold unfeeling light") leading to the title phrase. Sometimes the lyric relies on two syllable phrases ("grasp it, sense it … softly, deftly") as the music tiptoes carefully. Then in the release you get a long flowing lyric about letting your mind "journey through a strange new world" so that you can "leave all thoughts of the world you knew before." Here is a song lyric that manages to serve the music well even as it draws little attention to itself. And what of the music? Passages from Lloyd Webber's music have often been compared to that of Giacomo Puccini and "Music in the Night" is no exception. The music in the release is close to a recurring passage in Puccini's 1910 opera, *La fanciulla del West* (*The Girl of the Golden West*). The resemblance was strong enough that the Puccini estate filed lawsuit against Lloyd Webber; an agreement was settled out of court. Yet that section is only one part of the music for "The Music of the Night" and there is a lot of genuine Lloyd Webber in the song: the restrained opening, repeated musical phrases, the slow build to a new melody in the higher register, and the crashing resolution. It may sound like an opera aria but in terms of theatricality the music is pure Broadway operetta.

Song of the Season

The music for "The Music of the Night" was written some years before *The Phantom of the Opera* when Lloyd Webber composed it as a song for his fiancée Sarah Brightman. At the time it had a different lyric. While developing the number for the musical, Stilgoe and Black reworked the lyric into a solo for the Phantom. The song is arguably the most famous from the beloved score. Michael Crawford was the original Phantom in London and is heard on the cast recording. He also originated the role in New York but there was no Broadway recording. In 1992 he made a duet version of "The Music of the Night" with Barbra Streisand. There have been approximately 150 recordings of the song, including discs by Brightman, Richard Carlson, Marti Webb, Anthony Warlow, José Carreras, Marina Prior, Samuel Ramey, Jack Jones, Mirage, Colm Wilkinson, Peter Karrie, Sean McDermott, Katherine Jenkins, the Gabe Baltazar Quartet, Andrea Bocelli, and Marilyn Byrnes. Gerard Butler played the Phantom in the 2004 movie version of *The Phantom of the Opera* and sang the song to Emmy Rossum. During the long run of the musical on Broadway, some of the notable Phantoms included James Barbour, Ben Crawford, Steve Barton, Davis Gaines, Kevin Gray, Mark Jacoby, Norm Lewis, Marcus Lovett, Howard McGillin, Timothy Nolan, and Hugh Panaro.

Other notable songs from that season: "The Phantom of the Opera," "Masquerade," "All I Ask of You," "Prima Donna" from *The Phantom of the Opera*; "No One Is Alone," "Giants in the Sky," "Agony," ""On the Steps of the Palace," "No More" from *Into the Woods*; "I'll Always Remember the Song," "Romantic Notions," "Small Craft Warnings" from *Romance Romance*; "One Night in Bangkok," "Someone Else's Story," "I Know Him So Well," "You and I" from *Chess*; "Freedom Is Coming Tomorrow," "Africa Burning in the Sun" from *Sarafina!*; "Birds of Paradise," "Imagining You" from *Birds of Paradise* (Off-Broadway); "Ohio Afternoon," "Iris" from *Oil City Symphony* (Off-Broadway); "Good to Be Alive," "Times Like This," "Nice" from *Lucky Stiff* (Off-Broadway).

1988–1989 SEASON

For new works, the 1988–89 Broadway season is generally considered the worst since ... forever, I suppose. Only four book musicals opened all season and the critics fought over which was the worst. *Legs Diamond*, about the infamous gangster; *Chu Chem*, the "first Chinese-Jewish musical"; and the divorce jail musical *Welcome to the Club* were the top contenders. The satiric space-age comic strip musical *Starmites* from Off-Broadway amused some reviewers and patrons for two months and later was produced regionally. So where did audiences go for entertainment on Broadway? Revues featuring old songs were the only alternative and they did well with so little competition. The original cast of *Ain't Misbehavin'* returned and filled seats for nearly six months. Jerome Robbins re-created some of his most memorable production numbers from musicals he had directed and/or choreographed and it was titled *Jerome Robbins' Broadway*. Far more than a museum piece, the revue was a celebration of the best of Broadway as well as of Robbins himself. The show ran 634 performances but, with such a large cast and huge production costs, it never showed a profit. Running longer and doing better in box office numbers was *Black and Blue*, another celebration, this time of African American song and dance. If one wasn't interested in revues, there were some stars doing their acts for limited runs. Barry Manilow, Linda Ronstadt, Robert Klein, and Michael Feinstein were readily available. Or one could attend *Legends in Concert* in which stars such as Judy Garland, Liberace, Buddy Holly, and Nat King Cole were impersonated by clever performers. But even the lure of deceased stars could not attract an audience for more than three weeks.

Things were somewhat better Off-Broadway but many of the musicals there were also revues with old songs. *Suds* mixed 1960s songs with a soap opera setting; *The Taffetas* celebrated songs from the 1950s popularized by girl groups or female soloists; *Sweethearts* was a nostalgic look at the songs sung by Jeanette MacDonald and Nelson Eddy in the movies; and *The Middle of Nowhere* featuring songs by pop and Hollywood composer Randy Newman set in a Louisiana bus station. There were also revues with original songs, some of them quite accomplished. Richard Maltby, Jr., and David Shire's songs were featured in *Urban Blight*; *Laughing Matters* was yet another spoof of the theatre; and life in New York City was once again satirized in *Showing Off*. Joseph Papp presented two Old Testament musicals at the Public Theatre: *Genesis* musicalized some Medieval mystery plays and *Songs of Paradise* was performed in both Yiddish and English. None of these ran very long and only *The Taffetas* enjoyed a successful afterlife in regional theatres. Not one London musical opened on or Off-Broadway this season. Where was the British invasion when you needed it?

"Diva! (Hard to Be Diva)"
Music and lyric by Barry Keating
From *Starmites* (1989)
Introduced by Sharon McNight as Diva, and the Banshees

Song of the Season

Starmites is an example of how a small musical can develop and move into the limelight, even if only briefly. The show began Off-Off-Broadway in 1980, was presented Off-Broadway in 1987, and transferred to Broadway in 1989. It is a clever and diverting musical fantasy about a teenager (Liz Larsen) who lives in the world of comic books, in particular the sci-fi stories about the Starmites, the guardians angels of Innerspace. The villain in these comics is Diva (Sharon McKnight), the Queen of the Banshees, who is bigger-than-life physically and vocally. Her "I am" song is "Diva! (Hard to Be Diva)," a pop-R&B pastiche number with a little soul and gospel thrown in for good measure. Sharon McKnight sang it in a mock-Janis Joplin delivery in the Broadway production and it was a showstopper. Barry Keating wrote the vigorous music which sometimes went too fast for the facile lyric. Diva sings "My life may seem like heaven, babe, but boy it is hell!"[9] At other times, it gets a little eccentric, as the proclamation "I won't break the dishes—I'm a big-hearted girl!" Because it was such a lame season for new musicals, *Starmites* managed to get nominated for six Tony Awards, including Best Musical, but won none. Yet when "Diva!" was included in the Tony broadcast, it gave the little show a visibility it never would have gotten had it run over a year Off-Broadway. Regional productions soon followed and today there are three versions of *Starmites* that can be produced: a short Junior version for middle school, a full-length, edited version for high schools, and the original "adult" version for everyone else. There was no recording of the original Broadway production but nine years later some of the cast was brought back for a 1999 disc that also helped popularize the show. On that recording, "Diva!" is sung by Gwen Stewart who played one of the Banshees in the Broadway production.

Other notable songs from that season: "Starmites," "Little Hero," "Beauty Within" from *Starmites*; "The Music Went Out of My Life" from *Legs Diamond*; "Miss Byrd," "Life Story," "Don't Fall for the Lights" from *Urban Blight* (Off-Broadway); "When You Live in New York" from *Laughing Matters* (Off-Broadway); "How Things Change," "Rental Cruelty" from *Showing Off* (Off-Broadway).

1989–1990 SEASON

There were new musicals, revivals, and revues of quality this season, with hits both on and Off-Broadway. Surprisingly, these were mostly American efforts. Only two British musicals transferred to New York this season. Andrew Lloyd Webber's *Aspects of Love* ran four years in London but an unprofitable eleven months on Broadway. The satirical *Privates on Parade* was a modest success in the West End back in 1977. American producers were wary about the very-British "play with songs" and passed on it. But it showed up Off-Broadway this season and was a critical success but playgoers were hesitant and its two-month run at the Roundabout Theatre was not extended. The two home-grown musical hits were *Grand Hotel* and *City of Angels* running 1,018 and 878 performances. Although the two shows were quite different in tone and subject matter, both had superior scores, scintillating staging, and gifted performers. The other new book musicals on Broadway had embarrassingly short runs. *A Change in the Heir* ran only two weeks and *Prince of Central Park* and *Dangerous Games* each shuttered after four performances. Two biographical musicals boasted strong impersonations but could not attract an audience for more than a month each. Queen Esther Marrow was Mahalia Jackson in *Truly Blessed* and Julian Whitaker, Johnny Seaton, and Terry Mike Jeffrey played Elvis Presley at different ages in *Elvis: A Rockin' Remembrance*. Three revivals got a lot of attention. Pop star Sting played MacHeath in a revival retitled *3 Penny Opera*. Bob Gunton and Beth Fowler headed a reduced-sized cast in *Sweeney Todd: The Demon Barber of Fleet Street*, given an intimate production at the Circle in the Square. Tyne Daly was roundly applauded for her Mama Rose in a revival of *Gypsy* which ran a profitable 581 performances. A revival of sorts was *Meet Me in St. Louis*, the latest effort to turn a Hollywood musical classic into a workable stage show. The new version had some new songs by the original songwriters Ralph Blane and Hugh Martin and it was appealing enough to audiences to run 253 performances. The critics disparaged the musical and it lost a lot of money but *Meet Me in St. Louis* soon became a popular choice of regional theatres and schools and continues to receive dozens of productions each year.

The long-run champ Off-Broadway was *Forever Plaid*, a sly and tuneful revue in which the fictional four-guy-group called the Plaids gives a concert of 1950s and 1960s easy-listening standards. The humor was tongue-in-cheek and the songs were joyous so patrons kept it on the boards for over four years. It also has enjoyed a very active life in regional theatres. Two other first-rate revues also appealed to the critics and the public though not for more than eight months. *Further Mo'* was a delightful follow-up to the popular *One Mo' Time* and *Closer Than Ever* offered some superb new songs by Richard Maltby, Jr., and David Shire. Arguably the best musical of the Off-Broadway season was a new work: *Once on This Island*. Lynn Ahrens and Stephen Flaherty wrote a sparkling set of songs for this musical fable set on a remote Caribbean island. The Playwrights Horizons production played three weeks Off-Broadway then the next season moved to Broadway where it ran over a year. Finally, there was an Off-Off-Broadway entry worth

Song of the Season

noting. The musical drama *Hannah ... 1939* was set in a Prague garment factory where women labored under the eyes of the occupying Nazis. Its emotive book and songs were by Bob Merrill; sadly, it was his last full score.

"Love Changes Everything"
Music by Andrew Lloyd Webber;
lyric by Don Black, Charles Hart
From *Aspects of Love* (1990)
Sung by Michael Ball as Alex Dillingham

Aspects of Love was not the season's finest score but it did have the most visible hit song. "Love Changes Everything" is not a love song but rather a song *about* love as observed by the musical's central character Alex Dillingham (Michael Ball). He first sings it in the prologue of *Aspects of Love*. Alex then returns to the song as the years pass and his point of view changes. The lyric by Don Black and Charles Hart is a list of the ways in which being in love alters a person's perspective. The early lines are full of youthful hyperbole, singing that love changes. "Hands and faces, earth and sky" and "how you live and how you die."[10] Later lines have a more mature outlook: "Days are longer, words mean more ... Pain is deeper, than before." The lyric ends with a fatalistic tone, stating that love "will never ever let you be the same." Andrew Lloyd Webber's music repeats a beguiling six-note phrase followed by either an ascending or descending series of notes that gets rangy in both directions. The sheet music is marked "dramatico" yet the ballad has a moderate pace and does not require any bombast in order to be effective. Because portions of the song are repeated throughout the musical, the contagious melody is firmly planted in one's memory. Michael Ball played Alex in both the London and Broadway productions of *Aspects of Love* and his recording of "Love Changes Everything" went high on the charts and became Ball's signature song. Other early recordings were made by Marti Webb, Sarah Brightman, José Carreras, and Peter Cousens. Over the years there have been notable discs by Jonathan Antoine, John Barrowman, Il Divo, Acker Bilk, the Shadows, Jason Donovan, Audra McDonald, the Mantovani Orchestra, Nana Mouskouri, Sting, Christopher Peacock, and Tom Solomon. A 1993 TV-movie version of *Aspects of Love* featured Ball playing Alex and singing the song.

Other notable songs from that season: "Seeing Is Believing," "The First Man You Remember," "Anything But Lonely" from *Aspects of Love*; "Love Can't Happen," "Roses at the Station," "Who Couldn't Dance with You," "We'll Take a Glass Together" from *Grand Hotel*; "You're Nothing Without Me," "You Can Always

Count on Me," "Lost and Found," "With Every Breath I Take" from *City of Angels*; "Waiting for Life," "We Dance," "Mama Will Provide," "Forever Yours" from *Once on This Island* (Off-Broadway); "Privates on Parade," "The Price of Peace" from *Privates on Parade* (Off-Broadway); "Doors," "March of Time," "Patterns" from *Closer Than Ever* (Off-Broadway); "All Fall Down" from *Romance in Hard Times* (Off-Broadway).

Song of the Season

1990–1991 SEASON

Some excellent new musicals opened on and Off-Broadway this season, some of them finding an audience and enjoying a long run. None ran longer than *Miss Saigon*, a London megahit that repeated its success on Broadway. The musical was much in the news before it even opened. Actors Equity refused to give the two London stars, Lea Salonga and Jonathan Pryce, a contract on Broadway. Producer Cameron Mackintosh threatened to cancel the production and return the huge advance back to ticket holders. For a time there were a stand-off and tensions and further sales increased. In the end, Equity caved in, *Miss Saigon* opened to mixed notices but popular acclaim, and it ran an impressive 4,125 performances. Also chalking up a long run were *The Will Rogers Follies*, *The Secret Garden*, and *Once on This Island*, the last a transfer from Off-Broadway. A stunning production could not save *Shogun: The Musical* which struggled to run nine weeks, the same length of time the African American play with songs *Mule Bone* ran. The Yiddish revue *Those Were the Days* pleased audiences for sixteen weeks. *Buddy: The Buddy Holly Story* was a West End transfer with Paul Hipp reprising his performance as the pioneer rock-and-roll star. The bio-musical ran six months; in London, it ran an amazing fourteen years. Broadway may not have embraced *Buddy* but it later became a very popular choice for regional and summer theatres. A revival of *Fiddler on the Roof*, starring Topol who had been Teyve in the film version, also ran six months. *Peter Pan*, featuring Cathy Rigby, could have run that long but its limited engagement of forty-five performances was part of a tour. A revival of the Gershwins' 1926 *Oh, Kay!* was a lavish David Merrick production with an African American cast. It ran seventy-seven performances before it closed temporarily for revisions and cast changes. The new version began previews then Merrick pulled the plug on the revival and it never reopened.

Two outstanding new musicals opened Off-Broadway this season: Stephen Sondheim's *Assassins* and William Finn's *Falsettoland*. The Finn piece would be seen on Broadway the following season; the Sondheim work would not get to Broadway until thirteen years later. *Smoke on the Mountain*, a gentle spoof of gospel singers and Christian America, ran a year, as did the revue *And the World Goes 'Round* celebrating the songs of John Kander and Fred Ebb and bringing attention to director-choreographer Susan Stroman. Running three months longer were two unusual shows: *Song of Singapore* was a musical parody of *Casablanca* and other exotic Hollywood movies, and *Pageant* was a beauty contest with the girls played by men in drag and the audience voting on the winner.

"Lily's Eyes"
Music by Lucy Simon; lyric by Marsha Norman
From *The Secret Garden* (1991)
Sung by Mandy Patinkin as Archibald Craven,
and Robert Westenberg as Dr. Neville Craven

The only major change playwright-lyricist Marsha Norman made in her adaptation of Frances Hodgson Burnett's' popular novel *The Secret Garden* was to add a case of unrequited love. While Archibald Craven (Mandy Patinkin) mourns the death of his wife Lily, his brother Neville (Robert Westenberg) is also in despair because he too loved Lily but her affections were only for Archibald. This was perhaps added to increase the tension in the story but mostly it provided the situation for "Lily's Eyes," the finest song in the score and the best male duet heard in a Broadway musical in years. Actually, the duet is more a case of twin soliloquies because each man sings his own independent thoughts unheard by the other. The musical number is placed effectively in the plot. Both men have noticed that Archibald's orphaned niece Mary (Daisy Eagan) has hazel eyes just as Lily had. Seeing a young version of a loved one's eyes is both exhilarating and painful. Norman's lyric leads into the subject carefully. There has been a violent storm raging outside but when it subsides, there is a stillness in the house. Neville notes how "strangely quiet" it is in the verse and he is left "waiting, I think of her."[11] Archibald reflects how "this Mary, she leaves the room,/ Yet remains" and he also is thinking of Lily. The gentle and calm verse leads into a refrain that begins with a purpose then builds lyrically and musically. Archibald has very mixed emotions about recognizing Lily in Mary. He recalls "those eyes that closed and left me all alone," and admits that those eyes "will never ever let me go!" Neville at first is worried about how this recognition will affect his brother but soon he sings of his own torment. He sees "those eyes that loved my brother—never me" and remembers how Lily "never knew I longed/ To hold her close." By the song's conclusion, each man is in anguish, each wondering how things might have been: "To be alive and whole … in Lily's eyes!" Lucy Simon's music in "Lily's Eyes" is not in the Yorkshire folk song idiom as with much of the score but instead embraces Victorian operetta full throttle. The combination of baritone and tenor voices allows the harmonizing to become highly dramatic, Neville's voice ringing above Archibald at times and creating some intoxicating sounds. Because the number builds to such a climatic ending, "Lily's Eyes" stops the show. It is a thrilling moment. Because the number works best as a duet, most recordings feature two male singers. Mandy Patinkin and Robert Westenberg's recording on the original cast recording is masterful, as is the duo Philip Quast and Christian Patterson on the British cast album. On Broadway, Howard McGillin and Adam Grupper were replacements for Archibald and Neville and sang the duet. Because the song does not lend itself to female singers, most recordings have been by male artists. Among the notable discs are those by Anthony Warlow and Philip Quast, Dallyn Vail Bayles, David Pellegrene and Ethan Spell, Kane Alexander and Simon Gleeson, Brent Barrett and Ryan Silverman, Hayden Tee and John Owen-Jones, and John Riesen and Jonathan Estabrooks.

Other notable songs from that season: "Come to My Garden," "Where in the World," "Winter's on the Wing," "Race You to the Top of the Morning" from *The Secret Garden*; "Last Night of the World," "The American Dream," "The Movie in

My Mind" from *Miss Saigon*; "Will-a-Mania," "Favorite Son," "Give a Man Enough Rope" from *The Will Rogers Follies*; "What Would I Do?," "Holding to the Ground," "The Baseball Game" from *Falsettoland* (Off-Broadway); "Everybody Has the Right (To Be Happy)," "Unworthy of Your Love," "Another National Anthem," "Ballad of Booth" from *Assassins* (Off-Broadway); "You Gotta Do What You Gotta Do," "Sunrise" from *Song of Singapore* (Off-Broadway); "No Tears in Heaven," "I'm Using My Bible for a Roadmap" from *Smoke on the Mountain* (Off-Broadway).

1991-1992 SEASON

This was supposed to be the season dominated by the much-anticipated *Nick and Nora*, a musical adaptation of the popular *The Thin Man* films of the 1930s and 1940s. Despite a charming Joanna Gleason and Barry Bostwick as the title characters, everything went wrong in the musical's development and even weeks of previews could not fix the troubled show. When *Nick and Nora* finally opened, it was trounced on by the critics and closed after nine performances. Also folding before two weeks was up were the odd-ball variety program *André Heller's Wonderhouse*, the revue *The High Rollers Social and Pleasure Club*, and a rocking musical from Poland titled *Metro*. Two new musicals ran over a year on Broadway. *Jelly's Last Jam* was a high-style musical bio of jazz pioneer Jelly Roll Morton (Savion Glover and Gregory Hines) which was uncompromising in its depiction. Not quite as popular was *Five Guys Named Moe*, a revue from London utilizing the songs of swing composer-musician Louis Jordan. New to Broadway was *Falsettos* in which the Off-Broadway successes *March of the Falsettos* and *Falsettoland* were combined for an evening of provocative theatre. The Willian Finn piece ran 487 performances. It was a very profitable season for revivals on Broadway. A small-scale edition of Frank Loesser's *The Most Happy Fella* played in an intimate venue for seven months, Raul Julia was an impressive Don Quixote in a production of *Man of La Mancha* for three months, and Cathy Rigby returned in *Peter Pan* for a further six weeks. The season's two biggest hits were *Guys and Dolls* and *Crazy for You*. The former was a sparkling production of Loesser's popular musical with Nathan Lane and Faith Prince and director Jerry Zaks getting the most praise. *Crazy for You* was a revised version of the 1930 Gershwin musical comedy *Girl Crazy* with script changes and several Gershwin favorites added to the already-sterling score. *Guys and Dolls* ran 1,143 times and *Crazy for You* 1,622 performances, both surpassing their original productions. There were no runaway hits Off-Broadway although the satirical Shirley Temple-like *Ruthless!* did last nearly ten months. The London import *Return to the Forbidden Planet* was a silly sci-fi spoof using pop songs from the 1960s while the campy *Prom Queens Unchained* had an original score as it spoofed cheap horror flicks. Many song standards were heard in the Fred Astaire revue *I Won't Dance* but there were original songs for the music-drama *Groundhog* and the musical version of the cult film *Eating Raoul*. None of these were successful enough to be promising Broadway material but *Ruthless!* and *Return to the Forbidden Planet* did have many regional productions.

"I'm Breaking Down"
Music and lyric by William Finn
From *Falsettos* (1992)
Sung by Barbara Walsh as Trina

Song of the Season

Few Broadway musicals have as interesting a history as *Falsettos*. William Finn first explored the semi-autobiographical hero Marvin in the Off-Off-Broadway musical *In Trousers* in 1979. He wrote a whole new score for *March of the Falsettos* (1981) which concerned Marvin leaving his wife Trina for his lover Whizzer, much to the confusion of his son Jason. With the advent of the AIDS epidemic in the 1980s, Finn returned to the same characters in *Falsettoland* (1990) and the musical took on some very serious issues. *March of the Falsettos* and *Falsettoland* are each long one-act musicals so they were effectively combined under the new title *Falsettos*, first done in regional theatre and then on Broadway. The only holdover from *In Trousers* was the tour de force solo for Trina titled "I'm Breaking Down." This "new" number stopped the show and remains one of Finn's most dazzling musical numbers.

"I'm Breaking Down" comes fairly early in *Falsettos* but it has the power of an eleven o'clock number. Watching Marvin (Michael Rupert) and his lover Whizzer (Stephen Bogardus) go off together, Trina (Barbara Walsh) reacts with a panic attack in song. Much of Finn's lyric is a stream of conscience rant playing off words that trigger a new thought. She wants to be a "princess on a throne,/ To have a country I can call my own" then realizes she needs a king but in her case the king "is a queen."[12] The structure of the song is as chaotic as Trina yet both lyric and music do return to a repeated refrain "I'm breaking down/I'm breaking down." Finn has some delicious internal rhymes in the song, as with the couplet "The almost-virgin who sings this dirge/ Is on the verge of breaking down." And he manages to bring this tirade to some conclusion with Trina's realization that "The only thing that's breaking up/ Is my family./ But me, I'm breaking down." As frenzied as the song is, Finn's music is somewhat restrained and allows the lyric to shine. The composition is marked "swing" with 138 eighth notes per minute. The melody has a circus quality, cheerfully bouncing up and down to 4/4 time yet turning sharp on some awkward notes/words. Although "I'm Breaking Down" is an early work by Finn, it has his command of character and tone which makes his songs so distinctive. The song was first sung Off-Broadway by Alison Fraser and her performance is preserved on an original cast recording, as was Barbara Walsh's rendition on the original Broadway album of *Falsettos* and Stephanie J. Block on the recording of the 2016 Broadway revival. The solo piece is so tied into plot and character that other recordings of "I'm Breaking Down" are rare, though the number is frequently heard in cabaret acts.

Other notable songs from that season: "That's How You Jazz," "Lovin' Is a Lowdown Blues," "The Whole World's Waitin' to Sing Your Song" from *Jelly's Last Jam*; "Is There Anything Better Than Dancing?," "Look Who's Alone Now" from *Nick & Nora*; "I Hate Musicals," "Born to Entertain" from *Ruthless!* (Off-Broadway); "That Special Night," "Sherry's Theme," "Give Me Your Love" from *Prom Queens Unchained* (Off-Broadway); "One Last Bop," "Think About Tomorrow" from *Eating Raoul* (Off-Broadway).

1992–1993 SEASON

It took a while to get to Broadway, but John Kander and Fred Ebb's 1990 musical *Kiss of the Spider Woman* arrived in a compelling production directed by Harold Prince and featuring another memorable star turn by Chita Rivera. Despite its grim story, set mostly in a hellish Latin American prison, the musical was popular enough to run 906 performances. Running nearly as long was a stage version of the 1969 rock opera *The Who's Tommy*. Again, a masterly production directed by Des McAnuff made the production a must-see event. The season's other long-run entry was the British import *Blood Brothers*. The tragic musical about doomed twin brothers was disparaged by the press but audiences liked it enough for it to run 839 performances. The rest of the Broadway season consisted mostly of expensive new musicals with unprofitable runs. The highly anticipated *The Goodbye Girl* was fraught with problems and, even with stars Bernadette Peters and Martin Short, struggled to run over five months. The classy *Anna Karenina*, based on Tolstoy's novel, and *Ain't Broadway Grand*, a bio-musical about producer Mike Todd, ran six weeks and three weeks. Deserving a longer run was *My Favorite Year* which played its one-month engagement at Lincoln Center but was not extended. It was a disappointing season Off-Broadway for new works. The ambitious *Wings*, based on Arthur Kopit's play of the same name, explored the trials of a stroke victim as she undergoes rehabilitation. It was challenging material and found an audience for forty-seven performances. Dan Goggin, the creator of the ever-popular *Nunsense* musical and its spinoffs, offered *Balancing Act* about a struggling actor whose complicated personality was played by five actors. The curious came for seven weeks then the musical pretty much disappeared from view. The only bright spots Off-Broadway were revues with pre-existing songs. The most attention was placed on the Stephen Sondheim revue *Putting It Together* because it marked Julie Andrews' return to the New York theatre after thirty years. She was joined by a top-notch cast and the revue's limited run of three months was very popular. Mostly non-theatre songs were sung in *Back to Bacharach and David*, a collection of pop hits by Burt Bacharach and Hal David. It only survived eight and a half weeks. Even further from musical theatre were the silly ditties by Allan Sherman in which irreverent lyrics were set to classical and popular music. Titled *Hello Muddah, Hello Fadduh*, the revue found an audience nostalgic for the old novelty songs for over six months. Although the songwriter Jacques Brel had died in 1978, the revue of his work was still titled *Jacque Brel Is Alive and Well and Living in Paris*. It was revived Off-Broadway this season and pleased audiences for sixteen weeks. Composer Alan Menken, of *Little Shop of Horrors* and several successful Disney films, found his latest work produced Off-Off-Broadway. *Weird Romance*, with lyrics by David Spencer, offered two serious science fiction tales that were intriguing but oddly unsatisfying. Despite Menken's popularity, the musical ran its six-week run and has rarely been revived since then.

Song of the Season

> "Where You Are"
> Music by John Kander; lyric by Fred Ebb
> From *Kiss of the Spider Woman* (1993)
> Sung by Chita Rivera as Aurora, and the prisoners

The gay prisoner Molina (Brent Carver) escapes from his horrid situation by imagining that his favorite movie star, Aurora (Chita Rivera), appears to him for comfort and glittering entertainment. No song in the Kander and Ebb score better expressed this need to escape than "Where You Are." In Molina's imagination, Aurora appears in a stylish white outfit and sings and dances with the male prisoners serving as her back-up chorus. Molina introduces the song with the idea of escaping to another world "when you feel you've gone to hell in a hand basket."[13] Then Aurora takes over with an escapist philosophy: "You've got to learn how not to be/ Where you are." She suggests that one imagine himself/herself as "a movie star." Ebb's lyric has some of the self-denial of the Kander and Ebb song "Cabaret." Not only must you not see reality but "you've got to learn how not to do/ What you've done." As in "Cabaret," the music is painfully cheerful. Like much of the score, "Where You Are" is in the Latin American idiom. Most distinctive is the salsa rhythm but there are also touches of bossa nova and rhumba. Much of the musical number is a dance piece and offers Molina (and the audience) a glimpse of pizzazz in contrast to the oppressive prison setting. Chita Rivera played Aurora in the Toronto and London productions of *Kiss of the Spider Woman* before winning acclaim on Broadway. During the run she was replaced by María Conchita Alonso, Carol Lawrence, and Vanessa Williams. The London production was recorded and then the musical got a second Broadway recording featuring Williams, Howard McGillin, and Brian Stokes Mitchell. Aside from the two cast discs of *Kiss of the Spider Woman*, "Where You Are" has rarely been recorded. It is unfortunate, for this is one of Kander and Ebb's finest pastiche numbers.

Other notable songs from that season: "Kiss of the Spider Woman," "Anything for Him," "Dear One," "Gimme Love," "You Could Never Shame Me" from *Kiss of the Spider Woman*; "Tell Me It's Not True," "I'm Not Saying a Word," "Easy Terms" from *Blood Brothers*; "My Favorite Year," "Larger Than Life," "Twenty Million People" from *My Favorite Year*; "A Beat Behind," "I Can Play This Part," "This Is as Good as It Gets" from *The Goodbye Girl*.

1993–1994 SEASON

Seven American musical classics were revived on Broadway this season, most of them receiving critical acclaim and substantial runs. The revivals getting the most praise were a superb London production of *Carousel*, a sparkling remounting of *She Loves Me*, and the slightly revised *Damn Yankees*, each running approximately ten months. Running three and a half years was the return production of *Grease*, a musical that was still one of the most popular in schools and regional theatres. Robert Goulet, the original Lancelot in *Camelot*, played King Arthur in a revival that lasted seven weeks. Richard Chamberlain essayed Henry Higgins in a revival of *My Fair Lady* that ran twenty-one weeks. Finally, there was a return of the ever-popular *Joseph and the Amazing Technicolor Dreamboat* which pleased audiences for six months. For patrons looking for new works, the choice came down to two very different choices. The Disney company presented their first Broadway venture with a stage version of the movie *Beauty and the Beast*. The large and colorful production did not please the critics but the public thought otherwise. Without benefit of stars, *Beauty and the Beast* ran thirteen years. The alternative offering was *Passion*, Stephen Sondheim's most morose and bewildering musical. An odd romantic triangle was the center of the beautifully designed musical drama which met with mixed reviews and an indifferent public. Despite winning the Tony Award for Best Musical, *Passion* struggled to run 280 performances. The unfortunate short runs on Broadway were *The Red Shoes* (five performances) and *The Best Little Whorehouse Goes Public* (fifteen performances) but the most expensive failure of the season was *Cyrano: The Musical*. The Dutch musical version of *Cyrano de Bergerac* offered gorgeous production values but that wasn't enough to please the press or the public. The musical played to low-capacity houses but the producers stubbornly kept the show running for seventeen weeks, ending up losing $12 million.

Off-Broadway boasted a long-run champion this season though many argued that *Stomp* was not really a musical. The percussion program from London was clever and entertaining enough that it had no trouble finding an audience. After a hiatus brought on by the Covid pandemic, *Stomp* returned and continues to run as of this writing. When the much-anticipated sequel *Annie 2* closed out of town in 1989, the authors reworked the material and offered *Annie Warbucks* Off-Broadway. The script and score were both more than competent but the sequel lacked the charm of the original and closed after two hundred performances. A wacky revue titled *Howard Crabtree's Whoop-Dee-Doo* ran seven months on the strength of its imaginative and hilarious costumes designed by the Crabtree of the title. The uncompromising author-songwriter Michael John LaChiusa made a quiet but notable debut with two Off-Broadway musicals this season. *First Lady Suite* played only two weeks at the Public Theatre but the intriguing character study was roundly praised. At Lincoln Center, LaChiusa's complex *Hello Again*, about sexual encounters spread across decades of American history, ran only one hundred times but it was recorded, eventually caught on, and received many productions by adventurous theatres across the country, throughout Europe, and in Australia.

Song of the Season

> "Loving You"
> Music and lyric by Stephen Sondheim
> From *Passion* (1994)
> Sung by Donna Murphy as Fosca

A turning point in the musical *Passion* takes place in a railroad coach where the homely, sickly Fosca (Donna Murphy) has intruded once again into the life of the handsome Italian soldier Giorgio (Jere Shea). Since meeting Fosca, Giorgio has been polite then confused then annoyed with her. In this scene on the train, he becomes angry with the woman who persists in telling him how much she loves him. Giorgio coldly tells her to leave him alone and expressed his astonishment that she chooses to love someone who does not care for her. Fosca's reply is the song "Loving You," a simple but eloquent ballad. She explains that loving him "is not a choice … It's who I am … why I live."[14] Such a love is "not in my control" and what she will pursue "for what's left of my life." Fosca goes on to say that her love for him is the reason "I do the things I do." The lyric ends with her explanation that she would die for him. Although these words might appear to be bombastic rhetoric, Sondheim's music is calm and uncomplicated. Just as the lyric uses few rhymes, the music has a narrow range and few flourishes. The sheet music is marked "largo tranquillo" and the composition uses whole notes sparingly. "Loving You" has the quality of a period parlor song. (The musical is set in 1863.) It is during Fosca's singing of "Loving You" that Giorgio (and the audience) starts to soften toward her and one moves from pity to empathy. Donna Murphy's performance as Fosca was the highlight of *Passion* and her recording of "Loving You" on the original cast album is unforgettable. It did not take long for "Loving You" to become a favorite in cabarets and in concert. There was an early duet recording of the song by Nancy Wilson and Peabo Bryson, followed by discs by Mandy Patinkin, Marc Heller, Michael Ball, Michelle Nicastro, Sean McDermott, Johnny Mathis, Joan Vázquez, the Trotter Trio, Deborah Shulman, Melissa Errico, Barbra Streisand with Patrick Wilson, Eleri Ward, and Cyrille Aimée. Maria Friedman sang "Loving You" in the 1996 London production. Patti LuPone played Fosca in a celebrated concert version of *Passion* which was broadcast in 2005 and Judy Kuhn played her in a 2013 Off-Broadway revival.

Other notable songs from that season: "Happiness," "I Read," "No One Has Ever Loved Me" from *Passion*; "If I Can't Love Her," "Me," "Human Again" from *Beauty and the Beast*; "Hello Again," "In Some Other Life," "Listen to the Music," "The One I Love" from *Hello Again*; "It Would Have Been Wonderful," "Leave It to the Girls" from *Annie Warbucks* (Off-Broadway).

1994–1995 SEASON

The number of musicals on Broadway this season shrunk to nine and three of those were revivals. The only book musical to have a long run was Andrew Lloyd Webber's *Sunset Boulevard* but when it closed after 977 performances it still failed to make a profit. The only new work to make money was the revue *Smokey Joe's Cafe* which celebrated the pop-rock songs by Jerry Leiber and Mike Stoller, best known for writing many songs for Elvis Presley. Without stars or spectacle, the little revue ran four and a half years. It was a good season for revivals. Harold Prince staged a slightly revised version of *Show Boat* and it ran an impressive 946 performances. In addition to a top-notch cast and expert scenic design by Eugene Lee, *Show Boat* boasted fine choreography by Susan Stroman which helped unify the problematic second act of the musical. Two revivals from regional theatres arrived on Broadway and met with differing results. The LaJolla Playhouse in California offered a sprightly production of *How to Succeed in Business without Really Trying* featuring Matthew Broderick as the hapless hero. The Goodspeed Opera House in Connecticut brought its revival of *Gentlemen Prefer Blondes* to New York with KT Sullivan as Lorelei Lee. Exemplary reviews greeted *How to Succeed* and it ran 548 times; *Gentlemen Prefer Blondes* shuttered after three weeks. There was much more activity Off-Broadway this season, including a few musicals to enjoy long runs. The revues *Swingtime Canteen* entertained audiences with the Second World War-era songs for eight months and Vernel Bagneris' solo show *Jelly Roll!* ran a bit longer. New songs were heard in the gospel musical *Faith Journey*, the country-western spoof of Wagner's Ring Cycle titled *Das Barbecü*, the Jack the Ripper musical *Jack's Holiday*, and the sly *That's Life!* about being Jewish. Michael John LaChiusa offered the unusual musical fable *The Petrified Prince* and songwriter Andrew Lippa made a notable debut with the two-character Off-Off-Broadway music drama *John & Jen*. Of these new works, only *That's Life!* enjoyed a run over three hundred performances.

"As If We Never Said Goodbye"
Music by Andrew Lloyd Webber;
lyric by Don Black, Christopher Hampton, Amy Powers
From *Sunset Boulevard* (1994)
Sung by Glenn Close as Norma Desmond

While some argue that not much new was added in musicalizing the film classic *Sunset Boulevard*, the pivotal scene in the movie, in which Norma Desmond returns to a film studio for the first time in decades, is such an emotional moment that setting it to music has its power. "As If We Never Said Goodbye" is an opera aria of sorts. Not that the music is as demanding as opera but it gives the heroine a big dramatic moment in the second act in which she shows her fragility and foreshadows her eventual downfall into madness.

Song of the Season

Andrew Lloyd Webber's music begins tentatively (the sheet music is marked "tenderly") but slowly builds until Norma is joyous and triumphant as she contemplates returning to the movies and being a star again. Of course we know this is all delusion but it makes her exhilaration all the more pathetic. The lyric, by several hands, progresses forward effectively. It is based on the Alan Ayckbourn lyric "Half a Moment" from the failed 1975 London musical *Jeeves*. Librettist Christopher Hampton and lyricist Don Black adapted the words for Norma's visit to the studio and the lyric was then fine-tuned by Amy Powers. Just as the music starts quietly, so too is Norma's opening lines: "Don't know why I'm frightened … I know my way around here."[15] Soon she is reminiscing about the days when she was making films, recalling different details: "the cardboard trees, the painted scenes … the whispered conversations in overcrowded hallways … coming out of makeup … the early morning madness." In the release, she admits "you can't know how I've missed you." And in the finest line in the song, she notes, "In this ever-spinning playground/ We were young together." The song then becomes a yearning to make movies not as a career but as a way of recapturing her youth when both she and moviemaking were starting out together. Norma's ego is never far from the surface so when she proclaims "This world's waited long enough/ I've come home at last" it is clear how little she is in touch with reality. The lyric concludes as quietly as it began, realizing "Yes, everything is as if we never said goodbye" and pleading "Oh, please don't ever ever make me say goodbye."

"As If We Never Said Goodbye" was introduced by Patti LuPone in the 1993 London production of *Sunset Boulevard*. Glenn Close sang it in the New York production and she was succeeded by Betty Buckley, Karen Mason, and Elaine Paige. Close reprised her Norma Desmond in the 2017 Broadway revival of *Sunset Boulevard*. There were early recordings of "As If We Never Said Goodbye" by Barbara Streisand, Shirley Bassey, Elaine Paige, and Laurie Beechman. Subsequent discs of note were made by Brian Conley, Emile Pandolfi, Debra Bryne, Maria Friedman, Jason Manford, Danny Wright, David Osborne, Linda Eder, Stan Whitmire, Stephanie McKeon, John Barrowman, and Christopher West.

Other notable songs from that season: "With One Look," "New Ways to Dream," "Too Much in Love to Care" from *Sunset Boulevard*; "A Ring of Gold in Texas," "Turn the Tide" from *Das Barbecü* (Off-Broadway); "The Geshrunken Meshuggena Rag" from *That's Life* (Off-Broadway); "Tricks of the Trade" from *Jack's Holiday* (Off-Broadway); "The Road Ends Here" from *John & Jen* (Off-Off-Broadway).

1995–1996 SEASON

Only two new musicals this season enjoyed critical acclaim and long runs. Jonathan Larson's *Rent* moved up from Off-Off-Broadway and stayed twelve years. Equally innovative and exciting was *Bring in 'da Noise, Bring in 'da Funk*, Savion Glover's history of Black Americans told through tap and other forms of dance. It chalked up over one thousand performances. The Julie Andrews vehicle *Victor/Victoria* managed a run of 738 performances but the large Marquis Theatre was rarely filled and the show ended up in the red. What did make money this season were some expert revivals: Nathan Lane in *A Funny Thing Happened on the Way to the Forum*, Donna Murphy and Lou Diamond Phillips in *The King and I*, and Carol Channing (yet again!) in *Hello, Dolly!* What seemed like a revival was the Broadway debut of a stage version of the 1945 Rodgers and Hammerstein film *State Fair* that had been criss-crossing the country for quite a while. It ran only 118 performances on Broadway but was later a favorite with all kinds of theatre groups. Perhaps the most anticipated and, consequently, disappointing new musical was *Big* based on the popular Tom Hanks movie. It struggled for 173 performances and lost a bundle. Other musicals that failed to run include the edgy *Chronicle of a Death Foretold*, the revue *Swinging on a Star*, and the revival of *Company*. One-person shows were again in evidence: *Patti LuPone on Broadway*, (Red) *Buttons on Broadway*, and *The Many Voices of Danny Gans*. A unique show for two performers (Bill Irwin and David Shiner) called *Fool Moon* qualified (barely) as a musical because the duo performed songs with the Red Clay Ramblers. Off-Broadway, two important composer-lyricists made impressive debuts. Jason Robert Brown's *Songs for a New World* was a song cycle that displayed his versatility in several musical genres. Adam Guettel's *Floyd Collins* was based on a true story of a Kentucky man trapped in a cave and the media circus that surrounded the unsuccessful attempts to save him. Both Brown and Guettel were deemed highly promising. Andrew Lippa's *John & Jen* moved from Off-Off-Broadway to Off-Broadway where it ran three months. *Cowgirls*, a satiric musical that mixed country-western songs with classical musical, ran an impressive 319 performances. There were two sci-fi spoofs which were almost indistinguishable. *Zombies from Beyond* parodied 1950s alien invader movies while *Zombie Prom* was set in a high school overcome by aliens, often echoing *Grease* and *Little Shop of Horrors*. The former musical lasted nine weeks, the later half that.

"Seasons of Love"
Music and lyric by Jonathan Larson
From *Rent* (1996)
Sung by the ensemble

Song of the Season

Although it is often labeled a "rock musical," Jonathan Larson's score for *Rent* embraces a wide variety of music, from Latin to hip-hop. The hymn-like ballad "Seasons of Love" is definitely not in the rock mode but it blends beautifully with the other songs to make *Rent* so musically rich. The song is sung by the company at the beginning of the second act and is reprised briefly later in the act by the company with an extended lyric, and is heard again during the eulogy for Angel who has died of AIDS. In Larson's original script, "Seasons of Love" was just heard during Angel's memorial service. But after Larson died right before performances started Off-Off-Broadway, it was decided that the whole cast sing it at the top of Act Two as a tribute to the deceased composer-lyricist. The effect was so moving that it stayed that way in the show.

The music for "Seasons of Love" has a gentle gospel sound, particularly at the end when the tempo picks up and the musical and lyric phrases overlap. This effect keeps the song solemn but hopeful. The sheet music for the number is marked "steady, strong, accented." Larson's lyric asks how one can describe and evaluate a person's life. It starts with the number 525,600 which is the number of minutes in a year. Then the lyric suggests things that happen during that time (sunsets, midnights, cups of coffee) but ends up counting time and the seasons with how much one loved a friend. It is a potent lyric that avoids mawkishness because it is so clear-headed. The images are concrete: "truths that she learned ... in bridges he burned."[16] The lyric ends with a call for celebration and a desire to "remember a year in a life of friends." When sung by the cast at the beginning of Act Two of *Rent*, none of the major characters have died but several are HIV-positive. So, in essence, it is not characters singing about other characters but actors singing about the man who created *Rent*. The cast members drop their characters for a moment and we are hearing the song on another level. The track of "Seasons of Love" from the *Rent* recording was released as a single and made the charts in four different categories. Cast member Idina Menzel recorded the number as a single. Other recordings of note are those by Stevie Wonder, Sandy Lam, the Broadway Kids, the cast of *Glee*, Michael Ball, Lani Hall with Herb Alpert, Keith Nunnally, Richard Barratta, Afatia, David Tolley, Tammy Edwards, and Aaron Flores. "Seasons of Love" is performed hundreds of times each year in concerts, funerals, weddings, graduations, and so on. In the 2006 film version of *Rent*, "Seasons of Love" is sung by the eight principals, led by Jesse L. Martin and Tracie Thoms, at the beginning of the movie.

Other notable songs from that season: "I'll Cover You," "One Song Glory," "Without You," "Light My Candle," "Tango: Maureen" from *Rent*; "Stop, Time," "Fun" from *Big* (1996); "Living in the Shadows" from *Victor/Victoria*; "I'd Give It All for You," "Hear My Song," "The Stars and the Moon," "The New World" from *Songs for a New World* (Off-Broadway); "The Riddle Song," "The Call," "Is That Remarkable?," "Through the Mountain" from *Floyd Collins* (Off-Broadway); "Cowgirls," "We're a Travelin' Trio," "Saddle Tramp Blues" from *Cowgirls* (Off-Broadway).

1996–1997 SEASON

The critics didn't much care for the Broadway season's two long-run musicals but both *Jekyll & Hyde* and *Titanic* were audience shows and ran and ran. The Maury Yeston musical about the ill-fated ocean liner chalked up 804 performances and the Frank Wildhorn-Leslie Bricusse musical of Robert Louis Stevenson's *The Strange Case of Dr. Jekyll and Mr. Hyde* ran twice that. (Oddly, it still did not turn a profit until subsequent touring and international productions.) But there was more to appreciate in some less fortunate new musicals. Shakespeare's *Twelfth Night* was once again set to music, this time to song standards composed by Duke Ellington, and was titled *Play On!* The African American take on the old classic was charming and well performed but audiences only kept it alive for two months. The new John Kander and Fred Ebb musical *Steel Pier*, about a marathon dance during the Depression, had much to recommend it but it folded inside of ten weeks. The uncompromising *The Life*, with music by veteran composer Cy Coleman, was a vivid portrayal of life on the means streets of New York City. A fine score and potent performances helped the unlikely musical run fourteen months. *Juan Darién*, an intriguing theatrical piece that barely qualified as a musical, moved from Off-Broadway into a Broadway house for six weeks and dazzled patrons with its stunning visuals created by director-designer Julie Taymor. The season's three big revivals on Broadway this season were disappointing artistically and financially. *Once Upon a Mattress*, starring Sarah Jessica Parker as the hapless Princess Winnifred, lasted only five months; *Annie*, with Nell Carter as Miss Hannigan, ran two months longer; and *Candide*, with Jim Dale in the major roles, shuttered after twelve weeks. The season's only notable revue was *Dream*, a celebration of the songs co-authored by Johnny Mercer. It also lasted twelve weeks.

Off-Broadway offered fourteen musicals, some of them very successful. The revue *I Love You, You're Perfect, Now Change* dealt in every cliché regarding romantic relationships and audiences enjoyed the clichés for thirteen years Off-Broadway and long after that in regional theatres. A very different audience patronized another revue, *When Pigs Fly*, which featured songs and sketches about gay lifestyle and Right-wing fanatics. The show was a follow-up of sorts to *Whoop-Dee-Doo* and once again Howard Crabtree designed the outrageous costumes. *When Pigs Fly* ran three times as long: 840 performances. Politics also arose in another satiric revue, *A Brief History of White Music*, in which a cast of three African American singers mimicked white performers trying to sing Rhythm and Blues. The sly revue found an audience for nearly nine months. The creators of *Oil City Symphony* and *Smoke on the Mountain* turned their sense of parody to early radio in *Radio Gals* in which a retired Arkansas school teacher in 1927 gathers her former students together to broadcast hillbilly songs from her living room. Despite some glowing notices, *Radio Gals* lasted only five weeks but was picked up by regional theatres looking for an all-female revue. The finest new musical this season Off-Broadway was *Violet* at Playwrights Horizons. The tale of a scarred North Carolina girl and her journey to an Oklahoma televangelist in the hopes of being cured was a penetrating character study with an expert script and score. *Violet* marked the New York debut of composer Jeanine Tesori who would soon demonstrate her remarkable musical versatility. The intimate musical had a limited run of four weeks but soon was picked up by regional theatres and has seen dozens of productions each year.

"This Is the Moment"
Music by Frank Wildhorn;
lyric by Leslie Bricusse, Steve Cuden, Frank Wildhorn
From *Jekyll & Hyde* (1997)
Sung by Robert Cuccioli as Dr. Henry Jekyll

Jekyll & Hyde took a long road to Broadway, leaving demo, concept, and concert recordings of some of the songs along the way. Featured in all of them is "This Is the Moment," the hit song from the score. Dr. Henry Jekyll has been working on a formula that will explore the good and evil side of man. One night in his laboratory, he decides to use himself as the subject of the experiment. Before he drinks (or, in some versions of the musical, injects) the formula, Jekyll sings the bombastic "This Is the Moment" in which he revels in the importance of his experiment. Pop song composer Frank Wildhorn began working on *Jekyll & Hyde* in the 1980s with lyricist Steve Cuden. Over the years Leslie Bricusse was brought in to work on the libretto and contributed to the lyrics. Even Wildhorn himself is credited as one of the authors of the "This Is the Moment" lyric. The song is not well integrated to the character or plot, one of the reasons it travels so well outside of the context of the musical. Jekyll could be singing about any momentous thing, all of the images and metaphors being purposely vague. "This is the moment!," he sings, "This is the day,/ When I send all my doubts and demons/ On their way!"[17] He refers to his experiment as an "endeavor," a "precious chance," and "a final test." His labors leading up to it are labeled "dreaming and scheming" and he already sees success as inevitable. Without ever getting specific, the lyric is stirring and passionate as in a pop anthem. Of course, Wildhorn's music is certainly helpful. It begins quietly and slowly but soon starts changing keys and climbing for the expected crescendo that the song (and the situation) demands. "This Is the Moment" never fails to stop the show.

There were a handful of recordings of the song before the musical opened on Broadway. A demo disc was made in 1986 with Chuck Wagner singing the song. A concept album in 1990 featured Colm Wilkinson as Jekyll. After a very successful production at the Alley Theatre in Houston in 1990, the authors tried to get Broadway producers interested by producing a "complete" recording of the show with Anthony Warlow singing "This Is the Moment." Another production at the Fifth Avenue Theatre in Seattle in 1995 was followed by a touring version arranged with Robert Cuccioli as Jekyll. He reprised his performance in the 1997 Broadway production and during the long run he was replaced by Sebastian Bach, Robert Evan, Chuck Wagner, and

David Hasselhoff; the last mentioned was also featured in a 2000 video of the original production. In the brief 2013 Broadway revival of *Jekyll & Hyde*, Constantine Maroulis sang the role of Jekyll. Of the dozens of recordings made of "This Is the Moment" are covers by Frank Ferrari, Moody Blues, Rene Froger, Dave Willetts, You & Me, Michelle Nicastro, Sean McDermott, Donny Osmond, Will Martin, the Steve Goodman Trio, and James Bongiorno. The song has been translated into several languages, the most popular disc by Garry Hagger in Dutch as "Het mooiste moment."

Other notable songs from that season: "A New Life," "Someone Like You," "Take Me as I Am" from *Jekyll & Hyde*; "My Body," "The Oldest Profession," "Don't Take Much" from *The Life*; "In Every Age," "Lady's Maid," "Barrett's Song," "Autumn," "No Moon" from *Titanic*; "First You Dream," "Waiting to Ride," "Everybody Dance," "Leave the World Behind" from *Steel Pier*; "Hard to Say Goodbye," "Water in the Well," "Luck of the Draw," "On My Way" from *Violet* (Off-Broadway); "Laughing Matters," "Light in the Loafers" from *When Pigs Fly* (Off-Broadway).

Song of the Season

1997–1998 SEASON

It was a Broadway season of major triumphs and painful disappointments but the twelve musicals that opened this season offered diverse and fertile theatregoing. The two biggest surprises were *The Lion King* and *Ragtime*. The Disney tale was a beloved property with no human characters yet director-designer Julie Taymor reconfigured *The Lion King* into a stunning theatrical piece that had even the Disney-prejudiced critics cheering. E. L. Doctorow's massive novel *Ragtime*—with its many themes, historic and fictional events, and dozens of characters—was unlikely material for the confines of the stage. But again, a thrilling production staged by director Frank Galati and choreographer Graciela Daniele, as well as an expert adaptation by librettist Terrence McNally, made it come together. *Ragtime* ran two and a half years and *The Lion King* became a seemingly permanent landmark in Times Square. A surprise also was the revised revival of *Cabaret* which drew crowds for six years. The rest of the Broadway season was a mixed bag. The rousing operetta *The Scarlet Pimpernel* opened to weak notices, played for a few months, was revised and recast, opened again, and then did the same over again. The Frank Wildhorn musical eventually chalked up 640 performances but failed to show a profit. Running much less were the freak show musical *Side Show*, the comedy of manners musical *Triumph of Love*, the Paul Simon music-drama *The Capeman*, the "Retro Revue" *Street Corner Symphony*, and the stage version of the movie musical *High Society*. Faring better was the dance revue *Forever Tango* which pleased audiences for over a year. The season's other two revivals—*The Sound of Music* and *1776*—were well received but ran much less than *Cabaret*.

The highlight of the Off-Broadway season was the rock musical *Hedwig and the Angry Inch* which began Off-Off-Broadway then moved up to tally 857 performances in an Off-Broadway venue. The other long-run champ was the sarcastic revue *Secrets Every Smart Traveler Should Know* which made audiences laugh for two and a half years. Famous singers were impersonated in *Always ... Patsy Cline*, *Dinah Was* (about Dinah Washington), and *I Will Come Back* (about Judy Garland). Of the three, the Patsy Cline musical went on to receive hundreds of productions regionally. There was much to recommend in the AIDS-sensitive rock musical *The Last Session* and in Adam Guettel's song cycle *Saturn Returns: A Concert*. Songwriters Tom Jones and Harvey Schmidt looked back on their career in the revue *The Show Goes On*. The two veterans wittily commented on their past works and some young singers performed familiar Jones-Schmidt songs as well as those cut out of town. The revue began Off-Off-Broadway and was popular enough to move to a larger venue Off-Broadway for ten weeks.

"Ragtime"
Music by Stephen Flaherty; lyric by Lynn Ahrens
From *Ragtime* (1998)
Sung by the company

1980–1999 Seasons

Have two musicals in the same Broadway season ever begun with such an impact as *Ragtime* and *The Lion King* do? The opening numbers "Ragtime" and "Circle of Life" not only introduce the theme, tone, and rhythms of the two musicals but also encapsulate the essence of what follows. "Circle of Life" was written for the 1994 film *The Lion King* and is not, technically, a Broadway song. But "Ragtime" is pure theatre. McNally worked with songwriters Lynn Ahrens and Stephen Flaherty on an opening that presented the three major groups of people—the white upper class, the European immigrants, and the African Americans in Harlem—but also introduced several major characters. It was a tall order but it worked beautifully. The privileged family in New Rochelle seems to be content in their safe little world. They note, "The skies were blue and hazy, Rarely a storm, barely a chill."[18] But a "distant music" could be heard that was "Skipping a beat, singing a dream … Putting out heat, picking up steam." This leads into the Harlem section where one could hear "the music of something beginning/ An era exploding, a century spinning" and it was called ragtime. The immigrants are introduced with a different tone. Tateh banishes his past and "dreamed of a new life for his little girl." Eventually the three groups merge, find it awkward, then separate. Soon all are singing in unison: "In riches and rags/ And in rhythm and rhyme,/ The people called it ragtime … Everything was ragtime!" The song "Ragtime" is frequently interrupted by prose introductions, the characters often speaking of themselves in the third person. In addition to the white family in New Rochelle, Coalhouse Walker and Sarah in Harlem, and Tateh and his daughter on Ellis Island, the number also introduces African American educator Booker T. Washington, escape artist Harry Houdini, banking mogul J. P. Morgan, activist Emma Goldman, industrialist Henry Ford, and scandal celebrity Evelyn Nesbit with her lover Stanford White and her jealous husband Harry K. Thaw. Ahrens and McNally together created one of the most efficient and gripping opening numbers in the American musical theatre.

Flaherty's music is ragtime, of course, but not the vigorous, rapid kind of rag most known from many of Scott Joplin's vivacious piano pieces. Ragtime music is equally effective when played at a slower pace, as with Joplin's "The Entertainer." Flaherty's music starts with a lazy, elegant pattern for New Rochelle, moves into a brassier and swinging tempo for Harlem, then takes on a klezmer tone for the immigrants. The musical number builds but never speeds up, coming to an exhilarating climax through its composition dynamics rather than going faster. "Ragtime" is not reprised during the musical but it is heard briefly at the finale. Yet the song is the piece that remains with one, its insistent melody and rich harmonies working in such a way that this number is a musical on its own.

Other notable songs from that season: "The Wheels of a Dream," "New Music," "Back to Before," "Our Children," "Your Daddy's Son" from *Ragtime*; "Shadowland," "They Live in You," "Endless Night" from *The Lion King*; "Who Will Love Me as

I Am?," "Feelings You've Got to Hide" from *Side Show*; "Serenity," "Henchmen Are Forgotten" from *Triumph of Love*; "When I Look at You," "Into the Fire" from *The Scarlet Pimpernel*; "Satin Summer Nights," "Chimes" from *The Capeman*; "Origin of Love," "Tear Me Down," "Wicked Little Town" from *Hedwig and the Angry Inch* (Off-Broadway); "Children of the Heavenly King," "Icarus," "There's a Shout," "Pegasus" from *Saturn Returns* (Off-Broadway).

1998-1999 SEASON

Plenty of old standards were heard on and Off-Broadway this season and, with so many revivals, it was not a good year for new theatre songs. Happily, Broadway enjoyed a superb score with Jason Robert Brown's *Parade* and Off-Broadway shone with a wonderful score for William Finn's *A New Brain*. Unhappily, both musicals had short runs. But over time, both shows have been frequently produced regionally. *Parade* dealt with anti-Semitism in the South and *A New Brain* had its hero nearly dying of a brain tumor. Similarly serious subjects were to be found in *The Civil War*, *Footloose*, and *Bright Lights, Big City*. In fact, for musical comedy one had to turn to revivals of *Little Me*, *Annie Get Your Gun*, *On the Town*, *Peter Pan*, and *You're a Good Man, Charlie Brown*. Revues were prevalent this season, the biggest hit being *Fosse* in which the choreography of the late Bob Fosse was celebrated. The dance show ran over one thousand performances. Two revues featured African American performers and the song standards of the past associated with Black culture. *It Ain't Nothin' But the Blues* and *Rollin' on the T.O.B.A.* moved from Off-Broadway to the Street with mixed success. The former managed to run nearly eight months. The later, a recreation of Black vaudeville, closed in two weeks. (The title initials stood for "Tough on Black Asses," a summation of the difficulties African Americans experienced in touring vaudeville.) Other revues with old songs for the scores included *Band in Berlin*, about German-Jewish artists who moved from popularity to subjugation under the Nazis, and *The Gershwins' Fascinating Rhythm*. Both revues closed in two weeks. Both also came from regional theatres, something that could be said about more and more New York theatre. Finally, it was a season of one-person musical showcases. *An Evening with Jerry Herman*, *Mandy Patinkin in Concert: Mamaloshen*, *Charles Aznavour on Broadway*, *Sandra Bernhard: I'm Still Here Damn It!*, and *Marlene* (with Sian Phillips as Marlene Dietrich) all managed to find an audience.

"And They're Off"
Music and lyric by William Finn
From *A New Brain* (1998)
Sung by Malcom Gets as Gordon Schwinn, and ensemble

"And They're Off" can be described as a narrative number, a metaphor for an unhappy family, and even a torch song of sorts. It tells the story of a gambling father who loses the family fortune then abandons them. The metaphor is of horses racing, going in circles, and eventually losing the race. The torch quality comes in with the love-hate relationship Gordon (Malcolm Gets) has with his absent father. It is a remarkable song that works on more than one level. The music is gentle and idyllic as Gordon begins his narrative, observing "ponies in the sun" and seeing his "father bet the family fortune."[19] The family gave up lunch because "my father had a hunch." Then the words and music take on the

Song of the Season

hoof-beats of racing horses with "Ma would scoff,/ She would scoff./ Hear her scoff—And they're off!" The ensemble supports this refrain with a series of "La la la la la"s that relate to the excitement of the race even as they seem to be mocking the family. Even when the horse loses, the father is elated but the mother scolds him, "But Joe, the dumb horse lost!" His reply is stinging: "Sometimes joy has a terrible cost." The song then leaves the race track and centers on the domestic violence at home, resulting in the father leaving, never to return. Gordon sings "Daddy's off!" while the ensemble keeps the tempo moving with "La la la la la!" Gordon sings "We get letters from Maine/ Where he tries to explain/ Why he's off." His narrative is not a bitter one. He has mixed emotions, remembering "We also laughed a lot—That was a thing I often forgot to mention." The song climaxes with the horse race and the family downfall coexisting. "There is blood on the ground ... As the horses go round—And they're off!" Finn often used rapid wording and double-time pacing to demonstrate the pace of the city or the manic nature of the characters. But he scores "And They're Off" with a more controlled kind of tempo. (The sheet music says "Fast.") The speed comes from the horses motif yet the domestic tension is accented by those laughing "La la la la la"s. *A New Brain* was mostly complimented in its limited Lincoln Center production but it was not until the original cast album was released that the musical started to catch on. It has since seen many regional productions in North America, Great Britain, and Australia. "And They're Off" has not been much recorded but is a favorite song in cabarets, revues, and concerts.

Other notable songs from that season: "Sailing," "The Music Still Plays On," "Change," "Heart and Music" from *A New Brain* (Off-Broadway); "All the Wasted Time," "The Old Red Hills of Home," "You Don't Know This Man" from *Parade*; "My New Philosophy," "Beethoven Day" from *You're a Good Man, Charlie Brown.*

1999–2000 SEASON

The practice of moving Off-Broadway shows to the Street continued this season with mixed results. The dance program *Contact* was so popular in Lincoln Center's downstairs Off-Broadway venue that after 101 performances it moved upstairs, became a Broadway production, and ran over two years. On the other hand, the atmospheric little musical *James Joyce's The Dead* played a month at Playwrights Horizons before moving to Broadway where it floundered and closed after fourteen weeks. Two unconventional Off-Broadway works, Julie Taymor's 1996 fantasy *The Green Bird* and the multimedia program *Squonk*, also made the move to the Street for short runs. The Stephen Sondheim revue *Putting It Together*, first seen Off-Broadway in 1993, reappeared this season on Broadway with a starry cast headed by Carol Burnett. It ran thirteen weeks. The longest-running new work this season was *Aida*, a reworking of the classic Verdi opera with a pop/rock score by Elton John (music) and Tim Rice (lyrics). The Disney production ran five years. The latest screen-to-stage musical *Saturday Night Fever* was panned by the press but the disco musical was popular enough to run 500 performances. Running almost as long was the vivacious revue *Swing!*; running longer was the Irish dance show *Riverdance on Broadway*. More dance was enjoyed in the foreign import *Tango Argentino*, a show first seen on Broadway back in 1985. From South Africa came a very different production. *Kat and the Kings* was the tale of "colored" singers whose popularity in their homeland was crushed by racial laws. While *Riverdance* ran seventeen months, the other imports had to settle for much less. Michael John LaChiusa offered two demanding musicals on Broadway, not his usual venue. Lincoln Center produced his *Marie Christine*, a retelling of the Medea legend set in nineteenth-century New Orleans, for a one month engagement. Then later in the season, the Public Theatre presented LaChiusa's Roaring Twenties musical *The Wild Party* in a Broadway house for two months. Both musicals were very accomplished and featured outstanding players but critics (and audiences) admired them more than embraced them. There were three top-notch revivals on Broadway this season. *Kiss Me, Kate* entertained playgoers for two and a half years, *The Music Man* thrived for two years, and *Jesus Christ Superstar* was well received but only lasted four months.

Joseph Moncure March's poem "The Wild Party," which served as the source material for LaChiusa's musical, was also musicalized by Andrew Lippa and presented Off-Broadway for seven weeks. Comparisons were inevitable, LaChiusa's Twenties jazz music deemed more accurate but Lippa's version considered somewhat more accessible. The eccentric London musical *Shockheaded Peter* was self-described as a "junk opera" and, though it was only offered for two weeks, it eventually developed a cult following. Also very unorthodox was *The Donkey Show*, an imaginative disco musical version of *A Midsummer Night's Dream*. Audiences had no trouble enjoying the odd, colorful piece and kept it on the boards for four years. The other long-running Off-Broadway entries this season could not have been more different. *Our Sinatra* was a nostalgic revue featuring songs that the late Frank Sinatra popularized. The revue *Naked Boys Singing* was as its title announced, no more or no less. The Sinatra show ran three years; the unclothed revue ran eleven years. For many, the best songs heard Off-Broadway this season were those that Sondheim wrote in the 1950s for his musical *Saturday Night* which was never produced. The Off-Broadway theatre company Second Stage presented the piece of Sondheim juvenilia for six weeks and some wonderful new/old songs were finally heard in New York.

"Written in the Stars"
Music by Elton John; lyric by Tim Rice
From *Aida* (2000)
Sung by Adam Pascal as Radames, and Heather Headley as Aida

The romance of the Egyptian captain Radames and the Nubian slave Princess Aida is one of the great love stories in opera. It was not based on history or legend but was a completely fictional tale written by Antonio Ghislanzoni for Verdi's 1871 opera *Aida*. Like *Rent*, the classic Italianate music was changed to pop-rock; unlike *Rent*, the setting for this opera-to-musical retained the original Egyptian setting and character names. This invites comparisons to Verdi's opera, which is not what Elton John and Tim Rice intended. The most popular song from the score is "Written in the Stars" which comes at a pivotal moment in the musical. Radames (Adam Pascal) tells Aida (Heather Headley) that he is breaking off his engagement to the Pharaoh's daughter Amneris (Sherie Rene Scott) but, knowing such a move will ruin her father's chances of escape, Aida convinces him not to do so. In her verse, she tells Radames that they can never meet again and that she must be "someone you once loved, so long ago, so well."[20] In Radames' verse, he questions "How a perfect love can be confounded out of hand" and then moves into the refrain which asks "Is it written in the stars" that they were "given paradise but only for a day?" Aida later joins him in the duet which is a series of unanswerable questions, such as "Is this God's experiment in which we have no say?" Rice's lyric is modern in its sensibility but he used no contemporary expressions or anachronisms. It is a pop ballad that translates to many situations. John's music throughout *Aida* avoids any exotic or African tone as in his previous *The Lion King*. "Written in the Stars" is in the pop-rock mode but is rather restrained, the tempo being "moderately slow" and the crescendos not being bombastic. While *Aida* was in development, John recorded some of the songs with various artists to create a concept album. His recording of "Written in the Stars" with American singer LeAnn Rimes was made in 1999 and it went to the top of the singles chart. Rimes also recorded it as a solo in 2002. In the Broadway production of *Aida*, the duet was sung by Adam Pascal and Heather Headley who were replaced by Will Chase and Deborah Cox during the long run. A solo recording of "Written in the Stars" was made by Tom Michael and there have been duet versions by Matt Bogart and LaChanze, Frank Galan and Sandra Kim, and Marco Bakker and Willeke Alberti.

Other notable songs from that season: "Elaborate Lives," "Every Story Is a Love Story," "My Strongest Suit" from *Aida*; "When It Ends," "People Like Us," "Moving Uptown" from *The Wild Party* (Broadway); "Poor Child," "An Old-Fashioned Love Story," "Raise the Roof" from *The Wild Party* (Off-Broadway); "Way Back to Paradise," "I Will Love You," "Beautiful" from *Marie Christine*; "Michael Furey," "Wake the Dead," "Goldenhair," "The Living and the Dead" from *James Joyce's The Dead*; "If Your Shoes Don't Shine," "Lonely Girl," "Wild Time" from *Kat and the Kings*; "(What Do You Do on a) Saturday Night," "All for You," "Too Many People" from *Saturday Night* (Off-Broadway).

2000–2001 SEASON

Although *The Producers* was the runaway hit of the season, winning most of the kudos and awards, there were actually plenty of commendable musicals both on and Off-Broadway. Because tickets to *The Producers* were so difficult to get, other musicals benefited by so many patrons looking for alternatives. The silly musical comedy *The Full Monty*, for example, was able to run 778 performances. And a revival of the escapist musical *42nd Street* pleased audiences for three and a half years. Musicals with more substance had a difficult time of it. A commendable musical version of *Jane Eyre* struggled to last six months; the biographical *A Class Act*, about the late songwriter Ed Kleban, transferred from Off-Broadway to the Street where it floundered then closed after fourteen weeks; and a beautifully mounted *The Adventures of Tom Sawyer* shuttered inside of three weeks. The highly anticipated musical *Seussical*, in which tales by Dr. Seuss were set to songs by Lynn Ahrens and Stephen Flaherty, opened to mixed notices and went through revisions and cast changes in order to catch on with the public. Although *Seussical* ran less than six months and lost a bundle, the charming musical would later become a very popular choice for schools and regional theatres. The Broadway revivals this season were not as fortunate as *42nd Street*. *The Rocky Horror Show* was able to chalk up 436 performances in a small venue but *Bells Are Ringing*, despite a sparkling performance by Faith Prince, lasted only eight weeks, and a scaled-down revival of *Follies* only fourteen weeks.

Off-Broadway's biggest hit this season was the eccentric *Urinetown* which presented a future where a water shortage forced the public to "pay to pee." The show was so well received by the press and the public that after seven weeks it was eying Broadway. The biographical Janis Joplin musical *Love, Janis* ran almost as long by staying Off-Broadway. Similarly, the tabloid spoof *Bat Boy* found an audience Off-Broadway for seven months. Sixteen Off-Broadway musicals opened this season and the variety was impressive. Among the other notable entries were the satire of 1960s TV variety shows titled *Pete 'n' Keely*; the sci-fi musical *Time and Again*; the sassy Latinx revue *4 Guys Named José ... and Una Mujer Named Maria!*; the Roaring Twenties musical *The It Girl*; the Edward Gorey revue *Gorey Details*; the African American coming-of-age musical *The Bubbly Black Girl Sheds Her Chameleon Skin*; a revue of song standards called *American Rhapsody*; and revivals of *Godspell* and *Berlin to Broadway with Kurt Weill*. Only a few of these enjoyed substantial runs but, taken as a whole, it was clear Off-Broadway was thriving.

"Alone in the Universe"
Music by Stephen Flaherty; lyric by Lynn Ahrens
From *Seussical* (2000)
Sung by Kevin Chamberlain as Horton the Elephant,
and Anthony Blair Hall as JoJo

Although *Seussical is* an episodic musical encapsulating a variety of Dr. Seuss tales, there are some recurring characters who help unify the show and create some empathy with the stories. This is most effectively done with Horton the Elephant, the only one who believes in the invisible Whos, and young JoJo, the Who boy who communicates with Horton. The two first meet in the song "Alone in the Universe," an enticing ballad that is a musical highlight in the show. Like many of the musical numbers in *Seussical*, this one mixes spoken rhymed verse with sung lyrics. Lynn Ahrens' lyric captures Dr. Seuss' cadence and sensibility that it is difficult to tell where Seuss leaves off and Ahrens takes over. Horton has been guarding a leaf on which the tiny Whos live. The other animals laugh at him "for thinking a dust speck can speak" but Horton is adamant: "For I have found something/ That they'll never find."[1] The verse has a sense of wonder—"There are secrets on a leaf,/ In the water, in the air"—as Horton sees "hidden planets, tiny worlds, all invisible." Stephen Flaherty's music has been restrained to the point that it resembles recitative but in the refrain the music soars. A series of repeated notes is broken by descending or ascending phrases and the lyric also repeats sounds. The effect is like floating in the air. Although Horton is "alone in the universe," he has "found magic but they don't see it." The music and lyric get even more expansive in the release as Horton declares "I have wings!" and that he can "fly around the moon/ And far beyond the sky." The release is forceful enough that JoJo hears Horton and joins in singing the refrain, also lamenting that "No one notices anything/ Not one person is listening." Horton and JoJo introduce themselves to each other and discover that they both have "thinks" and imagine fantastical places like "Solla Sollew." The two new friends take comfort in knowing each has "One true friend in the universe/ Who believes in me." There are a lot of characters in *Seussical* but only in "Alone in the Universe" is there a warm relationship. Kevin Chamberlain played Horton in the Broadway production and Anthony Blair Hall was JoJo, replaced during the run by Andrew Keenan-Bolger, Cameron Bowen, and Aaron Carter. Although *Seussical* only ran 197 performances on Broadway and was a major financial failure, a revised version of the musical had two successful national tours followed by productions in London and South Africa. Today it receives hundreds of productions by all kinds of theatre groups.

Other notable songs from that season: "How Lucky You Are," "Oh, the Thinks You Can Think," "Solla Sollew," "It's Possible" from *Seussical*; "We Could Do It,"

"Where Did We Go Right?," "Keep It Gay," "That Face," "I Wanna Be a Producer" from *The Producers*; "Better," "Next Best Thing to Love" from *A Class Act*; "Breeze Off the River," "Big Ass Rock," "You Rule My World" from *The Full Monty*; "Run Freedom Run," "Follow Your Heart," "Don't Be the Bunny" from *Urinetown* (Off-Broadway); "Secret Soul," "Brave Enough for Love" from *Jane Eyre*; "Show You a Thing or Two," "Ruthie's Lullaby," "Three Bedroom House" from *Bat Boy* (Off-Broadway); "Beautiful Bright Blue Sky," "There Was a Girl" from *The Bubbly Black Girl Sheds Her Chameleon Skin* (Off-Broadway).

Song of the Season

2001–2002 SEASON

The theatre season in New York City was just starting to pick up steam, as it usually did in September, when the unthinkable happened. The terrorist attack on the World Trade Center on September 11 paralyzed the city in a way few could recall. Not since the assassination of President Kennedy in 1963 had the theatres on and Off Broadway gone dark from the shock. When shows started to reopen, patrons were wary of returning to the theatre. The city of New York was losing millions of dollars every day and a campaign was created to encourage playgoers to return to Broadway so that everyone could "get on with the show." It helped that the season's two biggest hits opened in a few weeks: the Off-Broadway transfer of *Urinetown* and the London mega-hit *Mamma Mia!* The quirky *Urinetown* ran for two and a half years and the ABBA jukebox success was a fixture on Broadway for fourteen years. The only other hit on the Street this season was *Thoroughly Modern Millie*, another stage version of a film musical but this one had some delightful new songs by Jeanine Tesori and Dick Scanlan and a colorful production featuring newcomer Sutton Foster. It ran a toe-tapping 903 performances. Some ambitious musicals found that post-9/11 audiences were not in an experimental mood. The French tragedy *Thou Shalt Not*, which musicalized Emile Zola's *Térese Raquin*, had a demanding score by Harry Connick, Jr., and powerful performances but audiences weren't buying; it closed after ten weeks. Similarly dark, but also quite accomplished, was *Sweet Smell of Success*, the Marvin Hamlisch and Craig Carnelia musical based on the Ernest Lehman novella that was the source material for the famous 1957 movie; it lasted eleven weeks. Two very different musicals from Britain had very different receptions in New York. The superb National Theatre revival of *Oklahoma!* (now with an American cast) was highly praised and ran nearly a year. The silly *By Jeeves*, which had already been produced regionally in the States, finally came to Broadway in a simple, intimate production, very atypical for an Andrew Lloyd Webber show. The musical farce, based on stories by P. G. Wodehouse, was dismissed by the critics and ignored by the public, closing in nine weeks. A revival of the Stephen Sondheim-James Lapine favorite *Into the Woods* ran nearly eight months.

The Off-Broadway musicals this season were either serious or satirical. For the latter, audiences enjoyed *Menopause: The Musical* with its predictable jokes and song standards altered to fit the subject matter. It not only ran four years in New York but repeated its success with regional theatres. Another musical satire, *Reefer Madness*, spoofed the infamous 1936 propaganda film of the same title. The sophomoric show only lasted three weeks but it too found life in regional productions. There was much more substance in *Tick Tick … Boom!*, a character piece composed of various songs written by the late Jonathan Larson. The intriguing three-character musical ran for six months. It was also picked up by regional theatres, as was Jason Robert Brown's two-character musical *The Last Five Years*. Deserving a run longer than its two weeks at Playwrights Horizons was *The Spitfire Grill*, an engrossing little musical set in a backwater town in Wisconsin and about the staff at the local diner. Like most of the Off-Broadway offerings this season, it found an afterlife in theatres across the nation.

Tom Jones and Harvey Schmidt returned to Off-Broadway for their rural musical *Roadside* but, aside from an entrancing title song, it found little favor and quickly closed.

"Gimme Gimme"
Music Jeanine Tesori; lyric by Dick Scanlan
From *Thoroughly Modern Millie* (2002)
Sung by Sutton Foster as Millie Dillmount

Jeanine Tesori and Dick Scanlan wrote a handful of pastiche numbers for the screen-to-stage musical comedy *Thoroughly Modern Millie*, perhaps the finest of them being "Gimme Gimme." The flapper Millie Dillmount (Sutton Foster) hopes to marry her rich boss Mr. Graydon (Marc Kudisch) but falls for the penniless Jimmy Smith (Gavin Creel). When she thinks Jimmy is cheating on her with another woman, Millie sings this Roaring Twenties version of a jazzy torch song. Scanlan's lyric is a series of short phrases rather than long and wordy lines. Millie is an efficient typist who takes shorthand and she sings in an abrupt and concise manner. She sums up the situation in the verse—"simple choice … nothing more … marry well … clever girl"—then in the refrain the word "gimme" is repeated effectively, acting as a kind of percussive instrument: "Gimme, gimme that thing called love!"[2] Also in the shorthand mode, the lyric sometimes turns nouns into verbs, as with "Aphrodite, don't forget me!/ Romeo and Juliet me!" Tesori's music starts out as a tentative slow jazz number but before long it turns into hot jazz, the vocals matching the brass in the accompaniment. By the final refrain, "Gimme Gimme" is a vibrant Charleston number and, although it is a solo and not an ensemble number, it calls out for dancing. The number is also the musical's eleven o'clock number that allows the performer playing Millie to stop the show.

Kristen Chenoweth was the first to sing "Gimme Gimme," both on a demo recording and in the early workshops of *Thoroughly Modern Millie*. The first full production of the show was in 2000 at the La Jolla Playhouse in California where Millie was played by Erin Dilly. But by the time the musical reached Broadway in 2002, understudy Sutton Foster was Millie; she was roundly praised and her celebrated career was launched with a bang. During the long run, Susan Egan replaced Foster and sang the song. "Gimme Gimme" is a popular choice in recitals, concerts, and cabarets, but there have been only a handful of recording, including those by Lisa Donahey, Ann Reburn, Lucie Jones, and Foster with Darcie Roberts.

Other notable songs from that season: "I Turned the Corner," "Not for the Life of Me," "Forget About the Boy" from *Thoroughly Modern Millie*; "I Cannot Hear the City," "Don't Know Where You Leave Off," "Don't Look Now," "Dirt" from *Sweet Smell of Success*; "I Need to Be in Love," "The Other Hours" from *Thou Shalt Not*; "By Jeeves," "Half a Moment," "That Nearly Was Us" from *By Jeeves*; "Our Little World" from *Into the Woods* (revival); "Why?," "No More," "Sunday," "Therapy" from *Tick, Tick … Boom!* (Off-Broadway); "The Next Ten Minutes," "Still Hurting," "A Summer in Ohio" from *The Last Five Years* (Off-Broadway); "A Ring Around the Moon," "When Hope Goes," "Way Back Home" from *The Spitfire Grill* (Off-Broadway).

2002–2003 SEASON

More than usual, playgoers turned to escapism and nostalgia in the years after 9/11. They got a taste of both with *Hairspray*, a rose-colored depiction of the early Sixties in which even racial strife is conquered by song and dance. The 1988 cult film favorite was softened for the stage and, given a first-rate production with sunny pastiche songs, *Hairspray* found plenty of fans and ran twelve years. There was nostalgia for later decades with *Movin' Out*, a dance show set to songs by pop composer-singer Billy Joel. It ran three years. All of the other new musicals on Broadway this season struggled to find an audience and folded before they could. The family musical *A Year with Frog and Toad* was perhaps too sweet and low-key for Broadway. A musical version of another film, *Urban Cowboy*, was a disappointment. The campy *Dance of the Vampires* had its fans but not enough of them. All three shows closed inside of nine weeks. The intriguing fantasy *Amour* had an affecting score by French composer Michel Legrand but was gone in two weeks. Broadway's only notable revue this season, *The Look of Love* celebrated the songs of Burt Bacharach and Hall David but shuttered in a month. There were some outstanding revivals which did find enough patrons to run several months. Brian Stokes Mitchell was a commanding Don Quixote in *Man of La Mancha*; Bernadette Peters' Mama Rose drew patrons to a revival of *Gypsy*; and film star Antonio Banderas was supported by a first-rate female cast in *Nine*. The most interesting revival was the rewritten version of *Flower Drum Song* with a libretto that turned the Rodgers and Hammerstein musical comedy into a musical play. A radiant cast was highly praised but the revival remained on the boards for only an unprofitable twenty-one weeks.

It was a busy season Off-Broadway where twenty musicals opened and, despite the fact that *Boobs: The Musical* ran longer than any other show, there was much to recommend in the diverse offerings. After scoring three major Broadway productions, Lynn Ahrens and Stephen Flaherty returned to Off-Broadway this season to present their new musical, *A Man of No Importance*, based on the 1994 Irish film of the same name. Terrence McNally did another expert adaptation, reworking into a musical the tale of a closeted gay man who finds a creative release in Dublin amateur theatricals. The musical was well received and Lincoln Center's limited run was extended to twelve weeks. A very different musical on a gay theme was the imaginative fantasy *Zanna, Don't!* which depicted a world in which heterosexuality is taboo. Michael John LaChiusa's *Little Fish* was an intimate character musical about exploring different relationships in contemporary Manhattan. At the Public Theatre, *Radiant Baby* was a bio-musical about pop artist Keith Haring and the disco scene of the 1980s. There were two other biographical musicals this season. *Jolson and Company* was a study of the famous entertainer while *Hank Williams: Lost Highway* told the story of the celebrated country-music legend using his songs. Two new African American musicals—*Harlem Song* and *Little Ham*—were set in Harlem during the "renaissance" of the 1920s. The latter ran nine weeks, the former twice that. One short section of Marcel Proust's multi-volume work *Remembrance of Times Past* was turned into the musical *My Life with Albertine* which ran for three weeks at Playwrights Horizons. A family musical version of Mark Twain's *The Prince and the Pauper* managed to catch on with the public. Attendance was so encouraging during the three-month summer engagement that the show was brought back for the holidays and ran another five weeks. Near the end of the season, an unorthodox little musical titled *Avenue Q* opened Off-Off-Broadway and was soon much talked about. Using the children's TV show *Sesame Street* as the source of its satire, *Avenue Q* used human and puppet characters to explore a group of neurotic young New Yorkers. The run at the Vineyard Theatre was extended to six weeks and plans were made to brave Broadway the next season.

"You Can't Stop the Beat"
Music by Marc Shaiman; lyric by Scott Wittman, Marc Shaiman
From *Hairspray* (2002)
Sung by Harvey Fierstein as Edna Turnblad, Jaret Winokur as
Tracy Turnblad, Matthew Morrison as Link Larkin,
Mary Bond Davis as Motormouth Maybelle, and company

The catchiest and most memorable song in the *Hairspray* score is not heard until the end of the musical. "You Can't Stop the Beat" is a dance number with several of the principal characters having solo sections which contribute to the general celebratory feel. Teenager Tracy Turnblad (Jaret Winokur) begins the song as her entry in the dance contest on the Baltimore TV program *The Corny Collins Show*. The lyric by Marc Shaiman and Scott Wittman is a list of forces of nature (an avalanche, the "motion of the ocean," the coming of the seasons, etc.) which can't be stopped. To these are added the need to sing and dance no matter what. Since the whole musical has been about the complications thrown in the way of 1960s segregation, the song ends up being about more than performance. Tracy declares "I just cannot stand still" because "the world keeps spinning 'round and 'round/ And my heart's keeping time to the speed of sound."[3] Tracy's boyfriend Link (Matthew Morrison) joins her for the propulsive refrain, the duo declaring the title phrase. Different characters are briefly featured as their lyric applies to their part of the story. Tracy's hefty mom Edna (Harvey Fierstein), for example, doesn't care how fat she grows and the African American activist Motormouth Maybelle (Mary Bond Davis) has her own perspective, singing "Yesterday is hist'ry and it's never coming back!" Like all of the songs in *Hairspray*, "You Can't Stop the Beat" is a pastiche of early 1960s pop music. Shaiman's music for this number is a fusion of rock and soul with a touch of gospel thrown in. The inspiration for this kind of music used comes from such pop classics as the Tina Turner hit "River Deep—Mountain High" and the disco favorite "Can't Stop the Music." "You Can't Stop the Beat" is a high energy and infectious finale that sends the audience home on a musical high. In the 2007 film version of *Hairspray*, the number was sung by Nikki Blonsky, as

Tracey, and the whole cast, though in a somewhat shortened version of the stage song. A 2016 live television version of *Hairspray* featured Maddie Baillio as Tracey who led the ensemble in the song. A recording by the cast of the television show *Glee* went high on the charts, and there have also been notable discs by Toxic Audio, BYU Noteworthy, and Adrian Hansel.

Other notable songs from that season: "Welcome to the 60s," "Timeless to Me," "Without Love," "I Know Where I've Been" from *Hairspray*; "Amour," "Ordinary Guy" from *Amour*; "He'll Never Know," "Alone" from *A Year with Frog and Toad*; "Total Eclipse of the Heart (Vampires in Love)" from *Dance of the Vampires*; "Love Who You Love," "The Man in the Mirror," "Art" from *A Man of No Importance* (Off-Broadway); "I Can Write Books," "I Think We Got Love," "Do You Know What It's Like?" from *Zanna, Don't!* (Off-Broadway); "Flotsam," "Simple Creature," "He" from *Little Fish* (Off-Broadway); "There's a Fine, Fine Line," "It Sucks to Be Me," "Everybody's a Little Bit Racist" from *Avenue Q* (Off-Off-Broadway).

Song of the Season

2003–2004 SEASON

It was a good season for making money on Broadway with six new musicals showing major profits. Despite negative out-of-town gossip and poor reviews, the fantasy musical *Wicked* was an audience favorite from the start. It continues to prove its appeal as it remains a seemingly permanent fixture on Broadway. But *Wicked* was not the sole winner in the tricky business of Broadway economics. The small but potent musical satire *Avenue Q* transferred to the Street and stayed six years. Also making a lucrative showing this season were three revivals. *Fiddler on the Roof*, with Alfred Molina as Tevye, ran two years; *Wonderful Town*, with Donna Murphy heading the cast, ran fourteen months; and the first Broadway production of the 1982 Off-Broadway success *Little Shop of Horrors* chalked up 372 performances. The quasi-biographical musical *The Boy from Oz*, about the late Australian singer-songwriter Peter Allen, ran a year on the strength of its star, Hugh Jackman. It was that rare case of the actor portraying another performer having more talent and audience draw than the subject of the musical. It took the dark musical *Assassins* twelve years to finally make it to Broadway but the production was so well received that it was worth the wait. All the same, *Assassins* was dissident stuff for Broadway and ran only thirteen weeks. Another applauded revival this season was *Big River*, a production of Los Angeles' Deaf West Theatre in which the characters were played by speaking and non-speaking performers. The limited run of eight weeks was well attended. Perhaps the most visually stunning Broadway production of the season was *Bombay Dreams*, a satirical look at Bollywood and how Hindu actors find sudden fame in the popular genre. The production originated in London where it ran two years; on Broadway it lasted only eight months. Also from London was *Taboo*, a musical about the Culture Club star Boy George with new and old songs by the iconic performer. What had been an intimate "fringe" musical in London was rewritten and turned into a full-scale Broadway spectacle. The critics were unkind and there were only enough Culture Club fans to keep *Taboo* on the boards for three months. Two other musicals that did not enjoy the good fortune of the season and deserved longer runs were *Never Gonna Dance* and *Caroline or Change*. The former was a clever and well-executed musical comedy based on the Fred Astaire-Ginger Rogers film *Swing Time*. Despite the glorious Jerome Kern-Dorothy Fields songs and the playful production, *Never Gonna Dance* got lost in the Broadway shuffle and lasted only ten weeks. The Jeanine Tesori-Tony Kushner musical *Caroline or Change* received rave reviews Off-Broadway at the Public Theatre and its thirteen-week engagement was a sellout. Similar praise for the Broadway production did not translate into ticket sales and the poignant and powerful musical closed after seventeen weeks.

It was a disappointing season for musicals Off-Broadway. The best entry, *Caroline or Change*, was whisked off to the Street where it failed to catch on. The only musicals that ran any longer than a few months were *Fame on 42nd Street* and *The Thing about Men*. The 1980 film *Fame* was a box office hit and became a very popular television show. Stage versions were produced in London and on US tours without much success so the property was turned over to amateur theatre groups. Retitled *Fame on 42nd Street*, the Off-Broadway musical found enough fans to run eight and a half months. Running a few weeks less was *The Thing about Men*, a sometimes clever tale of an unfaithful wife, a jealous husband, and a Bohemian artist. *Johnny Guitar*, a facile musical version of the 1954 Joan Crawford western of the same name, got some complimentary notices but New Yorkers only kept it running eight weeks. The campy western later found more success regionally. The same was true for *bare [sic]*, a "pop opera" about oversexed high schoolers putting on a production of *Romeo and Juliet*. There were two revues celebrating lesser-known songwriters: *Listen to My Heart: The Songs of David Friedman* and *They Wrote That?* with songs by Barry Mann and Cynthia Weil. An Off-Broadway season would not be complete without some silly musical revues and there were two notable ones. *Capitol Steps: Between Iraq and a Hard Place* found humor in current politics while *The Musical of Musicals: the Musical* offered the same trite tale as musicalized by the likes of Rodgers and Hammerstein, Jerry Herman, Stephen Sondheim, and Kander and Ebb.

"Defying Gravity"
Music and lyric by Stephen Schwartz
From *Wicked* (2003)
Sung by Idina Menzel as Elphaba, Kristin Chenoweth
as Glinda, and guards and citizens of Oz

The most famous song from Stephen Schwartz's score for *Wicked*, "Defying Gravity" is most known as a solo for a belt voice but in the musical it is a major production number involving the outcast Elphaba (Idina Menzel), her friend and rival Glinda (Kristin Chenoweth), and the ensemble. Near the end of the first act, Elphaba has discovered that the so-called Wonderful Wizard (Joel Grey) is far from good as he plans to subjugate the animal citizens of Oz. She defies the Wizard and vows to fight him even if it means she is considered evil and labeled the Wicked Witch. "Defying Gravity" begins as a duet as Elphaba and Glinda argue over her decision and Elphaba accuses Glinda of selling out to social pressures to conform. Elphaba argues that she has changed and is "through with playing by the rules/ Of someone else's game" as she moves into the celebrated refrain.[4] "It's time to try/ Defying gravity!" she sings. In a second duet section, Elphaba tries to convince Glinda to join her in her quest to see that "good" is achieved. Glinda recalls how "Dreams, the way we planned 'em/ If we work in tandem" but cannot bring herself to take the road of an outcast. So the two sing to each other, "I really hope you get it/ And you don't live to regret it;/ I hope you're happy in the end." Elphaba then launches into the most famous part of the refrain, announcing that "if I'm flying solo/ At least I'm flying free." At this point in the number, the citizens of Oz and the Wizard's guards enter. Elphaba enchants her broomstick and rises above the ensemble. With lights flashing, wind blowing, and smoke filling the stage, the song ends with

Song of the Season

Elphaba victorious, declaring that "nobody in all of Oz/ No Wizard that there is or was/ Is ever gonna bring me down!" She sings an extended vocal riff that is quite demanding as the citizens sing "Look at her, she's wicked!" And so ends one of the most thrilling Act One finales in the American musical theatre. Schwartz's music varies throughout the number as there are sudden key changes. The duet sections are syncopated at times but Elphaba's solo passages are rhythmically patterned as the music propels forward with determination. It is a very difficult song to sing accurately and is a harsh test of a singer's vocal control and power. In addition to the original cast album, Idina Menzel sang the song in the London production of *Wicked* then recorded "Defying Gravity" as a solo in 2007. There have been over fifty recordings of the song, including those by Julie Budd, Leslie Henstock, Debbie Gravitte, Kerry Ellis, Anthem Lights, Lucy Thomas, and the Midnite String Quartet. The cast of the TV series *Glee* sang "Defying Gravity" on two occasions. Over the years, the song has been sung in the Broadway production of *Wicked* by such performers as Shoshana Bean, Stephanie J. Block, Jackie Burns, Marcia Dodd, Eden Espinosa, Julia Murney, and Jennifer DiNoia.

Other notable songs from that season: "For Good," "Popular," "I'm Not That Girl" from *Wicked*; "Gonna Pass Me a Law," "Moon Change," "Lot's Wife" from *Caroline or Change*; "Everything Taboo," "Come On in from the Outside" from *Taboo*; "Salaa'm Bombay" from *Bombay Dreams*; "The Better Man Won," "The Greatest Friend" from *The Thing About Men* (Off-Broadway); "We Had Our Moments," "Tell Me a Lie" from *Johnny Guitar* (Off-Broadway); "Bare," "No Voice" from *bare* (Off-Broadway).

2004–2005 SEASON

Movies continued to inspire Broadway musicals and, if they were light enough fare, often succeeded. Such was the case with the season's two biggest hits. *Dirty Rotten Scoundrels* was a conventional musicalization of the 1988 film with sportive performances by John Lithgow and Norbert Leo Butz. *Spamalot* was more unconventional, turning the 1975 movie *Monty Python and the Holy Grail* into a wacky musical satire on just about everything. Both shows were endorsed by the critics. *Dirty Rotten Scoundrels* found audiences for a year and a half and *Spamalot* ran just under four years. Another screen-to-stage musical that hoped to join their ranks was *Chitty Chitty Bang Bang*. Even with its flying car and other expensive demands, the British musical fantasy was a moneymaker in London where it ran almost four years. An identical production, with a first-rate American cast, lost a bundle on Broadway when it closed in eight months. Off-Broadway provided the only new book musical to find success. After a regional production and a six-week run at the Second Stage Theatre, *The 25th Annual Putnam County Spelling Bee* moved to Broadway and stayed for two and a half years. The merry little musical then went on to be a favorite with all kinds of theatre groups across the country. Also enjoying a healthy post-Broadway life was the musical version of *Little Women* which was roundly dismissed by the press and struggled to run four months. Two jukebox musicals opened this season. *Good Vibrations* was about some young people on a road trip punctuated by songs by the Beach Boys. Songs popularized by Elvis Presley provided the score for *All Shook Up*, a slaphappy tale filled with all kinds of clichés. Both musicals failed to run very long on Broadway but *All Shook Up* soon saw hundreds of productions regionally. Such was not the case with Broadway failures *Dracula: The Musical* and *Brooklyn: The Musical*.

There were splendid revivals of *Pacific Overtures* and *La Cage aux Folles* this season but the return of *Sweet Charity* got mixed reactions. A new-old musical that also received uneven notices was *The Frogs*, a thirty-year-old curiosity based on an Aristophanes comedy. Stephen Sondheim added some new songs in the musical comedy tradition to his old score and the aquatic musical was given a skillful production by director-choreographer Susan Stroman. *The Frogs* ran its twelve-week engagement at Lincoln Center and has rarely been heard of since. For many critics and playgoers, the season's finest musical was also at Lincoln Center. *The Light in the Piazza* was based on a lesser-known novella and film about a mother and daughter finding new horizons and even love in Florence, Italy. Adam Guettel wrote the indelible score and Bartlett Sher staged the delicate production. The gentle musical was the surprise of the season, extending its run until it had played fifteen months.

Once *The 25th Annual Putnam County Spelling Bee* moved to Broadway, there was little of much interest Off-Broadway this season. The most ambitious musical was *Dessa Rose*, a grim tale of a Southern lady and her slave with a commendable score by Lynn Ahrens and Stephen Flaherty. There wasn't enough appreciation to extend the musical beyond its ten-week run at Lincoln Center. With a much lighter tone was *Captain Louie*, a family musical based on a children's book. With his behemoth *Wicked* packing them in on Broadway, Stephen Schwartz turned to Off-Broadway to score the unpretentious *Captain Louie* at the York Theatre. The vibrant score was reminiscent of Schwartz's *Godspell* even though the tale was much more naive. For those who wanted yet another *Nunsense* there was *Altar Boyz*, a spoof of Catholicism with four altar boys singing songs filled with religious jokes and double entendres. The juvenile show had no trouble getting easy laughs from playgoers for five years.

"Dividing Day"
Music and lyric by Adam Guettel
From *The Light in the Piazza* (2005)
Sung by Victoria Clark as Margaret Johnson

Adam Guettel's score for *The Light in the Piazza* is filled with the flavor of Italianate opera but the song that is most affecting is a Broadway ballad. "Dividing Day" is unique in that it is neither a love song nor a torch song but instead a bittersweet reflection about a marriage that is falling apart. The American tourist Margaret Johnson (Victoria Clark) is spending the summer in Florence with her grown daughter Clara (Kelli O'Hara) who is moderately mentally handicapped. When Clara falls in love with the local youth Fabrizio (Matthew Morrison), Margaret is at first alarmed but soon starts to realize that Clara has a chance for happiness she never thought possible. When Margaret tries to tell her husband Roy about the situation during a long distance phone call to the States, he is abrupt and not at all understanding. After Roy hangs up, Margaret reflects on her empty marriage in the poignant "Dividing Day." Guettel's lyric is addressed to the absent Roy with Margaret asking a series of difficult questions about when their marriage started to die. "Was it on the church step,?" she asks, or did "it go creeping slowly? When was your Dividing Day?"[5] The tone of the song is not passionate or angry yet still very expressive in its imagery. Margaret sees Roy "somehow wearing a frightening disguise" and notices "I can see the winter in your eyes" that tell her "We are together, but no more love, no more love allowed." "Dividing Day" has a finely crafted lyric that is restraint itself. Guettel's music is in 3/4 time and flows nicely. Just as Margaret is asking questions not easily answered, the melodic line rises with each inquiry. The song ends not with a flourish but with a lingering, unresolved coda: "When was, when was, when was Dividing Day?" Victoria Clark originated the role of Margaret and sang "Dividing Day" in the Seattle and Chicago tryout productions before opening on Broadway. Christine Andreas played Margaret in the US tour and Renée Fleming in a London production. "Dividing Day" has often been performed in concerts but there are only a few recordings, including the original demo by Guettel and heartfelt discs by Audra McDonald and Judy Kuhn.

Other notable songs from that season: "The Light in the Piazza," "Love to Me," "The Beauty Is," "Let's Walk" from *The Light in the Piazza*; "The Song that Goes Like This," "I'm All Alone," "You Won't Succeed on Broadway" from *Monty Python's Spamalot*; "Nothing Is Too Wonderful to Be True," "What Was a Woman to Do?," "Great Big Stuff" from *Dirty Rotten Scoundrels*; "I Love to Travel" from *The Frogs*; "Astonishing" from *Little Women*; "Pandemonium," "I'm Not That Smart," "The I Love You Song" from *The 25th Annual Putnam County Spelling Bee*; "We Are Descended," "At the Glen," "Fly Away" from *Dessa Rose* (Off-Broadway).

Song of the Season

2005–2006 SEASON

When Andrew Lloyd Webber, Elton John, and the Disney Company all have flops on Broadway in the same season, you know it was a tough time for making a buck. Only three new musicals turned a profit. In the case of the jukebox musical *Jersey Boys*, it was quite a profit indeed. The tale of Frankie Valli and the Four Seasons thrilled audiences for ten years on Broadway and toured successfully for longer than that. But being a jukebox musical filled with familiar tunes was no guarantee of a hit. John Lennon songs in *Lennon* and Johnny Cash favorites in *Ring of Fire* were not enough and both shows folded in seven weeks. What did do very well this season was the musical version of the popular book and film *The Color Purple* and the facile spoof of 1920s musicals called *The Drowsy Chaperone*. The former played 910 times and the drunken chaperone got laughs for 674 performances. There were fine rivals of *The Pajama Game*, *The Threepenny Opera*, and *Sweeney Todd*; only the last had a significant run. The rest of the season was rather dismal. Lloyd Webber's operatic *The Woman in White* lasted three months, Elton John's vampire musical *Lestat* ran only five weeks, and Disney's visually stunning *Tarzan* lost big time when it closed after 486 showings. Also failing to run were *The Wedding Singer*, *In My Life*, and *Hot Feet*.

There were no long-run hits Off-Broadway this season but there were some excellent musicals. *Grey Gardens* was an atypical entry in that it was a musical based on a documentary film. The 1975 movie, about the surviving mother and daughter of a once-wealthy family who were living in their decaying Long Island mansion, seemed unlikely material for a musical but a compelling libretto by Doug Wright and an outstanding score by newcomers Scott Frankel (music) and Michael Korie (lyrics) made for thrilling musical theatre. It helped that there were stunning performances by Christine Ebersole and Mary Louise Wilson, directed by Michael Greif. *Grey Gardens* was well attended during its two-month engagement at Playwrights Horizons, but when it transferred to Broadway the next season, it ran only 307 performances. Also of high quality were two musicals by John Michael LaChiusa. *See What I Wanna See* at the Public Theatre was a pair of intriguing musicals loosely based on Japanese short stories. *Bernarda Alba* at Lincoln Center was a tragic musical based on the Spanish classic play *The House of Bernarda Alb*a by García Lorca. Each musical ran five weeks. *The Great American Trailer Park Musical* ran twice as long. The farcical look at the inhabitants of a Florida trailer park enjoyed many subsequent productions regionally. The same thing happened to the revue *Almost Heaven: Songs of John Denver* which ran only eight weeks Off-Broadway. Five mini-musicals involving food made up the sometimes-clever *Five Course Love* and there were some entertaining things about *I Love You Because* which was very loosely based on Jane Austin's *Pride and Prejudice*. The two musicals ran nine weeks and fourteen weeks. An interactive musical experience titled *Bingo* was exactly what it said it was: patrons saw a musical and got to play bingo. The show found bingo players for twelve weeks.

"I'm Here"
Music and lyric by Brenda Russell,
Allee Willis, Stephen Bray
From *The Color Purple* (2005)
Sung by LaChanze as Celie

The eleven o'clock song in *The Color Purple* is not a splashy production number but a solo by the story's heroine as she realizes she has everything she needs to be happy and that she is proud of herself. Although the uneducated African American Celie (LaChanze) has been sexually and physically abused by her stepfather and her husband, by the 1940s she is free of them both and has her own women's pants business. Celie has been in love with the fiery Shug Avery (Elizabeth Withers-Mendes) but Shug has left her for a young man. At first Celie feels the loss, but soon realizes that she doesn't need to be loved by another but to love herself. "I'm Here" is a list song in which Celie recounts what she has: her house, her hands, her faraway sister Nettie, her absent children, and other things that bring her comfort. The lyric by Brenda Russell, Allee Willis, and Stephen Bray is a lovely piece of writing, inspired by the language of Alice Walker's book. Celie's grows in strength during the song and the lyric ends with a momentous realization that "I'm beautiful. And I'm here!"[6] The music by Russell, Willis, and Bray is a series of builds from careful, hesitant notes to a pounding crescendo in the gospel manner. The song allows the singer some jazz riffs as well as the traditional Broadway belt. "I'm Here" is a powerful number that shows how Celie has survived and grown over the course of the musical. It never fails to stop the show. LaChanze originated the role of Celie first in the Atlanta tryout production and then on Broadway. Cynthia Erivo played Celie in the 2013 London production and in the 2015 Broadway revival. Although "I'm Here" is a favorite of African American singers, it is heard frequently by various performers in cabarets and concerts. In addition to the cast albums, the song has been recorded by Jemma Rix and Alice Fearn.

Other notable songs from that season: "Too Beautiful for Words," "Push Da Button," "What About Love?" from *The Color Purple*; "All for Laura," "A Gift for Living Well," "I Believe My Heart" from *The Woman in White*; "Sure as the Sun Turns to Moon," "Waiting for This Moment" from *Tarzan*; "As We Stumble Along," "Show Off," "Love Is Always Lovely in the End" from *The Drowsy Chaperone*; "It's Your Wedding Day" from *The Wedding Singer*; "Another Winter in a Summer Town," "The Revolutionary Costume for Today," "Around the World," "Drift Away," "Jerry Likes My Corn," "Will You?" from *Grey Gardens* (Off-Broadway); "This Side of the Tracks," "It Doesn't Take a Genius" from *The Great American Trailer Park Musical* (Off-Broadway).

Song of the Season

2006–2007 SEASON

The London transfer of *Mary Poppins* was the runaway hit this season on Broadway. The expensive, mammoth musical ran twelve years. The only new American work to run over 600 performances was the Off-Broadway transfer of *Spring Awakening* which found an audience for three years. The two musicals couldn't have been more different, demonstrating how diverse the Broadway audience was becoming. Two escapist musical comedies—the backstage murder mystery *Curtains* and the stage version of the film *Legally Blonde*—didn't please the critics but audiences kept each on the boards for fourteen and sixteen months. Despite some commendable writing and performing, the other film-to-stage musical *High Fidelity* closed inside of two weeks. Deserving a better run also was the bio-musical *LoveMusik* about Kurt Weill (Michael Cerveris) and Lotte Lenya (Donna Murphy) which struggled to run over seven weeks. Running three weeks longer was *The Pirate Queen* with an impressive Stephanie J. Block as the title character. Two musical parodies were highly entertaining. *Kiki and Herb: Alive on Broadway* spoofed a singing lounge act and *Martin Short: Fame Becomes Me* was a self-mocking autobiography. The only jukebox musical this season was the misguided three-week failure *The Times They Are A-Changin'* featuring songs by Bob Dylan. It was quite a season for starry revivals with Kristen Chenoweth in *The Apple Tree*, Audra McDonald in *110 in the Shade*, and Raul Esparza in *Company*. But returns of *Les Misérables* and *A Chorus* had substantial runs without the benefit of stars. Two of the season's finest performances were those by Christine Ebersole and Mary Louise Wilson in *Grey Gardens* which transferred from Off-Broadway and managed to play seven months on the Street.

The Off-Broadway entries this season ranged from the large-cast Latinx musical *In the Heights* to the two-character parody *Gutenberg! The Musical!* Lin-Manuel Miranda's atmospheric depiction of the residents of Washington Heights used everything from traditional-sounding Spanish-language ballads to rap to bring the ethnic neighborhood to life. After selling out for twenty-three weeks Off-Broadway, *In the Heights* moved to the Street where it ran three years. *Gutenberg!* made fun of big-budget Broadway musicals by having two performers do a backers audition for their show about the inventor of the printing press. It ran only three months but later was picked up by small regional theatres. Two intriguing musicals also transferred to Broadway this season but with little success. The quirky *[title of show]* pleased audiences for ten weeks then made the big move to the Street and floundered after thirteen weeks. Even more unique was the autobiographical musical by Stew that was titled *Passing Strange*. It was praised at the intimate Public Theatre but lasted only four months in a Broadway house. Running just as long was the revue *Shout!* with 1960s songs sung by a cast of five women. Similarly, the film-to-stage horror musical *Evil Dead: The Musical* pleased fans of the gory movie for only sixteen weeks but was picked up by regional theatres that had plenty of stage blood. Of the many spoofs on and off the Street this season, perhaps the most clever entry was *Adrift in Macao* by

Christopher Durang (book and lyrics) and Peter Melnick (music). A satire on *film noir* movies set in exotic places, the tuneful little musical ran only three weeks and has yet to be widely discovered.

"96,000"
Music and lyric by Lin-Manuel Miranda
From *In the Heights* (2008)
Sung by Lin-Manuel Miranda as Usnavi, Christopher Jackson as Benny, Robin de Jesús as Sonny, Karen Olivo as Vanessa, Andréa Burns as Daniela, and company

---

Although there are several engaging characters in the musical *In the Heights*, it is the neighborhood of Washington Heights that is the major character. The song that best captures this ensemble feeling is the production number "96,000." When the struggling bodega owner Usnavi (Lin-Manuel Miranda) learns that someone bought the winning lottery ticket worth $96,000 at his store, he and some of the residents state what they would do with the money if they won. The number begins with Benny (Christopher Jackson) rapping about his dream of going to business school and becoming rich, "Richer than Nina's daddy, Donald Trump and I on the links, and he's my caddy."[7] Picking up on Benny's rap rhythm, Usnavi warns him of the dangers of money, foretelling that Benny will be "lying like Pinocchio." Daniela (Andréa Burns) has a different dream, living in Atlantic City with a Malibu breeze. Usnavi scolds Benny and Daniela for their "hypotheticals" and offers his more practical dream. He would pay off his bodega and give his "Abuela" (grandmother) Claudia some of the money. Then he would return to his home in the Dominican Republic. He sings, "Just fly me down to Puerta Plata, I'll make the best of it." The young Sonny (Robin de Jesús) takes a more radical viewpoint, arguing that the people in the barrio have to become more technically savvy. The music moves from rap to a flowing melody for Vanessa (Karen Olivo) as she sings about her dream of winning the lottery and living "downtown" in a "nice studio." Soon various other residents add their dreams and the number builds until it is all one loud declaration: "Once we start goin'/ We're never gonna stop!" Like much of the music in the *In the Heights* score, "96,000" mixes some traditional Latinx sounds with rap without changing the rhythm. Parts of the song are contrapuntal with two distinct melodies being sung at the same time. By the time the number is a full-fledged ensemble piece, the music is rapid and energetic. It is a thrilling character song for the neighborhood. In the 2021 film version of *In the Heights*, "96,000" was sung by Anthony Ramos as Usnavi, Corey Hawkins as Benny, Gregory Dias IV as Sonny, Melissa Barrera as Vanessa, Daphne Rubin-Vegas as Daniela, and the company.

Song of the Season

Other notable songs from that season: "In the Heights," "No Me Diga," "When the Sun Goes Down" from *In the Heights*; "Keys," "We Might Play All Night" from *Passing Strange*; "The Bitch of Living," "The Word of Your Body," "Mama Who Bore Me" from *Spring Awakening*; "Show People," "Coffee Shop Nights," "I Miss the Music" from *Curtains*; "Bend and Snap," "Blood in the Water" from *Legally Blonde*; "Practically Perfect," "Anything Can Happen," "Being Mrs. Banks" from *Mary Poppins*; "The Last Real Record Store on Earth," "Cryin' in the Rain" from *High Fidelity*; "A Way Back to Then," "What Kind of a Girls Is She?" from *[title of show]*; "Look Who's Evil Now," "All the Men in My Life" from *Evil Dead: The Musical* (Off-Broadway); "Sparks," "Ticky Ticky Tock," "Pretty Moon Over Macao" from *Adrift in Macao* (Off-Broadway).

2007–2008 SEASON

It was a season in which revivals on Broadway ran longer than most of the new musicals and, in some cases, rightfully so. This was not a very encouraging sign. Was Broadway becoming a museum featuring old works? It was not quite as bad as that but it was worrying. The finest, and most successful, of the revivals was Lincoln Center's *South Pacific*. There was nothing innovative or gimmicky about the Bartlett Sher production; it was just very very good. If there was anything unique about the revival, it was the use of a full orchestra in the oversized pit, giving the musical a sound too rarely heard on Broadway anymore. Audiences noticed the difference and *South Pacific* ran 996 performances. Patti Lupone shone as Mama Rose in a superb revival of *Gypsy* directed by author Arthur Laurents. It drew patrons for nearly a year. A solid production of *Grease* ran fourteen months and a limited engagement of *Sunday in the Park with George* from London was roundly praised. Regarding new works, the big disappointment of the season was *Young Frankenstein* which struggled to run 485 times. Despite strong performances and a lavish production, the stage version of the 1974 Mel Brooks film did not have the sparkle of his previous film-to-stage musical *The Producers*. The Disney company also had an expensive musical—*The Little Mermaid*—that lost money even after 685 performances. A bright spot in the season was *In the Heights* which transferred from Off-Broadway to the Street with success, running three years. Unfortunately the Broadway move for *Passing Strange* was not a good one and the intimate musical ran only 108 times. Another bright spot was the surprising *Xanadu*. Turning a flop movie into a Broadway success was far from the usual pattern but *Xanadu* was a satirical, campy delight. The show ran thirteen weeks and later found life in regional theatres. The poignant, small-scale musical *A Catered Affair* was lost in the shuffle and only managed a three-month run. Two musicals that were not well received by the critics or the public were *Cry-Baby*, another attempt to make a John Waters film into a musical like *Hairspray*, and *Glory Days* about trying to relive the days of high school glory. The former lasted two months and *Glory Days* closed on opening night.

The highpoint of the Off-Broadway season was the character musical *Next to Normal* which was well received when it ran a month at the Second Stage and made preparations to move to Broadway in the next season. A brilliant little expressionistic musical titled *Adding Machine* was also widely praised but it was too esoteric for the Street so it stayed Off-Broadway for nineteen weeks. *Walmartopia*, a not-so-subtle ribbing of the merchandising giant, lasted just as long. Finding an audience for seven months was *Celia: The Life and Music of Celia Cruz*. Stephen Flaherty and Lynn Ahrens offered *The Glorious Ones* about a *commedia dell-arte* troupe of players. Neither the press nor the public were very enthusiastic about it and the show shuttered after two months. For those who did not enjoy the frivolity of *Young Frankenstein* on Broadway, there was a deadly serious musical version of *Frankenstein* Off-Broadway. The chilling show pleased audiences for six weeks.

> "I Miss the Mountains"
> Music by Tom Kitt; lyric by Brian Yorkie
> From *Next to Normal* (2008)
> Sung by Alice Ripley as Diana

Next to Normal went through many productions and many changes before it ended up being the musical that won a Pulitzer Prize. Brian Yorkie's libretto and lyrics concerned mental illness and, in particular, housewife Diana Goodman (Alice Ripley) as she descends into depression and bipolar swings. How this affects her family is also central to the themes in *Next to Normal*. The reasons for Diana's illness (death of a son, an empty marriage, a resentful daughter) may have been pat but the emotional appeal of the musical was sincere. *Next to Normal* was first produced in 2006 at the New York Musical Theatre Festival then revisions were made during a month run at the Second Stage Off-Broadway. Further changes were made during a run at the Arena Stage in Washington, DC, before the musical opened on Broadway in 2009.

A number that was in the musical from the start was Diana's first-act solo "I Miss the Mountains." While much of the score by Yorkie and composer Tom Kitt was in the pop-rock mode, "I Miss the Mountains" is a Broadway ballad in the torch song tradition. It is also a very quiet song in a musical with a lot of shouting and angst. Diana has been put on various drugs to combat her bipolar disorder and she notices the difference in her emotions. Somewhat numbed by the medicine, she recalls a time when her feelings were more potent. Diana's observations are lucid in the verse as she looks at herself as if another woman who "flew higher" and was a "wild girl running free"; but now "I'm nowhere."[8] In the refrain, Diana is no longer an observer but is now expressing her feelings. "I miss the mountains/ I miss the highs and lows," she admits. Diana even confesses "I miss the pain." The lyric continues to state clearly her current situation ("My feet are on the ground") but with a sad realization that "Everything is perfect/ Nothing's real." The song ends with Diana's conclusion, "I miss the mountains … I miss my life." Kitt's music is very tentative in the verse, moving ahead in a hesitant manner. The refrain has a simple flowing melody reminiscent of an urban folk song. Musically restrained, the song slowly builds in the third refrain then pulls back for a quiet ending filled with remorse. "I Miss the Mountains," with its metaphor of mountain climbing, is perhaps the finest character song in a score that is filled with such numbers. Alice Ripley sang the song in the Off-Broadway and Broadway productions of *Next to Normal* and during the run she was replaced by Marin Mazzie. The number has been performed in cabarets and revues and there are recordings by Edin Espinosa and Lorie Line.

Other notable songs from that season: "I'm Alive," "A Light in the Dark" from *Next to Normal* (Off-Broadway); "The Brain," "Listen to Your Heart" from *Young Frankenstein*; "The World Above," "She's in Love," "I Want the Good Times Back" from *The Little Mermaid*; "One White Dress," "Don't Ever Stop Saying I Love You" from *A Catered Affair*; "The Music of the Machine," "I'd Rather Watch You" from *Adding Machine* (Off-Broadway).

Song of the Season

2008–2009 SEASON

It seemed like the 1980s again with a London blockbuster coming to Broadway and getting most of the attention. Most agreed that *Billy Elliot* was the best show of the season although the transfer of *Next to Normal* from Off-Broadway provided some artistic, if not financial, competition. For that, one had to look to another Off-Broadway transfer, *Rock of Ages*, the nostalgic celebration of rock songs from the 1980s. In fact, the rock revue ran nearly six years to *Billy Elliot*'s three years. (In London, Billy danced for more than fifteen years.) Some expected the American entry *Shrek the Musical* to be a long-run hit but the expensive stage version of the popular animated film went deep in the red when it lasted only a year. Ironically, *Shrek* was soon one of the most popular musicals in schools with hundreds of productions each year. Another screen-to-stage musical that looked promising was *9 to 5: The Musical* but it closed within four months. The adolescent musical *13* ran even less, and the two-character musical *The Story of My Life* only five performances. A propulsive production of *Hair* was the season's best revival. It was joined by returns of *Guys and Dolls, Pal Joey,* and *West Side Story*. There were some bright spots Off-Broadway this season, such as the exuberant *Fela!*, a jukebox musical about the Nigerian singer Fela Kuti. The song-dance piece played a month Off-Broadway but moved to the Street the next season and remained for a year. The campy musical *The Toxic Avenger* had enough fans of the movie to run seven months and enough patrons were nostalgic for pop songs from the 1950s and 1960s to let the revue *The Marvelous Wonderettes* play 545 times. The rest of the season's Off-Broadway entries had short runs, including the problematic Stephen Sondheim musical *Road Show*—which turned out to be his last—and the very fine character musical *Happiness* at Lincoln Center.

"Electricity"
Music by Elton John; lyric by Lee Hall
From *Billy Elliot* (2008)
Sung by David Alvarez/Trent Kowalik/Kiril Kulish as Billy Elliot

---

Among the many highlights of *Billy Elliot* is the song and dance solo "Electricity," a showstopper in the second act. When the working-class youth Billy auditions for the Royal Ballet School in London, the admissions committee ask him what he thinks about when he is dancing. Billy tries to verbalize his feelings in this list song which is hesitant at first but eventually expresses some deep-felt emotions. Although the song starts with Billy's admission "I haven't got the words," the lyric soon conjures up some vivid images, such as "forgetting, losing who you are" and the music letting you "disappear."[9] The refrain section uses the metaphors of "electricity" and " flying like a bird." The essence of the character of Billy is revealed in a later verse in which he admits being "angry ... scared ... all mixed up and mad as hell!" The song concludes with the simple declaration,

"Like electricity, electricity … Sparks inside of me/ And I'm free I'm free!" The lyric by Lee Hall is inspired by a short speech in his screenplay of *Billy Elliot*. Elton John's music starts as a pop ballad, tentative and halting at first. The music starts to flow without rests once Billy get more confident. The middle section of the number is a frenetic dance solo in which Billy releases all his pent-up emotions. The music has a disco beat but with snatches of Tchaikovsky's "Swan Lake" which had figured earlier into the plot. After the dance solo, Billy returns to the lyric and proclaims, "I'm free!" Three young performers alternated in the role of Billy when the musical opened in London in 2005 and Liam Mower was selected to sing "Electricity" on the cast album. When *Billy Elliot* opened on Broadway in 2008, David Alvarez, Trent Kowalik, and Kiril Kulish alternated as Billy. A live performance of the West End production was filmed in 2014 with Elliott Hannas as Billy. Composer John's recording of "Electricity" climbed the charts both in Britain and America. Later discs were made by The Tribute Co. and Collabro.

Other notable songs from that season: "Solidarity," "Expressing Yourself," "Shine" from *Billy Elliot*; "Big Bright Beautiful World," "I Know It's Today" from *Shrek the Musical*; "Brand New You," "Bad Bad News" from *13*; "Backwoods Barbie," "Shine Like the Sun" from *9 to 5: The Musical*; "The Best Thing That Ever Has Happened," "Addison's Trip" from *Road Show* (Off-Broadway); "You Tore My Heart Out," "Hot Toxic Love" from *The Toxic Avenger* (Off-Broadway).

Song of the Season

2009–2010 SEASON

With so many revivals and jukebox musicals this season, not many new songs were heard on Broadway. Instead patrons were treated to Elvis Presley, Jerry Lee Lewis, Johnny Cash, Carl Perkins, and Sam Phillips favorites in *Million Dollar Quartet*; dancing to Frank Sinatra hits in *Come Fly Away*; a staged version of the punk rock album *American Idiot*; and plenty of Stephen Sondheim songs in the autobiographical revue *Sondheim on Sondheim*. Original scores were heard in *Memphis*, about the segregated music business of the 1950s, and in *The Addams Family*, a campy musical based on the distinctive Charles Addams cartoons and the TV show in the 1960s. The Sondheim revue only lasted ten weeks; all the others above had substantial runs, *Memphis* being the most popular on Broadway and *The Addams Family* the most produced regionally. There were some commendable revivals this season but they met with mixed success. *A Little Night Music* and *La Cage aux Folles* each ran over ten months, *Promises Promises* found an audience for seven months, but the two best-reviewed revivals—*Finian's Rainbow* and *Ragtime*—struggled to run beyond two months.

There were three very different Off-Broadway entries of interest this season. The most successful was *Bloody Bloody Andrew Jackson*, a satiric reinvention of the controversial president as a rock idol in the populist movement. After selling out for six weeks at the Public Theatre, the anachronistic musical later moved to Broadway the next season for 120 performances. The novella and animated film *Coraline*, about a young girl who travels in and out of a parallel world, was given a brilliant musical staging Off-Broadway and its one-month engagement garnered a lot of praise. Not a likely prospect for Broadway, *Coraline* later received many productions regionally. An even more unlikely possibility for Broadway was *The Scottsboro Boys*, a powerful musical based on one of American history's darkest miscarriages of justice. But the reviews for the Susan Stroman production and the score by John Kander and Fred Ebb were so overwhelming that the show was moved to Broadway the next season. Despite another set of raves, *The Scottsboro Boys* floundered and closed after five weeks.

"Go Back Home"
Music by John Kander; lyric by Fred Ebb
From *The Scottsboro Boys* (2009)
Sung by Brandon Victor Dixon as Heywood,
Cody Ryan Wise as Eugene, and the Scottsboro Boys

Not only is the true story of the Scottsboro Boys very disturbing, the musical version of their tale was equally upsetting. When nine African Americans are accused of raping two white women, it soon becomes clear the females were prostitutes who lied to the police to protect themselves. What follows is years of trials and appeals as the nine men languish in jail. Librettist David Thompson and director/choreographer Susan Stroman decided to use the format of a minstrel show to tell this dark story. The long-gone theatrical entertainment known as minstrelsy is in itself very offensive to most audiences, even when the players are African American and not whites in blackface. *The Scottsboro Boys* fearlessly recreates the style and format of such shows, using the stereotypic clichés and songs for ironic (and sometimes painful) effect. The Kander and Ebb score is a marvel of pastiche, recreating Stephen Foster-like songs and ethnic dances of the Old South. Most of the numbers in *The Scottsboro Boys* are tied to plot and character but one song stands out as a tender and heartfelt ballad which recalls Foster's "Jeanie with the Light Brown Hair" and "Old Folks at Home." "Go Back Home" is an enticing song of yearning sung by the accused Heywood Patterson as he waits in jail for an uncertain future. Ebb's lyric avoids any thick Southern dialect since Heywood's thoughts are simple and unaffected: "Staring at the stars, I wonder … When I'm gonna go back home."[10] All nine men are overwhelmed by the circumstances they find themselves in. This is beautifully expressed by Heywood's "right before your eyes, things happen … Soon enough you're lost." As in Oscar Hammerstein's classic "Ol' Man River," Ebb relies more on identities than full rhymes, softening the words and giving them an understated sense of despair. Heywood wonders if someday he will get lucky and someone will say, "All right, Son … Hop a freight and go back home." But Eugene, the youngest of the accused, adds that he wouldn't wait for any train and would walk home if they's let him. The lyric repeats the lament, "Oh me, Oh, my … Time goes slow" before coming to the hope that one will see home again. John Kander's music is also understated, keeping to a narrow range and avoiding any operatic flourishes. When Eugene and the other men join Heywood in the refrain, there is the sense of a gospel folk song but "Go Back Home" is firmly in the Broadway tradition of an emotive ballad. *The Scottsboro Boys* was written in the early 2000s but possible productions were put on hold when Ebb died in 2004. The project was resurrected with a 2010 Off-Broadway production in which Brandon Victor Dixon played Heywood and sang "Go Back Home" on the cast album. When the musical moved to Broadway the next season, the role was played by Joshua Henry. The song has become popular with cabaret performers and the handful of recordings include those by Audra McDonald and composer Kander.

Other notable songs from that season: "You Can't Do Me," "Shout!," "Commencing in Chattanooga," "Southern Days" from *The Scottsboro Boys* (Off-Broadway); "The Music of My Soul," "Someday" from *Memphis*; "Just Around the Corner," "The Moon and Me" from *The Addams Family*; "I'm Not That Guy/I'm So That Guy," "The Saddest Song" from *Bloody Bloody Andrew Jackson* (Off-Broadway).

Song of the Season

2010–2011 SEASON

Where would the Broadway musical be without Hollywood and international movies? This year, the offerings would have been slim. Instead, there were screen-to-musical stage versions of the con-man film *Catch Me If You Can*, the holiday favorite *Elf*, the Spanish farce *Women on the Verge of a Nervous Breakdown*, the gospel-singing comedy *Sister Act*, and the Australian cult movie *Priscilla, Queen of the Desert*. The last two musicals arrived by way of London; they were the only two shows in the group to have substantial runs. The big winner this season with the press and the public was the satirical *The Book of Mormon*. Surprisingly, its irreverent songs, characters, and plot stirred up little controversy and the musical continues to entertain packed houses. A jukebox musical titled *Baby, It's You* featured 1960s songs to tell its tale of a fictional singing girl group; nostalgia for the songs helped the show to survive five months. *Wonderland*, an odd-ball, modern take on *Alice in Wonderland*, lasted only a month. The most ambitious musical of the season was *The People in the Picture* about performers in the Yiddish theatre during the Holocaust. It was potent storytelling and Donna Murphy was outstanding in the musical but audiences were not interested and the show closed after two months. There were only two revivals this season but they were both laudable. Daniel Radcliffe starred in *How to Succeed in Business without Really Trying* and Sutton Foster shone in a superior revival of *Anything Goes*. There were two notable Off-Broadway musicals, both having limited runs. *A Minister's Wife* at Lincoln Center was a musicalization of the George Bernard Shaw comedy *Candida*. The a cappella musical *In Transit* was well received and five years later it would show up on Broadway for 145 performances.

"I Believe"
Music and lyric by Robert Lopez, Matt Stone, Trey Parker
From *The Book of Mormon* (2011)
Sung by Andrew Rannells as Elder Price, and ensemble

Alternately satirical and sentimental, *The Book of Mormons* follows two missionaries of the Church of Jesus Christ of Latter-Day Saints who are sent to Uganda to convert the Africans to Mormonism. The script and the score by Robert Lopez, Matt Stone, and Trey Parker are sometimes blistering in the treatment of the Mormons' religious beliefs yet there is a tender, even sweet, aspect to the musical. This bi-polar tone is perhaps best demonstrated in the song "I Believe." Elder Price (Andrew Rannells) knows that the only way to convert the locals is to confront the warlord known as the General (Brian Tyree Henry) who rules and abuses the people of the village. Price sings this credo, which takes the form of a wacky list song, to screw up his courage and face the General. The verse for "I Believe" is mostly recitative with little melody as Price questions his own lack of faith because he is so scared. He fears that he will let down his family and his Church and admits that he is afraid of a "warlord who shoots people in the face."[11] Drawing strength from his religious belief that "my Lord is mightier/ And always has my back" the refrains are a list of Price's beliefs, starting with generalities—"I believe that the Lord God created the universe"—but soon the list includes peculiarities which Price accepts without question: "ancient Jews built boats/And sailed to America ... God lives on a planet called Kolob ... the Garden of Eden/ Was in Jackson County, Missouri ... in 1978 God changed his mind about black people." Gaining strength in singing these beliefs, Price walks into the General's compound and tries to convert the warlord, the song ending with Price's declaration, "And, dang it, a Mormon just believes!" The General is not impressed and has Price thrown out. Much of the power (and humor) in the song comes from its fervent music. Using a vigorous march tempo, the composition becomes a kind of anthem. The oft-used word "believe" is often held for several counts, suggesting a gospel flavor as well. The ensemble serves as backup singers and provides a mocking Mormon Tabernacle Choir sound on a small scale. Audiences laugh at Price's determined stance in "I Believe" which is not far from giggling at a religious hymn. Andrew Rannells originated the role of Price and was the first to record "I Believe." That original Broadway cast recording became the highest-charting Broadway cast album in over four decades. During the long run of *The Book of Mormon*, Rannells has been replaced by such performers as Ryan Bondy, Dave Thomas Brown, Kevin Clay, and Nic Rouleau.

Other notable songs from that season: "Hello!," "Turn It Off" from *The Book of Mormon*; "Take Me to Heaven," "Raise Your Voice" from *Sister Act*; "Live in Living Color," "Seven Wonders" from *Catch Me If You Can*; "Model Behavior," "Invisible" from *Women on Verge of a Nervous Breakdown*; "I Believe in You" from *Elf*.

Song of the Season

2011–2012 SEASON

The parade of screen-to-stage musicals continued this season with Broadway versions of *Leap of Faith, Ghost, Once,* and *Newsies*. Only the last two were hits. The stage adaptation of the Disney movie musical *Newsies* had found success regionally so it was brought to Broadway for a limited run. The response was so overwhelming that Disney made the show an open engagement and it ran for over 1,000 performances. So did *Once*, a little musical based on the little Irish film. After selling out its Off-Broadway engagement, *Once* moved to the Street and stayed for two and half years. The musical *Bonnie and Clyde* was not based on the famous film but taken from history. It only lasted a month but was later popular in regional theatres. Also running a month was *Lysistrata Jones*, a satiric musical based on Aristophanes' *Lysistrata* reset on a college campus, and *End of the Rainbow*, a drama with songs about the last days of Judy Garland (Tracie Bennett). The bio-drama was not based on a movie but became one in 2019. The two most expensive musicals of the Broadway season were *Nice Work If You Can Get It* and *Spider-Man: Turn Off the Dark*. The former was an original musical comedy using songs by the Gershwins and given a splashy Roaring Twenties-like production. Greeted with mixed reviews, *Nice Work If You Can Get It* struggled to run 478 performances and lost quite a bit of money. But that was pittance compared to the financial disaster *Spider-Man*. The high-tech fantasy made so many changes during its 182 preview performances that by the time it opened the cost was a record-breaking $75 million. The critics were not impressed but audiences came for three years. In the end, *Spider-Man* closed with a $60 million loss—another record. This season there were Broadway revivals of *Evita, Follies, Jesus Christ Superstar, Porgy and Bess, Godspell,* and *On a Clear Day You Can See Forever*. The last had a radically rewritten libretto and added songs but had trouble running beyond seven weeks. Although *Once* was the only hit to come from Off-Broadway, there were two intriguing musicals that garnered some attention during their limited runs. Maury Yeston's *Death Takes a Holiday*, based on the Italian play of the same name, concerned Death disguised as a prince on vacation in Italy. Michael John LaChiusa's *Queen of the Mist* told the true story of a 63-year-old teacher who goes over Niagara Falls in a barrel of her own design.

"Something to Believe In"
Music by Alan Menken; lyric by Jack Feldman
From *Newsies* (2012)
Introduced by Jeremy Jordan as Jack Kelly,
and Kara Lindsay as Katherine

The 1992 Disney live-action film *Newsies* was not well-reviewed by the critics and was a major financial failure at the box office. But it eventually became a favorite on home video and was a likely prospect for a stage production. The movie score by Alan Menken (music) and Jack Feldman (lyrics) included such theatrical songs as "Seize the Day," "Santa Fe," and "King of New York" which were retained for the stage version and the songwriters wrote several new numbers, including the love duet "Something to Believe In." Much of the *Newsies* score consists of vigorous songs of protest or pride but the musical quiets down for this ballad sung by the rebellious newsboy Jack Kelly (Jeremy Jordan) and the newspaper reporter Katherine Plumber (Kara Lindsay). She has been covering the newsboy strike and has fallen in love with Jack. The two have suffered abuse in the past but find strength in their love for each other. The duet is in the tradition of Menken's catchy pop numbers for Disney. The music has a strong melodic line and some expansive moments but maintains a driving beat that keeps it from becoming operatic. Feldman's lyric is direct, returning often to the song's premise: having someone believe in you allows one to believe in oneself. Katherine declares "I thought I knew what love was/ Now I'm learning what is true" and Jack calls her "an angel come to save me."[12] Together they realize that the world offers no promises but they have each other "For even a day … One day may be forever" and each has "something to believe in/ Now that I know you believed in me." Jordan and Lindsay recorded "Something to Believe It" on the original cast album of *Newsies* and sang it on the 2017 video version of the musical. During the run of the show, they were replaced by Corey Cott and Liana Hunt. In the 2022 London production, Michael Ahomka-Lindsay and Bronté Barbé sang the duet.

Other notable songs from that season: "That's Rich," "Watch What Happens" from *Newsies*; "Too Late to Turn Back Now" from *Bonnie and Clyde*; "When She Smiles" from *Lysistrata Jones*; "With You" from *Ghost the Musical*; "No More," "If the World Should End" from *Spider-Man: Turn Off the Dark*.

Song of the Season

2012–2013 SEASON

It took fifty-six years, but Rodgers and Hammerstein's television musical *Cinderella* finally arrived on Broadway this season. Ever since the 1957 broadcast, the musical had seen various stage versions regionally, not to mention two other TV productions. What opened on Broadway this season was a longer version of the original with some major plot changes and some added songs from the Rodgers and Hammerstein catalogue. The critics were not overly enthusiastic but audiences were, so *Cinderella* ran nearly two years, followed by hundreds of productions yearly by all kinds of theatre groups. There were five musicals this season based on movies, including *Hands on a Hard Body* which was inspired by a documentary film. *A Christmas Story* was presented for the holiday season (and has since returned to Broadway other years) and the cheerleading movie *Bring It On* played on Broadway for five months as part of a national tour. The two most successful screen-to-stage musicals were the London transfer *Matilda* and *Kinky Boots* based on a British film. The Roald Dahl-inspired *Matilda* ran nearly four years (the London production ran over seven years) and the Cyndi Lauper-scored *Kinky Boots* ran six years. Three biographical musicals were offered this season. *Scandalous: The Life and Trials of Aimee Semple McPherson* and *Chaplin* failed to run very long but the autobiographical *Motown* about record producer Barry Gordy was a hit at 738 performances. A refreshing revival of *Pippin* ran just as long and the return of *Annie* stayed over a year. A superb revival of *The Mystery of Edwin Drood* was not so fortunate, closing after seventeen weeks. The most intriguing Off-Broadway musical of the season was *Natasha, Pierre & the Great Comet of 1812* which musicalized one section of Leo Tolstoy's *War and Peace*. The immersive production was praised in two unconventional Off-Broadway venues and eventually made its way to Broadway in 2016. Michael John LaChiusa's musical version of Edna Ferber's novel *Giant* at the Public Theatre was also praised during its six-week run. Running just as long was the character musical *Murder Ballad*, but better reviewed was *Dogfight*, another musical based on a movie.

"Not My Father's Son"
Music and lyric by Cyndi Lauper
From *Kinky Boots* (2013)
Sung by Billy Porter as Simon/Lola,
Stark Sands as Charlie Price

The drag queen Lola (Billy Porter) and the young shoe manufacturer Charlie Price (Stark Sands) seem so very different from each other in the musical *Kinky Boots* but they realize that they both were major disappointments to their fathers in the song "Not My Father's Son." The songs in *Kinky Boots* include pop, funk, tango, and new wave but

Cyndi Lauper's "Not My Father's Son" is a gentle ballad and a character song in which Charlie and Lola (who reveals that his really name is Simon) bond emotionally. In the verse, Lola sings how he tried to be like his father but "It was never easy to be his type of man" and how "the best part of me/ Is what he wouldn't see."[13] The refrain states how different father and son are, realizing that each of them "couldn't be the one/ to echo what he'd done." In the release, Lola explains how he "found an escape" and perhaps "I went to extremes of leather and lace,/ but the world seems brighter six inches off the ground." Although Charlie did not "escape" and become a drag queen like Lola, he echoes Lola's sentiments about his own father, he and Lola harmonizing and turning the number into a heartfelt duet. Lauper's music is very tentative at first with several rests and a narrow range. As the number progresses, the music builds into a bluesy lament with a touch of a folk song but never gets too bombastic. The result is a tender song of recognition that lets Charlie and Lola work together toward their goal of making boots for drag queens. Porter and Sands sang "Not My Father's Son" on the original cast recording of *Kinky Boots* which climbed the charts. In London, Billy and Charlie were played by Matt Henry and Killian Donnelly who sang it on the West End recording. A solo version of "Not My Father's Son" was recorded by Greg Safel in 2015. When *Kinky Boots* was revived Off-Broadway in 2022 with some script changes, Calum Francis played Lola and Christian Douglas was Charlie.

Other notable songs from that season: "Everybody Say Yeah," "Hold Me in Your Heart" from *Kinky Boots*; "When I Grow Up," "Naughty," "Revolting Children" from *Matilda*; "Bring It On!," "One Perfect Moment" from *Bring It On: The Musical*; "The Life That You Wished For" from *Chaplin*; "Ralphie to the Rescue," "What a Mother Does" from *A Christmas Story*; "No One Else," "Dust and Ashes," "Sonya Alone," "Charming" from *Natasha, Pierre & the Great Comet of 1812* (Off-Broadway); "Private Property," "Topsy Turvy" from *Giant* (Off-Broadway); "Pretty Funny," "Come Back" from *Dogfight* (Off-Broadway).

Song of the Season

2013–2014 SEASON

Not for the first time or the last, a Disney adaptation and a jukebox musical were the season's long-run champions. Song favorites were heard in the biographical *Beautiful: The Carole King Musical* which ran five years. There were familiar songs and new ones in *Aladdin* which boasted a spectacular production; it ran over ten years. The only new work to have a substantial run was the sly *A Gentleman's Guide to Love & Murder*, a clever show with a Victorian pastiche score that amused audiences for over two years. There were the expected movie adaptations—*Bullets Over Broadway, Bridges of Madison County, Big Fish, Rocky*—but none of them ran long enough to show any profits. The same could be said about the concert piece *A Night with Janis Joplin*, the odd bio-musical *Soul Doctor: Journey of a Rockstar Rabbi*, the charming *First Date*, and the intriguing Idina Menzel vehicle *If/Then*. The only major revue on the Street this season was a recreation of a Cotton Club performance titled *After Midnight*. Thanks to several guest star appearances, it managed to run 272 times. The season's revivals did much better. The Off-Broadway musicals *Violet* and *Hedwig and the Angry Inch* were revived on Broadway with contrasting results. The Jeanine Tesori musical ran sixteen weeks but *Hedwig*, thanks to a star turn by Neil Patrick Harris and talented replacements, chalked up 507 performances. A cunning revival of *Cabaret* from London was a success with 388 performances but even more popular was a return of *Les Misérables* which stayed for two and a half years. Arguably the best musical of the season was *Fun Home* which ran three months at the Public Theatre then transferred the next season to Broadway for 582 performances. The Lisa Kron-Jeanine Tesori musical was based on a graphic novel by Alison Bechdel and was the first mainstream musical to feature a lesbian character. As on Broadway, there were musical versions of movies Off-Broadway, this season offering *Little Miss Sunshine, Far from Heaven*, and *Heathers*. Only the last found success regionally after its limited Off-Broadway run. Yet another biographical musical, *Here Lies Love*, concerned Imelda Marcos, the infamous First Lady of the Philippines. First a 2010 concept album by David Byrne and Fatboy Slim, it was turned into a musical and was presented in two different engagements at the Public Theatre and finally arrived on Broadway in June of 2023.

"Ring of Keys"
Music Jeanine Tesori; lyric by Lisa Kron
From *Fun Home* (2015)
Sung by Sydney Lucas as Small Alison and Beth Malone as Adult Alison

---

Fun Home is an autobiographical musical that takes the form of a memory play. The adult Alison (Beth Malone) looks back at her youth growing up with an overbearing gay father who later committed suicide, her wounded family, and the discovery of her sexuality. We see Alison as a ten-year-old girl (Sydney Lucas) and as a college student (Alexandra Socha), all three Alisons telling the story. In one of the most memorable scenes in *Fun Home*, Adult Alison recalls the time she was eating in a luncheonette with her father when a delivery woman comes in with a cart full of packages for the kitchen. The young girl immediately connects with this strong, "unfeminine" woman who dresses as she likes. Young Alison's description of the stranger—"the just right clothes you're wearing … Your short hair and your dungarees … And your lace up boots"—reveals an instant identification.[14] A detail that particularly impresses Alison is the woman's "keys, oh/ Your ring of keys/ Ring of keys." It is not so much a sexual attraction as it is a realization that what she thought was "s'pposed to be wrong" seems right and she admires how "you seem okay with being strong." Lisa Kron's evocative lyric ends with a repeated "I know you." Jeanine Tesori's music is initially tentative but soon turns into a confident and driving composition, much like a travel song in the way it is propelled forward. "Ring of Keys" does not have a wide range but it is a tricky song to sing, particularly for a young actress. Sydney Lucas played Small Alison in both the Off-Broadway and Broadway productions of *Fun Home* and is heard on the original cast recording which peaked in the Number 2 spot on the charts. In the 2018 London production, Brooke Haynes and Harriet Turnbull alternated as small Alison and Jenna Russell was adult Alison.

Other notable songs from that season: "Welcome to the Fun Home," "Changing My Major," "Days and Days" from *Fun Home* (Off-Broadway); "It All Fades Away," "Another Life," "To Build a Home" from *Bridges of Madison County*; "High Adventure," "Proud of Your Boy," "Somebody's Got Your Back" from *Aladdin*; "Be the Hero," "Daffodils," "Time Stops" from *Big Fish*; "Inside Out," "The Last One You'd Expect," "I've Decided to Marry You" from *A Gentleman's Guide to Love and Murder*; "You Don't Need to Love Me," "Some Other Me" from *If/Then*; "Happiness," "Keep on Standing" from *Rocky the Musical*; "Seventeen," "Freeze Your Brain" from *Heathers* (Off-Broadway).

Song of the Season

2014–2015 SEASON

Turning popular films into musicals continued to be risky business on Broadway. *Finding Neverland,* about the creation of the first production of *Peter Pan,* found an audience for fourteen months. *Honeymoon in Vegas,* on the other hand, struggled to run three months. Even the well-reviewed *An American in Paris,* with some outstanding dance numbers, ran a mere five months. The only new musical to enjoy a long run was *Something Rotten!,* a farce about an Elizabethan theatre troupe doing a musical. The critics were harsh but patrons came for two years. *Fun Home,* which moved to the Street this season, received another set of rave reviews, and played 583 times in the intimate Circle in the Square Theatre. All of the other new offerings had short runs. *The Last Ship,* by singer-songwriter Sting, folded in a month. So did a musical of *Doctor Zhivago,* based on the novel rather than the film, and the jukebox musical *Holler If You Hear Me* celebrating rapper Tupac Shakur. There was much to recommend in *It Shoulda Been You,* about two families brought together by a wedding, but it ran only seventeen weeks. Most disappointing (but not surprising), the dark musical *The Visit* managed to stay open for seven weeks. The John Kander-Fred Ebb musical, based on the German play of the same name, had seen productions in various cities since 2001. This mounting, directed by John Doyle, featured Chita Rivera and Roger Rees in an exquisite production but *The Visit* was not what audiences wanted. The season's Broadway revivals were a mixed bag. A superb *The King and I* with Ken Watanabe and Kelli O'Hara ran fourteen months at Lincoln Center, a raucous *On the Town* entertained theatregoers for nearly a year, and a delightful *On the Twentieth Century* with Kristin Chenoweth and Peter Gallagher saw healthy business during its limited run. Most critics and patrons disapproved of a revised *Gigi* that tried to be politically correct and a return of *Side Show* did no better the second time around. The biggest excitement of the season came, once again, from Off-Broadway. Lin-Manuel Miranda's *Hamilton* presented early American history in a bold and enthralling manner. It was a sellout at the Public Theatre then moved to Broadway the next season. The only other entries of interest Off-Broadway were *Fly By Night,* a rock musical set during the 1965 blackout in New York City, and *Pretty Filthy,* about making porn films in Hollywood.

"My Shot"
Music and lyric by Lin-Manuel Miranda
From *Hamilton* (2015)
Sung by Lin-Manuel Miranda as Alexander Hamilton,
Anthony Ramos as John Laurens, Okierette Onodowan as
Hercules Mulligan, Daveed Diggs as Lafayette,
Leslie Odom, Jr. as Aaron Burr, and the ensemble

The "I am" song for the title character in *Hamilton* is the rap number "My Shot" which is picked up by other characters as well. Lin-Manuel Miranda wrote the score and played Alexander Hamilton in the unorthodox musical which both celebrates and deconstructs American history. The eager immigrant Hamilton is impatient to succeed in his new homeland and makes no excuses for his bravado, repeatedly proclaiming "I am not throwing away my shot!"[15] Just like his country, Hamilton proudly describes himself as "young, scrappy and hungry." The rapid number gives some historical background—"A colony that runs independently./ Meanwhile, Britain keeps shittin' on us endlessly"—but always returns to Hamilton the individual who firmly believes that he "will lay down my life if it sets us free." His pluckiness is echoed by the French General Lafayette ("I dream of life without a monarchy"), the tailor Mulligan ("I know it's my chance/ To socially advance, instead of sewin' some pants"), and the abolitionist John Laurens ("we'll never be truly free until those in bondage have the same rights as you and me"). Their enthusiasm is mocked by Aaron Burr ("If you talk, you're gonna get shot") but they are undeterred, the song ending with a declaration "Rise up/ And I am not throwin' away my shot!" Like most rap music, the tempo is percussive with the title phrase emphasized by the vibrant orchestrations. The ensemble provides harmony under sections of the song, other times participating in a call-and-response. "My Shot" builds beautifully and sets the tone for the events that follow. The cast recording of the score for *Hamilton* climbed both the *Billboard* and the *Rolling Stone* charts. Miranda is heard on the original cast album and he appeared in the 2020 video of the production. Jamael Westman played Alexander Hamilton in the London production.

Other notable songs from that season: "The Room Where It Happens," "Satisfied," "You'll Be Back," "Helpless," "What'd I Miss?" from *Hamilton* (Off-Broadway); "I've Been Thinking," "I Love Betsy" from *Honeymoon in Vegas*; "Will Power," "Welcome to the Renaissance" from *Something Rotten*; "Yellow Shoes," "Love and Love Alone," "You, You, You" from *The Visit*; "Neverland," "When Your Feet Don't Touch the Ground" from *Finding Neverland*; "The Last Ship," "August Winds" from *The Last Ship*; "It Shoulda Been You," "A Little Bit Less Than" from *It Shoulda Been You*; "Fly By Night," "Stars I Trust" from *Fly By Night* (Off-Broadway).

2015–2016 SEASON

The most intriguing Broadway entry of the season was a musical about a classic musical. The title best describes the show: *Shuffle Along, or the Making of the Musical Sensation of 1921 and All That Followed*. An outstanding cast under the direction of George C. Wolfe was highly praised and its 100-performance limited run was well attended. Other original musicals of note were the folk drama *Bright Star,* set in rural North Carolina, and *Allegiance* about Japanese-American citizens put in interment camps during the Second World War. The latter ran four months and the banjo-strumming *Bright Star* lasted three months. As had become routine, there were plenty of shows based on movies. The most successful were *Waitress* and *School of Rock*, each running three and a half years. Less successful were the dark musical *American Psycho*, which closed after three weeks, and *Disaster!*, a spoof of Hollywood disaster movies of the 1970s. The charming musical fantasy *Tuck Everlasting* was also based on a film but struggled to run thirty-nine performances. The season's only jukebox offering on Broadway was the bio-musical *On Your Feet! The Story of Emilio and Gloria Estefan*; it pleased audiences for two years. It was another good season for revivals. A new production of *Fiddler on the Roof* featuring Danny Burstein and Jessica Hecht and a return of *The Color Purple* with Cynthia Erivo each ran eleven months. The Roundabout's sparking revival of *She Loves Me* was highly praised and ran seventeen weeks. Running just as long was a revival of *Spring Awakening*. *Dames at Sea*, the 1966 Off-Broadway musical spoof of Hollywood musicals, finally was produced on Broadway this season for two months. The offerings Off-Broadway were very diverse. *Daddy Long Legs*, an old-fashioned musical comedy from London, entertained patrons for five months and the bio-musical *Cagney* about movie legend James Cagney ran twice as long. The jukebox musical *Lazarus* used songs by David Bowie and the Yiddish musical *The Golden Bride* had a score comprised of traditional ethnic tunes and new songs. Michael John LaChiusa offered a follow-up to his *First Ladies Suite* with *First Daughter Suite* about offspring of US presidents. It ran a month at the Public Theatre. Running two months was the season's most captivating musical: *Hadestown*. The anachronistic version of two Greek myths was a sensation at the Public Theatre. The folk singer-songwriter Anaïs Mitchell wrote the music and lyrics as a concept album in 2010. Working with director Rachel Chavkin, Mitchell developed the piece for the stage and it was done regionally and in London before finally arriving on Broadway in 2019. The most powerful of the musical numbers in *Hadestown* was Hades' chilling "Why We Build the Wall," written a decade before Donald Trump was elected president but accurately describing the current situation.

"Everything Changes"
Music and lyric by Sara Bareilles
from *Waitress* (2016)
Sung by Jessie Mueller as Jenna, and the company

Late in the second act of *Waitress*, Jenna Hunterson (Jessie Mueller) has finally broken off her relationship with her ex-husband Joe and her recent attachment with Dr. Jim Pomatter and finds contentment in life with her young daughter Lulu. Jenna sings about her new freedom in the song "Everything Changes" in which fellow waitresses Becky and Dawn join her briefly with the ensemble. "I am changed, I am a mother," she sings in the verse.[16] The refrain is just as direct, acknowledging "my messy life" and realizing "I can feel myself believe/ Everything changes." There are also some distinct metaphors that demonstrate Jenna's newfound confidence, such as "an unsung melody is mine for safekeeping" and "my heart's at the wheel now." The music has the flavor of a country-western song but the beat is definitely one of a pop ballad. And, although the number builds, the song restrains itself from becoming a howling aria. Jessie Mueller played Jenna and she is heard on the cast album. Songwriter-actress Sara Bareilles was one of Mueller's replacements during the run and returned to the role of Jenna after the Covid interruption; she also played her in the video of the original production. Katharine McPhee was Jenna in the 2019 London production.

Other notable songs from that season: "A Soft Place to Land," "What Baking Can Do," "She Used to Be Mine" from *Waitress*; "Time," "Everything's Golden," "Everlasting" from *Tuck Everlasting*; "Ashville," "I Had a Vision" from *Bright Star*; "School of Rock," "You're in the Band," "Stick It to the Man" from *School of Rock*; "Things I Didn't Know," "The Color of Your Eyes" from *Daddy Long Legs* (Off-Broadway).

2016–2017 SEASON

Original musicals, meaning those not based on a movie, book, or whatever, had become a rare thing on Broadway but there were four notable ones this season. The most successful was *Dear Evan Hansen*, yet another musical centered on a misunderstood high school hero. Audiences connected to the musical and *Dear Evan Hansen* chalked up 1,672 performances. Running just about the same number of performances was the compelling *Come from Away* about strangers finding themselves becoming friends in the days following the attack on the World Trade Center in 2001. Chazz Palminteri's 2007 one-man memoir *A Bronx Tale* was a success on Broadway, was expanded into a movie, then returned to the Street as a musical. It stayed for 700 performances. *Bandstand* was about musicians searching for recognition during the postwar years and was most adulated for its vigorous dancing. Sadly, it couldn't turn a profit after five months. *War Paint*, about the cosmetic rivals Helena Rubinstein (Patti LuPone) and Elizabeth Arden (Christine Ebersole), ran a month longer but, despite its two popular stars, also lost a bundle. Five of the season's Broadway musicals were inspired by movies. Some had substantial runs but none turned a profit. Stephen Flaherty and Lynn Ahrens added some new songs to their film score for *Anastasia*. The Christmas classic *Holiday Inn* came to the stage with added Irving Berlin songs. The French film *Amélie* and the cult favorite *Groundhog Day* had much to admire but did not repeat the success of their screen originals.

The most satisfying musical adaptation this season came not from a movie but a book, one often considered the greatest of all novels, *War and Peace*. Dave Molloy dramatized and scored only a few chapters from Tolstoy's massive opus, giving it the title *Natasha, Pierre & the Comet of 1812*, and it was a thrilling experience. The creative staging by Rachel Chavkin, turning the performance space into a Russian supper club, was ingeniously done and the anachronistic score was admirable. The unconventional piece was first performed in some unconventional spaces Off-Broadway and regionally before it arrived on Broadway this season, pleasing audiences for 336 performances. Also arriving late from Off-Broadway was the 2010 a cappella musical *In Transit*; it only lasted two weeks. There were some laudable revivals this season both on and Off-Broadway. *Hello, Dolly!* was revived on the Street for the first time without Carol Channing. Bette Midler was the star (followed by Donna Murphy and Bernadette Peters) who helped the revival run fourteen months. Broadway revivals of *Miss Saigon* and *Falsettos* managed a run of 340 and 84 performances. *Sweeney Todd: The Demon Barber of Fleet Street* received its first Off-Broadway revival with a highly praised production from London. Also Off-Broadway, the recent *Tick, Tick ... Boom!* was revived for two months.

"You Will Be Found"
Music and lyric by Benj Pasek and Justin Paul
From *Dear Evan Hansen* (2016)
Sung by Ben Platt as Evan Hansen, and company

The adolescent musical *Dear Evan Hansen* has a terrific Act One finale with the song "You Will Be Found." Lying about his friendship with the suicide victim Connor Murphy, teenager Evan Hansen (Ben Platt) is talked into co-founding the Connor Project to keep the memory of the boy alive. The project is launched at a school assembly where Evan sings "You Will Be Found" and as he does so, students film his "speech" on their phones and it goes viral on the internet. Although Evan is indeed lying about his relationship with Connor, he is sincere in his sentiments. The lyric by Benj Pasek and Justin Paul speaks to anyone who has ever felt lost or overlooked. The song starts with a series of questions. "Have you ever felt like nobody was there? Felt forgotten, or like you can disappear?"[17] Evan then turns more confident and assures the students that there is always help somewhere, concluding with the knowledge that "when you're broken on the ground/ You will be found." The song is then picked up and sung by those seeing the video on the internet. The music by Pasek and Paul starts out like a folk ballad but it expends into a full-throttle chorale or anthem and brings the act to a stirring close. "You Will Be Found" was not in early versions of *Dear Evan Hansen* and another song was the first act finale. The new number was introduced during the 2016 Off-Broadway production and was already gaining attention by the time the musical opened on Broadway. Sam Smith and Summer Walker's cover of "You Will Be Found" was played during the closing credits of the 2021 film version; they also made a music video of the song which climbed the charts. In addition to many video versions, recordings of "You Will Be Found" have included those by Range a Cappella, the Bostonians, Peter Hollens, Jim Brickman, Nick Pitera, Voctave, Mat and Savanna Shaw, Joshua Vacanti, Anthem Lights, and Jennifer Nettles. There was even an illustrated children's book based on the song. Ben Platt played Evan Hansen in the Off-Broadway, Broadway, and film versions of *Dear Evan Hansen*. Sam Tutty played Evan in the 2019 London production.

Other notable songs from that season: "Waving Through the Window," "Sincerely Me," "If I Could Tell Her" from *Dear Evan Hansen*; "Times Are Hard for Dreamers," "The Girl with the Glass" from *Amélie*; "Me and the Sky," "I Am Here," "Welcome to the Rock" from *Come from Away*; "Everything About You," "Seeing You" from *Groundhog Day*; "This Is Life," "Love Will Come and Find Me Again" from *Bandstand*; "Out of Your Head," "In a World Like This" from *A Bronx Tale: The Musical*; "Beauty in the World" from *War Paint*.

Song of the Season

2017–2018 SEASON

There were some very expensive, highly spectacular musicals this season—most obviously the London hit *Charlie and the Chocolate Factory* and Disney's *Frozen*—but most agreed that the finest entry was the small-scale, intimate character musical *The Band's Visit*. The Roald Dahl fantasy about candy maker Willie Wonka ran 1,293 performances in the West End but the Broadway production, which made major (and damaging) changes, could not run a whole year. *Frozen*, on the other hand, had a ready and willing audience because of the popularity of the animated film and enjoyed full houses until the pandemic hit in 2020. Like both of the above, *The Band's Visit* was based on a movie, though a much less known one. But critical plaudits and word of mouth helped the affecting musical run 588 times. Also based on a film was *Mean Girls*, a musicalization of the catty high school tale that pleased audiences for nearly two years. Another stage adaptation, this time of the popular animated television show *SpongeBob SquarePants*, was given a clever production but struggled to run ten months. Of the three jukebox musicals on Broadway this season, the most successful was *Ain't Too Proud: The Life and Times of The Temptations* which ran nearly a year. *Summer: The Donna Summer Musical* and *Escape to Margaritaville*, filled with Jimmy Buffett songs, found fans for seven months and three months. The revue *Prince of Broadway*, celebrating the producing and directing career of Harold Prince, had a disappointing run of seventy-six performances.

There were some commendable revivals both on and off the Street. A lavish production of *My Fair Lady* at Lincoln Center featured Harry Hadden-Paton and Lauren Ambrose and was staged by Bartlett Sher. The critically acclaimed revival ran thirteen months. Running nearly as long was an atmospheric production of *Once on This Island* at the Circle in the Square. A solid revival of *Carousel* was less fortunate, closing after twenty-two weeks. Off-Broadway saw *Pacific Overtures* at the Classic Stage Company and *The Golden Land* at the National Yiddish Theatre Folksbiene. New works of note included *Desperate Measures*, Shakespeare's *Measure for Measure* set in the Old West; *Miss You Like Hell*, in which a Mexican mother and daughter take a road trip; and *Old Stock: A Refugee Love Story*, about two Jewish-Rumanian immigrants in 1908 Canada. The most offbeat musical entry was *KPOP* in which some South Koreans try to break into the American pop culture. The musical would show up briefly on Broadway in 2022.

"Omar Sharif"
Music and lyric by David Yazbek
From *The Band's Visit* (2017)
Sung by Katrina Lenk as Dina

As in the 2007 Israeli film it was based on, the musical version of *The Band's Visit* tells of an Egyptian orchestra touring in Israel and mistakenly finding themselves in a remote village where they were not scheduled to perform. The piece is a character study as Arab and Israeli characters meet and bond, most importantly the band's conductor Col. Tewfiq (Tony Shalhoub) and the cafe owner Dina (Katrina Lenk). Although they are two very different people, the Colonel and Dina find that they share a nostalgic link: the Egyptian singer-songwriter-actress Umm Kulthum, active from the 1920s to the 1970s, and the Arab movie star Omar Sharif who found international renown. In the song "Omar Sharif," Dina recalls growing up listening to Kulthum and seeing Sharif at the movies. David Yazbek's lyric is a wistful memory of youth as captured in these two images. In Dina's mind, they both arrived at her house like magic, "floating on the jasmine wind/ From the west, from the south."[18] Dina recalls how Kulthum and Sharif were like "Honey in my ear, spice my mouth." Listening to Kulthum on the radio and watching Sharif on their black-and-white TV, Dina and her mother would "sit there in a trance" and their "living room would become a garden." The descriptive nature of the lyric is very simple but potent. Kulthum is "Cleopatra" with the aura of "deep perfume" and Sharif is "the handsome thief" and the "pharaoh of romance." The fact that two Arabs would be so intoxicating to two Israelis underlines the theme of *The Band's Visit*. Yazbek's sublime music is not in the traditional Broadway mode. The music repeats with slight variations, giving the song a foreign folk flavor. Sometimes reminiscent of a Hebrew hymn, other times suggesting the rolling of an Arab chant, "Omar Sharif" is a scintillating experience. Katrina Lenk played Dina and sang "Omar Sharif" in the 2016 Off-Broadway production of *The Band's Visit* as well as the successful Broadway version. Miri Mesika played Dina in the 2022 London production.

Other notable songs from that season: "It Is What It Is," "Welcome to Nowhere," "Something Different" from *The Band's Visit*; "Stupid With Love," "Fearless," "Someone Gets Hurt" from *Mean Girls*; "The View From Here," "If Your Father Was Here" from *Charlie and the Chocolate Factory*; "The Ballad of Johnny Blood," "Life Takes You By Surprise" from *Desperate Measures* (Off-Broadway); "Over My Shoulder" from *I Miss You Like Hell* (Off-Broadway).

Song of the Season

2018–2019 SEASON

It took a while for *Hadestown* to get to Broadway but, once it did, it stayed. *Hadestown* was among the handful of recent musicals that were able to reopen after Covid. Another from this season was *Beetlejuice*, based on the popular 1988 movie. This season there were two major jukebox musicals: *Head Over Heels*, using songs by the Go-Go's, and *The Cher Show* featuring songs from the pop singer Cher's career. Original musicals did not do very well. *Gettin' the Band Back Together* folded in a month, *Be More Chill* hung on for 177 performances, and *The Prom* lost money running only 309 performances. Three movie favorites that were musicalized this season were expensive failures. *Tootsie*, *Pretty Women*, and *King Kong* could not compete with the vivid memory audiences had of the originals. There were only two revivals: a limited run of *Kiss Me, Kate*, with Will Chase and Kelli O'Hara as the battling co-stars, and a dark, small-scale version of *Oklahoma!* which emphasized the country-western aspects of the musical. The most applauded Off-Broadway musical this season was *The Girl from the North Country*, a British production of a jukebox musical with an American setting and score. Songs by Bob Dylan were used to tell the story of various citizens of Duluth, Michigan, during the Depression. After being praised in London, the musical was presented at the Public Theatre for three months and then transferred to Broadway the next season. Other original Off-Broadway musicals this season included *The Hello Girls*, about women serving during the First World War; the sci-fi folk musical *Rags Parkland Sings the Songs of the Future*; and *Midnight at the Never Get* with a selection of song standards sung in a smoky Greenwich Village club. The rarely seen *Carmen Jones* was revived at the Classic Stage Company, *Merrily We Roll Along* was given a revival at the Roundabout's Fiasco Theatre; and a Yiddish-language version of *Fiddler on the Roof* at the National Yiddish Theatre Folksbiene was well-received.

"Michael in the Bathroom"
Music and lyric by Joe Iconis
From *Be More Chill* (2019)
Sung by George Salazar as Michael Mell

The most talked about, imitated, and parodied song of the season did not come from one of the hit musicals but from the teenage fantasy *Be More Chill* which ran an unprofitable five months on Broadway. A mix of sci-fi and teen angst, the musical's central character was high-school misfit Jeremy (Will Connolly) who comes across a digestible supercomputer tablet called a Squib that turns into an internal guide that makes Jeremy popular. Such magic has its downside and the musical becomes an allegory for using drugs to improve your life. Jeremy's best friend is another loser, Michael

Mell (George Salazar), who realizes that Jeremy no longer needs his companionship. When the two go to a party, Jeremy deserts Michael who hides in the bathroom and goes into the hilarious and revealing soliloquy "Michael in the Bathroom." Joe Iconis' music alternates between a heavy rock pounding and a gentle, twinkling lullaby and his lyric is a panic attack with a stream of consciousness structure. He switches from "I wish I stayed at home in bed, watching cable porn" to suicide to the "wish I was never born."[19] There is an eccentric quality to the character and the song yet "Michael in the Bathroom" captures an honest anxiety that everyone has felt a one time. Make that more than once.

Be More Chill has had numerous productions since its Broadway run but it is the popularity of the cast recording that has made "Michael in the Bathroom" a cult favorite. The song was well enough known that during the Tony Awards ceremony in June of 2019, the number was parodied when host James Corden was joined by past hosts Sarah Bareilles, Josh Groban, and Neil Patrick Harris in a slightly altered version of the song set in a bathroom in Radio City Music Hall. The fact that the Tony audience immediately recognized the song is a testament to its sudden popularity. On the other hand, "Michael in the Bathroom" is too recent to say if it will retain its recognition. Because it is a character song, the number will not get numerous recordings. (Caleb Hyles' 2021 disc is noteworthy.) But it is very likely to be a song performers will return to for auditions, recitals, cabaret acts, and showcases. The teenage angst in "Michael in the Bathroom" will not date and a good song always has the chance of remaining a good song in the future.

Other notable songs from that season: "More Than Survive," "Voices in My Head" from *Be More Chill*; "Unruly Heart," "Dance with You" from *The Prom*; "What I Know Now," "Say My Name" from *Beetlejuice*; "Unstoppable," "Talk to Me Dorothy" from *Tootsie*; "Something About Her" from *Pretty Woman*; "Full Moon Lullaby/Shine" from *King Kong*.

Song of the Season

2019–2020 SEASON

In the summer of 2019, it looked like the Broadway season would be dominated by jukebox musicals in the fall and book musicals in the spring. But it was not to be. All theatres closed on March 12, 2020, because of the Covid-19 pandemic and the season was cut short. There were thirty-one productions (plays and musicals) playing on Broadway when the ban took effect; a few others were in previews. Of the musicals, a handful would never reopen. The show doing the most brisk business at the time was *Moulin Rouge!*, a stage version of the 2001 movie with a jukebox score. The lively, anachronistic musical about Paris in the 1890s opened in July so it was able to play six months before March of 2020. *Moulin Rouge!* was able to reopen in September of 2021 for an extended run. Other jukebox musicals to open that fall were *Jagged Little Pill*, based on the 1995 rock album by Alanis Morisette; the bio-musical *Tina: The Tina Turner Musical*; and the Bob Dylan musical *The Girl from North Country* which transferred from Off-Broadway. All three managed to reopen after the pandemic but didn't last very long. Folding before Broadway closed in March was *The Lightning Thief: The Percy Jackson Musical* based on a popular young adult novel of 2005. The tale of a youth who finds out he's a god and must find Zeus' thunderbolt played ninety-five times. The only Broadway revival to open that fall was a high-tech, mixed media production of *West Side Story*. The production received mixed notices, played for three weeks, was shut down in March, and never returned. The highlight of the truncated Off-Broadway season was the autobiographical musical *A Strange Loop* at Playwrights Horizons. The tale of an African-American homosexual trying to have his voice heard in the theatre was roundly applauded and ran five weeks. Its Broadway debut was delayed until April of 2022. Also of interest was *Soft Power*, a view of America from an Asian point of view. It was well received during its two-month run at the Public Theatre. The Signature Theatre offered *Octet*, a musical about internet addicts, and MCC Theatre produced *The Wrong Man* about an African American framed for a murder. Aside from *A Strange Loop*, all the Off-Broadway efforts disappeared in the pandemic.

"Memory Song"
Music and lyric by Michael R. Jackson
From *A Strange Loop* (2019)
Introduced by Larry Owens as Usher, and his Thoughts

Near the end of *A Strange Loop*, the African American homosexual Usher recalls various people and images growing up in "Memory Song." The number is a result of his parents' despair at their son who turns "his back on the Lord" because of his sexuality. Usher recalls growing up as "the one lone black gay boy" who refused to deny his sexual orientation for the sake of God. The lyric by Michael R. Jackson is scattered, more a stream of consciousness than a logical progression of ideas. Glimpses of gym class, going to church, watching soap operas on TV, and so on are interrupted by the refrain about "Sweet, sour memories ... This is my history. This is my mystery."[20] Jackson's music is steady without being angry. While there are some whole notes to savor, much of the lyric is spit out in tempo with few rests. The chorus of "Thoughts" harmonize with Usher on the repeated line "one lone black gay boy I knew who chose to turn his back on the Lord," the repetition becoming a mantra of sorts. Larry Owens played Usher in the Off-Broadway production; when the musical transferred to Broadway, the role was played by Jaquel Spivey. The original Broadway cast album won some awards and managed to stay on the charts for a time. The future of "Memory Song" is uncertain.

Other notable songs from that season: "A Strange Loop," "Today," "Exile in Gayville," "Second Wave" from *A Strange Loop* (Off-Broadway); "Put You in Your Place," "The Tree on the Hill" from *The Lightning Thief: The Percy Jackson Musical*; "It Just Takes Time," "Democracy" from *Soft Power* (Off-Broadway); "Refresh," "Beautiful" from *Octet* (Off-Broadway).

Song of the Season

2020–2021 SEASON

For the first time since the Civil War, no musicals opened in New York City during the 2020–21 season. Because of the Covid pandemic, there was no season as such. Some shows started reopening in April of 2021 but, in the following two months, no new musicals opened. It was the season that never was. Two musicals that were doing substantial business before the March 12 closing of all theatres—Disney's *Frozen* and the satiric *Mean Girls*—announced that they would not risk the uneasy state of theatregoing and would not return. Musicals that did brave the situation and reopened in April and May saw drastic drops in attendance as audiences were hesitant to go back to the theatre. Once the Covid vaccines were widely available, theatres required masks and proof of vaccination to attend a Broadway show. This policy was maintained well into 2022 when business was gradually getting back to normal. The financial damage caused by the pandemic was monumental. And even when musicals resumed performances, the momentum was lost. Even *The Phantom of the Opera*, for example, was rarely the sell-out that it used to be. So the 2020–21 theatre season remains a blank page in the history of American Musical Theatre.

2021–2022 SEASON

The first new musical to open on Broadway after the pandemic was the London hit *Six: The Musical*. The pop-rock musical about the six wives of Henry VIII was to open on March 12, 2020, the day all the theatres went dark. When it finally started playing in October, the concert-like show had no trouble finding an audience. Two musicals based on popular movies were in previews when the pandemic hit and finally opened this season to mixed reviews. Rob McClure was praised as the cross-dressing hero in *Mrs. Doubtfire* but the musical struggled to run ten weeks. Billy Crystal reprised his screen role in *Mr. Saturday Night*, about an aging comic hoping for a comeback. Crystal was the main attraction so the musical folded when he left after 116 performances. Also in previews when the pandemic closed all the playhouses was *Diana: The Musical* about the Princess of Wales. When it finally opened this season, the reviews were not favorable and it closed after four weeks. *Paradise Square*, about the draft riots in New York City during the Civil War, was well received by the press but some corrupt business dealings forced the show to close after thirteen weeks. Running only a month was *Flying Over Sunset*, an intriguing musical about some celebrities who experimented with LSD in the 1950s. The only two new musicals on Broadway this season to become hits were *MJ the Musical*, a jukebox bio-musical about Michael Jackson, and the transfer of *A Strange Loop* from Off-Broadway. A revival of *The Music Man* with Hugh Jackman and Sutton Foster got mixed notices but was an audience favorite for over a year. The first Broadway revival of *Funny Girl*, with Beanie Feldstein playing Fannie Brice, did spotty business until Lea Michele took over the title role and business then improved significantly. The season's other two revivals both came from London: a gender-shifting *Company* and a commendable *Caroline or Change* with Sharon D. Clarke reprising her towering performance from the West End. The standout musical Off-Broadway was *Kimberly Akimbo*, about a teenager (Victoria Clark) who ages quickly because of a rare medical condition. The compelling musical ran five weeks Off-Broadway then moved to the Street the next season. Two other interesting musicals Off-Broadway were *The Hang*, a jazz musical about a gay man who decides to host his own bizarre funeral, and *Harmony*, a musical by celebrated singer-songwriter Barry Manilow about the German singing group Comedian Harmonists of the 1920s. Harmony returned on Broadway in 2023. It should be pointed out that just about all of the above productions on and Off-Broadway had cast replacements and/or canceled performances when a member of the company got Covid. So it was harder than ever for producers to make top dollar even with a big hit show.

"Before I Go"
Music by Jeanine Tesori; lyric by David Lindsay-Abaire
From *Kimberly Akimbo* (2021)
Sung by Victoria Clark as Kimberly Levaco,
with Stephen Boyer as Buddy and Alli Mauzey as Patti

Song of the Season

David Lindsay-Abaire's 2001 play *Kimberly Akimbo* was an Off-Broadway success and had seen many productions regionally by the time the playwright teamed up with composer Jeanine Tesori to create a musical version of the comedy-drama. Kimberly Levaco (Victoria Clark) comes from a dysfunctional family who cannot deal with her unusual disease in which she physically ages four times faster than normal. Emotionally she is a teenager and goes through difficult times, getting more help from her teenage friends than her parents, the alcoholic Buddy and the bitter, pregnant Patti. Near the end of the musical, the family fighting ceases enough for Kimberly to sing "Before I Go," a gentle but assertive ballad in which she pleads for acceptance. "I was never the girl you intended," she sings.[21] "What you wanted wasn't me." Instead Kimberly sees their house as "haunted" by the "ghost of a girl I'll never be." She asks her parents to let the ghost "disappear" so that they can see her as she really is "while I'm still here." Having this rare disease means Kimberly "might be dying ... but I'm not dead." The parents sing a counter melody at the end of the song, showing the first signs of understanding. Lindsay-Abaire's lyric is unembellished and direct and Tesori's music has a folk quality in structure and in tone. After much angst in *Kimberly Akimbo*, the song "Before I Go" is a quiet moment but one that resonates with power. Victoria Clark played Kimberly with a heartbreaking kind of optimism at times, a fierce adolescent fury at other moments. Clark's penetrating performance was highly praised both Off-Broadway and when *Kimberly Akimbo* transferred to Broadway the next season. Although "Before I Go" has been heard in cabarets and concerts, it is too soon to see if the song will have a busy future in recordings.

Other notable songs from that season: "Better," "Anagram," "This Time," "Now" from *Kimberly Akimbo* (Off-Broadway); "Let It Burn," "Hard Times Come Again No More," "Someone to Love" from *Paradise Square*; "Flying Over Sunset," "The Music Plays On," "If Only I'd Known" from *Flying Over Sunset*; "About Time," "Just Pretend" from *Mrs. Doubtfire*; "My Wonderful Pain," "A Little Joy" from *Mr. Saturday Night*; "I Don't Need Your Love," "Heart of Stone" from *Six: The Musical*.

2022–2023 SEASON

If remembered for nothing else, 1922–23 will go down in history as the season *The Phantom of the Opera* closed. A mainstay on Broadway since 1988, the Andrew Lloyd Webber operetta reopened after the pandemic with a celebratory fanfare. The presence of the musical again playing to full houses was a sign that Broadway was indeed back. But it was not to last. After the first flush of success, the Majestic Theatre went over a year only occasionally playing to full capacity and the show lost money every month. When a closing was announced for February 2023, there was a surge in tickets sales so the closing date was pushed back to April. The mighty *The Phantom of the Opera* became another pandemic victim.

Another round of raves (and awards) greeted *Kimberly Akimbo* when it arrived on Broadway this season but the show for the tired businessman (if such a creature was still going to the theatre) was *Some Like It Hot*, a movie-to-stage musical that was highly pleasing. It was the second time the 1959 Billy Wilder film had been musicalized for Broadway (*Sugar* in 1972 was a modest success) and this time songs, cast, and book fell into place. The only other new musicals to run were *& Juliet*, a jukebox musical in which the fabled lovers do not commit suicide, and a broad musical comedy with a country-western score titled *Shucked*, about a rural town that gets desperate when its corn crop fails. The critics were mostly favorable in their notices for both shows and audiences responded with enthusiasm, turning the two sleepers into hits. The latest celebrity jukebox musical, *A Beautiful Noise: The Neil Diamond Musical*, was panned by the press but audiences came for several months. A great deal of anticipation was stirred up by the old/new musical *New York, New York* based on the problematic 1977 film. The handful of movie songs by Kander and Ebb (including the catchy title number) were augmented by some trunk tunes and new songs with lyrics by Lin-Manuel Miranda. The libretto took liberties with the unsatisfying screenplay but most critics felt the talented performers and sparkling production were let down by the weak libretto. But *New York, New York* was an audience show and they came for several months. The 2000 cult film *Almost Famous* was given new songs and arrived on Broadway where it was met with mostly negative reviews. Fans of the movie came for two months. Andrew Lloyd Webber's "adult" musical *Cinderella* changed its title to *Bad Cinderella* on its way from London to Broadway. It took a critical shellacking from the press and was soon gone.

There was a wide variety of revivals on Broadway this season. The all-female *1776* found little approval and quickly closed. On the other hand, a skillful revival of *Into the Woods* was popular enough that its run both Off-Broadway and on was extended a few times. Popular singer Josh Groban secured the success of *Sweeney Todd* on Broadway yet the well-reviewed production was a success in its own right. Among the production's assets were Annaleigh Ashford's Mrs. Lovett and the direction by Thomas Kail. Also praised by the press and public was a revival of the 1998 musical drama *Parade* featuring Ben Platt and Micaela Diamond. There was much interest in the revised revival of *Camelot* with a doctored book by Aaron Sorkin so there was much disappointment when it opened to mixed notices. Few of the libretto's problems were solved but most critics applauded the musical numbers. *K-Pop* or *KPOP*, a genre of electric pop music from South Korea which goes back to the 1990s, was heard briefly Off-Broadway in 2017 and arrived on Broadway this season. Even critics who applauded the invigorating songs could not recommend the random book; audiences came for only seventeen performances. Bob Fosse's 1978 *Dancin'* was revived (and slightly revised) on Broadway and the revue met with a mixed critical reaction. A revival of *Fiddler on the Roof* performed in Yiddish, first seen in 2018, returned to Off-Broadway to another round of plaudits. Also Off-Broadway, a revival of Stephen Sondheim's tricky musical *Merrily We Roll Along* had no trouble finding patrons with favorites Daniel Radcliffe and Jonathan Groff featured in the cast. Its run at the New York Theatre Workshop quickly sold out and plans were made to bring the revival to Broadway the next season. Also finding approval was a revival of *A Man of No Importance* at the Classic Stage Company. New works of interest Off-Broadway this season include: *Titanique*, a jukebox musical spoof of *Titanic* with songs popularized by Celine Dion; a musical version of the TV play and movie *The Days of Wine and Roses*; the surreal, racially slanted soap opera spoof *White Girls in Danger*; and the fantasy *Between the Lines* about a student caught between fiction and reality.

"Some Like It Hot"
Music by Marc Shaiman; and lyric by Shaiman, Scott Wittman
from *Some Like It Hot* (2022)
Sung by NaTasha Yvette Williams as Sweet Sue,
Adrianna Hicks as Sugar, J. Harrison Ghee as Daphne, and the Ensemble

---

Just as Marc Shaiman and Scott Wittman had captured the sound of early 1960s pop music in *Hairspray*, they created a pleasing pastiche score for *Some Like It Hot* in the jazz idiom. The title number, a list song that also serves as a tap dance production, is arguably the highlight of the score. It served as the Act One finale, sung by bandleader Sweet Sue and the ensemble in a supper club in Prohibition-era Los Angeles. The short verse invites patrons to the club by comparing it to life, offering items as if on a menu. The first refrain sets up the premise that different people prefer different joys, such as a tent in a rural setting to a beach on a Hawaiian island to a bungalow for two in the snow. But Sue suggests a warmer choice for those who, regardless whether they "like it rough" or "like it tame," like it hot because "hot is what I got for you."[22] What follows is a list of examples of things that are "hot," using foods "that burn your tongue" and "seafood salty." The lyric pays homage to the novel and movie *The Postman Always Rings Twice* and the Eugene O'Neill play *The Iceman Cometh* when Sue sings "though the postman might ring twice/ Some like the man who brings the ice/ He cometh with his block to stock my Frigidaire." The song concludes with "call me savage, call me wild/ But honey please don't call me mild" as she once again promises "hot is what I got for you." Sue's featured singer Sugar

(Adrianna Hicks) and the drag musician "Daphne" (J. Harrison Ghee) join in the singing before the number explodes in a vibrant tap number. The music is necessarily repetitive, often returning to the same jazz riff. Like many pastiche songs, "Some Like It Hot" may not have a life outside of the context of the musical. Or it may become a familiar favorite as "All That Jazz" in *Chicago*. But as part of *Some Like It Hot*, it delights and does its job very well.

Other notable songs from that season: "You Can't Have Me," "Ride Out the Storm," "Let's Be Bad" from *Some Like It Hot*; "Independently Owned," "Somebody Will," "OK" from *Shucked*; "A Simple Thing Like That," "I Love Music," "Cheering for Me Now" from *New York, New York*; "No Friends," "Everybody Coming Together" from *Almost Famous*; "Bad Cinderella," "Far Too Late" from *Bad Cinderella*.

AFTERWORD

As I write these final words, the Majestic Theatre on Broadway is under heavy construction and remodeling. Changes made to the stage, backstage, and below stage in 1988 for the arrival of *The Phantom of the Opera* are changing yet again. But all that is theatre architecture. I cannot help but think about all the songs that were first heard on Broadway from that stage since the playhouse opened in 1927. I hear strains of "On the Sunny Side of the Street," "You'll Never Walk Alone," "Younger Than Springtime," "Till There Was You," "Before I Gaze Again at You," "Anyone Can Whistle," "I Won't Send Roses," "Be a Lion," "Masquerade," and hundreds of other songs that could not be included in the discussion in these pages. The Majestic Theatre can change shape and even its name in the future but the songs live on, perhaps changing tempo or arrangement, but still the same at heart.

NOTES ON SONG LYRICS

1891–1899 Seasons

1. "Oh Promise Me." Lyric by Clement Scott, 1892. Geller, James J. *Famous Songs and Their Stories*. (New York: Garden City Publishing Co., 1940), 109.
2. "After the Ball." Lyric by Charles K. Harris, 1892. Furia, Philip, and Laurie Patterson. *The American Song Book: The Tin Pan Alley Era*. (New York: Oxford University Press), 2.
3. "Old Before His Time." Lyric by Sydney Rosenfeld, 1894. Bordman, Gerald, and Richard Norton. *American Musical Theatre: A Chronicle* (4th ed.). (New York: Oxford University Press, 2011), 150.
4. "(Private) Tommy Atkins." Lyric by Henry Hamilton, 1894. Ganzl, Kurt. *The British Musical Theatre, Vol. 1*. (New York: Oxford University Press, 1986), 478.
5. "El Capitan's Song." Lyric by Tom Frost, 1896. www.geniuslyrics/el-capitan
6. "I Love Thee, I Adore Thee. (The Serenade)" Lyric by Harry B. Smith, 1897. https://digitalcommons.library.umaine.edu/the-serenade
7. "The Tattooed Man." Lyric by Harry B. Smith, 1897. Bordman/Norton, 179.
8. "My Wild Irish Rose." Lyric by Chauncey Olcott, 1899. www.lyrics.com/my-wild-irish-rose
9. "When Chloe Sings a Song." Lyric by Harry B. Smith, 1899. https://sheetmusicsinger.com/when-chloe-sings-a-song.pdf

1900–1919 Seasons

1. "Tell Me, Pretty Maiden." Lyric by Leslie Stuart, © 1900. Geller, 181.
2. "Nancy Brown." Lyric by Clifton Crawford, © 1902. https://scholarsjunction.msstate.edu/nancy-brown
3. "In the Good Old Summer Time." Lyric by Ren Shields, © 1902. www.lyrics.com/in-the-good-old-summertime
4. "Toyland." Lyric by Glen MacDonough, © 1903. www.geniuslyrics/toyland
5. "Give My Regards to Broadway." Lyric by George M. Cohan, © 1904. Furia/Patterson, 46.
6. "You're a Grand Old Flag." Lyric by George M. Cohan, © 1906. Furia/Patterson, 59.
7. "The Streets of New York." Lyric by Henry Blossom, © 1906. www.geniuslyrics/the-streets-of-new-york
8. "I Love You So (The Merry Widow Waltz)." English lyric by Adrian Ross, © 1907. www.lyrics.com/i-love-you-so
9. "Shine On, Harvest Moon." Lyric by Nora Bayes, Jack Norworth, © 1908. www.lyrics.com/shine-on-harvest-moon

Notes on Song Lyrics

10. "Has Anyone Here Seen Kelly?" American lyric by William J. McKenna, © 1910. Geller, 202.
11. "Ah, Sweet Mystery of Life." Lyric by Rida Johnson Young, © 1910. www.lyrics.com/ah!-sweet-mystery-of-life
12. "Be My Little Baby Bumble Bee." Lyric by Stanley Murphy, © 1912. www.geniuslyrics/com.be-my-little-baby-bumblebee
13. "When Irish Eyes Are Smiling." Lyric by Chauncey Olcott, George Graff, Jr., © 1913. www.geniuslyrics.com/when-irish-eyes-are-smiling
14. "Peg o' My Heart." Lyric by Alfred Bryan, © 1913. www.geniuslyrics.com/peg-o-my-heart
15. "They Didn't Believe Me." Lyric by Herbert Reynolds, © 1914. Furia/Patterson, 113.
16. "I Love a Piano." Lyric by Irving Berlin, © 1915. Furia/Patterson, 128.
17. "Till the Clouds Roll By." Lyric by P. G. Wodehouse, © 1917. Furia/Patterson, 149.
18. "I'm Always Chasing Rainbows." Lyric by Joseph McCarthy, © 1917. Furia/Patterson, 160.
19. "Swanee." Lyric by Irving Caesar, © 1919. Furia/Patterson, 183.
20. "A Pretty Girl Is Like a Melody." Lyric by Irving Berlin, © 1919. Furia/Patterson, 174.

1920–1939 Seasons

1. "I'm Just Wild About Harry." Lyric by Noble Sissle, © 1921. Furia/Patterson, 210.
2. "April Showers." Lyric by B. G. DeSylva, © 1921. Gottlieb, Robert, and Robert Kimball. *Reading Lyrics*. (New York: Pantheon Books, 2000), 174.
3. "Nellie Kelly, I Love You." Lyric by George M. Cohan, © 1922. www.allmusicals.com/nellie-kelly-i-love-you
4. "Charleston." Lyric by Cecil Mack, © 1923. Gottlieb/Kimball, 32.
5. "Indian Love Call." Lyric by Otto Harbach, Oscar Hammerstein, © 1924. Asch, Amy. *The Complete Lyrics of Oscar Hammerstein*. (New York: Alfred A. Knopf, 2008), 55.
6. "Tea for Two." Lyric by Irving Caesar, © 1924. Gottlieb/Kimball, 223.
7. "Someone to Watch Over Me." Lyric by Ira Gershwin, © 1926. Kimball, Robert (ed.). *The Complete Lyrics of Ira Gershwin*. (New York: Alfred A. Knopf, 1993), 83.
8. "Ol' Man River." Lyric by Oscar Hammerstein, © 1927. Asch, 105.
9. "I Wanna Be Love by You." Lyric by Bert Kalmar, © 1932. Gottlieb/Kimball, 398.
10. "Ain't Misbehavin'." Lyric by Andy Razaf, © 1929. Gottlieb/Kimball, 247.
11. "I Got Rhythm." Lyric by Ira Gershwin, © 1930. Gottlieb/Kimball, 294.
12. "As Time Goes By." Lyric by Herman Hupfield, © 1931. Gottlieb/Kimball, 156.
13. "Night and Day." Lyric by Cole Porter, © 1932. Gottlieb/Kimball, 118.
14. "Smoke Gets in Your Eyes." Lyric by Otto Harbach, © 1933. Gottlieb/Kimball, 8.
15. "I Get a Kick Out of You." Lyric by Cole Porter, © 1934. Gottlieb/Kimball, 108.
16. "Begin the Beguine." Lyric by Cole Porter, © 1935. Gottlieb/Kimball, 103.
17. "My Funny Valentine." Lyric by Lorenz Hart, © 1937. Hart, Dorothy, and Robert Kimball (eds.). *The Complete Lyrics of Lorenz Hart*. (New York: Alfred A. Knopf, 1986), 229.
18. "I'll Be Seeing You." Lyric by Irving Kahal, © 1938. Gottlieb/Kimball, 359.

Notes on Song Lyrics

19. "September Song." Lyric by Maxwell Anderson, © 1938. Gottlieb/Kimball, 94.
20. "All the Things You Are." Lyric by Oscar Hammerstein, © 1939. Asch, 244.

1940–1959 Seasons

1. "Bewitched (Bothered and Bewildered)." Lyric by Lorenz Hart, © 1941. Hart/Kimball, 272.
2. "Everything I've Got (Belongs to You)." Lyric by Lorenz Hart, © 1942. Hart/Kimball, 285.
3. "Oh, What a Beautiful Mornin'." Lyric by Oscar Hammerstein, © 1943. Asch, 279.
4. "Speak Low." Lyric by Ogden Nash, © 1943. Gottlieb/Kimball, 354.
5. "If I Loved You." Lyric by Oscar Hammerstein, © 1945. Asch, 311.
6. "There's No Business Like Show Business." Lyric by Irving Berlin, © 1946. Kimball, Robert, and Linda Emmet. *The Complete Lyrics of Irving Berlin*. (New York: Alfred A. Knopf, 2001), 388.
7. "Almost Like Being in Love." Lyric by Alan Jay Lerner, © 1947. Gottlieb/Kimball, 526.
8. "Papa, Won't You Dance with Me?" Lyric by Sammy Cahn, © 1947. www.lyrics.com/papa-won't-you-dance-with-me
9. "Some Enchanted Evening." Lyric by Oscar Hammerstein, © 1949. Asch, 336.
10. "Diamonds Are a Girl's Best Friend." Lyric by Leo Robin, © 1949. Gottlieb/Kimball, 189.
11. "You're Just in Love." Lyric by Irving Berlin, © 1950. Kimball/Emmet, 434.
12. "They Call the Wind Maria." Lyric by Alan Jay Lerner, © 1951. Engel, Lehman. *Their Words Are Music*. (New York: Crown Publishers, 1975), 141.
13. "It's All Right with Me." Lyric by Cole Porter, © 1953. Gottlieb/Kimball, 110.
14. "Stranger in Paradise." Lyric by Robert Wright, George Forrest, © 1953. Gottlieb/Kimball, 491.
15. "Young and Foolish." Lyric by Arnold B. Horwitt, © 1955. Stein, Joseph, Will Glickman. *Plain and Fancy*. (New York: Random House, 1954), 33.
16. "On the Street Where You Live." Lyric by Alan Jay Lerner, © 1956. Gottlieb/Kimball, 533.
17. "The Party's Over." Lyric by Betty Comden, Adolph Green, © 1956. Comden, Betty, and Adolph Green. *The New York Musicals of Comden and Green*. (New York: Applause Books, 1997), 267.
18. "Seventy-Six Trombones." Lyric by Meredith Willson, © 1957. Gottlieb/Kimball, 349.
19. "I Enjoy Being a Girl." Lyric by Oscar Hammerstein, © 1958. Asch, 387.
20. "Do Re Mi." Lyric by Oscar Hammerstein, © 1959. Asch, 396.

1960–1979 Seasons

1. "If Ever I Would Leave You." Lyric by Alan Jay Lerner, © 1960. Gottlieb/Kimball, 531.
2. "Comedy Tonight." Lyric by Stephen Sondheim, © 1962. Sondheim, Stephen. *Finishing the Hat: Collected Lyrics 1954–1981*. (New York: Alfred A. Knopf, 2010), 83.

Notes on Song Lyrics

3. "What Kind of Fool Am I?" Lyric by Anthony Newley, Leslie Bricusse, © 1961. Gottlieb/Kimball, 603.
4. "People." Lyric by Bob Merrill, © 1963. Gottlieb/Kimball, 541.
5. "Sunrise, Sunset." Lyric by Sheldon Harnick, © 1964. Gottlieb/Kimball, 569.
6. "The Impossible Dream." Lyric by Joe Darion, © 1965. Richards, Stanley. *Great Musicals of the American Theatre, Volume 2*. (Radnor, PA: Chilton books, 1976), 506.
7. "Cabaret." Lyric by Fred Ebb, © 1966. Gottlieb/Kimball, 610.
8. "Aquarius." Lyric by James Rado, Gerome Ragni, © 1968. Richards, Stanley. *Great Rock Musicals*. (New York: Stein & Day, 1979), 391.
9. "Promises Promises." Lyric by Hal David, © 1968. Simon, Neil. *The Collected Plays of Neil Simon, Volume 1*. (New York: Penguin Books, 1986), 488.
10. "The Ladies Who Lunch." Lyric by Stephen Sondheim, © 1970. Sondheim (*Finishing the Hat*), 190.
11. "Day By Day." Lyric by Stephen Schwartz, etc., © 1971. www.allmusicals.com/godspell
12. "I Don't Know How to Love Him." Lyric by Tim Rice, © 1971. Richards, 266.
13. "Send in the Clowns." Lyric by Stephen Sondheim, © 1973. Sondheim (*Finishing the Hat*), 277
14. "In This Wide, Wide World." Lyric by Alan Jay Lerner, © 1974. www.allmusicals.com/gigi
15. "Time Heals Everything." Lyric by Jerry Herman, © 1974. Herman, Jerry, and Ken Bloom. *Jerry Herman: The Lyrics*. (New York: Routledge, 2003), 146.
16. "All That Jazz." Lyric by Fred Ebb, © 1975. www.allmusicals.com/chicago.
17. "Tomorrow." Lyric by Martin Charnin, © 1977. www.allmusicals.com/annie
18. "Old Friend." Lyric by Gretchen Cryer, © 1978. Cryer, Gretchen. *I'm Getting My Act Together and Taking It on the Road*. (Garden City, NY: Nelson Doubleday, 1977), 53.
19. "A Little Priest." Lyric by Stephen Sondheim, © 1979. Sondheim (*Finishing the Hat*), 356.
20. "Don't Cry for Me Argentina." Lyric by Tim Rice, © 1979. www.allmusicals.com/evita

1980–1999 Seasons

1. "Four Jews in a Room Bitching." Lyric by William Finn, © 1981. Finn, William, and James Lapine. *Falsettos*. (New York: Penguin Books, 1993), 5.
2. "And I'm Telling You I'm Not Going." Lyric by Tom Eyen, © 1981. www.allmusicals.com/dreamgirls
3. "Memory." Lyric by Trevor Nunn, T. S. Eliot, © 1982. www.allmusicals.com/cats
4. "I Am What I Am." Lyric by Jerry Herman, © 1983. Herman, 186.
5. "River in the Rain." Lyric by Roger Miller, © 1985. www.allmusicals.com/big-river
6. "Don't Quit While You're Ahead." Lyric by Rupert Holmes, © 1985. Holmes, Rupert. *The Mystery of Edwin Drood*. (Garden City, NY: Nelson Doubleday, 1986), 84.
7. "The Lambeth Walk." Lyric by Noel Gay, Douglas Furber, © 1937. Gottlieb/Kimball, 311.
8. "Music of the Night." Lyric by Charles Hart, Richard Stilgoe, © 1988. www.allmusicals.com/the-phantom-of-the-opera
9. "Hard to Be Diva." Lyric by Barry Keating, © 1989. https://lyricsondemand.com/s/starmites

Notes on Song Lyrics

10. "Love Changes Everything." Lyric by Don Black, Charles Hart, © 1990. www.allmusicals.com/aspects-of-love
11. "Lily's Eyes." Lyric by Marsha Norman, © 1991. Norman, Marsha. *The Secret Garden*. (New York: Theatre Communications Group), 53.
12. "I'm Breaking Down." Lyric by William Finn, © 1979. Finn/Lapine, 51.
13. "Where You Are." Lyric by Fred Ebb, © 1993. www.allmusicals.com/kiss-of-the-spider-woman
14. "Loving You." Lyric by Stephen Sondheim, © 1994, Sondheim, Stephen. *Look, I Made a Hat: Collected Lyrics 1981–2011*. (New York: Alfred A. Knopf, 2011), 172.
15. "As If We Never Said Goodbye." Lyric by Don Black, Christopher Hampton, Amy Powers, © 1994. www.allmusicals.com/sunset-boulevard
16. "Seasons of Love." Lyric by Jonathan Larson, © 1996. Hausam, Willey. *The New American Musical*. (New York: Theatre Communications Group, 2003), 179.
17. "This Is the Moment. " Lyric by Leslie Bricusse, Steve Cuden, Frank Wildhorn, © 1997. www.allmusicals.com/jekyll-&-hyde
18. "Ragtime." Lyric by Lynn Ahrens, © 1998. www.allmusicals.com/ragtime
19. "And They're Off." Lyric by William Finn, © 1998. www.allmusicals.com/a-new-brain
20. "Written in the Stars." Lyric by Tim Rice, © 2000. www.allmusicals.com/aida

2000–2023 Seasons

1. "Alone in the Universe." Lyric by Lynn Ahrens, © 2000. www.allmusicals.com/seussical
2. "Gimme Gimme." Lyric by Dick Scanlan, © 2002. www.allmusicals.com/thoroughly-modern-millie
3. "You Can't Stop the Beat." Lyric by Scott Wittman, Marc Shaiman, © 2002. www.allmusicals.com/hairspray
4. "Defying Gravity." Lyric by Stephen Schwartz, © 2003. www.allmusicals.com/wicked
5. "Dividing Day." Lyric by Adam Guettel, © 2005. Lucas, Craig. *The Light in the Piazza*. (New York: Theatre Communications Group, 2007), 42.
6. "I'm Here." Lyric by Brenda Russell, Allee Willis, Stephen Bray, © 2005. www.allmusicals.com/the-color-purple
7. "96,000." Lyric by Lin-Manuel Miranda, © 2008. www.allmusicals.com/in-the-heights
8. "I Miss the Mountains." Lyric by Brian Yorkie, © 2008. www.allmusicals.com/next-to-normal
9. "Electricity." Lyric by Lee Hall, © 2008. www.allmusicals.com/billy-elliot
10. "Go Back Home." Lyric by Fred Ebb, © 2009. https://www.musixmatch.com//go-back-home
11. "I Believe." Lyric by Robert Lopez, Trey Parker, Matt Stone, © 2011. www.allmusicals.com/the-book-of-mormon
12. "Something to Believe In." Lyric by Jack Feldman, © 2012. www.allmusicals.com/newsies
13. "I'm Not My Father's Son." Lyric by Cyndi Lauper, © 2013. www.allmusicals.com/kinky-boots
14. "Ring of Keys." Lyric by Lisa Kron, © 2015. www.allmusicals.com/fun-home

Notes on Song Lyrics

15. "My Shot." Lyric by Lin-Manuel Miranda, © 2015. www.allmusicals.com/hamilton
16. "Everything Changes." Lyric by Sara Bareilles, © 2016. www.allmusicals.com/waitress
17. "You Will Be Found." Lyric by Benj Pasek, Justin Paul, © 2016. www.allmusicals.com/dear-evan-hanson
18. "Omar Sharif." Lyric by David Yazbek, © 2017. www.allmusicals.com/the-bands-visit
19. "Michael in the Bathroom." Lyric by Joe Iconis, © 2019. www.allmusicals.com/be-more-chill
20. "Memory Song." Lyric by Michael R. Jackson, © 2019. Jackson, Richard R. *A Strange Loop*. (New York: Theatre Communications Group, 2020), 92.
21. "Before I Go." Lyric by David Lindsay-Abaire, © 2021. https://www.themusicallyrics.com/k/594-kimberly-akimbo
22. "Some Like It Hot." Lyric by Scott Wittman, Marc Shaiman, © 2022. https://themusicallyrics.com/s/585-some-like-it-hot-the-musical

BIBLIOGRAPHY

Alpert, Hollis. *Broadway: 125 Years of Musical Theatre*. New York: Arcade, 1991.
Atkinson, Brooks. *Broadway* (revised). New York: Macmillan Publishing Co., 1974.
Block, Geoffrey. *Enchanted Evenings: The Broadway Musical from Show Boat to Lloyd Webber* (2nd ed.). New York: Oxford University Press, 2009.
Bloom, Ken, and Frank Vlastnik. *Broadway Musicals: The 101 Greatest Shows of All Time*. New York: Black Dog & Leventhal Publishers, 2004.
Bordman, Gerald, and Thomas S. Hischak. *The Oxford Companion to American Theatre* (3rd ed.). New York: Oxford University Press, 2004.
Bordman, Gerald, and Richard Norton. *American Musical Theatre: A Chronicle* (4th ed.). New York: Oxford University Press, 2011.
Bowers, Dwight Blocker. *American Musical Theatre: Shows, Songs, and Stars*. Washington, DC: Smithsonian Press, 1989.
Campbell, Michael. *Popular Music in America: The Beat Goes On* (5th ed.). Boston, MA: Cengage, 2018.
DK. *Musicals: The Definitive Illustrated Story* (2nd ed.). London, UK: Dorling Kindersley Limited (DK) Publishers, 2021.
Engel, Lehman. *Their Words Are Music: The Great Theatre Lyricists and Their Lyrics*. New York: Crown Publishers, 1975.
Everett, William A., and Paul R. Laird (eds.). *The Cambridge Companion to the Musical* (3rd ed.). Cambridge, UK: Cambridge University Press, 2017.
Ewen, David. *Great Men of American Popular Song*. Englewood Cliffs, NJ: Prentice-Hall, Inc, 1970.
Ewen, David. *The Life and Death of Tin Pan Alley*. New York: Funk & Wagnalls, 1964.
Furia, Philip, and Michael Lasser. *America's Songs*. New York: Routledge Press, 2006.
Furia, Philip, Michael Lasser, and Laurie Patterson. *The American Song Book: The Tin Pan Alley Era*. New York: Oxford University Press, 2016.
Furia, Philip, Michael Lasser, and Laurie Patterson. *The Poets of Tin Pan Alley*. New York: Oxford University Press, 1992.
Ganzl, Kurt. *Ganzl's Encyclopedia of the Musical Theatre*. New York: Schirmer Books, 1993.
Geller, James J. *Famous Songs and Their Stories*. New York: Garden City Publishing Co., 1940.
Gershwin, Ira. *Lyrics on Several Occasions*. New York: Viking Press, 1973.
Grant, Mark N. *The Rise and Fall of the Broadway Musical*. Boston, MA: Northeastern University Press, 2004.
Green, Stanley, and Cary Ginell. *Broadway Musicals Show by Show* (9th ed.). Guilford, CT: Applause Theatre & Cinema Books, 2019.
Green, Stanley, and Cary Ginell. *Encyclopedia of the Musical Theatre*. New York: Dodd, Mead & Co., 1976.
Green, Stanley, and Cary Ginell. *The World of Musical Comedy*. New York: A.S. Barnes & Co., 1980.
Groce, Nancy. *New York: Songs of the City*. New York: Watson-Guptill Publications, 1999.
Grode, Eric. *The Book of Broadway: The 150 Definitive Plays and Musicals*. Minneapolis, MN: Voyageur Press, 2015.
Han, Charles. *Yesterdays: Popular Song in America*. New York: W. W. Norton & Co., 1983.

Bibliography

Hirsch, Foster. *Kurt Weill on Stage: From Berlin to Broadway.* New York: Alfred A. Knopf, 2002.

Hischak, Thomas S. *The American Musical Theatre Song Encyclopedia.* Westport, CT: Greenwood Press, 1995.

Hischak, Thomas S. *Off-Broadway Musicals since 1919.* Lanham, MD: Scarecrow Press, 2011.

Hischak, Thomas S. *The Oxford Companion to the American Musical: Theatre, Film and Television.* New York: Oxford University Press, 2008.

Hischak, Thomas S. *The Tin Pan Alley Song Encyclopedia.* Westport, CT: Greenwood Press, 2002.

Hischak, Thomas S. *Word Crazy: Broadway Lyricists from Cohan to Sondheim.* New York: Praeger Press, 1991.

Jackson, Arthur. *The Best Musicals from Show Boat to a Chorus Line.* New York: Crown Publishers, 1977.

Jones, John Bush. *Our Musicals, Ourselves.* Lebanon, NH: University Press of New England, 2003.

Kantor, Michael, and Laurence Maslon. *Broadway: The American Musical.* Guilford, CT: Applause Theatre & Cinema Books, 2020.

Kapilow, Rob. *Listening for America: Inside the Great American Songbook.* New York: Liveright Publishing Corp., 2019.

Kennedy, Michael Patrick, and John Muir. *Musicals.* Glasgow, UK: HarperCollins Publishers, 1997.

Lamb, Andrew. *150 Years of Popular Musical Theatre.* New Haven, CT: Yale University Press, 2000.

McMillan, Scott. *The Musical as Drama: A Study of the Principals and Conventions behind Musical Shows from Kern to Sondheim.* Princeton, NJ: Princeton University Press, 2006.

Miller, Scott. *Rebels with Applause: Broadway's Groundbreaking Musicals.* Portsmouth, NH: Heinemann Drama, 2001.

Mordden, Ethan. *Beautiful Mornin': The Broadway Musical in the 1940s.* New York: Oxford Press, 1999.

Mordden, Ethan. *Coming Up Roses: The Broadway Musical in the 1950s.* New York: Oxford Press, 1998.

Mordden, Ethan. *The Happiest Corpse I've Ever Seen: The Last 25 Years of the Broadway Musical.* New York: Palgrave Macmillan, 2004.

Mordden, Ethan. *Make Believe: The Broadway Musical in the 1920s.* New York: Oxford Press, 1997.

Mordden, Ethan. *Sing for Your Supper: The Broadway Musical in the 1930s.* New York: Palgrave Macmillan, 2005.

Morris, James R., J. R. Taylor, and Dwight Blocker Bowers. *American Popular Song: Six Decades of Songwriters and Singers.* Washington, DC: Smithsonian Press, 1984.

Norton, Richard C. *A Chronology of American Musical Theatre.* New York: Oxford University Press, 2002.

Patinkin, Sheldon. *No Legs, No Jokes, No Chance: A History of the American Musical Theatre.* Evanston, IL: Northwestern University Press, 2008.

Pender, Rick. *The Stephen Sondheim Encyclopedia.* Lanham, MD: Rowman & Littlefield, 2021.

Portantier, Michael (ed.). *The TheatreMania Guide to Musical Theatre Recordings.* New York: Backstage Books, 2004.

Raymond, Jack. *Show Music on Record: From the 1890s to the 1980s.* New York: Frederick Ungar Publishing Co., 1982.

Robinson, Mark A. *The World of Musicals: An Encyclopedia of Stage, Screen, and Song.* Santa Barbara, CA: Greenwood Press, 2014.

Schneider, Robert W., and Shannon Agnew (eds.). *Fifty Key Stage Musicals.* New York: Routledge, 2022.

Sheward, David. *It's a Hit: The Back Stage Book of Longest-Running Broadway Shows, 1884 to the Present*. New York: Watson-Guptill Publications-BPI Communications, Inc., 1994.

Singer, Barry. *Ever After: The Last Years of Musical Theatre and Beyond*. New York: Applause Theatre and Cinema Books, 2004.

Smith, Cecil, and Glenn Litton. *Musical Comedy in America* (2nd ed.). New York: Theatre Arts Books, 1981.

Sondheim, Stephen. *Finishing the Hat*. New York: Alfred A. Knopf, 2010.

Sondheim, Stephen. *Look, I Made a Hat*. New York: Alfred A. Knopf, 2011.

Stanley, Bob. *Let's Do It! The Birth of Pop Music: A History*. London: Faber & Faber, 2022.

Starr, Larry, and Christopher Waterman. *American Popular Music: From Minstrelsy to MP3*. New York: Oxford University Press, 2017.

Suskin, Steven. *More Opening Nights on Broadway*. New York: Schirmer Books, 1997.

Suskin, Steven. *Opening Night on Broadway: A Critical Quotebook of the Golden Era of the Musical Theatre*. New York: Schirmer Books, 1990.

Suskin, Steven. *Show Tunes: 1905-1985*. New York: Dodd, Mead & Co., 1986.

Swain, Joseph P. *The Broadway Musical: A Critical and Musical Survey*. New York: Oxford University Press, 1990.

Tawa, Nicholas E. *The Way to Tin Pan Alley: American Popular Song, 1866-1910*. New York: Schirmer Books, 1990.

Wilder, Alec, and Robert Rawlins (ed). *American Popular Song: The Great Innovators, 1900-1950* (3rd ed.). New York: Oxford University Press, 2022.

Wilmeth, Don. B., and Tice Miller (eds.). *Cambridge Guide to American Theatre*. New York: Cambridge University Press, 1993.

SONG INDEX

"The a la Girl" 24
"About Time" 344
"Absinthe Frappé" 30
"Ace in the Hole" 136
"Addison's Trip" 319
"Adelaide's Lament" 161
"Adrift on a Star" 189
"Adventure" 189
"Africa Burning in the Sun" 264
"After All, It's Spring" 164
"After the Ball" 4–5
"After You, Who?" 110
"Agony" 264
"Ah, Sweet Mystery of Life" 45–6
"Ah, Yes, I Love Thee" 5
"Ain't It the Truth" 179
"Ain't Misbehavin'" 99–101
"Alexander's Ragtime Band" 55, 59
"Alibi Baby" 83
"Alice Blue Gown" 72
"All Aboard for Dixie" 54
"All Alone" 86
"All Alone Monday" 92
"All at Once You Love Her" 173
"All Down Piccadilly" 44
"All Fall Down" 269
"All for Laura" 311
"All for the Best" 216
"All I Ask of You" 264
"All I Care About Is Love" 230
"All I Need Is the Girl" 182
"All of You" 170, 264, 293
"All That Jazz" 229–30, 347
"All the Children in a Row" 253
"All the Livelong Day" 236
"All the Men in My Life" 314
"All the Wasted Time" 290
"All Things to One Man" 255
"All the Things You Are" 127–8
"All Through The Night" 115
"Allah's Holiday" 60
"Allegro" 153
"Almost Like Being in Love" 148–9
"Alone" 303
"Alone in the Universe" 295
"Alone Together" 110
"Alone Too Long" 168

"Always, Always You" 188
"Always Do as People Say You Should" 17
"Always True to You in My Fashion" 156
"Amaryllis" 9
"America" 179
"The American Dream" 271
"Amour" 303
"Anagram" 344
"And I Am All Alone" 63
"And I Am Telling You I'm Not Going" 246–7
"And the Money Keeps Rolling In" 242
"And They're Off" 289–90
"And This Is My Beloved" 168
"Angels on Your Pillow" 253
"The Angelus" 13, 54
"Another Autumn" 164
"Another Hundred People" 214
"Another Life" 250, 329
"Another Little Girl" 57
"Another National Anthem" 272
"Another Op'nin', Another Show" 156
"Another Suitcase in Another Hall" 242
"Another Time, Another Place" 191
"Another Winter in a Summer Town" 311
"Any Dream Will Do" 233
"Any Old Place with You" 69
"Any Place I Hang My Hat Is Home" 147
"Any Time's Kissing Time" 66
"Anyone Can Whistle" 196, 348
"Anything But Lonely" 268
"Anything Can Happen" 314
"Anything Can Happen in New York" 153
"Anything for Him" 276
"Anything Goes" 115
"Anything You Can Do" 147
"Applause" 214
"The Apple Doesn't Fall Very Far" 253
"April in Paris" 110
"April Showers" 76–7
"April Snow" 144
"Aquarius" 207
"Are You Havin' Any Fun?" 129
"Army and Navy" 134
"Around the World" 311
"Art" 303
"Arthur in the Afternoon" 236
"Artificial Flowers" 189

Song Index

"As If We Never Said Goodbye" 279–80
"As Long As He Needs Me" 193
"As Time Goes By" 105–7
"As We Stumble Along" 311
"Ashville" 333
"Astonishing" 309
"At Long Last Love" 126
"At My Age" 253
"At the Glen" 309
"At the Red Rose Cotillion" 156
"At the Roxy Music Hall" 123
"At Ze Naughty Folies Bergere" 15
"Auf Wiedersehn" 59
"August Winds" 331
"Auld Lang Syne" 32
"Autumn" 285
"Autumn in New York" 115
"Away from You" 230
"A–Weaving" 250

"Babes in Arms" 120
"Babette" 236
"Baby, Dream Your Dream" 202
"Baby, Talk to Me" 185
"Back to Before" 287
"Backwoods Barbie" 319
"Bad Bad News" 319
"Bad Cinderella" 347
"Bali Hai" 156
"The Ballad of Booth" 272
"The Ballad of Johnny Blood" 337
"The Ballad of Sweeney Todd" 239
"Ballad of Uncle Sam" 126
"Baltimore Buzz" 75
"Bambalina" 79–80
"Barcelona" 214
"Bare" 306
"Barnum and Bailey Rag" 57
"Barrett's Song" 285
"The Baseball Game" 272
"Baubles, Bangles and Beads" 168
"Be a Lion" 227, 348
"Be a Performer" 193
"Be a Santa" 191
"Be Good or Be Gone" 247
"Be Italian" 247
"Be Kind to Your Parents" 170
"Be My Little Baby Bumble Bee" 48–9
"Be on Your Own" 247
"Be the Hero" 329
"The Beast in You" 182
"A Beat Behind" 276
"Beautiful" 253, 293, 341
"Beautiful Bright Blue Sky" 297
"Beauty in the World" 335

"The Beauty Is" 309
"Beauty School Dropout" 222
"Beauty Within" 266
"Because" 107
"Because You're You" 35
"Bedelia" 28
"Beethoven Day" 290
"Before I Gaze at You Again" 188, 348
"Before I Go" 343–4
"Before I Kiss the World Goodbye" 196
"Before the Parade Passes By" 196
"Begin the Beguine" 116–18
"Being Alive" 214
"Being Good" 204
"Being Mrs. Banks" 314
"Believe in Yourself" 227
"The Belle of New York" 15
"Belly Up to the Bar, Boys" 189
"Beneath the Skies" 9
"Bend and Snap" 314
"Bess, You Is My Woman Now" 118
"The Best in the World" 242
"The Best of All Possible Worlds" 175, 224
"The Best of Times" 253
"The Best Thing of All" 158
"The Best Thing That Ever Has Happened" 319
"The Best Things in Life Are Free" 95
"Better" 297, 344
"The Better Man Won" 306
"Bewitched (Bothered and Bewildered)" 131–3
"The Bicycle Song" 196
"Bidin' My Time" 104
"Big Ass Rock" 297
"The Big Beat" 224
"Big Bright Beautiful World" 319
"Big D" 173
"The Bilbao Song" 233
"Bill" 95
"Bird Upon the Tree" 182
"Birds of Paradise" 264
"The Birth of the Blues" 89
"The Bitch of Living" 314
"Black and Blue" 100–1
"Black Bottom" 89
"Blame It on the Summer Night" 261
"Blood in the Water" 314
"Blow, Gabriel, Blow" 115
"Blue Danube Blues" 78
"The Blue Room" 89
"Blue Skies" 92
"Body and Soul" 104
"Bongo on the Congo" 83
"Book Report" 205
"Born to Entertain" 274
"Bosom Buddies" 202

Song Index

"Boston Beguine" 164
"The Bowery" 1, 3
"A Bowler Hat" 230
"Boy, Do We Need It Now" 250
"The Boy Friend" 170
"The Boy from …" 202
"The Boy Guessed Right" 17
"A Boy Like That/I Have a Love" 179
"The Boys of Summer" 255
"The Brain" 317
"Brand New You" 319
"Brave Enough for Love" 296
"Breeze Off the River" 297
"Bring All the Boys Back Home" 219
"Bring Him Home" 261
"Bring It On!" 327
"Broadway Baby" 216
"Brother, Can You Spare a Dime?" 110
"Brotherhood of Man" 191
"Brown October Ale" 1, 3
"Brush Up Your Shakespeare" 156
"Buckle Down, Winsocki" 136
"Budweiser's a Friend of Mine" 38
"The Bully Song" 11
"The Bus to Amarillo" 239
"A Bushel and a Peck" 161
"Bustopher Jones" 250
"But Alive" 214
"But Not for Me" 104
"The Butterfly" 47
"Button Up Your Overcoat" 96
"By Jeeves" 300
"By My Side" 216
"By Myself" 123
"By the Mississinewah" 139
"By the Saskatchewan" 47
"Bye and Bye" 89
"Bye Bye, Baby" 158

"Cabaret" 203–4, 276
"Cabin in the Sky" 133
"Cadillac Car" 247
"California, Here I Come" 76, 78
"The Call" 282
"Call Me Savage" 196
"Camelot" 188
"Can-Can" 166
"Can This Be Love?" 104
"Can't Help Lovin' dat Man" 95
"Can't Stop the Music" 302
"Can't We Be Friends?" 96, 98
"Can't You Hear Our Country Calling?" 61, 63
"Carolina in the Morning" 79–80
"The Casino Girl" 19
"Cast of Thousands" 261

"Castle of Dreams" 72
"Celebration" 211
"Cell Block Tango" 230
"A Certain Girl" 208
"C'est Magnifique" 166
"Chain of Love" 219
"Change" 290
"Changing My Major" 329
"Charleston" 81–3
"Charming" 327
"Cheering for Me Now" 347
"Children and Art" 253
"Children of the Heavenly King" 288
"Children of the Wind" 261
"Chimes" 288
"Chin Chin Chinaman" 13
"Chinatown, My Chinatown" 47
"Chloe" 66
"Choo Choo Honeymoon" 211
"The Church Around the Corner" 75
"Circle of Life" 287
"City Lights" 236
"Civilization" 151, 153
"Clap Yo' Hands" 92
"Class" 230
"Cleopatterer" 66
"Climb Ev'ry Mountain" 184
"Close as Pages in a Book" 144
"Close Every Door to Me" 233
"The Cobbler's Song" 66
"Cocoanut Sweet" 179
"Coffee in a Cardboard Cup" 216
"Coffee Shop Nights" 314
"Colorado Love Call" 185
"Color and Light" 253
"The Color of Your Eyes" 333
"Colored Lights" 253
"The Colors of My Life" 242
"Come A-Wandering with Me" 191
"Come Back" 327
"Come Back to Me" 202
"Come Buy, Come Buy" 258
"Come Down, Ma Evenin' Star" 25–6
"Come Follow the Band" 242
"Come On in from the Outside" 306
"Come Rain or Come Shine" 147
"Come to Me, Bend to Me" 150
"Come to My Garden" 271
"Come to the Ball" 49
"Come Up to My Place" 144
"Comedy Tonight" 190–1
"Commencing in Chattanooga" 321
"Company" 214
"Composer Tango" 242
"Coney Island Boat" 168

Song Index

"Conga!" 166
"Consider Yourself" 193
"Cool" 179
"Corner of the Sky" 222
"Cotton Blossom" 94
"Could I Leave You?" 216
"Could You Use Me?" 104
"Count Your Blessings" 141
"The Country's in the Very Best of Hands" 176
"Cowgirls" 282
"The Cradle Will Rock" 123
"Crazy Rhythm" 95
"The Crickets Are Calling" 66
"Crinoline Days" 80
"Cross Your Heart" 92
"Cry the Beloved Country" 158
"Cryin' in the Rain" 314
"Cupid and I" 13
"Cuddle Up a Little Closer, Lovey Mine" 39, 41
"Cupid, Tell Me Why" 49
"A Cup of Coffee, a Sandwich and You" 89

"Daffodils" 329
"Dames at Sea" 211
"Dance a Little Closer" 250
"Dance with You" 339
"Dancing in the Dark" 107
"Darktown Is Out Tonight" 17
"Darn That Dream" 129
"Day By Day" 216
"Days and Days" 329
"Dear Friend" 193
"Dear Love" 199
"Dear Old Syracuse" 126
"Dear One" 276
"Deep in My Heart, Dear" 86
"Defying Gravity" 305, 306
"Democracy" 341
"The Desert Song" 92
"Diamonds Are a Girl's Best Friend" 157-8
"Diamonds Are Forever" 255
"Diary of a Homecoming Queen" 247
"Diga, Diga, Doo" 95
"Dime a Dozen" 250
"Dinah" 17, 83
"Dirt" 300
"Dis-Donc" 189
"Disneyland" 261
"Diva!" 265-6
"Dividing Day" 308
"Dixie Moon" 86
"Do Do Do" 92
"Do I Hear a Waltz?" 199
"Do It Again" 78
"Do Re Mi" 184-5

"Do You Hear the People Sing?" 261
"Do You Know What It's Like?" 303
"Doin' the New Low Down" 95
"Doin' What Comes Natur'lly" 147
"Dolly" 75
"Donny Didn't, Donny Did" 47
"Don't Be the Bunny" 297
"Don't Bother Me, I Can't Cope" 222
"Don't Cry, Bo-Peep" 28
"Don't Cry for Me Argentina" 240-1
"Don't Ever Leave Me" 101
"Don't Ever Stop Saying I Love You" 317
"Don't Fall for the Lights" 266
"Don't Know Where You Leave Off" 300
"Don't Let It Get You Down" 133
"Don't Look Now" 300
"Don't Marry Me" 182
"Don't Quit While You're Ahead" 257-8
"Don't Rain on My Parade" 196
"Don't Take Much" 285
"Don't Turn My Picture to the Wall" 52
"Don't Worry Darling" 255
"Door of Her Dreams" 86
"Doors" 269
"Down By the Erie" 57
"Down in the Depths" 120
"Down with Love" 123
"Dream Babies" 214
"Dreamless Rest" 15
"Drift Away" 311
"Drifting Along with the Tide" 78
"Drinking Song" 86
"Drop That Name" 176
"Drums in My Heart" 107
"Duet for One" 230
"Dulcinea" 202
"Dust and Ashes" 327
"D'ye Love Me?" 89

"Each Tomorrow Morning" 211
"Eadie was a Lady" 110
"The Eagle and Me" 144
"Ease on Down the Road" 227
"Easter Parade" 111, 113
"Easy Street" 233
"Easy Terms" 276
"Easy to Be Hard" 208
"The Echo Waltz" 211
"Edelweiss" 185
"El Capitan March" 10-11, 178
"El Capitan's Song" 10-11
"Elaborate Lives" 293
"Electricity" 318-19
"Embraceable You" 104
"Emmaline" 17

Song Index

"Empty Chairs at Empty Tables" 261
"Empty Pockets Filled with Love" 193
"The Enchanted Train" 83
"Endless Night" 287
"Epiphany" 238
"Everlasting" 333
"Every Day a Little Death" 222
"Every Day Is Ladies' Day to Me" 35
"Every Little Movement" 47
"Every Story Is a Love Story" 293
"Every Street's a Boulevard in Old New York" 166
"Everybody Calls Me By My Name" 247
"Everybody Coming Together" 347
"Everybody Dance" 285
"Everybody Has the Right" 272
"Everybody Is Awfully Good to Me" 24
"Everybody Ought to Have a Maid" 191
"Everybody Say Yeah" 327
"Everybody Step" 76, 78
"Everybody's a Little Bit Racist" 303
"Everybody's Doing It" 229
"Everybody's Got a Home But Me" 173
"Everybody's Got a Right to Be Wrong" 202
"Everything About You" 335
"Everything Changes" 332–3
"Everything Has Changed" 253
"Everything Taboo" 306
"Everything's All Right" 219
"Everything's Coming Up Roses" 182
"Everything's Golden" 333
"Ev'ry Time We Say Goodbye" 144
"Ev'rything I've Got Belongs to You)" 135–6
"Exactly Like You" 101
"Exile in Gayville" 341
"Expressing Yourself" 319

"F.D.R. Jones" 126
"Fabulous Feet" 253
"Face on a Dime" 147
"Falling in Love with Love" 126
"Falling Out of Love Can Be Fun" 158
"Fancy Forgetting" 170
"Fanny" 170
"Far from the Home I Love" 199
"Far Too Late" 347
"Faraway Boy" 185
"Fascinating Rhythm" 86
"Father to Son" 245
"Fatherhood Blues" 253
"Fathers and Sons" 236
"Favorite Son" 272
"Fearless" 337
"Feeling Good" 199
"Feeling I'm Falling" 96, 98
"Feelings You've Got to Hide" 288

"The Fellow That Played the Drum" 7
"Fifty Percent" 239
"Find Me a Primitive Man" 101
"Fine and Dandy" 104
"Finishing the Hat" 253
"The First Man You Remember" 268
"First Thing Monday Morning" 214
"First You Dream" 285
"Flag of My Country" 61
"Flash Bang Wallop" 199
"Flings" 176
"Flotsam" 303
"Fly Away" 309
"Fly By Night" 331
"Flying Over Sunset" 344
"Follow Your Heart" 297
"Foolish Heart" 141
"For Good" 306
"Forever Yours" 269
"Forget About the Boy" 299
"Forty-five Minutes from Broadway" 33
"Four Jews in a Room Bitching" 244
"Four Little Angels of Peace" 123
"Four Strikes Against Me" 253
"Frank Mills" 208
"Franklin Shepard, Inc." 247
"Freddy, My Love" 222
"Freedom Is Coming Tomorrow" 264
"Freeze Your Brain" 329
"Friendship" 129
"Fugue for Tinhorns" 161
"Full Moon Lullaby/Shine" 339
"Fun" 282
"Fun to Be Fooled" 115
"Funny Face" 95

"The Gaby Glide" 49
"A Game of Poker" 185
"The Games I Play" 245
"Gee, Officer Krupke" 179
"The Gentleman Is a Dope" 153
"The Geshrunken Meshuggena Rag" 280
"Get Happy" 101
"Get Me to the Church on Time" 173
"Get Out of Town" 126
"Getting Married Today" 224
"Getting to Know You" 161
"Giannina Mia" 52
"Giants in the Sky" 264
"A Gift for Living Well" 311
"Gimme Gimme" 299
"Gimme Love" 276
"The Girl Friend" 89
"The Girl on the Magazine Cover" 58
"The Girl That I Marry" 147

Song Index

"The Girl with the Brogue" 44
"The Girl with the Glass" 335
"Give a Little, Get a Little" 164
"Give a Man Enough Rope" 272
"Give Me Your Love" 274
"Give My Regards to Broadway" 29–30
"Glad to Be Unhappy" 118
"The Glamorous Life" 222
"Glitter and Be Gay" 176
"The Glow-Worm" 36, 38
"Go Back Home" 320–1
"Go Visit Your Grandmother" 216
"God's Country" 123
"The Gods on Tap" 261
"Going Up" 66
"Golden Days" 86
"Goldenhair" 295
"Gonna Build a Mountain" 192, 193
"Gonna Pass Me a Law" 306
"Good Morning, Dearie" 78
"Good Morning Starshine" 208
"Good News" 95
"Good Thing Going" 247
"Good Thing I Learned to Dance" 253
"Good to Be Alive" 264
"Goodbye, Becky Cohen" 47
"Goodbye Broadway, Hello France" 61, 63
"Goodbye Girls, I'm Through" 57
"Goodbye, Sweet Old Manhattan Isle" 33
"Goodnight, My Someone" 179
"Grand Old Ivy" 191
"Grant Avenue" 182
"The Grass Is Always Greener" 245
"A Great Big Girl Like Me" 30
"Great Big Stuff" 309
"Great Day" 101
"The Greatest Friend" 306
"Green Finch and Linnet Bird" 239
"Green-Up Time" 156
"Grizabella" 250
"Growing Up Catholic" 258
"Gus: the Theatre Cat" 250
"Guys and Dolls" 161
"Gypsy Love Song" 17

"Hair" 208
"Half a Moment" 280, 300
"Half a Moon" 92
"Half a Sixpence" 199
"Hallelujah" 92
"Happiness" 205, 278, 329
"The Happy Time" 208
"Hard Candy Christmas" 239
"Hard Times to Come Again No More" 344
"Hard to Be Diva!" 265–6

"Hard to Say Goodbye" 285
"Harlem on My Mind" 113
"Harrigan" 36, 38
"Has Anyone Here Seen Kelly?" 42–3
"Haunted Heart" 153
"Have Another Drink" 214
"Have I Told You Lately?" 191
"Have You Met Miss Jones?" 123
"He" 303
"He Always Comes Home to Me" 250
"He and She" 135
"He Goes to Church on Sunday" 35
"He Had Refinement" 161
"He Hasn't a Thing But Me" 118
"He Loves and She Loves" 95
"He Plays the Violin" 211
"Hear My Song" 282
"Heart" 170
"Heart and Music" 290
"Heart of Stone" 344
"Heat Wave" 111, 113
"The Heather on the Hill" 149, 150
"Heaven in My Arms" 129
"Heaven on Earth" 261
"Heaven Will Protect the Working Girl" 42, 44
"The Heidelberg Stein Song" 26
"He'll Never Know" 303
"Hello!" 323
"Hello Again" 278
"Hello, Dolly!" 195, 196
"Hello, Frisco, Hello" 59
"Hello Young Lovers" 161
"Helpless" 331
"Henchmen Are Forgotten" 288
"Her Face" 188
"Here I'll Stay" 156
"Here in My Arms" 88
"Here's Love" 196
"Here's That Rainy Day" 167, 168
"Here's to Your Illusions" 161
"Hernando's Hideaway" 168
"Herod's Song" 219
"Hey, Big Spender" 202
"Hey, Good-Lookin'" 139
"Hey, Look Me Over" 189
"Hey, Love" 193
"Hey, There" 168
"Hey There, Good Times" 233
"High Adventure" 329
"High and Low" 107
"High Flying Adored" 242
"High Jerry, Ho!" 5
"Highway 57" 247
"Hi-Ko, Hi-Ko" 30
"His Is the Only Music That Makes Me Dance"

Song Index

"Hold 'Em, Joe" 168
"Hold Me in Your Heart" 327
"Hold Me in Your Loving Arms" 59
"Holding to the Ground" 272
"Home" 216, 227
"Honey in the Honeycomb" 133
"The Honeymoon Is Over" 205
"Hooray for Captain Spaulding" 96, 98
"Hosanna" 219
"The Hostess with the Mostes'" 161
"Hot Tamales" 6–7
"Hot Toxic Love" 319
"A Houseboat on the Harlem" 86
"How Actresses Are Made" 19
"How Are Things in Glocca Morra?" 150
"How Do You Speak to an Angel?" 166
"How High the Moon" 129
"How Long Has This Been Going On?" 95
"How Lucky You Are" 296
"How Things Change" 266
"How'd You Like to Spoon with Me?" 31, 33
"How'm I Doing?" 255
"How's Chances?" 113
"Hugette's Waltz" 89
"Hulla-Baloo-Balay" 205
"Human Again" 278
"A Hundred Million Miracles" 182
"Hundreds of Girls" 227
"Hurrah for Baffin's Bay" 26
"Hurry! It's Lovely Up Here" 202
"A Hymn to Him" 173, 188

"I Ain't Down Yet" 189
"I Am Changing" 247
"I Am Easily Assimilated" 176
"I Am Here" 335
"I Am It" 233
"I Am Loved" 161
"I Am Only Human After All" 96, 98
"I Am What I Am" 252
"I Believe" 322–3
"I Believe in You" 191, 323
"I Believe My Heart" 311
"I Cain't Say No" 139
"I Can Cook, Too" 144
"I Can Do That" 227
"I Can Dream, Can't I?" 121, 123
"I Can Play This Part" 276
"I Can See It" 185
"I Can Write Books" 303
"I Cannot Hear the City" 299
"I Can't Do the Sum" 28
"I Can't Get Started with You" 118
"I Can't Give You Anything But Love" 95
"I Could Be Happy with You" 170

"I Could Get Married Today" 164
"I Could Have Danced All Night" 173
"I Could Write a Book" 133
"I Could've Gone to Nashville" 258
"I Did It for Defense" 139
"I Didn't Know What Time It Was" 129
"I Do Not Know a Day I Did Not Love You" 216
"I, Don Quixote" 202
"I Don't Care" 31, 33
"I Don't Know How to Love Him" 218
"I Don't Need Your Love" 344
"I Don't Remember Christmas" 233
"I Don't Remember You" 208
"I Don't Want to Know" 211
"I Dreamed a Dream" 261
"I Enjoy Being a Girl" 180–1
"I Feel Pretty" 179
"I Fought Every Step of the Way" 164
"I Found a Million Dollar Baby" 104
"I Get a Kick Out of You" 114–5
"I Get Embarrassed" 185
"I Got a Marble and a Star" 150
"I Got Lost in His Arms" 147
"I Got Love" 214
"I Got Lucky in the Rain" 156
"I Got Rhythm" 103–4
"I Got the Sun in the Morning" 147
"I Gotta Right to Sing the Blues" 110
"I Guess I'll Have to Change My Plan" 96, 98
"I Had a Vision" 333
"I Had Myself a True Love" 147
"I Happen to Like New York" 104
"I Hate Musicals" 274
"I Have Dreamed" 161
"I Just Can't Make My Eyes Behave" 35
"I Know Him So Well" 264
"I Know It's Today" 319
"I Know Now" 250
"I Know Where I've Been" 303
"I Know Your Kind" 182
"I Left My Heart at the Stage Door Canteen" 139
"I Like Ike" 161
"I Like the Likes of You" 113
"I Love a Film Cliché" 242
"I Love a Piano" 58–9
"I Love Betsy" 331
"I Love Louisa" 107
"I Love Music" 347
"I Love My Wife" 205
"I Love Paris" 166
"I Love the Name of Mary" 47
"I Love Thee, I Adore Thee" 12–13
"I Love to Dance" 239
"I Love to Travel" 309
"I Love You" 141

"I Love You So (The Merry Widow Waltz)" 36–7
"The I Love You Song" 309
"I Loved You Once in Silence" 188
"I Loves You, Porgy" 118
"I Married an Angel" 123
"I May Be Gone a Long Long Time" 61, 63
"I Miss the Mountains" 316
"I Miss the Music" 314
"I Need to Be in Love" 300
"I Never Has Seen Snow" 170
"I Never Know When to Say When" 182
"I Never Want to Go Home Again" 224
"I Never Wanted to Love You" 245
"I Read" 278
"I Say It's Spinach" 107
"I See Your Face Before Me" 123
"I Still Believe in Love" 239
"I Still Get Jealous" 153
"I Still See Elisa" 164
"I Talk to the Trees" 162, 164
"I Think We Got Love" 303
"I, To the World" 247
"I Turned the Corner" 299
"I Wanna Be a Producer" 297
"I Wanna Be Loved By You" 96–7
"I Wanna Get Married" 141
"I Want a Daddy Who Will Rock Me to Sleep" 72
"I Want It All" 253
"I Want the Good Times Back" 317
"I Want to Be a Lidy" 24
"I Want to Be a Military Man" 22
"I Want to Be a Popular Millionaire" 33
"I Want to Be Happy" 88
"I Want to Be with You" 199
"I Want to See a Minstrel Show" 70, 72
"I Want to Walk to San Francisco" 214
"I Want What I Want When I Want It" 33
"I Was a Florodora Baby" 75
"I Was Born in Virginia" 33
"I Will Love You" 293
"I Wish Him a Polite Good-Day" 13
"I Wish I Really Weren't, But I Am" 19
"I Wish I Were in Love Again" 120, 135
"I Wish It So" 182
"I Wonder What's the Matter with My Eyes" 41
"I Won't Grow Up" 170
"I Won't Let You Get Away" 224
"I Won't Send Roses" 227, 348
"Icarus" 288
"Ice Cream" 193
"I'd Do Anything for You" 193
"I'd Give It All for You" 282
"I'd Rather Watch You" 317
"Ida, Sweet as Apple Cider" 72
"If a Wish Could Make It So" 75

"If Ever I Would Leave You" 187–8
"If He Walked Into My Life Today" 202
"If I Can't Love Her" 278
"If I Could Tell Her" 335
"If I Had a Million Dollars" 214
"If I Had My Druthers" 176
"If I Loved You" 142–4
"If I Ruled the World" 202
"If I Were a Bell" 161
"If I Were a Rich Man" 199
"If Love Were All" 101
"If Mamma Was Married" 182
"If Only I'd Known" 344
"If the Rain's Got to Fall" 199
"If the World Should End" 325
"If There Is Someone Lovelier Than You" 115
"If They Could See Me Now" 202
"If This Isn't Love" 150
"If You Could See Her" 204
"If You Hadn't, but You Did" 164
"If Your Father Was Here" 337
"If Your Shoes Don't Shine" 293
"If You're in Love You'll Waltz" 92
"I'll Always Remember the Song" 264
"I'll Be Hard to Handle" 113
"I'll Be Here Tomorrow" 239
"I'll Be Seeing You" 121–3
"I'll Be Somewhere in France" 61, 63
"I'll Build a Stairway to Paradise" 79–80
"I'll Buy You a Star" 161
"I'll Cover You" 262
"I'll Follow My Secret Heart" 115
"I'll Go Home with Bonnie Jean" 150
"I'll Hit a New High" 104
"I'll Know" 161
"I'll Never Be Jealous Again" 168
"I'll Never Fall in Love Again" 210
"I'll Never Say No" 189
"I'll See You Again" 101
"I'm a Brass Band" 202
"I'm a Dumbell" 76, 78
"I'm a Jonah Man" 25–6
"I'm a Respectable Working Girl" 22
"I'm a Stranger Here Myself" 141
"I'm a Vamp from East Broadway" 75
"I'm Alive" 317
"I'm All Alone" 309
"I'm Always Chasing Rainbows" 65–6, 167
"I'm an Ordinary Man" 173
"I'm Breaking Down" 273–4
"I'm Calm" 191
"I'm Craving for That Kind of Love" 75
"I'm Falling in Love with Someone" 46
"I'm Flying" 170
"I'm Forever Blowing Bubbles" 72

Song Index

"I'm Getting Tired So I Can Sleep" 139
"I'm Glad to See You Got What You Want" 211
"I'm Going Back" 176
"I'm Gonna Wash That Man Right Out of My Hair" 156
"I'm Here" 311
"I'm in Love with Miss Logan" 164
"I'm Just Wild About Harry" 74–5
"I'm Not at All in Love" 168
"I'm Not Saying a Word" 276
"I'm Not That Girl" 306
"I'm Not That Guy" 321
"I'm Not That Smart" 309
"I'm on the Water Wagon Now" 28
"I'm Still Here" 216
"I'm Using My Bible for a Roadmap" 272
"Imagining You" 264
"The Impossible Dream" 201
"In a Little While" 185
"In a Simple Way I Love You" 236
"In a World Like This" 335
"In Arcady" 57
"In Buddy's Eyes" 216
"In Every Age" 285
"In My Own Lifetime" 216
"In Old New York" 34, 35
"In Some Little World" 208
"In Some Other Life" 278
"In the Good Old Summer Time" 25–6
"In the Heart of the Dark" 129
"In the Heights" 314
"In This Wide, Wide World" 223–4
"Independently Owned" 347
"Indian Love Call" 84–5, 118
"Inside Out" 329
"Into the Fire" 288
"Invisible" 323
"Iris" 264
"The Irish Have a Great Day To-Night" 63
"Is That Remarkable?" 282
"Is There Anything Better Than Dancing?" 274
"Isn't It a Pity?" 110
"Isn't It Great to Be Married" 60
"Isle of d'Amour" 54
"The Isle of Our Dreams" 35
"It Ain't Necessarily So" 118
"It All Fades Away" 329
"It Doesn't Take a Genius" 311
"It Is What It Is" 337
"It Just Takes Time" 341
"It Never Entered My Mind" 129
"It Never Was You" 126
"It Only Takes a Moment" 196
"It Shoulda Been You" 331
"It Sucks to Be Me" 303
"It Would Have Been Wonderful" 278

"Italian Street Song" 46
"It's a Hard-Knock Life" 233
"It's a Long Way to Tipperary" 61
"It's a Lovely Day Today" 160–1
"It's a Lovely Day Tomorrow" 129
"It's a Perfect Relationship" 176
"It's All Right with Me" 165–6
"It's Always Love" 219
"It's an Art" 236
"It's Delightful to Be Married" 35
"It's De-Lovely" 120
"It's Fun to Be Free" 139
"It's Good to Be Alive" 176
"It's Got to Be Love" 118
"It's Never Too Late to Fall in Love" 170
"It's Not Where You Start" 222
"It's Possible" 296
"It's the Going Home Together" 168
"It's You Who Makes Me Young" 211
"It's Your Wedding Day" 311
"I've a Shooting Box in Scotland" 60
"I've Been Thinking" 331
"I've Decided to Marry You" 329
"I've 'er Portrait Nex' to My 'eart" 15
"I've Got a Crush on You" 96, 98
"I've Got Five Dollars" 104
"I've Got My Captain Working for Me Now" 70, 72
"I've Got Rings on My Fingers" 39, 41
"I've Got to Be Me" 208
"I've Got Your Number" 193
"I've Gotta Crow" 170
"I've Grown Accustomed to Her Face" 173
"I've Never Been in Love Before" 161
"I've Still Got My Health" 133
"I've Told Ev'ry Little Star" 110
"Jasmine Lane" 86
"Jealousy Duet" 168
"Jeanine with the Light Brown Hair" 321
"Jerry Likes My Corn" 311
"The Jet Song" 179

"Joey, Joey, Joey" 173
"Johanna" 239
"Johnny One-Note" 120
"Johnny's Song" 120
"Jubilation T. Cornpone" 176
"June Is Bustin' Out All Over" 144
"Just a Housewife" 236
"Just a Little Joint with a Juke Box" 136
"Just Around the Corner" 321
"Just Don't Make No Sense" 219
"Just Go to the Movies" 242
"Just in Time" 176
"Just One of Those Things" 118
"Just Pretend" 344

"Ka-lu-a" 78
"Kansas City" 139
"Katie Went to Haiti" 129
"Keep It Gay" 297
"Keep Off the Grass" 24
"Keep on Standing" 329
"Keep Smiling at Trouble" 86
"Kelly from the Isle of Man" 43
"Keys" 314
"Kickin' the Clouds Away" 86
"The Kid Inside" 247
"Kids" 185
"King of New York" 325
"The Kinkajou" 92
"Kiss Me Again" 33
"Kiss of the Spider Woman" 276
"The Kiss Waltz" 47
"Knowing When to Leave" 210

"The Ladies Who Lunch" 213–14
"Ladies Who Sing with the Band" 141
"The Lady Is a Tramp" 120
"Lady of the Evening" 80
"Lady's Maid" 285
"The Lambeth Walk" 259–60
"The Land of Let's Pretend" 57
"Land of My Own Romance" 49
"The Land Where the Good Songs Go" 66
"Larger Than Life" 276
"Last Night of the World" 271
"The Last One You'd Expect" 329
"The Last Part of Every Party" 72
"The Last Real Record Store on Earth" 314
"The Last Round-Up" 113
"The Last Ship" 331
"Laughing Matters" 285
"Lazy Afternoon" 168
"The Leader of Vanity Fair" 26
"Leaning on a Lamppost" 261
"A Leap from the Earth to the Sky" 7
"Learn to Be Lonely" 250
"Leave It to Jane" 66
"Leave It to the Girls" 278
"Leave the World Behind" 285
"Leaving's Not the Only Way to Go" 255
"Left All Alone Again Blues" 72
"The Legend of the Frogs" 11
"Let It Burn" 344
"Let Me Come In" 214
"Let Me Entertain You" 182
"Let the Sunshine In" 208
"Let's All Be Americans Now" 61
"Let's Be Bad" 347
"Let's Be Buddies" 133
"Let's Do It" 96, 98, 230
"Let's Fly Away" 104

"Let's Go Back to the Waltz" 193
"Let's Have Another Cup of Coffee" 107
"Let's Not Talk About Love" 136
"Let's See What Happens" 208
"Let's Take a Walk Around the Block" 115
"Let's Take an Old-Fashioned Walk" 158
"Let's Walk" 309
"Letters I Write All Day" 28
"Lida Rose/Will I Ever Tell You?" 179
"Life Is" 211
"Life Is Happiness Indeed" 224
"Life Is Just a Bowl of Cherries" 107
"The Life of the Party" 208
"Life Story" 266
"Life Takes You By Surprise" 337
"The Life That You Wished For" 327
"Life Upon the Wicked Stage" 95
"Life's a Funny Proposition After All" 30
"A Light in the Dark" 317
"Light in the Loafers" 285
"The Light in the Piazza" 309
"Light My Candle" 282
"Like It Was" 247
"Lily's Eyes" 270–1
"Limehouse Blues" 83
"Lion Tamer" 224
"Lionnet" 158
"Listen to the Music" 278
"Listen to Your Heart" 317
"A Little Bit in Love" 166
"A Little Bit Less Than" 331
"A Little Bit of String" 13
"A Little Brains—A Little Talent" 170
"Little Girl Blue" 118
"Little Girl from Little Rock" 158
"Little Girls, Goodbye" 72
"The Little Gypsy Maid" 24
"Little Hands" 202
"Little Hero" 266
"A Little Joy" 344
"Little Old New York" 189
"A Little Priest" 237–9
"Little Rag Doll" 205
"Little Shop of Horrors" 250
"A Little Tin Box" 185
"The Little White House" 92
"Live for Today" 69
"Live in Living Color" 323
"The Living and the Dead" 293
"Living in the Shadows" 282
"Liza" 101
"Lonely Canary" 250
"Lonely Girl" 293
"Lonely House" 150
"Lonely Town" 144
"Lonesome on the Road" 236

Song Index

"Long Before I Knew You" 176
"Long, Lean, Lanky Letty" 57
"Long Live the King" 194
"Long Past Sunset" 253
"Look for a Sky of Blue" 185
"Look for the Silver Lining" 73, 75
"Look Over There" 253
"Look to the Rainbow" 150
"Look What Happened to Mabel" 227
"Look Who's Alone Now" 274
"Look Who's Dancing" 161
"Look Who's Evil Now" 314
"Look Who's in Love" 182
"Looking for Someone" 202
"Losing My Mind" 216
"Lost and Found" 269
"The Lost Barbershop Chord" 92
"Lost in the Stars" 158
"A Lot of Livin' to Do" 185
"Lot's Wife" 306
"Louisiana Hayride" 110
"Louisiana Purchase" 129
"Love and Love Alone" 331
"Love Can't Happen" 268
"Love Changes Everything" 268
"Love, Don't Turn Away" 196
"Love for Sale" 89, 104
"Love Has Come from Lotus Land" 22
"Love Held Lightly" 185
"Love in My Heart" 38
"Love Is Always Lovely in the End" 311
"Love Is a Dancing Thing" 118
"Love Is in the Air" 191
"Love Is Like a Firefly" 52
"Love Is Sweeping the Country" 107
"Love-Line" 199
"Love, Look Away" 182
"Love, Love, Love" 205
"Love Makes Such Fools of Us All" 242
"Love Makes the World Go Round" 188
"Love Me or Leave Me" 96, 98
"The Love Nest" 75
"Love Stolen" 230
"Love to Me" 309
"Love Who You Love" 303
"Love Will Come and Find Me Again" 335
"Love Will Conquer All" 211
"Love Will Find a Way" 75
"Lovely" 191
"Lovin' Is a Lowdown Blues" 274
"Lover, Come Back to Me" 96, 98
"Lovers on Christmas Eve" 233
"Lovie Joe" 47
"Loving You" 278
"Luck Be a Lady" 161
"Luck of the Draw" 285

"Lucky Day" 89
"Lucky in Love" 95
"Lucky to Be Me" 144
"Lud's Wedding" 230
"The Lusty Month of May" 188

"Ma Belle" 95
"Ma Blushin' Rosie" 22
"Ma Tiger Lily" 19
"Macavity" 250
"Mack the Knife" 168
"Mad" 250
"Mad About the Boy" 126
"Mad Dogs and Englishmen" 107
"Magic Moment" 191
"Magic to Do" 222
"Maisie" 24
"Make Believe" 95
"Make It Another Old-Fashioned, Please" 133
"Make Our Garden Grow" 176
"Make Someone Happy" 189
"Makin' the Rounds" 242
"Makin' Whoopee" 96, 98
"Mama, a Rainbow" 214
"Mama Who Bore Me" 314
"Mama Will Provide" 269
"Mame" 202
"The Man I Used to Be" 173
"The Man in the Mirror" 303
"Man of La Mancha" 202
"Mandy" 67, 69
"Manhattan" 86
"Many a New Day" 139
"March of the Falsettos" 245
"March of the Musketeers" 95
"March of the Toys" 27–8, 178
"March of Time" 269
"Maria" 179
"Marian the Librarian" 179
"Marriage Type Love" 166
"Marianne" 239
"Married" 204
"A Married Man" 199
"Marry the Man Today" 161
"Marry with Me" 219
"Marvelous Party" 126
"Mary's a Grand Old Name" 33
"The Mascot of the Troop" 33
"Masquerade" 205, 264, 348
"Matchmaker, Matchmaker" 199
"Maxim's" 38
"Maybe" 92
"Me" 278
"Me and My Girl" 261
"Me and My Town" 196
"Me and the Sky" 335

"Measure the Valleys" 224
"Meeskite" 204
"Memories of You" 104
"Memory" 249–50
"Memory Song" 340–1
"Men" 224
"Merely Marvelous" 182
"Merrily We Roll Along" 247
"Merry Little Minuet" 168
"The Merry Miller" 9
"The Merry Widow Waltz" 36–7
"The Message of the Violet" 26
"Michael Furey" 293
"Michael in the Bathroom" 338–9
"The Middle Years" 208
"Milk and Honey" 191
"The Miller's Son" 222
"Mine" 113
"Miss Byrd" 266
"Miss Lucy" 13
"Miss Marmelstein" 191
"Mister and Mrs. Fitch" 110
"Moanin' Low" 96, 98
"Model Behavior" 323
"Molasses to Rum" 209, 211
"Molly O!" 3
"Momma, Look Sharp" 209, 210–11
"Mon Homme" 78
"The Money Rings Out Like Freedom" 214
"Money to Burn" 199
"Monkey in the Mango Tree" 179
"Monotonous" 164
"The Moon and Me" 321
"Moon Change" 306
"Moon in My Window" 199
"The Moon Shines on the Moonshine" 75
"Moonbeams" 35
"Moon-Faced, Starry-Eyed" 150
"Moonfall" 258
"Moonshine Lullaby" 147
"More Than Survive" 339
"More Than You Know" 99, 101
"Morning Glow" 222
"The Most Beautiful Girl in the World" 118
"Most Gentlemen Don't Like Love" 126
"The Most Happy Fella" 173
"Mother Machree" 16, 47, 50
"Mountain Greenery" 89
"Mountain High—Valley Low" 147
"The Mounties" 86
"Move On" 253
"Movie in My Mind" 271
"Moving Uptown" 293
"Mr. Cellophane" 229, 230
"Mr. Dooley" 24
"Mr. Gallagher and Mr. Shean" 80

"Mr. Wonderful" 173
"Much More" 185
"Muddy Water" 255
"The Mummies" 24
"The Museum Song" 242
"The Music and the Mirror" 227
"The Music of Home" 185
"The Music of My Soul" 321
"The Music of the Machine" 317
"Music of the Night" 263–4
"The Music Plays On" 344
"The Music Still Plays On" 290
"The Music That Makes Me Dance" 196
"The Music Went Out of My Life" 266
"The Musical Moon" 49
"Mutual Admiration Society" 176
"My Alamo Love" 28
"My Blanket and Me" 205
"My Body" 285
"My Cup Runneth Over" 204
"My Father Fights for Uncle Sam" 61
"My Favorite Things" 185
"My Favorite Year" 276
"My Funny Valentine" 119–20
"My Heart Belongs to Daddy" 124, 126
"My Heart Is So Full of You" 173
"My Heart Stood Still" 95
"My Hero" 44
"My Home Town" 196
"My Husband Makes Movies" 247
"My Irish Molly-O" 30
"My Lucky Star" 96, 98
"My Mammy" 66
"My Man" 78
"My Man's Gone Now" 118
"My Most Important Moments Go By" 214
"My New Philosophy" 290
"My Own Morning" 204
"My Own United States" 26
"My Paradise" 60
"My Romance" 118
"My San Domingo Maid" 28
"My Ship" 133
"My Shot" 330–1
"My Sort of Ex-Boyfriend" 258
"My Strongest Suit" 293
"My Sword and I" 95
"My White Knight" 179
"My Wild Irish Rose" 16–17
"My Wonderful Pain" 344

"Namely You" 176
"Nancy Brown" 23–4
"Natural High" 236
"Naughty" 327
"Neapolitan Love Song" 60

Song Index

"Near to You" 170
"'Neath the Southern Moon" 46
"Nellie Kelly, I Love You" 79–80
"Nesting Time in Flatbush" 63
"Never" 236
"Never Will I Marry" 185
"Never, Never Land" 170
"Neverland" 331
"A New Argentina" 242
"New Fangled Preacher Man" 214
"A New Life" 285
"New Music" 287
"New Sun in the Sky" 107
"New Ways to Dream" 280
"The New World" 282
"New York, New York" 144
"Next Best Thing to Love" 297
"The Next Ten Minutes" 300
"Next to Lovin'" 227
"Nice" 264
"Nickel Under the Foot" 123
"Night and Day" 108–9
"Night Letter" 219
"Night of My Nights" 168
"Night Song" 199
"The Night was Made for Love" 107
"96,000" 313
"No Boom Boom" 211
"No Friends" 347
"No Me Diga" 314
"No Moon" 285
"No More" 264, 325
"No No Nanette" 88
"No One Else" 327
"No One Has Ever Loved Me" 278
"No One Is Alone" 264
"No Other Love" 166
"No Song More Pleasing" 230
"No Strings" 191
"No Tears in Heaven" 272
"No Time at All" 222
"No Voice" 306
"Nobody" 229
"Nobody But You" 69
"Nobody Else But Me" 147
"Nobody Makes a Pass at Me" 123
"Nobody Steps on Kafritz" 208
"Nobody Tells Me How" 236
"Nobody Told Me" 191
"Nobody's Chasing Me" 161
"Nobody's Heart" 136
"Normandy" 185
"Not a Day Goes By" 247
"Not for the Life of Me" 299
"Not My Father's Son" 326–7

"Not on Your Nellie" 208
"Not While I'm Around" 239
"Not Yet" 66
"Nothin' for Nothin'" 158
"Nothing" 227
"Nothing Can Stop Me Now" 199
"Nothing Counts but Love" 255
"Nothing Is Too Wonderful to Be True" 309
"Nothing More to look Forward To" 191
"Nothing, Only Love" 239
"November Song" 219
"Now" 344
"Nowadays" 230
"Now You Know" 247

"Of V We Sing" 136
"Off the Record" 123
"Off to the Races" 258
"Oh, By Jingo" 72
"Oh, Diogenes" 126
"Oh, Happy We!" 176
"Oh! How I Hate to Get Up in the Morning" 67, 69
"Oh, Johnny, Oh, Johnny, Oh!" 63
"Oh, Lady Be Good" 86
"Oh Me! Oh My! Oh You!" 75
"Oh, Promise Me" 1–2
"Oh, Rapture Unrestrained" 7
"Oh! Sweet Mystery of Life," 85
"Oh, the Thinks You Can Think" 296
"Oh, to Be a Movie Star" 205
"Oh, What a Beautiful Mornin'" 138–9
"Oh, What a Circus!" 241
"Oh, You Beautiful Girl" 49
"Ohio" 166
"Ohio Afternoon" 264
"OK" 347
"Oklahoma" 139
"Ol' Man River" 93–5, 255, 321
"Old Before His Time" 6–7
"Old Deuteronomy" 250
"Old Devil Moon" 150
"An Old-Fashioned Cake Walk" 80
"An Old-Fashioned Love Story" 293
"An Old-Fashioned Wedding" 200, 202
"Old Folks at Home" 68, 321
"Old Friend" 235
"The Old Red Hills of Home" 290
"The Oldest Established" 161
"The Oldest Profession" 285
"Omar Sharif" 336–7
"On a Clear Day You Can See Forever" 202
"On a Desert Island with You" 95
"On a Sunday By the Sea" 153
"On My Own" 261
"On My Way" 285

"On the Steps of the Palace" 264
"On the Street Where You Live" 171–2
"On the Sunny Side of the Street" 101, 348
"On This Night of a Thousand Stars" 242
"On Your Toes" 118
"Once in a Blue Moon" 83
"Once in a Lifetime" 192, 193
"Once in Love with Amy" 156
"Once Upon a Time" 191
"Once You Lose Your Heart" 261
"One" 227
"One Alone" 92
"One Boy" 185
"One Day More" 261
"One Extraordinary Thing" 239
"The One Girl" 96, 98
"One Hundred Easy Ways" 166
"The One I Love" 278
"One Kiss" 96, 98
"One Last Bob" 274
"One More Walk Around the Garden" 239
"One Night in Bangkok" 264
"One Night Only" 247
"One of the Boys" 245
"One Perfect Moment" 327
"One Room" 216
"One Song Glory" 282
"One White Dress" 317
"One Word from You" 49
"Only a Heartbeat Away" 261
"Only a Rose" 89
"Only Love" 211
"Only with You" 247
"Only You" 261
"Open a New Window" 202
"Ordinary Guy" 303
"Origin of Love" 288
"The Other Hours" 300
"Our Children" 287
"Our Language of Love" 188
"Our Little World" 300
"Our Private World" 236
"Our Time" 247
"Out of Breath" 96, 98
"Out of My Dreams" 139
"Out of Your Head" 335
"Over Here" 224
"Over My Shoulder" 337
"Over the Rainbow" 106
"Over There" 32

"Pack Up Your Sins" 79–80
"Pack Up Your Troubles in Your Old Kit Bag" 61
"A Pal Like You" 63
"Pandemonium" 309

"Papa, Won't You Dance With Me?" 152–3
"A Parade in Town" 196
"A Paradise for Two" 69
"Paris Is Paris Again" 224
"Paris Loves Lovers" 170
"Parisian Pierrot" 83
"The Party's Over" 175
"Patterns" 269
"Peg o' My Heart" 53–4
"Pegasus" 288
"People" 194–5
"People Like Us" 293
"People Will Say We Are in Love" 139
"Perfect Strangers" 258
"The Petals of the Plum Tree" 22
"The Phantom of the Opera" 264
"The Pickers Are Comin'" 227
"The Picture in the Hall" 261
"The Picture of Happiness" 189
"A Picture of Me Without You" 118
"Pine Cones and Holly Berries" 196
"Pinky Panky Poo" 26
"The Pipes of Pan" 44
"Pirate Jenny" 168
"Play a Simple Melody" 57
"Please Hello" 230
"Poems" 230
"Politics and Poker" 185
"Poor Child" 293
"Poor Little Person" 208
"Poor Little Rich Girl" 89
"Popular" 306
"Pore Jud Is Daid" 139
"Practically Perfect" 314
"Pretty as a Picture" 54
"Pretty Funny" 327
"A Pretty Girl Is Like a Melody" 70–2
"Pretty Lady" 230
"Pretty Moon Over Macao" 314
"Pretty Women" 239
"The Price of Peace" 269
"Prima Donna" 264
"Private Property" 327
"Private Tommy Atkins" 8–9
"Privates on Parade" 269
"Prohibition Blues" 67, 69
"Promises, Promises" 210
"Proud of Your Boy" 329
"Purlie" 214
"Push Da Button" 311
"Push De Button" 179
"Push Dem Clouds Away" 3
"Push Me Along in Your Pushcart" 22
"Put a Curse on You" 219
"Put a Penny in the Slot" 5

Song Index

"Put on a Happy Face" 185
"Put on Your Sunday Clothes" 196
"Put You in Your Place" 341
"Put Your Arms Around Me, Honey" 47

"A Quiet Girl" 166
"A Quiet Thing" 199

"Race You to the Top of the Morning" 271
"Rackety Coo" 60
"Rags" 261
"Ragtime" 286
"Ragtime Temple Bells" 57
"The Rain in Spain" 173
"Raining in My Heart" 211
"Raise the Roof" 295
"Raise Your Voice" 323
"Ralphie to the Rescue" 327
"The Rangers' Song" 92
"Razzle Dazzle" 230
"The Real American Folk Song" 69
"Real Live Girl" 193
"Red Hot Chicago" 101
"Red Sails in the Sunset" 118
"Refresh" 341
"Remember?" 222
"Rental Cruelty" 266
"Repent" 236
"Respectability" 182
"Reuben and Cynthia" 1, 3
"Revolting Children" 327
"The Revolutionary Costume for Today" 311
"Rhode Island Is Famous for You" 153
"Ribbons Down My Back" 196
"Rickety Crickety" 75
"The Riddle Song" 282
"Ride Through the Night" 191
"Ride Out the Storm" 347
"Ridin' High" 120
"The Riff Song" 92
"Right as the Rain" 144
"A Ring Around the Moon" 300
"A Ring of Gold in Texas" 280
"Ring of Keys" 328–9
"A Ring to the Name of Rosie" 83
"Rio Rita" 92
"Rise n' Shine" 110
"River Deep—Mountain High" 302
"River in the Rain" 255
"The Road Ends Here" 280
"The Road to Paradise" 66
"The Road You Didn't Take" 216
"Rock-a-Bye Your Baby with a Dixie Melody" 66
"Romantic Notions" 264
"Romany Life" 17
"A Room in Bloomsbury" 170

"The Room Where It Happens" 331
"A Room with a View" 96, 98
"A Room without Windows" 196
"Rose, Lucky Rose" 49
"Rose-Marie" 86
"Rose of the World" 41
"Roses at the Station" 268
"Row, Row, Row" 52
"Rum Tum Tiddle" 49
"Rumpty Tumpty" 9
"Run Freedom Run" 297
"Ruthie's Lullaby" 297

"'S Wonderful" 95
"The Saddest Song" 321
"Saddle Tramp Blues" 282
"Safety in Numbers" 170
"The Saga of Jenny" 133
"Sail Away" 191
"Sailing" 290
"Sailors' Song" 233
"Salaa'm Bombay" 306
"Sammy" 26
"Santa Fe" 325
"Satin Summer Nights" 288
"Satisfied" 321
"Saturday Night" 293
"Saturday Night in Central Park" 153
"Say It with Music" 76, 78
"Say My Name" 339
"School of Rock" 333
"Science Fiction Double Feature" 227
"The Sea Song" 168
"Seagull, Starfish, Pebble" 214
"Seasons of Love" 281–2
"Second Hand Rose" 78
"Second Wave" 341
"Secret Soul" 297
"A Secretary Is Not a Toy" 191
"See the Light" 216
"Seeing Is Believing" 268
"Seeing You" 335
"Seize the Day" 325
"Send in the Clowns" 220–1
"Sentimental Me" 86
"September Song" 124–6
"Serenade" 78, 86, 167
"Serenity" 288
"The Seven Deadly Virtues" 188
"Seven Wonders" 323
"Seventeen" 329
"Seventy-Six Trombones" 177–9
"The Shade of the Palm" 22
"Shadowland" 287
"Shaking the Blues Away" 95
"Shall We Dance?" 161

"Shalom" 191
"She Didn't Say Yes" 107
"She Loves Me" 193
"She Used to Be Mine" 333
"She Was a Miller's Daughter" 28
"The Sheep Song" 224
"Sherry" 205
"Sherry's Theme" 274
"She's in Love" 317
"Shine" 319
"Shine It On" 236
"Shine Like the Sun" 319
"Shine On, Harvest Moon" 39–40
"A Shine on Your Shoes" 110
"A Ship Without a Sail" 101
"Shoeless Joe from Hannibal, MO" 170
"Should I Speak of Loving You?" 233
"Shout!" 321
"Show Me" 173
"Show Off" 311
"Show People" 314
"Show You a Thing or Two" 297
"Shy" 185
"Side By Side By Side" 214
"The Sidestep" 239
"Sidewalk Tree" 224
"Simple" 247
"Simple Creature" 303
"Simple Little Things" 196
"A Simple Melody" 160
"A Simple Thing Like That" 347
"Sincerely Me" 335
"Sing for Your Supper" 126
"Sing Happy" 199
"Sing Me a Song of Social Significance" 123
"Sister" 247
"Sister Susie's Sewing Shirts for Soldiers" 57
"Sit Down, You're Rockin' the Boat" 161
"Silver Star of Love" 22
"Skid Row" 250
"Sleep, Laura, Sleep" 258
"A Sleepin' Bee" 170
"Sleepy Man" 230
"Slumber Deep" 28
"Small Craft Warnings" 264
"Small World" 182
"Smile" 261
"Smoke Gets in Your Eyes" 111–12
"So Far" 153
"So Far, So Good" 261
"So in Love" 156
"So Long, Dearie" 196
"So Long, Mary" 33
"Soft Lights and Sweet Music" 107
"A Soft Place to Land" 333

"Softly, as in a Morning Sunrise" 96, 98
"The Soldiers in the Park" 17
"Solidarity" 319
"Soliloquy" 144
"Solla Sollew" 296
"Some Enchanted Evening" 154–6
"Some Like It Hot" 346–7
"Some Other Me" 329
"Some Other Time" 144
"Some People" 182
"Some Sort of Girl" 57
"Some Sort of Somebody" 60
"Some Things Are Better Left Unsaid" 11
"Somebody Died Today" 214
"Somebody Loves Me" 86
"Somebody Will" 347
"Somebody's Got Your Back" 329
"Someday" 321
"Someone Else's Story" 264
"Someone Gets Hurt" 337
"Someone in a Tree" 230
"Someone Like You" 285
"Someone to Love" 344
"Someone to Watch Over Me" 90–1
"Something About Her" 339
"Something Different" 337
"Something Good Will Happen Soon" 214
"Something Seems Tingle-Ingleing" 54
"Something Sort of Grandish" 150
"Something to Believe In" 324–5
"Something to Remember You By" 104
"Something Wonderful" 161
"Something's Comin'" 179
"Sometimes I'm Happy" 92
"Somewhere" 179
"Somewhere That's Green" 250
"The Song Is You" 110
"Song of Love" 78
"Song of the Carbine" 13
"Song of the Vagabonds" 89
"Song of the Woodman" 120
"Song on the Sand" 253
"The Song That Goes Like This" 309
"Sonya Alone" 327
"Soon" 101
"Soon It's Gonna Rain" 185
"Sorry-Grateful" 214
"The Sound of Money" 191
"The Sound of Music" 185
"South America, Take It Away" 147
"South American Way" 127, 129
"Southern Days" 321
"Sparks" 314
"Speak Low" 140–1
"Splish Splash" 48

Song Index

"Spring Is Here" 123
"The Springtime Cometh" 161
"Standing on the Corner" 173
"Star Light, Star Bright" 11
"Starmites" 266
"Stars I Trust" 331
"Starting Here, Starting Now" 233
"Starlight Express" 261
"The Stars and the Moon" 282
"The Stately Homes of England" 126
"Staying Young" 185
"Steam Heat" 168
"Step to the Rear" 208
"Stick It to the Man" 333
"Still Hurting" 300
"Stonecutters' Song" 11
"Stools" 248, 250
"Stop That Rag" 44
"Stop Time" 282
"The Story Goes On" 253
"Stouthearted Men" 96, 98
"A Strange Loop" 341
"Strange Music" 144
"Stranger in Paradise" 167–8
"The Streets of New York" 34–5
"Strike Up the Band" 101
"Strong Woman Number" 236
"Stupid With Love" 337
"Style" 224
"Suddenly Seymour" 250
"A Summer in Ohio" 300
"Summer Nights" 222
"Summertime" 118
"Summertime Is Summertime" 164
"Summertime Love" 185
"Sunday" 253, 300
"Sunday in Cicero Falls" 144
"Sunday in the Park" 123
"Sunday in the Park with George" 253
"Sunny Disposish" 92
"Sunrise" 272
"Sunrise, Sunset" 198–9
"Sunset Tree" 208
"Sunshine Above" 9
"Sunshine Girl" 176
"Superstar" 219
"Supper Time" 111, 113
"Surabaya Johnny" 233
"Sure as the Sun Turns to Moon" 311
"The Surrey with the Fringe on Top" 139
"Swanee" 67–9
"Sweet and Low-Down" 89
"Sweet Italian Love" 47
"Sweet Transvestite" 227
"The Sweetest Sounds" 191

"Sweetheart, I'm Waiting" 11
"Sweethearts" 54
"Sympathy" 44, 52
"The Syncopated Walk" 57

"Take Back Your Mink" 161
"Take Care of This House" 230
"Take Him" 133, 135
"Take Me Along" 185
"Take Me as I Am" 285
"Take Me Back to Manhattan" 104
"Take Me Out to the Ball Game" 40
"Take Me to Heaven" 323
"Take, Oh Take Those Lips Away" 83
"Taking a Chance on Love" 133
"Talk About Yo' Luck (The Rabbit's Foot)" 15
"Talk to Me Dorothy" 339
"Talking to You" 196
"Tammany" 30
"Tango: Maureen" 282
"Tap Your Troubles Away" 227
"The Tattooed Man" 14–15
"Tea for Two" 87–8
"Tea in the Rain" 208
"Tear Me Down" 288
"Tell Me a Lie" 306
"Tell Me Again, Sweetheart" 24
"Tell Me It's Not True" 276
"Tell Me on a Sunday" 258
"Tell Me, Pretty Maiden" 21–2
"Ten Cents a Dance" 101
"Tender Shepherd" 170
"Thank Your Father" 101
"That Certain Feeling" 89
"That Face" 297
"That Haunting Melody" 49
"That Nearly Was Us" 300
"That Special Night" 274
"That's Him" 141
"That's How You Jazz" 274
"That's Rich" 325
"That's the Way It Happens" 166
"Theatre Party Ladies" 242
"Then You May Take Me to the Fair" 188
"Therapy" 300
"There But for You Go I" 150, 188
"There Is Nothin' Like a Dame" 156
"There Must Be Someone for Me" 141
"There Must Be Something Better Than Love" 158
"There She Is" 250
"There Was a Girl" 297
"There's a Fine, Fine Line" 303
"There's a Great Day Coming, Mañana" 133
"There's a Shout" 288
"There's a Small Hotel" 118

Song Index

"There's Always One You Can't Forget" 250
"There's More to the Kiss Than XXX" 69
"There's No Business Like Show Business" 145–6
"There's Nothing Like a Model T" 153
"They Call It Dancing" 76, 78
"They Call the Wind Maria" 162–3
"They Couldn't Compare to You" 161
"They Didn't Believe Me" 55–7
"They Live in You" 287
"They Were You" 185
"They Say It's Wonderful" 147
"They're Playing Our Song" 239
"Thief in the Night" 118
"Thine Alone" 53
"Things I Didn't Know" 333
"Things I Learned in High School" 247
"Think About Tomorrow" 274
"Thinking of You" 95
"This Can't Be Love" 126
"This Funny World" 92
"This Is a Great Country" 193
"This Is All Very New to Me" 170
"This Is as Good as It Gets" 276
"This Is Life" 335
"This Is the Army, Mr. Jones" 139
"This Is the Moment" 284
"This Must Be the Place" 255
"This Nearly Was Mine" 156
"This Side of the Tracks" 311
"This Time" 344
"This World" 224
"Thou Swell" 95
"Three Bedroom House" 297
"Three O'Clock in the Morning" 78
"The Thrill Is Gone" 107
"Thrill Me" 110
"Through the Mountain" 282
"Through the Years" 107
"Throw Me a Kiss" 40
"Throw Me a Rose" 63
"The Tickle Toe" 66
"Ticky Ticky Tock" 314
"Till the Clouds Roll By" 61–2
"Till There Was You" 179, 348
"Till Tomorrow" 185
"Time" 333
"Time Heals Everything" 226–7
"Time on My Hands" 104
"Time Stops" 329
"Time Warp" 227
"Timeless to Me" 303
"Times Are Hard for Dreamers" 335
"Times Like This" 264
"Tinkers' Chorus" 1, 3
"To Be Alone with You" 199
"To Build a Home" 329
"To Each His Dulcinea" 202
"To Keep My Love Alive" 140–1
"To Life" 199
"To Whom It May Concern" 258
"Today" 341
"Together Wherever We Go" 182
"Tom Tom Toddle" 75
"Tommy Atkins" 8, 9
"Tomorrow" 232
"Tomorrow Belongs to Me" 204
"Tonight" 179
"Too Beautiful for Words" 311
"Too Close for Comfort" 173
"Too Darn Hot" 156
"Too Good for the Average Man" 135
"Too Late to Turn Back Now" 325
"Too Long from Long Acre Square" 41
"Too Many Mornings" 216
"Too Many People" 293
"Too Many Rings Around Rosie" 88
"Too Much in Love to Care" 280
"Too-Ra-Loo-Ra-Loo Ral (That's an Irish Lullaby)" 16
"Toot, Toot, Tootsie" 76, 78
"Top Banana" 164
"Topsy Turvy" 327
"Total Eclipse of the Heart" 303
"The Touch of Your Hand" 113
"The Toy Monkey" 13
"Toyland" 27–8
"Tradition" 199
"Tramp! Tramp! Tramp!" 46–7
"The Tree on the Hill" 341
"Tricks of the Trade" 280
"Trina's Song" 245
"A Trip to the Library" 193
"Triplets" 123
"Trouble" 179
"Trouble Man" 158
"True Love Is Not for a Day" 24
"Try to Forget" 107
"Try to Remember" 185
"Tschaikowsky" 133
"Turn Back, O Man" 216
"Turn It Off" 323
"Turn the Tide" 280
"Twenty-Four Hours of Lovin'" 239
"The 20th Century Girl" 11
"Twenty Million People" 276
"Twilight in Barakeesh" 41
"Two Ladies" 204
"Two Ladies in the Shade of de Banana Tree" 170
"Two Lost Souls" 170

Song Index

"Uncle Sam, Tell Us Why You Are Waiting" 14
"Uncle Sam's Children" 61
"Under the Bamboo Tree" 26
"Under the Old Oak Tree" 30
"Unexpected Song" 258
"Unruly Heart" 339
"Unstoppable" 339
"Unworthy of Your Love" 272
"Up! Up! Up! in my Aeroplane" 44
"Use Your Imagination" 161
"The Varsity Drag" 95
"The View from Here" 337

"Vilja" 38
"Violets and Silverbells" 227
"Voices in My Head" 339

"The Wages of Sin" 258
"Wagon Wheels" 113
"Wait Till the Cows Come Home" 66
"Wait Till You See Her" 136
"Waitin' for the Evening Train" 196
"Waiting for Life" 269
"Waiting for the Girls Upstairs" 216
"Waiting for the Light to Shine" 255
"Waiting for the Sun to Come Out" 75
"Waiting for This Moment" 311
"Waiting to Ride" 285
"Wake the Dead" 293
"Walk Him Up the Stairs" 214
"Walking Away Whistling" 185
"Walking Happy" 205
"Waltz Me Around, Willie" 33
"Wand'rin' Star" 164
"Wanting You" 96, 98
"Warm All Over" 173
"Watch What Happens" 325
"Watching the Parade Go By" 233
"Water in the Well" 285
"Waving Through the Window" 335
"Way Back Home" 300
"Way Back to Paradise" 293
"A Way Back to Then" 314
"Way Down Town" 78
"Way Down Upon the Swanee River" 68
"Way Down Yonder in New Orleans" 79–80
"Way Out West" 120
"The Way to Treat a Lady" 13
"We Are Descended" 309
"We Are Not Strangers" 236
"We Belong Together" 110
"We Beseech Thee" 216
"We Could Be Close" 219
"We Could Do It" 296
"We Did It Before" 134
"We Dance" 269

"We Go Together" 222
"We Got It" 224
"We Had Our Moments" 306
"We Kiss in a Shadow" 161
"We Might Play All Night" 314
"We Need a Little Christmas" 202
"We Won't Take It Back" 153
"A Weekend in the Country" 222
"Weep No More, My Baby" 113
"Welcome to Holiday Inn" 222
"Welcome to Nowhere" 337
"Welcome to the Fun Home" 329
"Welcome to the Renaissance" 331
"Welcome to the Rock" 335
"Welcome to the 60s" 303
"We'll Stand By Our Country" 61
"We'll Take a Glass Together" 268
"Well, Did You Evah?" 129
"We're a Travelin' Tramp Trio" 282
"We're Alive" 182
"We're Gonna Have a Good Time" 233
"We're Having a Baby" 136
"West End Avenue" 224
"What a Mother Does" 327
"What About Love?" 311
"What Baking Can Do" 333
"What Can You Do with a Man?" 135
"What Chance Have I with Love?" 129
"What Did I Have That I Don't Have?" 202
"What Do the Simple Folk Do?" 188
"What Does He Want of Me?" 202
"What Ever Happened to Saturday Night?" 227
"What Good Would the Moon Be?" 150
"What I Did for Love" 227
"What I Know Now" 339
"What Is a Woman?" 205
"What Is This Thing Called Love?" 101
"What Kind of Fool Am I?" 192–3
"What Kind of Girl Is She?" 314
"What Makes Me Love Him?" 205
"What Takes My Fancy" 189
"What Was a Woman to Do?" 309
"What Would I Do?" 272
"What You'd Call a Dream" 255
"What'd I Miss?" 331
"Whatever Lola Wants" 170
"What'll I Do?" 83
"What's in the Air?" 208
"What's the Use?" 176
"What's the Use of Wond'rin'?" 144
"Wheels of a Dream" 287
"When a Fella's on the Level with a Girl That's on the Square" 38
"When Chloe Sings a Song" 18–19
"When Did I Fall in Love?" 185
"When Hearts Are Young" 80

Song Index

"When Hope Goes" 300
"When I Discovered You" 57
"When I First Saw You" 247
"When I Grow Up" 327
"When I Hear a Syncopated Tune" 69
"When I Look at You" 288
"When I'm Not Near the Girl I Love" 150
"When Irish Eyes Are Smiling" 16, 50–1
"When It Ends" 293
"When It's Apple Blossom Time in Normandy" 52
"When My Baby Smiles at Me" 72
"When She Smiles" 325
"When the Cat's Away the Mice Will Play" 19
"When the Children Are Asleep" 144
"When the Lights Are Low" 59
"When the Ships Come Home" 66
"When the Spring Is in the Air" 110
"When the Sun Goes Down" 314
"When Uncle Sam Is Ruler of the Sea" 61
"When You Hear Jackson Moan on His Saxophone" 63
"When You Live in New York" 266
"When Your Feet Don't Touch the Ground" 331
"When Your Lover Says Goodbye" 214
"When Your Pride Has Had a Tumble" 9
"When You're Right You're Right" 245
"Where Are Those People Who Did 'Hair'?" 236
"Where Did Robinson Crusoe Go with Friday on Saturday Night?" 60
"Where Did the Night Go?" 166
"Where Did We Go Right?" 297
"Where Do I Go?" 208
"Where in the World" 271
"Where Is Love?" 193
"Where Is the Life That Late I Led?" 156
"Where Is the Tribe for Me?" 199
"Where or When" 120
"Where You Are" 276
"Where's That Rainbow?" 92
"Which Witch?" 168
"Whip-poor-will" 75
"Who?" 89
"Who Are You Now?" 196
"Who Can I Turn To ?" 199
"Who Cares?" 107
"Who Couldn't Dance with You?" 268
"Who Dat Say Chicken in Dis Crowd" 17
"Who Is Sylvia?" 219
"Who Paid the Rent for Mrs. Rip Van Winkle?" 52
"Who Will Love Me as I Am?" 287
"A Whole Lotta Sunshine" 224
"The Whole World's Waitin' for Your Song" 274
"Who'll Buy?" 193
"Who's Been Sleeping in My Chair?" 182
"Who's That Girl?" 214
"Who's That Woman?" 216
"Whoever You Are" 210
"Why?" 72, 300
"Why Be Afraid to Dance?" 170
"Why Can't You Behave?" 156
"Why Do I Love You?" 95
"Why Do the Wrong People Travel?" 191
"Why Shouldn't I?" 118
"Why Was I Born?" 101
"Why We Build the Wall" 332
"Wicked Little Town" 288
"Wild Rose" 75
"Wild Time" 293
"Wildflower" 80
"Wilkommen" 204
"Will-a-Mania" 272
"Will He Like Me?" 193
"Will Power" 331
"Will You?" 311
"Will You Remember?" 66
"William's Song" 253
"Windflowers" 168
"Wintergreen for President" 107
"Winter's on the Wing" 271
"Wish You Were Here" 166
"With a Little Bit of Luck" 173, 188
"With a Song in My Heart" 96, 98
"With Every Breath I Take" 269
"With One Look" 280
"With So Little To Be Sure Of" 196
"With Style" 230
"With You" 325
"Without a Song" 99, 101
"Without Love" 282, 303
"Without You" 282
"A Wonderful Day Like Today" 199
"A Wonderful Guy" 156
"Won't You Charleston with Me?" 170
"Woodman, Woodman, Spare That Tree" 49
"The Word of Your Body" 314
"Words of Love Too Loudly Spoken" 7
"Words Without Music" 115
"The World Above" 317
"The World Is Your Balloon" 161
"World Weary" 96, 98
"Worlds Apart" 255
"The Worst Pies in London" 239
"Wouldn't It Be Loverly?" 173
"Written in the Stars" 292
"Wunderbar" 156

"(Ya Got) Trouble" 178, 179
"The Yama Yama Man" 41
"Yankee Doodle" 32
"Yankee Doodle Boy" 30
"Yankee Doodle Doings" 22

Song Index

"Yellow Drum" 219
"Yellow Shoes" 331
"Yes" 216
"Yesterdays" 113
"Yip-I-Addy-I-Ay" 38
"You and I" 264
"You and the Night and the Music" 115
"You Are Beautiful" 182
"You Are Love" 95
"You Are Never Away" 153
"You Are Woman" 196
"You Are You" 199
"You Can Always Count on Me" 268–9
"You Can Drive a Person Crazy" 214
"You Cannot Make Your Shimmy Shake on Tea" 70, 72
"You Can't Do Me" 321
"You Can't Fool the People" 136
"You Can't Get a Man with a Gun" 147
"You Can't Have Me" 347
"You Can't Stop the Beat" 302
"You Could Never Shame Me" 276
"You Do Something to Me" 101
"You Don't Know This Man" 290
"You Don't Need to Love Me" 329
"You Gotta Do What You Gotta Do" 272
"You Gotta Have a Gimmick" 182
"You Know and I Know" 57
"You Made Me Love You" 50, 52
"You Mustn't Be Discouraged" 196
"You Mustn't Kick It Around" 133
"You Never Can Tell" 57
"You Never Knew About Me" 63
"You Never Know" 126
"You Remind Me of My Mother" 80
"You Rule My World" 297
"You Said Something" 63
"You Say the Nicest Things, Baby" 156
"You Took Advantage of Me" 95
"You Tore My Heart Out" 319
"You Were Meant for Me" 83
"You Were There" 120
"You Will Be Found" 334–5
"You Won't Succeed on Broadway" 309
"You Wouldn't Fool Me, Would You?" 96, 98
"You, You, You" 331
"You'd Be Surprised" 70, 72
"You'll Be Back" 331
"You'll Never Get Away from Me" 182
"You'll Never Walk Alone" 144, 348
"Young and Foolish" 169–70
"Younger Than Springtime" 156, 348
"Your Arms Too Short to Box with God" 233
"Your Daddy's Son" 287
"Your Eyes" 95
"Your Land and My Land" 95
"You're a Builder-Upper" 115
"You're a Grand Old Flag" 31–2
"You're a Queer One, Julie Jordan" 143
"You're an Old Smoothie" 110
"You're Devastating" 113
"You're Here and I'm Here" 53–4
"You're in the Band" 333
"You're Just in Love" 159–60
"You're Lonely and I'm Lonely" 129
"You're Never Fully Dressed Without a Smile" 233
"You're Nothing Without Me" 268
"You're on the Right Road But You're Going the Wrong Way" 52
"You're the Cream in My Coffee" 96, 98
"You're the Top" 115
"You've Got That Thing" 101
"You've Got to Pick a Pocket or Two" 193
"You've Got What I Need" 202
"You've Got Possibilities" 202
"You've Got to Be Carefully Taught" 154

"Zing! Went the Strings of My Heart" 48, 115
"Zip" 133

TITLE AND NAME INDEX

A ... My Name Is Alice 251, 253
Abbott and Costello 127
Abbott, George 116, 131, 151, 160, 191, 248
About Town 34
Abyssinia 31
Ackerman, Loni 250
The Act 234, 236
Action in the North Atlantic 109
Adair, Beegie 57, 72, 112, 188
Adams, Cliff 179, 185
Adams, Lee 183, 200, 212, 237, 243
Adamson, Harold 154
Addams, Charles 320
The Addams Family 320, 321
Adding Machine 315, 317
Adler, Larry 126
Adonis 6
Adrift in Macao 312, 314
The Adventures of Tom Sawyer 295
Afatia 282
Afgar 73
After Midnight 328
After the Ball 5
Aguilera, Christina 158
Ahomka-Lindsay, Michael 325
Ahrens, Lynn 263, 267, 286–7, 296, 301, 307, 315, 334
Aida 291, 292–3
Aiken, Clay 193
Aimée, Cyrille 278
Ain't Broadway Grand 275
Ain't Misbehavin' 101, 234, 265
Ain't Supposed to Die a Natural Death 217, 219
Ain't Too Proud 336
Akers, Karen 221
Aladdin 328, 329
Alberghetti, Anna Maria 168
Alberti, Willeke 292
Albertson, Jack 131
Alda, Robert 159
Alexander, Jason 153, 191
Alexander, Kane 271
Alexander's Ragtime Band 72
Algeria 39, 41
The Algerian 6
Ali Baba and the Forty Thieves 64
Alice in Wonderland 209, 322

Alive and Kicking 157
All Aboard 53
All About Eve 212
All American 190, 191
All for Love 154
All Shook Up 307
All-Star Trio 69
All That Jazz 147
All the King's Horses 111
All the Way 110
Allegiance 332
Allegro 151, 153
Allen, Alana 214
Allen, Debbie 240, 256
Allen, Fred 79, 102
Allen, Harry 136, 185
Allen, Peter 237, 304
Allen, Sandra 181
Allen, Sasha 207
Allen, Woody 149
Alliance Orchestra of Gothenburg 11
Alonso, Maria Conchita 276
Alloway, Jackie 136
Allyson, June 63
Alma, Where Do You Live? 45
Almost Famous 345, 347
Almost Heaven: Songs of John Denver 310
Alone at Last 58
Along Fifth Avenue 154
Alpert, Herb 204, 210, 282
Altar Boyz 308
Alvarez, David 318, 319
Alvey, Bert 43
Alvin and the Chipmunks 232
Alvin Queen Trio 195
Always Leave Them Laughing 77
Always ... Patsy Cline 286
Always You 70
Ambassador 220
Ambassadors 82
Ambrose and His Orchestra 57, 260
Ameche, Don 153, 169
Amélie 334, 335
America 53
The American Idea 39, 41
American Idiot 320
An American in Paris 104

Title and Name Index

American Psycho 332
American Quartet 32, 80
American Rhapsody 295
Americana 90, 92
America's Sweetheart 102, 104
The Amen Corner 251
Ames Brothers 95
Ames, Ed 188, 201
Amour 301, 303
Anastasia 334
& Juliet 345
And the World Goes 'Round 230, 270
Anderson, Jessamyn 188
Anderson, Maxwell 124–5, 157
Andre Charlot's Revue 81, 83
André Weller's Wonderhouse 273
Andreas, Christine 155, 228, 240, 308
Andrews, Julie 91, 144, 169, 171, 185, 187, 188, 275, 281
Andrews, Nancy 157
Andrews Sisters 26, 49, 118, 146, 223
Angel 234
Angel in the Wings 151, 152
Angry Housewives 259
Animal Crackers 96, 98
Anja & Viktor 129
Anka, Paul 69, 149, 170
Ankles Aweigh 169
Anna Karenina 275
Annie 231–2, 283
Annie 2 277
Annie Get Your Gun 145–7, 200, 202, 289
Annie Warbucks 277, 278
Anthem Lights 306, 335
Antoine, Jonathan 268
Antz 149
Anya 200, 202
Anyone Can Whistle 194, 196
Anything Goes 114–15, 262, 322
Applause 212, 214
Apple Blossoms 70, 72
The Apple Tree 203, 205, 312
The Arcadians 42, 44
Arden, Eve 116, 127
Ari 215
Aristophanes 307, 324
Arlen, Harold 102, 108, 114, 121, 142, 169, 177, 183
Are You with It? 145
Arms and the Girl 157, 158
Arms, Russell 49
Armstrong, Louis 99–100, 104, 107, 112, 115, 161, 198, 204
Arnold, Charles 9
Aronson, Boris 212
Around the World 48, 145

Around the World in Eighty Days 145
The Art of Maryland 12
Arthur, Jean 157
Artists and Models 87
As the Girls Go 154, 156
As Thousands Cheer 111, 113
As You Were 70
Ash, Sam 72, 80
Ash, William 168
Asha-Louise 97
Ashford, Annaleigh 239, 345
Aspects of Love 267–8
Assassins 270, 272, 304
Astaire, Adele 64, 67, 70, 76, 102, 105, 108
Astaire, Fred 64, 67, 70, 72, 76, 84, 102, 105, 108–9, 112, 118, 273, 304
At Home Abroad 116, 118
At Home with Ethel Waters 167
At the Drop of a Hat 183
Atkins, Chet 26, 85, 161, 261
Atkinson, David 149, 202
Atlantic City 100
Atwell, Winifred 83
Auber, Daniel 115, 122
Aunt Hannah 19
Austin, Charlotte 100
Austin, Gene 100
Austin, Jane 180, 310
Austin, Patti 69
The Auto Race 36
Avenue Q 302–3, 304
The Aviator 123
Awakenings 66
Ayado, Chie 69
Ayckbourn, Alan 280
Ayres, Mitchell 161

Babbitt, Harry 161
Babes in Arms 75, 119–20
Babes in the Woods 197
Babes in Toyland 26, 27–8, 31, 240
Babes on Swing Street 54
Babette 27–8
Baby 54, 251, 253
Baby, It's You 322
Bacall, Lauren 212, 243
Bach, Kristina 204
Bach, Sebastian 284
Bacharach, Burt 209–10, 275, 301
Back Pay 57
Back to Bacharach and David 275
Bad Cinderella 345, 347
Bad Timing 123
Baga, Ena 181
Bagley, Eleanor 151

Title and Name Index

Bagneris, Vernel 279
Bailey, Mildred 118, 128, 149
Bailey, Pearl 158, 159, 169, 206
Baillo, Maddie 303
Bainter, Fay 48
Bajour 197, 199
Baker, B. J. 181
Baker, Chet 91, 120, 126, 128, 136, 149, 172
Baker, Josephine 54, 116, 223
Baker, Kenny 72, 128, 140
Baker, Paul 235
Baker, Phil 134
Baker Street 197, 199
Bakker, Marco 292
Balanchine, George 116
Balancing Act 275
Balgord, Linda 250
The Balkan Princess 45
Ball, Ernest R. 51
Ball, Lucille 187
Ball, Michael 198, 268, 278, 282
The Ballad of Buster Scruggs 44
"The Ballad of Tommy Atlins" 8
Ballard, Jordan 133
Ballard, Kaye 223
Ballet Ballads 151
Ballroom 237, 239
Ballyhoo of 1932 108, 110
Ballyhooligans 104
Bananas 46
Band in Berlin 289
Band of the Grenadier Guards 11
The Band Wagon 105, 107
Banderas, Antonio 301
The Band's Visit 336, 337
Bandstand 334, 335
Banjo Barons 32
Banjo Eyes 134, 136
Bar Harbor Society Orchestra 80
Barbara Carroll Trio 59
Barbé, Bronté 325
Barbour, James 188, 264
bare 305, 306
Barefoot Boy with Cheek 148
Bareilles, Sara 218, 332, 333, 339
Barer, Marshall 174, 183
Barfota Jazzmen 66
Barker, John 87–8
Barnabee, Henry Clay 23
Barnes, Mae 102
Barnum 240, 242
Barnum, P. T. 240
Barr, Roseann 181
Barratta, Richard 282
Barrera, Melissa 313

Barrett, Brent 271
Barrowman, John 109, 252, 268, 280
Barry, Barrel Fingers 30
Barry, Gene 252
Barry, Ken 147
Barry of Ballymore 45, 47, 50
Barry Sisters 198
Barrymore, Drew 28
Bart, Lionel 192
Barton, James 79, 102
Barton, Steve 264
Basie, Count 40, 139, 172, 195, 221
Bass, Paul 99–100
Bassey, Shirley 109, 149, 158, 175, 193, 201, 216, 218, 230, 241, 252, 280
Bat Boy 295, 297
Batman 200
Batman v Superman: Dawn of Justice 110
Battle, Hinton 243
Battling Buttler 81
Baum, L. Frank 25
Baurel, Henri 104
Bayes, Nora 39–40, 42, 43, 67
Bayles, Dallyn Vail 271
Be Kind Rewind 101
Be More Chill 338, 339
Beach Boys 307
Beach, Gary 252
Bean, Orson 167
Bean, Reathel 254
Bean, Shoshana 188, 306
Beard, Seymour 88
Beatty, Warren 147
Beaumont, Rose 24
Beatlemania 234
Beatles 206, 234
Beaton, Cecil 183
Beautiful 328
A Beautiful Noise: The Neil Diamond Musical 345
Beauty and the Beast 277, 278
The Beauty Spot 39
Because You're Mine 128
Bechdel, Alison 328
Bechet, Sidney 75, 100
Beebe, Ken 32, 40
Beechman, Laurie 218, 250, 280
Beehive 257
Beetlejuice 338, 339
Beggar's Holiday 148
The Beggar's Opera 223
Beiderbecke, Bix 95
Being Julia 57, 115
Belafonte, Harry 112, 167
Bell, Marion 148–9
Bell, Michel 95

Title and Name Index

The Belle of Brittany 42
The Belle of Mayfair 34
The Belle of New York 14–15
Bells Are Ringing 174–6, 295
Belmont, Joe 22
Belmonts 126
Ben Franklin in Paris 197, 199
Ben Webster Quartet 128
Bennett, Chris 188
Bennett, Michael 212, 225, 237, 247
Bennett, Sylvia 166
Bennett, Tony 100, 109, 115, 120, 122, 128, 141, 168
Bennett, Tracie 324
Benny Goodman Quartet 88
Benny Goodman Sextet 101
Benny, Jack 87, 102, 192
Benson, George 195
Benson, Jodi 92, 104
Bergen, Polly 66, 167, 175
Bergman, Ingrid 106
Bergsten, Cheryl 214
Berle, Milton 77, 136, 137
Berlin, Irving 55, 58–60, 61, 67, 70–2, 76, 93, 105, 111, 127, 137, 145–7, 157, 159–60, 192, 200, 334
Berlin to Broadway with Kurt Weill 141, 220, 295
Bernard, Al 69
Bernard, Sam 23, 27, 34, 61
Bernarda Alba 310
Bernardi, Herschel 199, 209
Bernstein, Leonard 142, 157, 165, 174, 177, 223
Besoyan, Rick 197
Besser, Joe 134
Best Foot Forward 134, 136
The Best Little Whorehouse Goes Public 277
The Best Little Whorehouse in Texas 237, 239, 256
Bethke, Veit 163
Betsy 90, 92
Bette Midler: Divine Madness 240
The Better 'Ole 67
Better Times 79
Between the Devil 121, 123
Between the Lines 346
Beyond Therapy 91
The Bicycle Girl 10
Bierco, Craig 179
Big 281, 282
Big Ben Banjo Band 43, 261
Big Boy 84, 86
Big Deal 75, 256
Big Deal on Madonna Street 256
Big Fish 328, 329
Big River 254–5, 304
The Big Show 61
Bilk, Acker 261, 268
Billion Dollar Baby 145

The Billionaire 25
Billy 209
Billy Barnes Revue 183
Billy Bishop Goes to War 240
Billy Budd 209
Billy Elliot 318–19
Billy Rose's Crazy Quilt 102, 104
Bingo 310
Birds of Paradise 262–3, 264
Birtill, Katie 227
Bishop, Julie 109
Bishop, Walter, Jr. 141
Bits and Pieces, XIV 197
Bitter Sweet 99, 101
Bittersuite 262
Black and Blue 265
Black Broadway 249
The Black Crook 1, 6, 167
Black Diamonds Band 11
Black, Don 249, 268, 280–1
Black, Jack 101
The Black Sheep 10–11
Blackbirds of 1928 93, 95
Blackburn Twins 134, 136
Blackhands 261
Blackman, Helena 181
Blackstone! 240
Blackwater Junction 185
Blade, Dina 109
Blaine, Vivian 72, 147, 152, 159, 213
Blair, Janet 175
Blake, Eubie 74–5, 102, 237
Blakey, Art 163
Blanchard, Steve 188
Blane, Ralph 134, 267
Blazing Saddles 115
Bledsoe, Jules 93–4
Blitzstein, Marc 157, 180
Bloch, Ray 163
Block, Stephanie J. 306, 312
Blonde 97
Blonde Ambition 241
Blonsky, Nikki 302
Blood Brothers 275, 276
Blood Red Roses 212
Bloody Bloody Andrew Jackson 320, 321
Bloomer Girl 142, 144
Blossom, Henry 34–5
Blossom Time 76, 78, 102, 140
Blow Dry 158
Blue Ambersol Quartette 80
Blue Bird Society Orchestra 261
Blue Champagne 158, 172
Blue Harlem 158
Blue Haze 112

Title and Name Index

The Blue Kitten 76
Blue Moon 34
The Blue Paradise 58, 60
Blue Skies 72
Bluebelles 195
Blues in the Night 248
Bluestein, Michael 216
The Blushing Bride 76
Blyden, Larry 217
Blyth, Ann 54, 86, 91, 168
Bob Cats 46, 83
Bobby Gordon Sextet 75
Boccaccio 228
Bocelli, Andrea 168, 264
Bock, Jerry 177, 183, 187, 192, 197–8, 203, 215
The Body Beautiful 177
Boe, Alfie 198
Bogardus, Stephen 244, 274
Bogart, Humphrey 106
Bogart, Matt 292
Boggess, Sierra 168
Boland, Mary 105
Bolcom, William 5, 59
Bolger, Ray 114, 135, 152, 209
Bolling, Claude 72
Bolton, Guy 55, 61–2, 64, 73, 81, 99
Bombay Dreams 304, 306
Bombo 76–8
Bond, Michael 179
Bond, Ridge 139
Bond, Sheila 151
Bondy, Ryan 323
Bongiorno, James 285
Bonnie and Clyde 324, 325
Boobs: The Musical 301
The Book of Mormon 322, 323
Boone, Pat 54, 72
Booth, Grahame Stuart 155
Booth, Shirley 159, 167, 180, 212
Bordoni, Irene 61, 76, 96, 127
Borg, Veda Ann 49
Borge, Victor 167
Born on the Fourth of July 32
Borodin, Alexander 167–8
Bostonians 335
Bostwick, Barry 273
Boswell, Connee 46, 118, 147
Boswell, Eve 170
Boswell Sisters 40
Botti, Chris 120
Bowen, Cameron 296
Bowie, David 332
The Boy Friend 169, 170, 212
The Boy from Oz 304
Boy Meets Boy 228

Boyer, Stephen 343
Boyle, Susan 201, 221, 250
The Boys and Betty 39
Boys and Girls Together 131
The Boys from Syracuse 124, 126
Bracken, Eddie 127
Bradlee, Scott 128
Bran Pie 66
Braswell, Charles 213
The Brave Little Toaster 77
Bray, Stephen 311
Brazzi, Rossano 156
Brecht, Bertolt 108, 231
Brel, Jacques 206, 275
Brett, Jeremy 172
Brewer, Teresa 40, 49
Brian, Donald 36–7, 48, 55–6
Brice, Carol 183
Brice, Elizabeth 48
Brice, Fanny 45, 48, 61, 96, 102, 111, 116, 119, 343
Brickman, Jim 335
Bricusse, Leslie 192–3, 283–4
The Bride Elect 14
Bridges of Madison County 328, 329
Bridgewater, Dee Dee 141
A Brief History of White Music 283
Brigadoon 148–50, 162
Bright Eyes 42
Bright Lights, Big City 289
Bright Star 332, 333
Brightman, Sarah 168, 250, 263–4, 268
Bring Back Birdie 243
Bring in 'da Noise, Bring in 'da Funk 281
Bring It On 326, 327
Brito, Phil 72
Broadway Brevities of 1920 75
Broadway Follies 243
Broadway Kids 282
Broadway Melody of 1940 118
A Broadway Musical 237
Broadway Opry '79 240
Broadway Rhythm 128
Broadway to Tokio 18
Broderick, Helen 105, 111
Broderick, Matthew 179, 279
Brole, Christian 244
Bromberg, Brian 141
A Bronx Tale 334, 335
Brooklyn: The Musical 307
Brooks, Albert 147
Brooks, David 148–9
Brooks, Harry 99–100
Brooks, Mel 190, 315
Brooks, Shelton 102
The Brother Bloom 118

Title and Name Index

Bravo, Giovanni 190
Brown Buddies 102
Brown, Dave Thomas 323
Brown, Deborah 85
Brown, Georgia 227
Brown, James 126, 193
Brown, Jason Robert 281, 298
Brown, Joe E. 87
Brown, Lew 87, 93, 96
Brown, Ruth 95, 122, 132
Brown, Teddy 100
Brubeck, Dave 100, 126, 128
Bruce, Carol 122, 132
Bruce Forsythe on Broadway 240
Bruneau, Ralph 251
Brunswick Light Opera Company 22
Brunswick Quartet 17
Bryan, Alfred 53
Bryan, Dora 158
Bryan, Hal 146
Bryant, Anita 185, 216
Brynner, Yul 159, 231, 254
Bryson, Arthur 102
Bryson, Peabo 278
Bubbling Brown Sugar 228
The Bubbly Black Girl Sheds Her Chameleon Skin 295, 297
Bublé, Michael 120
Bucchino, John 185
Buchanan, Jack 81
Buck and Bubbles 102
Buck White 212
Buckley, Betty 221, 235, 249–50, 280
Bucky, John 221
Budd, Julie 218, 306
Buddies 70
Buddy: The Buddy Holly Story 270
Buechner, Sara Davis 85
Buffalo Bills 51
Bullets Over Broadway 328
Burge, Gregg 243
Burke, Billie 111
Burlesque 158
Burlinson, Tom 110
Burnett, Carol 77, 184, 194, 291
Burnett, Frances Hodgson 271
Burnett, T-Bone 158
Burns, Andréa 313
Burns, David 105, 151
Burns, Jackie 306
Burr, Henry 40, 54
Burrows, Abe 159
Burstein, Danny 199, 332
Burton, Billy 80
Burton, Richard 187, 188, 243

Bushkin, Joe 59
Bussert, Meg 149
But Never Jam Today 209, 240
Butler, Gerard 264
Buttons on Broadway 281
Buttons, Red 281
Butz, Norbert Leo 307
Buzzell, Eddie 30
By Jeeves 298, 300
By Jupiter 134–6
By the Beautiful Sea 26, 167, 168
By the Light of the Silvery Moon 49
Bye Bye Birdie 183, 185, 243
Bygraves, Max 122, 204
Byrd, Charlie 207, 210
Byrd, Donald 141
Byrne, David 328
Byrne, Debra 280
Byrne, Pauline 168
Byrnes, Marilyn 264
BYU Noteworthy 303

Cabaret 203–4, 262, 286, 328
Cabin in the Sky 131, 133
Caesar, Irving 67–8, 87–8, 108
Caesar, Sid 151, 192
Cagney 332
Cagney, James 30, 32, 332
Cahill, Marie 23–4, 31, 39, 102
Cahn, Sammy 151–2
Cain, Jackie 191
Caiola, Al 141
Calendar Girl 158
California Split 54
Call Me Madam 159–61
Call Me Mister 145, 147
Callaway, Ann Hampton 123, 166
Callaway, Liz 210, 250
Calloway, Cab 77
Camelot 187–8, 246, 277, 345
Cameron, Violet 2
Camp 214, 247
Campbell, A. C. 17
Campbell, Glen 201
Campbell, Sharon 241
Can-Can 165–6
The Canary 67
Candida 322
Candide 174, 176, 223, 224, 283
Cannon, Ace 107, 155
Canova, Judy 116
Canterbury Tales 209, 211, 240
Cantor, Eddie 40, 61, 70, 81, 96, 134
The Capeman 286, 288
Capitol Steps 305

Title and Name Index

Capote, Truman 169, 217
Capp, Al 174
Captain Louie 307, 308
Carew, Leslie 260
Carey, Mariah 163
Cariou, Len 221, 237–9
Carle, Frankie 17, 204
Caribbean Carnival 152
Carlow, Blanche 22
Carlson, Richard 88, 264
Carmelina 237, 239
Carmen 140
Carmen Jones 140, 338
Carmines, Al 206, 209
Carnelia, Craig 259, 298
Carnival 187, 188
Carnival in Flanders 167, 168
Caroline, or Change 304, 306, 343
Carousel 142–4, 154, 169, 277
Carpenter, Carlton 97
Carpenter, Thelma 75
Carpenters 210, 241
Carr, Vicki 136, 204
Carreras, José 155, 201, 221, 264, 268
Carrie 262
Carrington, Katherine 105
Carroll, Barbara 136, 221
Carroll, Diahann 126, 169, 190
Carroll, Earl 81
Carroll, Harry 65
Carter, Aaron 296
Carter, Benny 91
Carter, Helena Bonham 239
Carter, Mel 201
Carter, Nell 283
Carver, Brent 276
Casa Loma Orchestra 17, 51
Casablanca 106, 107, 270
Cash, Johnny 5, 310, 320
The Casino Girl 18–19
Cass, Peggy 157
Cassella, Max 77
Cassidy, Jack 209
Castle, Vernon and Irene 50, 55
The Cat and the Fiddle 105, 107
Catch-22 126
Catch Me If You Can 44, 322, 323
The Catch of the Season 31
A Catered Affair 315, 317
Catlett, Walter 73
Cats 248–50
The Cat's Meow 75, 77
Causer, Bob 115
Cavallaro, Carmen 75
Cawthorn, Joseph 31, 56

Celebration 209, 211
Celebrity 104
Celia: The Life and Music of Celia Cruz 315
Cellier, Alfred 4
The Century Girl 61
The Century Revue 73
Cervantes, Miguel de 201
Cerveris, Michael 141, 239, 312
Chad and Jeremy 144
Chakiris, George 168
Chamberlain, Kevin 296
Chamberlain, Richard 277
Champion, Gower 112, 225
Champion, Marge 112
A Change in the Heir 267
Change Your Luck 102
Channing, Carol 100, 157–8, 165, 187, 194, 223, 234, 281, 334
Channing, Stockard 133
The Chaperone 75
Chaplin 326, 327
Chaplin, Sydney 175, 195
Charisse, Cyd 149
Charlap, Bill 128
The Charlatan 16
Charles Aznavour on Broadway 289
Charles, Ray 85, 91, 95, 100, 122, 139, 155, 198, 204
Charles, Walter 252
Charlie and Algernon 232, 243
Charlie and the Chocolate Factory 336, 337
Charlie Byrd Quintet 62
Charlie Byrd Trio 57
Charlot's Revue of 1924 81, 83
Charlot's Revue of 1926 87, 89
Charlotte Sweet 249–50
Charleston Chasers 69
Charlot, Andre 81
Charnin, Martin 192, 232
Chase, Will 292, 338
Chavalier, Maurice 30, 148
Chavkin, Rachel 332, 334
Checker, Chubby 83
Chee-Chee 96
Cheer Up 64
Chekhov, Anton 263
Chenoweth, Kristin 299, 305, 312, 330
Cher 112, 132, 201, 216, 338
The Cher Show 338
Chess 262, 264
Chevalier, Maurice 37, 69, 126, 192
Chiara, Claudio 170
Chicago 228–30, 347
Chilcoat, Johanna 247
Childish, Wild Billy 261
Children on Their Birthdays 123

385

Title and Name Index

Chin-Chin 55, 57
A Chinese Honeymoon 23–4, 27
Chitty Chitty Bang Bang 307
Cho, John 247
Chocolate Dandies 84, 86
The Chocolate Soldier 42, 44
Chordettes 40
A Chorus Line 215, 225, 227, 228, 312
Chrétien, Sarah 115
Chris and the Wonderful Lamp 18
Christie, Agatha 228
A Christmas Story 326, 327
Chronicle of a Death Foretold 281
Chu Chem 265
Chu Chin Chow 64, 66
Cinderella 50, 326, 345
Cinderella on Broadway 73
The Circus Girl 12–13
The Circus Princess 90
City of Angels 267, 269
The Civil War 289
Claire, Bernice 88
Claire, Ina 61
Clark, Bobby 79, 114, 119, 127, 137, 140, 154
Clark, Buddy 54
Clark, Petulia 107
Clark, Roy 163
Clark Sisters 75
Clark, Sonny 141
Clark, Victoria 144, 308, 343–4
Clarke, Sharon D. 343
Clary, Robert 162
A Class Act 296, 297
Clay, Kevin 323
Clayderman, Richard 172, 241
Clayton, Jan 5, 142–3
Clement, Frank 21–2
Cline, Patsy 286
Clooney, Rosemary 40, 122, 139, 147, 155, 161, 221
Clorindy 16–17, 25, 42
A Close Call 3
Close, Glenn 279, 280
Closer Than Ever 267, 269
The Club 231
Coburn, Charles 67, 126
Coca, Imogene 102, 111
Cochran, Charlie 122
Cochran's 1931 Revue 40
Coco 212, 214
The Cocoanuts 87, 90
Coffin, Hayden 9
Cohan and Harris Minstrels 39
Cohan, George M. 21, 25, 29–30, 31–2, 36, 39, 42, 48, 53, 55, 64, 79–80, 93, 121, 206
Cohan Revue of 1916 58

Cohan Revue of 1918 64
Cohen, Douglas J. 259
Cole, Jack 137
Cole, Nat King 5, 26, 149, 166, 170, 172, 175, 195, 265
Cole, Natalie 107, 166
Cole, Richie 107
Coleman, Cy 187, 192, 234, 283
Colfer, Chris 241
Collabro 319
Collett, Richard 156
Collins, José 53
Collins, Judy 120, 132, 216, 221, 241, 250
The Color Purple 310, 311, 332
Coltrane, John 141
Columbia Light Opera Company 13, 22
Columbia Vocal Gem Chorus 88
Comden, Betty 142, 162, 165, 174–5, 177, 187, 248
Come Fly Away 320
Come from Away 334, 335
Come Summer 209
Comedy in Music 167
A Comedy of Errors 124
Comedian Harmonists 343
Comin' Uptown 240
Como, Perry 28, 51, 66, 144, 155, 161, 172
Company 212–14, 281, 312, 343
Company Man 158
Coney Island 51
Confessions of a Dangerous Mind 147
Confetti 149
Conley, Brian 280
A Connecticut Yankee 93, 95, 135, 140–1
Connell, Jane 174
Connelly, Marc 81
Connick, Harry, Jr. 118, 147, 155, 166, 172, 185, 298
Conniff, Ray 207
Connolly, Will 339
Connor, Chris 104
Conor, Harry 23
Conrad, Lew 100
The Consul 157
Contact 291
Conversation Piece 114, 115
Convy, Bert 204
Conway, Russ 30, 69, 204
Cook, Barbara 5, 40, 59, 144, 159, 169, 177–8, 192, 217, 227
Cook, Joe 102
Cook, Will Marion 16, 25
Cooke, Sam 95, 100, 163
Cookson, Peter 165–6
The Cooler 149
Copeland, Joan 133

Title and Name Index

Copper and Brass 177
Copperfield 243
Coraline 320
Cordell, Larry 128
Corden, James 339
Cordials 193
Cornell, Don 168
Costa, Nikka 91, 232
Costello, Elvis 57
Cott, Corey 224, 255, 325
Cotton, Billy 75, 118, 260–1
Cotton Patch Gospel 246
The Count of Luxemburg 50
Countess Maritza 90
A Country Girl 25
Country Quartet 32
Courtin' Time 162
Cousens, Peter 268
Covington, Julie 241
Covington, Warren 88
Coward, Noel 96, 99, 114, 151, 194
Cowgirls 281, 282
Cox, Deborah 292
Coyne, Joseph 37
Crabtree, Howard 283
The Cradle Will Rock 121, 123, 151
Craig, Michael 195
Crain, Jeanne 77, 97, 100
Crane, Norma 199
Crawford, Ben 264
Crawford, Clifton 23–4
Crawford, Jesse 2, 46, 62
Crawford, Joan 305
Crawford, Lila 232
Crawford, Michael 250, 263–4
Crazy for You 92, 104, 273
Crazy Moon 123
Creager, Willie 85
Creel, Gavin 299
Crewe, Bob 5
Crimes and Misdemeanors 123
Criss Cross 90
Criswell, Kim 232
Croce, Jim 95
Crooks, Richard 46
Crosby, Bing 5, 26, 30, 32, 40, 51, 69, 77, 95, 100, 109, 122, 126, 139, 144, 160, 161, 166, 168, 172, 204
Crosby, Bob 46, 49, 83, 146
Crosby, Gary 160
Crothers, Scat Man 104, 126
Crouse, Russel 121
Crouse, Timothy 262
Crow, Sheryl 118
Cruz, Celia 315

Cry-Baby 315
Cry for Us All 212
Cryer, Gretchen 206, 212, 212, 234, 235
Crystal, Billy 343
Cubis, Tom 132
Cuccioli, Robert 230, 284
Cuden, Steve 284
Cugat, Xavier 117
Cullum, John 202, 225, 234
Cumming, Alan 158
The Curious Case of Benjamin Button 101
Curly McDimple 206
Curtains 312, 314
Curtis, Keene 252
Cyrano 220
Cyrano de Bergerac 277
Cyrano: The Musical 277

DaCosta, Morton 183
Daddy Long Legs 332, 333
Dahl, Roald 326
Dailey, Dan 30, 72
The Dairymaids 36
Dale, Jim 240, 283
Dalhart, Vernon 40
D'Antonio, Carmen 118
Daly, Tyne 267
Dames at Sea 209, 211, 257, 332
Damn Yankees 169, 170, 277
Damon, Stuart 183
Damone, Vic 72, 163, 168, 172, 188, 195
Dance a Little Closer 248, 250
Dance Flick 247
Dance of the Vampires 301, 303
Dancin' 234, 346
Dancing Around 55, 57
Dangerous Games 267
Dango, Fanny 22
Daniele, Graciela 286
Danieley, Jason 149
Daniels, Billy 115
Daniels, Danny 151
Daniels, David 169–70
Daniels, Frank 14–15, 23
Daniels, Joe 104
Dante, Nicholas 225
Dardanelle Trio 139
Darin, Bobby 104, 172, 175, 218
Darion, Joe 201–2
Darling, Jean 143
Darling of the Day 206, 208
Das Barbecü 279, 280
Daunno, Damon 139
David, Hal 209–10, 275, 301
Davies, Marion 22, 61

387

Title and Name Index

Davis, Bette 165
Davis, Jesse Bartlett 2, 12
Davis, Mark Jonathan 110
Davis, Mary Bond 302
Davis, Miles 100, 120, 128
Davis, Sammi 118
Davis, Sammy, Jr. 95, 118, 120, 144, 168, 171, 193, 197, 198, 223
Davis, Skeeter 97
Davison, John 252
Dawn, Hazel 61, 87
The Day Before Spring 145
A Day in Hollywood / A Night in the Ukraine 240, 242
Day, Dennis 17, 28, 51, 128
Day, Doris 49, 88, 152, 172, 175, 181, 185
Day, Edith 5, 61, 70, 85
Day, Spencer 172, 218
Days, Bill 109
Days, Maya 218
The Days of Wine and Roses 346
De Angelis, Jefferson 10, 29, 48
de Armas, Ana 97
de Cervantes, Miguel 201
de Jesús, Robin 313
De Koven, Reginald 1–2, 8, 14, 39
De Leath, Vaughn 75, 97
de Mare, Anthony 214
de Mille, Agnes 137
de Paul, Gene 174
de Rance, Haidee 57
de Shields, Andre 254
De Vol, Frank 175
Deakin, Julia 91
Deal of the Century 91
Dear Evan Hansen 334, 335
Dear Oscar 220
Dear Sir 84, 86
Dear World 209, 211
Dearest Enemy 87, 89
Dearie, Blossom 88, 91, 136, 214, 221
Dearman, Louise 227
Death Takes a Holiday 324
The Debutant 55
DeCarlo, Nick 88
Deconstructing Harry 128–9
Deer Tick 193
The Defender 25–6
D'Egidio, Nick 149
DeHaven, Gloria 169
Deiro, Pietro 11
Déja Vu 221
Deodato, Eumir 141
Delta Rhythm Boys 95, 118
De-Lovely 109, 115, 118

Demaresq, William 251
Demi-Tasse 68
Dench, Judi 204, 249
Denman, Jeffrey 59
Dennis, Denny 72
Denver, John 310
Denver, Karl 85
Depp, Johnny 239
The Desert Song 90, 92, 223
The Desk Set 109
Desmond, Paul 62
Desperate Measures 336, 337
Dessa Rose 307, 309
Destry Rides Again 180, 182
DeSylva, B. G. 73, 76–7, 87, 90, 93, 96
The Devil's Deputy 8
Devine, Loretta 75
Dewey, Phil 109
DeWolf, Billy 167, 174
Diamond Five 216
Diamond, Micaela 345
Diamond, Neil 345
Diamond Studs 226
Diamonds 254, 255
Diana: The Musical 343
The Diary of Anne Frank 257
Dias, Gregory, IV 313
Dick Meldonian Trio 46
Dickens, Charles 192, 200, 257
Dickson, Barbara 250
Die Fledermaus 50, 137
Diener, Joan 201
Dietrich, Marlene 289
Dietz, Howard 79, 96, 102, 105, 115, 116, 121, 142, 151
Diggs, Daveed 330–1
Dilly, Erin 299
Dinah Was 286
DiNoia, Jennifer 306
Dion 126
Dion, Celine 132, 346
Dirty Rotten Scoundrels 307, 309
Disaster! 332
Dishy, Bob 136, 183
Distel, Sacha 170
Divo, Il 268
Dixie, Henry E. 6
Dixie Jubilee Singers 95
Dixieland Ramblers 179
Dixon, Brandon Victor 320–1
Dixon, Harlan 59
Do Black Patent Leather Shoes Reflect Up? 246
Do I Hear a Waltz? 197, 199
Doctor Jazz 225
Doctor, Sam 4

Title and Name Index

Doctor Selavy's Magic Theatre 220
Doctor Zhivago 330
Doctorow, E. L. 286
Dodd, Jimmie 185
Dodd, Marcia 306
Dodd, Pat 261
Dogfight 326, 327
Doing Our Bit 64
The Doll Girl 53
The Dollar Princess 42
A Doll's House 248
A Doll's Life 248, 250
Dolly Sisters 48
The Dolly Sisters 66
Dolly Varden 23
Domingo, Placido 139
Dona Flor and Her Two Husbands 237
Donahey, Lisa 299
Donaldson, Walter 96
Donegan, Lonnie 175
Donica, Jordan 173, 188
The Donkey Show 291
Donlevy, Brian 114
Donnelly, Killian 327
Donovan, Jason 268
Don't Bother Me, I Can't Cope 220, 222
Don't Get God Started 262
Don't Play Us Cheap 217
Dooley, Ray 114
Doonesbury 251
Dorsey, Jimmy 104, 106, 115
Dorsey, Tommy 2, 104, 106, 115, 118, 122, 128
Doughboys 26
Doughboys in Ireland 51
Douglas, Christian 327
Douglas, Melvyn 180
Douglas, Mike 198
Douglass, Stephen 144
Dover Street to Dixie 74
Dowling, Eddie 70, 90, 114
Down for the Count 128
Down to Earth 247
Downey, Morton 51
Doyle, John 330
Dr. De Luxe 45
Dr. Syntax 8
Dracula: The Musical 307
Drake, Alfred 138–9, 144, 188
Draper, Paul 134
Drat! The Cat! 200
Dream 283
Dream City 34
The Dream Girl 84
Dreamgirls 246–7, 262
Dressler, Marie 10, 23, 42, 61

Dropstick Murphys 54
The Drowsy Chaperone 310, 311
Drummond, Jack 170
The Drunkard 212, 214
DuBarry Was a Lady 127, 129
Dubin, Al 243
The Duchess 48–9
The Duchess Misbehaves 145
Duchin, Eddy 109
Dude 220
Dudley Do-Right 85
Dudley, S. H. 9
Duff, Mary 43
Duffy's Tavern 51
Duke, Vernon 99, 108, 131, 134, 142
Dunbar, Dixie 114
Dunbar, Paul Laurence 16, 25
Duncan, Craig 17
Duncan, Sandy 240
Duncan, Todd 131
Dunham, Katherine 131
Dunne, Irene 5, 112
Durang, Christopher 313
Durante, Jimmy 102, 107, 119, 126
Durdan, Deanna 118
Dylan, Bob 155, 312, 338, 340
Dyson, Ron 207

Eagan, Daisy 271
The Earl and the Girl 31, 33
Earl Carroll's Sketch Book 116
The Earl Carroll Vanities 81, 87, 90, 96, 102, 105, 108, 110, 116, 127
Earl May Trio 95
Earl of Ruston 215
Early to Bed 141
Eating Raoul 273, 274
East of Eden 206
East Wind 105
Easter Parade 59
Eaton, Mary 40
Ebb, Fred 183, 197, 203–4, 206, 209, 215, 228–9, 234, 243, 251, 270, 275, 276, 283, 305, 320–1, 330, 345
Ebersole, Christine 240, 310, 312, 334
Ebsen, Buddy 111
Ebsen, Vilma 111
Eckroth, Rachel 207
Eckstine, Billy 107, 112, 161, 188, 195
The Ed Wynn Carnival 70
The Eddie Cantor Story 49
Eddy, Nelson 2, 46, 51, 85–6, 265
The Eddy Duchin Story 41
Eder, Linda 66, 122, 193, 201, 252, 280
The Education of H*Y*M*A*N K*A*P*L*A*N 206

Title and Name Index

Edwardes, George 8–9
Edwards, Sherman 209
Edwards, Tammy 282
Egan, Susan 204, 299
Eileen 61, 63
El Capitan 10–11
El Grande de Coca-Cola 220
Eldridge, Roy 88
Elf 322, 323
Eliscue, Edward 117
Eliot, T. S. 248, 249
Elliman, Yvonne 218
Ellington, Duke 88, 104, 148, 243, 260, 283
Ellington, Ray 260
Elliotts 69
Ellis, Anita 75, 97, 100
Ellis, Kerry 306
Ellis, Mary 84–5
Ellison, Sidney 22
Elsie, Lily 37
Elstree Calling 100
Eltinge, Julian 48
Elvis: A Rockin' Remembrance 267
The Emerald Isle 25
Emerson Dance Orchestra 80
End of the Rainbow 324
Engel, Lehman 136
Englander, Ludwig 6, 16, 23
The Enchantress 48–9
Epstein, Alvin 183
Erivo, Cynthia 311, 332
Erminie 6, 27
Errico, Melissa 149, 166, 221, 278
Errol, Leon 48, 61, 96
Erwin, Trudy 37, 139
Escape to Margaritaville 336
Esparza, Raul 312
Espinosa, Eden 306, 316
Estabrooks, Jonathan 271
Estefan, Emilio 332
Estefan, Gloria 332
Etting, Ruth 40, 77, 100
Eubie! 75, 237
Evan, Robert 284
Evans, Bill 141, 170
Evans, George 25–6
Evans, Greek 13
Evans, Niki 230
Evans, Paul 109
Evans, Wilbur 155
An Evening with Beatrice Lillie 165
An Evening with Jerry Herman 289
Everybody's Hobby 118
Everybody's Welcome 105–6
Everywoman 45

Evita 240–2, 324
Evil Dead: The Musical 312, 314
Excelsior, Jr. 10–11
Eyen, Tom 246–7

Fabian 26
Fabiani, Joel 235
Fabray, Nanette 131, 151–3, 159
Face the Music 105, 107
Fade Out—Fade In 194, 196
Fain, Sammy 121–2, 159, 183
The Fair Co-Ed 39
Fairbanks, Douglas 29
Fairbanks Twins 70
Faith Journey 279
Faith, Paloma 158
Faith, Percy 185, 218
Falsettoland 244, 270, 272, 273
Falsettos 244, 273, 274, 334
Fame 92, 304
Fame on 42nd Street 305
A Family Affair 190
Fancy Free 64
Fanny 169, 170
Fantana 29–30
The Fantasticks 184, 185, 209, 226
Far from Heaven 328
Farrell, Eileen 126
Fascinating Flora 34
The Fascinating Widow 48
Fay, Harry 43
Faye, Alice 43, 75, 152
Faye, Frank 67
Faye, Joey 151, 254
Fearless Frank 243
Fearn, Alice 311
Feinstein, Michael 40, 59, 104, 118, 227, 235, 265
Feist, Leo 53
Fela! 318
Felder, Hershey 92
Feldman, Jack 324–5
Feldstein, Beanie 343
Felts, Jimmy 126
The Fencing Master 5
Fenholt, Jeff 218
Ferber, Edna 183, 326
Ferguson, Maynard 95
Ferland, Danielle 77
Ferrari, Frank 285
Ferrer, José 194, 202
Ferry, Bryan 107
Festival 241
Fiddle-Dee-Dee 21–2
Fiddler on the Roof 197–9, 203, 231, 246, 270, 304, 332, 338, 346

Title and Name Index

Fields, Arthur 77
Fields, Benny 59
Fields, Billy 170
Fields, Dorothy 79, 93, 99, 157, 159, 304
Fields, Ernie 83
Fields, Gracie 139, 260
Fields, Herbert 99
Fields, Lew 12, 16, 18, 21, 23, 25, 27, 29, 31, 34, 36, 39, 43, 46, 48, 50, 53
Fields, W. C. 31, 58, 61, 81, 87, 96
Fierstein, Harvey 302
Fifth Dimension 207, 216
Fifty Miles from Boston 36, 38
Fifty Million Frenchmen 99, 101
The Fig Leaves Are Falling 209
Finding Neverland 330, 331
Fine and Dandy 102, 104
Finian's Rainbow 158, 150, 169, 320
Finn, William 243-4, 270, 273-4, 289-90
Finnerty, Paul 54
Fiorello! 183, 185, 214
Fioretta 96
The Firebrand of Florence 142
The Firefly 50, 52
The Fireman's Flame 121
First Date 328
First Daughter Suite 332
First Impressions 180
First Lady Suite 277, 332
Fisher, Eddie 77, 172, 192, 198
Fisher, Fred 53
Fisher, Irving 73
Fitzgerald, Ella 91, 100, 109, 115, 118, 132, 136, 141, 149, 166, 195, 204
Five Course Love 310
Five Guys Named Moe 273
The Five O'Clock Girl 93, 95
Five Satins 123
Flack, Roberta 172, 201
Flaherty, Stephen 263, 267, 286-7, 296, 301, 307, 315, 334
Flahooley 159, 161
Flamingos 95
Flanagan, Ralph 46
Fleischer, Dave 40
Fleming, Renée 128, 308
Fletcher, Douglas 170
Flo-Flo 64
Flora Bella 61
Flora, the Red Menace 197, 199
Flores, Aaron 282
Florodora 21
The Florodora Girl 22
Flory, Chris 170
Flower Drum Song 180-1, 301

Floyd Collins 281, 282
Fly By Night 330, 331
Flying Colors 108, 110
The Flying Deuces 41
Flying Down to Rio 117
Flying High 99, 101
Flying Over Sunset 343, 344
Flymo and The Vershons 95
Flynn, Jerome 100
Folies Bergere 127, 197
Follies 215, 216, 324
Follies of 1907 36, 38
Follies of 1908 39
Follow Me 61, 63
Follow the Band 100
Follow the Crowd 59
Follow the Girls 140-1
Follow Thru 96, 98
Fonda, Henry 111
Fontane Sisters 161
Fool Moon 281
Footloose 289
For Goodness Sake 76
Forbes, Matt 115
Forbidden Broadway 248
Forbidden Melody 119
Ford, Florrie 43
Ford, Helen 79
Ford, Mary 26, 132-3, 212
Ford, Nancy 206, 234, 235
Ford, Tennessee Ernie 204
Forever Plaid 267
Forever Tango 286
Forrest, Helen 66, 128
The Fortune Teller 16-17
Forty-five Minutes from Broadway 31, 33, 48
42nd Street 243, 248, 295
Forty-Year-Old Version 101
Fosse 59, 289
Fosse, Bob 74, 157, 228, 230, 234, 256, 346
Foster, Stephen 18, 68, 321
Foster, Sutton 115, 247, 298-9, 343
Four Aces 17, 40, 168
Four Freshmen 66, 141
4 Guys Named José ... and Una Mujer Named Maria 295
Four Jets 218
Four Lads 147
Four Preps 112, 170
Four Saints 179
4 Saints in 3 Acts 111
Four Seasons 310
1492, 4
Fountain, Pete 95, 104, 172

Title and Name Index

Four Sergeants 122
The Fourposter 203
Fowler, Beth 239, 267
Fox, Della 8, 10
Fox, Harry 58, 65–6
Foxy Grandpa 23
Foy, Eddie 23, 27
Foy, Eddie, Jr. 35, 102, 116
Franchi, Sergio 46, 85, 193
Francis, Calum 327
Francis, Connie 17, 26, 51, 104, 185, 210
Frank Merriwell 215
Frankel, Scott 310
Frankenstein 315
Franklin, Aretha 69, 95, 188, 195
Franzetti, Carlos 122
Fraser, Brendan 85
Fratantoni, Diane 250
Free for All 105
Freed, Stan 49
The Freelance 31
The French Doll 76, 78
The French Maid 14–15
Frey, Nathanial 157
Friedlander, Erik 210
Friedman, David 305
Friedman, Garry William 251
Friedman, Maria 193, 278, 280
Friml, Rudolf 50, 53, 58, 61, 70, 84, 87, 93
Fritz in Tammany Hall 31
Froger, Rene 285
The Frogs 307, 309
Frohman, Charles 56
From A to Z 183
Froman, Jane 88, 111
Frost, Tom 10
Frozen 336, 342
The Full Monty 295, 297
Fuller, Dean 174
Fuller, Penny 204
Fun Home 328, 329, 330
Funicello, Annette 28
Funny Face 93, 95, 248
Funny Girl 194–6, 343
A Funny Thing Happened on the Way to the Forum 190–1, 217, 281
Furber, Douglas 259–60
Furth, George 212, 234
Further Mo' 267

Gabe Baltazar Quartet 264
Gaga, Lady 109, 115, 132
A Gaiety Girl 8–9
Gaines, Davis 264
Galan, Frank 292

Galati, Frank 286
Gallagher, Helen 157, 162, 165, 169
Gallagher, Peter 330
Gambatese, Jenn 155, 185
The Game Is Up 197
Gans, Danny 281
Garde, Betty 138
Gardner, Ava 141
Gardner, Reginald 116
Garfunklel Art 155
Garland, Judy 26, 30, 59, 66, 69, 75, 77, 80, 104, 112, 147, 149, 265, 286, 324
Garner, Erroll 149
Garrett, Betty 136, 137
Garrett O'Magh 21
The Garrick Gaieties 84, 86, 87, 89, 96, 98, 102
Gary, John 51
Gaxton, William 127
The Gay Divorcee 108–10
The Gay Life 190, 191
Gay Men's Chorus of Los Angeles 252
Gay, Noel 259–60
The Gay Parisienne 12
Gaye, Marvin 57
Gayle, Crystal 166
Gaynor, Gloria 252
Gazarek, Sara 136
Gear, Luella 114, 127
Gee, Lottie 74
The Geezer 12–13
The Geisha 12–13
Geld, Gary 212
Geller, Herb 136
Genesis 265
Gensler, Lewis 90
Gentille, Linda 168
A Gentleman's Guide to Love & Murder 328, 329
Gentlemen Marry Brunettes 97, 100
Gentlemen Prefer Blondes 157–8, 223, 279
George, Boy 304
George Gershwin Alone 92
George M! 30, 33, 80, 206
George Washington Jr. 31–3
George White's Music Hall Varieties 108
George White's Scandals 70, 76, 78, 79–80, 84, 86, 87, 89, 90, 105, 107, 116, 127, 129
Georgy 212
Gershon, Gina 204
Gershwin, George 57, 61, 68, 84, 87, 93, 96, 99, 102–3, 108, 111, 117, 134, 248, 273, 324
Gershwin, Ira 84, 87, 93, 96, 99, 102–3, 105, 108, 111, 134, 142, 148, 248, 273, 324
The Gershwins' Fascinating Rhythm 92, 103, 105, 289
Gettin' the Band Back Together 338

Title and Name Index

Gets, Malcolm 136, 289
Getz, Stan 109
Geva, Tamara 102
Ghee, J. Harrison 346-7
Ghislanzoni, Antonio 292
Ghost 324, 325
Ghostley, Alice 162
Giant 326, 327
Gibbs, Arthur 83
Gibson, Deborah 181
The Giddy Throng 21
Gigi 223-4, 330
Gilbert, Simon 201
Gilbert, W. S. 1, 4, 6, 105, 111, 114, 119, 124, 140, 142, 151, 197, 203, 243
Gilda Radnor: Live from New York 243
Giles, Donna 247
Gilford, Jack 131
Gillespie, Dana 218
Gillespie, Dizzy 118, 149, 207
Gillette, Anita 204
Gillette, Ruth 28
Gilmore, Peter 172
Gilson, Deborah 204
The Gingham Girl 79
Gingold, Hermione 167, 183
Giordano, Vince 100
Giordano, Tyrone 255
The Girl and the Wizard 42
The Girl Behind the Counter 36
The Girl Behind the Gun 67
Girl Crazy 102-4, 273
The Girl Friend 87, 89
The Girl from Kay's 27
The Girl from Montmatre 50, 52
The Girl from Nantucket 145
The Girl from Paris 12
The Girl from the North Country 338, 340
The Girl from Up There 21
The Girl from Utah 55-7
The Girl in Pink Tights 167
The Girl in the Red Velvet Swing 21-2
The Girl Who Came to Supper 194
The Girl Who Smiles 58
Girlies 45
Girling, Nancy 22
The Girls Against the Boys 183
The Girls of Gottenberg 39
Give My Regards to Broadway 30
Glaser, Lulu 2, 8, 23, 31, 39
Gleason, Jackie 183
Gleason, Joanna 273
Glee 281, 303, 306
Gleeson, Simon 271
The Glorious Ones 315

Glory Days 315
Glover, Savion 273, 281
Goblin Market 256, 257
Godfrey, Lynnie 75
Godspell 215, 216, 295, 308, 324
Goggin, Dan 275
Go-Go's 338
Going Up! 64, 66, 231
Goldberg, Whoopie 191
The Golden Apple 167, 168
Golden Boy 197, 199
The Golden Bride 332
Golden Gate Orchestra 82
The Golden Land 256, 336
Golden Rainbow 206, 208
Goldilocks 180, 182
Goldman, James 190, 215
Goldman, William 190
Good Boy 96
Good-bye Cruel World 101
The Good Girl 123
Good Morning, Dearie 76, 78
Good Morning, Judge 69
Good News! 93, 95, 226
Good Times 73
Good Vibrations 307
The Goodbye Girl 275, 276
Goodman, Benny 104, 112, 116, 185
Goodman, Steve 285
Goodtime Charley 225
Goodwin, Wendy 198
Gordy, Barry 326
Gore, Lesley 170, 175, 193
Gorey Details 295
Gorme, Eydie 97, 198, 204, 206, 212
Gorney, Jay 99, 108
Gorshin, Frank 212
The Gospel at Colonus 262
Got to Go Disco 240
Gould, Jocelyn 166
Gould, Morton 157
Goulet, Robert 122, 144, 149, 163, 187, 188, 193, 198, 206, 277
The Governor's Son 21-2
Govich, Milena 204
The Grab Bag 84
Grable, Betty 51, 66, 127
Graff, George, Jr. 50-1
Graff, Randy 199
Graham, Martha 81
Grand Hotel 267, 269
A Grand Night for Singing 144
Grand Street Follies 81, 90
The Grand Tour 237, 239
Grant, Earl 95

Title and Name Index

Grant, Gogi 91
Grant, Peter 168
The Grass Harp 217, 219
The Grasshopper (La Cigale) 2
Grappelli, Stéphane 88, 104
Gravitte, Debbie 59, 181, 227, 250, 306
Gray, Alexander 88
Gray, Dolores 146, 162
Gray, Glen 17, 51
Gray, Kevin 264
Grayson, Kathryn 5, 112
Grease 220, 222, 277, 281, 315
The Great American Trailer Park Musical 310, 311
Great Day 99, 101
The Great Victor Herbert 46
The Great Waltz 114
The Great Ziegfeld 41, 66, 72
Greco, Buddy 57, 132, 136, 166
Green, Adolph 142, 162, 165, 174–5, 177, 187, 248
Green, Alice 57
The Green Bird 291
Green, Daisy 22
Green Grow the Lilacs 138
Green, Johnny 115
Green, Larry 132
Green, Martyn 124
Green, Mitzi 119
Green, Robson 100
Greenbank, Harry 8
Greenwich, Ellie 254
Greenwich Village 75
Greenwich Village Follies 70, 72, 73, 76, 78, 79, 81
Greenwillow 183, 185
Greenwood, Charlotte 55, 61, 159
Greer, Jo Ann 132
Greger, Max 218
Greif, Michael 310
Grenville, Beatrice 22
Grey Gardens 310, 311, 312
Grey, Joel 30, 33, 80, 206, 225, 305
Grieg, Edvard 142
Grier, David Alan 247
Griffen, Merv 169
Griffith, Corinne 57
Griffiths, Rachel 158
Grimes, Tammy 187
Grind 254, 255
Groban, Josh 201, 239, 339, 345
Groener, Harry 104
Groff, Jonathan 346
Groody, Louise 67, 87–8
Grossman, Larry 248
Grossmith, George 57
Groundhog 273
Groundhog Day 149, 334, 335

Grover, Mary 144
Grupper, Adam 271
Guaraldi, Vince 193
Guare, John 217
Guettel, Adam 281, 286, 307, 308
Guevara, Nacha 241
Guilty by Suspicion 158
Guittard, Laurence 139, 240
Gunton, Bob 191, 239, 267
Gutenberg! The Musical! 312
Guthrie, Tyrone 174
Guys and Dolls 159, 161, 169, 231, 273, 318
Gypsy 180–2, 225, 267, 301, 315
Gypsy Lady 148, 190

H.M.S. Pinafore 36, 142
Haarlem Nocturne 254
Hackett, Buddy 197
Hadestown 332, 338
Hadley, Jerry 168
Hagger, Garry 285
Hague, Albert 169–70, 183
Hair 206–8, 220, 318
Hairspray 301–3, 315
Hajos, Mitzi 67
Hale, Binnie 88, 106
Haley, Bill 100
Haley, Jack 127, 151
Half a Sixpence 197, 199
Hall, Adelaide 102, 107, 118, 128
Hall, Anthony Blair 296
Hall, Arthur 80
Hall, Bettina 102
Hall, Carol 256–7
Hall, Henry 115
Hall, Juanita 169
Hall, Lani 282
Hall, Lee 318–19
The Hall of Fame 23
Hall, Owen 8
Hallelujah, Baby! 203, 204
Halliday, Robert 102
The Ham Tree 31, 33
Hamilton 330–31
Hamilton, Henry 8–9
Hamilton, Roy 144, 201
Hamilton, Scott 172
Hamlisch, Marvin 197, 225, 298
Hammerstein, Arthur 97
Hammerstein, Oscar 70
Hammerstein II, Oscar 5, 70, 79, 84–5, 87, 93–5, 99, 105, 108, 116, 127–9, 134, 135, 137–8, 140, 142–4, 145–6, 151, 154–5, 159, 162, 165, 171, 180–1, 183–5, 281, 301, 305, 321, 326
Hampton, Christopher 280–2

Title and Name Index

Hampton Hawes Trio 193
Hampton, Lionel 122, 166
Hancock, Sheila 239
Hands on a Hard Body 326
The Hang 343
Hank Williams: Lost Highway 301
Hanks, Tom 281
Hanky-Panky 50
Hanley, James 90
Hanlin, Shaymus 149
Hanna, Phil 149
Hannah and Her Sisters 132
Hannah ... 1939 268
Hannas, Elliott 319
Hannon, Bob 128
Hansberry, Lorraine 223
Hansel, Adrian 303
Hanshaw, Annette 97
Happenings 104
The Happiest Girl in the World 187, 189
Happiness 318
Happy Days 70
Happy End 231, 233
Happy Hunting 174, 176
Happy New Year 240
The Happy Time 206, 208
Happyland 31
Haran, Mary Clare 136
Harbach, Otto 39, 42, 45, 48, 50, 53, 61, 64, 84–5, 87–8, 105, 111, 119
Harburg, E. Y. 99, 108, 114, 121, 131, 142, 148, 159, 177
Hardin, Melora 118
Hare, Ernest 77
Hargrove, Roy 141
Haring, Keith 301
Harlan, Byron G. 22
Harlem Nights 3
Harlem Song 301
Harmon, Linda 28
Harmonicats 54
Harmony 343
Harnick, Sheldon 177, 183, 187, 192, 197–8, 203, 215, 228
Harrell, Margi 72
Harrigan 'n Hart 254
Harrigan, Ned (Edward) 2, 254
Harris, Barbara 200, 203
Harris, Charles K. 4–5
Harris, Emmylou 158
Harris, Julie 200
Harris, Les 46
Harris, Marion 75, 88
Harris, Neil Patrick 328, 339
Harris, Niki 147

Harris, Sam 76
Harrison, Charles 17, 53, 66
Harrod, James 62
Harrold, Orville 45–6
Harry Allen Quartet 75
Hart, Charles 80, 263, 268
Hart, Lorenz 79, 84, 90, 93, 96, 99, 102, 116, 119, 120, 121, 127, 131–2, 134–5, 140, 162, 248
Hart, Moss 99, 105, 121, 131
Hart, Tony 254
Has Anyone Here Seen Kelly? 43
Hassard Short's Ritz Revue 84
Hasselhoff, David 285
Hatch, Tony 191
Hats Off to Ice 142
Hatzai, Steve 126
Havana 39
Have a Heart 61, 63
Haver, June 54
Hawkins, Coleman 126, 141
Hawkins, Corey 313
Haworth, Jill 203
Hayden, Michael 144
Hayden Quartet 17, 28
Hayes, Isaac 168
Hayes, Sean 210
Haymes, Dick 51, 57, 62, 66, 141, 146, 161
Haynes, Brooke 329
Haynes, Tiger 174
Hayton, Lennie 95
Hayworth, Rita 132
Hazel Flagg 165, 166
Hazell, Eddie 198
Hazelton, Tom 179
He Came from Milwaukee 45
Head, Murray 217
Head Over Heels 67, 338
Headley, Heather 292
Heads Up 99, 101
Healy, Dan 96–7
Healy, Ted 102
Hearn, George 239, 252
The Heart of Maryland 12
Heart of the Country 92
Heathers 328, 329
Heatherton, Ray 102
Hecht, Jessica 199, 332
Hedwig and the Angry Inch 286, 288, 328
Held, Anna 12, 23, 34, 36, 39, 61
The Helen Morgan Story 91
Helen of Troy, New York 81
Heller, Marc 278
Hellman, Lillian 157, 174
Hello Again 277, 278
Hello, Broadway 55, 57

Title and Name Index

Hello, Dolly! 1, 194, 194, 197, 206, 228, 234, 281, 334
Hello, Frisco, Hello 43
The Hello Girls 338
Hello Muddah, Hello Fadduh 275
Hello, Solly! 203
Hellzapoppin 125, 134
The Hen Pecks 45
Henderson, Bill 170
Henderson, Chick 118
Henderson, Florence 155, 169, 181, 194
Henderson, Joe 109
Henderson, Marcia 157
Henderson, Ray 87, 93, 96
Henderson, Skitch 152
Henning, Doug 223, 248
Henry, Brian Tyree 322
Henry, Joshua 144, 321
Henry, Matt 327
Henry, Sweet Henry 206, 208
Henshall, Ruthie 69, 104, 221
Henstock, Leslie 306
Hepburn, Katharine 109, 212
Her First Roman 209
Her Soldier Boy 61
Herbert, Evelyn 102
Herbert, Victor 8, 12–13, 14–15, 16, 27–8, 29, 31, 34–5, 39, 42, 45–6, 48, 50, 53, 55, 58, 61, 70, 73, 84–5, 148
Here Lies Love 328
Here's Howe 93, 95
Here's Love 194, 196
Here's Where I Belong 206
Herman, Jerry 190, 194, 226–6, 237, 251–2, 305
Herman, Woody 77, 136
Hermes House Band 252
A Hero Is Born 121
Herring, Steven 118
Hers to Hold 118
Hesitations 201
Hewitt, Colleen 216
Heyward, Dorothy 116
Heyward, DuBose 116
Heywood, Alice 241
Hicks, Adrianna 346–7
Higgledy-Piggledy 29–30
High Button Shoes 151–3
High Fidelity 312, 314
High Hatters 97
High Jinks 53–4
High Kickers 134
The High Rollers Social and Pleasure Club 274
High Society 166, 287
High Spirits 194, 196
Higher and Higher 127, 129

The Highwayman 14
Hildegarde 102, 122, 169
Hill, David 163
Hilliard, Bob 165
Hi-Lo's 141
Hines, Earl "Fatha" 72, 149
Hines, Gregory 243, 273
Hines, Maurice 256
Hip-Hip! Hooray 36, 58
Hipp, Paul 270
Hirsch, Louis 64
Hirt, Al 168, 210
His Honor, the Mayor 33
A History of the American Film 234
Hit the Deck! 90, 92
Hitchcock, Raymond 27, 48, 61
Hitchy-Koo 63
Hitchy-Koo of 1917 64
Hitchy-Koo of 1918 67
Hitt, Christine 40
Hobart, George V. 23
Hochberg, Adam 104
Hockridge, Edmund 166, 179
Hodge, Douglas 252
Hodnott, Lois 118
Hoffman, Dustin 147
Hogan, Luanne 77, 122
Hoity-Toity 23
Hokey-Pokey 48
Hold Everything 96, 98
Hold on to Your Hats 131, 133
Holgate, Ron 147
Holiday, Billie 100, 107, 109, 112, 122, 123, 141, 259
Holiday Inn 334
Holland, Curtis 75
Hollens, Peter 335
Holler If You Hear Me 330
Holliday, Jennifer 246, 247
Holliday, Judy 174–5, 192
Holly, Buddy 265
Hollywood Pinafore 142
Holman, Libby 96, 102
Holmes, Rupert 257–8
Holt, Will 251
Holtz, Lou 134
Home Sweet Homer 228
Honey Girl 70
Honeydew 73
The Honeymoon Express 50, 52
Honeymoon in Vegas 330, 331
Honeymoon Lane 90, 92
The Honeymooners 36
Honky Tonk Nights 259
Hood, Basil 37
Hooray for What! 121, 123

Title and Name Index

Hoosier Hot Shots 69
Hop 54
Hope and Glory 118
Hope, Bob 96, 116, 119
Hopkins, Miriam 81
Hopper, De Wolf 8, 10–11, 21, 23, 31, 42
Horn, Shirley 172
Horne, Lena 57, 91, 158
Horne, Marilyn 139
Horrocks, Jane 97, 161
Horton, Edward Everett 51
Horton, Robert 194
Horwitt, Arnold B. 169–70
Hoschna, Karl 39, 42, 45, 48, 50
Hot Butter 216
Hot-Cha 105
Hot Chocolates 99, 101, 102
Hot Feet 310
The Hot Mikado 124
Hot Rhythm 102
Hot Spot 192, 193
The House of Bernarda Alba 310
House of Flowers 169, 170
Houston, Cissy 232
Houston, Whitney 247
How Now, Dow Jones 206, 208
How to Steal an Election 209
How to Succeed in Business without Really Trying 190, 191, 279, 322
Howard Crabtree's Whoop-Dee-Doo 277, 283
Howard, Eugene 50, 61, 111
Howard, Willie 50, 61, 102, 111, 134
Howdy, Mr. Ice 164
Howe, Robert 9
Howerd, Frankie 191
Howes, Sally Ann 149, 221
Hoyt, Charles H. 1
Hubbard, Bruce 95
Hudgens, Vanessa 224
Hudson, Jennifer 247, 250
Hudson, Kate 230
Hue and Cry 221
Hughes, Langston 148, 177
Hughes, Mary Beth 100
Hughes, Patricia 149
Hugo, Victor 259
Huizinga, Ilse 172
Hullo, London! 40
The Human Comedy 251, 253
Humperdinck, Engelbert 122, 168, 207
Humpty Dumpty 29
Hunt, Liana 325
Hunt, Pee Wee 109
Hupfield, Herman 105–6
Hurly-Burly 16–17

Hurry Harry 220
Husbands 52
Husmann, Ron 166
Huston, Gil 163
Huston, Walter 124–6
Hutchinson, Leslie "Hutch" 118
Hutton, Betty 147
Hutton, June 49
Hyles, Caleb 339
Hyman, Dick 75, 139

I Can Get It for You Wholesale 190, 191
I Do! I Do! 203, 205
I Had a Ball 197
I Love My Wife 231, 233
I Love You Because 310
I Love You, You're Perfect, Now Change 283
I Married an Angel 121, 123
I Miss You Like Hell 336, 337
I Remember Mama 237
I Will Come Back 286
I Won't Dance 273
Ibsen, Henrik 248
The Iceman Cometh 346
Iconis, Joe 338–9
I'd Rather Be Right 121, 123
Idiot's Delight 248
The Idol's Eye 14–15
If/Then 328, 329
The Iliad 167
I'll Be Seeing You 122
I'll Say She Is 81
The Illustrator's Show 116
Illya Darling 203, 205
Im, Dami 247
I'm Getting My Act Together and Taking It on the Road 234, 235
I'm Solomon 206
Immerman, Connie and George 99
Imperials 201
In Caliente 51
In Circles 206
In Country 101
In Dahomey 25–6, 31
In Gay New York 10
In Posterland 26
In the Good Old Summertime 26
In the Heights 312–13, 314, 315
In Town 14–15
In Transit 322, 334
In Trousers 243, 274
Ingram, Rex 131
Ink Spots 17, 40, 168
Inside U.S.A. 151, 153
The International Cup 46

397

Title and Name Index

The International Revue 99, 101
Into the Light 259
Into the Woods 262, 264, 298, 300, 345
Ipi-Tombi 231
Irene 66, 70, 72, 220
Irish Eyes Are Smiling 49, 51
Irish Tenors 17, 51
Irma la Douce 187, 189
Irving, Ellis 146
Irwin, Bill 281
Irwin, May 10, 16
Is There Life After High School? 246, 247
Ishtar 147
The Isle o' Dreams 50–1
Isley Brothers 40
It Ain't Nothin' But the Blues 289
It All Came True 51
The It Girl 295
It Happened in Nordland 29–30
It Shoulda Been You 330, 331
It's a Bird … It's a Plane … It's Superman 200, 202
It's So Nice to Be Civilized 243
Ives, Burl 59

Jacinto, Ramon 201
Jacob, Bill 185
Jacob, Christian 62
Jack o' Lantern 64, 66
Jackie & Roy 216
Jackman, Hugh 139, 179, 304, 343
Jack's Holiday 279, 280
Jackson, Carrie 172
Jackson, Cheyenne 235
Jackson, Christopher 313
Jackson, Cliff 101
Jackson, Ethel 36–7
Jackson, Jermaine 149, 247
Jackson, Lorna Doone 13
Jackson, Mahalia 267
Jackson, Michael 128, 343
Jackson, Michael R. 340–1
Jacoby, Mark 264
Jacques Brel Is Alive and Living in Paris 207, 275
Jagged Little Pill 340
Jamaica 177, 179
James, Harry 118, 144, 166, 198
James, Joni 17, 51, 54
James Joyce's The Dead 291, 293
James, Paul 102
James, Sidney 152
Jamison, Judith 243
Jane Eyre 295, 297
Janek, Joni 72
Janis, Elsie 39, 61
Jansen, Marie 2

Jarrett, Keith 128
Jazz Messengers 163
The Jazz Singer 77, 93
Jay and the Americans 155
Jeanmarie, Zizi 115
Jeepers Creepers 26
Jeffrey, Terry Mike 267
Jekyll & Hyde 283, 265–6
Jelly Roll 279
Jelly's Last Jam 273, 274
Jenkins, Daniel 255
Jenkins, Gordon 62
Jenkins, Katherine 264
Jennie 194, 196
Jennifer 8 91
Jerome Kern Goes to Hollywood 112, 129, 256
Jerome Robbins' Broadway 153, 191, 265
Jerry's Girls 256
Jersey Boys 310
The Jersey Lily 27–8
Jessel, George 79, 102, 137
Jesus Christ Superstar 217, 218, 234, 248, 291, 324
The Jewel of Asia 25
Jiear, Alison 57
Jim Jams Jems 73
Jimmie 73, 75
Jimmy 212
Joel, Billy 301
John & Jen 279, 280, 281
John, Elton 91, 291, 292, 310, 318–19
John Murray Anderson's Almanac 167, 168
Johnny Guitar 305, 306
Johnny Johnson 119, 120
Johns, Glynis 220–1
Johnson, Bill 137, 146
Johnson, Chic 125, 134, 142
Johnson, J. Rosamund 131
Johnson, James C. 102
Johnson, James P. 82
Johnson, Judy 107
Johnson, Van 179
Johnson, William 171
The Johnsons 41
Johnston, Claire 97
The Jolly Bachelors 42–4
Jolson, Al 17, 30, 45, 48, 50, 55, 58, 64, 68–9, 75, 76–7, 87, 93, 131, 301
Jolson and Company 301
Jolson Sings Again 69, 75, 77
The Jolson Story 69, 77
Jones, Ada 40, 43, 49, 198
Jones, Allan 72, 128
Jones, Carolyn Lee 28
Jones, Catherine Zeta 221, 230
Jones, Dean 213

Title and Name Index

Jones, Etta 122, 144
Jones, Grace 232
Jones, Isham 82, 85
Jones, Jack 168, 221, 264
Jones, Leilani 254
Jones, Lucie 299
Jones, Quincy 172
Jones, Ricky Lee 91, 172
Jones, Salena 235
Jones, Shirley 144, 209
Jones, Sydney 8
Jones, Tom 183–4, 188, 194, 203, 209, 226, 241, 286, 299
Joplin, Janis 295, 328
Joplin, Scott 287
Jordan, Jeremy 324–5
Jordanaires 17
Jorgenson, Christine 181
Joseph and the Amazing Technicolor Dreamcoat 231, 233, 246, 277
Joy, Leonard 100
Joyce, Jimmy 185
A Joyful Noise 203
Juan Darién 283
Jubilee 116–18
Julia, Raul 202, 226, 273
Jumbo 116, 118
Juno 180, 182
Juno and the Paycock 180

Kahal, Irving 121–2
Kahn, Gus 96, 99, 117
Kahn, Madeleine 234
Kail, Thomas 345
Kalmar, Bert 81, 90, 93, 96–7, 99
Kames, Bob 28
Kamplain, Frank M. 69
Kanawa, Kiri Te 112
Kander, John 190, 197, 203–4, 206, 209, 215, 228–9, 234, 243, 251, 270, 275, 276, 283, 305, 320–1, 330, 345
Kane, Helen 96–7
Kanin, Garson 195
Kaplan, Jonathan 244
Karlin, Mirian 198
Karloff, Boris 157
Karnes, Bob 5
Karnilova, Maria 198–9, 209
Karns, Virginia 27
Karrie, Peter 264
Kat and the Kings 291
Katalina 133
Kate Kip, Buyer 16
Katinka 58, 60
Katja 90

Katz, Mickey 198
Kaufman, George S. 81, 99, 105, 121, 142, 148
Kaufman, Irving 53
Kaye, Danny 192, 215
Kaye, Judy 234
Kaye, Mary 149
Kaye, Sammy 107, 126
Kaye, Stubby 159, 254
Kean 190
Keanu 54
Kearns, Allen 81
Keating, Barry 265–6
Kedrova, Lila 251
Keel, Howard 139, 144, 147, 179, 183, 188
Keenan-Bolger, Andrew 296
Kelly 197
Kelly, Gene 104, 131, 149
Kelly, Jean Louisa 91
Kelly, John, T. 21
Kelly, Kitty 104
Kelly, Monty 185
Kelly, Nancy 170
Kelly, Patsy 102
Kelly, Paul Austin 43
Kendrick, Anna 214
Kennedy, Chilina 218
Kent, Barry 188
Kern, Jerome 5, 29, 31, 53, 55–6, 58, 61–2, 64, 70, 73, 76, 81, 87, 90, 93–5, 99, 105, 108, 111, 127–9, 162, 304
Kernan, David 191
Kerns, Grace 57
The Key 261
Kid Boots 81, 83
Kidman, Nicole 158
Kiki and Herb: Alive on Broadway 312
Kiley, Richard 155, 167–8, 190, 200, 201, 209, 234
Kilgore, Rebecca 75
Killer Diller 100
Kim, Sandra 292
Kimber, Kay 152
Kimberly Akimbo 343, 344, 345, 347
Kincaid, Bradley 51
The King and I 159, 161, 185, 231, 254, 281, 330
King, Carole 243, 328
King, Charles 48, 79–80
King, Dennis 84–5, 87
King, Donna 166
King, John Michael 171, 172
King Kong 338, 339
King, Morgana 136
The King of Cadonia 42
King of Hearts 237, 239
King of Schnorres 240

Title and Name Index

King, Wayne 46
The King's Carnival 21
Kingston Trio 163
Kingsway Strings 5
Kinky Boots 326, 327
Kipling, Rudyard 8
Kirke, Hazel 67
Kirkland, Jill 218
Kirkland, Kari 166
Kirkwood, Pat 43
Kirsten, Dorothy 46
Kismet 167–8, 234
The Kiss Burglar 64
Kiss Me, Kate 154, 156, 291, 338
Kiss of the Spider Woman 275, 276
Kissinger, Brittny 232
Kitt, Eartha 100, 109, 112, 141, 158, 162
Kitt, Tom 316
Kitty Grey 39
Kleban, Edward 225
Klein, Robert 265
Kline, Kevin 109, 243
Kloser, Gene 216
Klotz, Florence 234
Knickerbocker Holiday 124–6
The Knife 115, 259
Knight, Evelyn 152
Knight, Felix 46
Knight, June 117
Knights of Song 124
Koehler, Ted 108
Koffie 247
Kopit, Arthur 275
Korie, Michael 310
Kosta, Tessa 67
Kostelanetz, Andre 11, 232
Kowalik, Trent 318, 319
KPOP (K-Pop) 336, 346
Krakowski, Jane 158
Kral, Roy 191
Krall, Diana 109, 115, 149
Kramer, Jana 92
Krauss, Alison 255
Kreiger, Henry 246–7
Kreisler, Fritz 142
Kron, Lisa 328–9
Krueger, Benny 75
Krupska, Dania 166
Kudisch, Marc 299
Kuhn, Judy 139, 175, 278, 308
Kulish, Kiril 318, 319
Kulthum, Umm 337
Kuni-Leml 254, 255
Kunz, Charlie 43
A Kurt Weill Cabaret 254

Kushner, James 244
Kushner, Tony 304
Kuti, Fela 318
Kwamina 190, 191
Kwan, Nancy 181

La Belle Paree 46
La Cage aux Folles 251, 252, 307, 320
La Cigale (The Grasshopper) 2
La Fanciulla del West (The Girl of the Golden West) 263
La Gatta Cenerentola (Cinderella the Cat) 256
La Gross Valise 200
La La Lucille 67, 69
La Plante, Laura 95
La Plume de Ma Tante 180
La Strada 212, 214
LaBelle, Patti 195, 248
LaChanze 292, 311
LaChiusa, John Michael 277, 279, 291, 301, 310, 324, 326, 332
Ladies and Gentleman, Jerome Kern 256
Ladies First 67, 69
Lady, Be Good! 84, 86
Lady Billy 73
The Lady Comes Across 134
Lady Day at Emerson's Bar and Grill 259
The Lady in Ermine 79–80
Lady in the Dark 131, 133
The Lady of the Slipper 50
The Lady Slavey 10
Lady Teazle 29
Laffing Room Only 142
LaGuardia, Fiorello 137, 183
Lahr, Bert 96, 114, 119, 127, 162, 183, 194
Laine, Cleo 75, 213, 221, 258, 257–8
Laine, Frankie 100
The Lake House 149
Lam, Sandy 282
Lamas, Fernando 37, 86
Lamberti, Professor 137
The Lambeth Walk 261
Lamont, Robin 216
LaMott, Nancy 144
The Land of Joy 64
Lane, Burton 108, 131, 148
Lane, Lupino 260
Lane, Nathan 147, 191, 273, 281
Lane, Priscilla 75
Lang, Harold 162, 174
Lange, Arthur 80
Lange, Jessica 126
Langford, Frances 80
Langton, Diane 235
Lanin, Lester 136, 204

Title and Name Index

Lanning, Jerry 173
Lansbury, Angela 194, 200, 209, 225, 237–9, 251
Lanza, Mario 46, 57, 109, 128, 172
Lapine, James 298
Lapotaire, Jane 243
LaRosa, Julius 204
Larsen, Liz 266
Larson, Jonathan 281, 282, 298
Lassie 70
The Last Five Years 298, 300
The Last of the Hogans 2
The Last Session 286
The Last Ship 330, 331
Last Sweet Days of Isaac 212, 214
The Last Waltz 73
Late Nite Comic 262
Latessa, Dick 226
LaTouche, John 131, 134, 142, 148, 151
The Laugh Parade 105
Laughing Matters 265, 266
Laughlin, Anna 25
Lauper, Cyndi 326, 327
Laurence, Paula 137
Laurents, Arthur 180, 315
Lawrence, Carol 162, 174, 183, 276
Lawrence, Gertrude 81, 87, 90, 96, 131, 159
Lawrence, Lucille 3
Lawrence, Stephanie 97
Lawrence, Steve 194, 198, 204, 206
The Lawrence Welk Show 152
Lazarus 332
Leach, Billy 141
Leader, Joseph 163
Leader of the Pack 254
Leap of Faith 324
Leave It to Jane 64, 66
Leave It to Me! 124, 126
Lee, Brenda 122, 123, 166, 204
Lee, Eugene 223, 279
Lee, Gypsy Rose 119, 137
Lee, Peggy 54, 75, 107, 112, 218, 251
Lee, Thelma 199
Left Bank Bearcats 32
Legally Blonde 312, 314
Legend 88
Legends in Concert 265
Legrand, Michel 301
Legs Diamond 265, 266
Lehár, Franz 36–7, 50, 58
Lehman, Ernest 298
Leiber, Jerry 279
Leibert, Dick 3
Leigh, Carolyn 187, 192
Leigh, Jennifer Jason 204
Leigh, Mitch 201–2

Leigh, Vivien 192
Lemmon, Jack 97
Lemonides, Vanessa 97
Lemper, Ute 213, 230
Lend an Ear 154
Lenk, Katrina 336, 337
Lennon 310
Lennon, John 310
Lenya, Lotte 126, 141, 312
Leon, Viktor 37
Leonard, Jack 128, 128
Lerner, Alan Jay 148–9, 154, 162–3, 171–2, 187–8,
    223–4, 228, 237, 248
Les Misérables 261, 312, 328
Lessack, Lee 161
Lestat 310
Lester, Robie 175
Lester, Sonny 72
Let 'Em Eat Cake 111, 113
Let Freedom Ring 51, 137, 139
Let My People Come 231
Let the Good Times Roll 123
Let's Face It 134, 136
Let's Sing Yiddish 203
Lettermen 122, 170, 175
Letters, Will 42–3
Levene, Sam 159
Levey, Ethel 59
Levin, Ira 200
Lew Leslie's Blackbirds of 1930 102, 104
Lewis, Jerry Lee 320
Lewis, Leona 250
Lewis, Marcia 199
Lewis, Norm 264
Liam 91
Libby, J. Aldrich 4–5
Liberace 85, 123, 161, 265
The Liberty Belles 23
The Lieutenant 225
The Life 283, 285
Life Begins at 8:40 114, 115
The Light in the Piazza 307, 308–9
Light, Lively and Yiddish 215
The Lightning Thief 340, 341
Li'l Abner 174, 176
Liliom 143
Lillie, Beatrice 62, 81, 87, 116, 119, 151, 165, 174, 194
Lilo 165
Line, Lorie 316
Lindfors, Viveca 133
Lindquist, Per and Ulf 161
Lindsay, Howard 121
Lindsay, Kara 324–5
Lindsay, Robert 259–60
Lindsay-Abaire, David 343–4

401

Title and Name Index

Linehan, Maxine 51
Linger Longer Letty 70, 72
The Lion King 286, 287, 288, 292
The Lion Tamer 2
Lippa, Andrew 279, 281
Lipton, Celia 227
Listen Lester 67
Listen to My Heart: The Songs of David Friedman 305
Lithgow, John 307
Little Anthony 195
Little Boy Blue 48
The Little Cherub 34
Little Christopher Columbus 8–9
Little, Cleavon 115, 212
The Little Colonel 16
The Little Duchess 23
Little Fish 301, 303
The Little Foxes 157
Little Ham 301
Little Jesse James 81
Little Johnny Jones 29–30, 246
Little Mary Sunshine 183, 185, 197
Little Me 192, 193, 246, 289
The Little Mermaid 315, 317
The Little Millionaire 48–9
Little Miss Sunshine 328
Little Nellie Kelly 79–80
Little Nemo 39
A Little Night Music 220–2, 320
Little Orphan Annie 231
Little Shop of Horrors 246, 248–50, 275, 281, 304
The Little Show 96, 98
Little Simplicity 67
The Little Trooper 8–9
Little Voice 147
The Little Whopper 70
Little Women 307, 209
Liza 81
Lloyd Webber, Andrew 217, 218, 240–1, 248, 249–50, 262, 263–4, 267, 268, 279, 280, 298, 310, 345
Loesser, Frank 116, 154, 159, 171, 171, 183, 226, 231, 273
Loewe, Frederick 116, 148–9, 162–3, 171–2, 187–8, 223–4
Logan, Ella 30, 134
Lombard, Ramina 54
Lombardo, Guy 5, 70, 77, 141, 149, 152, 198
London, George 163
London, Julie 5, 49, 57
A Lonely Romeo 67, 69, 70
Long, Avon 75
Long Legged Letty 55
The Longest Day 261
Look for the Silver Lining 41

Look, Ma, I'm Dancin' 151
The Look of Love 301
Look to the Lilies 212
Looking for Comedy in the Muslim World 147
Lopeman, Mark 66
Lopez, Jennifer 195
Lopez, Robert 322
Lopez, Vincent 75
Lorca, García 310
Lorelei 158, 223, 224
Lorraine, Lillian 40, 48
Loss, Joe 54, 118
Lost in the Stars 157, 158, 217
Loth, Pauline 49
Loudon, Dorothy 59, 209, 239, 256
Louis the 14th 84
Louise's Diary 123
Louisiana Purchase 127, 129
Love, Bessie 43
Love Birds 73
Love, Janis 295
Love Life 154–6
The Love Song 84
Love! Valour! Compassion! 133
Lovely Ladies, Kind Gentlemen 215
Lovely to Look At 112
LoveMusik 141, 312
Love's Labour's Lost 147
Lovett, Marcus 264
Lowery, Fred 85
Lubich, Warren 11
Lucas, Sydney 328–9
Luce, Claire 108–9
Lucky Break 147
Lucky Lady 100
Lucky Stiff 263, 264
Luker, Rebecca 5, 185
Lund, Art 54
Lundy, Pat 216
LuPone, Patti 30, 115, 213, 239, 240–1, 251, 262, 278, 280, 315, 334
Lute Song 145, 147
Luther, Frank 103
Lyles, Aubrey 74
Lyman, Abe 77
Lynde, Paul 162
Lynn, Vera 40, 107, 122
Lynne, Gloria 85, 95, 170
Lynne, Jeff 132
Lysistrata Jones 324, 325
Lysistrata 324

Mabus, Joel 32
MacDermot, Galt 207, 217, 251
MacDonald, Jeanette 37, 46, 85–6, 265

Title and Name Index

MacDonald, Ray 63
MacDonald, W. H. 12
MacDonough, Glen 27–8
MacDonough, Harry 24, 26, 40, 51, 57
MacFarland, Seth 149, 166, 175
Mack and Mabel 225, 227
Mack, Andrew 51
Mack, Cecil 82
Mackintosh, Cameron 259
Macon, Uncle Dave 26
MacRae, Gordon 26, 46, 49, 88, 139, 144, 155, 188, 201
MacRae, Heather 88
The Mad Show 200, 202
Madame Sherry 45, 47
The Madcap Duchess 53
Maddox, Johnny 11, 49
Madonna 241
Mafia! 109
Maggie Flynn 209
Magic 46
Magic in the Moonlight 66
The Magic Melody 70
Magic Organ 152
The Magic Show 223, 224, 248
Maguire Sisters 170
Mahagonny 212
Mahler, Gustave 213
Maid in America 55
Maid Marian 2, 23–4
The Maid of the Mountains 67, 69
Majestic Dance Band 80
Make a Wish 159
Make Mine Manhattan 151, 153
Makowicz, Adam 70
Malone, Beth 328–9
Maltby, Richard, Jr. 231, 251, 265, 267
Mame 200, 202, 251
Mamma Mia! 298
Mamoulian, Rouben 117, 137
Mamzelle Champagne 34
Man of La Mancha 200–2, 234, 273, 301
A Man of No Importance 301, 303, 346
Man on the Moon 225
The Man Who Owns Broadway 42
Man with a Load of Mischief 205
Mancini, Henry 179
Mandy Patinkin in Concert: Mamaloshen 289
Manford, Jason 280
Mangione, Chuck 188
Manhattan Jazz Quartet 104, 120
Manhattan Mary 93
Manhattan Rhythm 248
Manhattans 232
Manilow, Barry 30, 97, 107, 212, 250, 265, 343

Mann, Barry 305
Manners, J. Hartley 53
Manning, Bernard 57
Manning, Bob 166
Manning, Irene 49
Mantovani Orchestra 268
The Many Voices of Danny Gans 281
March of the Falsettos 243–4, 274
March of the Wooden Soldiers 28
Marco Spada 122
Marcovicci, Andrea 112, 136, 170
Margie 77
Marie Christine 291, 293
Marilyn: An American Fable 251
Marinka 145
Marjorie 84
Marks, Roger 161
Marlene 289
Marlowe, Gloria 169–70
Marlowe, Rita 122
Maroulis, Constantine 285
The Marriage Market 53–4
Marrow, Queen Esther 267
Marsalis, Wynton 175
Marsh, Howard 102
Marshall, Henry I. 48–9
Marshall, Kamilah 132
Martin, Dean 54, 170
Martin, Hugh 134, 159, 267
Martin, Jesse L. 282
Martin, Lynn 40
Martin, Mary 115, 124, 140–1, 147, 149, 154–5, 169, 184, 194, 203
Martin, Millicent 191
Martin Short: Fame Becomes Me 312
Martin, Tony 128, 168
Martin, Virginia 174
Martin, Will 285
The Marvelous Wonderettes 318
Marx Brothers 81, 87, 90, 96
Marx, Peter 147
Mary 73, 75
Mary Poppins 312, 314
Mason, Karen 28, 149, 158, 280
Massey, Daniel 192, 224
Massey, Ilona 137
Masteroff, Joe 192
Masters, Frankie 128
Mathis, Johnny 28, 168, 170, 195, 201, 232, 250, 278
Matilda 326, 327
A Matinee Idol 42
Matthau, Walter 169
Matthews, Roger 74
Matz, Peter 218
Mauzey, Alli 343

403

Title and Name Index

The Mavoureen 3, 6
May, Edna 31
May, Marty 145–6
Maye, Marilyn 204
Mayor 254, 255
Maytime 64, 66
Mazar, Debie 77
Mazzie, Marin 316
Mazzy, Jimmy 75
McAnuff, Des 255, 275
McArdle, Andrea 232
McBroom, Amanda 221
McCarthy, Joseph 65, 70, 90
McCauley, Jack 137, 151–2
McCauley, Joseph 105
McClure, Rob 343
McCorkle, Susannah 147, 158
McCormack, John 2, 17, 51
McCoy, Bessie 48
McCullough, Paul 79, 114
McCutcheon, Bill 174
McDermott, Sean 264, 278, 285
McDonald, Audra 75, 123, 268, 308, 312, 321
McElroy, Michael 255
McGillin, Howard 264, 271, 276
McGovern, Maureen 28, 104
McGrath, Bob 185
McGregor, Ewan 161
McGuire, William Anthony 99
McHugh, Jimmy 93, 99, 154
McIntyre, Lily 22
McKenna, Dave 221
McKenna, William 42–3
McKenzie, Julia 191, 227
McKenzie, Sarah 88
McKeon, Stephanie 280
McKnight, Sharon 265–6
McLean, Don 28
McNair, Barbara 181
McNair, Sylvia 62
McNally, Terrence 286, 287, 301
McNulty, Chris 170
McPartland, Jimmy 179
McPhail, Douglas 80
McPhee, Katharine 333
McRae, Carmen 141, 175
Me and Bessie 228
Me and Juliet 165, 166, 180
Me and My Girl 259–61
Me First and the Gimme Gimmes 241
The Me Nobody Knows 212, 214, 215, 251
Mean Girls 336, 337, 342
Mears, Martha 109
Measure for Measure 336
Mecca 73

The Medium 148
Meet Me in St. Louis 267
Meet the People 131
Mehldau, Brad 170
Meilhac, Henri 37
Melchior, Lauritz 2
Meldrum, Verity-Anne 216
Melnick, Peter 313
Melville, Herman 209
Memphis 320, 321
Memphis Bound 142
Mendes, Camila 230
Mendes, Sergio 109
Menken, Alan 275, 324–5
Menopause: The Musical 298
Menotti, Carlo 148, 157, 169
Menuhin, Yehudi 88
Menzel, Idina 282, 305–6, 328
Mercenary Mary 84
Mercer, Frances 127
Mercer, Johnny 57, 99, 108, 174, 183, 283
Mercer, Mabel 170
Mercer, Marion 197
Mercouri, Melina 203
Merlin 248
Merlin, Joanna 198
Merlino, Gene 188
Merman, Ethel 72, 102–3, 114–15, 119, 127, 131, 137, 145, 158, 159–60, 174, 180, 200
Merrick, David 169, 192, 203, 226, 243, 270
Merrill, Bob 174, 183, 187, 194–5, 268
Merrill, Helen 62, 134, 144
Merrill, Robert 85, 144
Merrily We Roll Along 246, 247, 338, 346
The Merry Countess 50
Merry-Go-Round 90
The Merry Malones 93
The Merry Monahans 66
The Merry Widow 36–8, 39, 45, 56, 140, 200, 240
The Merry Widow Burlesque 36, 38
Merrymen 185
Mesika, Miri 337
The Messenger Boy 23–4
Metro 273
Mexican Hayride 140–1
Michael, George 166
Michaels, Marilyn 126
Michele, Lea 230, 241, 343
Michell, Keith 201
Mickey Mouse 3
The Middle of Nowhere 265
Middleton, Ray 145–6
Midler, Bette 223, 334
Midnight at the Never Get 338
The Midnight Sons 39, 41

Title and Name Index

Midnite String Quartet 232, 250, 306
A Midsummer Night's Dream 197, 291
Mielziner, Jo 165
Mihanovich, Sandra 252
The Mikado 124, 134
Mike Flowers Pops 241
Milk and Honey 190, 191
Miller, Ann 240
Miller, Flournoy 74, 102
Miller, Glenn 54, 118
Miller, Marilyn 55, 58, 61, 70, 73, 87, 102, 111
Miller, Mitch 43–4
Miller, Mulgrew 218
Miller, Nina 28
Miller, Reed 57
Miller, Roger 254–5
Miller, Sienna 204
Million Dollar Quartet 320
Mills Brothers 17, 88, 260
Mills, Irving 100
Mills, Stephanie 251
Milton, Billie 43
A Minister's Wife 322
Minnelli, Liza 40, 100, 197, 204, 223, 227, 230, 234
Minnie's Boys 212, 214
Miracle on 34th Street 194
Miracles 141, 172
Mirage 250, 264
Miranda, Carmen 75, 127, 134
Miranda, Lin-Manuel 312, 313, 330–1, 345
Misery 123
Miss Dolly Dollars 31
Miss Hook of Holland 36
Miss Innocence 39, 41
Miss Liberty 157, 158
Miss 1917 54, 66
Miss Saigon 270, 271, 334
Miss Springtime 61, 63
Miss You Like Hell 336, 337
Mitchell, Anaïs 332
Mitchell, Brian Stokes 147, 188, 202, 276, 301
Mitchell, Guy 161
Mitchell, James 163
Mitchell, Louis 75
MJ the Musical 343
Mlle. Mischief 39
Mlle. Modiste 31, 33
The Mocking Bird 25
Moffo, Anna 46, 85
Molaskey, Jessica 75
Molina, Alfred 199, 304
Molloy, Dave 334
Molly 223
Molly Darling 79
Molnar, Ferenc 143

Mamma Mia! 298
Moms and Dads 17
Moncure, Joseph 291
Monda, Richard 49
Monder, Ben 139
Monk, Debra 213
Monk, Julius 197
Monk, Thelonious 88, 104, 112
Monkeybone 97
Monro, Matt 175, 201
Monroe, Asher 91
Monroe, Marilyn 97, 158
Monroe, Vaughn 2, 40, 46, 115, 163
Monsieur Beaucaire 70
Montalban, Ricardo 169
Montand, Yves 91
Monte Carlo 14
Monte Cristo, Jr. 67
Montgomery, Dave 21, 25, 34, 42, 55, 64
Monty Python and the Holy Grail 207
Monty Python's Spamalot 207, 209
The Monuments Men 110
Moody Blues 285
Moody, Ron 251
Moog Machine 207
Moon Over Parador 118
The Mooney Shapiro Songbook 243
Moonlight in Havana 51
Moonshine 31
Moore, Garry 153, 149
Moore, Melba 212
Moore, Victor 102, 127
Morgan, Corinne 28
Morgan, Dennis 17, 40, 51, 72
Morgan, Frank 105
Morgan, Jane 30, 49, 70, 144, 174
Morgan, Jaye P. 69
Morgan, Lorrie 28
Morgan, Marion 49
Morgan, Russ 260
Morgan, Vanessa 230
Morisette, Alanis 340
Mormon Tabernacle Choir 11, 32, 139, 201, 323
Moross, Jerome 151
Morris, Audrey 227
Morris, Joan 5, 59
Morrison, Matthew 221, 302, 308
Morrison, Van 115, 175
Morrow, Doretta 167–8
Morrow, Karen 258
Morton, Alicia 232
The Most Happy Fella 171, 173, 240, 273
Mostel, Zero 190–1, 198–9, 217, 231
Mother Earth 220
Mother Goose 27

Title and Name Index

The Motor Girl 42
Motown 326
Moulin Rouge! 158, 340
The Mountebanks 4, 5
Mouskouri, Nana 268
Movin' Out 301
Mower, Liam 319
Mr. & Mrs. Bridge 46
Mr. Bluebeard 25
Mr. Bug Goes to Town 49
Mr. Holland's Opus 91
Mr. Lode of Koal 42
Mr. President 192, 193
Mr. Saturday Night 101, 343, 344
Mr. Strauss Goes to Boston 145
Mr. Wix of Wickham 29
Mr. Wonderful 171, 173
Mrs. Doubtfire 343, 344
Mrs. Henderson Presents 129
Much Ado about Nothing 140–1
Mueller, Jessie 144, 332, 333
Muenz, Richard 188
Mulder, Karen 252
Mule Bone 270
Mulligan, Gerry 104, 120, 128, 141, 149
Munger, Mary 204
Munro, Ronnie 260
Munsel, Patrice 144
Munshin, Jules 159
Murder at the Vanities 111, 113
Murder Ballad 326
Murney, Julia 306
Murphy, C. W. 42–3
Murphy, Donna 141, 278, 281, 304, 312, 322, 334
Murphy, George 80
Murphy, Rose 97
Murphy, Sally 144
Murphy, Stanley 48–9
Murray, Billy 30, 32, 40, 43, 49, 59, 80
Murray, George F. 51
Music Box Revue 76, 78, 79, 81, 83, 84, 86
Music in My Head 152
Music in the Air 108, 110, 162
Music Is 231, 233
Music Maids 104
The Music Man 177–9, 243, 291, 343
Musical Chairs 240
The Musical of Musicals 305
My Fair Lady 171–3, 187, 197, 228, 246, 277, 336
My Favorite Year 275, 276
My Golden Girl 70
My Lady 21
My Lady's Maid 34
My Life with Albertine 301
My Maryland 93, 95

My One and Only 248
My Sister Eileen 165
My Wild Irish Rose 17, 51
Myers, J. W. 24, 26
The Mystery of Edwin Drood 256, 257, 326

Nabors, Jim 69, 163, 201
Naked Boys Singing 291
Naked Eyes 210
Nancy Brown 24, 25
Nash at Nine 220
Nash, Johnny 95
Nash, Ogden 140
Natasha, Pierre & the Great Comet of 1812 326, 327, 334
Natwick, Mildred 215
Naughty Marietta 13, 27, 45–7, 240
Neagle, Anna 88
Neapolatan Trio 2
Neff, Hildegarde 169
Nellie Bly 145
Nelson, Paula 255
Nelson, Willie 91, 100, 122, 126, 128, 175
Nero, Franco 188
Nero, Peter 136
Nesbitt, James 75
Nesmith, Michael 118
Nettles, Jennifer 139, 232, 335
Neuwerth, Bebe 59, 230
Never Gonna Dance 304
New Americana 108, 110
A New Brain 289, 290
New Deal Rhythm Band 161
New Faces of 1934 111
New Faces of 1936 116
New Faces of 1952 162, 164
New Faces of 1956 174
New Girl in Town 174, 176
The New Moon 96, 98, 140
New Orleans Syncopators 11
New York City Gay Men's Chorus 235
New York, New York 345, 347
The New Yorkers 102, 104
Newley, Anthony 141, 192–3
Newman, Randy 265
The News 256
Newsies 324–35
Newton-John, Olivia 221, 241
Next to Normal 315, 316–17, 318
Nicastro, Michelle 278, 285
Nice Work If You Can Get It 92, 324
Nicholas Brothers 116
Nichols, Red 54, 57, 75
Nick and Nora 273, 274
Niesen, Gertrude 112, 116

Title and Name Index

Night and Day 109, 115, 118
The Night Boat 70, 72
A Night in Paris 97
A Night in Spain 90
Night of January 16 257
A Night with Janis Joplin 328
Niles, Barbara 218
Nilsson, Harry 66, 107
Nina Rose 102
Nine 246, 247, 301
9:15 Revue 99, 101
9 to 5 318, 319
The 1940s Radio Hour 123, 240
The Ninth Configuration 46
Nite Club Confidential 251
Nixon, Marni 158, 251
No-Frills Revue 262
No More Peace 121
No No Nanette 87–8, 215, 231
No Strings 190, 191
No Way to Treat a Lady 261
Nob Hill 51
Noble, Ray 17
Nobody Home 55, 57
Nobody's Darling 66
Noises Off 147
Nolan, Lloyd 132
Nolan, Timothy 254, 264
Nordstrom, Clarence 65
Norman, Lucille 46
Norman, Marsha 270, 271
Normand, Mabel 225
Northrop, Pat 162
Norworth, Jack 39–40
Nothing Sacred 165
Now Is the Time for All Good Men 206, 208
Nunn, Trevor 249
Nunnally, Keith 282
Nunsense 256, 257, 275, 308
Nype, Russell 159–60

Oakie, Jack 43, 66
Oba Oba 262
O'Brien, Joanne 161
O'Brien, Pat 51
O'Casey, Sean 180
O'Connell, M. J. 59
O'Connor, Caroline 227
O'Connor, Donald 66, 161, 248
O'Connor, Grace 170
O'Connor, Sinéad 97, 132, 241
Octet 340, 341
O'Day, Anita 88, 100, 132, 141
Odds and Ends 64
Odom, Leslie, Jr. 175, 330–1

O'Donnell, Ace 26
The Odyssey 167
Of Thee I Sing 105, 107, 111, 162
Of V We Sing 134, 136
Offenbach, Jacques 84, 187
The Office Boy 27–8
Offspring 88
Ogden, Cathi 110
Oh, Boy! 61–3
Oh, Brother! 246, 247
Oh, Calcutta! 212, 215, 231
Oh, Captain 177
Oh, Coward! 220
Oh, I Say! 53
Oh, Joy! 62
Oh, Kay! 90–2, 270
Oh, Lady! Lady! 64, 66
Oh, Look! 65–6
Oh My Dear! 67
Oh! Oh! Delphine 50
Oh, What a Lovely War! 57, 197
Oh, You Beautiful Doll 54
O'Hara, John 131
O'Hara, Kelli 92, 175, 308, 330, 338
O'Hara, Maureen 153
O'Hara, Paige 227, 232
O'Horgan, Tom 206, 217
Oil City Symphony 262, 264, 283
Oklahoma! 65, 73, 135, 137–9, 200, 212, 240, 298, 338
Olcott, Chauncey 6, 16–17, 50–1
Old Dutch 42
Old Possum's Book of Practical Cats 249
Old Stock: A Refugee Story 336
The Old Town 42
Oldfield, Mike 104
Oldham, Derek 85
Oliver! 192, 193, 251
Oliver, Edna May 61–2
Olivetti, Eva 95
Olivo, Karen 313
Olivor, Jane 66, 155
Olsen, Ole 125, 134, 142
Olsen, Robert 46
Olympus on My Mind 261
On a Clear Day You Can See Forever 200, 202, 324
On the Town 142, 144, 217, 289, 330
On the Twentieth Century 234, 236, 330
On Your Feet 332
On Your Toes 116, 118, 169, 248
Once 324
The Once and Future King 187
Once on This Island 267, 269
Once Upon a Mattress 183–4, 185, 283
One for the Money 124

Title and Name Index

110 in the Shade 194, 196, 312
One Mo' Time 240, 267
One Sunday Afternoon 26
One Touch of Venus 140–1
O'Neal, William 145–6
O'Neill, Eugene 174
O'Neill, Jonjo 44
Only Fools Are Sad 217
The Only Girl 55
Onodowan, Okiertte 330–1
Onward Victoria 243
Orbach, Jerry 147, 210
The Orchid 34–5
Orlando, Tony 104
Osborne, Bobby 163
Osborne, David 280, 280
O'Shea, Michael 35
Osmond, Arthur 43
Osmond Brothers 49, 207
Osmond, Donny 30, 285
Osmond, Marie 144
O'Sullivan, Maureen 132
Oswald, Virginia 149
O'Toole, Peter 201
Our Sinatra 291
Out of Blue 123
Out of This World 159, 161
Ovation 147
Ovenden, Julian 168
Over Here! 223, 224
Over the Top 64
Owen, Reginald 217
Owen-Jones, John 271
Owens, Larry 340, 341
Oxford, Earl 114
Oy, is Dus a Leben! (*Oh, What a Life!*) 137

Pace, Johnny 136
Pacific Overtures 228, 230, 307, 336
Page, Patti 77, 126
Pageant 270
Paige, Elaine 112, 144, 232, 241, 249–50, 280
Paint Your Wagon 152–63
Painter, Eleanor 67
Painting the Clouds with Sunshine 52
Paisley, Brad 104
The Pajama Game 167, 168, 177, 223, 310
Pal Joey 131–3, 162, 318
Palma, Frank 4
Palmer, Peter 149
Palminteri, Chaz 334
Panabaker, Kay 91
Panama Hattie 131, 133
Panaro, Hugh 264
Pandolfi, Emile 214, 280

Papa's Wife 18–19
Papp, Joseph 206, 256, 259, 265
Parade 289, 290, 345
Paradise Square 343, 344
Paragon Ragtime Orchestra 62
Pardon My English 108, 110
Paris 96
Paris-Manhattan 133
The Parisian Model 34–5
Park 212
Park Avenue 148
Parker, Charlie 104, 109, 118
Parker, Sarah Jessica 85, 283
Parker, Trey 322
Parks, Larry 75
A Parlor Match 12
Parrott, Nicki 77, 136
Parsons, Estelle 243
Parton, Dolly 115
Pascal, Adam 292
Pasek, Benj 334–5
The Passing Show of 1894 6–7
The Passing Show of 1912 50
The Passing Show of 1913 53
The Passing Show of 1914 55
The Passing Show of 1915 55, 58
The Passing Show of 1916 61, 63
The Passing Show of 1918 66
The Passing Show of 1919 70, 72
The Passing Show of 1922 79–80
Passing Strange 312, 314, 315
Passion 277, 278
Patinkin, Mandy 66, 122, 155, 259, 270, 271, 278
Patterson and Jackson 100
Patterson, Christian 271
Patterson, Meredith 59
Patti LuPone on Broadway 281
Paul, Justin 334–5
Paul, Les 26, 132–3
Pavlova, Anna 61
Payne, John 66
Peace 209
Peacock, Christopher 268
Peerce, Jan 2, 188
Peerless Quartet 69
Peg 251, 253
Peg o' My Heart 53, 54
Peggy from Paris 27
Peggy-Ann 90, 92
Peil, Mary Beth 254
Pellegrene, David 271
Pen, Polly 256–7
Pendleton, Austin 198
Penner, Joe 102
Pennies from Heaven 41

408

Title and Name Index

Penningron, Ann 61, 87, 102
The People in the Picture 322
Pepe 126
The Perfect Fool 76
Perkins, Carl 320
Peronne, Patrick 110
Perryman, Jill 191
Personals 257
Pete 'n' Keely 295
Peter Pan 157, 169, 170, 240, 273, 289, 330
Peters, Bernadette 80, 144, 147, 209, 221, 225–6, 256, 275, 301, 334
Peters, Roberta 85, 144
Peterson, Caleb 95
Peterson, Oscar 57, 95, 109, 118, 195
The Petrified Prince 279
Petsch, Madelaine 230
Pettersson, Johanna 175
Pfeiffer, Michelle 91
The Phantom of the Opera 262–4, 342, 345, 348
Philemon 226
Phillips, David 32
Phillips, Lou Diamond 281
Phillips, Sam 320
Phillips, Sian 289
Phillips, Sunny 216
Phoenix, Whitney 250
Piaf 243
Piaf, Edith 112
Pickens Sisters 109
Pickwick 200, 202
The Pickwick Papers 200
Pieces of 8 218
Piff! Paff!! Pouf!!! 27
Pilita 218
The Pink Lady 45, 47
Pinocchio 124
Pins and Needles 121, 123, 125
Pinter, Harold 213
Pinza, Ezio 154–5, 169
Pioneer Days 34
Pipe Dream 171, 173, 180
Pipino il Breve (*Pippin the Short*) 256
Pippin 220, 222, 326
The Pirate Queen 312
The Pirates of Penzance 243
Pitch, Harry 158
Pitera, Nick 335
Pitney, Gene 172
Pitter Patter 73
Pizzarelli, Bucky 221
Pizzarelli, John 104, 221
Plain and Fancy 169–70
A Plantation Act 77
Platinum 237

Platt, Ben 334–5, 345
Platters 3, 40, 107, 112, 126
Play Me a Country Song 248
Play On! 283
Pletcher, Tom 72
Plunkett, Maryann 259–60
Polonaise 145
Poppy 81, 83
Porgy 116
Porgy and Bess 116, 118, 134, 140, 165, 231, 324
Porter, Billy 172, 326–7
Porter, Cole 57, 58, 79, 96, 99, 102, 108, 114–15, 116–18, 119, 124, 127, 131, 134, 137, 142, 145, 154, 159, 165–6, 191, 230, 262
The Postman Always Rings Twice 346
Potter, S. 8–9
Pousse-Café 200
Powell, Eleanor 116, 118
Powell, Jane 57
Powell, Janet 75
Powers, Amy 280
Powers, Tom 62
Present Arms 93, 95
The President's Daughter 215
Presley, Elvis 118, 201, 267, 279, 307, 320
Presnell, Harve 104, 163
Preston, Robert 177–9, 197, 203, 225–6
Pretty Filthy 330
Pretty Mrs. Smith 55, 57
Pretty Woman 338, 339
Previn, André 57, 59
Price, Leontyne 198
Pride and Prejudice 180, 310
The Prima Donna 39
Prima, Louis 75, 83, 161
Primary Colors 32–3
Prince Ananias 8–9
Prince, Faith 153, 175, 273
Prince, Harold 192, 197, 200, 203, 212, 215, 223, 225, 228, 234, 241, 248, 254, 275, 279, 336
The Prince and the Pauper 302
Prince Igor 167
Prince Kam 6–7
Prince of Broadway 336
Prince of Central Park 267
The Prince of Pilsen 25–6, 27
Prince's Dance Band 80
Princess Flavia 87
Princess Nicotine 6
The Princess Pat 58, 60
Prior, Marina 264
Priorities of 1942 134
Priscilla, Queen of the Desert 322
Privates on Parade 267, 269
Proby, P. J. 163, 193

Title and Name Index

The Producers 295, 297, 315
Prom 338, 339
Prom Queens Unchained 273, 274
Promenade 209
Promises, Promises 209–10, 320
Proust, Marcel 301
Prowse, Juliet 166
Pryce, Jonathan 270
Pryor, Arthur 40, 68, 77
Puccini, Giacomo 250, 263
Puckett, Riley 51
Pump Boys and Dinettes 246, 247
Purlie 212, 214
The Purple Road 50
Putting It Together 275, 291

The Quaker Girl 48
Quast, Philip 155, 271
Queen High 90
The Queen of Moulin Rouge 39
Queen of the Mist 324
Questel, Mae 97
Quilley, Denis 239
Quinn, Aileen 232
Quinn, Anthony 251

Radcliffe, Daniel 322, 346
Radiant Baby 301
Radio Days 126
Radio Gals 283
Rado, James 207
Raggedy Ann 259
Ragni, Gerome 207
Rags 261
Rags Parkland Sings the Songs of the Future 338
Ragtime 21, 286, 287, 320
Raimondi, Barbara 170
Rainbow 96, 98
The Rainbow Girl 64
Rainbow 'Round My Shoulder 100
The Rainmaker 194
Raisin 223, 224
A Raisin in the Sun 223
Raitt, John 142–3, 147, 163, 188, 203
Ralph Sharon Trio 59
The Ramblers 90, 92
Ramey, Samuel 95, 109, 139, 144, 264
Ramin, Sid 69
Ramírez, Carlos 118
Ramona 115
Ramos, Anthony 313, 330–1
Rand, Ayn 257
Randall, Tony 177
Randolph, Boots 107, 122, 207
Range a Cappella 335

Rannells, Andrew 244, 322, 323
Rap Master Ronnie 254
Rapp, Louis 77
Rappold, Marie 2
Rastelli, José 46
Ravel, Maurice 250
Ravens 126
Rawls, Lou 139, 221, 232
Ray, Johnnie 100
Ray, Sean 235
Raye, Martha 131
Rayner, David 261
Razaf, Andy 99–100, 102
Reading, Bertice 158
Really Rosie 243
Reardon, John 174
Reburn, Ann 299
Red Clay Ramblers 281
Red, Hot and Blue! 119, 120
The Red Mill 27, 34–5, 145
The Red Shoes 277
The Red Widow 48
Redbone, Leon 100
Reddy, Helen 161, 175, 218
Redhead 180, 182
Redmond, William M. 24, 26
Reds 32
Reed, Alyson 204
Reed, Lou 126
Reed, Nancy 152
Reefer Madness 298
Rees, Jerry 77
Rees, Roger 330
Reese, Della 66, 158, 161, 168
Reese, William 80
Regan, Phil 51, 54, 80
Reggae 240
Regina 157, 158
Reid, Don 117
Reilly, Charles Nelson 28, 200
Reiner, Carl 151
Reinhardt, Django 88, 100, 109, 126
Reinking, Ann 225
Reisman, Leo 85, 100, 109, 115
Relative Values 149
Relyea, Marjorie 22
Remembrance of Times Past 301
Remi, Salaam 158
Renard, Jacques 106
Renard, Paul 80
Rent 281–2, 292
Replay 232
Respect 123
Return to Me 52, 91
Return to the Forbidden Planet 273

Reuben, Sharon 188
Reveille with Beverly 109
Revenge with Music 114, 115
Revill, Clive 203
Rex 228, 230
Reynolds, Burt 100
Reynolds, Debbie 66, 97, 220
Reynolds, Herbert 55–6
Reynolds, Mark 54
Rhapsody 142
Rhapsody in Black 102
Rhapsody in Blue 69, 104
Rhodes, Kimmie 46
Rice, Elmer 148
Rice, Tim 217, 218, 240–1, 249, 291, 292
Rich, Fred 103, 106
The Rich Mr. Hoggenheimer 34
Richard, Cliff 216
Richard Lennox Trio 132
Richardson, Ian 228
Richardson, Natasha 204
Richardson, Ron 255
Riddle, Nelson 139, 204
Riesen, John 271
Rieu, André 179
Rigby, Cathy 270, 273
Riggs, Lynn 138
The Right Girl 73
Right This Way 121–3
Rimes, LeAnn 292
Rines, Joe 260
Ring, Blanche 25–6, 39, 61
Ring, Justin 51
Ring of Fire 310
Ringo, Shiina 97
Ringwald, Molly 204
The Rink 251, 253
Rio Rita 90, 92
Ripley, Alice 214, 235, 316
Riso, Rick 109, 149
Ritchard, Cyril 169
Ritter, Tex 126
Rittman, Trudy 185
Rivera, Chita 169, 197, 228–9, 258, 256, 275, 276, 330
Riverdance on Broadway 291
Rivers, Joan 197
Rix, Jemma 311
Road Show 318, 319
Roadside 299
The Roar of the Greasepaint—The Smell of the Crowd 197, 199
The Roaring Twenties 75
Rob Roy 8–9
The Robber Bridegroom 228, 230, 231

Robbins, Jerome 142, 151, 160, 191, 197, 265
Roberta 111–13
Roberti, Lyda 102
Roberts, Bob 40
Roberts, Darcie 299
Roberts, Joan 112, 138
Roberts, Kenny 85
Roberts, Pernell 163
Roberts, Tony 210
Robertson, Dick 32, 57, 103
Robertson, Guy 102
Robertson, Liz 235
Robeson, Paul 2, 105
Robin, Leo 157–8
Robin Hood 1–3, 6, 8, 23
Robinson, Bill "Bojangles" 100, 102, 124, 142
Robinson, Chris 144
Robinson Crusoe, Jr. 58, 60
Robinson, Smokey 141
Robeson, Paul 93–5
Rock 'n' Roll: The First 5,000 Years 248
Rock of Ages 318
Rockabye Hamlet 228
The Rocketeer 118
Rocky 328, 329
The Rocky Horror Show 225, 227, 295
Rodgers, Mary 183, 192
Rodgers, Richard 79, 84, 87, 90, 93, 102, 116, 119, 120, 121, 127, 131–2, 134–5, 137–8, 140, 142–4, 145–6, 151, 154–5, 159, 162, 165, 171, 180–1, 183–5, 190, 197, 215, 228, 237, 248, 281, 301, 305, 326
Rodney, Dion 77
Roger, Elena 241
Rogers Brothers 18
The Rogers Brothers in Central Park 21
The Rogers Brothers in Paris 29–30
The Rogers Brothers in Wall Street 18
Rogers, Eileen 115
Rogers, Ginger 102–3, 109, 112, 304
Rogers, Harlan 128, 128
Rogers, Kenny 120, 221
Rogers, Roy 40
Rogers, Will 58, 61, 87
Rollin' on the T.O.B.A. 289
Rollins, Sonny 112, 166
Roly-Boly Eyes 70, 72
Roly Poly 50, 52
Romance in Hard Times 267, 269
The Romance of Athlone 16–17
Romance, Romance 262, 264
Romberg, Sigmund 53, 58, 61, 64, 73, 76, 84, 87, 90, 93, 96, 102, 105, 116, 119, 134, 142, 167
Rome, Harold 121, 159, 165
Romeo and Juliet 177, 305

Title and Name Index

Ronstadt, Linda 91, 120, 243, 265
Rooney, Mickey 104, 240
Rosalie 93, 95
Rosalinda 137
Rose, Billy 102
Rose, Earl 59, 118, 147
Rose, George 209, 243
The Rose Maid 48
Rose-Marie 84–6, 137
The Rose of Algeria 42
The Rose of Stamboul 76
Rose of Washington Square 41, 66, 75
Roselli, Jimmy 30, 51, 69
Rosenfeld, Sydney 6–7
Rosenthal, Anthony 244
Ross, Adrian 36–7
Ross, Annie 136
Ross, Diana 132, 207
Ross, Murray 252
Ross, Shirley 127
Ross, Steve 118
Rossetti, Christina 256
Rossum, Emmy 264
Roth, Lillian 107
The Rothschilds 215, 216
Rouleau, Nic 323
The Rounders 18
Routledge, Patricia 206, 228
Rowles, John 207
Roy, Harry 260
Roy's Tiger Ragamuffins 260
Royal Canadians 5
The Royal Vagabond 67
Roza 262
Rubens, Paul 21–2, 27
Rubin-Vega, Daphne 313
Ruby, Harry 81, 90, 93, 96–7, 99
Ruffins, Kermit 100
Ruffner, Dave 179
Rugelwere, Yvette 85
Ruggles, Charles 61, 67, 81
A Runaway Girl 16–17
Runaways 234, 236
The Runaways 25
Running for Office 25, 36
Running Wild 81–2
Rupert, Michael 243–4, 274
Russell, Brenda 311
Russell, Dana 214
Russell, Jane 97, 100, 213
Russell, Jenna 329
Russell, Leon 120
Russell, Lillian 2, 6, 10, 18–19, 21, 23, 25, 48
Russell, Luis 104
Russell, Rosalind 102, 165

Russell Wooding's Jubilee Singers 99
Ruthless 273, 274
Ryan, Peggy 66
Rydell, Bobby 77
Ryley, Charles 8
Ryskind, Morrie 99, 105

Sadie Thompson 142
A Safe Place 91
Safel, Greg 327
Said, Mario 210
Sail Away! 190, 191
The Saint of Bleecker Street 169
Saker, Bob 147
Salazar, George 338–9
Sally 73, 75, 151
Sally in Our Alley 25–6
Sally, Irene and Mary 79
Salonga, Lea 54, 181, 232, 270
Salvant, Cécile McLorin 136
Salvation 212
The Sambo Girl 31, 33
Sammy Stops the World 193
San Basilio, Paloma 241
San Francisco Gay Men's Chorus 252
San Toy 21–2
Sanderson, Julia 29, 48, 55–6, 92
Sandler, Adam 147
Sandra Bernhard: I'm Still Here Damn It! 289
Sands, Stark 326–7
Sands, Tommy 28
Sandy Wexler 147
Santley, Joseph 67
Sarafina! 262, 264
Sarandon, Susan 91
Saratoga 183, 185
Saratoga Trunk 183
Sargent, Kenny 17
Satisfiers 66
Saturday Night 292, 293
Saturday Night Fever 291
Saturn Returns 286, 288
Saunders, Gertrude 82
Savará 237
Savo, Jimmy 102
Sawyer, Ivy 67
Say, Darling 177
Say It with Flowers 43
Sayer, Cynthia 77
Scaggs, Boz 132, 141
Scandalous 326
Scanlan, Dick 298–9
The Scarlet Pimpernel 287, 288
Scheff, Fritzi 48
Scherzinger, Nicole 241

Title and Name Index

Schmidt, Harvey 183–4, 194, 203, 209, 226, 286, 299
The School Girl 29
School of Rock 332, 333
Schoras, Chiara 75
Schubert, Franz 76
Schulz, Charles 249
Schwartz, Arthur 79, 96, 102, 105, 114, 116, 121, 148, 151, 159
Schwartz, Stephen 215, 216, 220, 305–6, 308
Scolari, Peter 193
Scorsese, Martin 234
Scott, Bobby 149
Scott, Clement 2
Scott, Hazel 104, 134
Scott, Sherie Rene 292
Scott, Walter 8
The Scottsboro Boys 320, 321
Scrambled Feet 240, 242
The Sea Gull 263
Seaton, Johnny 267
Second Generation 216
The Second Little Show 102
The Secret Garden 270–1
The Secret Life of Walter Mitty 197
Secrets Every Smart Traveler Should Know 286
Sedaka, Neil 122, 198
See America First 58, 60
See My Lawyer 123
See What I Wanna See 310
Seeley, Blossom 59
Seesaw 220, 222
Segal, Vivienne 58, 87, 131–3, 162
Sella, Robert 173
Selph, Chad 101
Selvin, Ben 72, 83
Sendak, Maurice 243
Sennett, Mack 225
September Affair 126
Serbedzija, Rade 156
The Serenade 12–13
Sergeant Bru 29–30
Sergeant Pepper's Lonely Hearts Club Band 225
Sesame Street 302
Set to Music 124, 126
Seurat, George 251
Seuss, Dr. 295
Seussical 295, 296
Seven Brides for Seven Brothers 248
The Seven Lively Arts 142, 144
Seventeen 162, 164
1776 209, 211, 286, 345
Seventh Heaven 169
70, Girls, 70 215, 216
Sex in the City 158

Sex in the City 2 133
Sex Tips for Modern Girls 259
Shades of Harlem 254
Shadows 241, 250, 268
Shaiman, Marc 302, 346
Shakespeare's Cabaret 243
Shakur, Tupac 330
Shaloub, Tony 337
The Shanghai Gesture 66
Sharif, Omar 337
Shaw, Artie 57, 85, 88, 116, 118, 126, 128, 168
Shaw, Elliot 80
Shaw, George Bernard 322
Shaw, Hollace 127
Shaw, Mat and Savanna 335
Shaw, Oscar 90, 106
Shaw, Woody 141
Shawn, Dick 101
She Loves Me 192, 193, 277, 322
Shea, Jere 278
Shearing, George 172
Sheehan, Ciarán 17
Shelley, Joshua 151
Shelter 220
Shelton, Anne 122, 123
Shenandoah 225, 227
Sher, Bartlett 307, 315
Sheridan, Ann 40
Sherman, Allan 275
Sherman, Hiram 127
Sherry! 203, 205
Sherwood, Lew 109
Sherwood, Robert 248
She's a Good Fellow 67
She's My Baby 93
Shevelove, Bert 217
Shew, Bobby 141
Shields, Brooke 204
Shields, Ren 25–6
Shine On Harvest Moon 40, 49
Shiner, David 281
Shire, David 231, 251, 265, 267
Shirley, Bill 54, 172–3
Shockheaded Peter 291
The Sho-Gun 29–30
Shogun: The Musical 270
Shoot the Works 105
Shore, Dinah 57, 88, 91, 112, 161, 166, 185
Short, Bobby 107
Short, Martin 275
A Shot in the Dark 75
Shout! 312
Show Boat 5, 93–5, 105, 111, 137, 145, 147, 154, 248, 279
Show Girl 99, 101, 187

Title and Name Index

The Show Goes On 286
The Show Is On 119, 120
Show Time 137, 142
Showing Off 265, 266
Shrek the Musical 318, 319
Shriner, Herb 151
Shubert Brothers 29, 45, 50, 53, 55, 58, 64, 102, 111, 116
Shubert Gaieties 70
Shucked 345, 347
Shuffle Along 73–5
Shuffle Along, Or The Making of the Musical Sensation of 1921 and All That Followed 75, 332
Shulman, Deborah 278
Shutt, Arthur 59
Side By Side By Sondheim 191, 231
Side Show 286, 288, 330
Siegel, Arthur 174
Silk Stockings 169, 170
Sillman, Leonard 111, 162, 174
The Silver Slipper 25
Silverman, Ryan 271
Silvers, Louis 76–7
Silvers, Phil 127, 151, 162, 187, 191, 217
Simmons, Jean 221
Simms, Ginny 115, 128
Simms, Margaret 99–100
Simon, Carly 120, 128, 132
Simon, Lucy 270, 271
Simon, Neil 174, 192
Simon, Paul 286
Simple Simon 99, 101
Simply Heavenly 177
Simply Irresistible 133
Sims, Zoot 104, 126, 136, 163
Sinatra, Frank 88, 91, 95, 97, 107, 109, 115, 118, 120, 122, 123, 132, 139, 144, 147, 149, 155, 166, 221, 291, 320
Sinbad 64, 67–8
Since I Don't Have You 123
Sincerely Yours 52
Sinclaire, Denzel 57
Sing for Your Supper 124, 126
Sing, Israel, Sing! 203
Sing Out, Sweet Land 142
Singin' in the Rain 256
The Singing Girl 18
The Singing Kid 69, 77
Sissle, Noble 74–5
Sister Act 322, 323
Sister Mary 18
Sitting Pretty 81, 83
Six Hits and a Miss 104
Six: The Musical 343, 344
1600 Pennsylvania Avenue 228, 230

Skinner, Emily 218, 235
Sky High 84
Skyscraper 200, 202
Skyliners 123, 144
Slayton, Bobby 77
The Sleeping Beauty and the Beast 23
Slezak, Walter 102, 169
Slim, Fatboy 328
Small Wonder 154
Smile 261
Smiles 102, 104
Smith 220
Smith, Anna Nicole 158
Smith, Bessie 228
Smith, Celina 232
Smith, Ethel 179
Smith, Harry B. 1, 12, 14, 16, 18–19, 23
Smith, Kate 17, 40, 51, 103, 123
Smith, Keely 168, 193
Smith, Maggie 174
Smith, Queenie 87
Smith, Rex 243
Smith, Rufus 147, 162–3
Smith, Sam 335
Smith, Sheridan 247
Smith, William C. 95
Smith, Willie "The Lion" 75, 88, 104
Smoke on the Mountain 270, 272, 283
Smokey Joe's Cafe 279
Smothers Brothers 163, 201
Smuin, Michael 262
Snoopy 248, 250
Snyder, Terry 30
So Long, 174th Street 228
So Long, Letty 63
So This Is Love 75
Socha, Alexandra 329
A Society Circus 31
Soft Power 340, 341
Soileau, Leo 17
Solomon, Tom 268
Some Like It Hot 97, 217, 345, 347
Someone to Watch Over Me 91
Somebody's Sweetheart 67
Something for the Boys 137, 139
Something Rotten! 330, 331
Something's Afoot 228
Sondheim on Sondheim 191, 320
Sondheim, Stephen 177, 180, 190–1, 197, 212, 213, 215, 220–1, 223, 225, 228, 237–9, 251, 262, 275, 277, 278, 291, 292, 298, 305, 307, 318, 320, 346
Song and Dance 256, 257
Song of Norway 142, 144
Song of Singapore 270, 272
Song of the Flame 87

Title and Name Index

Songs for a New World 281, 282
Songs of Paradise 265
Sons o' Guns 99, 134
Soon 215
Sophisticated Ladies 243
Sorkin, Aaron 345
Sothern, Ann 102, 106
Sothern, Georgia 137
Soul Doctor 328
The Sound of Music 183–5, 286
Sousa, John Philip 5, 10–11, 14, 16, 26, 31, 262
South, Eddie 72
South Pacific 155–6, 315
Southern, Jeri 112, 115, 141, 166
Sparks, Ned 67
Speed Racer 133
Spell, Ethan 271
Spencer, David 275
Spencer, Kenneth 95
Spewack, Bella and Samuel 154
Spice of 1922 79–80
Spider-Man: Turn Off the Dark 324, 325
Spielberg, Robin 30, 144, 232
Spivey, Jaquel 341
SpongeBob SquarePants 336
Sporting Days 39
Spring Awakening 312, 314, 332
Spring Is Here 96, 98
The Spring Maid 45
The Spring Chicken 34
Springfield, Dusty 185, 210
The Spitfire Grill 298, 300
Squonk 291
St. Denis, Teddie 260
St. Louis Woman 145, 147
Stafford, Jo 28, 66, 122, 123, 128, 149, 170
Stage Mother 51
Stamper, Dave 40
Stander, Lionel 162
Stanley, Frank 40
Star! 91
Star and Garter 137
A Star Is Born 69
Starlift 51
Starlight Express 261
Starmites 265, 266
Starr, Kay 100, 161
Starr, Ringo 109
Stars in Your Eyes 44, 125
Stars on Ice 138
Starting Here, Starting Now 231, 233
State Fair 281
Steel, John 71–2
Steel Pier 283, 285
Steele, Shayna 133

Steele, Squeek 163
Stein, Gertrude 111
Stein, Leo 37
Steinbeck, John 206
Steinberg, Jeff 107
Stepping Stones 81, 83
Stevens, April 85, 88
Stevens, Ray 85, 85
Stevens, Risë 28
Stevenson, Robert Louis 283
Stew 312
Stewart and Gillen 26
Stewart, George Rippey 163
Stewart, Gwen 266
Stewart, Larry 17
Stewart, Paula 183
Stewart, Rod 109, 115, 132
Stewart, Sandy 62
Stilgoe, Richard 263
Sting 91, 267, 330
Stitt, Sonny 100
Stoll, George 69
Stoll, Natasha 28
Stoller, Mike 279
Stomp 277
Stone, Dorothy 81
Stone, Emma 204
Stone, Fred 21, 25, 34, 42, 55, 64, 81
Stone, Judy 216
Stone, Matt 322
Stone, Peter 190, 209
Stop! Look! Listen! 58–9
Stop the World—I Want to Get Off 192–3
Stordahl, Axel 149
Storm, Gale 152
Stormy Weather 100
The Story of My Life 318
The Story of Will Rogers 69
Stothart, Herbert 70, 73, 84, 96
Stott, Maggie 51
The Strange Case of Dr. Jekyll and Mr. Hyde 285
A Strange Loop 340–1, 343
Straus, Oscar 36, 42, 73
Strauss, Johann 50, 114, 121, 137
Street Corner Symphony 286
Street Scene 148, 150, 240
The Streets of Paris 127, 129
Streisand, Barbra 66, 91, 104, 107, 128, 132, 141, 144, 194–5, 213, 221, 232, 250, 264, 278, 280
Strider 240
Strike Me Pink 108
Strike Up the Band 99, 101
Stritch, Elaine 151, 162, 180, 213
Stroman, Susan 279, 321
Stromberg, John 16, 18–19

415

Title and Name Index

Strouse, Charles 183, 200, 212, 232, 237, 243, 248
Stuart, Leslie 21–2
Stuart, Kirt 161
Stuart, Ralph 127
The Student Prince 84, 86, 102, 140
Studebakers 181
Styne, Jule 151–2, 157–8, 162, 165, 174–5, 177, 180, 187, 194–5
Subways Are for Sleeping 190, 191
Suds 265
Sugar 217, 219, 345
Sugar Babies 240
Sugarpie and the Candymen 132
Suicide Fleet 66
Suki, Yama 181
Sullivan, Arthur 1, 4, 6, 105, 111, 114, 119, 124, 140, 142, 151, 197, 203, 243
Sullivan, Jo 144, 169
Sullivan, KT 28, 158, 166, 279
Sullivan, Maxine 46, 100, 122, 152
The Sultan of Sulu 25
Summer, Donna 241, 336
Summer: The Donna Summer Musical 336
The Summer Widowers 45
Sunday in the Park with George 253, 315
Sunny 87, 89
Sunny River 134
Sunny Side of the Street 115
Sunset Boulevard 279, 280
The Sunshine Girl 50
Sunshine, Marion 59
The Supremes 132, 195, 207
The Survivor 118
Suzuki, Pat 107, 172, 180–1
Swanson, Adam 75
Swanson, Marcella 28
Sweeney Todd: The Demon Barber of Fleet Street 215, 267, 310, 334, 345
Sweet Adeline 99, 101
Sweet and Low 102
Sweet Charity 200, 202, 256, 307
Sweet Smell of Success 298, 300
The Sweetheart Shop 75
Sweethearts 53–4, 88, 265
Swenson, Bob 126
Swenson, Inga 174, 194
Swenson, Ruth Ann 168
Swift, Kay 102
Swimming Upstream 52
Swing! 121, 123, 291
The Swing Mikado 124
Swing Shift 123
Swing Time 304
Swinging on a Star 281
Swinging the Dream 127, 129

Swingtime Canteen 123, 279
Swit, Loretta 258
Syncopation 46
Szot, Paulo 156

Taboo 304, 306
The Taffetas 265
Taft, Harry 11
Tagle, Anna Maria Perez 216
Take a Chance 108, 110
Take Me Along 183, 185, 254
Taking My Turn 251
The Talk of New York 36, 38
Talva, Galina 160
Tamara 111–12, 122
Tango Argentino 256, 291
Tanguay, Eva 23, 31
Tanner, Tony 193
The Tap Dance Kid 251, 253
Tarzan 310–11
The Tattooed Man 15
Tatum, Art 88, 100, 128
Taylor, Elizabeth 221
Taylor, James 95, 139, 149
Taylor, Laurette 48, 53–4
Taymor, Julie 283, 286, 291
Tea for Two 88
Tebelak, John-Michael 216
Teddy and Alice 262
Teddy Wilson Quartet 126
Tee, Hayden 271
Teek, Angela 92
The Telephone 148
Tell Me More! 84, 86
Temby, Nathan 235, 252
Tempest, Marie 6
Temple, Shirley 206, 273
Templeton, Fay 10, 16, 21, 23
Tempo, Nino 85, 88
Temptations 69, 95, 109, 155, 201
Ten Percent Revue 262
The Tenderfoot 27–8
Tenderloin 187, 189
Tennessee Tooters 83
Térese Raquin 298
Terfel, Bryn 155, 163, 172
Terris, Norma 5, 102
Tesori, Jeanine 284, 298–9, 304, 328–9, 343–4
Texas, Li'l Darlin' 157
Texasville 126
Texsmith, Vaughn 22
That's Life! 279, 280
Their Finest 41
There's No Business Like Show Business 72, 146
These Foolish Things 110

Title and Name Index

They Wrote That? 305
They're Playing Our Song 237, 239
Thielemans, Toots 168
The Thin Man 273
The Thing About Men 304–5, 306
The Third Little Show 105, 107
13 318, 319
This Is the Army 137, 139
This Was Burlesque 246
This Year of Grace 96, 98
Thomas, Bob 80
Thomas, Lucy 306
Thompson, Charlie 85
Thompson, David 321
Thompson, Kay 166
Thoms, Tracie 282
Thomson, Virgil 111
Thoroughly Modern Millie 46, 298, 299
Those Were the Days 270
Thou Shalt Not 298, 300
Three Cheers 96
3 Guys Naked from the Waist Down 254
Three Little Maids 27–8
Three Little Words 97
The Three Musketeers 93, 95
Three Postcards 259, 261
Three to Make Ready 145
Three Twins 39, 41
Three Waltzes 121
Three Wishes for Jamie 162
The Threepenny Opera 108, 167, 168, 228, 267, 310
Three's a Crowd 102, 104
Through the Years 105, 107
Thumbs Up! 114, 115
A Thurber Carnival 183
Thurber, James 197
Tick Tick ... Boom! 298, 300, 334
Tickets, Please! 157
Tickle Me 73, 75
Tierney, Harry 70, 90
Tijuana, Brass 210
Till the Clouds Roll By 57, 95, 112, 128
Tillie's Nightmare 42, 44
Tilton, Martha 161
Timbuktu! 234
Time and Again 295
A Time for Singing 200
The Times They Are A-Changin' 312
Tin Men 128
Tina: The Tina Turner Musical 340
Tinney, Frank 48, 61
Tintypes 33, 243
Tip-Toes 87, 89
Tip-Top 73
Titanic 283, 285, 346

Titanic, Jinx 97
Titanique 346
[title of show] 312, 314
Titmus, Phyllis 66
To Live Another Summer, To Pass Another Winter 217
To Whom It May Concern 256, 258
Todd, Dick 122
Todd, Michael 124, 137, 275
Tolley, David 282
Tolstoy, Leo 275, 326, 334
Tom Jones 36
Tombes, Andrew 105
Tommy 275
Tonight at 8:30 119, 120, 151
Tonight's the Night 57
Too Many Girls 127, 129
Tootsie 338, 339
Top Banana 162, 164
Top-Hole 84
Top o' the Morning 51
Topol 198, 199, 270
The Toreador 23–4
Tormé, Mel 62, 109, 132, 166, 188
Touch and Go 157
The Tourists 34
Tovarich 192
Town and Country 158
Town Topics 58
Townsend, Ed 172
Townsend, Peter 118
Toxic Audio 303
The Toxic Avenger 318, 319
Tozzi, Giorgio 156
Transatlantic Coffee 41
Trask, Diana 181
Traubel, Helen 171
Travis, Merle 69
Treacher, Arthur 137
Treasure Girl 96, 98
A Tree Grows in Brooklyn 41, 159, 161
Treeminisha 228
Trent, Jackie 218, 232
Trentini, Emma 45–6, 50
The Tribute Co. 319
Tricks 220
A Trip to Chinatown 1, 3, 4–5, 6
A Trip to Japan 42
A Trip to Mars 6
A Trip to Swaddades 126
Trotter, John Scott 122
Trotter Trio 191, 278
Troup, Bobby 57, 120
Triumph of Love 286, 288
Truly Blessed 267

Title and Name Index

Tuck Everlasting 332, 333
Tucker, Sophie 134
Tumble Inn 67
Tune, Tommy 231, 248
Turnbull, Harriet 329
Turner, Lana 37
Turner, Tina 340
Tunick, Jonathan 212
Turturro, John 97
Tuscaloosa's Calling Me ... But I'm Not Going 228
Tusser, Thomas 76
Tutty, Sam 335
Twain, Mark 301
Twelfth Night 206, 231, 283
The 25th Annual Putnam County Spelling Bee 307, 309
Twiddle-Twaddle 31
Twiggy 248, 261
Twillie, Carmen 123
Twirly-Whirly 25–6
Two Against the World 40
Two By Two 215, 216
Two for the Show 127, 129
Two Gentlemen of Verona 217, 219
Two Little Girls in Blue 73, 75
Two on the Aisle 162, 164
Two's Company 165
Tyler, Bonnie 247
Tyler, Judy 171
Tyner, McCoy 104
Tyrell, Steve 107
Tymes 195

U2 109
Udell, Peter 212
Uggams, Leslie 77, 203, 209, 256
Under Many Flags 50
Undercover 27
Underwood, Carrie 185
The Unsinkable Molly Brown 187, 189
Up and Down Broadway 45, 47
Up in Central Park 142, 144
Up in One 237
Up She Goes 79
Ups-a-Daisy 96
Upstairs at O'Neals' 248, 250
Uptown ... It's Hot 256
Uranowitz, Brandon 244
Urban Blight 265, 266
Urban Cowboy 301
Urban, Joseph 58, 73, 79, 200
Urinetown 295, 297, 298
Utopia (Limited) 6–7
The Utter Glory of Morrisey Hall 237

Vacanti, Joshua 335

The Vagabond King 87, 89, 140
Vale, Jerry 198, 210, 218
Vallée, Rudy 97, 106
Valli, Frankie 310
Van and Schenck 70
Van, Bobby 157, 169
Van Brunt, Walter 17, 54, 59
Van Dyke, Dick 179, 243
Van Peebles, Melvin 217
Vandross, Luther 201
Vaudeville Days 51
Vaughan, Frankie 30, 155, 204
Vaughn, Billy 85, 210
Vaughn, Sarah 32, 46, 91, 100, 112, 126, 129, 132, 141, 161, 216
Vázquez, Joan 278
Velasquez, Regine 193
The Velvet Lady 67
Ventures 207
Venuta, Benay 49, 135
Venuti, Joe 104, 221
Vera Violetta 49–49
Verdi, Guiseppe 291, 292
Verdon, Gwen 157, 169, 174, 200, 228
Vereen, Ben 254
Very Good Eddie 58, 60, 228, 231
Very Warm for May 127–9
Vestoff, Virginia 183
Via Galactica 220
Victor Arden-Phil Ohman Orchestra 103
Victor Light Opera Company 22, 28, 35, 57, 88
Victor Military Band 9
Victor Salon Orchestra 46
Victor/Victoria 281, 282
Vidnovic, Martin 149
Vidgen, Jack 247
Village Stompers 195
Vincent, Gene 54
Vincent, Leslie 100
Vinton, Bobby 72
Violet 283, 285, 328
The Visit 330, 331
Voctave 335
Vogues 201
Voltaire 174, 223

Wagner, Chuck 284
Wagner, Robin 234
Wainwright, Loudon, III 100
Wait a Minim! 200
Waitress 332, 333
Waits, Tom 166
Wake Up and Dream 99, 101
Walk a Little Faster 108, 110
Walk Down Mah Street! 209
Walker, George 25, 31

Title and Name Index

Walker, Margaret 22
Walker, Nancy 136, 148, 151, 177, 183, 187
Walker, Summer 335
Walking Happy 203, 205
Wallace, Lee 254
Waller, Thomas "Fats" 88, 99–100, 234
Wallis, Quvenzhané 232
Wallis, Shani 75, 201
Walmartopia 315
Walsh, Barbara 273–4
Walsh, Bradley 109
Walters, Charles 117
Walston, Ray 169
Walton, Jim 230
A Waltz Dream 36
Wang 27
War and Peace 326, 334
War Paint 334, 335
Ward, Eleri 278
Warfield, David 16, 21
Warfield, William 95
Waring, Fred 32, 155, 179
Warlow, Anthony 252, 264, 271, 284
Warren, Adrienne 75
Warren, Harry 243
Warren, Jeff 161
Warren, Ron 197
Wars of the World 55
Warwick, Dionne 109, 195, 210
Washington, Dinah 100, 132, 286
Watanabe, Ken 330
Watch Your Step! 55, 57
Waters, Ethel 40, 102–3, 111, 116, 131, 167
Waters, John 315
Watts, Andre 104
Wayburn, Agnes 22
Wayburn, Ned 68
Wayne, Carl 147
Wayne, David 206
Webb, Clifton 61, 67, 96, 102
Webb, Marti 250, 252, 264, 268
Weber, Joe 12, 16, 18, 21, 23, 25, 27, 29, 31, 34, 36, 48, 50
Weber, Kay 115
Webster, Ben 128
Webster, Paul Francis 183
Wedderburn Oldtimers Orchestra 80
The Wedding Singer 310, 311
Weidman, John 228, 262
Weil, Cynthia 305
Weill, Kurt 108, 119, 124–5, 140–1, 142, 148, 154, 157, 212, 231, 312
Weird Romance 275
Welch, Elisabeth 82, 106, 112
Welcome to the Club 265
Welk, Lawrence 5, 172

Welland, Laura 170
Welles, Orson 145
Wenrich, Percy 73
We're No Angels 52
West, Charles 202
West, Christopher 280
West, Lydia 22
West, Mae 49, 67
West Side Story 177, 179, 190, 240, 318, 340
Westenberg, Robert 270–1
Westman, Jamael 331
Weston, Paul 149, 170
What Makes Sammy Run? 194, 196
What's a Nice Country Like You Doing in a State Like This? 220, 257
What's in a Name 70
Wheatley, Anna 62
Wheeler, Hugh 223
When Johnny Comes Marching Home 25–6, 61
When Pigs Fly 283, 285
When Sweet Sixteen 48
When the Boys Meet the Girls 104
Where's Charley? 154, 156, 226
Whirl-i-Gig 18–19
Whirl of Society 48
The Whirl of the World 53
Whitaker, Julian 267
Whitcomb, Ian 75, 77
White Christmas 59
The White Eagle 93
White, George 70
White Girls in Danger 346
The White Hen 34
The White Horse Inn 119
White, Lilias 75, 247
White, T. H. 187
Whiteman, Paul 75, 77, 82, 85, 95, 109, 115, 128
Whitfield, Wesla 126, 170
Whiting, Jack 102, 127, 131
Whiting, Margaret 77, 91, 120, 188, 251
Whiting, Richard 105
Whitman, Slim 46, 85
Whitmire, Stan 122, 195, 280
Whittaker, Roger 188, 221
Whoop-Dee-Doo 27
Whoop-Up 180
Whoopee! 96, 98, 237
The Who's Tommy 275
Whyte, Ronny 62
Wicked 304, 306–7
Wickes, Mary 240
Wickman, Dick 179
The Widow Jones 10–11
Wilber, Richard 174
Wild About Harry 75
Wild Card 46

419

Title and Name Index

The Wild Party 291, 293
The Wild Rose 23–4
Wildcat 187, 189
Wilder, Billy 345
Wildhorn, Frank 283, 284, 286
Wiley, Lee 91, 107
Wildflower 79–80
Wilkinson, Colm 188, 201, 264, 284
The Will Rogers Follies 270, 272
Williams, Andy 54, 172, 193, 207
Williams, Bert 25, 31, 42, 45, 48, 61, 70, 229
Williams, Bonnie Lou 54
Williams, Frances 105–6, 106, 114
Williams, Hank 301
Williams, Hank, Jr. 100–1
Williams, Joe 170
Williams, Michelle 204
Williams, NaTasha Yvette 346
Williams, Roger 66, 152, 198, 201
Williams, Vanessa 276
Willie Tyler Band 32
Willis, Allee 311
Willitts, Dave 285
Willson, Meredith 177–9, 187, 194
Wilson, Bob 83
Wilson, Christina 43
Wilson, Dooley 106–7, 131
Wilson, Eileen 141
Wilson, Francis 8, 10, 23
Wilson, Harvey 66
Wilson, Jackie 69
Wilson, Julie 149, 213
Wilson, Marie, L. 22
Wilson, Mary Louise 310, 312
Wilson, Nancy 122, 132, 170, 278
Wilson, Patrick 139, 278
Wilson, Robin 218
Wilson, Stan 163
Wilson, Teddy 104, 126
Winans, BeBe 32
Wind in the Willows 256
Windsor, Annie 261
Wine, Women and Song 137
Winehouse, Amy 91
Wing 250
Wings 275
Winninger, Charles 66, 80
Winokur, Jaret 302
The Winsome Widow 48–9
Winters, Lawrence 95
Winters, Shelley 212
Wisdom, Norman 203
Wise, Cody Ryan 320
Wish You Were Here 165, 166
The Witches of Eastwick 91

Withers, Ivy 144
Withers-Mendez, Elizabeth 311
Wittman, Scott 302, 346
The Wiz 225, 227, 251
The Wizard of Oz 25–6, 27, 34, 225, 251
The Wizard of the Nile 10–11
Wodehouse, P. G. 61–2, 64, 73, 81, 298
Wolfe, George C. 332
Wolfe, Karin 223–4
Wolpe, Lenny 254
The Woman in White 310–11
Woman of the Year 243, 245
Women on the Verge of a Nervous Breakdown 322, 323
Wonder Boy 102
Wonder, Stevie 195, 282
Wonder Wheel 77
Wonderful Town 165, 166, 304
Wonderland 31, 322
Woods, Renn 207
Woods, Sheryl 5
Wopat, Tom 147
Words and Music 136
Working 234, 236
Working, Julian 149
A World of Pleasure 58
Worth, Billie 161
Wright, Danny 221, 280
Wright, Doug 310
Wright, Finbar 51
Wright, George 69
Wright, Robert 167–8
The Wrong Man 340
Wyatt, Eric 188
Wylie and the Wild West 85
Wyman, Nicholas 173
Wynn, Bessie 27–8
Wynn, Ed 58, 61, 67, 76, 102, 105, 121, 131
Wynn, Nan 57, 75

Xanadu 315
Xavier, Charles 28

A Yankee Circus on Mars 29
The Yankee Consul 27–8
Yankee Doodle Dandy 28, 32, 80
The Yankee Girl 42
The Yankee Prince 36
Yanks 123
Yarnell, Bruce 147
Yarrington, Steve 158
Yazbek, David 336, 337
A Year with Frog and Toad 301, 303
The Yearling 200
Yellen, Jack 102

Title and Name Index

Yellowjackets 104
Yeo, Julian 77
Yerke's Novelty Five 69
Yeston, Maury 283, 324
Yip Yip Yaphank 67, 69
Yokel Boy 127
Yorkie, Brian 316
You & Me 285
You Never Know 124, 126
You Said It 102
Youmans, Vincent 57, 73, 79, 87–8, 90, 96, 99, 105, 117
Young, Alan 100
Young at Heart 91
Young, Faron 126
Young Frankenstein 46, 315, 317
The Young Philadelphians 52
Young, Rida Johnson 45–6, 64
Young Victor 126, 163, 169
Young, Will 129
Your Arms Too Short to Box with God 231, 233, 248
Your Own Thing 206, 207–8
You're a Good Man, Charlie Brown 203, 205, 289, 290
You're in Love 61
Yours, Anne 257
Yvette 123

Zadora, Pia 252
Zaks, Jerry 262, 273
Zann, Lois 161
Zanna Don't! 301, 303
Zappa, Frank 51
Ziegfeld, Florenz 12, 18, 36, 39–40, 48, 53, 70–2, 73, 81, 105, 111
Ziegfeld Follies of 1909 42, 44
Ziegfeld Follies of 1910 45, 47
Ziegfeld Follies of 1911 48–9
Ziegfeld Follies of 1912 50, 52
Ziegfeld Follies of 1913 53–4
Ziegfeld Follies of 1914 55
Ziegfeld Follies of 1915 58–9
Ziegfeld Follies of 1917 61, 63
Ziegfeld Follies of 1918 64, 67, 69
Ziegfeld Follies of 1919 70–2
Ziegfeld Follies of 1920 75
Ziegfeld Follies of 1921 76, 78
Ziegfeld Follies of 1922 40, 79, 80
Ziegfeld Follies of 1923 81, 83
Ziegfeld Follies of 1925 87
Ziegfeld Follies of 1927 93, 95
Ziegfeld Follies of 1931 105
Ziegfeld Follies of 1933–1934 111, 113
Ziegfeld Follies of 1936 116, 118
Ziegfeld Follies of 1942 137
Ziegfeld Follies of 1957 174
Ziegfeld Girl 66
Ziegfeld's American Revue 90
Ziemba, Karen 230
Zien, Chip 244
Zola, Emile 298
Zombie Prom 281
Zombies from Beyond 281
Zoot Suit 237
Zorbá 209, 211, 251
Zorbá the Greek 209, 251
Zorina, Vera 127, 169

ABOUT THE AUTHOR

Thomas S. Hischak is an internationally recognized author and teacher in the performing arts, and one of the foremost authorities on American musical theatre. He is author of over forty nonfiction books about theatre, film, and popular music, notably *The Oxford Companion to the American Musical*; *The 100 Greatest American Plays*; *The Rodgers and Hammerstein Encyclopedia*; *Through the Screen Door: What Happened to the Broadway Musical When It Went to Hollywood*; *Theatre as Human Action*; *The Tin Pan Alley Encyclopedia*; *Off-Broadway Musicals since 1919*; *Word Crazy: Broadway Lyricists*; *American Literature on Stage and Screen*; *1939: Hollywood's Greatest Year*; *The Abbott Touch: Pal Joey, Damn Yankees, and the Theatre of George Abbott*; *Musicals in Film: A Guide to the Genre*; *The Mikado to Matilda: British Musicals on the New York Stage*; *The Thornton Wilder Encyclopedia*; *The Oxford Companion to American Theatre (with Gerald Bordman)*; *The Disney Song Encyclopedia*; and *Musical Misfires: Three Decades of Broadway Musical Heartbreak* (the last two with Mark A. Robinson).

Hischak is also author of more than fifty published plays that are performed throughout the United States, Canada, Great Britain, and Australia. Hischak is a Fulbright scholar who has taught and directed in Greece, Lithuania, and Turkey. From 1983 to 2015, he was Professor of theatre at the State University of New York (SUNY) at Cortland, where he has received such honors as the 2004 SUNY Chancellor's Award for Excellence in Scholarship and Creative Activity and the 2010 SUNY Outstanding Achievement in Research Award. Four of his books have been cited as Outstanding Nonfiction Books by the American Library Association, and *The Oxford Companion to the American Theatre* was cited as an Outstanding Reference Work by the New York City Public Library in 2008. His playwriting awards include the Stanley Drama Award (New York City) for *Cold War Comedy* and the Julie Harris Playwriting Award (Beverly Hills, California) for *The Cardiff Giant*. Hischak is currently on the adjunct faculty of Flagler College (St. Augustine, Florida) where he teaches courses on theatre and film. www.thomashischak.com